1989

Educating
Special
Learners

Educating Special Learners

THIRD EDITION

G. Phillip Cartwright
University of California, Davis

Carol A. Cartwright
University of California, Davis

Marjorie E. Ward
The Ohio State University

Wadsworth Publishing Company
Belmont, California
A Division of Wadsworth, Inc.

Education Editor: **Suzanna Brabant**
Production Editor: **Deborah Cogan**
Managing Designer: **Andrew Ogus**
Print Buyer: **Barbara Britton**
Designer: **Vargas/Williams/Design**
Copy Editor: **Thomas Briggs**
Compositor: **TypeLink, Inc.**
Cover: **Vargas/Williams/Design**

Printed in the United States of America 85
1 2 3 4 5 6 7 8 9 10———93 92 91 90 89

Library of Congress Cataloging-in-Publication Data

Cartwright, G. Phillip (Glen Phillip), 1937–
    Educating special learners / G. Phillip Cartwright,
Carol A. Cartwright, Marjorie E. Ward—3rd ed.
        p.   cm.
    Includes bibliographies and index.
    ISBN 0-534-09570-4
    1. Special education—United States.
I. Cartwright, Carol A.,   1941– .   II. Ward,
Marjorie E.   III. Title.
LC3981.C37   1989   88-15633
371.9—dc19   CIP

Cover Art

The artwork on the cover of this book is a tempera painting by Cedric Johnson. The print is from the Creative Growth studio in Oakland, California. A community program, Creative Growth is dedicated to the idea that all people, no matter how severely disabled mentally, physically, or emotionally, can gain strength, enjoyment, and fulfillment through creative endeavor and can produce work of high artistic merit. Creative Growth programs include artistic development and personal integration through creative experience in the visual arts. Creative Growth offers professional instruction and support in drawing and painting, ceramic sculpture, printmaking, and fiber arts.

For more information write or call:
Creative Growth
355 24th Street
Oakland, CA 94612
(415) 836-2340

Part Opening Photographs
Part I: Photo by Joseph Bodkin.
Part II: Photo courtesy of HDS/U.S. HHS.
Part III: Photo by Stephen Coon. Courtesy of *Centre Daily Times.*

CONTENTS

PART I   Major Influences Shaping the Education of Exceptional Children   3

CHAPTER 3
Definitions and Classification Schemes   57

PART II   Characteristics of Exceptional Children   75

CHAPTER 4
Visual Handicaps   77

CHAPTER 7
Physical Handicaps and Health Problems   179

CHAPTER 8
Mental Retardation   217

CHAPTER 9

Learning Disability   249

CHAPTER 10

Emotional Disturbance   277

PART III   Identification, Assessment,
and Teaching   441

CHAPTER 15
Identification and Assessment   443

A Special Note:
What You Should Get from This Book

As you read the book, you will widen your understanding of some exceptional behaviors and how they affect a child's classroom and home environment. You will see characteristics that are so similar—yet so different—that you will be confused. You will read about children who have been given four or five different labels—and what happened as a result. And you will come to understand how terribly important careful assessment is in your professional life as a teacher. We hope you will discover that a teacher is not merely a dispenser of lesson plans or content, but is actually part investigator, part counselor, part diplomat, part problem solver, and part legal advocate. As an illustration of some of the problems facing teachers, consider the following description of a real child we will call Linda.

Linda seems inattentive most of the day. She often leaves her seat and interrupts other children. She seems bothered by the teacher's questions and has a certain testy manner about her. Her school work is spotty, and she frequently misses assignments. Linda is becoming a topic of conversation among the chil-

dren. Some call her dummy; *others are unwilling to join her reading group or play with her. Yesterday Joey clapped his hands behind her to awaken her from one of her daydreams. The whole class laughed, and she rushed out of the room crying, "I don't like school!"*

Is Linda emotionally disturbed? Educably mentally retarded? Is her poor school performance a result of an inability to read letters? A learning disability? Is she hard of hearing and, thus, simply unable to pay attention and keep up? Or is she of such superior intelligence that she finds this classroom an incredibly miserable experience?

By the time you finish the last page of this book, you will know how to deal with problems presented by children like Linda, and you will realize that *you can cause things to happen*—you don't have to deal just with the effects of others' actions. This book is an invitation to be the "compleat teacher." We hope it will have an impact on you that will cause you to have special impact on special children.

PREFACE

At least one out of every ten children will require special education services at some time during his or her school years. *Educating Special Learners* is an introduction to those children and the services they will receive. For some readers, this book may be the only formal contact they have with special education and exceptional children. For others, it will serve as a springboard to more advanced studies.

In our discussions throughout the book, we stay fairly close to the definitions, categories, and services that are mandated by Public Law 94–142, the Education for All Handicapped Children Act of 1975. This federal law, which went into effect in 1978, is the most ambitious and pervasive education legislation ever enacted. And, in spite of pointed but unsuccessful political attempts to weaken—even repeal—the law, P.L. 94–142, and related legislation enacted in the 1980s, remains a driving force behind efforts to improve the quality of life of handicapped children.

Put simply, P.L. 94–142 requires the coordinated efforts of many disciplines to provide a free, appropriate education for all the nation's handicapped children and youth. The responsibility for direct instruction of handicapped children will fall to teachers—regular teachers, special education teachers, physical education teachers, art and music teachers, and others. They will not, however, be alone in their efforts. Psychologists, speech therapists, counselors, and other professionals will work together with teachers to plan and provide the best education possible for all handicapped children. Regardless of the role that

you, the reader, will play in providing services to exceptional children or to other persons, you will need to know certain key concepts, ideas, facts, and figures. We hope this volume lays down a satisfactory foundation.

The context of special education has changed drastically during the last decade. Part I of this text, "Major Influences Shaping the Education of Exceptional Children," describes the settings in which handicapped and gifted youngsters can and should be educated. Part I covers legal and humanistic issues, definitional problems, and variety of services available for handicapped children and their families.

Part II, "Characteristics of Exceptional Children," presents the main facts and theories, promises and problems—the "what is" and "what should be" about exceptional children. Part II discusses gifted and talented children, as well as the legal categories of handicaps and other groups that are of concern to educators.

Part III, "Identification, Assessment, and Teaching," draws the facts and theories together and gives readers specific skills in dealing with atypical persons. Although every aspect of identifying, diagnosing, teaching, and using technology with all ages and all levels of handicapped and gifted youngsters cannot be covered thoroughly in a single volume, Part III provides basic information that is generic to many teaching situations and to many children.

Some instructors might wish to cover the material in the text in a different order than our chapter sequencing. In general, we think the flow is best if the sequence of the three parts is pre-served. However, with some preplanning, an instructor can rearrange the order of chapters within parts, especially in Part II.

Several things were important to us as we wrote this book. Often, such working procedures and details are not explained to readers, but because they have shaped the book to such a large extent, we want to share them with you.

1. Several years ago we were responsible for developing a course of study for regular educators on the needs of handicapped children. At latest count, nearly 25,000 regular and special education teachers and college students majoring in special education, regular education, and many other fields have taken the course. Their feedback has been invaluable in helping us address what we believe will be your needs as you use the book.
2. We know that teachers are sometimes impatient with discussions of theory; they prefer to learn about practical ideas. We agree that the practical ideas are necessary, but some understanding of theory is important, too. If you know the theory, you can often generate hundreds of practical ideas on your own—you don't need a prepackaged bag of tricks.
3. In some chapters, various technical and/or medical terms are used. We have found it necessary to understand the meanings of some of these terms in order to converse easily with parents and other professionals. Therefore, they are included and defined.
4. Special attention is given to deaf-blind and multihandicapped students in Chapter 14. Also included in Chapter 14 are other groups that concern teachers but are not identified as handicapped according to federal and state regulations. We are not trying to create new categories of exceptionality by including these groups; we simply want to make you aware of their special needs.
5. We find special education to be a dynamic field. Nearly everywhere we turn these days we find positive references to handicapped individuals. We've tried to share some of this excitement with you by including "boxes" in the chapters. These boxes contain information that is supplementary to the main text and that adds human interest.

As you read this book it will become evident to you that a particular point of view has guided our writing. To state it quite simply, we believe that handicapped youngsters should be educated in a setting as close to normal as possible. Accomplishing this goal will require cooperation between regular and special educators—and that's where you come in.

We have had direct teaching experiences with the legal categories reported in this text, except for the physically handicapped. Consequently, we asked our colleague, Dr. Patricia Seibel, of the Pittsburgh Public Schools, to prepare the chapter on that subject. In addition, we asked Dr. Elisa Klein, of the University of Maryland, to write the chapter on the gifted and talented because of her recent training and experiences with gifted youngsters. These two chapters reflect the many years of training and experience the authors have had in those areas.

This third edition brings us up to date on many issues and reassures us that the provision of education services to all handicapped youngsters is not just a passing fad. We studied the results of P.L. 94–142 and related legislation and litigation. Important new developments in these areas, as well as in the more traditional educational and scientific areas, are included in this new edition. And we reviewed systematically all the major journals and texts relevant to each of the chapters in the book.

In addition to updating all chapters, we have expanded our coverage of such areas as parent-related issues (including genetic counseling), early childhood education, and multi- and severely handicapped children. We have also expanded our coverage of special groups and minorities. And we have expanded the coverage of the impact of high technology on individuals with disabilities.

We wish to thank those people who gave us permission to use their stories in this book. Most of the names used in the case studies are fictitious and do not refer to specific individuals.

Numerous individuals have contributed to the three editions in many different ways. We acknowledge the help of the following talented people, including graduate students, faculty, and staff who helped with content and research: Alex Johnson, Sally Mascitelli, Elizabeth Hrncir, Cecelia Ward, Bo In Chung, Chris Richardson, Marci Weiner, Annie Mandelker, Jerry Luckovich, Art Pentz, Barbara Polka, Ann Krise, Debbie Reynolds, Phyllis Allegretto, Patrick Schloss, Cathie Ellen, Elizabeth McLean, and Steve Bugaj. We appreciate the help of James Collins and Wayne Secord, faculty members in the Department of Educational Services and Research at Ohio State University, who reviewed chapters in the manuscript. Janis Leitzell and Glenda Carelas typed some of the original manuscript. Carolyn Harbolis, Ruth Kilhoffer, Becky Young, Charlotte Fisher, and Karen Bruno helped out with galleys and page proofs. Barbara Andolina, Jan Becker, Pauline Elias, Pat Hunt, and Nancy Silverman helped us collect children's materials and shared their experiences teaching exceptional children. Maureen Smith and Anjali Misra were extremely helpful to us during this most recent revision, performing innumerable tasks and doing much original research and writing. We are grateful to them for their efforts and their willingness to help. Jack Vesnesky, Michael Behe, and the children and teachers in Central Intermediate Unit 10 provided us with interesting photographs.

We would also like to acknowledge the contributions of the reviewers of the third edition: Betty Bitner-Corvin, Arkansas Technical University; Richard Schick, Mansfield University of Pennsylvania; Carol Downs Taylor, San Jose State University; and Melinda Fassett Welles, University of Southern California.

Special thanks go to Suzanna Brabant, Education Editor at Wadsworth, who helped us prepare this third edition.

Finally, we are much indebted to Roger Peterson, who encouraged us to begin, and complete, the manuscript. His guidance was excellent; his patience was appreciated; and his friendship is valued.

G. P. Cartwright
C. A. Cartwright
M. E. Ward

Part I describes the settings in which handicapped and gifted youngsters can and should be educated. It covers legal and humanistic issues, definitional problems, and the variety of services that are available for children with handicaps and their families.

PART I

Major Influences Shaping the Education of Exceptional Children

CHAPTER 1

Legal and Humanistic Forces

Did You Know That . . .

- federal law entitles all children to a free, appropriate public education, regardless of how severely handicapped they may be?

- mainstreaming does not mean placing all children with disabilities in regular classes?

- education of children and youths with disabilities is an important issue in public policy and has had political as well as economic effects on our nation?

- federal law guarantees that all persons with disabilities shall have equal access to programs, jobs, and housing?

- parents and lawyers have been leaders in promoting laws to treat persons with disabilities fairly?

- the word *mainstreaming* does not even appear in Public Law 94–142, which is often called the "mainstreaming law"?

- many states require special programs for gifted and talented youngsters?

- children suspected of being handicapped must be tested in their native languages?

- parents must be consulted before a child is categorized as "handicapped" or placed in special education programs?

I proceed, gentlemen, briefly to call your attention to the *present* state of insane [and retarded] persons confined within this Commonwealth, in *cages, closets, cellars, stalls, pens! Chained, naked, beaten with rods, and lashed* into obedience. . . . I have seen many [persons] who, part of the year, are chained or caged.

(Dix, 1843, in Rosen, Clark, & Kivitz, 1975, pp. 6–7)

In 1843, Dorothea L. Dix, a crusader for human rights, presented a moving speech to the legislature of Massachusetts. Her message, a small part of which is given above, implored the legislature to concern itself with the plight of "insane and idiotic" persons confined in almshouses and prisons. Dix reported in painful detail the grim, filthy quarters in which human beings were chained and the abusive methods used to control these unfortunate people.

Although the work of Dorothea Dix marks neither the beginning nor the end of the development of concern for the welfare of others, it does illustrate that such feelings were a matter of public record well over a century ago. Unfortunately, the lives of persons with disabilities often were not immediately altered by the impassioned pleas of Dorothea Dix and her contemporaries. Positive changes came only over a very long period of time and usually only when forced by court actions.

Humanists such as Dorothea Dix were responsible for initially calling attention to problems in the care and education of persons with disabilities. In the twentieth century, parent groups such as the National Association for Retarded Citizens were instrumental in applying pressure on state and national legislative bodies to change legislation that did not provide suitable housing and treatment for persons with handicaps. Although parents and professional workers were keenly aware of abuses of, and poor programs for, the handicapped, it took a partnership between parents and lawyers to bring about positive change.

As an educator in the 1990s, you have inherited a major responsibility. After well over a century of agitation, lawsuits, and state and federal

Treatment of persons who were mentally ill or retarded in the eighteenth and nineteenth centuries was often cruel and inhumane. (*Aliéné enchaîné à Bedlam,* Esquirol, 1838. Courtesy of the National Library of Medicine.)

In spite of a severe spinal injury, this young woman participates actively in all aspects of high school life. (Courtesy of Wide World Photos.)

laws, it is now the law of the land (**Public Law 94–142**, which will be discussed later in this chapter) that *all* citizens, regardless of a handicap, must be treated fairly and equally with respect to education. Regardless of how severely handicapped a child is, it is our job as educators to see to it that that child receives a free, appropriate public education—one suitable to his or her needs. Furthermore, Sections 503 and 504 of the Vocational Rehabilitation Act of 1973 guarantee that all persons with handicaps, young and old, shall have equal access to programs, jobs, and housing. Thus, educators' responsibilities are consistent

with, and part of, a far-ranging humanistic and legal movement.

NORMALIZATION AND MAINSTREAMING

Society's attitudes toward persons with disabilities is undergoing a gradual change. Although the transformation is far from complete, people with disabilities are far more likely to be treated fairly and humanely. The changing attitude is anchored by two important concepts: *normalization* and *mainstreaming*.

Normalization

Early advocates for the handicapped pleaded that persons with disabilities be allowed to grow up in as normal an environment as possible. The increasing influence of parents in the process of deciding what was best for their handicapped children resulted in a strong reaction against overcrowded institutions. Parents began to ask for more homelike surroundings for their children, even for those children who required considerable physical care. The trend in the past decade thus has been to **deinstitutionalize** persons with handicaps.

J. W. Putnam and R. H. Bruininks (1986) described deinstitutionalization as practices that reduce and prevent the need for persons with disabilities to live in large institutional environments. These practices promote more normal living environments in smaller settings that are less isolated from community life. Deinstitutionalization has had a major impact upon schools: The number of students with severe handicaps, formerly served in institutional settings, who are now enrolled in special education programs has increased substantially.

The effort to provide surroundings, opportunities, and programs much like those provided for more normal children and adults has become known as **normalization**. The idea behind normalization originated in Denmark, and it was in the Scandinavian countries that the practice of normalization was first implemented successfully (Wolfensberger, 1972). H. R. Turnbull (1986) defined normalization as "a proposition that handicapped persons should live and be treated like nonhandicapped persons as much as possible and that their differences from nonhandicapped people can be reduced by minimizing the degree to which they are treated different" (p. 11).

Bruininks and G. Warfield (1978) collected from various professional publications the follow-

The principle of normalization should be extended to all aspects of the lives of persons who are handicapped, including recreation. (Courtesy of the Easter Seal Society for Crippled Children and Adults of Pennsylvania.)

ing suggestions for implementing normalization. They indicate that these normalization principles can be used to enhance the effectiveness of services for persons with handicaps.

- Plan and manage services for retarded people that require attention to normative cultural patterns.
- Allow retarded persons to experience normal routines of the day (e.g., dressing, eating in normal-sized groups) and normal routines of the life cycle (e.g., activities appropriate to one's age) that generally accompany increasing maturity.
- Respect choices and desires, and provide normal economic and civic privileges.

BOX 1.1

BARRIER-FREE LIVING

Kathy Vaczi was involved in a car accident that left her paralyzed from the waist down. Despite this obstacle, she completed college and began a teaching career. As part of her plans for completely independent living, Ms. Vaczi designed and built a barrier-free home. To outsiders, her home appears no different from any other in the neighborhood. However, it has many special features. For example, it is built on a cement slab, which eliminates the need for ramps and railings. Windows can be opened by cranks located at their bases. The grill and sink in the kitchen are 26 inches from the floor, allowing her to roll her wheelchair under each. Kitchen cabinets have sliding shelves that can be pulled out. Building the house cost no more than a standard home; however, careful planning has enabled Ms. Vaczi to achieve the independence enjoyed by other homeowners.

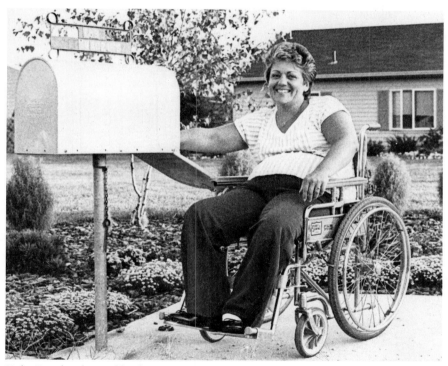

Kathy Vaczi has designed her home to minimize physical barriers. She is able to live independently because of careful planning.

Source: Vaczi, K. L. (1984, Fall). No telltale signs for Kathy. *Accent on Living*, pp. 66–70. Information and photo courtesy of Katherine L. Vaczi-Shawaryn.

BOX 1.2
SENSITIZING THE NEXT GENERATION

Some literature for children includes handicapped characters or stories about handicapped people and how they have managed to live a fairly normal life in spite of their problems. An article that appeared in a children's magazine illustrates how children can learn about handicapping conditions. In the process, they are likely to become more accepting of the handicapped. These knowledge and attitude changes will go a long way toward achievement of the goals of normalization in the years to come. "My Friend Eric," by H. M. Myer, appeared in *Jack and Jill* magazine, February 1978, *40*(2), 34–35.

My Friend Eric

I would like you to meet a very special friend of mine. His name is Eric Lilliequist. He is eleven years old and lives in Boulder, Colorado, with his mother and dad and sister Maria.

The first time I saw Eric he was zooming down a steep hill on skis with a grin a mile wide across his face. His bright red hair was sticking out from under his knit cap. He was wearing yellow goggles. But it was something else he was wearing that caught my eye. Over his parka he had on a bright orange vest, and printed on this vest were the words BLIND SKIER!

Yes, Eric is completely blind. He was born blind, but that hasn't stopped him for a single minute. Even though he lives in a world of total darkness, there are few things he doesn't try to do. . . .

Every Sunday during the winter Eric boards the ski bus for the two-hour ride to Winter Park Ski Area high up in the Rocky Mountains. There he is met by his ski instructor, Cricket Counce. She has been teaching Eric for two years. This was hard because she couldn't *show* him how; she had to *tell* him how. They ride the ski tow up the mountain just like everyone else. But the big difference is coming down the hill. Cricket stays right behind Eric and tells him which way to go and when to turn. . . .

Eric also plays the piano. He has to practice just like anyone who wants to learn to play well, but he has to memorize each note because, of course, he can't read music.

But Eric does read books. All of his books are printed in Braille. . . .

Eric reads every issue of *Jack and Jill* from cover to cover. He gets his copy written in Braille. It is his favorite magazine. He can hardly wait each month for it to come. . . .

Eric must work very hard at everything he does, but he still is a happy person. I am very proud to have Eric as a friend, for he truly is special.

Source: From *Jack and Jill* magazine, copyright © 1978 by the Saturday Evening Post Company, Indianapolis, Indiana. Adapted by permission of the publisher.

- Provide education, training, care, and residential living in facilities of normal size and appearance.
- Whenever possible, use generic services rather than separate ones.

(pp. 191–192)

Mainstreaming

A corollary to normalization is **mainstreaming**— the concept and practice of educating children with handicaps in an environment as nearly normal as possible. Mainstreaming seeks the integration of children with learning, behavioral, and/or physical problems into regular education settings and programs unless their problems are so severe that they cannot be accommodated in regular programs. Many educators and parents view mainstreaming as one of the most important changes in education in recent years. Most certainly, the inclusion of many children with handicaps in regular classrooms will have a profound impact on regular education for many years to come.

In 1976, the Council for Exceptional Children

(CEC), the leading professional organization that deals with the educational problems of exceptional children and youths, announced its official definition of mainstreaming and the philosophy underlying it. Following are the major elements of the CEC position:

- Exceptional children have a wide variety of special educational needs, varying greatly in intensity and duration.
- There is a recognized continuum of educational settings that may, at any given time, be appropriate for a particular child's needs.
- Each exceptional child should be educated in the least restrictive environment in which his or her needs can be satisfactorily met.
- Exceptional children should be educated with nonexceptional children.
- Special classes, separate schooling, or other removal of an exceptional child from education with nonexceptional children should occur only when the intensity of the child's special needs is such that they cannot be satisfied in an environment including nonexceptional children even when supplementary aids and services are provided.
(Official Actions, 1976, p. 43)

Though mainstreaming does not mean that *all* students with handicaps will be integrated into regular education, it does mean that many more children than ever before will be placed in regular education. In fact, the U.S. Department of Education (1984) reported that fewer than 7 percent of all children and youths with disabilities are educated in either separate schools or separate environments. Of the 93 percent who are in regular schools, nearly two-thirds receive their education in the regular classroom with their nonhandicapped peers.

The word *mainstreaming* does not actually appear in P.L. 94–142. Underlying the concept is the idea of the **least restrictive environment**. If placements were possible on a continuum from most segregated (restricted) to most integrated (not restricted), we would want to place the child in the setting as close as possible to the "most inte-grated" end of the continuum. For the majority of children with special needs, that means placement in regular education.

Studies of the effects of special classes for youngsters with handicaps have had an impact on the development of mainstreaming. Research conducted in the 1950s and 1960s indicated that children who were segregated into special classes were not learning any better than their counterparts who remained in regular class situations. In fact, some studies showed that mildly handicapped children who remained in regular classes actually made greater academic gains than did similarly handicapped children who were placed in special classes. More recent studies, however, offer conflicting data regarding the impact of mainstreaming upon the academic and social development of students with disabilities. Some authors report the successful integration of students with handicaps (Macy & Carter, 1978), whereas other authors draw less positive conclusions (Gottlieb, 1981; Heller, 1983; Johnson, 1983). W. Stainback and colleagues (1985), in their review of the literature, reported that the only consistent finding is that mainstreaming works if regular classroom teachers are able to adapt instruction for students with a wide range of disabilities. Other factors that may contribute to the success of mainstreaming, as identified by S. J. Salend (1984), include:

1. developing specific criteria for mainstreaming (e.g., the ability to interact positively with others, obey class rules, and display proper work habits)

2. preparing students with disabilities for the social and academic demands of the mainstream setting

3. preparing nonhandicapped students to interact positively

4. communicating among the professionals involved (e.g., regarding the student's academic and social development, as well as medical/prosthetic information)

5. evaluating student progress

6. providing in-service training that enhances teachers' skills and promotes positive values

For the same reasons that have prompted de-institutionalization of persons with disabilities, that is, *humanistic reasons,* many persons have felt it is more civilized to treat children with disabilities as normally as possible. Thus, mainstreaming received support from those who believed that all children, regardless of handicap, should be treated with dignity and kindness. A second driving force toward the development of mainstreaming was the combination of court cases (litigation) and federal and state laws (legislation) that mandated mainstreaming. These developments will be discussed in more detail in the next section.

LITIGATION AND LEGISLATION

Although most educators are uncomfortable with the notion that lawyers have had a greater influence on recent educational events than have teachers, the facts seem to support that observation. In the final analysis, there are certain legal bases upon which the American educational system rests. Lawyers and legislators know these bases well and operate within the legal and judiciary system. Although the *logical* reason for the provision of education and other services to the handicapped has been a humanistic one, the *compelling* reason has been the legislation and court decrees requiring such services. In short, we now have free public education for children with disabilities because it is the law of the land.

There are several areas of law that regulate and mandate education and other civil issues. One area is **constitutional law**—law that emanates from the United States Constitution as a result of court rulings and interpretations of specific aspects of the Constitution. Although the Constitution does not specifically state that education is a fundamental right, court decisions as well as the Fifth and Fourteenth amendments to the Constitution provide equal protection under the law.

This means that a child cannot be excluded from education because of race, creed, or religion, or because of a handicap.

A second source of law is the legislative branch of government. The U.S. Congress passes laws that must be obeyed by the nation as a whole, and federal financial support for education is the result of such laws.

These sources of law establish, often quite precisely, the nature of an educational program that must be provided to a child with a disability. The sources of law are often lumped together in the phrase "litigation and legislation," but there are significant differences between the two. **Legislation** refers to the passage of laws by the U.S. Congress or state legislatures. **Litigation** refers to court action and usually involves a lawsuit of one kind or another. Both laws and lawsuits have played very important roles in the development of state and federal policy toward the education and welfare of the people with handicaps. The courts and the Congress have not only mandated that children *shall* be served, they have also frequently specified *how.*

Litigation

In 1954, in the landmark *Brown* v. *Board of Education* case, the U.S. Supreme Court ruled that under the Fourteenth Amendment it was unlawful to discriminate against a class of persons for an arbitrary or unjustifiable reason. In the ruling, Chief Justice Earl Warren wrote: "In these days it is doubtful that any child may reasonably be expected to succeed in life if he is denied the opportunity of an education. Such an opportunity, where the state has undertaken to provide it, is a right which must be made available to all." Though the specific ruling applied to black Americans, its application to the handicapped is obvious.

As late as 1958, a local court (with or without parental permission) could place a child with mild mental retardation in a residential institution when it thought that lower intelligence rendered the child unlikely to profit from public school classes. Consequently, children with handicaps were denied a classroom in which to learn, and the schools were made to feel no responsibility to create programs for those children.

A California **class action suit** (one brought on behalf of all members of a group) in 1970, *Diana* v. *State Board of Education,* ended in a **consent agreement** between the two opposing parties stipulating that children are to be tested in their primary language. Interpreters may be used when a bilingual examiner is not available. This suit was brought on behalf of a group of nine Mexican-American children who had been labeled mentally retarded because they received low scores on standardized intelligence tests. The court ruling has been interpreted as applicable to individuals who are deaf, blind, and physically handicapped as well as to those individuals whose primary language is not English.

Two federal district court rulings the following year dealt directly with the rights of individuals who are mentally retarded. In *Wyatt* v. *Aderholt* (1971), the court ruled that institutionalized persons who are mentally retarded have a constitutional right to adequate treatment. Guidelines for individual treatment plans, minimum educational standards, provisions against involuntary servitude (individuals were being "farmed out" or being used as institutional peons and not given any wages), a humane psychological environment, and a least restrictive setting necessary for **habilitation** and training were included in the ruling.

The second suit, which originated in Pennsylvania (*PARC, Bowman et al.* v. *Commonwealth of Pennsylvania,* 1971), alleged that children who were retarded had been denied access to education and due process. The resulting consent agreement provided that these children are entitled to free public programs of education and training commensurate with the children's abilities. Such placements shall be in regular public school classes when possible instead of in self-contained special education classes or schools. In addition, the consent agreement stipulated periodic reevaluations of the children at least every two years and the right to a hearing and access to procedural due process. **Due process** refers to

procedural safeguards such as obtaining parental permission for testing a child or changing a child's education program placement. The provision for placement in a regular public school class has had a far-reaching effect for teachers of all subjects and for the teacher preparation programs offered by colleges of education.

A class action suit in the District of Columbia in 1972 (*Mills* v. *Board of Education of the District of Columbia*) carried the PARC ruling further by obtaining an acknowledgement of the right to an education for all children with handicaps, not just those with mental retardation. It specifically assured the child's constitutional right to procedural due process and to appropriate educational placement.

In the late 1970s, Pennsylvania was once again at the leading edge of the deinstitutionalization/ normalization movement. Two court orders emanated from the Federal District Court in Pennsylvania. One case, *Halderman* v. *Pennhurst* (1977), resulted in the closing of a state-run institution for the retarded, Pennhurst, and the establishment of group homes for its residents. The court order was significant partly because it established the precedent of group homes and partly because it dealt with individuals who were severely handicapped. One unit of the institution contained 153 residents, all of whom were nonambulatory. The average age of this group was twenty-eight; the average length of institutionalization was fourteen years; the average IQ was only 9.

Subsequent appeals were made to the U.S. Court of Appeals and to the U.S. Supreme Court. The Appellate Court agreed that conditions at Pennhurst were such that residents were being denied adequate education and habilitation. The higher court, however, believed that conditions at Pennhurst could be improved so that the institution would be an appropriate placement for some individuals with severe handicaps. Thus, that section of the original court ruling that Pennhurst be closed was vacated, or overturned (*Halderman* v. *Pennhurst,* 1979). This case was pursued, and in 1981, the U.S. Supreme Court issued its decision (*Pennhurst* v. *Halderman,* 1981). Although the highest court did not disagree that conditions at

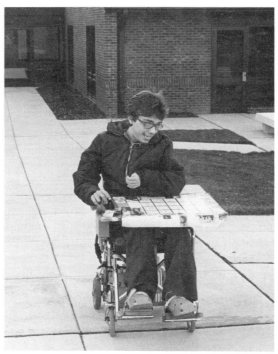

Some students who are severely handicapped can profit from year-round programs, and this fact has been recognized by the courts in *Battle* v. *Commonwealth of Pennsylvania* (1980). (Photo by J. A. Bensel. Courtesy of the Maryland School for the Blind.)

Pennhurst had been dangerous and inadequate for habilitation, it did not order its closing. The court agreed, in effect, that conditions should be improved and that individuals who are severely and profoundly retarded are entitled to adequate habilitation. By 1987, Pennhurst had ceased to exist as a large facility but served a few clients in small group settings.

One dramatic impact of the suit was the return of many of Pennhurst's school-age residents to public school programs in Philadelphia and surrounding counties. The schools involved were faced with the need to develop high-quality programs for youngsters with severe developmental disabilities and to find people trained to teach in such programs.

The second landmark Pennsylvania suit of the late 1970s was *Armstrong* v. *Kline* (1979). In this case, the counsel for the plaintiff argued that Gary Armstrong's disabilities were so great that he needed more schooling than the traditional 180-day school year. If Gary received no education or training during the summer, he regressed academically. Furthermore, the regression was so great that it took a good deal of the next school year to help him regain or recoup the academic losses sustained over the summer. Thus, a new term entered the educational jargon. The problem of losing ground over the summer has come to be known as the **regression/recoupment phenomenon**. The federal court ruled that the school and the state education department were not providing an appropriate education for Gary and ordered the state to begin offering an **extended school year** to Gary and to all children with handicaps who were in need of summer programs. In *Battle* v. *Commonwealth* (1980), the Third Circuit Court of Appeals confirmed the lower court's ruling. Thus, many schools are now faced with the task of developing year-round programs for children and youths with severe disabilities.

The ruling in the *Armstrong* case promises to have a profound effect on the philosophy and practice of education, especially as applied to the financing of public education. There is not yet a firm body of information from which to develop criteria for use in determining which children should be eligible for extended school year (ESY) programs and what types of programs should be made available for them. M. L. Kabler, T. M. Stephens, and R. T. Rinaldi (1983) reviewed the available evidence and concluded that "educational issues surrounding the benefits for extending the school year are far from resolved for both handicapped and nonhandicapped students" (p. 109). They point out that although the ESY is intuitively attractive, no research base as yet supports the idea. Fortunately, studies now being done do support it. For example, J. McMahon (1983) did a controlled study of the effects of an ESY program on twenty-six students with severe handicaps. He found that when educational programming is interrupted, as for a summer session, "regression increases and improvement decreases; . . . when an ESY program is provided, the opposite appears true. . . . This cycle appears to be the regression/ recoupment disability syndrome described for this unique population" (p. 459).

Other court cases dealt with the issue of expulsion of students with disabilities. *Stuart* v. *Nappi* (1978) involved the expulsion of a learning disabled student with a history of learning problems. A federal court ruled that school expulsion of a child with a handicap constituted a denial of the right to an appropriate education. A child's placement could be changed, however, after a staff conference that included parents. Similarly, in *S-1* v. *Turlington* (1979), seven students who were mentally retarded had been expelled early in the 1977–78 school year and for all of the 1978–79 school year because of alleged misconduct. They maintained their retardation was the cause of their behavior. A Florida court agreed and ruled that students with disabilities cannot be excluded from their educational programs because of actions resulting from a handicap.

Four other cases of great importance to the education of special learners, all of which were related to provisions described in P.L. 94–142, the Education of All Handicapped Children Act, passed in 1975 and amended in 1986, also have reached the Supreme Court. P.L. 94–142 will be described in detail in the next section; the four cases clarifying its provisions are presented here.

The first case was *Board of Education of the Hendrick Hudson Central School District* v. *Rowley,* 458 U.S. 176 (1982). Amy Rowley was an eight-year-old child with a profound hearing impairment enrolled in a third-grade public school classroom. School officials had denied her parents' request that Amy be provided with a sign language interpreter. Her parents, in turn, filed suit alleging the district's refusal violated Amy's right to a free, appropriate public education.

The *Rowley* case was heard at the Federal District Court (*Rowley* v. *Board of Education,* 1980a). It was appealed to the Second Circuit Court of Appeals (*Rowley* v. *Board of Education,* 1980b) and finally resolved by the Supreme Court (*Board of Education* v. *Rowley,* 1982). The lower courts had ruled that the school district was obligated to provide a sign language interpreter for a child with a hearing impairment, even though the child was making above-average progress in a regular class. The interpreter was needed, the courts said, to ensure that the child was receiving a free, appropriate public education as mandated by law. The Supreme Court overturned the lower courts' rulings and stated that "since the child was receiving substantial specialized instruction and related instruction at public expense, she was receiving an appropriate education . . . and was not entitled to a sign language interpreter" (McCarthy, 1983, p. 520).

In *Smith* v. *Robinson* (1984), the Supreme Court addressed the issue of the cost of attorneys' fees incurred by parents who filed a lawsuit charging violation of their child's rights under P.L. 94–142. Tommy Smith, an eight-year-old boy disabled by cerebral palsy and a variety of other physical and emotional handicaps, was placed by his local education agency in a hospital program. After one year, the parents were notified that the local education agency (LEA) would no longer fund Tommy's program. The Smiths appealed and were granted an injunction in 1976 that was upheld by the Rhode Island Supreme Court in 1978. In 1981, they were awarded $8,000 as reimbursement for attorneys' fees incurred while obtaining the injunction. In 1982, the Federal District Court awarded the Smiths $32,109 as reimbursement for costs incurred during the state administrative process, a decision later overturned by the Federal Court of Appeals for the First Circuit. The Supreme Court agreed to hear the case in 1983. One year later, the Supreme Court upheld the decision of the Court of Appeals and overturned the reimbursement. The Court reasoned that no specific provision under P.L. 94–142 allows for such fees. R. A. Luckasson (1986), in an analysis of the Supreme Court's decision, warned that "to insist that families of handicapped children bear the entire burden of legal fees while allowing reimbursement of fees in other civil cases places special disability on these individuals" (p. 388). N. Wolf (1985) suggested that parents who are unable to afford attorneys' fees may be unable to ensure the protection of their child's rights. Fortunately, since the *Smith* v. *Robinson* decision, P.L.

94–142 has been amended to include a provision for attorneys' fees.

On the same day it ruled in *Smith* v. *Robinson,* the Supreme Court also announced its decision in *Irving Independent School District* v. *Tatro* (1984). Amber Tatro was born with spina bifida, which resulted in a bladder condition requiring clean intermittent catheterization (CIC). This procedure involves washing a small catheter, inserting it into the bladder, allowing the urine to drain, removing the catheter, and wiping the bladder region. Amber required the procedure be performed every three to four hours to prevent the development of a chronic kidney infection. The school district in which Amber was a student refused to administer CIC on the basis that it was a medical procedure. Her parents disagreed, arguing that CIC was necessary to ensure Amber's right to an appropriate education as guaranteed by P.L. 94–142. They sued, requesting the school district to provide CIC and seeking compensatory damages and attorneys' fees. The case finally reached the Supreme Court, which ruled that CIC was indeed a supportive service that enabled a child with a disability to benefit from special education. Once again, however, the Court did not award attorneys' fees. This decision was reversed on August 5, 1986, when P.L. 99–372, the Handicapped Children's Protection Act, was signed. This bill authorized reimbursement of legal fees and expenses to parents who won a court action.

The last major case involving provisions of P.L. 94–142 was *Burlington School Committee of the Town of Burlington, Massachusetts* v. *Department of Education of Massachusetts* (1985). Eight-year-old Michael Panico was experiencing learning difficulties and was enrolled in a private school for students with learning disabilities by his father without approval of school officials. A hearing officer ruled the private facility was appropriate for Michael and ordered the school district to reimburse Mr. Panico and to pay tuition and transportation expenses. School officials appealed the ruling, arguing that the father waived his right to reimbursement because he placed Michael without their approval. The case eventually went to the Supreme Court, which ruled that expenses for a private school placement made by a parent of a child with a disability may be reimbursed if the Court ultimately decides the placement is appropriate under the provisions of P.L. 94–142.

Despite the lack of rulings universally in favor of students with disabilities, recent decisions of the Supreme Court represent attempts to protect the rights of these children as guaranteed by P.L. 94–142. These decisions reinforce the tremendous strides made in the development of suitable programs and facilities during the last decade.

Legislation

Although many state and federal laws have had an impact on education, there are several critical federal laws with which you should be familiar. These laws are applicable in all states.

The Mental Retardation Facilities and Community Mental Health Centers Construction Act of 1963 (Public Law 88–164) authorized the construction of research centers and facilities for persons who are mentally retarded, the construction of community health centers, and the training of teachers of children who are mentally retarded or mentally ill or otherwise handicapped. The act also authorized the creation of the Division of Handicapped Children and Youth, as part of the Department of Health, Education and Welfare. In short, the act was the federal government's official recognition of the problem of mental retardation and mental illness in the United States.

The 1965 Elementary and Secondary Education Act (ESEA; Public Law 89–10) contained provisions for compensatory education for educationally disadvantaged children. The General Provisions and Definitions section of this legislation (Title VI) provided some of the bases for subsequent laws concerning education of children with handicaps.

Four years later a new law passed by the U.S. Congress gave a strong legislative boost to education services for youngsters with handicaps. Public Law 91–230 repealed the Title VI provision of ESEA and replaced it with the Education of the Handicapped Act. This law centralized all pre-

The concept of the least restrictive alternative means that children with handicaps are to be educated with nonhandicapped children to the extent possible. (Photo by Joseph Bodkin.)

vious legislation dealing with education of children with handicaps and administration of educational programs for such children.

The federal government passed Public Law 93–380, Title VI B—Education of the Handicapped Amendment—in 1973. Also called the **Mathias Amendment**, this piece of legislation focused on the one area that would be most likely to ensure state cooperation—the pocketbook. The law requires that, in order to retain eligibility to receive federal funds for the education of children with handicaps, a state must meet specific provisions.

Under P.L. 93–380, full educational opportunities for all children with handicaps and procedures for due process were made mandatory. Furthermore, the concept of **least restrictive alternative** was defined to mean that these children are to be educated with nonhandicapped children unless the nature and severity of the handicap are such that education in regular classes with the use of supplementary aids and services cannot be achieved satisfactorily. Finally, reflecting the ruling of the *Diana* case, P.L. 93–380 provided that

the evaluative materials used to classify and place children with handicaps could not be racially or culturally discriminatory.

Also passed in 1973 was P.L. 93–112, the Rehabilitation Act of 1973, which guarantees that people with handicaps must have the same access to facilities and programs as people without handicaps. Sections 503 and 504 of this act represent a civil rights statement for people with handicaps and prohibit discrimination against them. A state agency violating this prohibition can lose all federal education and rehabilitation funds intended for that agency. As a result, the last decade has witnessed many changes in physical facilities (ramps, curb cuts), as well as greater participation by persons with handicaps in travel, schooling, and public programs of many kinds. Because of P.L. 93–112, persons with sensory and physical disabilities are able to get around more easily and to take advantage of a variety of new opportunities.

The Rehabilitation Act of 1973 was amended by Congress when it passed the Rehabilitation Act Amendments of 1986 (P.L. 99–955). A major provision in this act called for transition serv-

BOX 1.3

COLLEGE STUDENTS WITH DISABILITIES

The enactment of the Rehabilitation Act of 1973 (P.L. 93–112) has resulted in greater participation by individuals with handicaps in all aspects of everyday life. An excellent example is the enrollment of students with handicaps into colleges and universities.

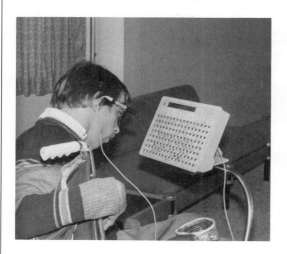

Ernie Eggers is a student at Kent State University in Kent, Ohio. He has cerebral palsy, but that hasn't prevented him from participating in the academic and daily activities of university life. Mr. Eggers enrolled at Kent State when he was twenty-six years old. This was a drastic change from the residential care facility in which he resided for ten years. Cerebral palsy does limit his abilities to maneuver and communicate; however, a powered wheelchair and an augmentative communication device help him achieve some measure of independence.

Utako Matsutani, who is blind, is a graduate student at Penn State. She is participating in a project involving the use of a voice synthesizer and special computer programs. This equipment enables her to hear what she has typed. Ms. Matsutani currently keeps the equipment in her dorm room so that she can type her class assignments and update her notes. She is able to take her own notes during class, thus eliminating the time-consuming task of transcribing them into Braille from tape recordings.

Sources: (*Left*) The college campus scene (1985, Fall). *Current Expressions*, p. 1. Information and photo courtesy of Prentke Romich Company.

(*Right*) Erb, C. (1986, October 23). Talking computer makes learning, working easier. *Centre Daily Times*, pp. 1, 8. Information, and photo by Steve Coon, courtesy of *Centre Daily Times*.

ices for youths with severe handicaps. This provision evolved out of concern for youths who were enrolled in existing special education programs but who were not being taught skills necessary for successful adjustment in employment, independent living, and recreational settings. The Rehabilitation Act Amendments call for the establishment of a transition plan for each student with a severe disability two years prior to completion of his/her formal education. This plan is the result of cooperative efforts between educators, parents, and adult service providers. The impact of this act is discussed in more detail in Chapter 13.

PUBLIC LAW 94–142

This brings us to the legislation that has had the greatest impact of all laws dealing with the handicapped. Public Law 94–142 (Education for All Handicapped Children Act of 1975) was the official recognition by the federal government that the more than 8,000,000 American children with handicaps had special educational needs that were not being fully met. Specifically, it stated that more than four million of them did not receive appropriate educational services and that one million of them were being excluded entirely from the public school system. The law placed responsibility for correcting these conditions in the hands of state and local agencies. The Office of Special Education and Rehabilitative Services, Department of Education, is the federal agency charged with implementing this law.

P.L. 94–142 stated further that many children with handicaps who were in public schools were not succeeding because their needs had gone undetected. Adequate resources, advanced teacher training, and improved diagnostic and instructional procedures, the law suggested, were the means by which states should remedy these inadequacies.

P.L. 94–142 aimed to assure that all children with handicaps have available a free, appropriate education and that their rights, as well as those of

their parents, be protected. It also established criteria by which to judge the effectiveness of efforts made to implement it. Finally, it provided financial and planning help for the states and localities in meeting these new standards.

Having been "passed in perpetuity" and by huge margins (404–7 in the House; 87–7 in the Senate), this act can be negated or repealed only by an act of Congress. Therefore, children with handicaps and their parents can be sure that their educational rights are finally guaranteed.

P.L. 94–142 was thus the culmination of litigation and legislation that began at least thirty years ago. In Table 1.1, you can review the major precursors that led to this milestone legislation. In Table 1.2, the major provisions within P.L. 94–142 are traced back to their origins in earlier litigation or legislation.

Definitions

A number of terms vital to the vocabulary of those who work with individuals who are handicapped were used in the P.L. 94–142 legislation. Most important was the "official" definition of **handicapped**: those children evaluated and diagnosed "as being mentally retarded, hard-of-hearing, deaf, speech impaired, visually handicapped, seriously emotionally disturbed, orthopedically impaired, other health impaired, deaf-blind, multihandicapped, or as having specific learning disabilities, who because of those impairments need special education and related services" (U.S. Office of Education, 1977a, p. 42478).

Special education is defined as "specially designed instruction, at no cost to the parent, to meet the unique needs of a handicapped child, including classroom instruction, instruction in physical education, home instruction, and instruction in hospitals and institutions" (U.S. Office of Education, 1977a, p. 42480). Transportation and such developmental, corrective, and other supportive services as are required to enable a child with a handicap to benefit from special education are considered **related services**. Also included as related services are speech pathology and audiol-

TABLE 1.1

LITIGATION AND LEGISLATION

Litigation

1. *Brown v. Board of Education of Topeka, Kansas, 347 U.S. 483 (1954)*
   It was alleged that separate educational facilities for black students violated their rights under the Fourteenth Amendment of the U.S. Constitution. The plaintiffs felt it was unlawful to discriminate against a class of persons for an arbitrary or unjustifiable reason.

2. *Diana v. [California] State Board of Education, C-70 37 PFR (1970)*
   Nine Mexican-American public school students ages eight through thirteen alleged that they had been inappropriately placed in classes for students with retardation on the basis of biased, standardized intelligence tests. The plaintiffs came from home environments in which Spanish was the only or predominant language spoken.

3. *Wyatt v. Aderholt, 334 F. Supp. 1341 (1971) (originally Wyatt v. Stickney)*
   It was alleged that the two Alabama state mental hospitals and a home for people with mental retardation involved in the case were grossly understaffed and that the programs of treatment and habilitation afforded the residents were extremely inadequate.

4. *PARC, Bowman et al. v. Commonwealth of Pennsylvania, 334 F. Supp. 279 (1971)*
   It was alleged that the retarded plaintiffs had been denied access to education and, furthermore, that the plaintiffs had been deprived of due process provided by the U.S. Constitution.

5. *Mills v. Board of Education of the District of Columbia, 348 F. Supp. 866 (1972)*
   A class action suit was filed in 1971 in the District of Columbia to compel the school board to provide appropriate education for students with mental retardation, physical handicaps, emotional disturbances, hyperactivity, and other handicaps.

6. *Stuart v. Nappi, 443 F. Supp. 1235 (D. Ct., 1978)*
   Plaintiffs argued that expulsion of a learning disabled youth with a history of learning difficulties constituted a denial of the right to an appropriate education.

7. *S-1 v. Turlington, No. 78-8020 (S.D. FL, 1979)*
   Seven students with mental retardation alleged that their misconduct was the result of their handicap and that subsequent expulsion by the school was a denial of their right to an appropriate education.

---

ogy, psychological services, physical and occupational therapy, recreation, early identification and assessment of disabilities in children, counseling services, and medical services for diagnostic or evaluation purposes. School health services, social-work services in schools, and parent counseling and training also fall into this category.

These services are available as a **free, appropriate public education (FAPE)**, which means they "are provided at public expense, under public supervision and direction, and without charge" (U.S. Office of Education, 1977a, p. 42478). The

FAPE provision also guarantees that these services meet standards of the state educational agency; include preschool, elementary, or secondary school education in the state involved; and be provided in conformity with an **individualized education program (IEP)**.

As suggested by the Rowley case, the P.L.94–142 definition of a free, appropriate public education is nebulous. R. D. Kneedler (1984) attempted to clarify this concept by describing seven essential features of a free, appropriate public education. They include:

8. *Board of Education* v. *Rowley, 458 U.S. 176 (1982)*
   Parents of a child with a profound hearing impairment filed suit alleging the school district's refusal to provide a sign language interpreter violated their daughter's right to a free, appropriate public education.

9. *Smith* v. *Robinson, 104 C. St. 3457 (1984)*
   Parents sought reimbursement of legal fees incurred during a lawsuit charging violation of their child's rights under P.L. 94–142.

10. *Irving Independent School District* v. *Tatro, 104 S. Ct. 3371 (1984)*
    Parents of a child born with spina bifida charged that clean intermittent catheterization was a supportive service necessary if their daughter was to benefit from special education.

11. *School District of Burlington, MA* v. *Department of Education of MA, 105 S. Ct. 1996 (1985)*
    The parents requested reimbursement for expenses incurred as the result of private school placement for their learning disabled son.

Legislation

1. *Public Law 88–164,* Mental Retardation Facilities and Community Mental Health Centers Act of 1963

2. *Public Law 89–10,* Elementary and Secondary Education Act of 1965—Title VI

3. *Public Law 91–230,* Elementary, Secondary, and Other Educational Amendments of 1969

4. *Public Law 93–380,* Title VI B—Education of the Handicapped Amendment (Mathias Amendment) of 1973

5. *Public Law 94–142,* Education for All Handicapped Children Act of 1975

6. *Public Law 98–410,* Education of Handicapped Act Amendment of 1983

7. *Public Law 99–955,* Rehabilitation Act Amendments of 1986

8. *Public Law 99–457,* Education of the Handicapped Act Amendments of 1986

9. *Public Law 99–372,* Handicapped Children's Protection Act of 1986

1. instruction that is specifically designed to meet the unique needs of a student with a handicap

2. instruction that is based upon an adequate evaluation of a child's needs

3. related services, if necessary

4. an IEP developed cooperatively by the educational agency and parents

5. services in accordance with the IEP

6. services reasonably calculated to enable the student to meet reasonable goals

7. an annual review of progress

Provisions in the Law

Individualized Education Program. Whereas FAPE guarantees the education will be paid for by the state, the IEP assures parents that education will indeed be specialized for each child. It re-

TABLE 1.2

EVOLUTION OF THE CONCEPTS OUTLINED IN PUBLIC LAW 94–142

Provisions	Litigation Evolved from	Legislation Originally Outlined in	Refined or New Concept in P.L. 94–142
Free, appropriate public education (FAPE)	*Brown* v. *Bd. of Ed.*, 1954 *PARC et al.* v. *Commonwealth of Pennsylvania*, 1971 *Mills* v. *Bd. of Ed. of D.C.*, 1972	P.L. 93–380	Refined: fuller definition
Right to education	*Brown* v. *Bd. of Ed.*, 1954 *PARC et al.* v. *Commonwealth of Pennsylvania*, 1971 *Mills* v. *Bd. of Ed. of D.C.*, 1972	P.L. 93–380	Refined: fuller definition, includes IEP
Definitions			
Handicapped	None	P.L. 93–380 (does not include categories deaf-blind, multihandicapped, or specific learning disabilities)	Refined: changes *crippled* to *orthopedically impaired* and adds deaf-blind, multihandicapped, and specific learning disabilities
Special education	None	None	New language
Related services	*PARC et al.* v. *Commonwealth of Pennsylvania*, 1971	None	New language
Individualized education program (IEP)	*PARC et al.* v. *Commonwealth of Pennsylvania*, 1971	None	New language
Procedural due process	*PARC et al.* v. *Commonwealth of Pennsylvania*, 1971 *Mills* v. *Bd. of Ed. of D.C.*, 1972	P.L. 93–380	Refined
Least restrictive alternative or least restrictive environment	*Wyatt* v. *Aderholt*, 1970 *PARC et al.* v. *Commonwealth of Pennsylvania*, 1971 *Mills* v. *Bd. of Ed. of D.C.*, 1972	P.L. 93–380	Refined
Nondiscriminatory testing	*Diana* v. *State Bd. of Ed. of California*, 1970	P.L. 93–380	Refined
Native language	*Diana* v. *State Bd. of Ed. of California*, 1970	P.L. 93–380 (provisions but no specific language)	Refined and new language
Confidentiality of information	None	Family Rights and Privacy Act of 1974 (Buckley Amendment)	Refined

quires that a statement specifying instructional goals and any special education and related services the child may need be written and reviewed annually by a team consisting of a school representative, the child's teacher, parent or parents, and the child, where appropriate. The IEP must include (1) the present educational levels of the child; (2) a statement of annual goals, including short-term instructional objectives; (3) a statement of specific services, if needed; (4) the programs to be followed; (5) the date when special services are to begin and the expected duration of these services; and (6) the tests and other requirements or information used to gauge the child's progress to determine if the instructional objectives are being met. The IEP must be developed in consultation with one or both parents who, if they are not satisfied with the IEP, may request a revision or a hearing by an impartial hearing officer.

Although the development of an IEP requires a great deal of effort and adds considerable work to the educator's workload, its establishment offers many advantages. Turnbull (1986) justifies its development on the following grounds:

1. It is a method for assessing a student and providing appropriate programming that potentially minimizes violations of due process and equal protection.

2. It enables teachers to better help a student develop his/her potential.

3. It facilitates monitoring of a student's progress.

4. It recognizes the individuality of each child.

5. It has the potential of strengthening a child's program because of the cooperative link between parents and educators.

Least Restrictive Environment. Successful implementation of an IEP assumes the existence of a variety of program settings that can be used to provide education for children with handicaps in the least restrictive environment. This provision of the law is sometimes referred to as mainstreaming and is often misunderstood. Nowhere in P.L.

94–142, or in the federal regulations, do the words *mainstream* and *mainstreaming* appear. Even *least restrictive environment* appears only in the regulations and not in the law itself. Although not all children with handicaps will be able to participate as fully in the mainstream of education as their nonhandicapped peers do, it is expected that many of these children can be moved from rather segregated settings into less isolated, or less restrictive, settings where they can interact more freely and in more normal ways with their peers. Serving the child in the least restrictive environment is the proper way of referring to the mainstreaming intent. It does not mean that *all* children with handicaps will be "dumped" into the regular classrooms of our public schools, as some have feared. But it does mean that many of these children who are able to function there will be integrated into regular classes.

Nondiscriminatory Testing. Public Law 94–142 also incorporated the nondiscriminatory testing concept of the Mathias Amendment. It stated specifically that (1) in all direct contact with the child (including evaluation), communication would be in the language normally used by the child, and not that of the parents (if there is a difference between the two) and (2) if a person is deaf or blind, or has no written language, the mode of communication would be that normally used by the person (such as sign language, braille, or oral communication).

Confidentiality. In addition, the law recognized the right of children with handicaps and their parents to *confidentiality of information and record keeping*. It clearly outlined procedures for (1) notifying parents about state or local programs set up to identify, locate, or evaluate children with handicaps; (2) inspecting and reviewing any educational records relating to their children; (3) amending records if information in them is inaccurate or misleading or violates the privacy or other rights of the child; and (4) requesting a hearing to challenge the accuracy of such records. To assure this confidentiality, the act provides for one official in each agency, school, or institution to train and instruct those persons responsible for storage of information.

Prior to this act, the privacy rights of the general student population were legislated by the **Buckley Amendment** (Family Rights and Privacy Act of 1974), which resulted from growing evidence that students' records were being misused across the nation. The amendment outlined three types of confidential record keeping to protect the rights of the student. Type A includes basic information the school needs in order to classify the student. Type B includes information necessary for the safety of the child, such as pharmacological data (in other words, data not relevant to the planning of an educational program). Information potentially useful but whose accuracy or completeness has not been verified is Type C; when verified, this information must be moved to Type B or destroyed. For example, a note from a teacher to a psychologist stating that the teacher *believes* a child to be emotionally disturbed is Type C information. Similarly, a newspaper clipping announcing a student's arrest for vandalism is potentially useful but is Type C information until the student is convicted or cleared. If the student is cleared, the original clipping should be removed from the file.

Public Law 94–142 requires that children be tested in their native language. In some cases, it may be necessary to use sign language, as illustrated here. (Courtesy of Public Information, The Pennsylvania State University.)

Due Process. Certain rights of parents are also guaranteed by P.L. 94–142 and other recent legislation and court decisions. Parents have a right to have their child evaluated and to be informed of the results of the evaluation. Parents must be consulted about the child's educational program prior to its implementation, and they have the right to have the program reviewed periodically to assess its success.

If the situation arises in which parents disagree with the school's evaluation or program, the parents have the right to an impartial due process hearing to decide the matter. In other words, parents have the right to expect that due process will be followed throughout the screening, assessment, and programming phases of their child's case. Most importantly, parents have the right to be kept continually and accurately informed by

the school about what is happening to their child, and they have the right to an impartial hearing if they think these rights have been violated or if they disagree with the decisions made about their child.

An impartial, due process hearing is not a part of civil or criminal court proceedings. Rather, it is set up by the state department of education. In this hearing, parents have the right to be represented by a lawyer, to give evidence, to cross-examine, and to receive a written transcript of the hearing and a written decision about the disposition of the case. An impartial hearing officer, appointed by the state education agency, conducts the hearing and renders a decision. Such a decision may favor the school or the parents, or it may represent a compromise. Parents or schools may

BOX 1.4

PUBLIC LAW 94–142 VOCABULARY: IMPORTANT CONCEPTS EMANATING
FROM THE EDUCATION FOR ALL HANDICAPPED CHILDREN ACT OF 1975

- Access
- Confidentiality
- Due process
- Education for All Handicapped Children Act
- Extended school year (ESY)
- Free, appropriate public education (FAPE)
- Handicapped
- Individualized educational program (IEP)

- Least restrictive environment
- Mainstreaming
- Nondiscriminatory testing
- Paren participation
- Regression/recoupment
- Related services
- Right to education
- Special education

appeal such decisions to the head of the state education agency. If satisfaction is not achieved through this appeal process, the next step is to take the case to the civil courts.

Amendments to P.L. 94–142

Since it was enacted in 1975, P.L. 94–142 has been amended twice—in 1984 (P.L. 98–410) and in 1986 (P.L. 99–457). The more recent amendments have focused on the availability of services for young children with handicaps and their families. Previously, local and state education agencies were required to provide educational programs for young children with handicaps who were between three and five years of age only if these agencies offered such programming to nonhandicapped children in this age group. The new law stipulates that all eligible children between the ages of three and five years must receive services by 1990. Each three- to five-year-old child served under this program has the same rights and protections afforded to school-age children. In addition, P.L. 99–457 includes an initiative that assists state and local agencies in the development and implementation of comprehensive programs for infants through two. The impact of these amendments upon young children with handicaps and their families is discussed in greater detail in Chapter 12. *131,746*

CONCERNS ABOUT MAINSTREAMING

Often when a new law is passed or a new idea receives a lot of publicity, a backlash sets in. So it is with mainstreaming. The definitions, understandings, and applications of the term vary so much that some persons have rebelled against the very notion. Special teachers are concerned with the amount of time required to prepare individualized education plans for children with handicaps, meet with their parents, hold conferences with other teachers, and so on.

Cost. A very significant concern of school administrators and taxpayers is the cost of educating children in the least restrictive environment. It is much more costly to educate severely handicapped youngsters than it is to exclude them from school. The average cost of educating children with handicaps is approximately double that of educating nonhandicapped children. The cost of transporting these youngsters from their homes to special facilities is enormous when viewed from a national perspective. Millions of dollars have been spent in retraining special teachers to work with children who are seriously handicapped and to help regular educators cope with students who are mildly handicapped. The total state, local, and federal funds spent in the decade following the enactment of P.L. 94–142 in 1975 are in excess of 40 billion dollars.

Concerns of Parents. Some parents are adamantly opposed to educating youngsters with handicaps in the same classroom as nonhandicapped youngsters. The parents of the nonhandicapped believe that their children might be shortchanged—that teachers would be forced to spend an inordinate amount of time with the handicapped to the detriment of the nonhandicapped. And some parents of children with handicaps believe that their children could not get the individual attention in regular classes that they would get in smaller special classes serving only these children.

Concerns of Regular Educators. We have spoken with numerous regular teachers who fear that they will be deluged with children who are severely retarded or physically handicapped. They fear that mainstreaming means that most, if not all, such youngsters will be returned to or placed in regular classes. A chemistry teacher asks, "How can I teach the chemistry lab if I have to worry about a child with cerebral palsy? How can such a child be expected to use the apparatus? What is my legal liability if a handicapped child is injured in my class?"

Other regular teachers feel that they are already overtaxed with the so-called nonhandicapped and that the placement of youngsters, even those with mild handicaps, in their classes will prevent them from doing an adequate teaching job with any youngsters.

One of the chief fears of regular educators is that of being forced to absorb antagonistic, disturbed youngsters in regular classes. Discipline is always a problem (especially at the junior high level, it seems), without the added difficulty of coping with a youngster's behavior problem.

The concerns of regular educators are valid, to a great extent. Indeed, teachers' reactions were so varied that the American Federation of Teachers (AFT) drew up guidelines for implementing the law at the local level (Rauth, 1981). These guidelines were similar to those adopted by the Council for Exceptional Children in their call for a recognized continuum of educational settings and their recognition of the need for related and supportive services. Also stressed in the guidelines was the importance of initial and continuing training for both regular and special education personnel who work with children and youths with disabilities.

In addition, a better understanding of the least restrictive environment and mainstreaming may allay some of the fears. Clearly, there never was any intent to "dump" all children with handicaps back into regular classes. Although many children with mild handicaps *will* be spending more time with their peers in regular classes, the law requires that proper training be given to all professionals involved and that related services be made available to the children as required. Assistance for regular educators may come from special aides assigned to work with children with handicaps, or it may come from additional special services that have not been available in the past. Many special training programs continue to be available to help regular educators become more comfortable working with children with handicaps and to provide the necessary teaching and management skills.

Reverse Mainstreaming. A different kind of backlash, a very positive one, is also starting to be seen. *Reverse mainstreaming,* as it is known, apparently was developed by a special class teacher, on her own, without benefit of a large federal grant. In this program, elementary-age, nonhandicapped students come into a special class of severely and profoundly retarded youngsters on their own time to play with the retarded youngsters and to help them acquire social and self-help skills (Poorman, 1980). The response to the program has been so overwhelming that the teacher, Mrs. Christine Poorman, who teaches in the State College, Pennsylvania, Area School District, has established a brief training program for regular teachers and nonhandicapped children to give them certain kinds of background information about the children who are retarded. The nonretarded children are scheduled for certain periods of the day and actually participate in the educational program for the children in the special class. The result is much greater acceptance of children with handicaps by the regular school population and a better educational program for all.

Regular Education Initiative. The federal government and many leaders in special education have called for a Regular Education Initiative to create fundamental changes in education provided for students, particularly those with mild to moderate disabilities (Lilly, 1986; Wang, Reynolds, & Walberg, 1986; Will, 1986). This initiative is based on the premise that the removal of students from regular settings into special settings for services has failed to meet their educational needs (TED Executive Committee, 1986). Supporters of the initiative contend these students can be effectively taught in regular education programs with a variety of support services. The first part of the initiative calls for the use of strategies that promote systematic and organized integration in the regular classroom and that prevent identification of a student as handicapped. The second part provides limited time waivers of certain rules and regulations for both federal and state authorities. These waivers allow selected state and local agencies to implement these strategies on a trial basis. The federal government has made several million dollars available to test the effectiveness of the Regular Education Initiative. Most likely it will be several years before the most effective practices emerge from this initiative and become part of the regular education programs in the nation's schools.

HOW FAR HAVE WE COME?

This chapter has traced the litigative and legislative history of the rights of children with disabilities over the last quarter-century. Humanistic forces at the heart of recent laws and court actions—deinstitutionalization and normalization—were described.

You might be ready to conclude, to paraphrase the popular ad, that "we've come a long way baby,"

and you are certainly correct. However, these excerpts from a letter to the governor of Massachusetts, written in 1857 by Samuel G. Howe, a surgeon and humanitarian, are worth noting. Howe was writing to protest the governor's veto of a bill that would have increased the number of state beneficiaries at the School for Idiotic Children.

Boston, June 30, 1857

In one sense, Public Charitable Institutions, like all prisons and other penal establishments, are evils; and are maintained only to avoid greater ones.

Being called upon lately to give advice about the establishment of Institutions for the Blind and the Deaf Mutes in a new State, I have counselled a course, different from the one I, myself, followed many years ago. It is to dispense with any great costly building, having common dormitories, dining-rooms, chapel, and the like. To make no preparation for any great common household at all; but to build a simple building, with all the conveniences for instructing classes, and make provision for boarding the pupils in private families. In a word, to reduce the Institution, as we would any machine, to the simplest possible form. . . .

I would advise modification of several of our public Institutions; curtailment of operation in some cases, and total discontinuance of the establishment in others.

(Howe, 1857, in Kirk & Lord, 1974, p. 5)

A century and a quarter later, B. Nirje was saying the same thing—evidence, unfortunately, that in the last hundred years we have not made the gains that might have been desirable. In a 1976 report by the President's Committee on Mental Retardation, Nirje made a plea, much like Samuel G. Howe's 1857 proposal, for the elimination of large residential institutions for individuals with retardation and for the establishment of small group homes:

If retarded persons cannot or should not any longer live in their family or own home, the

BOX 1.5

PROJECT SPECIAL FRIEND

"Reach for it, Johnny, reach for it," said two sixth graders at Lemont elementary school, as they dangled a graham cracker morsel just above the supine youngster who wanted the cracker badly enough to stretch a thin arm for it.

That was hard for Johnny, a profoundly mentally retarded child who can't sit, stand, walk or talk. Although not many years ago he would have been left alone to vegetate, he is now being taught to reach and grasp, to feed himself, to be more alert.

Helping him and his classmates learn are boys and girls from regular classes in the school building, who have volunteered to be part of "Project Special Friend," a program devised by Christine Poorman, teacher of the special class.

"It's mainstreaming in reverse, and may be a break-through in education," says Mrs. Poorman.

Mainstreaming involves educating handicapped children with normal children so far as is possible. Strongly advocated by educators these days, mainstreaming could never work for her students, Mrs. Poorman decided early this school year. With their differing and very basic needs, they are severely and profoundly retarded, and could never be candidates for the regular classroom, she decided.

To solve the problem, she brought the regular classes to her students. This was done after consultation with Jack Bailey, her supervisor from the Central Intermediate Unit, which sponsors the class; Carl Morris, building principal; other teachers in the building; and finally, the building's students.

"We wanted to help children become aware of all kinds of differences in other children and to accept those differences," she said. "We also hoped to squelch the fears and myths which surround special children."

It's working, according to Lettie Houtz, a sixth grade teacher in the building. "There's such an attitude change," she said. "Nobody really knew or understood what the children's problems were, and there was some fear of them (because they're 'different').

"Now my students no longer call it 'that room,' and when they see some of the special children they no longer avoid them. Instead, they call out 'Hi,' and talk to the children. It's a very positive reaction."

Another teacher, Mark King, agreed. "My kids enjoy going to help, and some even miss recess to go. And they come back all excited about helping."

The response is good, says Mr. Morris. "It's very stimulating," he said. "How quickly the helping children pick up the professional vocabulary describing their activities—for instance, they come back to the classroom talking about 'visual motor skills.'"

"It's been a super experience. Our kids have really perked up," said Mr. Bailey. "Those helpers are really a super bunch of kids."

The students themselves say it's fun. "A real fun experience," one said. "You learn a lot while you watch them learn. It's really worthwhile."

"It's fun to work with people who don't make you feel inferior," said another student. Others said, "It's sad and kind of scary, but once you get to know them it's ok. . . . I felt kind of funny at first but I feel better now. . . . They'll have a lot more friends now. We're willing to be friends."

"They help you as they show what they can do. . . . It's good to get to help them learn to do things that are easy for you but hard for them . . . you can see the different problems they have and see the different ways they can communicate."

"It's neat."

The project started with only a few students volunteering to help the special children. But interest mounted as the helpers returned to their classrooms and shared experiences. Now 83 regular

Source: *Centre Daily Times*, State College, Pa., March 1979. Written by Alice Kountz. Reprinted by permission.

students take turns participating in the program. "We don't have enough time slots to accommodate everyone," says Mrs. Poorman.

"We usually have five or six helpers for three half-hour periods every school day, averaging about 15 helpers per day," she said. "Some of the helpers give up their free time (recess) to work with our children."

It takes a lot of work and planning on the teacher's part, Mrs. Poorman emphasized. "We not only plan for our children and the continuous changing of three groups, but we plan for the ability of the individual children to work with each child in our room.

"But the progress seen not only by us but by others makes it all worthwhile," she said. As one observer commented, "It looks like a busy little factory with so much learning going on."

Factory it is. While two boys are working with Johnny, encouraging reaching and grasping, others are helping Eric learn to play ball, two more are encouraging Mary Beth to follow directions ("Put it down, Mary Beth," after she'd had a sip of water from a cup), and another team is timing Jeffrey while he puts a puzzle together.

"We think it's most important to utilize the vitality, ingenuity and special willingness of the students here at Lemont to benefit their special friends," Mrs. Poorman said. "That energy and willingness to accept and help are there, just waiting to be used."

Before the program started, teachers felt that it might be too upsetting for the special children and might be impossible to organize. They also feared that the student helpers would participate only out of curiosity and would lose interest, using the project only to get out of going to classes.

"Instead, we've found an increase in interest as the months go on," Mrs. Poorman said. "There's a

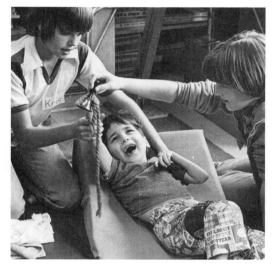

Project Special Friend. (Photo by Thelma Robinson. Courtesy of *Centre Daily Times.*)

true concern about what and how much our students are learning.

"Each helper is striving to get his special friend to learn something new from him—and not only to complete a task, but to complete it correctly.

"And to top it off, we see a definite sign of progress in our (special) children, who are developing social awareness."

homes provided should be of normal size and situated in normal residential areas, being neither isolated nor larger than is consistent with regular mutually respectful or disinterested social interaction and integration.

(Nirje, 1976, p. 174)

What will our great-grandchildren be saying about this topic?

SUMMARY

From the early 1800s to the present day, groups of concerned parents and others have lamented and protested the sometimes inhumane treatment received in large institutions by people labeled as retarded and insane. Through the outspoken efforts of humanists like Dorothea Dix and Samuel Gridley Howe, and later, through the work of parent groups such as the National Association for Retarded Citizens and the National Association for Children with Learning Disabilities, the public at large became more informed about the needs of children and adults with handicaps.

Eventually, provision of care and education for *all* citizens with handicaps became a legal issue. It could be said that the 1960s were the years of rapid growth in the strength of parent groups. The 1970s was the decade of the lawyers. The efforts of professional groups and parents' groups, combined with the work of lawyers, turned the issue of appropriate care and education of individuals with handicaps into a civil rights issue. A look back at the 1970s reveals a remarkable series of lawsuits (litigation) and laws (legislation) that have forever changed the way the United States deals with children and adults who are disabled. In essence, it is now the law of the land that all persons, regardless of the type or severity of their handicap, must be given access to appropriate education, housing, transportation, and jobs. It is against the law to deny any person such access simply on the basis of handicap.

Individuals with disabilities and their advocates argue that everyone should be permitted to grow up and live in as normal and unrestrictive an environment as possible. They should be permitted freedom of choice of housing, jobs, and education, with no more constraints than are placed on nonhandicapped persons. This concept, called normalization, was borrowed in part from the Scandinavian countries and popularized here by advocates such as Nirje and Wolfensberger.

Normalization in education was given the force of law with the passage of Public Law 94–142, the Education for All Handicapped Children Act of 1975. This law guarantees that all children with handicaps are entitled to a free, appropriate public education, that such an education will be individually prescribed, and that they will be educated in as normal and unrestrictive an environment as possible. Furthermore, the type or severity of handicap cannot be used as an excuse to deny access to education; *all* children, even those with profound mental retardation and severe physical handicaps, can and should benefit from an education or training program geared to their needs.

The least restrictive environment concept has been popularized under the term *mainstreaming*. This term is often misunderstood. Some people fear that it means the wholesale return of all children with handicaps to the regular classroom and the expectation that regular teachers will teach all children without any extra help or training. That is neither the intent nor the result of the law. The law requires only that youngsters with handicaps be educated with normal youngsters to the extent possible and in the environment or setting that places the least restriction on their education and normalization.

Suggestions for Further Reading

Abeson, A., Bolick, N., & Hass, J. (1975). *A primer on due process.* Reston, VA: Council for Exceptional Children. This paperback is brief and to the point, covering the intricacies of due process and legal issues in lay terms.

Bilken, D., Bogdan, R., Ferguson, D., Searl, S., & Taylor, S. (1985). *Achieving the complete school: Strategies for effective mainstreaming.* New York: Teachers College Press. This text describes practical issues arising from the placement of students with disabilities into regular school programs.

Blatt, B., & Kaplan, F. (1966). *Christmas in purgatory: A photographic essay on mental retardation.* Boston: Allyn and Bacon.

If you ever need to be convinced that "man's inhumanity to man" is more than a catch phrase, this book will do it. In grim detail, it shows the conditions under which retarded individuals were forced to exist as "residents" in large institutions, even as late as the 1950s and 1960s.

Department of Health and Human Services. (1981). *Your rights as a disabled person.* Department of Health and Human Services.

Individuals who are disabled or who are the parents or guardians of a person with a disability will find this pamphlet very informative. It describes the rights guaranteed by law to people with disabilities.

Meisel, C. J. (1986). *Mainstreaming handicapped children— Outcomes, controversies and new directions.* Hillsdale, NJ: Lawrence Erlbaum.

This book presents an overview of issues and attitudes surrounding the concept of mainstreaming.

Public Law 94–142 (Education for All Handicapped Children Act of 1975); and regulations for its implementation.

You would expect a federal law to be pretty dull reading, and you would be right in most cases. Parts of P.L. 94–142 are fascinating, however, and written in a language easily understood even if you are not a senator or a lawyer. You can obtain a copy of the law and the regulations for implementing it by writing to your U.S. senator or congressperson. (The regulations were published in the *Federal Register* on August 23, 1977.)

Rosen, M., Clark, G., & Kivitz, M. S. (Eds.). (1975). *The history of mental retardation: Collected papers* (Vols. I & II). Baltimore, MD: University Park Press.

Scheerenberger, R. (1982). Treatment from ancient times to the present. In P. Cegelka & H. Prehm (Eds.), *Mental retardation: From categories to people.* Columbus, OH: Merrill.

An overview of education and treatment programs with emphasis on shifting treatment philosophies.

Shore, K. (1986). *The special educator's handbook: A comprehensive guide for parents and educators.* New York: Teachers College.

A comprehensive easy-to-read guide to the provisions of P.L. 94–142.

Shrybman, J. (1982). *Due process in special education.* Gaithersburg, MD: Aspen Systems.

Description of all phases of due process hearings, including roles and responsibilities of all participants.

Turnbull, H. R. (1986). *Free appropriate public education: The law and children with disabilities.* Denver, CO: Love.

Description of the current legal status of right to education for students with handicaps. All relevant court cases and laws through 1984 are reviewed.

Warfield, G. J. (Ed.). (1974). *Mainstream currents: Reprints from exceptional children 1968–1974.* Reston, VA: Council for Exceptional Children.

Numerous reports and essays preceded the passage of the so-called mainstreaming law, P.L. 94–142. This series of reprints captures the flavor of the debates and reproduces classic articles on many issues related to free, appropriate education for handicapped children.

Ysseldyke, J., & Algozzine, B. (1982). *Critical issues in special and remedial education.* Boston: Houghton Mifflin.

"A straightforward, objective analysis of the major conceptual and practical issues that face professionals involved in special and remedial education" (p. vii).

Relevant Journals

Exceptional Children

This bi-monthly journal is published by the Council for Exceptional Children and includes reviews and empirical reports regarding major issues and trends in special education.

The Journal of Law and Education

The Jefferson Law Book Company publishes this journal, which provides descriptions and analyses of recent litigation and legislation.

CHAPTER 2

Human Services and Placements

Did You Know That . . .

- one of the highest costs of educating children with handicaps is providing transportation?

- if the parents of a child with a handicap and the public school agree, the school may pay all the costs (including transportation) to send the child to a private school?

- children with disabilities are educated in a variety of settings, not just special classes?

- for some children with disabilities, the least restrictive education environment may be a full-time residential program, but for others the best placement may be in a regular class?

- public schools often work closely with state agencies such as vocational rehabilitation to provide uninterrupted service for persons with handicaps?

- special education teachers are often part of child-study teams, along with social workers, physicians, psychologists, speech therapists, recreation specialists, and others?

C

hapter 1 stressed that children with handicaps are entitled by law to a free, appropriate public education in the least restrictive environment. No single type of environment or setting is appropriate, however, for all children with handicaps. Rather, laws and good education practice dictate that a range of placements or settings must be available for these children. The first part of this chapter explains how the concept of the least restrictive environment is actually implemented. It describes the predominant settings and types of programs that have been developed for children with handicaps.

The second part of the chapter extends the concept of least restrictive environment to non-school services for persons with a variety of problems. Just as schooling for children should be flexible and unrestrictive, so should provision of services be flexible and easy to find and use. As you will see, although many services are available to help children and adults with disabilities, all too often those services are inflexible or poorly coordinated.

EDUCATIONAL PROGRAMS AND PLACEMENTS

Cascade of Services

There are many ways to describe educational placements and least restrictive environments. The most popular scheme for the range of placements that should be available for children with handicaps was outlined by Maynard Reynolds (1962). Evelyn Deno (1970) expanded upon Reynolds' idea and referred to the framework as "The Cascade System of Special Education Service." Both Reynolds and Deno suggested that the best way to assure appropriate placements for children with handicaps is to provide a continuum of services ranging from complete regular class attendance to total instruction in a residential or hospital setting. Teachers, parents, and administrators have embraced this concept; indeed, it is regarded as standard in most parts of the country.

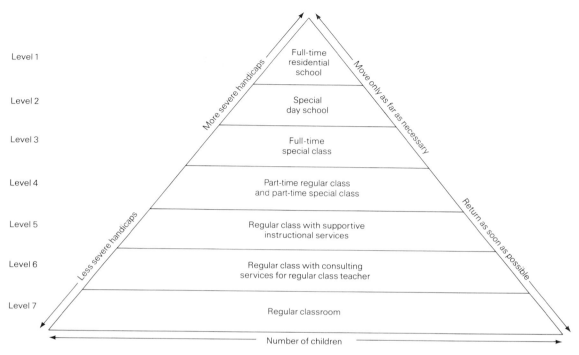

Figure 2.1. Cascade of Special Education Services. (Adapted from E. Deno, "Special Education as Developmental Capital," *Exceptional Children,* 1970, *37,* p. 235; and M. C. Reynolds, "A Framework for Considering Some Issues in Special Education," *Exceptional Children,* 1962, *28,* p. 368. By permission of The Council for Exceptional Children.)

The Cascade continuum predates P.L. 94–142, but the work of Reynolds, Deno, and numerous others (e.g., Dunn, 1968; Lilly, 1970, 1971) anticipated and helped lay the groundwork for that important law. An adaptation of Deno and Reynolds' Cascade is shown in Figure 2.1. The **Cascade model** suggests three things:

1. A variety of educational alternatives should be available to youngsters with handicaps.

2. Relatively more youngsters are appropriately placed in least restricted environments (e.g., regular classes, part-time special classes).

3. Youngsters should be able to move freely between levels, with the greatest emphasis placed on moving them into less restricted environments.

The Cascade model (as adapted) presents seven levels on the continuum of special education services. The varying widths of the levels signify the proportion of children to be served in each level—more children should be served in the lower levels (5–7) than in the upper levels (1–4). The idea of the Cascade is that children with handicaps should naturally gravitate down the Cascade of Services to the level (environment) that is most appropriate and least restrictive. The natural flow should be from the more restrictive environments, like institutional schools and full-time, special day schools, toward the least restrictive settings, like the regular class.

The Cascade model is more than a model or theory; it is a system that is actually used to help school personnel make the best placements for children who are handicapped. In practice, terminology varies from state to state or district to district, and gradations in placement criteria might permit a child to be placed in one level of the Cascade in one state and in another level in another state, at least initially. In general, though, the field of education has embraced the concept of the Cascade model. As an example of the model's acceptance, consider a study by R. L. Peterson and colleagues (1983), who found that, in spite of some overlap in the levels, the model has become a "basic feature of special education" (p. 404).

The following sections describe the most frequent placements for children with handicaps according to the Cascade continuum.

Full-Time Residential School

The most restrictive placement is a full-time residential school. This type of placement was much more common in the first half of the century. Today, only the most severely handicapped youngsters live and go to school in an institutional, residential setting.

When we think of a residential school, we typically envision an institution for youngsters, often even infants, who are severely mentally retarded or mentally ill. Also included in this category would be residential schools for students who are deaf. Many educators in the area of deafness believe that the child who is severely or profoundly hearing impaired is best placed with other youngsters who are similarly impaired. This facilitates the creation and maintenance of a twenty-four-hour environment geared to language stimulation.

For some youngsters, full-time residential placement is the best alternative. However, the concept of full-time residential placement has changed substantially in the last ten years. No longer is it considered a good practice to place a youngster in an institution with two thousand other people in a functional but impersonal facility on a few acres of ground. Rather, full-time residential placement at its best is a small, home-like situation with as few as four and up to perhaps a dozen individuals residing in a house in a conventional residential neighborhood. For most

Some students with handicaps are appropriately educated in residential schools where their needs can best be met. (Photo by J. A. Bensel. Courtesy of the Maryland School for the Blind.)

individuals with moderate or severe retardation who do not have serious medical problems, a group home is preferable to the traditional institutional setting. In those cases where the individual's health or physical condition dictate it, a hospital environment may be necessary. Also, a more restrictive environment may be necessary for an individual whose behavior is self-destructive or overly aggressive, in order to maintain the safety of both the individual and others. In either case, society must provide the education appropriate to those individuals. In fact, the law requires it.

Special Day School

The second most restrictive educational environment is a full-time special day school. During the late 1950s and early 1960s, it was felt that a logical

BOX 2.1

CASE STUDY: SAMUEL

Samuel, age sixteen, has an IQ of approximately 30. He has slight cerebral palsy, which causes him to walk with a jerky motion, but he can get around on his own and is able to feed himself with some difficulty. Samuel lives in a group home with five other moderately and severely retarded teenage boys. The group home is staffed with a full-time housemother and housefather who are relieved by weekend houseparents. In addition, other staff members are available at various times throughout the week to assist in bathing, feeding, and recreation. Monday through Friday the boys are transported by the public school bus to a regular public school building, where they are a part of the special class. Although these youngsters do require a great deal of individual attention and care and are living in a residential institution of sorts, their best education placement is not an institutional school; it is a program provided within the public schools.

BOX 2.2

CASE STUDY: WILLIAM

William is fifteen years old and has an IQ of approximately 30. He lives in a state institution for the mentally retarded. At one time, this institution housed some 2,200 residents; now the total residential population is down to about 400 individuals. Those who remain are the most seriously handicapped residents. Although William has some receptive communication skills (that is, he can understand a few words such as *William* and *juice*), he has such serious physical handicaps that he is unable to care for any of his bodily needs. Furthermore, he was born with a cleft lip and cleft palate and is prone to upper respiratory problems. His physical health is frail, and he is on medication virtually all the time. His case is such that he requires full-time medical care as well as care for his other needs. William's best placement is in the school attached to the institution. His school program focuses on communication, especially helping him acquire some means of expressing his needs.

extension of the special class was a special school. Some school districts established centers for learners with handicaps. The reasoning was simple and straightforward: If individuals with handicaps were grouped together in the special school, that school could be designed and equipped to be more applicable to their needs. This would be especially true for youngsters with physical handicaps and for those with vision and hearing problems. In the late 1970s, though, there was a movement away from separate schools. In fact, many states have now prohibited this practice. Again, however, some educators argue that an educational program should include a total milieu enhancing either language or mobility and communication.

For some youngsters, especially those with serious physical disabilities, the special school may, indeed, be the most appropriate and least restrictive environment. For others, however,

When necessary, children with handicaps are educated in special classes in special or regular schools. (Courtesy of Easter Seal Society for Crippled Children and Adults of Pennsylvania.)

such as children with moderately severe behavior problems, the value of a special school is questionable. In cases where the special school is warranted, it is likely that youngsters from several different neighborhoods or even different school districts may be brought together with special transportation arrangements. Such travel across district lines can mean a much longer school day, and thus the possibility of fatigue attributable to travel and the longer hours must be considered when a special school placement is contemplated for youngsters with handicaps. Although the cost of modifying regular classroom buildings might be high, the current practice is to modify existing neighborhood schools to accommodate children who are physically handicapped, blind, hearing impaired, or severely retarded and to include these children in special classes in regular schools. Thus, full-time day schools are becoming increasingly less common as the placement of youngsters in regular schools becomes more widespread.

Full-Time Special Class

By far the most popular style of educating children with mild and moderate handicaps has been the full-time special class. In this environment, youngsters spend their entire school day in the classroom with a single special education teacher who is responsible for all aspects of the education program, including lunch in some cases. During the 1950s and 1960s, the number of special classes in the public schools in the nation increased dramatically. School districts were often judged not by the quality of their programs but by the number of special classes they established.

The assumption behind special classes was that the homogeneity in grouping was of substantial educational benefit. In fact, no solid evidence supported the contention that youngsters who were mildly or moderately handicapped were best educated in special class situations. In a classic essay published in 1968, Lloyd Dunn, a leader in

BOX 2.3

*SEVERELY RETARDED YOUNGSTERS IN A REGULAR
JUNIOR HIGH SCHOOL*

One of the authors has visited a junior high school in a large metropolitan area that is noted for its strong academic program. On the first floor of this school is a special class for individuals who are severely retarded. There are seven youngsters enrolled in this program. The youngsters have measured IQs in the 20s. Two of the seven do not have adequate control of bowel and bladder functions. Two are severely handicapped physically and are confined to wheelchairs. None of them can read, although two can identify boys' and girls' bathrooms. The education program for these youngsters consists almost entirely of self-care and social skills. For most of the day, they are in a two-room suite that is set up much like a home, with furniture and a kitchen area.

The youngsters do go to the regular lunchroom for their meals, although they need assistance with the trays. Also, they are part of the school routine at functions such as assembly programs, special meetings, presentations, and the like. Two of the youngsters attend a music class, and all receive physical education adapted to their individual needs. Thus, although the youngsters are separated for academic programs, there have been serious attempts to help them become a part of the school in other ways. The nonspecial students in this school have accepted the special youngsters after an initial period of curiosity and even some mild teasing.

special education for the last thirty years, critically examined this practice. As a result of his questioning and critiques by a great many other people involved in working with children with handicaps, the education profession began to question seriously the practice of providing full-time special classes for so many youngsters. The Dunn article proved to be the harbinger of the mainstreaming movement, as the philosophy of isolating youngsters with mild handicaps for educational purposes has come under serious discussion.

Although the absolute number of special classes for youngsters with handicaps probably has not changed significantly in the last few years, the characteristics of the youngsters in those classes have changed. You will note on the Cascade model in Figure 2.1 that one of the arrows pointing from top to bottom suggests that youngsters should be moved down into the less restrictive environment as rapidly as possible. That

concept has begun to be realized. Whereas in the past, even youngsters with mild retardation were placed in special classes, the trend now is to move such youngsters into a less restrictive environment such as a part-time special class or a regular class with supportive services and to move youngsters who formerly would have been enrolled in special day schools or institutions into the full-time special classes. Even youngsters who are profoundly retarded and nonambulatory have now taken their places in full-time special classes in regular public schools.

Today, youngsters enrolled in full-time special classes have much greater interaction with regular class youngsters than in past years. It is much more common for special class youngsters—even those with severe handicaps—to be integrated with non–special class youngsters in lunchroom, recreation, and other nonacademic activities. Special class youngsters with mild or moderate physical handicaps can be integrated into the regular

Prevention of disabilities, as shown by the use of safety glasses, is as important as the provision of special services. (Courtesy of the National Society to Prevent Blindness.)

This youngster spends part of his day in a regular class. The special education teacher helps him keep track of his assignments. (Photo by Joseph Bodkin.)

school environment more fully than can those with severe physical handicaps. Those capable of competing in nonacademic settings are involved to the extent possible in physical education, art and music, shop, and other activities.

Part-Time Regular Class

At this point in the continuum of the Cascade of Services (Figure 2.1), the distinction between the various levels becomes somewhat hazy. Levels 4, 5, and 6 of the Cascade provide increasing flexibility and increasing amounts of interaction with the regular class environment. Level 4—part-time special class and part-time regular class—is designed for youngsters who have special problems but who can benefit from a substantial number of regular education services. For example, children with visual impairments may spend much of the day in regular classes, with a portion of their day

spent in a special class with other children who are blind. The special class component would be devoted to such activities as training in braille reading or use of reading devices such as the Optacon or Kurzweil Reading Machine and in mobility training (skills required to move about the home and school community). Youngsters who are mildly retarded may be assigned to a regular homeroom and attend many nonacademic school activities with their regular class peers but go to a special class for their academic subjects.

Regular Class with Supportive Instructional Services

During the 1960s, the resource room concept became popular for youngsters with learning disabilities. Such youngsters often have difficulty in one or more academic subjects but can function effectively in other aspects of the school curricu-

A consulting teacher helps the regular class teacher solve problems presented by handicapped children enrolled in regular classes. (Photo by Joseph Bodkin.)

lum. Resource rooms were developed to assist them in improving reading or mathematics skills or to provide them with additional help with assignments given in regular classes. The resource room concept has also been used with children who are visually or hearing impaired. Some resource rooms are set up so that children with visual impairments can dictate their homework or can have readers read the class assignments for them.

Generally, the resource room is for academic support. In some cases, however, it is used as a way of releasing youngsters with behavior problems from tension that may build up during the day. In the resource room, they can work with very small groups or on an individual basis with a teacher or an aide.

Regular Class Placement with Consulting Services for Regular Teachers

The function of some special educators is consulting with regular class teachers. For some youngsters who have mild behavior or learning problems, no instructional services are provided outside the regular class, but certain modifications in their programs are carried out by the regular classroom teachers. Ideally, consultation for these teachers is provided by consulting teachers, resource room teachers, or itinerant teachers who visit the school once or twice per week. Consultation services include making suggestions for major and minor program modifications, preparation of special materials to be used in conjunction with regular class assignments, and preparation of special materials for remedial or enrichment purposes. Usually, the consulting teacher does not actually remove a youngster from the direct care of the regular classroom teacher.

Clearly, the inclusion of youngsters with mild handicaps in the regular class for total instruction by the regular classroom teacher represents additional responsibilities for the teacher, and consulting services may be of considerable assistance. The use of teacher aides for assistance with mainstreamed children is also becoming increasingly common. When teacher aides are available, the consulting teacher may work with both the regular teacher and the aide to develop special instructional strategies and materials for implementation by the aide.

Regular Classroom

The least restrictive alternative for education of all youngsters is regular class placement. Even here, some youngsters with handicaps will receive some special services. For example, speech therapy services are offered to a large number of children who have essentially no educational problems other than speech difficulties. School health services, adapted physical education and

BOX 2.4
A DAY IN THE LIFE OF A RESOURCE ROOM TEACHER

Ms. Arkin has a resource room in an elementary school. This school has one first grade, one second grade, two third grades, and three each of grades four, five, and six. The school also has classes for children who are mildly and severely mentally retarded. Today, Ms. Arkin is scheduled to see a total of twenty different youngsters who will spend varying amounts of time in her resource room.

The youngest child, Mary Ann, is a first grader. She spends ten to fifteen minutes per day working individually with Ms. Arkin on visual perceptual motor skills. Mary Ann has trouble differentiating certain letters and finds it difficult to trace letters and shapes. Ms. Arkin will have a series of activities to help Mary Ann acquire the kinds of skills she needs to begin to read. Other than this perceptual motor problem, Mary Ann is a quite capable young girl; she is of normal intelligence and is well accepted by her classmates.

Most of Ms. Arkin's day will be spent with small groups of fourth, fifth, and sixth graders who have mild to moderate reading problems and who cannot keep up with their classmates in reading. Ms. Arkin works with these youngsters on either an individual or a small-group basis to strengthen their reading skills and to provide some assistance in translating difficult reading assignments into less complex assignments. One boy has a serious problem in mathematics comprehension. Ms. Arkin works with him on a very basic level establishing certain number concepts and relationships. All of these youngsters spend most of their day in their regular classes.

Part of Ms. Arkin's day is spent working with three children who are educable mentally retarded. These youngsters are being considered for placement back into the regular class situation. Ms. Arkin is working with them on two dimensions: social and academic. Socially, she is helping the youngsters acquire the skills necessary for them to be reintegrated successfully into the regular class. After having spent three years in special classes, they will need to acquire certain habits that are much more critical in regular classes than in the special class situation. For example, these youngsters will need to be more independent in a class of thirty than in a class of ten or fifteen, and they will be expected to be more responsive to group instruction. Academically, Ms. Arkin is working to prepare the youngsters for the transition into the regular class by giving them assignments parallel to those currently given in the classes to which they will be transferred. The change of assignment from special class to regular class will be smoothed by having the children continue working with Ms. Arkin on all of the academic subjects. Then as they become acclimated to the regular class situation, they will be expected to begin working with their regular class peers in some less demanding academic programs.

Finally, Ms. Arkin will spend a portion of the day talking with regular class teachers about the problems of children who are currently obtaining services in the resource room or who have had such services in the past but are now receiving all their education in the regular classes.

recreation, and some counseling services are provided more or less routinely in most schools. Such services are available to all children and are not limited to those with handicaps.

A continuing concern of many regular educators is that they are not trained to deal with the problems of children with handicaps. M. Rauth (1981) has spelled out the concerns of the American Federation of Teachers and suggested that more training for regular educators is needed before they shoulder the additional burden of trying to provide extra services for children with a variety of identified handicaps. In response to this real concern of teachers, most states have now mandated two levels of additional training for regular classroom teachers and other instructional personnel.

First, many states now require additional coursework and experience with youngsters with handicaps before a person qualifies for the teaching certificate or license. Most college and university teacher-education programs now require coursework and/or demonstration of certain competencies related to the education of learners with handicaps before the bachelor's degree is issued.

Second, a great deal of time and attention has been given to helping teachers who are already on the job. Special courses and consultation, often called in-service education, are now required in many states. In-service education is designed to help regular teachers acquire the information and skills they need to work with children with handicaps in their schools or classes.* Another aspect of the training needs is to help children with handicaps work together with their nonhandicapped peers. A. B. Kennedy and S. K. Thurman (1982) discuss some of the implications of integrating children with handicaps and nonhandicapped children, especially with respect to social behavior.

In summary, most children ideally should be educated in levels 5 through 7 of the Cascade of Services model. Children with relatively severe problems will be educated in environments that may be more restrictive. The goal is to move youngsters to successively less restrictive levels. Once again, the concept of normalization becomes evident: Youngsters with handicaps have the right to an appropriate education in a setting as nearly normal as possible. At the same time, they have the right to other kinds of services besides schooling. The next section will introduce some services that should be available to children and adults with disabilities.

---

*D.A. Powers (1983) has provided a set of guidelines to assist in the development of these programs.

HUMAN SERVICES FOR SPECIAL LEARNERS

It is a rare week when at least one of the authors does not receive a phone call or a letter from a parent seeking help for a child with a handicap. The help sought may vary from parent to parent, but there is often a common thread to the requests: "To whom, or to which agency, can I go to get help for my child?" As you read this chapter, keep in mind that you are very likely to be asked the same question if you are involved in education on a continuing basis. From the parents' point of view, there seem to be a lot of agencies supported by local, state, and federal governments, but each agency has a very narrowly defined focus. Parents often get referred from agency to agency, and only after they have again filled out the same detailed personal forms are they told, "Oh, we can't help you. You'll have to go to XYZ Agency."

The problem is not lack of available services, it's finding the appropriate services. The array of services available to help people of all ages with all types of problems is truly bewildering. Most of these services are available from publicly supported agencies.

Some services and agencies are controversial—for example, birth-control and abortion clinics—whereas others, such as the schools, are so common that people accept their services without a second thought. Many other services and agencies fall somewhere in between. Theoretically, social, medical, and rehabilitation services are designed to provide aid from "the cradle to the grave." Prenatal and religious services may even extend those limits.

The states and cities seek to provide extensive full-range services. The various agencies providing the services should be available to help people, and these agencies should be flexible enough so that the help is easy to find and use. Too often, the maze of services and agencies is impenetrable to the person encountering the bureaucracy for the first time. The lines are too long, or the forms are too confusing, or the staff doesn't seem to want to answer the questions the potential client wants to ask. Under such difficult, and sometimes humiliating, conditions, it is no wonder that many persons simply give up. The least restrictive environment concept would dictate that the services and agencies be modified to fit the clients, not the reverse.

Let us hasten to add, however, that much attention in recent years has been given to the coordination of human services. Greater emphasis is being given to training professionals in all fields to interact positively and knowledgeably with professionals in other disciplines. Let us hope that your experiences with other agencies will be increasingly positive and result in better services for all.

Full Range of Service

The President's Committee on Mental Retardation has considered quite carefully the variety of services needed by persons who are retarded throughout their lives. That committee suggests that three areas of service should be available to persons with handicaps and their families. Table 2.1 lists the three areas of service and provides some examples of each.

The Multidisciplinary Team Approach

The current thrust is to provide a continuum of services to meet the needs of persons with handicaps within the communities in which they reside. Many professional disciplines work to provide the continuum of services, each offering services related to its area of expertise. When two or more types of service providers work together to identify and provide for the needs of persons with handicaps, it is sometimes referred to as the interdisciplinary or multidisciplinary approach. This approach has been especially useful with individuals who are more severely handicapped and who require a variety of services. Service providers working together can combine services more effectively than can service providers work-

TABLE 2.1

THREE AREAS OF SERVICE AVAILABLE TO PERSONS WITH HANDICAPS AND THEIR FAMILIES

Protective Services

- equal protection and due process of law
- personal representations or advocacy
- employment safeguards
- income maintenance

Developmental Services

- pre- and postnatal maternal and child care
- general and special health services
- education and training, including early childhood programs
- social and recreational programs
- vocational training

Supportive Services

- family services
- social-work services
- mobility and transportation
- old-age services
- genetic counseling

ing independently. You are likely to encounter the following disciplines when working with children with disabilities in an education setting:

social work
medicine
physical therapy
occupational therapy
special education
adapted physical education
therapeutic recreation
rehabilitation counseling
speech therapy
psychology
nutrition
dentistry

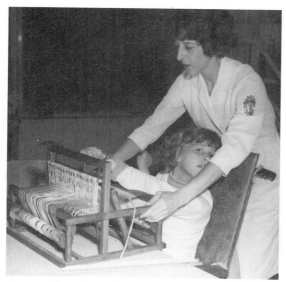

One member of a multidisciplinary team, an occupational therapist, is shown here working with a student who is physically handicapped. (Courtesy of Easter Seal Society for Crippled Children and Adults of Pennsylvania.)

Clearly, the involvement of a particular discipline will vary according to the extent of problems within that discipline's specialty area. In addition, some disciplines, such as special education, recreation, nutrition, and social work, may have continuing, close association with a specific child or group of children. Other areas—psychology and dentistry, for example—may assist on initial in-depth assessment and program planning for a child and then withdraw from a case. The **low incidence handicaps** (severe retardation, serious physical handicap, blindness, deafness) usually involve more professional groups than do the **high incidence handicaps** (mild retardation, behavior problems, learning disability). Figure 2.2 identifies some of the professionals who should

be members of a multidisciplinary team according to the handicapping condition displayed by a youngster.

There are two main decisions a team must make about a child: (1) Is the child handicapped? and (2) If the child has been identified as handicapped, what is the appropriate placement for that child? Both these decisions must be made with the input of the parent or parents and with the advice of a multidisciplinary team. The first question can be answered with the aid of guidelines set forth in state and federal laws (see Chapter 3 and the chapters devoted to the various disability groups). Fewer guidelines exist to answer the second question, so that considerable professional judgment as well as negotiation and discussion with the parents is involved.

Much attention has been given to the procedures whereby children with handicaps are placed in settings appropriate for them. J. W. Bajan and P. L. Susser (1982) report that many of the problems involved in educating youngsters with handicaps revolve around the need for prompt placement of youngsters in mutually agreeable settings. Current practice demands a team approach to decision making, with the parent (and, when appropriate, the child) being a part of the team making the decision about placement within the Cascade of Services. B. R. Gearheart and M. N. Weishahn (1984) recommend that multidisciplinary team members consider four categories of variables when determining the least restrictive placement for a youngster with a handicap. These categories are summarized in Table 2.2.

Consideration of these variables is a lengthy, difficult process; in fact, it often leads to disagreement between parent and school. Furthermore, the team approach is an expensive one in terms of personnel time, and it suffers from a lack of well-defined procedures. When E. J. Bradford and J. G. Hickey (1982) reviewed New York City's placement procedures, they found that as knowledge of special education increases, the likelihood decreases that a team member will recommend a more restrictive placement. The fact that most

Handicapping Condition

Multidisciplinary Team Member	Deaf	Deaf-Blind	Hard-of-Hearing	Mentally Retarded	Multihandicapped	Orthopedically Impaired	Other Health Impaired	Seriously Emotionally Disturbed	Specific Learning Disability	Speech Impaired	Visually Handicapped
Administrator	X	X	X	X	X	X	X	X	X	X	X
Audiologist	X	X	X								
Occupational Therapist						X					
Parents	X	X	X	X	X	X	X	X	X	X	X
Physical Therapist						X					
Physician					X	X	X				
Regular Educator	X	X	X	X	X	X	X	X	X	X	X
School Nurse					X	X	X				
School Psychologist				X	X			X	X		
Social Worker					X			X			
Special Educator	X	X	X	X	X	X	X	X	X	X	X
Speech & Language Pathologist	X	X	X							X	
Ophthalmologist		X			X						X

Figure 2.2. Those professionals who should be included on the multi-disciplinary team established for a child who is handicapped are denoted by an "X."

state regulations require persons of varying disciplines to serve on teams increases the probability that placement of children will continue to be a sensitive issue, and as different agencies become involved in the placement and schooling process, the situation becomes even more sensitive and potentially troublesome. For example, in 1983, the results of all due process hearings held in Illinois over a twenty-seven-month period were reviewed. The results showed that 67.5 percent of the hearings resulted in disagreement on the placement of the child in question. The average number of hours spent by school district personnel on the cases was seventy-three (Kammerlohr, Henderson, & Rock, 1983).

In spite of what seems like a lot of personnel time and opportunity for disagreement both among professionals and between parents and schools, the prevailing idea of multidisciplinary planning and team decision making is still valid and workable. It works on behalf of the child and to the child's direct benefit, at least in the majority

TABLE 2.2

VARIABLES TO CONSIDER WHEN DETERMINING THE LEAST RESTRICTIVE PLACEMENT FOR A YOUNGSTER WITH A HANDICAP

Student Variables

- age
- nature and degree of impairment
- academic status
- intellectual ability
- additional handicapping conditions

Parent Variables

- willingness to participate in the decision-making process
- willingness to monitor their child's development

Teacher Variables

- professional training
- prior experience
- flexibility
- ability to work cooperatively with parents and other professionals

Administration Variables

- degree of commitment to the premise that all children, regardless of their disability, are entitled to an education in the least restrictive environment

of situations. Studies of the Cascade model (e.g., Peterson et al., 1983) point out overlaps among the various levels of the model but indicate that the continuum provides well for children with varying types and severities of handicaps. H. Knoff (1983) showed that the information most important for placement decisions came from different sources and tapped the expertise of different disciplines. Other researchers and writers have reported on the effectiveness of team decisions and identified key features of the process (Berquist, 1982; Holland, 1982; Maher, 1983; Pfeiffer, 1982; Ysseldyke, Algozzine, & Allen, 1982). In general, the key features reported to be most helpful in the team decision making process are (1) frequent communication among team members, (2) respect for opinions of other team members, and (3) working from a common set of procedures, definitions, and regulations.

Private School Placement

One of the continuing areas of disagreement is whether a child should be placed in a private day or residential facility at school district expense. Many parents believe that such a placement is superior to a public school placement and, of course, they want the best schooling possible for their children. On the other hand, public school personnel believe they can provide excellent education services at a lower cost. Costs of educating youngsters in private facilities, especially residential ones, are considerably higher than educating them in more conventional public school placements. Nevertheless, those youngsters with very serious medical or behavioral problems or those who require constant nursing or other supervision may best be placed in a private school or facility. Often, there is disagreement between parent and school, with parents arguing for private school placement and the public school arguing against it.*

Related Services: P.L. 94–142

P.L. 94–142 mandates multidisciplinary assessment of children and requires related services to be provided, as needed, to children with handicaps. **Related services** refers to:

> transportation and such developmental, corrective, and other supportive services as are required to assist a handicapped child to benefit from special education, and includes speech pathology and audiology, psychological services, physical and occupational therapy, recreation, early identification and assessment of disabilities in children, counseling services, and medical services for diagnostic and evaluation purposes. The term also includes school health services, social work services in schools, and parent counseling and training.
>
> (United States Office of Education, 1977a, p. 42479)

This organization scheme is most directly related to the school situation. In fact, related services means those services that are most important to a child's education program. It is the school's responsibility to locate and provide related services when those services are determined to be

necessary for a child's education program. Therefore, if a parent has a school-age child with a handicap, the first place to seek help for the child is the public school (except for emergency or long-range medical or dental care). If a particular service, such as physical therapy or speech therapy, is included in a child's IEP (individual education program), then the school must provide that service at no cost to the child or parents.

Transportation.   As you will note from the list of related services presented earlier, all services except transportation are provided by highly skilled professionals. Although transportation as a service seems straightforward and easy to provide, transporting children with disabilities is no simple task. In some cases, two persons—a driver and an attendant—must be used to transport children who are severely handicapped or behaviorally disordered. Sometimes, long distances are involved. Consequently, the costs are often much greater than one might expect. As an example, consider one large, urban school district with a population of approximately twenty thousand youngsters with handicaps. The instructional budget for these children was approximately $40,000,000 in 1984. That is, the school district spent $40,000,000 or about $2,000 per child on teachers' salaries, instructional supplies, speech and hearing services, assessment, medical services, and the like. Transportation costs, excluding costs for services available to all children, amounted to an additional $4,000,000. Thus, transportation increased the per pupil cost by 10 percent.

Other Agencies

In addition to the school, parents may turn for help to three other types of agencies: state agencies, voluntary agencies, and private agencies.

State Agencies.   Included in this category are those helping agencies that are supported primarily by federal and state taxes. They include agencies such as Vocational Rehabilitation Centers,

---

*For an interesting series of articles discussing the problems of private school placements, see D. Audette (1982), Bajan and Susser (1982), L. Grumet and T. Inkpen (1982), and R. L. Guarino (1982).

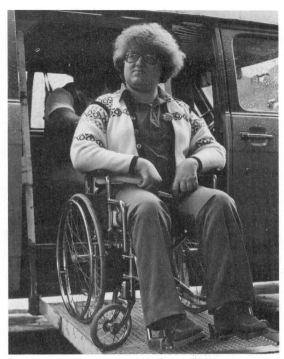

Public Law 94–142 requires that students who are handicapped shall be provided with transportation services if needed. (Photo by Patricia Seibel.)

plans such as Medicare, and county-based (but state-related) services such as Mental Health/Mental Retardation (MH/MR) offices. These agencies are operated by state or county employees and are supported through budgets provided by state and federal legislatures. The types of services provided range from specific health care to food and housing subsidies. The services can be for a single incident or for long-range care. For example, some municipalities and counties provide a twenty-four-hour drug crisis center, staffed and prepared to assist school-age youngsters as well as adults with an acute drug or alcohol problem at any time. The same counties usually provide nursing homes for adults who are seriously handicapped, for the aged, and for persons who are chronically ill. Also, an agency such as MH/MR

can provide psychological evaluation and counseling for all youngsters.

Voluntary Agencies. Unlike state agencies, voluntary agencies receive much of their support, in terms of both time and money, from voluntary contributions. These agencies depend quite heavily on volunteer workers who donate a few or many hours a week to the agency, doing anything from scrubbing floors or answering the telephone to providing free medical or dental care. Some financial support is obtained from state agencies and some from charity organizations such as the United Way. Clients of these agencies pay for the services to the extent that they are able. Some of the more well-known voluntary agencies are listed later in this chapter.

Private Agencies. Private agencies are supported primarily by fees paid by the clients who receive the services. In some cases, the fees are paid by a third party, usually an insurance company or a state agency. The range of services offered by private agencies is somewhat more restricted than that of state agencies, and the types of services are determined almost exclusively by the needs of the local citizens.

The lines dividing these three types of agencies are somewhat blurred. Most private agencies receive some public support, either directly or indirectly. For example, many children once were excluded from the public schools because they were too disruptive, too retarded, or too physically handicapped to fit in. The parents' only alternative, other than no school at all, was to place these children in expensive private schools. Some private schools provided instruction for youngsters with handicaps, but the entire cost of the schooling was borne by the parents. In the 1970s, the number of such private schools increased dramatically. Why? After the 1971 PARC consent decree, public schools could no longer exclude children who are profoundly retarded, seriously disturbed, or severely disabled from the public education system. A great many schools found that it was more economical for them to pay tuition to private schools than to make physical

BOX 2.5

TRANSPORTATION: A BIG PROBLEM

One of the surprises of P.L. 94–142 was the tremendous expense of transporting children with disabilities to and from school. This vignette illustrates the problem of transportation—especially of youngsters with serious physical disabilities.

It is early morning. Swirling Texas Gulf Coast fog is making the drive into this large southwest city even slower than usual. In the inbound lane is a large bus painted the familiar school bus yellow. But there, almost all similarity to other school buses and their passengers stops.

This is a wheelchair van. Inside are four young handicapped children strapped into their wheelchairs. Their breathing is regulated by the chest respirators they each wear. As the nurse on the bus surveys her charges, she notices Janie's distress. Janie's respirator has stopped functioning because, as it is later learned, the battery used during travel had not been recharged on schedule.

It is well that the nurse looked at Janie. Her weak vocalizations would never have attracted attention in the noise of the bumper-to-bumper traffic. The nurse braces herself between the wheelchair and the wall of the bus, squeezing an Ambu-Bag with one hand and suctioning a mucus plug from the tracheostomy tube with the other hand. Ordinarily a patient with respirator problems would be taken to a hospital emergency department, but in this traffic it would be hard to reach one; moreover, Janie's parents had given explicit written directions that in a medical emergency Janie is to be taken to Children's Hospital, which is 10 miles away in another direction, in traffic that forces the bus to a complete stop for minutes at a time.

The emergency procedures used by the nurse sustain Janie until the bus reaches the school, where the chest respirator is plugged into an electrical outlet. The battery is recharged for the trip home.

This is one example of a problem in serving severely handicapped children in an urban public school system. Dramatic? Yes. Unique? Unfortunately, no. Other school districts can match the experiences of the transportation and special educa-

Source: Shell, P. M. Straining the system: Serving low-incidence handicapped children in an urban school system. *Exceptional Education Quarterly,* 1981, 2(2), pp. 1–10. Used with permission of the publisher, PRO-ED.

adaptions to their buildings, expand their special services, and so on. Thus, many private schools now receive a portion of their operating expenses from public rather than private sources.

Finding the Right Agency

How does a parent go about finding help from the many services available? In spite of sincere attempts by many agencies to cooperate with each other and to refer clients to other agencies, finding the right source of help remains a problem for parents. Persistence is required, but perhaps the following guidelines may be of some assistance.

First, don't overlook the school as an invaluable resource and referral mechanism. The law requires that the school be responsible for providing a variety of services related to education, including medical diagnosis, physical therapy, and speech therapy. If these or other services (e.g., counseling) seem to be required for a child, the parents should insist that the school make the services available. The school is obligated to make a thorough evaluation of the child's capabilities and provide all the related services that a multidisciplinary team agrees are essential for the child.

Even if the school is not the right agency to provide a particular service (income maintenance, for example), most schools have social

tion departments of the Houston School District. There have been several life-threatening emergencies in Houston involving respirators of young handicapped children that stopped working while buses were en route to school or home in peak traffic on the major freeway loop around the city. Transportation is only one, albeit a visible, area of school district operations greatly affected by the increasing number of low-incidence, severely handicapped children.

. . . because of the mandate to serve handicapped children in the least restrictive environment and the thrust for deinstitutionalization and normalization of children formerly served in state residential schools, more and more profoundly handicapped children are actually being served on local public school campuses. For example, on a junior high school campus in Houston there is a 14-year-old boy in an infant seat, wearing Pampers, bottle fed. In the same district there are other children who are fed through gastrostomy tubes. There are several children in chest respirators who also have tracheos-

tomy tubes. There are children who require catheterization. There are a great many children left incontinent because of cerebral palsy or spinal chord accidents, who must be changed and bathed and dressed during the course of each school day.

. . . Indeed, following the incident described at the beginning of this article, the Houston School District spent an additional $9,000 refitting one of the wheelchair vans to carry severely involved children in respirators and children who must be transported lying prone on a stretcher. This bus has emergency life support systems, including oxygen, suction equipment, and a back-up power system for respirators. It is operated by aides and drivers trained as emergency medical technicians. It was necessary for a transportation department administrator to seek legal advice about whether the van described earlier should be licensed as a school bus or as an ambulance.

workers on the staff whose job it is to be familiar with the many agencies at the local and state level. The school social worker or guidance counselor thus should be able to offer good advice.

Second, local priests, rabbis, or pastors may be able to provide emergency counseling or assist a family in locating necessary services.

Third, just as there are often free or low-cost clinics for persons with medical problems, legal-aid services are often available. Legal services agencies are not as widespread as medical clinics, but they are increasing in number yearly. Legal-aid services can be found listed with attorneys or the county bar association.

Finally, most government agencies have coun-

ty or local offices that attempt to coordinate the efforts of the public agencies through an implicit, if not a formal, referral service. Usually, the main telephone number or first listed number is staffed by someone familiar with the various agencies in the area. The Yellow Pages of the telephone book carry listings under *Government* such as *City, Town,* or *Borough; County; State;* and *United States.* Under *County Government,* for example, you may find such agencies or offices as:

Information Resources and Development
  Service
Adult Foster Home Care
Agency on Aging

BOX 2.6
FEDERAL HELP FOR PERSONS WITH DISABILITIES

The role of the federal government in providing services to the handicapped is described in a pamphlet entitled "Pocket Guide to Federal Help for the Disabled Person." As the pamphlet points out, a great deal of the federal money and services go to states, and the states, in turn, make decisions about how to spend the money, within certain regulations and guidelines. For this reason, the pamphlet does not pinpoint exactly what services will be available in any specific location. The pamphlet does serve the purpose of alerting parents and guardians, as well as handicapped individuals themselves, about the principal government services for which they may be eligible. Individuals are advised to contact the Office of Information and Resources for the Handicapped in Washington, D.C., if they are having difficulty locating services. They are also told:

Keep in mind that every year new programs begin and some old ones dissolve, particularly at the state and local levels. Keep in touch with your contacts and stay as aware as you can, through reading and talking to knowledgeable people, of what is happening in the area of services to the handicapped. There are many excellent voluntary organizations, as well as state, local, and Federal offices that can help you. Numerous newsletters are produced by groups of and for the handicapped.

The twenty-four-page booklet is packed with information. Addresses and telephone numbers of federal agencies are provided; for some topics, region-by-region data are given. Information about the following topics is included in the pocket guide.

- *Developmental disabilities program*—This program serves those with mental retardation, cerebral palsy, and other severe, chronic mental or physical impairments that have their onset in childhood.
- *Vocational rehabilitation*—Each state has an agency to help handicapped persons become employable.
- *Education*—Those seeking services are directed to information about their rights under P.L. 94–142. Special sources of information regarding education are listed, such as Closer Look Information Center, Head Start, Schools for the Blind, Library Services for Special Groups, Schools for the Deaf, and Federal Student Financial Aid.

Source: Office of Information and Resources for the Handicapped, "Pocket Guide to Federal Help for the Disabled Person," U.S. Department of Education, Washington, D.C.: U.S. Government Printing Office, 1983.

Children's Services
Community Services
Domestic Relations
Drug and Alcohol Crisis Center
Employment and Training
Juvenile Officer
Mental Health and Mental Retardation
Public Defender
Veterans Affairs
Youth Services
Medical Emergency

Under *State Government* you may find some of the same listings, as well as the following:

State Health Department
Drug Control
Employment Security
Unemployment Compensation
Vocational Rehabilitation
Public Welfare

Finally, under *United States Government,* you may find listings for local offices like the following:

Federal Job Information Center
Social Security
Occupational Safety and Health Administration

- *Employment*—One of the responsibilities of the more than 2,400 local employment security offices in the United States is helping handicapped job seekers. Help is also available from federal job information centers (at least one in every state), the Governor's Committee on Employment of the Handicapped (most, but not all, states have such a committee), and the Small Business Administration.
- *Financial assistance*—The two federal programs that provide direct financial assistance to disabled persons are the Social Security Disability Insurance Benefits program (continuing monthly income when earnings are reduced due to disability) and the Supplemental Security Income program (minimum monthly income for those whose disabilities prevent them from holding gainful employment).
- *Medical assistance*—Major federal sources of medical assistance for disabled persons are Medicare; Medicaid; Crippled Children's Services; and Early Periodic Screening, Diagnosis and Treatment Program (EPSDT). Additional information is available from the Health Care Financing Administration in Washington, D.C.

- *Civil rights/legal assistance*—A disabled person has rights, guaranteed by law, to education, employment, health care, senior citizen activities, welfare, and any other public or private services that receive federal assistance. Responsibility for enforcing federal laws prohibiting discrimination falls to the Office for Civil Rights.
- *Housing*—Loans are available to help handicapped individuals adapt their homes to their needs, and rent assistance is available to low-income families. The U.S. Department of Housing and Urban Development (HUD) has more information.
- *Tax benefits*—The Internal Revenue Service allows certain medical and dental expenses to be deducted from the earned income of the disabled person or his or her parents.
- *Transportation*—The major goal is to make transportation systems more accessible to handicapped travelers. The President's Committee on Employment of the Handicapped provides a list of guides to accessible places to stay, eat, visit, and tour.

Voluntary agencies that may be of assistance include such local, state, or national organizations as:

American Association on Mental Deficiency
Association for Retarded Citizens
Council for Exceptional Children
Association for Children with Learning Disabilities
American Foundation for the Blind
Alexander Graham Bell Association for the Deaf
Easter Seal Society for Crippled Children and Adults
United Cerebral Palsy Association
Goodwill Industries

Even with all the agencies available, it still seems difficult to get the best match between agency and client. Fortunately, professionals in all the agencies are gradually becoming more knowledgeable about services provided by related agencies. You will undoubtedly be called on to help someone solve a problem with a child if you remain in a human-services field; you can be of great assistance to others by becoming acquainted with services provided by the agencies in your community, county, and state.

SUMMARY

The concept of least restrictive environment is applicable to education as well as to the whole range of human services for individuals with handicaps. Reynolds (1962) and Deno (1970) have given us the most popular description of the various education placements or settings that should be available for the education of handicapped children. This Cascade of Special Education Services portrays the options that can ensure that, despite the severity of a handicap, each child can be served in the least restrictive environment most appropriate for his or her needs. The seven levels, or settings, ranging from most to least restrictive, are:

1. full-time residential school

2. special day school

3. full-time special class

4. part-time regular class and part-time special class

5. regular class with supportive instructional services

6. regular class with consulting services for regular teacher

7. regular classroom

Although a wide range of publicly and privately financed services are available to help children and adults with handicaps and their families, the coordination of the services is a problem. Often, parents must cope with a mountain of forms or seemingly contradictory information in order to find the right agency to assist them. The problem is not the lack of services, at least in the major population areas. Rather, it is finding the right agency at the right time to help with a particular problem.

In general, there is a continuum of services that can be used by persons with handicaps and their families. According to the President's Committee on Mental Retardation, three broad catego-

ries of services should be available to all persons: protective services, developmental services, and supportive services. Ideally, these services are provided by a team of professionals from different disciplines (e.g., medicine, psychology, education, social work). Two or more disciplines working together to provide services is called the interdisciplinary or multidisciplinary approach.

Public Law 94–142 stipulates that only after a multidisciplinary assessment can a child become eligible to receive special and related services. Related services are those that are ancillary to a child's educational program and include such services as transportation, speech therapy, physical therapy, and counseling.

Suggestions for Further Reading

Anderson, K., & Milliren, A. (1983). *Structured experiences for integration of handicapped children.* Gaithersburg, MD: Aspen Systems.

A practical guide designed to help students and staff prepare for successful mainstreaming of children with handicaps.

Anderson, W., Chitwood, S., & Hayden, D. (1982). *Negotiating the special education maze: A guide for parents and teachers.* Englewood Cliffs, NJ: Prentice-Hall.

A practical, step-by-step guide to assist parents and teachers in advocating for children with special needs.

Deno, E. (1970). Special education as developmental capital. *Exceptional Children, 37,* 229–237.

Reynolds, M. C. (1962). A framework for considering some issues in special education. *Exceptional Children, 28,* 367–370.

These two articles are widely quoted as sources for the introduction and development of the Cascade model of special education services.

Dunn, L. M. (1968). Special education for the mildly retarded—Is much of it justifiable? *Exceptional Children, 35,* 5–24.

This article has had an immediate and long-lasting effect on contemporary thought in special education. It questioned the wisdom of placing children with mild handicaps in segregated special classes and helped lay the groundwork for later litigation and legislation on behalf of individuals with handicaps.

LaCour, J. (1983). Interagency agreement. *Exceptional Children, 49*(3), 265–267.

LaCour recounts some of the problems of interagency agreement and makes some suggestions for improvement.

Ortis, A. (1984). Choosing the language of instruction for exceptional bilingual children. *Teaching Exceptional Children, 16,* 208–212.

Placement of youngsters with handicaps may require special considerations if English is not their primary language. This article surveys these special placements and teaching problems.

Programs for the Handicapped. Washington, D.C.: Special Education and Rehabilitative Services, U.S. Department of Education.

This is a free publication, published every other month for professional people working in special education and rehabilitation. It covers a variety of topics but focuses on current issues, legislation, and recent publications.

Relevant Journals

Exceptional Children
The Council for Exceptional Children publishes this influential bi-monthly journal that addresses most aspects of the education of exceptional individuals.

Journal of Special Education
The most scholarly journal in the field of special education, the *Journal of Special Education,* published by Grune and Stratton, was founded by Dr. Lester Mann. There are no "sacred cows" or popular ideas that escape careful scrutiny and research by this quarterly journal.

CHAPTER 3

Definitions and Classification Schemes

Did You Know That . . .

- knowing that a child has been classified as retarded (or disturbed, hearing impaired, and so on) does not necessarily help a teacher provide a good education program for the child?

- children labeled as handicapped may acquire negative self-images, and their teachers may expect less of them?

- children who are handicapped often have more than one discrete handicap or problem?

- children may be classified as handicapped in one situation but not be handicapped in other situations?

- a disability may produce different behaviors in different children?

- similar behaviors may be found in children with different disabilities?

- although professional people (e.g., teachers, psychologists) use many different definitions, the official, legal definitions of handicapping conditions appear in state and federal laws?

- most problems of children with handicaps fall within the following functional developmental domains: cognitive, motor, social, and language?

A central theme of this book is that *no two children are alike; children should be viewed first as individuals and only second as handicapped.* Furthermore, a child should participate in a particular educational program, therapy, or the like only if that child's unique characteristics clearly call for that approach or treatment. In other words, the education program should be dictated by a child's unique characteristics rather than by his or her membership in a group such as the mentally retarded.

If that point of view is held widely in the field of special education, why, you may ask, is there such an interest in categorizing and labeling children? Why has the system and practice of categorizing children as retarded, disturbed, crippled, blind, and so on continued to be so prevalent, especially if educators prefer to view youngsters as individuals rather than members of a category? Why have we devoted an entire chapter to definitions and classification systems? In fact, there are some positive dimensions to labeling as well as some negative ones. We will begin, however, by looking at some arguments against labels.

THE LABELING CONTROVERSY

Categories and Labels: Cons

Although most educators believe that all children should be treated as distinct individuals, they also believe that certain definitions are not only helpful, they are essential. Unfortunately, the category system does not always aid the educator. Often, not much is gained from using the category system, and we stand the risk of unfairly penalizing or stigmatizing children by labeling them. We would like to toss out the outmoded practice of labeling and categorizing children and replace it with a completely individualized approach to education. Merely affixing a definition or "label" to a child does not automatically result in better services for the child, nor is the label pinned to a child necessarily appropriate at all times and in all situations. For example, educators have discovered

This young man has a disability but not a handicap. He participates actively in many sports and is a frequent winner in athletic contests. (Photos by Patrick Little.)

the hard way that some children who have been labeled as mentally handicapped often are handicapped only in the academic atmosphere of the middle-class school. Often, such children turn out to be self-supporting citizens once they leave the school situation. In school, special class youngsters may excel in art, music, or athletics, or even in certain academic situations. Thus, the impact of a disability may be stronger in one situation than in another. There has been a tendency in the past to categorize children on the basis of apparent disabilities that are most obvious in the school situation and to group them on the basis of those disabilities. Theoretically, this produces a more homogeneous group of youngsters, and the teacher's job is made easier. Unfortunately, this procedure has not always been successful, for several reasons.

A considerable body of information about the effects of labeling on children has been accumulated over the past two decades. Although the evidence is contradictory in some instances, there does seem to be some agreement that labeling can cause problems.* G. P. Cartwright and C. A. Cartwright (1978) reviewed the effects of categorization and labeling of children. Some of the possible consequences they found include the following:

▪ Some labeling systems are so coarse that it is relatively easy to label as handicapped a child who really isn't handicapped.

*For excellent reviews of research studies on the effects of labeling, look up Algozzine and Mercer (1980), and Ysseldyke and Algozzine (1982). For some studies on this topic, see Schloss and Miller (1982), Palmer (1983), and Salvia (1980).

BOX 3.1

DO YOU THINK OF YOURSELF AS HANDICAPPED?

Handicap is a matter of degree. All of us are handicapped in some ways. The woman who is unattractive or obese is handicapped in casual social contacts—that is, her looks cause her to be at a disadvantage in such situations. The man who is very short is handicapped—i.e., placed at a disadvantage by his height, in obtaining certain kinds of jobs which entail impressing clients. The person whose IQ is 110 may be handicapped in a Ph.D. program in which most of the other students have IQs over 125. The child who is tone deaf may be handicapped in his music classes. The child who is very active physiologically and physically may be handicapped throughout his school career because school activities are largely sedentary. We recognize the disadvantages such characteristics cause individuals. We may even say, "She is really handicapped by her looks," or, "That child is going to have a real problem in school." Yet we don't think of these individuals as handicapped. We think of them as people with selected characteristics that place them at a disadvantage. But at some point along the continuum of characteristics that cause people to be at a disadvantage we begin to refer to people as handicapped people; not as people with disabilities or impairments. When we think of a person as someone with characteristics that are likely to be of a disadvantage to him, we still perceive him primarily as someone generally similar to ourselves. When we label and begin to think of a person as handicapped, we see him as different and apart from ourselves. His primary identification for us becomes his impairment or disability. His abilities, his similarities with other people, are lost to us, or become something that surprises us when we cannot ignore them.

Source: Shirley Cohen, *Special People,* © 1977, p. 8. Reprinted by permission of Prentice-Hall, Inc., Englewood Cliffs, NJ.

- Labeled individuals may acquire a lowered or negative self-concept.
- People who work with a child labeled as handicapped may have needlessly lowered expectations of what the child really can accomplish.
- Children not formally labeled as handicapped, but who have minor problems, may be excluded from needed services because they are *not* labeled.
- Most category and label systems are inadequate for instructional purposes; that is, they do not tell us anything about how to teach a child.
- Labels often create stereotypic images. The public may feel that all persons given a particular label will exhibit all behaviors associated with that label, or that all persons so labeled form a homogeneous group.

Categories and Labels: Pros

The federal government has exercised a great deal of leadership in recent years in rapidly expanding services for persons who are handicapped. In order to accomplish its goals, the government established, and has continued to use, "categories" of exceptional children. In addition to governmental regulations, there are several compelling reasons for continuing to use some traditional terms and concepts.

First, much of the information relevant to the study of children with problems is tied to the category system. For many years, research—medical, psychological, educational—has been strongly based on identification of children by diagnostic category. Total rejection of the long-standing category system might easily result in the loss of valuable and relevant information about groups of children who share certain common characteristics.

Second, the existing category structure is a convenient (though often imprecise) communication system that is used as a kind of shorthand by professional workers. Total elimination of categories would tend to inhibit this often useful shorthand.

Third, even if a totally new and extremely useful alternate classification system were developed, a lengthy transition period from the old to the new would be required. Because one of the purposes of the book is to help you communicate with other persons who work with people who are handicapped, it is necessary to acquaint you with the existing system as well as potential systems so you will be able to speak the language of those already working in the field.

Finally, various private and public funding sources and support agencies are bound either by law or by interest to provide funding or services only for certain handicapping conditions. Abandonment of the traditional categories might eliminate or severely curtail the availability of funds or services to certain categories of handicaps.

In short, most educators are not satisfied with the traditional category system, but they are stuck with it, at least to some extent. Ideally, we should be able to utilize the best aspects of the traditional category system while also using the best features of other emerging classification approaches.

THE PROBLEMS WITH DEFINITIONS

At the present time, state and federal laws require that definitions of handicaps be used, if for no other reason than to facilitate allocation of funds. (Actually, the allocation of funds is a very big reason; by 1983, federal aid for educating the handicapped exceeded $1 billion.) It may seem a simple task to define the various handicapped

groups and get on with the business of educating the youngsters; in fact, it is a very difficult task.

Consider for a moment what is required of a good definition of, say, mental retardation. The definition should communicate in a few words the essential characteristics of people who are mentally retarded. It should include persons who are retarded and exclude those who are not. It should be timely and helpful, a tool or shorthand to facilitate communication among people in a variety of disciplines. A good definition might suggest a course of action or help provide a useful summary of behaviors.

In practice, it is extremely difficult to find or construct definitions that are useful, communicative, and acceptable to all or even most persons interested in the problem. For example, Cartwright and Cartwright (1978) attempted to compile a list of definitions of mental retardation. They found thirty-five different definitions and noted that their list was not exhaustive. Among other things, they found:

- The definitions vary widely in their usefulness; that is, some are operational in nature, others are not.
- Some definitions overlap other conditions; that is, a definition of severe mental retardation might not exclude behaviors resulting from autism or severe emotional disturbance.
- Even "good" definitions are not equally useful or acceptable to members of different professional groups.
- The point of view held by a person or professional group largely determines the type of definition that is most useful or acceptable to that person or group.

LEGISLATIVE DEFINITIONS

Clearly, it is beyond the scope of this book to report all existing definitions of all handicaps. This chapter will cover the definitions of hand-

BOX 3.2
THE POWER OF LABELS

Kurt Vonnegut's best-selling novel *Slapstick* is not about handicapped individuals, but two of the central characters in the book, Eliza and Wilbur Swain, are portrayed at one time as being retarded and later as exceptionally gifted. For teachers, the important message that surrounds the transition of Eliza and Wilbur concerns expectancies and self-fulfilling prophecies. Here's what happened in the story:

Eliza and Wilbur are twins. When they were born, they were so ugly that their parents thought they were monsters and arranged to have them taken away and cared for by nurses and aides. Their parents expected them to die by the time they were fifteen years old and wanted only to make them fairly comfortable in the meantime. Their physical needs were completely taken care of by others, and they were never expected to become independent or learn anything. Actually, Eliza and Wilbur were very intelligent. On their own, they discovered all the secret passages in the old mansion where they lived. Most important, they had discovered the library and taught themselves to read, acquiring extensive knowledge by reading many of the books in the well-stocked library.

By accident, on their fifteenth birthday, they hear their parents discussing them and learn that their parents are anxious for them to die. At one point in the conversation, their mother says that she might have some hope if she could see just one tiny spark of intelligence in her children. That, it turns out, is all that Eliza and Wilbur need. Never before had they been informed that someone was interested in their being intelligent. Some of their reactions to

learning of their mother's desire for a small spark of intelligence are described in the passages here.

In one discussion, they tell why they have kept their abilities secret: "We did not itch to display our intelligence in public. We thought of it as being simply one more example of our freakishness . . ." (p. 42).

They decide to inform their parents about their intelligence by making a banner:

> DEAR MATER AND PATER:
> WE CAN NEVER BE PRETTY BUT WE CAN BE
> AS SMART OR AS DUMB AS THE WORLD REALLY
> WANTS US TO BE.
> YOUR FAITHFUL SERVANTS,
> ELIZA MELLOW SWAIN
> WILBUR ROCKEFELLER SWAIN   (p. 70)

You can imagine the shock and disbelief expressed by those who know them, especially their parents. Eliza and Wilbur are astonished at the reaction and apologize: "'We simply did not realize,' Eliza said, 'that anybody wanted us to be intelligent'" (p. 73).

We think Vonnegut conveys the terrible consequences of lowered expectations better than do many specialized discussions of research results. But the message of both is the same: We cannot *assume* low ability; we should *expect better* and arrange the circumstances so that the child has the *opportunity* to do better. And there's another message here, too: One characteristic (or label), such as ugliness, does not ensure that other characteristics, such as mental retardation or mental illness, exist.

Source: Kurt Vonnegut, *Slapstick*. New York: Delacorte Press, 1976.

icaps as determined by federal law. Each of the chapters in this book devoted to handicapping conditions will provide additional or elaborated definitions to enhance understanding of the conditions being discussed.

The United States Office of Education has defined handicapped children as those

1. who have been evaluated in accordance with certain specified procedures

2. who have been found to have one or more of the impairments listed below

3. who, because of the impairments, need special education and related services

Eleven categories of impairment have been identified. They are:

deaf
deaf-blind
hard-of-hearing
mentally retarded
multihandicapped
orthopedically impaired
other health impaired
seriously emotionally disturbed
specific learning disabilities
speech impaired
visually handicapped

(U.S. Office of Education, 1977a, p. 42478)

The legislative definition clearly is educational in orientation. The inclusion of the phrase "need special education and related services" means that children are "labeled" retarded or disturbed only to assure that they will become eligible for special services. Possession of a mild hearing disability, for example, does not mean that a youngster should forever be labeled as handicapped. The designation should be applied *only* in those instances when the hearing impairment is of such an intensity and form that the child needs special services. Incidentally, in spite of some attempts to change the federal law, these definitions remain essentially unchanged.

Evaluation Procedures

The legislative definition is also somewhat operational in that references are made to procedures that should be followed in **evaluation** of a child as having a handicap. Specifically, the *Federal Register* of August 23, 1977, (pp. 42496–7) requires that certain procedures and safeguards be observed. The following statements are paraphrased from the list of regulations given in that *Federal Register*.

1. Procedures and materials used for purposes of evaluation and placement of children must *not* be racially or culturally discriminating.

2. A full, *individual* evaluation of a child's educational needs must be conducted *before* that child is placed in any special education program.

3. Tests and other evaluation materials
   a. must be administered in the child's native language.
   b. must be administered properly by trained personnel.
   c. must assess specific educational needs.
   d. must be so administered as to take into account a child's impaired sensory, manual, or speaking skills.

4. No single test or procedure can be used as the *only* criterion for determining an appropriate educational program for a child. Also, placement of a child cannot be based only on the results of a test that yields a single general intelligence quotient.

5. Evaluation of a child must be made by a multidisciplinary team including at least one teacher or other specialist in the area of suspected disability.

6. The child must be assessed in all areas related to the suspected disability, including, where appropriate, health, vision, hearing, social and emotional status, general intelligence, academic performance, communicative status, and motor abilities.

7. Evaluation procedures must be conducted every three years or more often as needed.

8. Placement of a child must be reviewed annually.

(U.S. Office of Education, 1977a, pp. 42496–7)

The fact that the Congress chose to make the regulations fairly explicit with respect to evaluation procedures is an acknowledgement that differing results would be obtained if different states or school districts used varying evaluation procedures. The federal regulations were designed to ensure that some commonalities would occur between states. Explicit, operational procedures provide consistency and give assurances that chil-

BOX 3.3
THE "CONTEST" OF LIVING

According to the dictionary, a handicap is some form of contest in which difficulties are placed upon superior competitors or advantages given to inferior ones so as to equalize their chances of winning. What a marvelous, truly democratic concept! What a pity that we apply it only to games. There is another meaning of the word "handicapped." It refers to something that hampers a person's functioning and places him at a disadvantage. At least 10 percent of our population may be thought of as handicapped. It is in the everyday lives of these people that the concept of giving advantages to disadvantaged contestants is desperately needed. The contest is living. The goal is a decent life. Unfortunately, there are often no advantages given to these disadvantaged competitors, or the advantages provided are more than offset by the special burdens that are placed upon them.

Source: Shirley Cohen. *Special People*, © 1977, p. 2. Reprinted by permission of Prentice-Hall, Inc., Englewood Cliffs, NJ.

dren identified as handicapped in one state would also be identified as handicapped in another state. Those basic regulations remain in effect today.

Categorical Definitions

The federal regulations also provide definitions for each of the eleven impairments or categories listed in the USOE definition of handicapped children. Basic definitions are given here; fuller coverage of the conditions is found in other chapters in this book.

1. **Deaf.** A hearing impairment which is so severe that the child is impaired in processing linguistic information through hearing, with or without amplification, which adversely affects educational performance.

2. **Deaf-Blind.** Concomitant hearing and visual impairments, the combination of which causes such severe communication and other developmental and educational problems that they cannot be accommodated in special education programs solely for deaf or blind children.

3. **Hard of Hearing.** A hearing impairment, whether permanent or fluctuating, which adversely affects a child's educational performance but which is not included under the definition of "deaf" in this section.

4. **Mentally Retarded.** Significantly subaverage general intellectual functioning existing concurrently with deficits in adaptive behavior and manifested during the developmental period, which adversely affects a child's educational performance.

5. **Multihandicapped.** Concomitant impairments (such as mentally retarded–blind, mentally retarded–orthopedically impaired, etc.), the combination of which causes such severe educational problems that they cannot be accommodated in special education programs solely for one of the impairments. The term does not include deaf-blind children.

6. **Orthopedically Impaired.** A severe orthopedic impairment which adversely affects a child's educational performance. The term includes impairments caused by congenital anomaly (e.g., clubfoot, absence of some member, etc.), impairments caused by disease (e.g., poliomyelitis, bone tuberculosis, etc.), and impairments from other causes (e.g., cerebral palsy, amputations, and fractures or burns which cause contractures).

7. **Other Health Impaired.** Limited strength, vitality, or alertness, due to chronic or acute health problems such as a heart condition, tuberculosis, rheumatic fever, nephritis, asthma, sickle cell anemia, hemophilia, epilepsy, lead poisoning, leukemia, or diabetes, which adversely affects a child's educational performance.

8. **Seriously Emotionally Disturbed.**
   a. The term means a condition exhibiting one or more of the following characteristics over a long period of time and to a marked degree, which adversely affects educational performance:
      (1) An inability to learn which cannot be explained by intellectual, sensory, or health factors;
      (2) An inability to build or maintain satisfactory interpersonal relationships with peers and teachers;
      (3) Inappropriate types of behavior or feelings under normal circumstances;
      (4) A general pervasive mood of unhappiness or depression; or
      (5) A tendency to develop physical symptoms or fears associated with personal or school problems.
   b. The term includes children who are schizophrenic or autistic. The term does not include children who are socially maladjusted, unless it is determined that they are seriously emotionally disturbed.

9. **Specific Learning Disability.** A disorder in one or more of the basic psychological processes involved in understanding or in using language, spoken or written, which may manifest itself in an imperfect ability to listen, think, speak, read, write, spell, or do mathematical calculations. The term includes such conditions as perceptual handicaps, brain injury, minimal brain dysfunction, dyslexia, and developmental aphasia. The term does not include children who have learning problems which are primarily the result of visual, hearing, or motor handicaps, of mental retardation, or of environmental, cultural, or economic disadvantage.

10. **Speech Impaired.** A communication disorder, such as stuttering, impaired articulation, a language impairment, or a voice impairment, which adversely affects a child's educational performance.

11. **Visually Handicapped.** A visual impairment which, even with correction, adversely affects a child's educational performance. The term includes both partially seeing and blind children.

(U.S. Office of Education, 1977a, pp. 42478–9)

Statistics released by the Department of Education report the number of children between the ages of three and twenty-one who fell into these categories for the 1985–1986 school year (Education of the Handicapped, 1986). These statistics are included in Table 3.1. Note that the categories of deaf and hard-of-hearing have been combined. Also, these figures are approximate because special education enrollment includes students between ages three and twenty-one whereas public school enrollment includes students in kindergarten through twelfth grade.

Handicapped Infants and Toddlers. Under P.L. 94–142, the eleven categories of handicapping conditions include primarily school-age youngsters. More recent legislation has recognized the need to provide intervention early in the life of a child with a handicap. Specifically, P.L. 99–457, the Education of the Handicapped Act Amendments of 1986, includes provision for infants and toddlers with handicaps. It describes these children as:

Individuals from birth to age 2, inclusive, who need early intervention services because they
(a) are experiencing developmental delays, as measured by appropriate diagnostic instruments and procedures in one or more of the following areas: cognitive development, physical development, language and speech

TABLE 3.1

ESTIMATED NUMBER AND PERCENTAGE OF STUDENTS IN EACH CATEGORY
OF IMPAIRMENT*

Category	Number**	Percentage of Students with Handicaps**	Percentage of Students in Public Schools***
Learning disabled	1,843,964	44.81	4.69
Speech impaired	1,106,621	26.89	2.81
Mentally retarded	595,616	14.48	1.51
Emotionally disturbed	332,963	8.10	.85
Multihandicapped	68,970	1.68	.18
Other health impaired	50,478	1.23	.13
Orthopedically impaired	47,977	1.17	.12
Hard-of-hearing and deaf	46,380	1.13	.12
Visually handicapped	20,427	.49	.05
Deaf-blind	910	.02	.002
Total	4,114,675	100.00	10.462

*These figures are for the fifty states.
**Based on special education enrollment of students ages three to twenty-one.
***Based on total U.S. enrollment of 39,350,000 in kindergarten through
   twelfth grade.

development, psychosocial development, or self-help skills, or

(b) have a diagnosed physical or mental condition which has a high probability of resulting in developmental delay.

(P.L. 99–457, p. 1146)

The implications of these amendments are discussed in Chapter 12.

Gifted and Talented. So far, we have said nothing about children who are gifted and/or talented. Most of the federal laws we deal with are designed to provide equal educational opportunity for children who are handicapped. For the most part, youngsters who are gifted are served by other laws and, frankly, are not as often identified for special treatment as are children who are disabled. Nevertheless, youngsters who are gifted and talented are a special class of exceptional individuals and often need special education.

The federal definition of children who are gifted and talented was passed into law in 1978

through the Gifted and Talented Children's Act of 1978. It reads as follows:

> . . . "gifted and talented children" means children, and whenever applicable, youth, who are identified at the preschool, elementary, or secondary level as possessing demonstrated or potential abilities that give evidence of high performance capabilities in areas such as intellectual, creative, specific academic, or leadership ability, or in the performing and visual arts, and who by reason thereof, require services or activities not ordinarily provided by the school.
>
> (P.L. 95–561, Section 902)

INTERRELATIONSHIPS AMONG HANDICAPS

It should be obvious by now that there are reasons both for continuing the practice of categorizing children and for modifying the practice. This

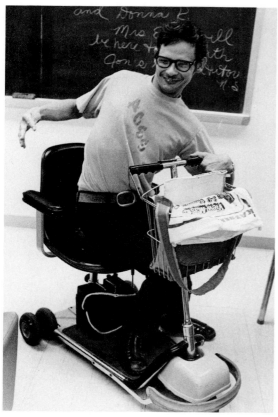

Sam has cerebral palsy and experiences serious motor and speech problems. Nevertheless, he is academically talented and performs very well in his university courses. (Photo by Joseph Bodkin.)

In addition to learning problems, this child has a vision problem and has difficulty interacting with other people. (Courtesy of HDS/U.S. HHS.)

section introduces an important concept: It is dangerous to label a child as having a certain disability or handicap simply because he or she exhibits one or more traits associated with that condition.

At this stage, it is important to obtain a clear understanding of the differences between a disability and a handicap. The term **disability** refers to an objective, measurable, organic dysfunction or impairment, such as loss of a hand or paralysis of speech muscles or legs. The term **handicap** refers to environmental or functional demands placed upon a person with a disability in a given situation. A handicap is the effect a disability has on an individual's functioning in specific circumstances. Whereas a disability is always with the individual, a handicap is not. Handicaps are situation-specific; that is, a person with a disability may be handicapped in one situation but not in another. Persons who are visually impaired may be more handicapped when traveling in unfamiliar terrain than are sighted persons. On the other hand, persons who are visually impaired may have an advantage over sighted persons in occupations where eyesight is not important. For example, some persons who are blind may work well in film-processing plants, where it is essential that certain operations be carried out in total darkness.

Similarly, a child's physical disability may not be a handicap in many situations. A mathematically precocious boy with IQ of 130 would not be considered handicapped in calculus class even though he is paralyzed from the waist down. All the teacher needs to do is to make room for the wheelchair; no other special considerations are necessary. Additional discussions of disability and handicap are found in Chapter 7.

There are three major problems with overzealous categorization:

1. Children who are handicapped often have more than one discrete handicap or problem.

2. A disability may produce different behaviors in different children.

3. Similar behaviors may be found in children with different disabilities.

Related Handicaps

It is almost inevitable that children who are handicapped will feel a certain amount of frustration when they are unable to compete with their more normal peers in certain activities. The frustration may result in a characteristic style of behavior and may lead to additional emotional problems. For instance, a child with a physical disability may be unable to compete in certain physical activities, such as baseball, during recess. If this child's normal peers place a high value on this activity and spend their free time talking baseball and playing the game, the child who is handicapped may become quite frustrated. This frustration may become generalized and make the child lose confidence in his/her other normal abilities.

For example, John S. was born with a club foot. Although early surgery helped, at age nine John is a little clumsy and cannot keep up with his peers in sports. Although his school work is above average, he is not popular with his peers or his teachers because of his inappropriate behavior. In a word, he is a pest! He fights, pinches, and makes others unhappy in a variety of ways. John's inappropriate behavior very well may stem from his own feelings of inadequacy and inability to keep up with his more athletically inclined peers.

Varying Behavior

A disability may produce different behaviors in different children. It is often quite difficult to pinpoint the cause of a behavior or set of behaviors. Indeed, it is unwise to assume that we know precisely why a certain child displays a particular behavior. Conversely, it is difficult to know exactly which behaviors will result from a specific disability. For instance, consider brain injury. Some years ago, it was a fairly common practice to label some children as "brain injured" and to set up special classes for them. We now know that this was not a good practice because brain injury in children can result in quite different behaviors, depending upon, among other things, such factors as (1) the location of the lesion (injury) on the brain, (2) the severity of the injury, and (3) the age of the child when the injury occurred.

Mental retardation, hyperactivity, hypoactivity, blindness, and cerebral palsy are all possible effects of brain injury. It is easy to see that each will be associated with quite distinctive behaviors.

Let us look at two children who are mentally retarded who behave quite differently. Bill is an aggressive child who is always fighting. The major source of his problems may be the fact that his mental retardation or slow learning ability prevents him from keeping up with his peers in school, and so he acts aggressively in an attempt to gain some status in an area unrelated to academics. Mary is also mentally retarded, but she is shy and withdrawn. She never participates in class because she is so far behind the other children. She has a few friends her own age, but she is more relaxed with younger children.

Clearly, it is unfair to the children to stereotype them and to assume that all children who carry the same label are alike.

As mentioned earlier, there is a potential relationship between **hyperactivity** and brain injury. The child who is hyperactive is fidgety, often out of his/her seat, and highly distractible, finding it hard to concentrate for very long. That child often seems unable to focus on relevant stimuli and is distracted by irrelevant details. A popular belief is that brain injury is the cause of hyperactivity and, furthermore, that hyperactivity is a reliable and valid indicator of brain injury. Unfortunately, little scientific evidence supports these conclusions. Many children who are hyperactive show no neurological evidence of brain injury. Also, many children with brain injury are not hyperactive. In fact, certain forms of brain injury may be related to hypoactivity, which is just the opposite of hyperactivity. In addition, some evidence suggests that brain injury may be the cause of certain forms of mental retardation, blindness, deafness, cerebral palsy, epilepsy, and other disabilities. Then again, these disabilities may be caused by factors other than brain injury. Consequently, it is often impossible to identify a precise cause-and-effect relationship between brain injury and particular disabilities.

Similar Behavior

Children with different disabilities may exhibit similar behaviors. For instance, children who are emotionally disturbed may exhibit the same behaviors as those who are mentally retarded, although their behaviors result from different mechanisms and causes. Judging from one set of behaviors, we could not make a firm and accurate diagnosis of the etiology of the condition. For example, both children who are mentally retarded and children who are emotionally disturbed can be hyperactive, poor achievers in school, and not well liked by others. Therefore, we must exercise caution before we assume that a child has a certain disability just because he or she exhibits one or more symptoms of that disability. There is such

overlapping of symptoms from different disabilities that psychologists and physicians often have difficulty accurately diagnosing a given problem.

In some cases, such as mental retardation and emotional disturbance, the resulting behaviors may in fact be due to a third factor, such as brain injury. Brain injury may produce some forms of mental illness and some forms of mental retardation. Most educational personnel do not have the training to make diagnoses about mental retardation or to distinguish mental retardation attributable to disease from that caused by brain injury or cultural-familial conditions. It is much more fruitful for educators to deal with the specific behaviors they wish to change or improve than to conjecture about the supposed source of the condition.

For example, consider the case of John S. discussed in the previous section. He exhibits disturbed behavior that we attribute to feelings of inadequacy based on his inability to compete well with his peers. Bill T. acts a lot like John S. Although he is not physically handicapped and is a fair athletic competitor, Bill is always in trouble and seems to go out of his way to pick a fight. He is not popular with his classmates because of inappropriate behavior. Tests show that he is quite far behind his peers in school. In fact, he will be placed in a resource room program for slow learners as soon as possible. Although their behaviors are the result of different problems (mental retardation and physical disability), it is likely that similar methods will be used to help the two boys control their behavior.

GENERIC CLASSIFICATION: AN ALTERNATIVE TO TRADITIONAL CLASSIFICATION SCHEMES

Clearly, the traditional system of labeling children as having certain disabilities is not useful to all people on all occasions. For administrative purposes, most states will continue to use some form of categorical system. Similarly, the category system will continue to be used by many professional groups. For instructional purposes, however, it is much more helpful to consider alternatives to traditional classification schemes. One alternative is to use no labels at all and treat each child as an individual, building an instructional program for that child based upon his or her unique set of strengths and weaknesses. Another alternative is to group children into matching groups depending on the subject matter or skill being taught. Any such classification system depends in large measure on a careful analysis of a child's academic, physical, and personal strengths and weaknesses. This approach has come to be known by many names, the most common of which are generic, cross-categorical, and noncategorical.

Regardless of the terminology employed, the philosophy is similar and the goal is the same—to provide the best education or treatment program possible for each child. Still, because so many diverse sources and kinds of information about special learners are available, all the generic systems require some way to relate the many bits of information and concepts to a readily communicable model or design. We have chosen to illustrate one method that we have found to be especially helpful.

Developmental Domains

Some years ago, Benjamin Bloom (1956) developed what he called a "Taxonomy of Educational Objectives." In his classic work, he proposed a system whereby all the education-related tasks taught in schools would be classified in three functional domains: cognitive, affective, and psychomotor. That classification system proved to be popular and useful as a way not only of organizing educational objectives but also of classifying children's problems. Over the next twenty years, other writers adopted Bloom's classifications, and some added a fourth domain: language. It can be argued that language is properly a function of cognition,

but there is a certain utility to the separation of the two domains. Thus, we choose to introduce four functional **developmental domains**: the cognitive, motor, social, and communication domains.

The *cognitive,* or intellectual, domain is most clearly identified with the academic aspects of education. This domain includes the construct that is so hard to define and measure: **general intellectual ability.** Traditionally, youngsters who are retarded were viewed as deficient in cognitive skills, and consequently, they were thought to be incapable of learning certain academic subjects. This traditional view has somewhat limited use, but it is true to some extent. More recent thinking, on the other hand, suggests that some youngster's lack of success in the cognitive domain lies as much in the definition and presentation of academic tasks as in the child's innate lack of ability.

Also included within the cognitive domain are specific academic achievements, such as reading comprehension and decoding and arithmetic computation and reasoning. Children with specific learning disabilities often have problems in specific academic areas. In fact, the U.S. Office of Education definition of learning disabilities includes references to problems in specific academic areas that are *not* primarily the result of mental retardation.

The *motor* domain includes the ability to use gross and fine motor skills in order to move about the environment. Children with mild or serious muscular, skeletal, and/or coordination problems find it difficult in some situations to take care of themselves independently. Blind youngsters, though perhaps having no muscular, skeletal, or coordination problems, also may find it difficult to move freely in their environment.

The *social* domain deals with an individual's social ability: for instance, establishing and maintaining satisfactory interpersonal skills; displaying behavior within reasonable social expectations; and personal adjustment—freedom from irrational fears, compulsion, and so on.

The *communication* domain covers facility

Handicapping Condition

Domain	Deaf	Deaf-Blind	Hard-of-Hearing	Mentally Retarded	Multihandicapped	Orthopedically Impaired	Other Health Impaired	Seriously Emotionally Disturbed	Specific Learning Disability	Speech Impaired	Visually Handicapped
Cognitive				X	X				X		
Motor		O			X	X	X				O
Social	O	O	O	O	X	O		X			
Communication	X	X	X		X			O		X	X

Figure 3.1. The relationship between a handicap and domains of functioning. The "X" indicates the domain typically affected the most. The "O" indicates a domain that may be affected to a lesser extent.

with language and the ability to communicate at a level commensurate with one's general intellectual and physical capabilities. Communication is a basic human characteristic; the inability to communicate deprives an individual of the essence of human interaction. Youngsters who are deaf, blind, speech impaired, or learning disabled often face problems in this domain.

Finally, there are interactions among the domains. As we saw in the previous section, "Interrelationships Among Handicaps," problems in the cognitive, motor, or communication domains often spill over into the social domain.

The relationship is quite simple in some cases: Youngsters who are mentally retarded by definition have problems in the cognitive domain. Youngsters who are orthopedically or otherwise health impaired clearly have problems in the motor domain. Emotional disturbance falls within the social domain, and hearing impairment within the communication domain. Blindness, however, cuts across at least two domains—motor and communication: motor, because persons who

are blind may face mobility restrictions, and communication, because of their inability to read conventional print under normal circumstances. Learning disability has historically been a catchall category; the various forms and symptoms of learning disability cut across all four domains. Figure 3.1 illustrates the impact of a handicapping condition on each domain.

In summary, analysis of functional behaviors within the four developmental domains can be a useful tool for describing relevant behaviors of individual children and for developing education programs for youngsters with problems. It provides a frame of reference shared by most professionals who work with children who are handicapped. There are differences of opinion about the utility of the system, but most professionals use its terms and categories. The usefulness of a given system is judged by the extent to which it helps its users communicate with others in the same or related fields. Precise communication of a child's needs is the first step toward the provision of services to meet those needs.

SUMMARY

Definitions and classifications imply the affixing of labels to children. Most educators believe that indiscriminate labeling should be avoided and, most importantly, that *no two children are alike* and labeling invites finding similarities or likenesses when none exist. Thus, most educators believe that children should be viewed first as individuals and only second as handicapped. Some educators fear that labeling a child as handicapped may cause teachers and others to have lowered expectations about what the child can actually accomplish and lead the child to feel less worthy or to have lowered expectations about what he or she can or can't do. Pinning a label to a child does not mean the child will always receive better services. In fact, knowing a child's category or label tells us almost nothing about what the child needs in the way of education programs.

On the other hand, considerable knowledge about human abilities is related to the traditional category system, and over the years, a kind of shorthand based on this system has developed among certain professional disciplines. This shorthand enables people to communicate easily and rapidly (although often somewhat imprecisely). In addition, some state and federal laws are tied specifically to certain categories, and elimination of the category system might eliminate or severely curtail the availability of funds or services to certain children.

According to the United States Congress, children who are handicapped are children who, having been evaluated in accordance with certain specified procedures, have been found to have one or more of the impairments listed and consequently to need special education and related services. The categories of impairment are mentally retarded, hard-of-hearing, deaf, speech impaired, visually handicapped, seriously emotionally disturbed, orthopedically impaired, other health impaired, deaf-blind, multihandicapped, and specific learning disabilities. Two other classes of exceptional individuals that may re-

quire special services are youngsters who are gifted and talented and infants and toddlers who are handicapped.

Because of some abuse and misuse of testing and evaluation procedures, the federal government also has defined the procedures that should and should not be followed when determining if a child has a handicap. Educators are cautioned not to assume a child who is categorized as having a particular handicap is just like every other child who is similarly labeled. The following cautions should be noted:

1. Children who are handicapped often have more than one discrete handicap or problem.

2. A disability may produce different behaviors in different children.

3. Similar behaviors may be found in children with different disabilities.

In addition to the traditional classification scheme that appears in U.S. law, another scheme often used by educators and other professional groups classifies education-related problems into one or more of four developmental domains: cognitive, motor, social, and communication.

Suggestions for Further Reading

Bloom, B. (1956). *Taxonomy of educational objectives: The classification of educational goals.* New York: Longmans.
This is the classic work that led to much rethinking of planning and procedures for educating children. Bloom introduced the idea that education goals could be classified as cognitive, affective, or psychomotor.

Cartwright, G. P., & Cartwright, C. A. (1978). Definitions and classification approaches. In J. T. Neisworth & R. M. Smith (Eds.), *Retardation: Issues, assessment, and intervention.* New York: McGraw-Hill.
Although this chapter was developed specifically for a book dealing with mental retardation, the concepts it raises are applicable to all handicapping conditions.

Hobbs, N. L. (1975). *The futures of children.* San Francisco: Jossey-Bass.

Hobbs, N. L. (1976). *Issues in the classification of children* (Vols. 1 & 2). San Francisco: Jossey-Bass.

This three-volume set is the product of a federally funded study of the problems of labeling and classifying children. Approximately ninety researchers and writers from many different disciplines collaborated to produce a definitive and far-reaching analysis of issues in the classification of children.

Rosenthal, R., & Jacobsen, L. (1968). *Pygmalion in the classroom*. New York: Holt, Rinehart and Winston.

This book is suggested not for the excellence of its research design (which has been criticized by research specialists), but for the provocative theory it proposes: Children labeled as retarded do not achieve as well as those children of equal intelligence who are not so labeled. The "Rosenthal phenomenon" is often quoted by persons who are opposed to labeling children for instructional purposes.

Ysseldyke, J. E., & Algozzine, B. (1982). *Critical issues in special and remedial education*. Boston: Houghton Mifflin.

Chapter 4 of this book, "Issues in Identification," contains an excellent review of the problems, and pros and cons, of classification and labeling.

Relevant Journals

Exceptional Children

This journal is published six times a year by The Council for Exceptional Children in Reston, Virginia. Articles related to definition and classification of children frequently appear.

The Journal of Special Education

This journal, published by Grune and Stratton, occasionally includes articles pertaining to issues of classification and definition.

Part II presents the predominant facts and theories, promises and problems—the "what is" and the "what should be"—about exceptional children. It covers the gifted and talented in addition to those whose disabilities fall within the legal categories of handicaps, as well as other groups— especially young children and their families and the adult handicapped—who are of concern to educators.

PART II

Characteristics of Exceptional Children

Visual Handicaps

Did You Know That . . .

- many children and adults who are labeled blind may actually have useful vision?

- most children who are visually handicapped are presently attending schools in their own neighborhoods with sighted children?

- teachers' attitudes, expectations, and reactions to students who have little or no vision can influence how those students feel about themselves, their capabilities, and their associations with the sighted world?

- attempts to determine the number of people who are blind yield widely differing figures because there is so little agreement on what constitutes blindness?

- people with little or no vision do not automatically develop superior auditory and tactile senses?

The setting is the state fair grounds on a hot, humid August afternoon, with the sun pouring rays of light and heat over the tightly packed bleachers. Paul and Cindy, each balancing melting ice cream cones and half-empty boxes of popcorn, wiggle between the obstacle course of knees and feet to their seats with their parents in the center section across from the bandstand.

The youngsters had been eagerly counting off the days until this trip to the fair, although each day that brought closer the excitement of the exhibits and competitions also brought closer the first day of school, now just two weeks away. Both dates generated anticipation, the former of delight and the latter of apprehension. Paul worried about how his fourth-grade classmates would react to his closed-circuit television and his tinted thick lenses. Cindy, Paul's cousin, wondered if her eighth-grade friends would still treat her as one of the gang now that she would be using braille, taped texts, and her Optacon for reading this year. The parents of both children were also concerned about the degree of acceptance their children would meet as the new school year began and what growth the children would show in social and academic skills during the year. So much would depend upon the teachers Paul and Cindy were to have and how prepared and willing they would be to welcome children with special needs but with the same desire and potential to learn as the other children in the class. These questions, and long-range uncertainties, however, were crowded out for the moment by the entrance of the marching band that opened the afternoon program.

If you were a spectator seated near Paul and Cindy and their parents, what would your reactions be to these two active youngsters at the fair? Probably you wouldn't even notice them or their parents among the crowd, unless you happened to note Cindy's constantly wandering, uncoordinated eye movements or Paul's heavy spectacle lenses. Their concerns about school would not be apparent, just their animated responses to the activity and bustle around them. Would you

Some students use the Optacon for reading and then take notes on the brailler, as this student is doing. (Courtesy of the Wisconsin School for the Visually Handicapped.)

wonder about what these children could actually be seeing? How would you react to them or other children whose vision was limited if they were in your school or your classes? What would be your expectations for them at the fair or at school once you learned that Paul could see nothing very clearly five inches beyond his nose and Cindy could only tell the difference between light and dark, distinguish light sources, and pick out large moving objects? And what would you expect from their parents?

Paul and Cindy are among the over 46,000 school-age children in the United States who have little or no useful vision (*American Printing House for the Blind Annual Report,* 1987). Although they are a relatively small group among the total number of children with handicaps in this country, children and young adults with visual impairments deserve the same professional concern and expertise as children with other types of disabilities so that they can develop fully their capabilities during their school years. Vision is responsible for a great deal of human communication, and a reduction or absence of this sense can

lead to significant changes in patterns of activity and social interaction.

The questions we raised about your reactions to and expectations for children like Paul and Cindy will emerge again in this chapter as we talk about the way we see; definitions; causes of limited vision; identification of school children with impaired vision; characteristics of children who are visually handicapped in areas of cognitive, language, motor, and social development; and appropriate educational programs.

HOW WE SEE

Normal vision is the result of a very carefully synchronized complex of intricate structures, coordinated muscle activities, photochemical reactions, and electrical impulses. Efficient use of vision, however, is greatly dependent upon the state of the whole human being. We cannot accurately predict how a person will use what vision he or she possesses, but we can try to understand the process of seeing, the kinds of problems that can occur, the human capabilities we as educators can call into play, and the environmental adjustments we can make to enhance the process.

The process of seeing requires the presence of light, something to reflect that light, a functional organ of sight to pick up or sense that light, and a brain to receive and give meaning to the impulses transmitted by the organ. When the cells of the retina are stimulated by light rays that have passed through the various structures of the eye (see Box 4.1), the resulting chemical reaction brings about the release of electrical impulses, which travel along the optic nerve to the brain. The brain then acts upon these impulses to interpret them. At this point, we enter the realm of perception, "the ability of the person to make sense and to organize impressions reaching him via the sense organs" (Faye, 1970, p. 169).*

Visual performance is dependent to a large extent on how well the brain combines the visual images with auditory and other sensory input. The skills used to get visual images transmitted as electrical impulses to the brain involve:

- fixing and focusing on an object
- tracking or following a moving object
- accommodating or adjusting for objects at different distances
- converging or directing both eyes to a near point or object at close range

The perception of visual images "is a decision process that is related more to the child's learning capabilities than to condition of the eyes" (Barraga, 1983, p. 24). The development of visual perception follows a sequence; it seems to progress through various levels that gradually become more complex (Barraga, 1964, 1986):

1. awareness of light, color, contour, edges, and angles

2. form perception of three-dimensional objects

3. form perception of objects represented in pictures and other visual displays

4. sorting and categorizing, identifying and organizing by class

5. symbolic representation of letters and words

6. symbolic representation of expressed ideas

DEFINITIONS

You have already read about the difficulties and dangers inherent in classification and labeling systems. In addition to the problems common to any such system, the terminology used to denote the state of having little or no sight is further complicated by the fact that the same terms are defined in very different ways. In *The Unseen Minority: A Social History of Blindness in America* (1976), a comprehensive volume commissioned by the American Foundation for the Blind (AFB) to commemorate their fiftieth anniversary as well as to record the history of blindness in the United States, F. A. Koestler stated that at least sixteen different definitions are given to the word *blind*. A further problem is the emotional overtones that cloak the words used to describe the absence or loss of sight. There is much truth to the statement made in 1949 by Lloyd Greenwood, who was blinded during the war, that "more people are blinded by definition than by any other cause" (Schloss, 1963, p. 111).

Personal Definitions

Human beings throughout history have shown a wide range of attitudes toward those with limited or no sight. Frequently, they attribute to these "less fortunate" people the feelings and reactions they think they would find in themselves in similar circumstances (Bartel & Guskin, 1980; Scholl, 1986b; Wright, 1983). Even today, thoughts of

---

*Perception in general, and visual perception in particular, are beyond the scope of this discussion. For a basic introduction to this fascinating area, see J. J. Gibson (1966) and J. E. Hochberg (1964). We will summarize by quoting Hochberg: *In short, we do not see objects directly, nor do we "see" the retinal image, nor do we "see" the excitation of the optic nerve. At most, we can say that what we "see" is the final effect on the projection area of the cerebral cortex. (p. 15)*

dependency, uselessness, punishment, darkness, evil, and the supernatural arise among those not acquainted with persons without sight who are functioning and contributing members of society. Some people may have a positive attitude toward *individuals* who are blind, but they may react quite differently to the *concept* of blindness. B. Lowenfeld (1975) has identified four attitudes people commonly display toward those who are blind: pity, because "the blind" are often viewed as helpless; fear, because blindness may be catching and because visions of the perceived sense of helplessness may be aroused; guilt, because one's own position is more fortunate for no apparent reason or merit; and discomfort, because there is a certain amount of uncertainty about how to initiate interaction with a person who does not see you.

The attitudes toward, the expectations for, and the reactions to individuals with handicapping conditions to a great extent help determine the way those individuals feel about themselves, their capabilities, and their interactions with others (Barraga, 1983; Scholl, 1986b). In *The Making of Blind Men,* Robert Scott reports his study of agencies and organizations providing services for the blind. Having worked from a sociological perspective, Scott (1969) states:

> The disability of blindness is a learned social role. The various attitudes and patterns of behavior that characterize people who are blind are not inherent in their condition but rather, are acquired through ordinary processes of social learning. . . . Blind men are made, and by the same processes of socialization that have made us all. (p. 14)

One way people define blindness, then, is through their own emotional responses and expectations in the absence of knowledge or direct experience.

Definitions for Legal and Administrative Purposes

The definitions used to determine eligibility for rehabilitation services, tax exemptions, disability benefits, and Social Security payments for the blind date from 1934. At that time, the Section of Ophthalmology of the American Medical Association, at the request of the Illinois Department of Public Welfare, developed definitions that could be incorporated into statutory laws and regulations (Schloss, 1963). The AMA definition, with slight modification, quickly gained acceptance and is still used today for many official purposes. According to this definition, **blindness** is "central visual acuity for distance of 20/200 or less in the better eye with correction or, if greater than 20/200, a field of vision no greater than 20 degrees at the widest diameter" (Hatfield, 1975).

Notice that the emphasis is on distance visual acuity and visual field. **Visual acuity** is a measure of the resolving (or refracting) power of the eyes to bend light rays so they come to a point of focus on the retina and enable us to see fine detail at varying distances. Normal visual acuity is recorded as 20/20. The top numeral indicates the distance from the letter or symbol on the familiar eye chart, usually the Snellen Chart (see photo). The bottom numeral indicates the distance from which a person with normal vision could read the test letter or symbol. In other words, a visual acuity of 20/200 means that a person must be only twenty feet away to read the symbol on the Snellen Chart that a person with normal vision would be able to read from a distance of two hundred feet. Visual acuity accurately measured with the Snellen Chart tells us how an individual responds to certain kinds of visual stimuli under specific ambient and direct lighting conditions and with careful consideration of both distance from and height of the chart. The acuity obtained, however, tells us little about how an individual might use vision in the everyday events of home and school.

Visual field is the entire area we can see at one time without shifting our gaze. Visual field is reported in degrees. Some individuals have such very restricted fields that we say they have "tunnel vision," a situation that may make it difficult for them to move around freely from place to place, particularly in crowded or unfamiliar areas. Those persons with a field restricted to 20° or less are considered blind for legal purposes.

BOX 4.1
THE EYE AND THE PROCESS OF SEEING

The eyeball, or globe, takes up about one-fifth of the orbit, the bony pear-shaped cavity in the face that, with fatty and connective tissues, provides a protective housing. The six extraocular muscles that control the movements of the eyeball attach to the globe and are anchored in the orbit as well. Additional protection for the globe comes from the eyelids, lashes, and brows, as well as from the tears that constantly bathe the inner surfaces of the eyelids and the front of the eyeball.

The eyeball is made up of three main layers. The transparent cornea and opaque tough sclera form the outer protective layer. The middle layer contains the iris, the ciliary body, and the vascular choroid. The choroid nourishes the sensory retina, the inner nerve layer of the eyeball.

Figure 4.1 illustrates the major structures of the eye that enable light rays to enter and activate the seeing process. Light first penetrates the cornea, approximately one millimeter thick and the size of a small watch crystal. The cornea is the most powerful refractive medium of the eye; that is, it accomplishes most of the bending of the light rays toward a point of focus.

Light rays continue from the cornea through the anterior chamber, which is filled with aqueous humor, a clear liquid secreted by the ciliary body. The aqueous humor helps regulate the intraocular pressure. Any condition that interrupts the even flow of aqueous humor from the posterior chamber (the area between the lens and the iris) through the pupil into the anterior chamber and on to the Canal of Schlemm can result in a dangerous increase in intraocular pressure. The result is glaucoma, a major cause of blindness in the United States.

Light rays in the aqueous humor continue through the pupil, an opening the size of which is controlled by action of the muscles in the iris. The iris acts as a sensitive diaphragm to limit the amount of light that passes through the pupil to the back portion of the eye.

Next, light rays pass through the biconvex crystalline lens. Here the rays are further refracted so that in the normal eye they come to a point of focus on the retina. The lens is held in place by suspensory ligaments. The lens curvature is altered by action of the ciliary muscle on the suspensory ligaments, which in turn cause a greater or lesser bulging of the lens surface. The greater the bulge or curvature, the stronger the refractive power. This action of the ciliary muscle, suspensory ligaments, and lens to focus light rays is known as accommodation. The ability to accommodate allows us to see objects clearly at a distance as well as close by. The ability decreases with the aging process, which explains why many adults over age forty experience some difficulty focusing on close objects or reading print held at the distance to which they have been accustomed. The lens may also become opaque and prevent the clear passage of light rays in a condition known as cataract, a major cause of blindness among adults.

From the lens, the rays proceed through the gel-like vitreous body. The vitreous body, about 99 percent water, accounts for almost two-thirds of the weight and volume of the eyeball and helps maintain its form and internal pressure.

Finally, light rays reach the retina, where, in the normal eye, they come to a point of focus (see Figure 4.2). The retina contains some 126 million photoreceptor or rod and cone cells that produce a chemical reaction when stimulated by light, that portion of the electromagnetic spectrum visible to humans. The 120 million rods are distributed throughout the retina but are more numerous in the periphery. They are most sensitive to movement and low levels of

Source: Information in this box is based on Newell and Ernest (1974) and Vaughan and Asbury (1986).

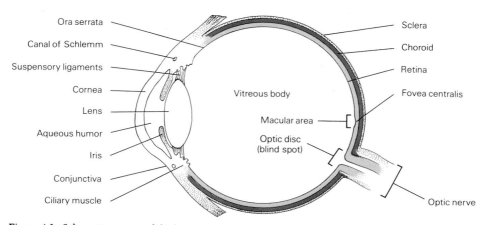

Figure 4.1. Schematic section of the human eye. (With permission of the American Optometric Association, 243 No. Lindbergh Blvd., St. Louis, MO 63141.)

illumination. Clustered tightly together in the macular region, the area of central (as opposed to side, or peripheral) vision, are most of the six million cone cells. These cells are sensitive to color and high levels of illumination, and they enable us to discriminate fine detail. Only cone cells are located in the fovea, the area giving us our sharpest central vision. The retina is an extension of brain tissue; if it is damaged, it cannot be regenerated or replaced.

When rods and cones are stimulated by light, the resulting chemical reaction leads to the release of electrical impulses, which are transmitted along the optic nerve and pathways to the occipital lobe of the brain in ways that are not all clearly understood.

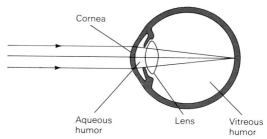

Figure 4.2. Path of light rays from environment to retina. (Adapted from *Human Eye* [Southbridge, Mass.: American Optical Corporation], 1976, p. 17; Courtesy of American Optical Corporation.)

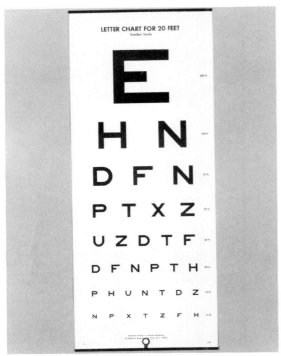

LETTER CHART FOR 20 FEET
Snellen Scale

The Snellen Chart. (Courtesy of the National Society to Prevent Blindness.)

The definition used for **partial vision** has usually been 20/70 or less in the better eye after correction (Hatfield, 1975). In other words, at a distance of twenty feet, a person with 20/70 acuity can read the symbols on the chart that a person with normal vision could read from seventy feet. Again, this definition takes into account only distance acuity. The term *partially sighted* is still found sometimes, but less and less as we recognize the importance of usable vision for educational purposes (*International classification of impairments, disabilities, and handicaps*, 1980: Scholl, 1986a).

Definitions for Educational Purposes

There are many visual behaviors in addition to looking at distant objects. At one time, people

believed that those with poor vision who continued to try to see would increase the danger of further vision loss. But once eye specialists realized that this was not true except in rare cases, they directed more attention to the ways individuals could use whatever vision they possessed in a variety of settings. In her study with children considered blind for legal purposes, N. Barraga (1964) showed that with carefully designed and sequenced instruction, visual performance or efficiency could actually be improved, although the measured near-vision acuity might not show significant change.

Definitions that reflect a concern for effective and efficient use of functional vision are being used more frequently in decisions about appropriate educational settings and instructional programs for school children with impaired vision. **Functional vision** denotes "how people use whatever vision they may have" (Barraga, 1983, p. 24). The federal regulations for Public Law 94–142 define visually handicapped for school purposes in such a way that functional vision is primary: "Visually handicapped means a visual impairment which, even with correction, adversely affects a child's educational performance. The term includes both partially seeing and blind children" (U.S. Office of Education, 1977a, p. 42479). Not all children, or adults, who have visual impairments will necessarily have difficulty with their functional vision. For this reason, we reserve the term *visually handicapped* for "the broad range of children who require special education programs and services because of their visual limitations" (Scholl, 1986b, p. 29).

For the remainder of this chapter, we will use the following set of definitions, which are based on assessment of functional vision:

▪ **Visually handicapped.** The total group of children who require special educational provisions because of visual problems (Barraga, 1983, p. 22); a child "whose visual impairment interferes with his optimal learning and achievement, unless adaptations are made in the methods of presenting learning experi-

TABLE 4.1

SUMMARY OF DEFINITIONS OF BLINDNESS AND LOW VISION

	Legal/Administrative			Educational/Functional
Terms	*Clinical*	*Vocational*	*Economic*	
Blind	Corrected visual acuity of 20/200 or less or field restriction to 20 degrees or less (Hatfield, 1975, p. 4)	"Impossible for a person to do work at which he had previously earned a living"; 20/60 to 20/200 (Schloss, 1963, p. 112)*	"Absence of ability to do any kind of work, industrial or otherwise, for which sight is essential"; less than 20/200 or severe field loss (Schloss, 1963, p. 112)*	Total loss of sight *or* light perception without projection (Faye, 1970, p. 3) Can be educated through braille and related media with little or no residual vision employed (Halliday, 1971, p. 11) No vision or no "significant usable vision" (Colenbrander, 1976b, p. 4)
Legally blind	"An outmoded term" (Faye, 1976, p. 9)			Inability to perform tasks that normally require gross vision without increased reliance on other senses (Colenbrander, 1976a, p. 6) Inability to read ordinary newsprint even with the help of glasses (Public Health Service, reported in Graham, 1963, p. 130)
Low vision	Partially seeing; visual acuity from 20/70 to 20/200 in the better eye after correction (Hathaway, 1959, p. 17)			Significant visual handicap but with significant usable residual vision (Colenbrander, 1976b, p. 4) Inability to perform tasks normally requiring detailed vision without special visual aids (Colenbrander, 1976a, p. 6) Useful vision for many tasks but adjustments possibly necessary in light, contrast, and distance; auditory and tactile aids useful as supplements to visual materials for some school activities (Barraga, 1983, p. 22–23)

*Adopted by American Medical Association 85th Convention, 1934.

Many children with low vision must hold their materials close to their faces to see them. (Courtesy of the Wisconsin School for the Visually Handicapped.)

ences, the nature of the materials used, and/or in the learning environment" (Barraga, 1983, p. 25).

- **Blind.** Having either no vision or, at most, light perception (the ability to tell light from dark) but no light projection (the ability to identify the direction from which light comes) (Faye, 1970; Barraga, 1983).
- **Low-vision.** Limited distance vision but some useful near vision at a range of several feet; function varies with light, task, and personal characteristics; adjustments are possibly necessary in lighting, size of print or objects, and distance (Barraga, 1976, 1983).
- **Visually limited.** Having useful vision for most educational purposes but with some limits in function under average conditions; may need some adjustments, as for those with low vision (Barraga, 1983).

The definitions in Table 4.1 summarize those used for legal or administrative, educational, economic, and vocational purposes. Think back to

our earlier descriptions of Paul and Cindy. Both are blind for administrative purposes, but what about for educational purposes? On the basis of the rather limited information about them, how would you describe the functional vision of these children? How many others are there like Paul and Cindy in school?

THE EXTENT OF THE PROBLEM

Any estimate of the size of the visually handicapped population is subject to question for a variety of reasons, not the least of which is that many persons with what others consider to be limited vision do not view themselves as visually handicapped and "have no particular zeal to be counted" (Bledsoe & Williams, 1967). Aside from the human desire to be one of the "in" group, crude census procedures, problems in sampling, and variety in definitions used to collect data all influence the accuracy of the figures obtained and extrapolated (DeSantis & Schein, 1986; Schein & DeSantis, 1986). A fundamental problem has been the lack of agreement on just what constitutes blindness. Unless it is explicitly stated, readers can never be absolutely certain whether the term *blind* as used in the various reports denotes total blindness, legal blindness, or some level of functional blindness.

In spite of the difficulties, however, attempts have been made to determine the number of people who are blind on all continents. The World Health Organization estimates that there are at least 28 million totally blind persons in the world, with the number increasing each year (Vaughan & Asbury, 1986). Estimates of the number in the United States alone run from 400,000 to 10 million (Wood, 1968; Vaughan & Asbury, 1980). The United States Public Health Service, on the basis of the National Health Interview Survey for 1978, reported 11,415,000 people with some type of vision impairment affecting one or both eyes. Of that number, 1,391,000 are unable to read newsprint even with glasses (*Sight Saving Review,* 1979). This figure includes some individuals whose functional vision might be improved, in some cases to within the normal range, with well-fitted lenses, surgery, medication, or some combination of these measures.

If we limit the estimate to include only those people whose vision is below the normal range after correction, the figure drops considerably. Using the definition for administrative or legal purposes—20/200 or less in the better eye after correction or a field restricted to 20° or less—the National Society to Prevent Blindness (NSPB) has recently revised its estimates of the size of the blind population to be 498,000 in the United States, Puerto Rico, and the Virgin Islands (*Vision Problems in the United States, A Statistical Analysis,* 1980).

As for school-age children, figures vary greatly. Each January, the American Printing House for the Blind (APH) conducts an annual registration of school-age children who qualify for service under the definition of blindness for legal purposes. The APH registration figures shown in Table 4.2 indicate a steady rise over the past 12 years to a total of 45,930 in 1986. This increase reflects, among other things, better reporting and registering procedures and greater awareness of school programs for the visually handicapped since passage of P.L. 94–142. Of course, there are many among that number whose *functional* vision does not warrant the label "blind" in any way; and there are some whose acuity (better than 20/200) excludes them from registration but whose visual function is not well developed.

Now, let's compare the figures reported by the United States Department of Education, Special Education Programs (SEP), with the APH figures (Kirchner, 1985). In 1980–81, SEP reported the number of children who are visually handicapped to be 35,759, and in 1981–82 to be 33,577. During those same years, the APH registration figures for only those children considered blind and deaf-blind for legal purposes were 33,920 and 34,939, respectively. SEP totals are for *all* children who are visually handicapped and deaf-blind, not just

TABLE 4.2

SCHOOL-AGE BLIND CHILDREN REGISTERED WITH THE AMERICAN PRINTING HOUSE FOR THE BLIND

Year	Number of Children
1974	25,809
1975	27,320
1976	28,995
1978	32,465
1980	34,814
1982	38,249
1984	44,313
1985	45,221
1986	45,930

Source: From annual reports published by the American Printing House for the Blind, Louisville, Kentucky.

those youngsters with visual handicaps whose visual acuity was 20/200 or less after correction. It is reasonable to expect that, because those children with acuity of 20/200 or less are a subset of the larger group of visually handicapped, SEP figures should be larger than APH figures. In fact, they were *less* in 1981–82, which should raise doubts about the accuracy of counting and reporting procedures and should encourage caution in projecting future needs for facilities, personnel, and equipment.

Another elusive but significant figure that carries implications for educators working in nursery school and preschool settings is the number of preschool children (to age five) with impaired vision. In a survey of 250 programs reporting services for preschool children with visual handicaps and centers serving children who are deaf-blind, the American Foundation for the Blind obtained responses from 125 programs, 95 of which actually had preschoolers with visual handicaps enrolled. The number of children with visual handicaps reported was 3,860 (Felix & Spungin, 1978). Because many children in that age group who are visually handicapped attend regular public and private preschool programs not surveyed in this study, both the total number of children served and the number to be served remain unknown.

Let's return to the APH figure for 1986— 45,930 children with vision 20/200 or less or a severe field restriction. Although in relation to other groups of students who are handicapped that figure may seem small, it does not begin to convey the degree of effort required to provide appropriate instructional programs for those children in suitable educational settings. Each student has a myriad of characteristics that set him or her apart from others in the "group" of visually handicapped, just as you may be distinguished from your colleagues and family by your unique skills, behaviors, and idiosyncrasies. R. E. Hoover, the developer of the long-cane technique used for mobility training of many persons who are blind, has wisely observed that only "in the minds of authorities are the blind ever assembled" (Hoover, 1967, p 1).

CAUSES OF
IMPAIRED VISION

Major causes of congenital and acquired visual impairment vary from age group to age group, from country to country, and from one period of history to another as international politics, widespread epidemics, wars, and new technological and medical advances enter the scene. At present in developing countries, major causes of blindness are infectious disease, malnutrition, and vitamin A deficiency (Jan, Freeman, & Scott, 1977; Vaughan & Asbury, 1986). The tragic fact is that much more could be done to prevent the loss of vision that results from these conditions.

In the United States, the major causes of blindness among adults are related to the aging process: retinal degeneration, retinal damage related to diabetes, glaucoma, and senile cataract (Kupfer, 1979). A survey of available eye reports for a sample of 3,885 children who are legally blind registered at the American Printing House for the Blind in 1968–69 showed that the major causes of blindness among school students at that

time were prenatal conditions, injuries and poisonings, tumors, and infectious diseases, including rubella or German measles (Hatfield, 1975).

Prenatal Influences. These were responsible for almost half the blindness among school-age children. Most of these prenatal influences are hereditary and include congenital cataracts, albinism, congenital glaucoma, myopia or nearsightedness, and retinitis pigmentosa. The pattern of transmission for some of these conditions can be determined, so couples who seek **genetic counseling** to obtain information regarding the likelihood of producing offspring with genetically determined disabilities in many instances can make informed decisions regarding their plans to have children. Genetic counseling cannot eliminate the problem of defective, missing, or misplaced genetic material that has played or may in the future play havoc in the development of the fertilized egg. Such counseling and studies of families to discover the presence or absence of specific conditions can, however, yield valuable information concerning probabilities of producing offspring with similar conditions (Milunsky, 1977; Siegel, 1976).

Injuries and Poisoning. These accounted for the second-largest number of children with impaired vision. Retrolental fibroplasia (RLF), now more commonly called retinopathy of prematurity (ROP), caused most of the cases among children in the APH sample. Before 1954, many premature infants of low birth weight were given high concentrations of oxygen over long periods of time in order to maintain life. The risk involved for many of these tiny and fragile infants was not recognized until 1954, and since that time the incidence of RLF has dramatically decreased among that group of infants typical of those premature infants in the 1950s. But today, as high-risk premature infants of much lower birth weight than those in the early 1950s are kept alive, even with carefully monitored procedures and equipment necessary to try to preserve life, some infants still develop the signs of what is now referred to as ROP.

BOX 4.2
MULTICENTER RESEARCH ON RETINOPATHY OF PREMATURITY

Retinopathy of prematurity (ROP) typically develops in the eyes of premature infants of low birth weight. At highest risk are premature infants under 1500 grams (about 3½ pounds) with evidence of intraventricular hemorrhage. Because many more of these tiny babies are now surviving, the total number of children with ROP is increasing. According to U.S. census statistics, the survival rate for infants under 2.2 pounds at birth had risen to about 35 percent in 1983, up from 8 percent in 1950. Preliminary data from more recent studies suggest that the survival rate may be close to twice that rate. Although the exact cause and mechanism for the development of ROP are still not known, factors such as oxygen, even at room concentration, and bright lights have been suggested as possible contributors to compound problems in the premature retina.

In an attempt to find a way to stop or reduce the abnormal proliferation of blood vessels in the peripheral retina of the eyes of these infants, as well as to determine the natural history of ROP (the progression or course of the disease if left untreated), the National Eye Institute has recently funded a study of ROP that involves the cooperation of twenty-four medical centers. Babies under 1251 grams at birth are referred for monitoring of both eyes. If one eye shows evidence of ROP that meets the criteria for therapeutic intervention, then random assignment is made to treatment or control. Treatment in this study is cryotherapy, the application of extreme cold to destroy the portion of the peripheral retina where abnormal vascular growth occurs. If both eyes are affected and meet criteria for randomization, one eye only is randomly selected for treatment. Periodic follow-up will continue for at least one year to determine outcomes from photographs of the posterior retina of both treated and nontreated (control) eyes.

This clinical study of the natural history of ROP using the recently developed uniform classification system for staging ROP and randomized trial of cryotherapy for intervention holds promise for increasing our basic knowledge of ROP. It also should enable ophthalmologists to identify predictors of adverse outcomes for functional vision and to evaluate the effectiveness of cryotherapy as an intervention technique for the management of ROP.

Source: Palmer, E. A., & Phelps, D. (1986). Multicenter trial of cryotherapy for retinopathy of prematurity. *Pediatrics, 77* (3), 428–429.

In addition to instances of eye damage related to administration of oxygen in the presence of other factors, other substances also can lead to eye problems. Certain drugs for treatment of diseases like malaria can be toxic to eye tissue, as can the lead in paint that some children manage to eat. Fortunately, the eye damage often is only temporary (Vaughan & Asbury, 1986).

The percentage of students with impaired vision due to injury, although seemingly small, can be misleading—many eye injuries involve only one eye, and as long as vision in the other eye remains within the normal range, the student would not be considered blind. The National Society to Prevent Blindness estimates that about 90 percent of eye injuries might have been prevented in the first place. Protective eye wear for participants in sports, enforcement of safety rules and procedures in laboratories and shops, and careful supervision of playground activities would all help to reduce the estimated 167,000 eye injuries that occur annually in the five–seventeen age group (National Society to Prevent Blindness, 1976).

Among the approximately 40 million young adults and adults who participate in racquet sports (squash, racquetball, tennis, handball, paddleball, and badminton), the number of eye injuries has reached almost epidemic proportions (Thackray, 1982). Clearly, an eye that sustains a direct hit from a hard ball traveling at speeds of over one hundred miles per hour is at high risk. Protective eye wear can prevent eye injury, but only if it is worn, something many players resist. Teachers, especially those involved in physical education programs, can significantly reduce loss of vision due to eye injuries by promoting the use of protective eye wear among children—and among professional colleagues.

Neoplasms. These tumors ranked third among the causes of impaired vision in school-age children. Most were retinoblastomas, malignant tumors originating in the retinal layer. Many are probably inherited, although some do result from a new genetic mutation (Newell & Ernest, 1974; Vaughan & Asbury, 1986). Other tumors may occur in the brain or pituitary gland and cause damage to the optic nerve and pathways to the occipital lobe of the brain.

Infectious Diseases. German measles, or rubella, in the mother during pregnancy was responsible for the greatest percentage of damage from infectious diseases. During the first trimester of pregnancy, the structures of the eye form and are very vulnerable to attack by virus infection, which apparently interferes with transcription of genetic information. Varying degrees of hearing impairment, cardiac malformation, and mental retardation frequently accompany eye defects resulting from maternal rubella. Vaccination against rubella can help prevent the spread of this contagious and potentially devastating disease but will not, of course, bring relief to those children who already bear its effects. What is not generally realized is that the viral infection may persist and render the child contagious for several years after birth (Newell & Ernest, 1974; Vaughan & Asbury, 1986).

General Systemic Diseases. Blindness in school-age children due to such conditions as central nervous system disorders and multiple sclerosis was relatively infrequent in the APH sample.

Unfortunately, in the sample studied, the cause of about one-third of the cases was either not known or not specified. A large portion of this group probably can be attributed to RLF cases for which no supporting information was reported and to other cases for which no diagnostic information was available.

CHARACTERISTICS OF CHILDREN WITH VISUAL HANDICAPS

One of the first characteristics of children who are visually handicapped is, by "definition," less than normal vision. There are five major ways that visual impairment, defined as "any optically or medically diagnosable condition in the eye(s) or visual system that affects the structure or functioning of the tissues" (Barraga, 1983, p. 23), *may* affect functional vision to render it less than normal:

1. Vision may be blurred for close work only, blurred for distant vision only, or fuzzy overall. **Refractive errors** are common causes of reduced visual acuity and the lack of sharply focused, clear vision. Refractive errors include nearsightedness, farsightedness, and astigmatism.

   In nearsightedness, or **myopia**, which affects approximately 70 million Americans (Kupfer, 1979), the eyeball is usually too long, which causes light rays to be focused at a point in front of the retina. Only objects held very close to the eyes appear clear. For some, the point of best near vision may be just inches from the face.

   In farsightedness, or **hyperopia**, the eyeball is generally too short, the curvature of the cornea rather flat, or the refractive power of the lens weaker than normal. Light rays are focused at a theoretical point behind the retina, and near objects do not appear as distinct as distant objects. In extreme cases, both near and distant vision are affected.

   In **astigmatism**, the curvature of the cornea is generally irregular, which means some light rays may come to a focus in front of the

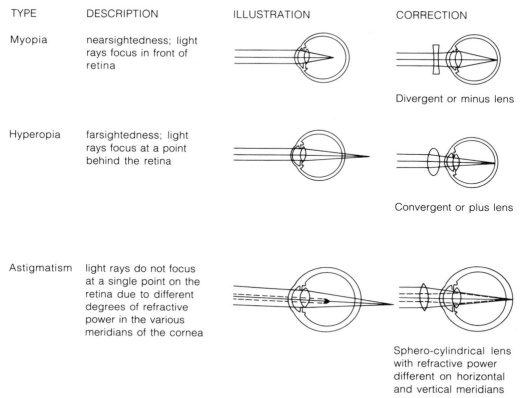

Figure 4.3. Refractive errors and how they can be corrected with lenses.

retina, some on the retina, and some at the theoretical point behind it. Vision can be distorted or blurred, and intensive close work may lead to fatigue and headache.

Fortunately, most refractive errors can be corrected with spectacle or contact lenses. Some individuals, however, have such severe refractive errors that functional vision remains below normal even after correction. Many of the low-vision children in regular classes have severe refractive errors.

2. Visual field may be restricted. Central vision in the macular area of the retina is most suited for detection of detail and color. Peripheral vision is sensitive to motion and the presence of light. Thus, damaged areas of the retina may lead to reduced peripheral vision, loss of central vision, or sporadic patches of vision throughout the field. Field defects may occur in one or both eyes and be symmetrical or irregular; they may affect reading efficiency, safe travel, and the degree to which magnification can be beneficial (Faye, 1970).

3. Color vision may be deficient. Red-green discrimination difficulty is the most common color vision defect. Problems with color vision occur in approximately 7 percent of males but only .05 percent of females.

4. Adaptation to light and dark may be very slow or deficient. A certain decrease in rapid adaptation from dark to light and light to dark occurs with the aging process in the normal eye.

5. The eyes may be extremely sensitive to light, or **photophobic**. People with albinism usually

experience discomfort in bright light, and students who are albinos may function better if they are permitted to sit in darker areas of the classroom.

These major functional vision defects, singly or in combination, can greatly influence other areas of development and performance. Lowenfeld (1971) has identified three primary areas in which visual impairment can lead to difficulty: cognitive development, motor development, and social development.

Cognitive Development

Visual input plays a large role in the development of concepts, in the stimulation and direction of behavior, and in the general provision of information for a child who is sighted to organize the outside world in his or her own thoughts. Children whose visual input is limited, distorted, or essentially nonexistent must rely on other sensory input to construct ideas of what impinges upon them and surrounds them. Hearing and touching; feeling parts to imagine or construct the idea of a whole, or enveloping a small object and then sensing distinct parts; substituting the known qualities of heat, sounds, textures, or feeling for the unknown qualities of color; or using sound cues to determine distance and motion—all these acts can help children who are congenitally blind assimilate information from the environment and adjust their thinking and behavior in response. The range and variety of their experiences, however, may be quite limited in both number and quality compared with those of children with sight or even of children with low vision or students who are adventitiously blinded (students who become blind sometime after birth).

Range and variety of experiences also play a vital role in the development of language in all of its forms—listening, speaking, reading, and writing (Harley, Henderson, & Truan, 1979; Elstner, 1983; Scholl, 1986a). Language acquisition actually has its roots in the first weeks and months of life, as is also true of cognitive, motor, and social development. All of these areas of development are interrelated and can complement, or even impede, each other as a child gains (or has limited) experiences by acting on, interacting with, and accommodating to the people and things in the environment (Urwin, 1983; Millar, 1983). The question of how a child develops spatial and visual concepts when vision is lost, limited, or absent raises interesting points for discussions regarding the use of visual terms such as *look* and *see*. Because they are an integral part of our everyday language, these visual terms are, and should be, used by individuals who are visually handicapped and by those around them. Children without vision can come to an understanding of such terms by using other than visual information and may find that language itself can function to extend access to the world beyond the range of touch and hearing (Garman, 1983; Urwin, 1983; Werth, 1983; Scholl, 1986a).

Motor Development

Without vision, the motor development of a child who is blind may proceed slowly. Before safe, efficient, and independent movement within the environment must come recognition of body parts; an understanding of directionality, laterality, position in space, and position in relation to objects within space; and the skills required to sit, crawl, stand, and finally walk (Hart, 1980; Tooze, 1981). S. Fraiberg and her associates (1977) were able to observe instances of delay in independent walking among the ten infants followed in their studies of otherwise normal children who were blind. Although the prerequisites to independent travel were present, the visual lures—the visually interesting and intriguing and beckoning faces and objects—were not. Although reaching toward interesting sounds was eventually a stimulus to independent exploration for infants who were blind, they did so several months later than infants with sight reached toward visual stimuli. With limited experience, little incentive, and in some cases little encouragement, some low vision and blind children may arrive at school age with poor orientation skills, inadequate body awareness and coordination, and

Beeper softballs emit beeping sounds so people with limited or no vision can hear when the ball is coming near them. Beeper softball is one of many games sighted youngsters and youngsters with limited vision can play together. (Photo by Steve Coon. Courtesy of Centre Daily Times.)

little desire or know-how to move about safely in unfamiliar areas.

The amount of research that has been reported on the physical condition and cardiovascular efficiency of school-age youngsters who are visually handicapped is sparse (DePauw, 1981), but at least one study did indicate that many children who were blind in a modern and well-organized school were less physically fit and exhibited more obesity, weaker upper limbs, and lower exercise tolerance than did the children who were sighted (Jankowski & Evans, 1981). To remedy these problems in these children and to avoid their development in others, we need to be sensitive to the types and amounts of physical activities in which students with visual handicaps participate.

Social Development

Closely tied to both cognitive development and mobility skills are the personal and social factors that are vulnerable to the effects of visual impairment. Attitudes of parents, peers, and teachers

apparently play an important role in determining ideas of self for some students who are visually handicapped, although they are less important for others. Wide differences in personality characteristics can be observed among children who are both low vision and blind, just as in the sighted population. Making social contacts may demand more effort from the visually handicapped because the systems of nonverbal communication may not be operating effectively. Success in school tasks, independence in mobility, and satisfying relationships with family and friends, all in an atmosphere of mutual acceptance and recognition of the inherent worth of each human being, can facilitate the development of a healthy, unique personality. Programs that teach social skills can be successful in promoting satisfactory social contacts (Van Hasselt, Simon, & Mastantueno, 1982; Scholl, 1986a).

Having limited or no vision does not obliterate or eradicate other qualities and reduce persons who are visually handicapped to a homogeneous group. Although some children will be recognized early as needing special assistance or adjustments so they can function in school, and some will be moved to various settings other than the regular classroom to enhance their development and learning, still others will slide by unnoticed unless an alert teacher observes behaviors that indicate a need for careful evaluation and eye examination. In the next section, we consider how teachers can recognize signs of possible eye trouble in children.

IDENTIFICATION

The identification of children with impaired vision depends to some extent on the severity of the impairment. Infants who do not seem to react or respond to faces and brightly colored toys or mobiles may arouse the suspicions of alert parents. Some conditions, such as cataracts or retinoblastoma, will cause the pupil of the eye to appear milky. Other conditions will result in a noticeably small or a very large eyeball. But sometimes, particularly in the case of low-vision and visually limited children or when only one eye is involved, the early months slip by without recognition that vision is not normal.

Screening

In 1972, in an attempt to identify preschoolers having even mild visual impairment, the National Society to Prevent Blindness initiated a large-scale vision screening program. With the help of the mass media and the energies of trained local volunteers from service clubs and community organizations, the society has distributed over 9 million copies of the Home Eye Test, and many children with a "lazy eye" have been identified and referred for care before the point when there is little hope for improvement (National Society to Prevent Blindness, 1983b).

A recently developed Home Eye Test for Adults provides screening tests for distance vision, near vision, and macular degeneration along with a glaucoma survey (Appleton, 1982). Although this screening test should in no way be

This parent is screening his preschool child with a Home Eye Test made available by the National Society to Prevent Blindness. (Courtesy of the National Society to Prevent Blindness.)

considered a substitute for a professional eye examination by an eye care specialist, this test for adults, coupled with the one for preschoolers, provides a convenient and quick way to alert parents and other adults to the possibility of eye problems in young children and in themselves. Often, it becomes the responsibility of the teacher to spot signs of eye problems in school-age children.

Signs of Possible Eye Problems

Too often, children who are visually limited (in Barraga's terms) may not be noticed until the third

TABLE 4.3

SIGNS OF POSSIBLE EYE TROUBLE

Appearance

Crossed eyes
Red-rimmed, encrusted, or swollen eyelids
One eye higher in relation to other
Eyes do not move smoothly in all directions of gaze
Inflamed or watery eyes
Recurring styes

Behaviors

Rubs eyes excessively
Shuts or covers one eye, tilts head or thrusts head forward
Has difficulty reading or doing other work requiring close use of the eyes
Blinks more than usual or is irritable when doing close work
Unable to see distant things clearly
Squints eyelids together or frowns when looking at objects
Loses place frequently when reading

Complaints

Eyes itch, burn, or feel scratchy
Dizziness, headaches, or nausea following close eye work
Blurred or double vision
Eyes hurt in bright light

Source: National Society for the Prevention of Blindness (1977).

or fourth grade, when the size of print in school books is typically decreased and the page layout in texts and workbooks becomes more complex. For this reason, classroom teachers need to be alert to signs of eye problems in all the students in their classes; Table 4.3 summarizes these signs. In addition, some causes of visual impairment do not become manifest until the child is several years old or in school. Mild refractive errors, for example, may not be caught until children start doing more close eye work. Children who exhibit clusters of these signs frequently over a period of time should be referred for further evaluation. Usually, the referral goes to the school nurse, the supervisor of special education, or the supervisor of a program for the visually handicapped. In some school districts, all referrals pass through the principal first.

Referral and Follow-up

Referrals can be a waste of time unless there is a well-organized procedure for follow-up. In some school districts, parents are asked to take eye report forms with them for the eye specialist to complete and return to the school. Sometimes in the case of children who are blind and low-vision returning for reexamination by specialists in eye clinics or private offices, the special teacher of the visually handicapped will accompany the parent and child in order to help clarify the child's present level of visual function and to obtain information from the eye specialist.

Teachers and other school personnel can expect to have contacts and/or correspondence with the following health professionals who provide eye care for low-vision and blind youngsters:

- **Ophthalmologist.** Sometimes known as an oculist, an ophthalmologist is a medical doctor who further specializes after medical school and residency in the diagnosis and treatment of eye conditions. The ophthalmologist can use and prescribe drugs, perform surgery, do refractions, prescribe lenses, and carry out other types of medical treatment.
- **Optometrist.** An optometrist is a licensed nonmedical practitioner trained to measure refractive errors and eye muscle disturbances. In the majority of cases, the optometrist's treatment is limited to the prescribing and fitting of lenses. Some optometrists, as well as some ophthalmologists, focus their practice on low-vision care and specialize in examining low-vision patients to determine what aids, if any, might enhance their usable vision for close work, travel, or distance sightings.
- **Optician.** An optician is trained to grind lenses according to prescription, fit spectacle lenses into frames, and adjust frames to the wearer.
- **Orthoptist.** An orthoptist is a technician trained to carry out eye exercise programs under medical supervision to try to improve fusion and muscle balance and to stimulate the use of central vision in individuals whose foveal area of the macula in the retina for some reason has not been adequately stimulated.

Children who have been examined by eye specialists may be referred to low-vision clinics to see if special lenses, magnifiers, closed-circuit television systems, or other electronic aids may help increase the efficiency of their visual performance for certain tasks. For example, Paul, whom we saw at the state fair, visited a university low-vision clinic. After experimenting with several hand-held magnifiers, as well as with several types of spectacle lenses, he chose to try a hand-held magnifier for his school work. Because Paul's myopia may progress as he grows older, his present aid may be helpful for only a limited time. People using low-vision aids will often abandon them because they have not learned to use them prop-

The specialist is watching for any signs that may be indicative of vision problems. (Courtesy of Association for Retarded Citizens.)

erly or because their level of visual function has changed and the aid is no longer in fact an aid. Follow-up visits to low-vision clinics are essential to eliminate these problems and to reassess the usefulness of aids as eye conditions change and as users develop their skills and broaden their interests.

Of course, not all the children identified in screening programs or by teachers are candidates for programs for the visually handicapped. Screening is only a gross check to separate those youngsters whose performance meets a predetermined standard from those whose performance does not and who, therefore, need a professional eye examination. Screening is not diagnostic; it is the first sift. Further evaluation may show that performance is within the normal range but bears regular checking; or it may be that spectacle or contact lenses, medication, surgery, or some combination of these measures will alleviate the problem and lead to visual performance within the normal range. For some children, however, even with the best possible correction, vision remains low. These are the children who will require educational assessment of visual function so that they are placed in appropriate instructional programs.

EDUCATIONAL PLACEMENTS

You will remember that Paul and Cindy were mulling over what lay ahead for them as another school year approached. Both will return to regular classes, where the majority of students registered at the American Printing House for the Blind are enrolled. In 1986, more than 70 percent of students who were visually handicapped attended day-school programs of some type; the rest were placed in residential schools or training centers.

The first programs for children with visual handicaps were offered by residential schools. The first private residential schools for the blind opened in 1832 in Massachusetts (New England Asylum for the Blind, now Perkins School for the Blind) and in New York (New York Institute for the Blind). The following year, the Pennsylvania Institution for the Instruction of the Blind, now Overbrook School for the Blind, was founded in Philadelphia. In 1837, the first state residential school for blind children opened in Columbus, Ohio.

These and other residential schools established in the following years provided much of the education available to blind children for the next hundred years (Lowenfeld, 1973). There are presently fifty state and private residential schools for the blind in the United States and Puerto Rico and many other smaller private schools with programs for youngsters who have visual handicaps and multiple handicaps.

The trend toward integrating children who are blind or low-vision into regular education programs throughout the country began in the early 1900s, when day-school programs were first started. The first public school class for children who were blind opened in Chicago in 1900. Five

years later, in Cincinnati, special classes were established for these children. These classes were harshly criticized as "little institutions," however, and some years later, Cincinnati changed to Chicago's cooperative plan for integrating the children into the regular classroom for their instruction whenever possible (Lowenfeld, 1975). Classes for children who were blind increased in major cities, and the development of itinerant programs made it possible for blind children in more rural areas to remain in their local communities for school.

Once educators and parents had been assured by the medical profession that use of poor vision would not lead to further loss of vision, the number of children with low vision in public school classes began to increase. Prior to that time, classes for children who were partially seeing were frequently called "sight conservation" classes, and their teachers were "sight conservationists." Today, those terms and the philosophy they reflect are disappearing, as more professionals recognize the potential for increasing visual efficiency through low-vision stimulation and sight utilization.

The common types of educational programs for students who are blind or who have low vision in the United States today range from attendance in home school district regular classes to residential placement (Barraga, 1983; Tuttle, 1986):

- *Regular class placement,* with teacher-consultant providing materials and help to the classroom teacher and to others working with the student who is handicapped
- *Itinerant teacher program,* with the student who is handicapped remaining in the regular classroom but receiving tutoring in special subjects, such as listening skills or Optacon, from a traveling teacher who serves several schools
- *Resource room program,* where the student who is handicapped remains with classmates except for instruction or assistance in specific subjects from a resource teacher in a specially equipped room

In the following program options, the students are no longer listed on the roster of the regular class teacher but instead, for administrative purposes, are considered members of a special class:

- *Cooperative or part-time special class,* in which the students are registered in a special class for the visually handicapped but participate with students in the regular class as much as is feasible, given their instructional needs
- *Full-time special class,* or self-contained classroom, in which students are enrolled for all their instruction
- *Residential school,* in which students live at the school and attend classes on campus but participate whenever possible in local public or private school programs in the surrounding community

Selection of a particular type of program in what is the least restrictive environment for a particular child must be based on careful consideration of many factors. Although some advocates still staunchly support the benefits of one program over another, so far no research has demonstrated that any one type of program is unquestionably superior to the others. "The practical approach, therefore, suggests a continuing study of the child and his total situation together with a careful evaluation of the facilities available to him" (Taylor, 1973, p. 173). The goal today should be the same as it was more than twenty years ago when Lowenfeld, long a leader in the education of children who are blind, wrote that education "must aim at giving the child who is blind knowledge of the realities around him, the confidence to cope with these realities, and the feeling that he is recognized as an individual in his own right" (Lowenfeld, 1981, p. 44).

Careful study of the child to determine the appropriate placement and program should include, but not necessarily be limited to:

1. *Level of visual function.* In addition to an ophthalmological examination with reports of near and distant visual acuity, the record should contain a report of how the student functions visually in the classroom and in other school settings such as the playground or cafeteria. A number of factors can affect the level of visual functioning. These include
   a. age of onset of impaired vision
   b. degree of loss
   c. nature of condition—improving, stable, fluctuating, or deteriorating
   d. chronological age
   e. presence of other handicapping conditions, such as hearing loss
   f. motivation, an elusive factor to pinpoint but critical to performance

2. *Physical examination.* This is essential to rule out or pick up any additional physical problems, such as neurological problems or heart defects.

3. *Psychological evaluation.* Most formal, standardized intelligence, achievement, and aptitude tests have been normed on sighted groups. Alterations in testing procedures, changes in item wording, or elimination of items will invalidate the norms for the student who is blind or low-vision. An analysis of performance, item by item, however, can provide extremely useful information regarding levels of performance to the psychologist or diagnostician who is a good observer. A source of help is *The School Psychologist and the Exceptional Child* (Scholl, 1985).

4. *Observations and reports from qualified teachers.* Reports—ideally from both the regular class teacher and the teacher of students with visual handicaps—will present current levels of performance in academic subjects, social behavior, and mobility.

5. *Concerns of parents.* Federal regulations require that parents or parent surrogates be an integral, not nominal, part of discussions and decisions made on behalf of the child. When appropriate, the student may also participate in these discussions.

CURRICULUM FOR STUDENTS WITH VISUAL HANDICAPS

Although the elements found in the regular school curriculum are important for children who are low-vision and blind, the previous discussion makes clear that certain areas call for greater emphasis and structured effort to a degree not necessary for normally sighted youngsters. These areas might be referred to as the "plus curriculum," even though that particular term was originally applied to the knowledge and skills that competent teachers of visually handicapped students should master (Abel, 1959; Taylor, 1959). The elements of this "plus curriculum" can be clustered under six major headings (Barraga, 1973, 1983; Scholl, 1968; Taylor, 1973).

1. *Personal Competence, Self-adjustment, and Daily Living Skills.* Learning skills in self-care and management of the daily routines of family, school, and community life begins for all of us in infancy. Whereas sighted children can learn by imitation and from the behaviors modeled by family members and other children, children who are blind or low-vision may totally miss such opportunities for incidental learning. Dressing, eating, looking at speakers during conversation, ways of sitting and standing—these and many other social behaviors are a part of the appropriate curriculum for many children who are visually handicapped.

Much of the way we act and react to others is derived from the reactions of others to us, and much of that reaction is nonverbal. Again, such feedback may be diminished, distorted, or absent for students with visual handicaps who must, therefore, learn socially appropriate behaviors and reactions from direct instruction. Sex education comes under this heading; in fact, this is an area where much remains to be done in all fields of special education. Topics such as marriage and family life, reproduction, and genetic transmission of disease have not been brought up in many educational programs for the handicapped until

After mastering basic mobility skills, students are ready to take to the streets. (Photo by J. A. Bensel. Courtesy of the Maryland School for the Blind.)

recently (Burleson, 1975), although the students have made such subjects topics of their own discussions.

2. *Orientation and Mobility.* Orientation, or the location of oneself within the environment and in relation to objects within the environment, begins for the sighted child during infancy. Objects and faces gradually attract attention and take on meaning and function, and rudiments of eye-hand coordination appear during the first few months of life. Separation of self as a unique entity continues as the sighted child begins to crawl toward intriguing toys and to explore cupboards and crannies. Children who are visually handicapped from birth may miss the visual lures to independent movement and control of environmental objects and space, although, as Fraiberg (1977) and her colleagues have demonstrated, sounds eventually can take on stimulus characteristics and

BOX 4.3

THE SONICGUIDE INCREASES ENVIRONMENTAL AWARENESS

The major systems to aid mobility of individuals who are blind are the human guide, the long cane, the dog guide, and electronic travel aids. Electronic travel aids, the newest of the systems, emit signals that bounce back and are translated into either vibrations or auditory signals with particular pitches and patterns that can be interpreted by the user to indicate obstacles within a specific range. The Sonicguide is an example of an electronic travel aid.

The Sonicguide, an electronic mobility aid and environmental sensor, can enhance and extend the independent travel of blind individuals. Used in conjunction with a long cane or dog guide, the Sonicguide allows safer, more confident, and more efficient travel. As a training tool for basic orientation and mobility, concept and spatial awareness training with children, and low vision training, the Sonicguide improves an individual's understanding of the environment and his ability to move through it.

For the individual user, the Sonicguide is an effective aid to orientation and mobility skills in familiar areas, indoors or outdoors. It provides information about the distance of an object ahead of the Sonicguide user and the object's location within and beyond the length of a normally used long cane. The ten to fifteen foot effective range of the Sonicguide allows the blind traveler to avoid contact with and navigate around objects above ground level and at head height, such as awnings, sign posts, drinking fountains, or other pedestrians. For example, at a street crossing, the Sonicguide user can often locate landmarks that can assist with correct alignment and position on the corner, locate obstacles on the street itself, and frequently while crossing, locate the up-curb or other orientation clues on the opposite corner. Since the Sonicguide does not detect dropoffs, such as a down-curb, the use of a long cane or dog guide is essential.

The availability of specific and extended orientation information decreases the stress of travel and makes the user more self-confident and relaxed in his general movement. As one Sonicguide user states, "I feel that the Sonicguide, together with a

Source: Reprinted with permission of Wormald International Sensory Aids, Bensenville, Illinois 60106.

provoke a child to move and explore. Techniques for safe and efficient travel eventually need to be included in the instructional program so students can become self-sufficient and independent in familiar areas and know how to move about safely in unfamiliar areas (Hill, 1986). This is absolutely essential for those students in vocational and academic programs who expect to be employed after technical training or college.

Various aids to travel are available, including dog guides, the Hoover or long cane, and electronic devices such as laser canes and sensors. None of these aids, however, can substitute for the basic orientation skills an individual must possess in order to use the aids.

Progress toward independent travel can be enhanced if the student who is blind has good reason to want to travel alone. An example of one type of motivation to develop skills is found at the Ohio State School for the Blind (OSSB). Students in mobility are permitted off campus to go to McDonald's once they have mastered certain cane skills and have learned how to cross at light-controlled intersections. The McDonald's near OSSB has distributed menus transcribed in braille for blind customers who are not familiar with what is available in their restaurants. Most students from the school are now well acquainted with the menu, and all are treated just like the other customers by the counter employees.

3. Communication Skills. Communication includes listening, speaking, reading, and writing. In addition to instructional activities and experiences to establish a solid language base and good listening skills for communication, teachers of

cane, turns mobility into a craft—this is a significant change and improvement."

Apart from information about distance and location of objects, the Sonicguide also provides helpful information about the nature of objects within its beam. It is possible, for example, to distinguish between a brick wall, a glass store front, or shrub hedge. Meaningful landmarks can be identified from other objects without direct contact. Familiar areas become more meaningful, and independent familiarization in new travel situations is more easily accomplished. The Sonicguide allows many users to develop an aesthetic feeling for environmental features previously unknown or undetected.

A combination of increased environmental information and interaction, expanded travel ability, and improved self-confidence can provide the Sonicguide user with a personally meaningful travel awareness and understanding. In many employment, social, and recreational situations, the Sonicguide can produce greater independence and an increased scope of activities.

This blind pedestrian can avoid obstacles with the help of the Sonicguide system.

children with visual handicaps have an armory of aids and equipment that can help many students with reading and writing tasks (Mellor, 1981). These are described in a later section.

4. Vocational Guidance and Career Development. Until fairly recently, these curriculum components were not stressed even in regular education programs for sighted children. Changes in the job market, increases in the amount of training required for jobs in what were once considered rather menial positions, the closing off of some job possibilities and the creation of new ones as a result of technological advances, and the development of new products and sales markets have made it very clear that prevocational skills and vocational guidance for all students merit attention. In addition, the impetus Commissioner of Education Sidney Marland, Jr., gave in 1971 to career education in his proposal to reorder education programs led to action at the federal level as well as in the private sector (Wurster, 1983).

Today, with the increasing rate of change brought about by developments in microelectronics, the idea of career development as a continuing process has taken on great importance. As H. G. Shane (1987), in his intriguing discussion of what he calls the impact of microbioelectronic technology on teaching, learning, and life in the home and the workplace, has pointed out, it is unlikely that many young people today will follow one lifelong career. Instead, as opportunities for new jobs and positions appear and as old jobs become obsolete or are relegated to robots or other machines, individuals will need to anticipate career and other changes and design strategies to cope

BOX 4.4

THE SEEING EYE

Mrs. Dorothy Harrison Eustis, founder of The Seeing Eye, Inc., was a dog fancier particularly fascinated by German shepherds. In 1923, she established Fortunate Fields, a breeding program in Vevey, Switzerland, where she and Elliot (Jack) Humphrey, a well-known animal trainer, genetically bred shepherds for their working qualities. The dogs proved the success of the breeding system by working for the Swiss army, the Swiss police, and the Red Cross.

Word of Mrs. Eustis' shepherds spread to the United States, and, as a result, *The Saturday Evening Post* asked her to write an article about Fortunate Fields. Rather than tell of Fortunate Fields, however, she decided to write about a place she had visited in Potsdam, Germany, where the Germans were training their shepherds to lead blinded war veterans. Mrs. Eustis' article appeared in November 1927, and she was instantly deluged with mail from blind people in the United States who asked how they could obtain a dog to guide them. One letter in particular touched Mrs. Eustis because it was different from all the rest. It was from a young man in Nashville, Tennessee, named Morris Frank who told Mrs. Eustis that if she would train a dog to lead him, he would return to America and show how free and independent a blind man could be with the help of a dog. Mrs. Eustis invited Morris to her home in Switzerland, where he trained with Buddy, one of Mrs. Eustis' German shepherds. Morris Frank and Buddy returned to the United States, and Morris kept his word.

Soon, Mrs. Eustis realized the important role that dogs could play in the lives of blind people, and in January 1929, she and Mr. Humphrey returned to America and established The Seeing Eye in Nashville, Morris Frank's home town. Because the climate in Tennessee was not conducive to the instruction of dogs and blind people, The Seeing Eye moved in 1931 to Morristown, New Jersey, where the school remains today.

In 1986, 341 German shepherd and Labrador retriever puppies were whelped at The Seeing Eye's Scientific Breeding Station. All pups born at the Breeding Station are placed with 4-H families for their first year of life to learn basic obedience and socialization. At twelve to fourteen months of age, the dogs return to The Seeing Eye to receive formal training. A team of twelve highly skilled instructors works with the dogs for twelve weeks teaching them not only how to guide but also how to intelligently disobey a command. "Intelligent disobedience" is the hardest thing to teach the dogs, but it is the most important ability in guide work. The dog learns to use its own judgment to avoid danger despite being told to execute a command that the blind person may not realize could lead to trouble.

After the twelve-week training period, the dogs' temperaments and characteristics are matched to the needs of an incoming class of eighteen blind students. The students, who come from all over the United States and Canada, stay at The Seeing Eye for twenty to twenty-seven days to learn to live and work with their new dogs. The students are required to pay a fee of $150 for their first Seeing Eye dog; because the typical working life of a dog is ten years, the fee is $50 when students return for replacement dogs. Both fees include the dog, the dog's initial equipment, the student's room and board, the instruction, and round-trip air transportation to and from The Seeing Eye from anywhere in the United States and Canada. Naturally, the student fee does not cover the true cost of obtaining a Seeing Eye dog, but the school believes that students should contribute a small part in order to strengthen their will to do something for themselves and not to be the objects of charity. The rest of the money comes from private donations. The Seeing Eye is a national nonprofit philanthropy. In 1986, 223 blind students graduated from The Seeing Eye program.

The Seeing Eye reports that the greatest difficulty for dog guide users is public interference. People who distract a working dog by trying to pet it or feed it disrupt the concentration and communication

Source: Text prepared by Lori Schulz, Public Information Office, The Seeing Eye, Inc., Morristown, NJ.

Pups are cared for by 4-H families until ready for formal training. This pup still has some growing and learning to do. (Photo by E. James Pitrone. Courtesy of The Seeing Eye, Inc.)

Angela Barnett and Anne Musgrave and their Seeing Eye dogs. (Photo by E. James Pitrone. Courtesy of The Seeing Eye, Inc.)

between master and dog, which endangers the lives of both.

It is estimated that only 2 percent of the blind population uses dog guides. One reason, of course, is that not everyone likes dogs or is willing to take on the responsibility of caring for one. The other reason is that only a small percentage of blind people have actually lost enough vision to warrant the use of a dog. Those people that use dogs, however, find great independence and freedom as they travel at a three- to four-mile-per-hour pace through their communities and beyond for work and recreation.

For example, Miss Angela Barnett, one of 121 women who graduated from The Seeing Eye in 1986, explains, "Since I live alone, I depend on Zim to get where I want to go." Miss Barnett is active in The Pilot Club, an organization of business and professional women devoted to community service. She is a graduate of St. Mary's University in San Antonio, Texas, and she looks forward after further study to a career in real estate. Her Seeing Eye classmate, Mrs. Anne Musgrave, works as a community services manager for the Ontario March of Dimes in Toronto. In addition to her work outside of the home, Mrs. Musgrave is the busy mother of three children ages two to twelve. Mrs. Musgrave and her Seeing Eye dog, Feather, travel all over Toronto by bus, subway, and light-rail transit.

with the rapid acceleration of change. Students also will need to find ways to gain access to available information, many times in forms other than print hard copy. Accompanying the difficulties with quick and easy access to information that some students with limited vision have is the problem of the sheer volume of information to be sorted and processed. If we continue to generate information at the present rate, the prediction is that by the 1990s, the rate at which we accumulate information will double every two years (Shane, 1987, p. 24). Just keeping current will be a daily challenge!

The implications for students who are visually handicapped seem obvious. Not only do they need teachers who are aware of the social context and work force into which they will go, these students need to develop the skills, as well as the attitude and perspective, to prepare themselves for the certainty of uncertainty and flux around them (Simpson, 1986). They also need to learn what their career options are and how they will prepare for them. Knowledge of career possibilities, requirements, and the work skills necessary to satisfy employer expectations are integral parts of the instructional programs for all students and warrant special attention for students who are visually handicapped (Scadden, 1984).

The reality of the situation, however, is that all individuals who are visually handicapped will likely not be employed in the competitive market. But even these individuals need to learn, to the extent possible, some personally and socially useful activities (Scholl, 1973) that might lead to supported employment, work in a sheltered workshop, or simply to fuller participation in the activities of daily living.

5. Special Aids and Equipment. Before we briefly describe some of the more commonly used aids and equipment, we should stress that such devices do not "solve" the problems of communication or mobility or writing, nor are they substitutes for vision; they simply provide alternative ways to read, write, or move about. The attitude of teachers and sighted students toward special materials and aids used by students who are visually

handicapped can greatly influence whether or not a particular student develops skill in using the device. Not all students should use, can use, or will want to use all the devices and aids currently available. The selection must be made after due consideration of each student's levels of function, needs, age, and long-term goals.

Among the more commonly used equipment and aids are the following:

- *Tape and cassette recorders.* These are used for taking notes, playing taped texts, and responding orally to test questions. Some tape recorders have variable speed controls so users can adjust the speed of the tape and, in effect, compress or reduce the time of the original recording. Compressed speech recordings can be prepared in other ways as well, some of which eliminate the change in pitch that accompanies faster speeds. Many students, particularly at the secondary level and beyond, find the ability to use compressed speech a valuable addition to their store of study skills.
- *Record players and Talking Book machines.* Record players and Talking Book machines, distributed through the Library of Congress and its regional branches, are used for recorded texts, magazines, and recreational reading.
- *Typewriters.* Typewriting can ease the writing task for children with low vision, whose handwriting is frequently difficult to read, and for students who are blind, who are thus enabled to prepare homework and correspond with sighted individuals.
- *Braille.* **Braille** is a system for reading and writing based on a combination of six dots within a cell two dots wide and three dots high (see Figure 4.4). Today, there are braille codes for literary, music, scientific, and mathematical materials. Braille can be embossed with a braillewriter—most frequently the Perkins brailler developed in 1950 at Howe Press, Perkins School for the Blind—or with a slate and stylus, the braille equivalent of the paper and pencil.
- *Large-type materials.* Some students, though

The six dots of the Braille cell are arranged and numbered thus: 1 4 2 5 3 6

The capital sign, dot 6, placed before a letter makes it a capital. The number sign, dots 3, 4, 5, 6, placed before a character, makes it a figure and not a letter.

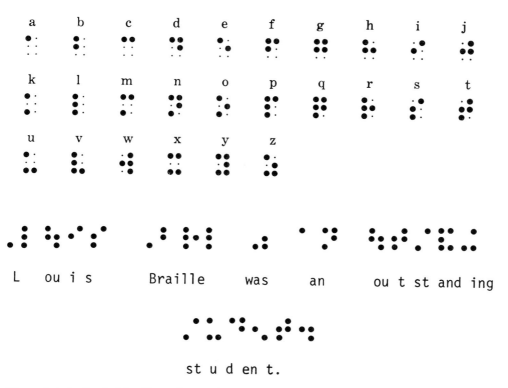

Figure 4.4. In Grade 1 braille, each print letter has a braille symbol. In Grade 2, certain letter combinations can be contracted.

not all, find reading enlarged type easier and more efficient than reading regular print. A number of factors can influence the choice of regular or large type: spacing between lines, distance between words on a line, length of lines, size of margins, style of print, width of strokes in letters, and quality of paper. Individual lighting requirements also can influence the choice of regular or large-type materials. The recommended procedure is to determine whether or not large-type materials make the reading task easier; if not, they should not be used.

▪ *Optical aids*. Low-vision aids include magnifiers, clip-on lenses, telescopic lenses, and other special lenses to aid reading and travel.

BOX 4.5
LOUIS BRAILLE AND THE BRAILLE SYSTEM OF EMBOSSED WRITING

Louis Braille, born in 1809 in Coupvray, not far from Paris, lost his vision at age three as the result of an accident in his father's harness shop. After attending the local school with his brothers and sisters for several years, Louis was enrolled at the National Institution for the Blind in Paris. He continued at the school as an instructor after his graduation. Because of poor health, however, he had to return to Coupvray, where he died in 1852.

The embossed system of writing we call braille was developed while Braille was at school in Paris. Charles Barbier, an officer in Napoleon's army, had devised a system for sending military messages at night by means of raised dots. His system for *écriture nocturne* eventually became known to Braille, who realized the possibilities it held for the blind. He decreased Barbier's twelve-dot cell to six dots and developed a code that permitted the sixty-three dot combinations possible with a six-dot cell to take on different meanings depending upon their position in a sequence of cells. Braille's literary code was published in 1834. Braille also developed a code for music transcription.

Grade 1 braille is letter-for-letter transcription of print to braille.

Except for a few beginning reading books, most materials are published in Grade 2 contracted braille, in which some whole words, parts of words, and punctuation are represented by special cell combinations.

Blind students usually write braille with a Perkins brailler, a sturdy ten-pound machine (11½″ × 14″) that is easily carried from class to class. Extension keys are available for students who have difficulty with control of wrist or finger muscles.

Some students, particularly those at the secondary level, use a slate and stylus, the braille equivalent of paper and pencil for print writers. Slates vary from postcard size to the full thirty-eight cell size for 11″ × 11½″ paper. The slate and stylus require writing from right to left; the paper is clamped into position between the plates of the slate, and the braille dots are embossed one at a time by pushing the stylus into the grooves of the cells on the slate. Students have generally mastered most of Grade 2 braille before they begin extensive use of the slate and stylus.

Perkins brailler. (Courtesy of American Printing House for the Blind.)

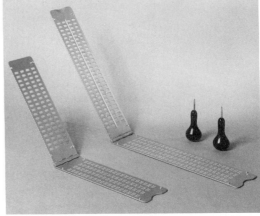

Slate and stylus. (Courtesy of American Printing House for the Blind.)

BOX 4.6
KURZWEIL READING MACHINE

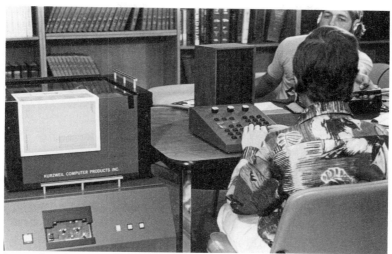

Kurzweil Reading Machine with direct translation from print to voice output. (Photo by J. A. Bensel. Courtesy of the Maryland School for the Blind.)

The Kurzweil Reading Machine (KRM), a computer-based device, converts printed material into synthetic English speech at rates up to 225 words per minute. Books, memos, letters, and other clearly printed material are placed one page at a time on the reading surface. As the scanning mechanism under the surface moves across the page one line at a time, the written words are converted into spoken words. Voice-control keys permit adjustments in "voice" pitch and quality; other control keys allow adjustments for margins, some variation in type styles and spacing, spoken punctuation, spelling of words, and so on. With accessory parts, the KRM will read computer terminals as well.

Students need careful instruction in use and care of their aids. The critical lens-to-object distance, the restricted field, the lighting requirements, and the unusual appearance of some aids are deterrents to use for many individuals.

- *Electronic reading devices.* These include the Kurzweil Reading Machine (see Box 4.6), a computer-based machine that converts print to intelligible English speech; the Optacon, an optical-to-tactile conversion device (see Box 4.7); and various closed-circuit television systems that permit visual reading and writing for those with useful vision.

- *Miscellaneous.* Other aids include the abacus, talking calculators, tactile maps and globes, biology models, simple machine models, and so on. Complete listings of tangible aids and appliances are available from the American Printing House for the Blind and the American Foundation for the Blind.

6. Vision Stimulation. Students who retain the ability to distinguish between light and dark can learn to use even that limited information to aid mobility. Many students with the ability to discriminate colors, to detect moving objects, and/or to recognize gross outlines can learn to use what-

BOX 4.7
OPTACON

The Optacon, an OPtical-to-TActile-CONversion device, consists of a miniature camera, highly sophisticated electronic circuitry housed in a small case, and a tactile array where a vibrating pattern of the visual image from the camera appears. As an Optacon user moves the camera smoothly across a line of print with the right hand, the photoreceptor cells in the camera send the data they sense through the circuitry, where the image of each letter is converted to a vibrating pattern of that letter. The user rests the left forefinger on the array of 144 pins and feels the vibrating letter pattern as it moves under the finger.

The Optacon user must learn to track the line of print evenly with the camera and identify the letter patterns (not braille) in order to read. If the original letter is not clear or if the letter strokes are smudged or too close together, the vibrating pattern the finger feels will not be precise enough for the Optacon reader to detect the critical features that lead to accurate identification.

With training and much practice, some Optacon users have developed reading rates of 30 to 50 words per minute. Although this rate is not very fast in comparison to print reading (250 to 275 words per minute on the average for adults), braille reading (90 to 120 words per minute average for good high school students), or speaking (about 175 words per minute), many Optacon users have reported that the independence an Optacon offers outweighs the possible disadvantages of the comparatively slow reading rates. Some users have, for the first time, been able to read their own mail, kitchen labels, and library and textbooks; use card catalogs and reference materials in the library; and, with special Optacon camera lenses, read computer terminals and proofread typing while the paper is still in the typewriter.

Along with braille, tapes, records, and both human and electronic readers, the Optacon provides another access to printed materials for those who can master the necessary skills.

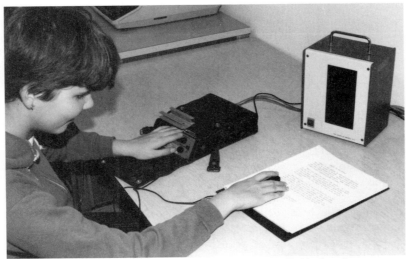

The Optacon provides another access to print for the functionally blind student. Here a student is reading his story tactually. The visual display is for the teacher's benefit during instruction. (Courtesy of the Wisconsin School for the Visually Handicapped.)

Reading with the Optacon, using a tracking aid and visual display. (Courtesy of *Akron Beacon Journal.*)

The Optacon enables a student to have direct access to printed materials. (Photo by J. A. Bensel. Courtesy of the Maryland School for the Blind.)

Closed-circuit TV helps some students read with less difficulty. Note the limited amount of text on the screen when the degree of magnification is high. (Courtesy of the Wisconsin School for the Visually Handicapped.)

ever vision they do have to better advantage. To do so, many will require structured programs of vision stimulation and utilization activities. Barraga (1986) has described the interrelation of motor and perception skills and has developed an assessment instrument, the Visual Efficiency Scale, to determine levels of visual function within broad categories. This scale has recently been reworked and is now available from APH as the Program to Develop Efficiency in Visual Functioning. The program includes an assessment instrument and ideas for activities to increase those areas of function in which a visually handicapped student has demonstrated difficulty.

COMPUTER TECHNOLOGY FOR THE VISUALLY HANDICAPPED

We have previously mentioned some aids and equipment for students who are visually handicapped that incorporate computer technology. Devices such as the Kurzweil Reading Machine

with its synthetic speech output; the Optacon, which converts an optical image to a tactile image; and laser canes are examples. But there is another set of devices that allow students who are visually handicapped to have the same direct access to information displayed on computers as their sighted co-workers do. At present, many functionally blind employees already use computers daily in their work. G. L. Goodrich (1984) has identified over thirty job titles, from attorney to physicist to secretary to tax analyst to word processor, that are held by blind computer users. There are five major ways that individuals who are visually handicapped can access information from computers: synthetic speech, hard copy braille, refreshable braille, large-print computer configurations, and use of optical aids.

1. *Synthetic speech* or voice output devices provide access to text displays. Voice synthesizers vary in intelligibility of speech, control of speaking rate, pitch of "voice," rules for English pronunciation of words with different accented syllables that depend on sentence structure, capabilities for review and data entry, and cost. Synthetic speech output is especially useful for word-processing tasks but less so for reading complex screen or page layouts. So far, speech synthesizers do not handle graphic displays (Kelly, 1987).

2. *Hard copy braille* printers can be attached to personal computers or to larger systems and configurations. Their primary purpose is to produce permanent braille copy on paper for the braille reader (Goodrich, 1984). Braille translation programs that produce Grade 2 braille from print text enable the sighted person to input print text that is then fed to a translator program. After on-line proofing, the braille translation can then be printed out or, more accurately, embossed by a braille printer in regular Grade 2 braille. Many volunteer braille transcribing groups have begun to use this procedure for the production of braille materials.

3. *Refreshable braille* or paperless braille refers to a set-up whereby braille is stored on a regular audio cassette tape and then played out on a device that presents a braille display strip of twelve to thirty-two braille cells at a time, depending upon the type and model of the playback unit. With a unit such as TSI's VersaBraille, the user can either input his own braille and use the unit for word processing or down load from a microcomputer to which the VersaBraille has been linked and then read out the information on the braille display instead of on a visual monitor. The VersaBraille unit can be used as a part of a configuration with a microcomputer, printer, braille embosser, and voice synthesizer that allows for braille input and output, braille input with print output, print input with braille output, or speech output of the print text.

By linking a microcomputer to a synthetic speech unit and high resolution monitor and with special software, a student can obtain both large print and speech output. (Courtesy of the Wisconsin School for the Visually Handicapped.)

4. With high-resolution monitors and the right software, it is possible to get *large-print text* of various sizes to ease the reading task for computer users with low vision. Of course, the amount visible at one time decreases as the size of type increases, but this is true for any enlargement of materials onto a display of fixed size.

5. *Optical aids* such as are used for noncomputer reading tasks may be just as helpful to some computer users as are large-print software programs. Again, as the degree of magnification increases, the amount of text visible at one gaze lessens. Locating a cursor, finding a new place on a display, or getting an idea of a complete screen layout may be difficult for the beginning user (Goodrich, 1984).

All of these ways to gain access to computer text have advantages and disadvantages associated with them. Selection of a particular means of access will depend on what the user wants to do, for how long, and with what equipment and resources.

Many teachers of youngsters who are visually handicapped have faced the difficult question of how to introduce their students to computers. The American Printing House for the Blind has developed the TAlking Literacy Kit for the Apple IIe (TALK: IIe) to acquaint students, and teachers, with the capabilities of the Apple IIe. The Echo Speech Synthesizer, required to use TALK: IIe, consists of a set of twelve computer parts that includes a microchip, transistor, and floppy disc so the students, and teachers, can see what helps make a computer work.

With the rather startling and certainly rapidly appearing capabilities for hyperminiaturization even beyond that possible with the silicon chip and integrated circuit, the use of laser beams in place of electronic current, and ongoing research to extend further the power of the mind, it is difficult to envision just what aids and devices might lie within reach of the student of the twenty-first century. The National Technology Center (NTC), established in 1986 by the American Foundation for the Blind, should be of particular help to teachers and counselors who work with students and clients with limited vision and who attempt to keep up with the new developments in technology. The Center, located at AFB in New York City, has three major components: a national information system and network that will build a database of devices and products available for children and adults who are low-vision or blind, provide consumer evaluation studies of these devices, and suggest ways users have found to adapt equipment for specific needs; an evaluation laboratory where personnel will work with consumers and manufacturers to evaluate existing products and propose new ones; and an engineering group that will work closely with the evaluation laboratory in the design of new devices.*

TEACHER CONSIDERATIONS

You may have already thought about how Paul and Cindy might perform on the tasks and skills mentioned in the six areas of curriculum for visually handicapped. If you look back at the excerpts from their thoughts, you can see that they are aware of the impressions they make on their peers, and you can discern the degree of importance they place on these impressions. If you were one of their teachers, how would you respond to these questions?

- What would you infer about their mobility and communication skills since both are enrolled in regular classes with itinerant services on a regular basis?
- Although nothing was mentioned about pre—vocational training or career education, what would you expect fourth- and eighth-grade students in regular classes to be learning about such topics? What *should* they be learning, and how, at those grade levels?
- From the descriptions provided, you know that Cindy can distinguish light and dark and that Paul reads print with some magnification. Where do these students fit on the sequence of

visual performance levels? What would you expect them to do visually in your class?

It is important for teachers to sort out their own reactions to, expectations for, and feelings toward students with visual or other impairments in order to assist all of their students, nonhandicapped as well as handicapped, in coming to grips with the difficult situations that inevitably arise during the process of growing up. We offer the following general suggestions for classroom teachers who will have visually handicapped children as members of their classes.

1. Accept the child as indeed a member of the class. Your attitude will rub off on the other children in the class and will also affect the way the child who is visually handicapped reacts toward being there.

2. Ask the consulting or resource teacher for information about the child's level of visual functioning as well as his or her academic and social functioning. You should be given such information before the child's arrival, but if not, ask for it. Armed with that information and your own careful observations and assessment, you and the child can decide on the best seating arrangements, lighting conditions, and desk and chair height.

3. Provide space for special equipment and books that do not fit in the student's desk. Expect the student to organize materials for learning, but don't be surprised if, like other children, he or she needs reminding at times to keep things in order.

4. The majority of children who are visually handicapped in regular classes have low vision. Encourage use of low vision by careful selection of instructional materials according to:

   a. effective use of color
   b. good contrast
   c. type size and spacing
   d. page layout

   In an effort to be visually appealing, some

---

*The evaluation laboratory staff has issued its first in a series of reports on products available for computer users. This first report examines reactions to six synthetic speech screen-access programs for the IBM PC or compatible systems (Schreier et al., 1987).

textbooks actually are cluttered with busy art work, contain colored type on top of illustrations, and have irregular page layouts that can cause confusion in locating important information. Your attention to the appearance and design of textbooks and other instructional materials can make visual tasks less difficult for many normally sighted students as well as for low-vision students.

5. Hold the same expectations for behavior and performance for your student with limited vision as you do for your other students. Although the materials your student who is visually handicapped uses may not be the same as those for other students, and the form in which work is prepared may be different, the quality of the student's work should be at the level you would expect from any other child with similar capabilities.

Providing appropriate educational programs for children and youth with limited or no vision requires the professional cooperation and collaboration of personnel from both special and regular education. Although so much of what we do depends upon what we "see," not all "seeing" is necessarily done with the organ of sight. The challenge to educators is to provide for those students for whom visual input is absent, limited, or distorted the learning environment, experiences, and materials appropriate for them to develop all their capabilities and to use all their senses as effectively as possible.

SUMMARY

Over 46,000 school-age children with visually handicapping conditions are presently attending classes in residential and day schools in the United States. Although some of these children are called blind for administrative reasons, the majority have a degree of useful vision. For instructional purposes, therefore, we consider children with some useful vision—even at only close range—to be low-vision students. Only those students who have no sense of vision or at most the ability to distinguish light from dark are considered blind.

The way students who are low-vision or blind feel about themselves and their capabilities can be influenced by those significant persons around them—their parents, peers, and teachers. Teachers must be aware of their own attitudes toward blindness and low vision as abstractions, as well as of their attitudes toward and reactions to an individual child who is low-vision or blind who might be placed in their classes.

The complex and intricate process of seeing can be disrupted by various causes, including prenatal conditions resulting in hereditary or congenital defects that may be manifest at birth or some time later in life and injuries, poisonings, tumors, and diseases. The resulting effect on functional vision may be poor near vision, blurred distant vision, a restricted field of vision, deficient color vision, or poor adaptation or sensitivity to light.

Reduced functional vision, particularly during the developmental period, can significantly affect the cognitive, motor, and social development of children. Early identification becomes critical, and classroom teachers are frequently in the best position to identify those children with useful but less than normal vision.

Children who are visually handicapped may attend school in residential or day-school programs. Placement decisions must be carefully made for each child, with consideration given to level of visual function, presence of other handicapping conditions, present levels of academic and social functioning, age, previous school history, and parental concerns. In addition to the regular school curriculum, students who are visually handicapped may need special instruction to develop competence in daily living skills, language and communication, orientation and mobility techniques, and use of special aids and equipment. Vision stimulation, vocational guidance, and career education are also important elements in an appropriate program for students who are low-vision or blind.

Teachers who have students with visual handicaps in their classes should work with the consulting, itinerant, or resource room teacher to determine appropriate instructional procedures, provide adequate space for storage of books and equipment, encourage the use of any residual vision, and expect behavior and performance at the level required of other students in the class.

Suggestions for Further Reading

Barraga, N. (1983). *Visual handicaps and learning* (rev. ed.). Austin, TX: Exceptional Resources.
In this well-organized revision of an earlier work, Barraga provides an excellent discussion for regular and special educators and any other school personnel interested in the developmental and learning processes of children with impaired vision. Her opening vignettes introduce the reader to the diversity and variability of behavior and levels of function among children with limited or no vision; later chapters cover ways to design appropriate instructional settings and programs to accommodate variations. In the closing chapter, Barraga identifies issues confronting teachers whose goals are to help children move toward greater independence and participation in a sighted world.

Koestler, F. (1976). *The unseen minority: A social history of blindness in America.* New York: David McKay.
In this very interesting and well-documented social history of the blind in the United States during the past fifty years, Koestler traces the changes in attitudes toward blind persons, the development of agencies and organizations serving the blind, the effects of technological advances on educational and rehabilitation programs, legislation, and the accompanying changes in business and commercial opportunities. Her account is peopled with the fascinating men and women who led the activities that have brought us to the present in the history of blind people in America.

Lowenfeld, B. (1981). *Berthold Lowenfeld on blindness and blind people: Selected papers.* New York: American Foundation for the Blind.
These more-than-twenty papers selected from almost forty years of Lowenfeld's work with, and on behalf of, visually handicapped children not only portray a fascinating panorama of changing attitudes and developing programs for visually handicapped, they also point to many opportunities for professionals today to help visually handicapped individuals gain knowledge of the realities around them, build confidence in their abilities to cope with these realities, and be recognized as individuals in their own right. This book covers psychological, social, historical, and educational aspects of services to the visually handicapped and concludes with a discussion of challenges confronting education and rehabilitation personnel in the years ahead.

Mellor, C. M. (1981). *Aids for the 80s: What they are and what they do.* New York: American Foundation for the Blind.
This succinct little book provides a quick overview of the various travel, reading, and low-vision aids available for visually handicapped persons today. The author describes direct-translation reading machines, optical and electronic low-vision aids, and paperless braille and computer braille production and includes discussion of questions regarding development costs, market size, sources of funds for purchase of aids, and the basic criteria for evaluation—usefulness, durability, and cost effectiveness.

Scholl, G. (Ed.). (1986). *Foundations of education for blind and visually handicapped children and youth.* New York: American Foundation for the Blind.
Considered the major comprehensive text for educators of children who are visually handicapped, this book represents the work of over twenty contributing authors whose chapters provide an overview of theory and practice in education of children with visual handicaps and youth from birth to age twenty-one. The twenty-two chapters cover definitions, development, components of high-quality education programs, and special curriculum considerations. An especially interesting feature is the time line on the front and back inside covers that traces significant events from the 1700s, when educational programs were first established for children who are blind, to the 1980s, when the first braille embosser was attached to a microcomputer to facilitate braille transcription and production.

Schulz, P. J. (1980). *How does it feel to be blind? The psychodynamics of visual impairments.* Los Angeles: Muse-Ed.
Schulz writes about the range of emotional reactions to loss of sight by newly blinded individuals and their families. Then he discusses forms of adjustment to blindness. Finally, he considers whether a person who has once had useful vision ever gets used to being blind. Schulz, a counselor and consulting psychologist, has been blind since age sixteen.

Warren, D. H. (1984). *Blindness and early childhood development* (rev. ed.). New York: American Foundation for the Blind.
Warren, in this second edition of his 1977 book, reviews in very readable fashion the available literature on the effects of visual impairment on motor, perceptual, cognitive, language, social, and personality development. After pointing out some of the more common weaknesses in the research to date and making suggestions for further research, Warren proposes a "hierarchical model," which calls for careful selection and detailed description of individuals used in research studies.

Relevant Journals

Journal of Visual Impairment and Blindness
Published ten times a year by the American Foundation for the Blind, 15 West 16th Street, New York, NY 10011.

Education of the Visually Handicapped
A quarterly journal of the Association for Education and Rehabilitation of the Blind and Visually Impaired.

Organizations for Parents and Professionals

Association for Education and Rehabilitation of the Blind and Visually Impaired
206 North Washington Street, Room 320
Alexandria, VA 22314

The Council for Exceptional Children
Division of the Visually Handicapped
1920 Association Drive
Reston, VA 22091

National Association for Parents of the Visually Impaired
P.O. Box 180806
Austin, TX 78717

National Federation of the Blind
Parents of Blind Children Division
1800 Johnson Street
Baltimore, MD 21230

CHAPTER 5

Hearing Handicaps

Did You Know That . . .

- the United States Department of Education has reported that approximately five out of every thousand school children have at least a mild hearing loss?

- a leading cause of deafness among children could be significantly reduced if more people were immunized against German measles?

- teachers of children who are deaf frequently disagree as to what mode of communication is best for a child with a profound hearing loss?

- hereditary deafness accounts for about half of all cases of deafness among school-age children?

- increasing volume may do nothing more for the person who is deaf than make unintelligible sounds unintelligible at a greater intensity?

- hearing may fluctuate and result in inconsistencies in day-to-day school performance?

- hearing is not something we can observe directly; we must look for behaviors that indicate its presence?

I magine a classroom of busy children all working, or pretending to work, on the assignment you have just explained to them—except for one child who never seems to pay attention unless you are speaking to him directly. He is always the last to settle down when the class is called to order, he often does not follow directions others find clear, and he frequently asks someone around him what to do next. Or perhaps you notice another student who usually completes written assignments once she understands what to do but who never volunteers to answer in class and quite often does not respond when called upon. These behaviors could be the result of many factors that affect children. One factor that few teachers would automatically consider is hearing impairment.

Children with little or no hearing present a most complex challenge to teachers. A hearing loss or deficit is not something that can be pointed to or observed directly; rather, it must be inferred from behavior that is seen. Later on in this chapter, we will describe certain tests that can verify loss of hearing, but clues that suggest the possibility of a hearing problem can be found in observable behavior.

In the past, few children with known hearing problems were admitted to regular classrooms. The current emphasis on appropriate integration with support service has meant shifts in program location, student placements, and greater possibilities for regular class participation on the part of students with hearing impairments. It is important for elementary and secondary school personnel to know that with early identification, follow-up, intervention, and instruction, many children with impaired hearing do develop language, achieve academic success, build solid social relationships, and establish communication with others in their environment.

Communication for all of us is a two-way operation, an active process that enables the exchange of messages between sender and receiver (Lindgren, 1969; Owens, 1986). For the communicator to determine the effectiveness of a message, there must be an audience to receive the message and then provide feedback. This process underlies social interactions and enables social relationships to develop. Feedback plays an influential role in guiding the further exchange of messages between communicator and receiver or audience.

The verbal portion of communication relies on hearing, language, and speech production. The effectiveness and efficiency of verbal communication can be reduced as a result of difficulty in any one area, and the entire process may break down completely if serious problems exist in one or a combination of areas.

In this chapter, we will concentrate on the hearing component of the communication process. While we do not mean to suggest that hearing is the most important of the components of communication, we do want to show just how critical hearing is to the development of normal language and speech and to illustrate what schools can do for children whose hearing is limited or absent. Our concerns are the types and signs of hearing impairment and the implications for instruction of children with impaired hearing who are in regular classroom settings.

HOW WE HEAR

The ear is a delicate mechanism designed to receive sound waves, convert them to electrical impulses, and send those impulses along the neurological pathway to the brain for processing and interpretation. Sound waves enter the outer ear and cause the tiny bones of the middle ear to vibrate. The movement of these tiny bones leads to movement of fluid in the inner ear. This motion activates the delicate nerve endings that send impulses to the brain (see Box 5.1).

When we consider the precision and complexity of the conversion of acoustical energy to mechanical and hydraulic energy and then to electrical impulses transmitted to the brain, we can better understand the potential for hearing loss if injury, disease, or structural anomaly affect any portion of the inner, middle, or outer ear.

Types of Hearing Loss

Hearing loss can occur at a number of places in the hearing mechanism, and the location of the problem provides one way to classify hearing impairment. Most hearing losses are either conductive or sensorineural (Beadle, 1982). In **conductive hearing loss**, sound waves are reduced in intensity before they reach the inner ear. Infection, trauma, wax build-up, trapped water, growths, or some combination of conditions may result in a blocked passage leading to the middle ear or in prevention of movement of the three small ossicles (bones) in the middle ear. If the source of the impediment can be eliminated, hearing may improve. If the blockage cannot be cleared, then amplification to increase the volume of the sound, or the intensity of the acoustical energy entering the ear, may improve hearing to some extent.

In **sensorineural hearing loss**, the problem is with reception of sound in the inner ear or transmission of the electrical impulses along the auditory nerve to the brain. Although sound waves may reach the inner ear, they may not be transmitted correctly if the inner ear structures are damaged. Speech may be perceived as distorted even with amplification. Most sensorineural losses are permanent.

In some cases of impaired hearing, problems arise with the transmission of electrical impulses from the brain stem to and within the auditory cortex due to tumor, abscess, stroke, or other kind of brain damage (Beadle, 1982). With this **central auditory dysfunction**, the major difficulty is interpreting what comes from the auditory nerve. As with sensorineural loss, amplification usually offers no significant assistance.

Degree of Hearing Loss

Hearing impairment can also be classified according to the degree of loss in terms of frequency (or pitch) and intensity (loudness). Hearing tests can measure sensitivity to variations in frequency at certain levels of intensity.

Frequency is determined by the cycles per second (cps), or hertz (Hz). The average fre-

BOX 5.1
THE PROCESS OF HEARING

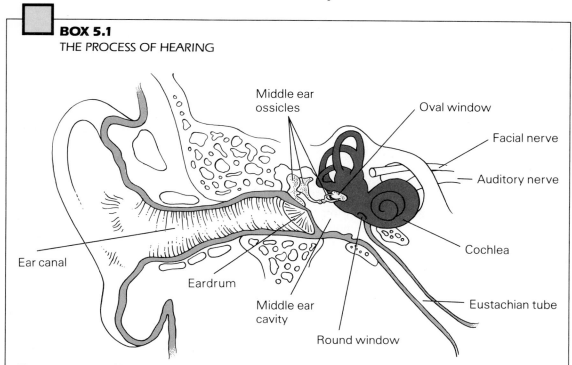

Figure 5.1. Section of human ear. (From K. R. Beadle, "Communication Disorders—Speech and Hearing." In E. E. Bleck and D. A. Nagel (Eds.), *Physically Handicapped Children: A Medical Atlas for Teachers,* 2nd ed. New York: Grune and Stratton, 1982, p. 135. By permission.)

Sound waves enter the outer ear canal as acoustical energy and move into the middle ear, where they bump against the eardrum, or tympanic membrane. These sound vibrations, which are actually variations in air pressure, set the eardrum in motion; in this manner, acoustic energy is converted to mechanical energy. The motion of the eardrum activates the three small ossicles (bones) of the middle ear—the malleus, incus, and stapes. The stapes, the innermost bone, is connected to the oval window, a delicate membrane that seals off the inner ear. As the oval window moves in reaction to the movement of the stapes, the fluid of the inner ear is set in motion. This hydraulic energy activates the minute auditory nerve endings, called hair cells, that join to form the auditory or eighth cranial nerve. The hair cells relay what are now electrical impulses to the brain for processing and interpretation.

quency range for normal hearing lies roughly between 16 and 16,000 cps; however, the critical area for speech reception falls between 250 and 4,000 cps (Harrison, 1985).

Intensity of sound is expressed in decibels. A **decibel (dB)** indicates the pressure, or power, of one sound relative to an arbitrary standard sound or reference point. Thus, 0 dB does not mean absence of sound; rather, it indicates sound exactly equal to the reference point. A sound at 60 dB is 60 dB higher in level than the reference point. The point at which an individual responds

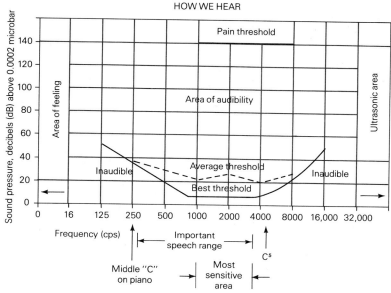

Figure 5.2. Graph showing area of audibility and sensitivity of the human ear. The best threshold separates audible from inaudible sounds. This level is generally the reference level for sound-level meters. The average threshold of hearing lies considerably above the best threshold and is the reference level used in audiometers calibrated to the ASA standards. (From Sataloff and Michael, *Hearing Loss,* 1973, p. 17. Courtesy of Charles C. Thomas, Publisher, Springfield, Illinois.)

to sound at least half the time is that person's **threshold of hearing,** or hearing level (Keith, 1976).

Figure 5.2 illustrates the area of audibility and sensitivity of the human ear. Because the average threshold indicated on the graph is derived from tests of many individuals, a particular individual may have a hearing threshold that exceeds or falls below the average threshold. A person with a threshold of 10 dB should have less sensitivity, or a higher threshold, than a person with a − 10 dB threshold. A person with a low threshold of hearing, in other words, has more acute hearing than does a person with a high threshold, just as a person whose pain threshold is low feels sensations as pain before a person whose pain threshold is higher.

Figure 5.3 and Table 5.1 list some common sounds in the environment in addition to speech sounds and their usual pitch and intensity range. Note that some sounds can actually reach an in-

tensity that causes pain for the individual and increases the risk of damage to the sensitive structures of the middle ear. For this reason, workers subjected to loud noises, as are typical in construction or around airport gates, are frequently required to wear ear covers for protection.

To clarify the relationship between intensity and frequency in human hearing, we can use the volume and station knobs on a radio. If you turn the volume knob clockwise, the volume increases. Turn it counterclockwise and, although the sound is still clear and intelligible, the volume decreases until you can no longer detect it; it falls below your threshold of hearing, the point at which you become aware of sound. Now if you set the volume knob at a comfortable level and alter the position of the station knob (which changes the frequency), you will pick up interference such as static, two stations, or noise, all of which interfere with discrimination of words. Such are the

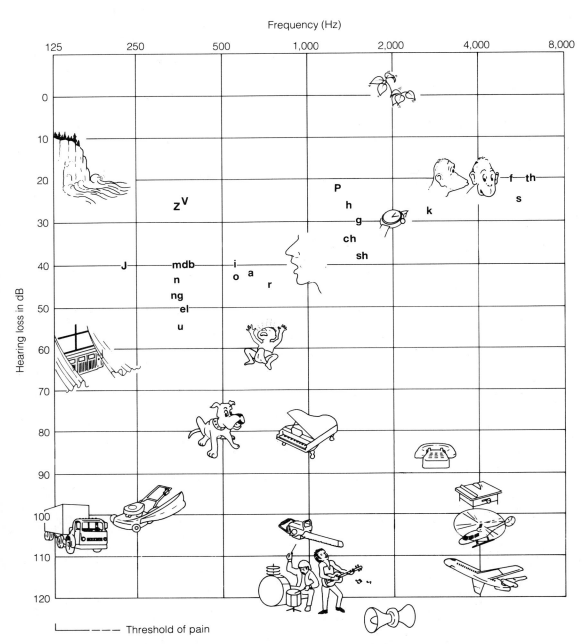

Figure 5.3. Frequency spectrum and intensity of everyday sounds, including English-language speech sounds. Note that the ability to hear leaves rustling in a soft breeze requires a lower threshold of hearing than does the ability to hear a baby crying. (From Northern, J. & Downs, M. (Eds.) (1984). *Hearing in children* (3rd ed.). Baltimore, MD: Williams & Wilkins. Used with permission.)

TABLE 5.1

NOISE LEVELS OF COMMON SOUNDS

Source	Perception/Hearing	Sound Level in dB SPL
Whisper	Just audible	10
Rustle of leaves		30
Normal conversation	Comfortable	50
Auto traffic		60
Window air conditioner	Loud	80
Snowmobile/motorcycle		95
Power lawn mower	Very loud	100
Pneumatic jackhammer/chain saw		110
Rock music		115
Oxygen torch	Uncomfortably loud	120

Source: From Northern & Lemme (1986), p. 418. Used with permission of the publisher.

problems faced by a person who has losses in the frequency range and/or in the decibel range necessary for discriminating speech sounds. For some, the sounds are perhaps clear but not loud enough; for others, sound is present but distorted; for still others, both volume and clarity are problems.

Level of Function

Although the *degree* of hearing loss can be determined fairly accurately and is particularly important for diagnostic purposes, classification according to *level of function* is usually more helpful to those involved in planning and providing instructional programs for children who are hearing impaired. One such functional classification system separates levels of function according to decibel loss within the frequency range critical for comprehension of speech sounds (1,000–3,000 cps). We can match these levels with some characteristics of hearing and behavior and suggest possible implications for educational programs (see Table 5.2). We stress, however, that an individual displaying any one or even several of the characteristics does not necessarily have hearing at the level where that behavior cluster is found. Table

5.2 shows a general picture of groups with significant hearing impairment, not a portrait of any particular individual within the group.

In closing this discussion of levels of hearing, we emphasize that location and type of loss as well as level of function are all important considerations when decisions are to be made about appropriate educational programs. More attention will be given to this topic in later sections.

HEARING IMPAIRMENT

Earlier, we pointed out that an *impairment* is a physical, observable condition of tissue that can affect the function of the organ or organ system of which that tissue is a part. Hearing impairment indicates some damage or malformation of the hearing mechanism. As a result of such impairment, there may be a hearing *disability* (an absence or decrease in the capacity to receive speech and other sounds of various frequencies and/or intensities). How people function in specific settings with what hearing they have determines the extent of their *handicap*. When you ask, "What is

TABLE 5.2

HEARING LEVELS AND GENERAL CHARACTERISTICS

Level of Loss	dB Area of Loss	Hearing Characteristics	Typical Education Services
	0–24	Normal hearing	Regular education
	25–35	Children: *may* have some difficulty with faint speech sounds and with discrimination of certain sound combinations Adults: essentially normal	Regular education; perhaps speech therapy
I	36–54	Some difficulty with soft or faint speech sounds Some difficulty in hearing speech at a distance	Regular education Favorable seating and lighting Amplification for some Speech therapy and/or lipreading
II	55–69	Difficulty with loud and soft speech Difficulty with telephone conversation Some problem in understanding strangers	Regular education with support services but some special class or special school Speech/language therapy Amplification
III	70–89	May identify vowels but have trouble with consonants Hear only shouted or amplified speech Possible deterioration in speech if no monitoring or therapy	Regular education with support services but frequently special class/special school placement appropriate Speech/language therapy to prevent deterioration
IV	90 and beyond	Severe handicap May hear loud sounds Must rely primarily on other than auditory input Prelingual deafness: possibly poor speech quality Postlingual deafness: risk of deterioration in speech without monitoring	Usually special education services required with special class placement not uncommon Speech/language therapy Educational assistance

Source: *American Annals of the Deaf* (1975); Downs (1976); Pearson, Kell, & Taylor (1973).

wrong with her hearing?" you are asking about the impairment. When you ask, "How severe is the loss?" you focus on the disability. When you ask, "How does she manage in school?" you are inquiring about functioning in a particular setting and about the effects of the disability—the degree of handicap—in that setting.

The term **hearing impaired** for most professionals in the field is a generic term that refers to both hard-of-hearing and deaf individuals (Moores, 1987; Northern & Lemme, 1986). The terms *hard-of-hearing* and *deaf* focus on the degree of impairment. A child considered hard-of-hearing does have speech and oral language and can process verbal information, generally with some type of amplification, but often there will be some adverse effects on school performance (Moores; 1987). The federal regulations for P.L. 94–142

This child is having his hearing evaluated with amplification. Notice how unobtrusive his hearing aid is. (Photo by Joseph Bodkin.)

describe **hard-of-hearing** as a "hearing impairment, whether permanent or fluctuating, which adversely affects a child's educational performance but which is not included under the definition of deaf" (U.S. Office of Education, 1977a, p. 42478).

A child who is **deaf** may lack speech and oral language and will have some difficulty in processing verbal information, with or without amplification, efficiently for educational purposes (Moores, 1987). In fact, the federal regulations for P.L. 94–142 describe deafness as a "hearing impairment which is so severe that the child is impaired in processing linguistic information through hearing, with or without amplification, which adversely affects educational performance" (U.S. Office of Education, 1977a, p. 42478). Amplification can be helpful for some children who

are deaf; but even with amplification, the child who is deaf will, by definition, have problems processing auditory input, and the results will be detrimental to school performance.

Both the severity of the hearing loss and the age at which it occurs are important concerns of teachers who work with children who are deaf. The degree of loss may fluctuate, with the result that under certain environmental conditions such as in a noisy room or in physical states such as tiredness, the hearing disability may be much more handicapping than under other circumstances. This fluctuation can cause some uncertainty and ambiguity in the performance of tasks for which auditory input is required.

The age at which the hearing loss occurs is important because of the possible effects on development of normal language and speech. **Prelingual deafness**, deafness that occurs before the child has acquired language, can have serious consequences for initial development of both language and speech. The child who has never heard the sounds of his or her native tongue will have much more difficulty mastering language skills and speech than will the child who has had at least some useful hearing before the age of two or three. Severe hearing loss after basic language and speech skills have been well established is called **postlingual deafness**. People with postlingual deafness are sometimes called deafened or adventitiously deaf.

Incidence of Hearing Impairment

As is true of the other traditional categories of children with handicaps, estimates of the school-age population of hearing impaired vary according to the definition used and the date of the estimate. The development of highly sensitive and carefully calibrated devices for detecting and measuring hearing losses has led to the identification of more affected children. More and better screening programs, coupled with observations by parents and teachers alerted to the behavioral signs of possible hearing loss, have also contributed to the number recognized and served.

The National Information Center on Deafness (*Deafness: A fact sheet,* 1984) at Gallaudet University estimates that approximately 16 million Americans have some degree of hearing impairment. About 2 million of that group might be considered deaf by functional standards; that is, they do not pick up or understand speech sounds or common environmental noises even with amplification. In 1975, what was then the United States Office of Education (USOE), now the Department of Education, estimated that about .58 percent of the school-age population had some hearing impairment. Of that figure, .08 percent were considered deaf. That places the incidence of impaired hearing at approximately five out of every thousand children. Other studies have estimated that 5 percent, or five out of a hundred, of school-age children have at least mild hearing loss. Given the intricacy and delicacy of the structures that enable us to hear, it is surprising that the incidence of hearing loss is not much greater.

CAUSES OF IMPAIRED HEARING

Although some hearing impairments are **congenital**, others can occur adventitiously at any age after birth and may come on suddenly or insidiously. Unfortunately, the cause of impaired hearing remains unknown for as much as 30 percent of the school-age hearing impaired population.

Table 5.3 outlines the common known causes of **peripheral** and **central hearing loss** among the general population. For school-age children, the major causes are heredity, maternal rubella, cytomegalovirus (CMV), mother-child blood incompatibility, meningitis, and complications of prematurity (Moores, 1987).

Heredity. Hereditary deafness covers over 150 types of hearing loss that occur either alone or as part of a syndrome (Moores, 1987). In most instances, the condition is transmitted through recessive genes, which means the parents may have normal hearing themselves but be carriers of the defect.

Rubella. Maternal rubella, a virus disease, accounted for most of the congenital nonhereditary hearing impairment among children in the 1960s, when rubella epidemics swept across the country. If a pregnant woman contracts rubella or is immunized against rubella during her first trimester of pregnancy, the fetal cells that at that time are forming the delicate eye and ear structures are especially vulnerable to attack by the rubella virus. The result can be damage to ears and eyes as well as to the heart and central nervous system. Because the disease or reaction to immunization may be very mild and not even recognized or identified by the mother, the possibility of birth defect may not be thought of until the baby has arrived, at which time the defects may still not be very obvious. As more of the population receives immunization against rubella, the number of children who suffer devastating damage should decrease.

Cytomegalovirus. Researchers are now beginning to understand better how CMV, an infectious disease caused by a herpes virus, can affect hearing. CMV can attack any age group but can be particularly devastating to a baby *in utero* or to a newborn. CMV infection may not cause noticeable symptoms, or it may resemble a cold. Infants who are affected before birth, however, run the risk of suffering serious problems such as microcephaly, liver and spleen enlargement, deafness, neurological damage, and retardation. The virus can be transmitted through the placenta or picked up during passage through the birth canal. The earlier the infection occurs in the developing child, the greater the possibility of damage. Some children infected by this virus develop hearing losses several years after birth for no apparent reason. Only in the last few years, since about 1980, have researchers begun to recognize and study CMV as a major cause of deafness (Moores, 1987).

TABLE 5.3
SOME CAUSES OF HEARING LOSS

Peripheral Loss

Conductive

- Possible causes: Wax in ears
  Infection in ear canal
  Ruptured or perforated eardrum
  Foreign body in canal
  Otitis media
- Result: Faulty or blocked passage of sound pressure waves to inner ear

Sensorineural

- Possible causes:

Meningitis	Multiple sclerosis
Infection	Measles
Drugs	Otosclerosis
Mumps	Acoustic trauma
Direct head injury	Vascular disorders
Occupational noise	Neuritis
Hereditary deafness	Vestibular disorders
Virus infections	Presbycusis
Systemic disease	Unknown causes

- Result: Poor or blocked transmission through inner ear and/or auditory nerve damage

---

Central Auditory Dysfunction

- Possible causes: Mostly still a mystery but can be result of damage or malfunction in central
  nervous system between lower brain stem and cerebral cortex
  Tumor
  Abscess
- Result: Faulty interpretation of what is heard even though sensitivity may be normal

---

Source: Compiled from information in Berlin (1972); Sataloff and Michael (1973);
and Reynolds and Birch (1977).

Blood Incompatibility. The most common form of mother-child blood incompatibility involves the Rh factor where the mother's body builds up antibodies that destroy cells in the baby she carries. Fortunately, procedures such as the use of a vaccine or prenatal blood transfusions can be carried out to reduce the risk of problems if the condition is recognized in time.

Meningitis. The most common cause of adventitious hearing impairment is meningitis, a viral infection accompanied by a very high fever. Any damage to hearing from this disease is irreversible and may result in profound hearing loss, so prevention of the disease and rapid treatment when it has been diagnosed are vital. Antibiotics and other medicines have reduced the threat of meningitis, but the disease still accounts for between 5 and 7 percent of the deafness in the school-age population.

Prematurity. Complications leading to hearing impairment related to prematurity, especially in infants of low birth weight, will likely increase as neonatologists develop techniques to maintain the lives of more premature infants. Frequently, a hearing loss is only one of the problems that appears in these tiny infants. In Chapter 4, we discussed the high risk these babies have of damage to the retinas of the eye; the structures for and the process of hearing are also vulnerable.

IDENTIFICATION OF IMPAIRED HEARING

At the beginning of this chapter, we described two hypothetical students whose behavior evidenced signs of possible hearing loss. In some children, of course, the explanation for suspicious behavior may be preoccupation or inattention, but assuming such simple causes without further evaluation may result in devastating delays in securing care for a child's real problem.

Parents and teachers are generally the first to suspect that something is wrong with the hearing in children whose losses are mild. Children may not realize they have poor hearing if what and how they hear is the way it always has been, but such mild undetected losses can mean frustration and inefficient use of school time. Parents and school personnel thus must recognize signs of possible hearing loss in children not already identified as hearing impaired and signs of hearing difficulty in children for whom they know adjustments are necessary. Table 5.4 summarizes these warning signs.

Common behavior signs may cluster, or they may be evident only in particular situations. Such information can help professionals identify the type and location of hearing loss if one actually does exist. Although most of us occasionally exhibit many of these signs, a child who exhibits such signs frequently or in a variety of situations should be referred to a specialist in order to diagnose, or rule out, a hearing problem. The presence of physical signs may likewise suggest the need for a complete hearing examination. There are also some complaints that may be related to hearing loss and that call for investigation. As is the case with behavior signs, these physical signs and common complaints may occur occasionally in all of us, but when they cluster and appear frequently, it is time for a more formal evaluation.

Formal evaluation to determine the presence and degree of hearing loss includes those tests that measure hearing awareness, those that measure the integrity of the auditory system, and those that attempt to detect the electrical activity of the inner ear and acoustic nerve in response to auditory stimuli (Harrison, 1985; Northern & Lemme, 1986; Tucker & Nolan, 1986). In clinics and in many schools, measures of hearing sensitivity or acuity are made by using pure-tone audiometry. The individual wears earphones, and the audiologist tests each ear alone with tones of predetermined frequencies and intensities to check the hearing threshold of the various frequencies. The threshold of hearing, as well as the point at which hearing drops off, can be reported. In some instances, to bypass the middle ear system, the pure tones are introduced through a vibrator placed on the skin over the hard mastoid bone behind the ear lobe. Because the vibrations from the tone can spread through the head to the nontest ear, the audiologist will use masking noise to cover any tone that reaches the nontest ear. The results of pure-tone audiometry can be reported on **audiograms**, as illustrated in Figures 5.4 and 5.5. These audiograms contain only the results of the air conduction test, during which a tuning fork is held next to but not touching the ear. Note that the reference point for 0 dB on each audiogram differs from side to side. Two reference points are used—American Standards Association (ASA), which is primarily for human hearing threshold and ranges, and International Standards Organization (ISO), which is mainly for environmental and industrial noises.

Speech audiometry involves tests to determine the thresholds at which an individual can hear speech, or, in case of infants or young children, environmental sounds such as rattles. These tests include such tasks as discriminating consonant and paired vowel sounds and responding to directions on auditory cues.

TABLE 5.4

POSSIBLE SIGNS OF EAR TROUBLE

Behavior Indicators

Inattention
Turning head or ear toward speaker
Failure to follow spoken instructions, especially in group setting
Requests for repetition of spoken words, particularly questions
Speech problems
Reluctance to volunteer in class or in any group discussion
Withdrawn behavior
Unusual concentration on speaker's face or mouth
Inconsistent or inappropriate responses
Better work in small group or one-on-one
Use of gestures
Reliance on classmates for directions and assignments

Physical Signs

Ear discharge (running ears)
Mouth breathing
Frequent use of cotton in ears
Tired, strained expression early in day

Complaints

Earache
Ringing or buzzing in ears
Head noise
Stuffy feeling in ears
Sores in ears
Frequent colds, sore throats, and/or tonsilitis

Source: Berlin (1972); Geyer and Yankaver (1971).

A number of rather crude screening procedures are also used at times. These include the whisper test, during which the student stands approximately fifteen feet from the teacher/observer, faces away, and repeats words whispered by the observer; and the coin-click test, in which the student, again facing away, tries to tell when coins are clicked. These procedures add data to the collection, but they are not nearly as conclusive or reliable as standardized and controlled procedures.

Measures of the integrity of the structures of the ear are known as acoustic immittance or acoustic impedance techniques. They require that a small microphone be sealed in the ear canal. The reflection of sounds introduced through the microphone can tell the audiologist about the mobility of the eardrum and the capacity of the muscle that is attached to the stapes bone in the middle ear to contract in response to loud sounds.

Electrophysiological audiometric procedures involve sophisticated equipment used to determine the electrical potential in response to sound of parts of the inner ear and acoustic nerve that

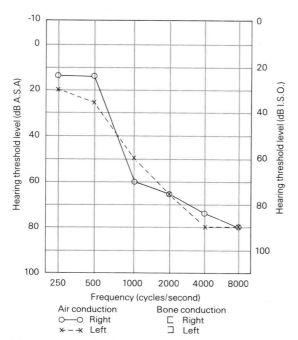

Figure 5.4. Descending audiometric pattern characteristic of sensorineural loss. (From Sataloff and Michael, *Hearing Loss,* 1973, p. 141. Courtesy of Charles C. Thomas, Publisher, Springfield, Illinois.)

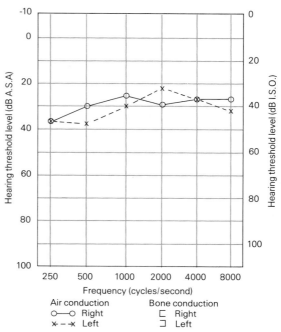

Figure 5.5. Essentially flat audiometric pattern characteristic of conductive loss. (From Sataloff and Michael, *Hearing Loss,* 1973, p. 141. Courtesy of Charles C. Thomas, Publisher, Springfield, Illinois.)

leads to the brain. In the inner ear or cochlea are located the tiny nerve endings that stimulate impulses in the VIIIth cranial or auditory nerve that leads to the brain and the site where the impulses are interpreted as meaningful sounds. Measures can be made of electrical activity occurring in the cochlea, along the acoustic nerve, and in the brain.

With these specialized procedures, it is possible to gather information about an individual's level of awareness of sound, the efficient passage of sound through the middle ear to the inner ear, and the capacity for the transmission of the electrical impulses from the inner ear along the auditory pathways to the brain. Such data, coupled with the observations of auditory function gathered by parents and teachers, can provide helpful information when the time comes to design appropriate instructional programs for children with impaired hearing.

EDUCATIONAL ALTERNATIVES FOR CHILDREN WITH HEARING IMPAIRMENTS

In Chapter 2, you read about the alternatives included in the continuum of services to be provided for children who are handicapped according to P.L. 94–142. Table 5.5 shows the enrollment in residential school and day classes for deaf children for selected years since 1975. In 1984, the majority of youngsters were going to day-school programs, and many of those were spending part or, in some cases, all of their time in regular classes with hearing classmates. Enrollments have shifted during the past several decades as public awareness and attitudes, medical skills and technology, educational expertise, and, more recently, federal mandates have increased the pos-

TABLE 5.5

ENROLLMENT IN SCHOOLS AND CLASSES FOR THE DEAF DURING SELECTED YEARS

	1975	1980	1982	1984
Residential students	15,952	12,702	12,573	10,645
Day students	36,533	36,876	33,684	38,907
Total students	52,485	49,578	46,257	49,552
Multihandicapped students	10,365	10,366	9,061	10,135
Total schools and classes	745	576	643	793

Source: Adapted from *American Annals of the Deaf, 121* (April 1976), p. 144; *126* (April 1981), p. 191; *128* (April 1983), p. 210; *130* (April 1985), p. 132.

sibilities for early diagnosis, treatment, and intervention. The number of children who are deaf in programs for the multiply handicapped jumped from 473 (*American Annals of the Deaf,* 1969) to 10,135 in 1984. It is interesting to note the fluctuations in total numbers of children during the last ten years.

Invariably, the question arises as to the relative merits of day-school programs and residential school programs. The question, however, ought to be: What are the relative merits of each in light of the needs of each particular child? In order to respond to that question, we need to know how hearing impairment can affect learning.

Effects of Hearing Impairment on Learning

One of the most important considerations in determining an appropriate education for children with hearing impairments is their level of language. The development of language skills and the formulation of basic concepts by children both deaf and hard-of-hearing are influenced by several major factors (Avery, 1967; Northern & Lemme, 1986).

Nature of Hearing Defect. The inability to hear very low-pitched sounds or extremely high-pitched sounds or musical tones, though unfortunate, does not have the profound effect on language acquisition and communication skill that inability to hear sound within the speech range

has. A major consideration, then, is whether or not the hearing loss is within the speech range.

Age at Onset. The earlier a hearing loss occurs, the more serious may be the effect on language and speech acquisition in prelingual children and on language maintenance in older children and adults.

Degree of Loss. Total loss or absence of hearing across frequencies within the speech range has serious effects on the development of language and speech in very young children, whereas children with a mild loss may still be able to develop language and speech spontaneously. Amplification of sound is beneficial for some but not all, as was discussed earlier. Hearing aids increase the intensity of *all* sounds, not just those of a particular sound source, and a user must learn to adjust the aid as the sounds of the environment change.

Cognitive Function. Some studies have indicated that intelligence is distributed in the deaf population as it is in the hearing population, and that the average IQ of persons who are deaf is similar to that of hearing persons (Avery, 1967; Willis & Faubion, 1979). D. R. Frisina (1967), in his review of the research, concluded that although differences in cognitive function between individuals who are deaf and those with normal hearing may be suggested, both limited language facility and the manner in which intelligent behavior is measured can influence an individual's

Hearing testing is done by trained professionals who use an audiometer and other instrumentation. (Photo by G. P. Cartwright.)

proficiency in expressing or revealing his or her intellectual capabilities. Because so much of the test performance depends on language skill, test results obtained with instruments heavily based on verbal performance are very limited. Current test instruments and procedures may not provide an adequate picture of the strengths and weaknesses of a child's learning potential. D. F. Moores (1987), after an extensive review of research on deafness and cognitive functioning, has concluded that

> Given the present state of knowledge, the most parsimonious approach would be to conclude that the evidence suggests that deaf and hearing children are similar across a wide range of areas traditionally related to the study of cognitive and intellectual abilities. The great difficulty encountered by deaf children in academic subject matter is most likely not caused by cognitive deficiencies. In fact, it is safe to say that educators of the deaf have not capitalized on the cognitive strengths of deaf children in the academic environment. (p. 165)

As for academic performance, which also relies heavily on language skill, children who are hard-of-hearing generally are behind their hearing peers, and children who are deaf may function at a retarded level. In young children whose hearing loss may not yet have been detected, difficulties with language comprehension, speech production, and manipulation of abstract ideas may be mistaken for evidence of mental retardation. For that reason, many special education programs include hearing tests as one step in the evaluation process of all children referred for special services, not just those suspected of hearing loss.

Presence of Other Handicapping Conditions. When hearing is poor, even greater reliance is placed on vision. Children who have poor or no vision in addition to impaired hearing present a great challenge to parents and teachers. Such children, particularly if their problems stem from rubella, may also have motor problems, central nervous system disorders, and cardiac defects. These children who are multihandicapped gener-

BOX 5.2
"HUH?"

Sometimes we do not hear what someone has said to us because we do not pay attention or because other sounds mask what we are trying to hear. But other times, in the absence of these factors, we still do not hear what a speaker has said to us. Such is certainly the case for many who have some degree of hearing loss and for whom the usual environmental sounds like the wind or the air conditioner fan or conversations going on nearby can interfere with the clear reception of a speaker's voice.

Rather than say "Huh?" here are some suggestions for handling those somewhat awkward situations when part of a conversation is missed. Teachers may want to help their students with impaired hearing learn to temper their "Huh's?" with some of these alternatives:

- I didn't catch that.
- Could you say that again . . . (more slowly, using different words, facing me, etc.)
- I'm not sure I understood you.
- Did you say . . . ?
- Do you mean . . . ?
- Correct me if I'm wrong, but you said . . .
- I understood you until . . . , then I lost you!
- It would help me to understand you better if you would . . .
- Tell me the main topic.
- Please rephrase that for me.
- I have difficulty hearing, could you please . . . (be specific in your instructions)

Source: Buoata, J. (1986). What do you say after you've said "huh"? *The Voice, 2(4).*

ally require extensive educational services that are appropriately provided in special class settings.

Nature and Amount of Stimulation Provided. Children who have normal hearing learn much incidentally from the sounds and sights of their environment. Children with limited or no hearing, by contrast, may miss this incidental learning unless parents and teachers plan carefully to enable them to make sense out of the world around them. Parents and teachers form a vital team whose cooperative efforts are essential to the full development of potential in such children.

INSTRUCTIONAL CONSIDERATIONS

One of the major concerns of regular classroom teachers about the integration of a student with hearing impairments into a regular class is the possible difficulty in communication—"How will I talk to him?" "How will she know what we are discussing?" "What if I want to show a film?" "Will he hear the bell?"

From all you have read so far about the potentially detrimental effects of hearing impairment on language development, you can understand the importance of stimulating language production and establishing some means for the child to express wants and needs. But to do this effectively, we must clearly distinguish between the child who is hard-of-hearing who depends on an auditory-verbal system to a large extent and the child who is deaf whose communication relies on a primarily visual system (Ross, 1981). Hard-of-hearing children need to learn to use effectively whatever hearing they have. Children who are deaf, in contrast, must learn to use other input channels, chiefly the visual, to establish and maintain contact and interact with the people around them. These two groups of children will develop and rely on different modes or combinations of modes of communication. These various modes can be described as primarily manual, primarily oral, and essentially the combination of the two, called total communication.

Manual Communication

Manual communication is a generic term that refers to systems of hand symbols that convey specific ideas, concepts, or words. In many cases, the hand positions resemble the objects or actions they represent. The manual symbols also may resemble many natural gestures for expressions and emotions.

One form of manual communication is **finger-spelling**, in which each letter of a word is presented using the American Manual Alphabet (see Figure 5.6). Fingerspelling is language-based; that is, words of a particular language are spelled. Although fingerspelling may be used exclusively, it usually supplements signing when the user does not know the sign for a particular word or if the word has no sign (Willis & Faubion, 1979).

At the opposite extreme of fingerspelling in a specific language is **American Sign Language**, or **Ameslan**. Ameslan is a separate natural language with its own rules for use (Schein, 1984b). The signs are hand/motion configurations that convey meaning by the shape of the hand, the position relative to the rest of the body, and the motion. Other qualities such as the speed of delivery, direction, vigor, and facial expression of the signer all help to refine meaning. Signs, therefore, are not exactly the manual analog for spoken words, even though we may talk about how to "sign a word." In the United States, Ameslan is the third most frequently used non-English language behind Spanish and Italian (Wilbur, 1979). Some colleges and universities, including Harvard, Brown, and MIT, have now approved Ameslan as an acceptable option for students to meet foreign language requirements. Although this mode of communication provides a way to exchange information, ideas, feelings, and thoughts, signing also separates those who rely upon it exclusively from communication with people who have not mastered the language of signs. For school-age young-sters, Ameslan is not commonly used as the language for instruction; rather, English-based sign systems are more commonly used (Moores, 1987; Schein, 1984b).

English-based sign systems, referred to as Manual English (Schein, 1984b), follow the English-language syntax or word order. Among the more commonly used varieties of Manual English systems are Seeing Essential English, Signing Exact English, and Signed English. As previously mentioned, some form of Manual English is most frequently used in school programs for children who are deaf. One reason is the relative ease with which it can be learned compared to Ameslan. Another is the fact that English is the language of the majority of people in the United States (Schein, 1984b).

Oral Communication

With **oral communication**, speech becomes the main channel for communication. Those who learn to speechread or lipread can increase their understanding of the spoken word by drawing cues from the shape of the speaker's lips and jaws.

Not all youngsters who are deaf, or adults for that matter, can master the motor skills required for clear speech production in the absence of useful hearing. Nor can they all learn speech- or lipreading, which to some extent requires a good understanding of the structure of language. Consequently, some educators of the deaf have emphasized the advantages of alternatives to exclusively oral communication for some students who are deaf.

Cued speech is a speech-based system of communication in which hand locations and shapes supplement lip movements to make the more than forty **phonemes** of spoken English distinguishable from one another. The four hand positions and eight configurations provide a phonetic analogue of the spoken language and carry no meaning unless they are used with speech. Cued speech was developed in the mid-1960s at Gallaudet University but is not widely used. Its primary function is to enhance development and compre-

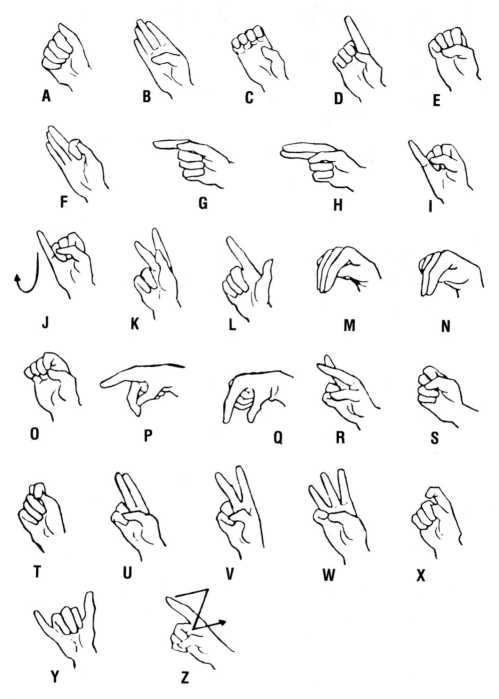

Figure 5.6. The manual alphabet as seen by the person who is hearing impaired.

BOX 5.3
AMERICAN SIGN LANGUAGE

The teacher models for his student the sign for *correct*. (Photo by Joseph Bodkin.)

American Sign Language, known also as Ameslan or ASL, is the fourth most used language in the United States, preceded by English, Spanish, and Italian, and followed by French, German, and Yiddish (American Speech and Hearing Association, 1974; Wilbur, 1979).

Ameslan employs both signs and fingerspelling. It is not merely a manual form of English; rather, it is a separate language with its own system and rules for formation of signs (Wilbur, 1976, p. 432). Meaning is conveyed in a variety of ways, including speed and vigor of delivery, size of the sign, the place the sign is made in relation to the body, the direction of movement, facial expression, head and shoulder movements, shape of mouth and cheeks, movement of the tongue, movement and focus of the eyes, and the overall emotion of the signer (Fant, 1977). Of course, signers who fingerspell English words produce English along with the sign, but the signs themselves make up a separate visual language of movement or relationship.

Ameslan comes originally from a French sign system developed by Abbé de l'Epée, who established the first school for the deaf in Paris in 1760.

Thomas Hopkins Gallaudet, an American, traveled to Europe in the early 1800s to learn about the education of deaf children and returned home greatly impressed by de l'Epée's sign method, which he found popular in France.

In 1817, Gallaudet founded the first school for deaf children in the United States in Hartford, Connecticut. His son Thomas later opened a church for deaf people in New York City, and his son Edward eventually became president of the Columbia Institution for the Deaf and the Dumb and the Blind in Washington, D.C. In 1894, the institution was renamed Gallaudet College in memory of Thomas Hopkins Gallaudet, who had introduced the language of signs into educational programs for deaf children. In 1986, Gallaudet College was again renamed and became Gallaudet University. Gallaudet University today is the only private liberal arts school for deaf students in the country. In addition to the liberal arts program, the university has a special research program in education of the deaf and a teacher preparation program to train teachers of deaf individuals.

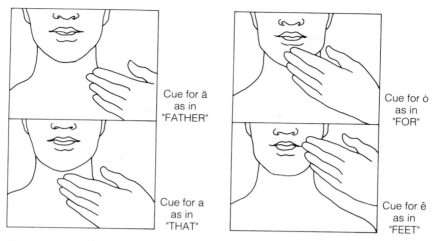

Cue for ä
as in
"FATHER"

Cue for ȯ
as in
"FOR"

Cue for a
as in
"THAT"

Cue for ē
as in
"FEET"

Figure 5.7. Cued speech vowel cues. (From Schein, J. D. (1984). *Speaking the language of sign: The art and science of signing.* Garden City, NY: Doubleday, p. 96.)

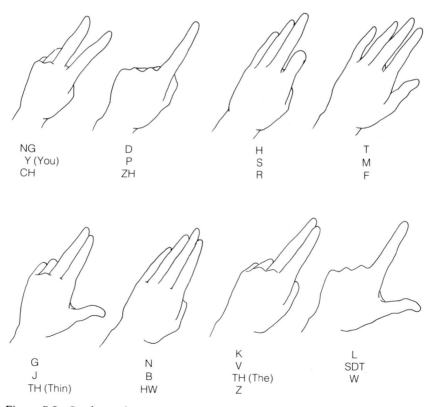

NG
Y (You)
CH

D
P
ZH

H
S
R

T
M
F

G
J
TH (Thin)

N
B
HW

K
V
TH (The)
Z

L
SDT
W

Figure 5.8. Cued speech consonant cues. (From Schein, J. D. (1984). *Speaking the language of sign: The art and science of signing.* Garden City, NY: Doubleday, p. 97.)

BOX 5.4
TAKE A CUE FROM CHRISTY!

Christy Neth was born with normal hearing on October 29, 1974. Her initial development in all areas seemed average or above-average. By age two, she was speaking in five-word sentences, sometimes even more, knew her telephone number and address, and could identify a variety of animals and tell which ones would bite.

At age twenty-five months, on the day before Thanksgiving, Christy complained of an upset stomach and spiked a fever of 104.6 degrees. A visit to the doctor's office later that day resulted in directions for medication and sponge baths to bring the fever down and instructions to call if any changes were observed. Christy developed leg pains, and her fever dropped only to 102 degrees even with the medicine. Because she seemed worse, the doctor, upon seeing her the first thing the day after Thanksgiving, sent Christy to Children's Hospital where she was diagnosed as having H. flu meningitis. After two weeks in the hospital, Christy was discharged.

On the afternoon she came home, Christy's mother noticed that she did not respond to her baby brother's crying or to the barks of the family dog. During the next few weeks, audiometric testing that included an evoked auditory response indicated that Christy now had a profound hearing loss. At 250 Hz, she had a 75 dB threshold; at 500 Hz, she had a 115 dB threshold; and above 125 dB, she showed no response to 125 dB, which was the limit of the testing equipment.

At age two years and ten months, Christy entered a class for hearing-impaired children in the school district adjacent to her own district of residence. Her parents reported that she "entered the class speaking and left after summer school the following year not speaking."

Christy's parents made the difficult decision to send her to a residential school in another state. "Sending our daughter 500 miles away to go to

school at a young age of 3 was the most difficult thing we her parents ever did. We felt that if Christy was to succeed in life she must have the best education possible."

During the three years Christy was away from home, her parents learned about Cued Speech and asked that Christy be taught the eight hand positions and their various placements and be encouraged to use Cued Speech in school. The school personnel adamantly refused and also would not approve having a tutor teach Christy Cued Speech outside school at her parents' expense.

Christy's parents enrolled her the next year for first grade in a local private Christian school where she spent one-half of her day in a language program and the other half in the regular class. Her language skill level was that of a three-year-old when she began school. She made progress during the next three years and mastered Cued Speech.

Christy's parents then asked their local school district to permit Christy to attend the local public school with a Cued Speech interpreter or else pay for her to go to a public school program for deaf children in another district. Up to this time, Christy's parents had paid for all tuition fees, language and speech therapy, and costs of the Cued Speech interpreter. Christy entered Groveport Ele-

Source: This material is used with permission of the Neth family. Photos courtesy of the Neth and Burnett families.

Christy and her friend share a funny incident with the help of Cued Speech.

mentary School for fourth grade. Her interpreter taught Cued Speech to her classmates, and one of her teachers traveled to Gallaudet College (now Gallaudet University) in Washington, D.C., to learn Cued Speech. Her parents report, as Christy comes to the end of her first year in Groveport-Madison Middle School South,

All the teachers and support personnel at Groveport Elementary were excellent in their acceptance of Christy. In one conversation with Christy's principal, Mr. Tom Stevenson, he mentioned that he wished Christy had been with them since the first grade. Christy progressed beyond our wildest expectations, winning the Presidential Academic Excellence Award at the end of her fifth-grade year. In two years she had only one B; the rest were A's. This year she entered Groveport-Madison Middle School South and has continued her academic excellence. Because of all the students that cue to Christy she is adapting and growing like any normal child. We are often amazed at her use of slang and some types of language which she must be getting from her peers.

Christy was just tested by the school district for the special services diagnostic team. She scored at or above grade level in all categories and two or more years above in language skills. This is from a student who upon entering first grade had a language skill level of a three-year-old.

We, her parents, are proud of Christy's accomplishments to date, and it is our fondest hope that other children will also be given the opportunity, which Christy has had, to learn. We realize that it is up to each individual to determine at what level they are willing to work at and achieve, but with Cued Speech deaf children have the same opportunity as hearing children and their success or failure is due to themselves, not an inability to perceive or understand our language.

Christy has agreed to let us share with you the essay she wrote recently for a class assignment.

(continued)

(continued)

> My hero is a very special man named Dr. Orin Cornett. He invented something new for deaf kids called cued speech. You use 8 different hand shapes and four places around your mouth to show a deaf person exactly what you say. I know cued speech works because I am deaf and I use cued speech. When someone cues to me, I understand exactly what they say. I can see what others hear.
>
> Because of Dr. Cornett and cued speech I can go to a regular school, Groveport Elementary. I have many friends that cue to me and an interpreter cues what my teacher, Mr. Timmons, says. I have made the honor roll.
>
> Thank you Dr. Cornett for being my hero and making me so happy.

Figure 5.9. Christy's essay.

hension of verbal language (Cornett, 1975).

The Rochester Method, another speech-based system of communication, combines speech with fingerspelling. The speaker fingerspells each word as it is spoken. The method takes its name from the school in Rochester, New York, where it was first consistently used in the United States (Furth, 1973).

The fact remains that understanding of and ability to use spoken language are essential skills for youngsters placed in regular classes for their instruction. D. Ling and his colleagues concluded that "the extent to which a hearing-impaired child can benefit from placement in a regular class depends primarily upon that child's ability to understand and employ spoken language" (Ling, Ling, and Pflastier, 1977, p. 209).

Total Communication

An approach to teaching children who are deaf that many educators espouse today is **total communication**. Total communication can refer to the philosophical position regarding the development of communication skills that advocates the use of whatever enables the child who is deaf to communicate with others (Moores, 1987). We also use it to indicate the combined use of speech, signing, gestures, speechreading, fingerspelling, and even writing and reading in an attempt to extend the communication capabilities of the child who is deaf.

The decision to instigate a total communication system for a particular child must be based on a variety of factors, among which are the child's

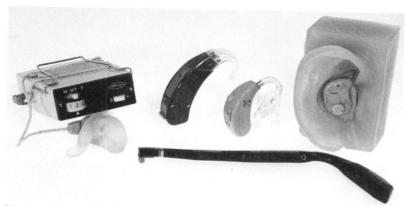

Hearing aids are classified according to where they are worn on the body. The hearing aids on the left are over-the-ear or ear-level aids. The aid at the upper right is an all-in-the-ear hearing aid. The aid at the lower right is a body aid. (Photo by Hans Hake. Aids courtesy of the Ohio State University Speech and Hearing Clinic.)

prelanguage skills and potential to learn and to use a symbolic communication system, the child's repertoire of natural gestures, the child's ability to coordinate muscles necessary for speech production, and the support in the child's environment that will foster the use of signs (Lombardino, Willems, & MacDonald, 1981).

A controversy over the merits of oral communication, manual communication, and total communication has been going on for some time. Some educators of children who are deaf have insisted that only one approach be incorporated into their programs. Others, however, have stressed the necessity of considering the capabilities of each child in question rather than espousing one method for all children. If a child has no useful hearing and is not learning oral language, then alternative modes may be essential in order for that child to make and maintain contact and exchange ideas with others. For children who have useful hearing, however, effort should go into the development of good oral language skills. Careful evaluation of each child is critical, for as Ling and others point out, "Absence of appropriate evaluation can readily lead to 'oral' failure, 'manual' failure, or 'total' failure, as the case may be" (1977, p. 212).

TECHNOLOGICAL DEVELOPMENTS FOR STUDENTS WITH IMPAIRED HEARING

In recent years, technological advances in electronics have led to the development of a variety of aids and equipment that have improved communication opportunities and alleviated to some extent some of the problems that can occur in education programs for both students who are deaf and students who are hard-of-hearing (Kelly, 1987). These developments can be classified for purposes of this discussion as language/speech aids, environmental situation aids, and microcomputer adaptations and applications.

Language/Speech Aids. Hearing aids are perhaps the most common form of aids to enhance reception and expression of language in spoken form. Some hearing aids are worn behind or in the ear, some can be mounted in the earpiece of spectacle eyeglass frames, and some are body aids that have a set of controls in a pack worn on the chest or on the back. (The latter location helps prevent the child from playing with the controls.) Some

Captioned TV programs help the hearing impaired follow dialog. (Courtesy of National Captioning Institute.)

People who are deaf can communicate on the telephone by means of the TTD, a teletypewriter connected to a telephone by a special adapter. The person receiving the call must also have a TTD hook-up. Messages are typed out as they are received from the sender. (Photo by Joseph Bodkin.)

aids are binaural; that is, an aid is worn in each ear, and each aid has its own microphone, receiver, and set of controls.

For a limited number of carefully selected children who have profound hearing losses and who cannot be assisted by any amplification a hearing aid might provide, cochlear implants may be an option. Presently, cochlear implants are considered investigative and still rather controversial for children (Schein, 1984a), although for some children, the results have been promising. The implant might be considered an analog of a pacemaker for the heart. The electrodes that are surgically inserted are activated by auditory stimuli picked up by a microphone. The signal that is transmitted represents sounds at a preset frequency range, not the full range of speech sounds that would be received by a person with normal hearing. The signal results in impulses being sent along the auditory pathway to the brain. With practice, the person can learn to use the variation in the intensity and rhythm of the signal to improve his ability to understand what others are saying and to be more aware of his own voice quality and sounds in the environment.

Environmental Situation Aids. Other systems are also available to help improve reception and expression of spoken language. In some classrooms for youngsters who are hearing impaired, the teacher and students use an FM sound system. The teacher wears a microphone that transmits on an FM frequency to which the students' receivers are preset. No wires or separate amplifiers are necessary. Such systems can be used indoors or outdoors and allow for much greater physical freedom than did older systems that required microphones and receivers to be connected by wires.

Another device that can aid in language and speech development and that also can help an individual who is profoundly deaf become more aware of environmental sounds is a vibrotactile device (Sheely & Hansen, 1983). The device consists of a microphone, usually clipped to the collar, an electronic sound receiver/analyzer in some type of pocket carrier that is often worn at the waist, and a wrist vibrator that is activated when sounds are picked up. Vibrotactile devices translate sounds into patterns of vibration so that, with training, the individual first can become aware of sound at the basic level and then can discriminate voiced and voiceless sounds, separations between words and phrases and sentences, and characteristics of voice quality. These devices can increase awareness of sound and improve lipreading skills, reception of spoken language, and quality of expressive language. With any of these language/speech aids, the goals are maximal use of listening skills, increased intelligibility of spoken language, and greater integration and independence within mainstream society (Cole & Gregory, 1986).

Aids for children and adults who are hearing impaired that increase awareness of specific environmental situations include blinking or strobe lights activated by fire alarms, alarm clocks, ringing of telephones or door bells, and the crying of a baby. Captioned TV programs and captioned films also help the hearing-impaired viewer follow action and dialogue while watching news, films, or other television or movie productions. Telecommunication devices for deaf people (TTDs) enable individuals who otherwise could not use telephones to communicate with each other or with hearing individuals who have the necessary equipment. Many human-services offices, libraries, and agencies today have TTD numbers listed on letterhead along with regular telephone numbers so individuals with hearing impairments will see how to access services or information just as hearing individuals can.

Computer Aids. Perhaps the most dramatic technological developments have occurred in the application of computer technology to improve the communication skills of those with impaired hearing. Microcomputer software has been used for speech training, math instruction and practice, language development and evaluation, reading instruction, and vocabulary and concept development (Kelly, 1987; Messerley, 1986; Rose & Waldron, 1984). Interactive videos for self-instruction, graphic displays of voice production to improve spoken language, and on-line message

This "pocket size" TALK TONE by Audiotone can be attached to a telephone receiver. The device converts the telephone push-button tones to letters, numbers, symbols, and words! (Courtesy of Audiotone, Inc.)

boards for information exchange, such as through CompuServe's Handicapped Users' Database program, are additional applications to enhance communication. Teachers are advised to be cautious in the selection of software for use with students who are hearing impaired because technical and instructional quality as well as the quality of the content sequence and design can vary widely even within one program. K. Kettler (1985) has outlined critical features to evaluate in the selection of commercially available software; these are summarized in Table 5.6.*

---

*Gallaudet University has recently published *Software Shopper,* a catalog of courseware with annotations for over four hundred public domain programs suitable for hearing-impaired students as well as for other students. The intent is to update the catalog periodically (Software Shopper available, 1987).

TABLE 5.6
FACTORS IN THE SELECTION OF COMMERCIAL SOFTWARE FOR STUDENTS WITH IMPAIRED HEARING

Technical Factors

Documentation
Ease of operation
Well-designed screen displays
Effective graphics
Sound as option, if available
Remedial branching
Record-keeping and student data management functions
Capability for content alteration for individualizing instruction

Content Factors

Match between software and curriculum objectives
Accurate and error-free displays
No stereotypical references
Careful sequencing of materials to promote learning and retention

Instructional Factors

Clearly presented instructional objectives
Concise instructions appropriate for target user group
Consistency in reading, vocabulary, and language levels
Degree of student/teacher control of pace, sequence, difficulty, and stop/start points
Immediate remedial feedback
Motivating features appropriate for instruction
Opportunities for student to respond and interact with content

Source: From Kettler (1985), pp. 357–360.

TEACHER CONSIDERATIONS

Since the passage in 1975 of P.L. 94–142, the need for in-service programs for regular class teachers who are to incorporate children with special needs into their classes has become evident. Ling and others (1977) have observed that "preparation and support of the regular classroom teacher and orientation of the normally hearing pupils in the regular class are essential to successful mainstream educational placement" (p. 210).

Teachers who anticipate having a child with a hearing impairment in their classes need some basic information before profitable instructional planning can occur. This information should cover the extent of the child's hearing loss, previous educational background and experiences at school and at home, a report of psychosocial behavior including relationships with classmates and other peers as well as adults, and an estimate of academic achievement and potential. The teacher will also need to know what resources are available in the school and in the district (Teitelbaum, 1981).

In-service training can occur in special meetings, conferences, formal workshops, or informal discussions with teachers of the hearing impaired and other teachers. Unfortunately, many times other topics or issues take precedence. The following suggestions are included here to give classroom teachers some specific pointers on proce-

Hearing impaired students "see what they say" with the Video Voice Speech Training System. Named as one of the hundred most significant technological advances of 1984, the system received an IR 100 Award in the recent Annual Industrial Research and Development Competition in Chicago. (Courtesy of Micro Video Corporation, Ann Arbor, Michigan.)

dures when a child with a hearing impairment becomes a member of the class.*

1. Assign the child a favorable seat, removed from noise sources and close to the area where you instruct. A hearing aid helps only partially and cannot be expected to make this child a normal hearer.

2. Establish positive attitudes toward the child who is hearing impaired; you are a model for the other children in your class.
   a. Provide a buddy system in which another child helps to communicate classroom activities.

   b. Help the class to understand hearing and hearing loss by having specialists discuss the ear, hearing, hearing loss, hearing aids, noise, famous hearing impaired people, and the like.
   c. Encourage the child who is hearing impaired to participate in class activities. Do not expect less work from that child.

3. Speak naturally and face the child. Children with impaired hearing often rely heavily on visual cues to aid understanding.
   a. Rephrase instructions if necessary.
   b. Introduce new topics clearly with a short sentence or key word so the child can follow changes in activities.
   c. Be sure the child who is hearing impaired understands when questions are being asked.

4. Help the child with the hearing impairment to keep in touch with lesson content through written instructions and summaries.
   a. Place a simple lesson outline on the board.

*Most of these suggestions are adapted from a handout prepared by the Board of Education of the City of New York, Bureau for Hearing Handicapped Children. They were reprinted in J. Davis (Ed.) (1977). *Our forgotten children: Hard-of-hearing pupils in the schools*, Minneapolis, Minn.: National Support Systems, University of Minnesota, pp.41–42. Reprinted by permission.

BOX 5.5
"WHAT DO I DO IF THE HEARING AID WON'T WORK?"

1. If the hearing aid whistles check to see if
   a. the earmold fits
   b. the battery is the wrong type or the battery contacts are corroded
   c. the cord connections are broken
   d. the receiver is broken

2. If the hearing aid is "dead" check to see if
   a. the battery is dead, is the wrong type, or is in backwards
   b. the aid is in the telephone position
   c. the cord is broken

3. If the hearing aid is weak check to see if
   a. the battery is weak or the wrong type
   b. the volume or tone control is on the wrong setting
   c. the cord is broken

4. If the signal goes on and off, check to see if
   a. the battery contacts are corroded
   b. the cord or its contacts are broken
   c. the receiver is broken

5. If the aid sounds noisy or distorted, check to see if
   a. the battery is weak or the terminals are corroded
   b. the tone setting is in the wrong place
   c. the cord contacts are loose
   d. the earphone is broken, the wrong type, or clogged with wax
   e. the earmold is clogged with wax

Source: Jane R. Madell, *Pointers for Parents*. Reprinted with the permission of the New York League for the Hard of Hearing.

---

b. Give written tests whenever possible, making sure that they are at a level the child can read and comprehend.
c. Write key words or phrases on the board as the lesson progresses.
d. Write homework assignments on the blackboard.

5. Be aware of any speech and language problems the child who is hearing impaired may have.
   a. If you have difficulty understanding the child, ask him or her to repeat.
   b. Do not call attention to the child's speech errors in the classroom; record and share them with the speech clinician.
   c. Realize that the child may have limited vocabulary and syntax, both receptively and expressively. Failure to understand may be related to this language deficit as well as to the inability to hear normally.

6. Because the means of amplification used is essential to the child's success, check the hearing aid daily to be sure it is functioning. Encourage the child to tell you if the aid is not working properly, then consult with the appropriate support personnel (usually the audiologist).

7. When reporting to the parents of a child who is hearing impaired, who may be anxious about their child's ability to cope in a regular classroom, be sure to discuss the child's strengths as well as weaknesses. Be honest with parents.

8. Use support personnel (speech clinician, audiologist, resource room teacher) as consultants. They are available to provide special services for the child (speech and language therapy, academic tutoring, monitoring of amplification) and to answer your questions.

9. Work cooperatively with the notetaker if one has been assigned to help the child who is hearing impaired. In addition to taking notes on lectures and discussions, notetakers can cue or alert students to special announcements made over the PA system or to announcements made during study time when

the hearing-impaired child may not be watching the teacher. Notetakers may be drawn from volunteers, paraprofessionals, or students from upper classes (Wilson, 1981).

10. Work cooperatively with the child's interpreter or interpreter/tutor if one has been provided. Rate of delivery of information may need to be adjusted to allow for adequate time for manual presentation of information to the student.

Two final points will serve to sum up this discussion of instructional considerations.

First, concentrate efforts and concern on the child and the child's capabilities rather than on ears and disabilities. For instructional purposes, there are three areas that require particular effort on the part of the child and are usually of concern to the regular class teacher (Caccamise, 1974):

1. *Acquisition of a language base.* Children who are hearing impaired coming into a regular classroom will most likely have or show evidence of developing a strong language base or they would probably not be candidates for such placement.

2. *Communication skills.* We generally think of the spoken word as the main avenue for communication. There are, however, other ways to communicate. Children who are hearing impaired in regular classrooms will be refining their skills in communicating with hearing persons.

3. *Substitution.* Children with hearing impairments in regular classrooms can be taught to use visual and other information effectively. They can be taught to compensate for lack of auditory information and to substitute other kinds or combinations of information.

Language acquisition and development, skills for communicating with hearing persons, and efficient use of all information available are major factors in decisions about appropriate programs and placements for children with hearing impairments. They remain important factors throughout the school years, although their relative importance may fluctuate from time to time.

Second, educating children who are hearing impaired in regular classrooms requires a team effort. You should have the assistance of other professionals. Their special training, coupled with your training and skills as a classroom teacher, will increase the opportunities for successful participation of children who are hearing impaired in regular class activities. In addition, it will facilitate the development of positive attitudes and communication among all the children. Such specialized professionals might be those with special education preparation, medical skills, or counseling skills. It will be important to maintain a clear understanding of role distinctions and areas of responsibility for the various team members and to develop open lines of communication so that help is available when and where it is needed. Among those with whom regular class teachers may work on behalf of students who are hearing impaired are the following professionals, who should contribute to team efforts at both elementary and secondary levels:

▪ **Teacher of hearing impaired**. A trained professional with knowledge about language development, strategies for stimulating language development, and skill in various modes of communication. The teacher of the hearing impaired can work directly with a child with a hearing loss and can also be a resource for the regular class teacher and other team members.

▪ **Audiologist**. A professional trained to use audiometric equipment and other devices to measure the degree of hearing loss and to determine the effect of that loss on functional hearing. The audiologist can prescribe hearing aids for those helped by amplification of sound.

▪ **Otologist**. Medical doctor who specializes in treatment of diseases of the ear. The otologist can diagnose causes of hearing problems and recommend medical and surgical treatment.

▪ **Otolaryngologist**. Ear, nose, and throat specialist who, like the otologist, can treat diseases of the ear and provide medical and surgical treatment.

- **Speech/language pathologist** or **clinician.** Professional trained to determine the nature of speech and language problems and their remediation.
- **School psychologist.** Professional trained to administer individual tests and evaluate performance to determine the nature of problems in learning and behavior.
- **Principal.** Professional who provides administrative leadership for a school and sets the tone for the entire school program; without the principal's support and encouragement, the integration of any child with special needs in school becomes almost impossible.

The guidance counselor and vocational rehabilitation counselor also play important roles on the team as consultants, interpreters, and advisers to team members and can help them understand the needs of students who are deaf or hard-of-hearing.

Hearing impairment presents a very real challenge both to the children who must learn to live in a hearing world and to the teachers who strive to help them.

SUMMARY

The verbal portion of communication relies on knowledge of a language system, useful hearing, and clear speech. Impaired hearing, in addition to reducing sensory input, can affect the development of language and the production of speech and thus greatly disrupt the entire communication process.

A child with a hearing impairment who has some oral language and speech and who can receive verbal information, often with amplification, is called hard-of-hearing. The child who lacks speech and oral language and who has difficulty receiving verbal information efficiently for educational purposes is considered deaf. The degree of hearing loss, fluctuation in hearing efficiency or function, and age of onset are of particular concern to teachers because of the serious

consequences for initial language development. Approximately five out of every thousand children of school age have at least a mild hearing loss.

Most peripheral hearing losses are either conductive, resulting from some impediment to the passage of sound waves to the middle ear, or sensorineural, resulting from problems with reception of sound waves in the inner ear or transmission of the electrical impulses along the auditory nerve to the brain. Some individuals have central auditory dysfunction and have difficulty understanding what they hear.

Hearing losses can be classified according to degree of loss in terms of frequency and intensity. The critical range for normal speech lies roughly between 1,000 and 3,000 cycles per second (cps). Intensity of sound, expressed in decibels (dB), refers to the volume needed for an individual to hear sounds of various frequencies. An individual's hearing threshold or hearing level is the decibel level at which that person becomes aware of sound at least half the time. Tests of frequency and intensity are usually done by audiologists, and results are reported on audiograms.

For instructional purposes, hearing losses can also be classified as to effects on function within the frequency range critical for speech sounds. Children whose loss is 90 dB or beyond usually require intensive speech and language programs to help them develop modes of communication; frequently, these students are in special classes for children who are deaf.

Major causes of hearing loss among school-age students are maternal rubella, meningitis, and hereditary causes, the latter accounting for about half of all cases among school children.

Regular class teachers, from their excellent vantage point for observation of children, should be alert to behaviors, physical signs, and complaints that, when they appear with regularity, might be indicators of hearing problems. Many times, children with mild losses are considered inattentive, uninterested, slow, lazy, or stubborn, and their underlying problem remains undetected and unattended, with potentially serious effects on initial language development, speech production, and social interaction.

Children with impaired hearing attend public and private residential and day-school programs. Decisions as to the appropriate placement for a particular child must be based on the nature of the hearing defect, age of onset, degree of hearing loss, level of intellectual function, presence of other handicapping conditions, and levels of language and speech development.

Various modes of communication can be employed by individuals with impaired hearing. Among those frequently used are systems of manual communication and oral communication, as well as the combination of modes, called total communication. As is the case with selection of school placement, no one mode of communication is the best for all children; the decision as to which to teach must be made for each child. The same is true for the selection of any technological aids and equipment to improve communication and alleviate educational problems that might arise. Although aids to enhance language and speech production or to increase awareness of spoken language and environmental sounds may increase opportunities to participate with others in school, work, recreation, and community activities, any aid must be selected with the specific needs of the particular child in mind.

Teachers who have children with hearing impairments in their classes can expect to become part of a team made up of various professionals, including specially trained teachers of the hearing impaired, speech/language therapists, audiologists, psychologists, administrators, and medical personnel. The team effort should focus on the child, the child's capabilities and skills, and ways to increase those capabilities and skills.

Suggestions for Further Reading

Griffin, B. (1978). *My child comes with directions.* Washington, DC: Alexander Graham Bell Association for the Deaf.
Betty Griffin has written an appealing pamphlet in workbook format so that information about a particular child with a hearing impairment can be summarized for a teacher or any other professional. Information covers medical and educational background, speech and language development, special needs, how and when to help, and what to do if a hearing aid develops problems.

Lloyd, L. (Ed.). (1976). *Communication assessment and intervention strategies.* Baltimore, MD: University Park Press.
An extensive examination of communication disorders and strategies to remediate communication problems in developmentally disabled children, this volume provides detailed discussions by twenty-eight specialists on language assessment and behavior analysis and management, set in the context of a model for communication described in the first chapter. A later chapter on parent involvement presents a clear look at approaches to working with parents and contains specific suggestions for promoting effective and active parent participation in programs for developmentally disabled. Although broader in scope than just the area of hearing impairment, the book also offers detailed information on audiology, amplification systems, and systems of manual communication.

Moores, D. (1987). *Educating the deaf: Psychology, principles, and practices* (3rd ed.). Boston: Houghton Mifflin.
Moores' third edition of his comprehensive text covers in fourteen chapters the history of treatment and education of children and adults who are deaf in the United States as well as in other countries, major causes of hearing impairment in the past and present, effects of deafness on cognitive development and mental health, modes of communication for deaf people, and intervention strategies for developing communication skills. Particularly interesting portions deal with the impact of P.L. 94–142 on educational placement and services for students who are deaf, postsecondary education and the economic status of deaf people, and the development of the deaf community. For both the casual reader curious about deaf people and the serious student whose professional goal is work with children or adults who are deaf, this text serves as a rich resource.

Ross, M., & Nober, L. W. (Eds.). (1981). *Educating hard-of-hearing children.* Washington, DC: Alexander Graham Bell Association for the Deaf; Reston, VA: Council for Exceptional Children.
The nine chapters in this compact publication focus on the special educational needs of children who are hard-of-hearing, a group the authors view as frequently overlooked and lost. Information is aimed primarily at speech/language pathologists but has been presented in such a way as to show how the responsibilities of teachers, parents, audiologists, and speech/language pathologists are interrelated. Classroom teachers and others working directly with hard-of-hearing youngsters will find this book to be interesting, informative, and practical. It provides perspective and direction for teaching children who are hard-of-hearing in regular classes.

Relevant Journals

American Annals of the Deaf
Founded in 1847 and published five times a year by the Conference of Educational Administrators Serving the Deaf and the Conference of American Instructors of the Deaf as the official organ of each Conference (5034 Wisconsin Avenue, N.W., Washington, DC 20016).

Journal of Education of the Deaf
The official organ of the American Deafness and Rehabilitation Association, published four times per year (814 Thayer Avenue, Silver Springs, MD 20910).

The Volta Review
Published seven times a year as the journal of the Alexander Graham Bell Association for the Deaf, established in 1890, to encourage speech, speech reading, and the use of residual hearing (3417 Volta Place, N.W., Washington, DC 20007).

Organizations for Parents and Professionals

Alexander Graham Bell Association for the Deaf
3417 Volta Place, N.W.
Washington, DC 20007

American Deafness and Rehabilitation Association
814 Thayer Avenue
Silver Springs, MD 20910

Convention of American Instructors of the Deaf
5034 Wisconsin Avenue, N.W.
Washington, DC 20016

Council for Exceptional Children
Division for Children with Communication Disorders
1920 Association Drive
Reston, VA 22091

International Parents Organization
Alexander Graham Bell Association for the Deaf
3417 Volta Place, N.W.
Washington, DC 20007

National Association of the Deaf and
National Association of Parents of the Deaf
814 Thayer Avenue
Silver Springs, MD 20910

CHAPTER 6

Communication Disorders: Language and Speech

Did You Know That . . .

- language is silent?

- we communicate with symbols that are linked together according to an agreed-upon set of rules?

- the communication of thoughts, ideas, and feelings via speech can be reduced by "noise in the transmission" in the form of speech that calls attention to itself, is unclear, or causes distress in the listener or speaker?

- language and speech development have their beginnings with the cries and coos of infants?

- children with speech problems have the highest rate of cure and dismissal?

- we can communicate without words?

Communication skills are essential for full participation today in the activities of family, school, work, church, and the extended national and international community. Communication skills in listening, speaking, reading, and writing enable us to share ideas, information, and feelings and to respond to what others express. Yet, while we may agonize for hours over how we will express our ideas through the string of words and sentences we write, most of us give little thought to the production and sequencing of the words that we speak or to the analysis of the sounds that we hear. The actual production of sounds that we send out or pick up and interpret as words and ideas, however, is no small accomplishment in itself, as any person who has a communication problem in speech or language will affirm. And the way we assemble our words into sentences upon analysis suggests how complex a task it is to communicate clearly with words.

Suppose you heard the messages below spoken in the course of your daily activities. On the basis of these statements alone, would you be prepared to say which speakers, if any, had language or speech problems? On what would you base your decisions?

Calvin: Thum people think I thoud thpeak like my thithter Thynthia or my brother Tham. My mother liketh me even when I thound thilly.

Jake: In February we stawted south foah miles along the water. Our idear was to reach the fawm by dawk.

Mindy: I wuh-wuh-wuh-wa-wan-wanto-g-g-go-home!

Carol: Ga-ga-ga-ga goooooo eeeee babababa bo do da?

Did you understand these messages? And did you understand all the symbols used above to convey the messages? Did each speaker send only one message? Is understanding the message sufficient for clear communication?

By the end of this chapter, you will have had the opportunity to consider these questions in the context of school settings. We want to be certain you receive *our* message, which has to do with the

BOX 6.1

MATCHING MINDS AND MACHINES FOR A MIRACLE

We who are TABs can communicate our ideas and feelings in many ways. But what about people who are not TABs? Read on . . .

The highest form of human expression, said Phillip Cartwright, "is the bringing together of great minds and the most sophisticated technology on behalf of a single handicapped individual."

This is no lofty ideal. As professor-in-charge of special education at Penn State, Dr. Cartwright devotes a great deal of his time to trying to coordinate the minds and machines that can perform minor miracles in everyday life.

The kind of miracles that allow people like Juanita Decker to communicate feelings and study science and math. The kind of miracles that allow paralyzed individuals to communicate through a computer which allows them to pick pre-selected words and phrases through the movement of their eyes.

There are many success stories woven into Dr. Cartwright's cloak of technology. They sparkle amid the coarse fiber of scientific data.

"I remember one case, where a disabled youth—he was 16—had no reliable motor behavior (use of his arms, legs, or even vocal cords). Everyone thought he was retarded, but his parents said no," Dr. Cartwright recalled. "He did have some head movement that was reliable, and someone, somehow, figured out that he knew Morse code."

A switch, which he taps with his head, feeds the Morse code signals into a computer which prints out the words.

"This was the first time anyone gave him some means of speech," Dr. Cartwright said. "The first thing he spelled out was 'I love you, mom.' Now he's a college student and a sports writer."

Many people shy away from contact with the handicapped, he said, simply because they don't understand what they are going through.

He explains it like this:

"Imagine that you are paralyzed, from the nose down. You can't use your arms or legs. You can't speak or write. And you have an itchy nose. You can't tell someone that you itch. You can't scratch it. Even if you can get someone's attention with your eyes, how do you let them know that you want your nose scratched? That's just a drop in the bucket of frustrations that handicapped people have to bear."

Patience, Dr. Cartwright said, is one thing necessary to help break down the barriers between handicapped persons and what they call "TABs," or Temporarily Abled Bodies.

He said patience is important with someone who is trying to communicate, especially when the words are hard to distinguish or come very slowly and laboriously.

He had several suggestions for those who want to better understand and help their disabled neighbors:

√ "If you saw a drunk walk into a lamp post downtown, you'd most likely stop and ask if he was all right or needed help. You can do the same thing for a disabled person." If a blind person or someone in a wheelchair appears to be having trouble, offer your help. Ask "May I help you? What can I do for you?" Never simply start pushing a chair or guiding someone without first asking his permission.

√ When talking with someone who has a hearing impairment, do not look away or gaze out a window. Reading lips and expressions is very important to someone who has trouble hearing. Many people who are deaf also can read lips. It is a good idea to watch that you are not standing or sitting where a bright light (such as sunlight streaming through a window) will make it difficult for someone to watch your face as you talk.

√ Do not assume that people cannot hear or talk, just because they have other disabilities. Often, people will address the person accompanying a blind person or someone in a wheelchair, rather than talking directly to the handicapped individual.

√ Do not patronize a disabled person. Many people talk to people with disabilities as if they were very young or lacking intelligence. "Baby-talk" is especially distressing, he said.

—Kathie Dwyer McCann

Source: Reprinted with permission of *Centre Daily Times*.

human communication system and the problems some individuals have with language and speech production. In this chapter, we will emphasize the verbal expression of language and look at some of the more common difficulties that school children display when they express themselves through language and speech. We will also describe a classic model that allows us to illustrate breakdowns in communication resulting from speech and language problems as well as from sensory and motor impairments. But first, we want to say a brief word about the development of language and the production of speech so you will be aware of the normal sequence of events and be in a better position to identify children who show signs of difficulty or delay.

LANGUAGE AND SPEECH DEVELOPMENT AND PRODUCTION

The beginnings of language and speech lie in the cries, coos, and gurgles that accompany the infant's waking hours. These crying and comfort sounds set the stage for the later coordination of muscle activity essential for the articulation of clear phonemes and syllables. Gradually, we begin to hear the **babbles**, the combinations of consonant and vowel sounds, that are repeated over and over, particularly when the baby is alone and content. About the sixth month, at the time when many parents are thrilled because their offspring is smiling at them regularly, comes more babbling, in what seems like attempts to get attention or to respond when spoken to. Vocal play sounds contain syllable repetitions and take on inflections similar to those of adult speech, even the inflections of other languages (Van Riper, 1978). Carol, whose speech sample you read earlier in the chapter, has reached this stage in language development and is content to lure anyone within hearing distance to listen to her outpouring of verbiage.

Along with the babbling, babies will begin to imitate their own sounds and those of others; in other words, their own sounds serve as stimuli for

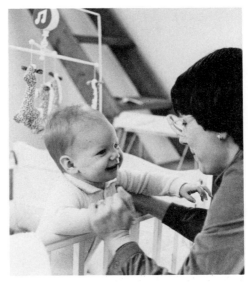

Vocal play with repetition and imitation of sounds is an important part of early language development. (Photo by Joseph Bodkin.)

production of more sounds, and the sounds of others also stimulate them to imitate or echo the pleasing sounds they have heard (Eisenson, Auer, & Irwin, 1963).

As early as eight or nine months of age, a baby may utter a real word of one or two syllables, delighting the family and reinforcing the idea of budding genius. Any time between nine and eighteen months, however, is the normal time for the appearance of the first words. From then on, in the presence of adequate language and speech models and in the absence of organic problems or environmental deprivation, the normal child's vocabulary will grow dramatically, coordination of muscles to produce sequences of sounds will improve, and more complex language structures will emerge and give listeners one index of intellectual development and mastery of surroundings.

Not all speech sounds are accurately articulated by a certain age; rather, they are produced, practiced, and improved over time, ideally with good speech and language models available (McLean & Snyder-McLean, 1978). Figure 6.1 shows the average ages and upper limits of customary consonant production. You will note that some consonant sounds may not be well estab-

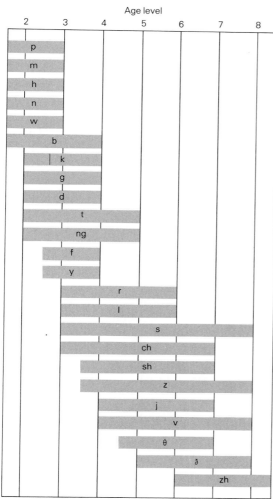

Figure 6.1. Average age estimates and upper age limits of customary consonant production. The solid bar corresponding to each sound starts at the median age of customary articulation; it stops at an age level at which 90 percent of all children are customarily producing the sound. (From E. K. Sander, in "When Are Speech Sounds Learned?" *Journal of Speech and Hearing Disorders,* 1972, 37 (1), 55–63. Used with permission of the author.)

lished until a child is six to eight years old—this is *normal*. Vowels and diphthongs, in contrast, can usually be recognized in the babbles and verbal play of normal infants and should pose little problem in production by school age (Van Riper & Emerick, 1984).

We can summarize the early stages of pre-language and language development as crying and comfort sounds, babbling, **lalling, echolalia, vocal play,** and on to production of first words. Gradually, as experience increases and practice continues in the presence of good language models, these early language skills are refined and integrated. This integration enables children to acquire and use language competently.

The actual production of the phonemes of any language requires a source of energy, a vibrating body, and a resonator (Thomas, 1958). In humans, the energy for speech comes during breathing out, or exhalation. During inhalation, air travels through the mouth or nose, through the pharynx and larynx, into the trachea, and into the lungs. During exhalation, muscles of the diaphragm and ribs force the air back out of the lungs and trachea and across the muscular vocal bands or folds in the larynx (see Figure 6.2). The force of the exhaled air, the degree of vocal fold mass and tension, the frequency of vibration, and the relative approximation, or proximity, of the vocal folds together determine the sound that travels into the resonating cavities of the throat, mouth, and nose.

A very intricate musculature allows the speaker to exert a fair amount of voluntary control to regulate and adjust how these resonating cavities are used as air is expelled. Voice quality is determined in part by how air is permitted to pass through these resonators. Changes in position of the tongue, soft palate, lips, and jaw produce the distinctive sounds of a language. The fine muscle coordination required to make the rapid changes and properly sequenced and timed adjustments requires practice on the part of the child and patience on the part of listeners.

You can readily understand how certain organic defects could result in problems with speech production. Clefts of the hard and/or soft palate and the lip can affect both voice quality and articulation. Severe dental malocclusion may make production of certain consonants difficult. Hearing impairment severe enough to limit significant feedback of the speech of others as well as one's own speech may also affect both articulation and voice quality. Those afflicted with cerebral

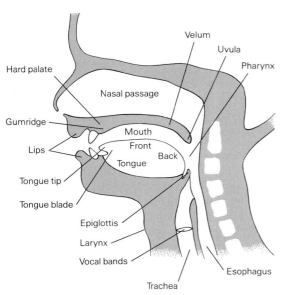

Figure 6.2. Passages of the nose, mouth, and throat through which air passes to the lungs. (From C. K. Thomas (1958), *An introduction to the phonetics of American English.* New York: Ronald Press, p. 15. Used with permission.)

palsy, depending on the type and degree of involvement, may have problems in articulation and voice as well as language.

A THEORY OF COMMUNICATION

Language has been described as a set of symbols agreed upon by members of a social community and used according to relatively standardized rules for the purpose of exchanging information (Blake & Haroldsen, 1975; Owens, 1986; Littlejohn, 1983). The symbols of a particular language—verbal, written, or representational—are the units that, alone or in sequence, carry messages formulated in one mind to the mind of another. The rules and symbols agreed upon by the members of one social community who use a particular language may differ quite a bit from the rules and symbols used in another social community, so much so that verbal communication between the two groups is limited if not impossible. For many American tourists, travel in a foreign country can illustrate very dramatically the breakdown in communication between individuals or groups who do not share a common set of verbal symbols and rules.

Various theories and models of the communication process have been formulated (Littlejohn, 1983) in attempts to clarify how messages are transferred from source to source or, for our purposes, from mind to mind(s). We have chosen to elaborate upon Claude Shannon's model (1949), however, because Shannon's model is considered a classic in information theory and because it provides a framework for introducing our discussion of information exchange. Shannon, along with his colleague Warren Weaver at Bell Telephone Laboratories, was especially concerned with the technical engineering problems of transmitting messages. Shannon proposed that an information *source* prepares a *message* that a *transmitter* sends across a *channel* by some *signal* or series of signals that a *receiver* then picks up and reconstructs for the *destination* (Shannon, 1949). The process may break down at many points because of technical interference or noise, distortions or static in the signal, or errors in transmission. One of the goals of speech/language pathologists who work with youngsters with speech problems that interfere with communication is to reduce or eliminate the undesirable effects of noise.

Figure 6.3 illustrates an instance of human-to-human communication with some noise introduced into the transmission. The accuracy of the interpretation the listener gives to Ronald's message is dependent to some extent on the listener's background of experience with both the set of name symbols of the English language and the expectations set up by the first part of the message, which offers a cue that a "name" is to follow.

Weaver (1949) suggested that message transmission may be considered at three different levels:

1. *Level A.* How accurately can the symbols of communication be transmitted?

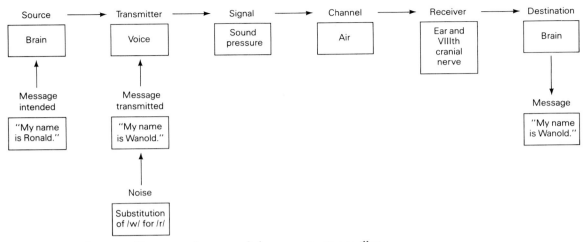

Figure 6.3. A diagram of human-to-human verbal communication to illustrate disparity between message intended and message received. (Based on Shannon & Weaver, 1949, p. 5.)

2. *Level B.* How precisely do the transmitted symbols convey the desired meaning?

3. *Level C.* How effectively does the received meaning affect conduct in the desired way?

Level A tackles the technical problems of accuracy of transmission and reduction of undesirable channel noise. Channel noise refers to such varied interference as static, smeared print, vertical or horizontal rolls on the TV screen, elaborately illuminated letters, background conversations, crying or barking, and other disturbances of signal fidelity (Blake & Haroldsen, 1975).

Level B is concerned with the problems of semantics or interpretation. Examples of semantic noise when humans talk include (Blake & Haroldsen, 1975)

1. words or subjects too difficult for the receiver to understand

2. differences in connotations and/or denotations attached to words by sender and receiver

3. confusing sentence patterns

4. confusing message organization

5. cultural differences between sender and receiver

Level C concerns the effect the message has on the listener's conduct and can include any emotional loading or consideration of style or judgment about quality. All three levels are interrelated.

To illustrate these problem levels, let's use Ronald and his message. His message, as transmitted, contained the substitution of an initial /w/ for the intended /r/ in *Ronald*. That error in transmission may not adversely affect the meaning the person receiving the message gives to it. But what might be the effect on the receiver even if he or she does translate *Wanold* as *Ronald*? That effect, as well as an indication of the understanding of the content of the message, is revealed in the behavior, or lack of behavior in some cases, that follows. This feedback is one of the unique characteristics of human communication (Etkin, 1963) that enables the receiver, who then becomes the sender in responding to the message received, and the sender, who then assumes the receiver role, to decide whether or not to modify the next message or the form of the next message. The message content may remain the same, but the original sender may select alternative symbols to express the next message if the receiver's response indicates uncertainty.

For example, a very young child might imitate the symbol as received and indeed call *Ronald*,

Wanold. A teacher or speech clinician might mentally note to check the frequency with which Ronald substitutes /w/ for /r/ and in what situations and in which positions the substitution occurs. Another adult might simply observe that Ronald is still talking "baby talk." But other third graders might make "Wanold" the butt of their jokes. This example points out both the importance and the interrelationship of the three levels of communication we mentioned earlier: the accurate transmission of symbols, the match between message sent and message received, and the effect of the message received on the receiver.

Let's look at another example. In response to your reply to a question, a teacher might say, "I find your statement contains certain inaccuracies." A brutal translation of that reply might be "That's wrong." Someone might even say bluntly, "You are wrong." Notice the subtle message added to the second translation: "That's wrong" points to the message, whereas "You are wrong" points to the person who originated the message and carries an emotional loading quite different from the original. In some verbal interactions, such a response introduces some undesirable material, or noise, that can influence the efficiency and effectiveness of any further communication if the receiver feels under attack as a person.

Aspects of Oral-Verbal Communication

Having established a model for the basic process of communication and illustrated that more is involved than just clear transmission of a signal, we are now ready to talk about some aspects of communication that are essential for understanding when humans speak to each other. Table 6.1 lists those aspects with their elements and descriptions.

Language. First, of course, in human oral-verbal communication comes **language**, the agreed-upon set of symbols and rules for their use. Elements of language include phonology, the sounds of a particular language; and morphology, the rules for combining the sounds of that language.

Syntactic and semantic rules of a language provide for putting sound units together in words and then putting those words in an order that conveys the intended meaning.

Pragmatics as an element of language refers to how we choose to use language in a particular situation. The way we speak in an elementary school classroom to convey the message that lunch time has arrived usually will be quite different from the way we would communicate that idea to a gym class or to seventh graders or to a group of students in a high school science laboratory. Some students may master the sounds, syntax, and semantics of language but have problems with pragmatics.

Speech. Another aspect of human oral-verbal communication is **speech**. To produce speech, an individual must have breath control; vocal cords that can vibrate as air is exhaled during respiration; cavities in which the sound emitted by the vibrating vocal cords can resonate; and muscle control to position the tongue, lips, palate, and teeth so the sound is shaped or momentarily stopped to enable the listener to recognize the sounds as particular phonemes. In English, for example, as previously noted, we have approximately forty phonemes that can be discriminated from one another.

Speech also encompasses **fluency**, the smooth "flow" of speech associated with rhythm, phrasing, speed, and inflection (Shames, 1986). All of us, on occasion, when tired, angry, anxious, frustrated, or stressed in some other way, or perhaps when talking about a topic that is difficult or unfamiliar or upsetting, will have moments when we struggle for the right word or for the best way to explain or phrase our thoughts. Our occasional repetitions, extended hesitations, and interjections generally are accepted as evidence that we are considering carefully what we say. When production of speech sounds is characteristically labored, noticeable, and distracting, then fluency in speech production is decreased. The line between this aspect of speech production and elements of paralinguistics to be discussed in the next section is not easily drawn; the main distinction in fluency

TABLE 6.1

ASPECTS OF ORAL-VERBAL COMMUNICATION

Aspects	Elements	Description
Language		Socially agreed-upon set of symbols and rules for their use for transmitting information
	Phonology	Sounds of the language and their characteristics
	Morphology	Structure of words and the use of inflections to indicate number, gender, case, and time
	Syntax	Grammar or rules for ordering words in a particular language
	Semantics	Rules for determining meaning of words and relationships between word units to convey meaning
	Pragmatics	Consideration of language form in social context; usage
Speech		Verbal-oral means of transmitting ideas, thoughts, meaning, intent
	Respiration	Breathing; inhalation and expiration of air
	Phonation	Production of sound by vibration of vocal cords
	Resonance	Characteristics of voice quality due to reverberation, reflection, and absorption of sound in the cavities above the larynx
	Articulation	Pronunciation of words and sentences controlled by placement of tongue, lips, soft and hard palate, and teeth
	Fluency	Degree of smooth, effortless production of sound
Paralinguistics		Prosody; signals or cues to attitudes and feelings of speaker
	Intonation	Pitch variation
	Stress	Accent of syllable or word for emphasis
	Rate of delivery	Speed of utterance
	Pause	Temporary stop or rest between morphemes, words, phrases, sentences, or larger semantic units
	Pitch at end of utterance	Highness or lowness of tone of voice
	Cadence	Melodic or rhythmic quality of speech
Nonlinguistics		Elements that convey meaning but are not part of the linguistic code; elements of nonverbal communication
	Body position	
	Gesture	
	Eye contact	
	Facial expression	
	Head movement	
	Distance from listener	
Metalinguistics		Indicators of status of communication exchange that reflect relationship between participants: acceptability of form and content of language for situation
	Attitude of dominance, submission, or equality	
	Use of listener's name, polite phrases, or routines	

Sources: Curt (1984); Littlejohn (1983); Owens (1986); Shames & Wiig (1986); Van Riper & Emerick (1984).

Learning to communicate is a critical skill. (Courtesy of Association for Retarded Citizens.)

is the effortless and uninterrupted flow of speech as deemed appropriate for the context of the conversation.

Paralinguistics. A third aspect of human communication is made up of **paralinguistic** elements that suggest the attitudes or feelings of the speaker. These elements include intonation patterns; stressed syllables or words to give emphasis over and above any stress called for by morphological rules or correct pronunciation; rate of speech flow; and use of pauses, again to a degree greater or lesser than pauses normally made between words, phrases, or longer word strings; variations in pitch and volume; and overall melody or rhythm of the speech utterance.

Nonlinguistics. A fourth aspect of the human communication process is **nonlinguistic** elements, which help convey the meaning and feeling underlying our spoken word but which are nonverbal contributions that are not part of the linguistic code. Our gestures, smiles, touches, body position, eye contact, eye movement, facial expressions, head movements, and distance from our listener all contribute to the impact of the words we say (Curt, 1984; Littlejohn, 1983). A raised eyebrow, roll of the eyes, shrug of a shoulder, extending of the arms, nod of the head, or step back can each carry its own message. In most cases, these nonverbal features are at least congruent with the message of our words and at best highly significant in clarifying or intensifying our message. For those who understand this "silent language" (Hall, 1959), the perceived mismatch of nonverbal and verbal messages sometimes can reveal an inconsistency or insincerity in the spoken message. But consider the disadvantage placed upon a speaker who has limited vision and who may not see any of the nonverbal cues. Or, as can occur when speakers represent different language and cultural backgrounds, the use of the nonlinguistic features of one language and culture within another culture and with another language may confuse the intended message or actually change it completely. We will elaborate on this point in Chapter 14 in our discussion of cultural diversity and its impact on education in our public schools today.

Metalinguistics. The final aspect of human communication we will mention is the **metalinguistic** aspect, which is somewhat similar to pragmatics, that is, appropriate language given the particular situation. Metalinguistic elements, however, go beyond to reflect the "status of communication" (Owens, 1986, p. 28), the attitude or degree of respect and the relationship between the participants. Use of such conversational conventions as "Would you please . . . ?" "Oh, my dear!" "Hey, will ya . . . ?" and "Good grief!" are all clues to the degree of familiarity of the speakers and the formality of their verbal exchanges. Metalinguistic features or linguistic strategies may be difficult for some youngsters to learn as they become young adults, and lack of sensitivity to such features can interfere with communication in ways quite separate from any problems that might occur in the language, speech, paralinguistic, and nonlinguistic aspects of communication (Secord, 1986; Wiig, 1986).

We have presented a model in which to consider the human communication process and have reviewed critical aspects that contribute to clear communication between individuals and among groups who share the same language. We are now ready to talk about some of the problems found in the language and speech of school children and youths.

SPEECH AND LANGUAGE PROBLEMS

Speech has been defined as the "medium that employs an oral linguistic code that enables one human being to express feelings and to communicate thoughts to another human being" (Eisenson, Auer, & Irwin, 1963, p. 6). **Speech problems** are those associated with the production of the oral symbols of language, whereas **language problems** are difficulties with the linguistic code, or rules and conventions for linking the symbols and symbol sequences. The two are not necessarily discrete sets of problems.

When does a speech or language difficulty reach problem status? Charles Van Riper, a pioneer in the field of speech pathology who for thirty years was himself a stutterer, has provided one answer for that question:

> Speech is abnormal when it deviates so far from the speech of other people that it calls attention to itself, interferes with communication, or causes the speaker or his listeners to be distressed. (Van Riper & Emerick, 1984, p. 34)

Van Riper's key factors in determining whether or not a person's speech is defective are the extent to which the speech is (1) conspicuous, (2) interfering, or (3) unpleasant. In terms of the communication model, there is noise in the transmission. Of course, age, cultural norms, and expectations of the group the speaker represents must be considered.

Our concern here is particularly with the children who become classified as speech impaired. The term **speech impaired**, as one category of handicapped children included under P.L. 94–142, describes someone with "a communication disorder, such as stuttering, impaired articulation, a language impairment, or a voice impairment which adversely affects a child's educational performance" (U.S. Office of Education, 1977a, p. 42479). We can summarize the problems suggested by the federal definition as those of language that include delays in development of language and those of speech that include absence of speech as well as problems of articulation, voice, and fluency.

Articulation

Articulation errors are those resulting in faulty production of the phonemes, the distinctive sounds of a language. In English, there are over forty standard phonemes to master, and we also must learn to recognize the slight variations in each phoneme, the allophones. For example, the /p/ sound in *pile* is slightly different from the /p/ sound in *up*. In the former, there is a slight puff of air that follows the separation of the lips as they move to the position for the *i* or /ai/. In *up*, we may choose to keep the lips together if the word ends a sentence rather than releasing the bit of compressed air. Both productions of /p/ are acceptable allophones in the *p* class (Thomas, 1958).

Articulation errors are of three types (Van Riper & Emerick, 1984):

1. Substitution of one phoneme for another, as *mudder* for *mother*

2. Distortion of a phoneme, as *shoup* for *soup*

3. Omission of a sound, as in *mik* for *milk*

Speakers sometimes add a sound to a word, as when our New England friends say they have an "ideer." Such additions reflect variations in dialect and are not properly considered speech problems. Other additions, such as "shlumber" for "slumber," not typical of any English dialects can be considered distortions.

Children with articulation problems make up the majority of the case loads of speech clinicians who work in school programs. Among this group we would have to include Calvin, whose speech sample you read at the beginning of the chapter. Some might also try to put Jake in this group, but Jake's New York speech is representative of one of the many interesting and intriguing dialects in the United States. Jake's case points up the necessity of careful listening and of knowing the critical features of regional dialects before labeling speech as deviant or deficient.

Voice

Voice problems involve the resonant quality of speech. An individual's voice can show a wide range of variations in pitch, volume, and quality (or timbre), all of which are the result of muscle activity and as such reflect changes in muscle tone. Voice quality can be a clue to mood, emotional state, and attitude (Van Riper & Emerick, 1984).

Both too high and too low a pitch are relative descriptions, dependent on such factors as the age, sex, and physical state of a particular individual. An unexpected flip-flop in pitch, which frequently occurs in adolescent boys, can be extremely disconcerting. Lack of pitch variation, an ailment prevalent among the professorial ranks according to many students, and extremes in pitch variation, resulting in the stereotypic inflections ascribed to some elementary school teachers, are equally irritating (Van Riper & Emerick, 1984).

Voice intensity also must be judged in context. A very loud voice might be appropriate in the gym but ordinarily is not in a classroom. Colds or excessive screaming may lead to temporary loss of voice, or aphonia. In some individuals, there are organic causes for aphonia, and in a few cases, emotional factors play a part.

Voice quality is difficult to define precisely, because it refers to attributes that distinguish one voice from another of the same pitch and volume. Terms used to describe voice quality frequently reflect a listener's subjective evaluation of voice characteristics (rich, rasping, mellow, whining), and another listener may react differently to the same voice (Van Riper & Emerick, 1984). Van Riper (1978) has written that only a few terms have gained widespread use: *hypernasal, harsh* or *strident* or *rasping, breathy, falsetto, throaty,* and *denasal* (as when one has a head cold).

Fluency

As previously noted, fluency has to do with the smooth flow or rhythm of speech. The major types of fluency problems are stuttering and cluttering, which are manifest in more than 2 million people in this country (Van Riper & Emerick, 1984).

Stuttering. For many years, **stuttering** has challenged professionals, and yet the research on stuttering is still "long, vast, and inconclusive" (Eisenson, 1971, p. 200). Stuttering, which most often begins between ages two and six, occurs "when the forward flow of speech is interrupted abnormally by repetitions or prolongations of a sound, syllable, or articulatory posture, or by avoidance and struggle behaviors" (Van Riper & Emerick,

This device, a voice light, helps children learn to control voice intensity. As the voice gets louder, the light gets brighter. (Photo by Joseph Bodkin.)

1984, p. 262). The critical features, as Van Riper emphasizes, are the abnormal number and length of the repetitions and prolongations. We all repeat and hesitate in our speaking at times, and young children frequently block or repeat or struggle with certain sounds or words. But a stutterer may repeat a syllable so many times it becomes necessary to take another breath or hesitate for several seconds before finally firing out the word, and posture may be fixed and contorted in the struggle to speak.

Stuttering has been attributed to many factors, among them emotional conflicts, neurophysiological defects, genetics, neuroses, disturbances in thought processes, expressions of anxiety in stressful situations that become conditioned, and parental misdiagnoses of normal disfluencies and their subsequent inappropriate correction (Shames, 1986; Van Riper & Emerick, 1984). Treatment methods vary considerably. Some use psychotherapy and work on what are thought to be the underlying emotional causes and problems of the stutterer. Others, using classical and operant conditioning, try to reinforce and strengthen nonstuttering behavior to a point where the stuttering behavior weakens and decreases. A third approach is to teach the stutterer

to stutter "without struggle or avoidance," to stutter in new ways that will be more fluent and not interfere with communication. Van Riper is associated with this third approach, which is often used with confirmed stutterers.

With young children whose nonfluency is not yet entrenched, clinicians generally work with parents as well as the children to reduce the frustration and penalties attached to instances of hesitancy or repetitions and to strengthen normal speech flow. Situations of uncertainty, stress, and pressure to respond alone in front of others can lead to stuttering episodes. Some children, as well as adults, experience no difficulty in choral reading or singing. For instance, before we should label Mindy, whose speech sample appeared at the beginning of this chapter, as a stutterer, it would be imperative to consider, among other factors, Mindy's age (five), the situation (her first morning at kindergarten), the frequency and duration of her repetitions of sounds in other settings, and her level of awareness of and reactions to any instances of hesitating or repeating.

Cluttering. Another fluency problem, which may be confused with stuttering, is **cluttering**. Although the person who clutters may repeat, the

BOX 6.2
HOW WOULD YOU FEEL IF YOU LIVED ON THE OTHER SIDE OF THE BLOCK?

You may think *you* feel uncomfortable at first as you wait for a person who stutters to hurtle at last over the block and finish the sentence. But what do you suppose the individual's feelings are?

"Slowly. Speak slowly. More slowly. Take it easy!" my mother would say, with a slowing gesture of her hand, but without patience. "Think of the words before you say them. Think of them one at a time."

But I did think of them one at a time, those words. I thought of them: and the words—one by one—loomed up in front of me like cliffs, and after the spasm in my mouth and four gulps of saliva, I would stop, blocked. Then I would start again more slowly and I would choose other words; I tried to take them by surprise, from the side, these words, catch them and say them before they too could turn into cliffs. The worst were the words that I knew had stopped me other times.

"Have you studied your history?" my mother said, since I liked that subject very much. "Do you know it?"

"Yes–yes, I've lear—" I gulped—"learned it."

"Where are you?"

"The . . . the . . . fall . . . of the . . ." I gulped, gulped again. "Roman . . ."

"Good. You know it then?"

" . . . Empire." How silly, I thought, I could have stopped with "Roman." I had to learn, learn to economize.

And, very slowly, I really learned to save many words. But it always seemed I hadn't learned enough, and I was determined to become more clever and sly, to evade and trick that enemy that was both inside me and outside me, but who I thought proudly, was more outside me than inside.

Source: Alessandra Lavagnino, *The Lizards.* Translated by William Weaver. English translation copyright © 1972 by Harper & Row, Publishers, Inc. Pages 15–16. Reprinted by permission of the publisher.

distinguishing elements here are excessive speed of verbal output; disorganized sentence structure; and slurring, telescoping, or even omitting syllables or sounds. Van Riper likens the clutterer's speech to what happens when a beginning typist's speed exceeds control and the keys pile up on top of each other. Some clutterers tend to speak more clearly when they concentrate on their speech, whereas stutterers generally produce less fluent speech the harder they try (Eisenson, 1971).

Language Disorders

Language disorders encompass absence of language, delayed language, deviations and interruptions in language development, and disorders acquired after language has been established.

We can examine language disorders from several perspectives to get an idea of how complex the factors can be that affect our language competence (Leonard, 1986). From the developmental perspective, we focus on observed language development of a child in comparison to other children of similar age. From the etiological perspective, we can consider what might have contributed to or caused the language disorder. And from a functional perspective, we can try to identify the elements of language with which the child seems to have the most trouble.

Developmental Perspective. If we look at language disorders in children in light of what is considered typical language development, we find some children whose development in language competence is progressing but at a much slower rate than would be expected, even after allow-

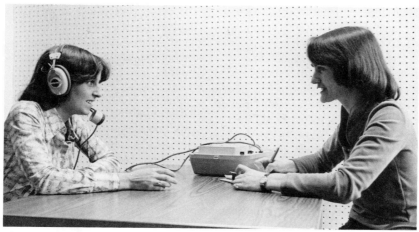

The student with the earphones is demonstrating a delayed feedback device used to control stuttering. (Photo by Joseph Bodkin.)

ing for the range of differences we can anticipate within normal development. Some of these youngsters may eventually reach a level of language competence that falls within the expected range. Others may never catch up. Still others will show extreme delays in the use of various types of word combinations (questions, imperatives, and so on) or word formations (-*ing* endings). In extreme cases, no language emerges and there is an absence of functional language for purposes of communication.

Etiological Perspective. Another way to classify language disorders is according to their suspected cause, even though it must be emphasized that children whose problems are attributed to the same cause very likely will display language characteristics both of other children whose difficulties are theoretically due to some other cause and of still other children whose language is considered normal. In etiological terms, many youngsters demonstrate what has been called a specific language impairment; that is, they appear to perform within normal limits in all or most areas of functioning except language. The cause of this specific language impairment is frequently thought to be brain damage, but that theory is

very difficult to substantiate unless brain tissue is examined directly during autopsy. Other causes of specific language impairments are thought to be related to weak perceptual or cognitive abilities, the amount of language stimulation available during the early months and years of life, and/or the quality of the interactions youngsters have had with those around them.

Other cases of specific language impairment are associated with mental retardation, emotional conflicts, and autism. With mental retardation and autism, there is controversy regarding what might be cause and what effect. Results of studies with children drawn from both groups suggest that qualitative differences may occur in the way people respond to retarded youngsters and children whose behavior appears to be autistic. These reported differences in responses to verbal interaction could influence the course of development and refinement of language skills.

Children with emotional conflicts, schizophrenia, or autistic behavior may use little language, may use a private language, or may repeat words and phrases to accompany bizarre body movements. Children who are mentally retarded will gradually show evidence of lagging behind the norm in language development and in their abilities to master the complexities of language structure and linking of abstractions. Severe mental retardation is associated with delayed language development (Eisenson, 1971).

Some language disorders result from neurological defects or brain damage following head trauma, vascular accident, or serious illness, which may impair auditory perception, ability to recognize written or verbal symbols, and muscle coordination necessary for speech production. When language competence is impaired or reduced in these ways, we use the term *acquired aphasia*. **Aphasia** refers to the loss of ability to understand language, produce comprehensible language in the form of speech and/or writing, or use language appropriately in a social context. The severity of the problem is related to the developmental age at which the injury or illness occurs and the extent of the damage to the brain, although a direct correspondence between site and extent of damage and the severity of aphasia has not yet been clearly demonstrated (Leonard, 1986; Van Riper & Emerick, 1984). Children who have extreme difficulty with reading may be called dyslexic. Children whose major problem is with forming the written letters or symbols of the language may be called dysgraphic.

You have probably already thought about some of the causes of delays in language development as you read about children with sensory impairments. Children who are deaf frequently have serious difficulty learning the structure of the language, the accurate production of sounds, and the subtle colorings and inflections that add to the meaning of verbal messages. Sylvia Ashton-Warner (1963) has captured the significance of hearing and being heard: "For it is not so much the content of what one says as the way in which one says it. However important the thing you say, what's the good of it if not heard or, being heard, not felt?" (p. 17). The language organization and speech of children with lesser degrees of hearing impairment may also reveal problems, although the age at which the hearing loss is sustained and the level of the child's language development at the time play a part in determining the efficiency of communication skills. Limited vision or no vision can also influence a child's language, particularly in the areas of basic concept development, depth of experience, and repertoire of overall experiences that form the base on which language can be built.

Functional Perspective. A third way to classify childhood language disorders is according to the elements of language that give the child the most difficulty (Leonard, 1986; Wiig, 1986). A child may have a very limited repertoire of words or lexicon from which to draw. Or a child may have difficulty retrieving a word to a much greater extent and with more frequency than is normal.

Other elements that may cause problems for children are in the production of sounds or phonology that may reflect motor and/or word organization difficulties; in syntax, or the ordering of words to express the intended message; or in morphology and the way words are formed with prefixes, suffixes, and other inflections to indicate number, time, quality, possession, and so on. Other children may have major difficulty with pragmatics, or the appropriate use of language in a social situation; they do not seem to follow a line of thought through a conversation. Words are formed, spoken, ordered, and yet do not really communicate a message or respond to the content of another speaker's message.

Speech/language pathologists face a large task when they take on the assessment of language disorders and plan individualized therapy programs for children. Of course, not just language disorders in young children should be of primary concern (Secord, 1986). Problems with semantics, pragmatics, and the selection of how to respond in a given situation in sometimes rather subtle ways can continue to influence the effectiveness and clarity of interpersonal communication of adolescents and young adults as well.*

---

*E. H. Wiig (1986) and W. A. Secord (1986) have elaborated upon the significance of language disorders in adolescents and the impact these disorders can have on learning and the development of linguistic strategies necessary to determine how to formulate responses in given social contexts.

BOX 6.3
THE STORY OF HILARY

Hilary was fortunate. At age four years and ten months, her bilateral sensorineural hearing loss was diagnosed, and her bilateral conductive loss was surgically corrected. Her parents, in reviewing Hilary's early development, tried to identify the signs that should have pointed to the need for intensive investigation and examination much earlier. In what follows, her mother explains the problems in early identification of children with hearing losses serious enough to interfere with language and social development but not severe enough to draw attention until their insidious influences are well established.

Two, three, or even four years had passed before we found out what was wrong with Hilly. Why? Because nothing she did until the week before she was tested was really bizarre, or even very unusual for a child her age.

The fact that Hilary is probably a bright child, growing up in a relatively unconfusing household, surrounded by many playmates, could account for her speaking ability at the time she was tested. She might not always have had the amount of sensorineural loss that she had when it was discovered, but Hilary has probably been dealing with a hearing problem for a long time and has been compensating by lip-reading and using contextual clues. . . .

Her preschool teachers and our friends, the other adults in her life, were mostly people experienced with children who were accepting of Hilary in spite of her unwillingness to even look at them sometimes. In another environment, she might have been labeled a brat and met with frequent rejection. Because she spent her early childhood in the midst of people who were kind to her and who seldom made demands she couldn't meet, she arrived at age five able to trust most grown-ups. In addition to having

developed some degree of proficiency in her language, Hilary was fairly well adjusted, making the suspicion of hearing loss seem unwarranted.

Another reason for our great slipup was that we had had no experience with and little information in our educational backgrounds about hard of hearing children. The usual array of parents' handbooks sits on my shelves. They contain information on fevers, the use of pacifiers, proper diet, what is normal at various stages, but little information on hearing loss. There is advice on why parents should have various handicaps diagnosed early, by professionals, but nothing on what to look for if you have a mild, fleeting suspicion.

If a hearing loss causes retarded speech, it can be picked up that way, but if the child manages to learn to talk anyhow, even though he or she is operating nowhere near his or her potential, it is likely to go undiagnosed. Certainly books and pamphlets have been written on the subject, but one has to seek them out. By the time parents have suspicions that are serious enough to send them to a large library, they have probably called for professional help. . . .

Suppose Hilary had not been blessed with at least normal intelligence, or were unattractive, or had four siblings to compete with? Hers could have been a sad story. Hil is in good shape. She is working hard at her language therapy and loves public school kindergarten, but she has a lot of catching up to do. Who is to say how much she has lost because she could not hear during those crucial years? How many other children are nervous with people and cannot remember the simplest nursery rhyme at age four or five because their ears are blocked or because they do not have their hearing aids yet? I hope that there will be one or two fewer because of Hilary's story.

Source: S. L. Wooding, "Hilary's Story." Reprinted by permission from *Young Children*, Vol. 35, No. 2 (Jan. 1980), pp. 31–32. Copyright © 1980, National Association for the Education of Young Children, 1834 Connecticut Avenue, N.W., Washington, DC 20009.

Extent of the Problems

Youngsters with speech and language disorders, about 4 to 5 percent of the school-age population, make up the second largest group of children termed handicapped in the United States. Until recently, before the creation of the learning disability category of handicapped children, children with speech and language disorders constituted the largest group of youngsters receiving special services. Recent figures reported to Congress under P.L. 94–142 and P.L. 89–313 indicate that 1,130,569 children were actually receiving services for communication disorders, excluding hearing impairments, in 1983.

Estimates of prevalence and incidence are difficult to determine and vary greatly. One reason is that it is difficult to determine the total number of children affected and to discover how many of those identified have only articulation problems as opposed to voice, language, or fluency problems. Children with more than one problem may be counted more than once. We have already mentioned that hearing loss, mental retardation, visual impairments, and emotional problems can affect the development of language and speech. But deviations in the normal development of language and speech may also affect intellectual performance, achievement, and social behavior.

The group of youngsters with speech and language disorders, perhaps more than other groups, has a significant turnover, as many children with mild articulation problems who are diagnosed in the early school years receive speech therapy, make progress, and are dismissed.

CHARACTERISTICS OF CHILDREN WITH SPEECH IMPAIRMENTS

From the previous discussion of factors contributing to language development, the complexities of speech production, the process of communication, and common causes of impaired speech, it will come as no surprise to you to learn that the characteristics of the large group of children called speech and language impaired vary widely. A list of intellectual, motor, and social/emotional behaviors *shared* by the entire group would indeed be short.

A few generalizations can be made, however. Within the school population, speech problems seem to be more common among boys than among girls, especially in the early grades. This is particularly true in the case of stuttering (Shames, 1986). D. A. Barbara (1965) reported that from four to eight times as many boys as girls are stutterers. He suggested that one reason for this might be the greater environmental stress and social competition that boys meet earlier than girls. Others have proposed that boys may just be more vulnerable than girls (Van Riper & Emerick, 1984). It will be interesting to see whether this situation changes and stuttering behaviors appear more frequently among girls if social attitudes and expectations for girls continue to change.

Emotional reactions to having impaired speech may show up as anxiety, frustration, guilt, and hostility (Van Riper & Emerick, 1984). These reactions are thought to be in response to the rejection and the not always unintentional hurts aimed at those whose speech is not normal. In time, response sets may be formed so that the hurts of the past are expected, and the anticipation feeds the emotional fuel to heat up feelings even more. Some children do not seem, at least overtly, very troubled by their speech difficulties; for others, the situations that call for verbal interactions are highly charged. There seems to be a relationship between personality problems and speech or language deficiency; but whether that is a result or a cause of the deficiency, or has any connection to it at all, is not clear (Eisenson, 1971).

Identification

Much has already been suggested about signs of language and speech problems. The definition we have given provides the major indicators teachers can use to identify those children who need to be referred for complete assessment of speech and language.

1. Is speech conspicuous?

2. Is speech interfering with communication?

3. Is speech unpleasant to the speaker or to the listener?

Once again, it is important to remember that these questions must be considered in light of age, setting, and cultural norms.

Another set of signs teachers can be alert for include both objective and subjective considerations (Eisenson, 1971):

1. Speech is not audible.

2. Speech is not readily intelligible.

3. Speech is vocally unpleasant.

4. Speech is visually unpleasant.

5. Speech is labored in production or lacking in conventional rhythm and stress.

6. Speech is linguistically deficient.

7. Speech is inappropriate to the individual (in content or manner of production) in terms of age, sex, and physical development.

8. The speaker responds to his or her own speech as if one or more of the above conditions were present.

Teachers who are aware of these signs of potential problems can create opportunities and a nonthreatening atmosphere for children to exercise all their communication skills. Those who can work cooperatively with speech/language pathologists to help children with manifest deviations are valuable members of educational teams. Although the majority of speech impaired children, particularly those with articulation problems, will be found during the elementary school years, teachers who work with junior and senior high school students also need to be sensitive to the therapeutic and emotional needs of their pu-

pils with speech impairments and with language problems such as those at the level of metalinguistics mentioned earlier.

Assessment

Assessment procedures may take a variety of forms but essentially are designed to gather information regarding language form (syntax), content (semantics), and pragmatics (usage) and regarding speech in terms of articulation, fluency, and voice. If problems are suspected in a child's language or speech abilities, referrals for professional evaluation should be made to a speech/language pathologist, who is trained to carry out extensive assessment procedures (Scholl, 1985). The particular procedures, however, will in part be selected according to the type of problem that is suspected (Shames & Wiig, 1986; Van Riper & Emerick, 1984).

For example, to assess language competence, spontaneous and/or elicited speech samples are necessary so judgments can be made about both comprehension and performance. During the assessment process, the speech/language pathologist might select norm-referenced and criterion-referenced tests to use to determine a child's language skills in comparison with other children of the same age and to identify which specific skills that child has mastered and which are causing difficulty. Test items typically check receptive as well as expressive language and involve responding to questions and following directions. To determine if aphasia is the cause of the language difficulty, the speech/language pathologist generally uses tasks and/or tests specifically designed to coax out the nature and extent of the difficulty with verbal, gestural, and graphic skills and competence with simple math, time, and money problems (Van Riper & Emerick, 1984).

To identify speech problems, the speech/language pathologist usually selects tests and tasks focused on articulation, voice, or fluency, depending upon the reason for the referral. If articulation problems are suspected, the speech/language pathologist presents identification and discrimination tasks to stimulate production of phonemes in

A speech/language pathologist makes a careful evaluation of a child's speech and then carries out a systematic program to help the child improve areas of weakness. (Photo by Joseph Bodkin.)

various positions and checks the structures and movements of the oral cavity necessary for articulation. If a voice problem is suspected, a detailed history of voice use and signs of possible voice abuse is essential along with a medical examination to rule out any physical cause for the problems. When disfluency is the reason for a child's referral, a determination of how much disfluency, under what conditions, and subsequent to what events is important. An essential part of the assessment in this case is a discussion with the child's parents about their perceptions of the child's problem and their responses to it.

Classroom teachers and other teachers not specifically trained in speech and language can play a very important role on the multidisciplinary team by being aware of the signs and cues in speech production and language competence that suggest possible problems for their students. If patterns of problems appear with frequency and consistency in the speech and/or language of any children, those children and the documentation of their speech and language performance should be called to the attention of the speech/language pathologist for closer investigation.

The ACS SpeechPAC/Epson is a portable communication device with computer capabilities. Typed input is spoken out in male, female, or child voice. Sentences can be stored in memory for future recall. (Courtesy of Adaptive Communication Systems, Inc., Pittsburgh, Pa.)

Use of Technology

Individuals with language and/or speech problems and the speech/language pathologists who try to help them may find some of the recent technological developments, especially computer technology, useful in several ways. First, speech/

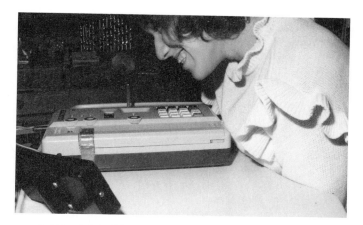

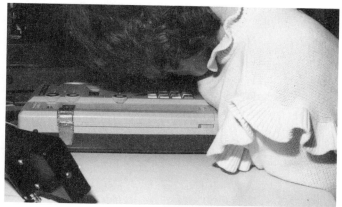

Belle operates an electronic speech synthesizer with her nose or chin for some of her communication needs. The Phonic Mirror HandiVoice simulates the human voice with 888 words, 45 phonemes, 13 morphemes, and 26 letters as well as 16 commonly used phrases. (Photos by G. P. Cartwright.)

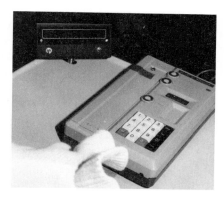

language pathologists can use the computer to help with phonologic analysis of language samples. G. L. Bull and G. E. Rushakoff (1987) suggest that in the future, computers should be able to process oral language samples to produce written transcripts and an analysis of the language and speech elements of that sample.

For therapy sessions, the computer at present can be used to show graphically intonation patterns and variations in pitch and volume. Some speech/language pathologists program computers to generate materials that can supplement mate-

rial used during therapy sessions. Others find computers useful in managing client records and therapy data. The common word-processing features of microcomputers are helpful for producing reports and summaries of data.

For individuals who do not speak, the computer is currently being used and holds promise in the future for greater use as an augmentative communication aid. The user can input by typing or pressing preprogrammed keys on a regular or modified keyboard, by touching a screen, or by interrupting an electronic signal in some way,

BOX 6.4
GIRL SPEAKS FIRST WORDS VIA COMPUTER

Children usually say their first words between the ages of nine and eighteen months. Here is a case where a young lady said her first words at age seventeen years, thanks to the matching of minds and machines.

"I am Vicki Karuso" is a simple enough four-word phrase. But in 17 years Vicki Karuso has not been able to say those or most other words.

Vicki has had cerebral palsy since birth and is so severely handicapped that she has almost no control over her body and can speak only a few almost unintelligible words.

Wednesday, for the first time in her life, Vicki was able to "speak" by pressing her head against an electronic switch which helped her choose words that were then spoken by a talking computer.

"I am Vicki Karuso," she tapped out with her head.

A smile exploded across her face as she heard the words come out of a speaker, and she quickly tapped out "I want water. I like to talk," from the computer's vocabulary.

"This is fantastic," said Mary Abler, whose 14-year-old daughter, Jane, has been working most of this year with the Michigan State University professor who developed the computer system that Vicki first used Wednesday.

"Just think of the unanswered questions of all the people who cannot talk. Just think of finding a way for them to communicate," Mrs. Abler said.

Both Vicki and Jane are patients at the Plymouth Center for Human Development, a facility run by the state Department of Mental Health for retarded people who have half or less normal intellectual ability.

The two took part in an equipment demonstration for special education teachers in the Northville school system.

There were other demonstrations—and other victorious results. Jane Abler, who has virtually no control over her body as a result of a delivery room accident in which oxygen was briefly cut off to her brain, was strapped into a special chair and linked up to a series of pulleys which enabled her to move a spoon into her mouth.

This is the first step toward learning to feed herself, and Wednesday was the first time Jane had

Source: By William Grant, Free Press Education Writer. Reprinted with permission from the *Detroit Free Press*, Vol. 145–No. 178, October 30, 1975.

perhaps with a head nod or muscle contraction, to indicate what output is desired. Output may be in the form of synthetic or prerecorded speech, pictures, or letters as in regular typing. Although creating messages may take some time, users have the ability to form their own messages and communicate at least to some extent in their own style.

EDUCATIONAL PROGRAMS

For a long time prior to federal and state mandates, many school districts and cooperative education units voluntarily employed speech clinicians to screen and provide speech correction for their students. In 1908, for example, a program for children with defective speech was started in New York City.

Under the federal regulations for P.L. 94–142, speech pathology is one of the related services that handicapped children might require to have their unique educational needs met appropriately. The regulations define speech pathology services as

1. identification of children with speech or language disorders

2. diagnosis and appraisal of specific speech or language disorders

been able to lift a spoon from a table to her mouth.

The computer "speech synthesis system" which brought the smile to Vicki Karuso's face was developed by John Bryson Eulenberg, a professor of computer science at MSU.

Eulenberg has been working for some time with computers that speak and has even used a computer to order a pizza.

For most of this year he has been working on different systems which let handicapped people who have control over any part of the body—the head or a portion of one limb—operate a switch which selects words a computer can then speak for them.

The system demonstrated Wednesday will be used by Northville teachers in the coming year with a small number of students at the Plymouth center.

"This is the most exciting thing to happen in the Northville schools in our whole 100-year history," said school Superintendent Raymond Spear.

"We are only in the world because we can communicate with each other," said Eulenberg. "It is everybody's right to be able to communicate and now the technology makes it possible."

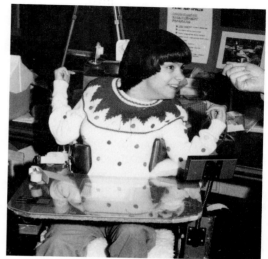

Vicki Karuso is completing high school with the assistance of a sophisticated computer system. The system, customized by Michigan State University's Artificial Language Laboratory, allows Vicki to communicate by using computer-generated speech.

3. referral for medical or other professional attention necessary for the habilitation of speech or language disorders

4. provision of speech and language services for the habilitation or prevention of communicative disorders

5. counseling and guidance of parents, children, and teachers regarding speech and language disorders

The number of speech/language pathologists and audiologists who belong to the American Speech, Language, and Hearing Association (formerly the American Speech and Hearing Asso-

ciation), the major professional organization for speech pathologists, has increased tremendously—from 1,600 in 1950 to 23,000 in 1975 when P.L. 94–142 was signed, to over 40,000 in 1986.

Teacher Considerations

During the course of a school year, the regular classroom teacher, particularly in the elementary grades, is likely to meet children with a wide variety of expressive language skills. What can a teacher realistically be expected to do to foster language development and good speech, given all his or her other responsibilities? Actually, much

BOX 6.5
COMPUTERIZED AIDS OFFER VOICE TO NONVOCAL-HANDICAPPED

What must it be like to have some thought or quip or bit of information to share with another person and no way to express it? Fortunately, the development of computerized communication aids has enabled some people like Michael Williams to speak for themselves.

In March 1980, at the age of 42, Michael Williams found his voice. It did not emanate from within—that capability was permanently impaired by cerebral palsy—but from a Phonic Mirror HandiVoice, a newly developed voice output communication aid (VOCA) that is beginning to free many from the netherworld of nonvocal persons.

With his "fiendishly clever" portable voice synthesizer, Williams reports that he no longer suffers the terrible isolation of the nonvocal. People no longer talk over him or around him. They talk to him. If he wants to, he can answer. Questions like "Can he hear me?" and "Does he understand?" are a thing of the past. And with his more advanced home computer, Williams can pursue his work as a freelance writer.

The significance of this technological breakthrough can hardly be understated. As social beings, communication is our most important faculty. Without it, individual potential is severely restricted. Computerized communication devices represent a giant step forward for millions of neurologically and neuromuscularly impaired people.

But as miraculous as they may seem, VOCAs did not appear from the heavens. They are the result of years of painstaking effort by scientists, engineers, manufacturers, teachers, social workers, and others, and they have barely scratched the surface. The new aids are limited in function and quite costly, and a good deal more research and analysis will be needed to determine future development. The potential benefits are there, however, and those in the field are eagerly optimistic that computerized communication aids will one day be widely available to the nonvocal handicapped.

Source: Reprinted from *Programs for the Handicapped*, U.S. Department of Education.

of the usual school schedule, directly or indirectly, involves language development and use of speech. With such rich opportunities to observe the expressive language of students, the teacher can contribute in many ways to the overall speech and language program of the school. These contributions can take the form of

1. referrals to the speech/language pathologist for any child who seems to have speech or language problems

2. promotion of a classroom atmosphere conducive to unpressured verbal interaction, with stimulation and opportunities for speech in a variety of situations

3. reinforcement for children who are using newly developed speech patterns

4. exchange of information with speech/language pathologists regarding performance of children in speech or language programs

Special mention should be made of those students who may need to rely on augmentative modes of communication and who participate in the regular school program. Teachers' attitudes toward and reactions to these students can set the tone for the way the other students respond to the use of alternative modes of communication. Among the alternative modes are gestures, American Sign Language or some form of manual

Michael Williams dines out in style with the use of his voice output communications aid (VOCA). (Photo by Carole Krezman, from *Communication Outlook*.)

English, pointing systems or sound-interruption systems with communication boards, special symbol systems such as Blissymbols, and typing on a regular typewriter or microcomputer. An individual whose larynx has been removed because of severe injury or disease, typically cancer, may be able to learn esophageal speech that requires precise control of air intake and release or to use a pneumatic or electronic artificial larynx. Some individuals have been successful in producing alaryngeal speech subsequent to surgical procedures that involve reconstruction or incorporation of some external device along with surgical modification of the pharynx.

The mode or modes selected depends to a great extent on the capabilities and any other disabilities the individual has in motor skills, intellectual function, and hearing. For example, a youngster with cerebral palsy who does not have control of hand or arm movement but who has achieved head control may be able to make needs and wants known with a communication or language board. A child with sufficient arm and head control may opt for a typewriter or microcomputer. Some children may use a system of gestures or perhaps a sign language.

The ability to carry on a conversation with another person is one of the unique characteristics of human beings. Children whose language development or speech production is significantly impaired face a difficult life without the skills to communicate clearly and in a pleasing, or at least "acceptable," manner. Charles Van Riper, who has worked for forty years in speech correction, summed up the reason for and the essence of his efforts and those of others who labor to aid the speech-handicapped "join or rejoin the human race" (Van Riper, 1978, p. 8):

> The potential in any living thing is immense, but to release that potential, someone must often intervene. (*Notes on Charles Van Riper's Speech Correction*, 1978, p. 6)

Teachers who are alert to signs of speech and language difficulties in young children and who know the difficulties and threats that breed exasperation for those who stutter, the embarrassment and mocking that often greet those with voice problems, and the mistaken notions and blank stares given in response to those with language deficiencies will perhaps reap the rewards that come from helping others reach toward higher levels of speech and language function.

SUMMARY

Humans convey messages with written, representational, or verbal symbols following an agreed-upon set of rules that may vary considerably from one language to another. In any language, however, the sender prepares a message, which the transmitter sends across a channel by some signal or series of signals, which a receiver picks up and reconstructs at the destination.

The communication process may break down because of "noise" in the system. In oral communication, that noise may take the form of speech that calls attention to itself in a negative fashion, that interferes with the message, or that causes uneasiness or distress in the speaker or listener.

The common causes of speech problems in youngsters of school age are errors of articulation, problems of voice production and fluency, and language disorders. Articulation errors result from faulty production of sounds. Voice problems show wide variations in pitch, volume, and quality reflecting changes in muscle tone. The major types of fluency problems are stuttering and cluttering. Language disorders include absence of language, delays or deviations in language development, and disorders acquired after language has been established.

The beginnings of language and speech normally are found in the cries and babbles of the infant. As the baby grows and develops in other areas, sounds gradually become combined and eventually are recognizable as words. With time, experiences, oral language practice, and good models for speech, the normal child learns the rules for use of the symbols that make up his or her native language.

Some children have problems with normal language development and production of speech because of organic defects such as cleft palate and/or lip, cerebral palsy, brain damage, loss of the larynx, or hearing loss.

It is estimated that 4 to 5 percent of the school-age population has some speech or language disorder. Although this group is large, the turnover is high; many young children who receive help make progress as they move through the elementary grades and are replaced by younger children just entering school programs.

Regular classroom teachers have an excellent vantage point from which to observe children and watch for signs of speech and language problems. Chief among such indicators is speech that calls attention to itself, is unclear, or is unpleasant to the listener and/or speaker. Signs of language problems include absence of speech, delays in development, and symbol confusion.

Children with speech and language disorders are usually referred to a speech/language pathologist. The alert teacher and skilled pathologist as a team can contribute greatly not only to the improvement of speech and language in children experiencing problems but also to the establishment of a classroom atmosphere that will facilitate language and speech development of all children.

Suggestions for Further Reading

Shames, G. H., & Wiig, E. H. (Eds.) (1986). *Human communication disorders: An introduction* (2nd ed.). Columbus, OH: Merrill.

Shames and Wiig, with contributions from fourteen colleagues, have compiled an extremely informative and readable introductory text for initial exploration of careers in speech/language pathology, audiology, and related fields. In Part I, readers are introduced to basic information about communication, language, speech, the physical process of producing speech, and the professions focusing on problems in communication. In Part II, readers learn about disorders that can occur in speech, voice, and language. In Part III, the communication differences and disorders of special groups are considered in chapters on hearing and auditory disorders, language differences, cleft palate, neurogenic disorders, cerebral palsy, and adult aphasia. The editors emphasize in the introduction that, although they have broken apart elements of the human communication process in an attempt to increase our understanding of it, they recognize the unity of body and mind in individuals who participate in the complex process of communication. Readers should find throughout the technical discussions of anatomy, speech and language disorders and disabilities, and language differences that, indeed, all the authors recognize and respect the efforts required for clear communication and give high regard to those individuals for whom it is difficult, as well as to those who would serve to alleviate human communication disorders.

Shannon, C. E., & Weaver, W. (1949). *The mathematical theory of communication*. Urbana, IL: University of Illinois Press.

In this classic book, Shannon outlines his theory of communication as he developed it originally for Bell Laboratories, and Weaver amplifies the theory to show its applicability to various kinds of communication. This book is fascinating reading, especially for the reader interested in a mathematical treatment of a communication model.

Van Riper, C., & Emerick, L. (1984). *Speech correction: An introduction to speech pathology and audiology*. Englewood Cliffs, NJ: Prentice-Hall.

In this seventh edition of a classic text in speech correction, Van Riper and Emerick place speech pathology in the context of communication, describe the various speech and language disorders that can adversely affect communication, and then discuss the functions of speech/language pathologists and the settings in which they frequently work. The authors' experiences, professional expertise, and humor permeate all fourteen chapters.

Relevant Journals

Journal of Childhood Communication Disorders
Published twice a year by the Division for Children with Communication Disorders, Council for Exceptional Children, 1920 Association Drive, Reston, VA 22091

Journal of Communication Disorders
Published six times a year by Elsevier Science Publishing Company, Inc., 52 Vanderbilt Avenue, New York City, NY 10017

Journal of Rehabilitation of the Deaf
Published quarterly by the American Deafness and Rehabilitation Association, Rt. 5, Box 535A, Morganton, NC 28655

Journal of Speech and Hearing Disorders
Published quarterly by the American Speech-Language-Hearing Association, 10801 Rockville Pike, Rockville, MD 20802

Journal of Speech and Hearing Research
Published quarterly by the American Speech-Language-Hearing Association, 10801 Rockville Pike, Rockville, MD 20802

Language, Speech, and Hearing Services in the Schools
Published quarterly by the American Speech-Language-Hearing Association, 10801 Rockville Pike, Rockville, MD 20802

Organizations for Parents and Professionals

American Speech-Language-Hearing Association
10801 Rockville Pike
Rockville, MD 20802

Division for Children with Communication Disorders
Council for Exceptional Children
1920 Association Drive
Reston, VA 22091

Division for Children with Learning Disabilities
Council for Exceptional Children
1920 Association Drive
Reston, VA 22091

CHAPTER 7

Physical Handicaps and Health Problems

Patricia Seibel
Pioneer School, Pittsburgh, PA

Did You Know That . . .

- a physical disability may or may not be a handicap?

- two individuals with the same medical diagnosis may be as different as day and night in their functioning ability?

- as far as we know, there is no direct relationship between intelligence and severity of physical disability?

- the major goal of professionals working with children who are physically handicapped is to alter the environment so the children can function?

- a physical disability, by itself, is no reason for special class placement; placement should be based on learning characteristics and needs?

- if individuals with disabilities are not able to compensate for environmental or functional demands in given situations, they will be handicapped in those situations but not necessarily in all situations?

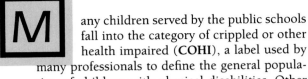

Many children served by the public schools fall into the category of crippled or other health impaired (**COHI**), a label used by many professionals to define the general population of children with physical disabilities. Other labels used to describe this population include

crippled
physically handicapped
physically disabled
nonambulatory
having organic problems
orthopedically handicapped
developmentally delayed

For the purposes of this chapter, the term **physically disabled** will be used to describe individuals who have nonsensory physical impairments, limitations, or health problems. Although loss of sight and hearing are certainly physical disabilities, they are discussed in Chapters 4 and 5. Here, visual and auditory problems will be considered only as they are associated with or secondary to other physical disabilities.

DISABILITY OR HANDICAP?

As we saw earlier, a physical disability may or may not be a handicap to a person. The term *disability* refers to an objective, measurable, organic dysfunction or impairment. Loss of a hand or paralysis of speech muscles, legs, or arms are examples of physical disabilities. Usually, a physician is involved in the diagnosis of a physical disability because it is a medical condition. A *handicap,* by contrast, refers to the effect a disability has on an individual's functioning in specific circumstances. Someone who uses a wheelchair because of paralysis caused by cerebral palsy certainly has a physical *disability,* but that person may not be *handicapped* in everything he or she does in life. Let's use Jerry and Sharon as examples.

Jerry has been diagnosed as having cerebral palsy (a physical disability). He has good use of his upper extremities (arms and hands), but he cannot walk and uses a wheelchair. In terms of using the public transportation in the town where he lives, Jerry is handicapped because he is unable to walk up and down the steps of the bus and there is no special entrance for wheelchairs. On the other hand, Jerry has discovered that his disability (paralysis of his legs) is *not* a handicap on his job as a computer programmer, because there he needs to use only his arms and hands.

Sharon had cancer of the bone when she was six years old and had to have her right leg amputated (a physical disability). An artificial limb was fitted for Sharon, and she was taught how to use and care for her new leg. Her severe physical disability has proven not to be a handicap for Sharon at all! She runs, plays baseball, climbs trees, swims, and does all of the other things a "normal" nondisabled child her age does.

It is important to remember that even the most severe physical disability may not be a handicap in specific situations. Many of the environmental factors that create handicaps for individuals with physical disabilities can be modified to accommodate the disabled. Barrier-free environments will be discussed later in this chapter.

It is both difficult and unfair to treat children with physical disabilities as a homogeneous group. Even within specific disability groupings, such as cerebral palsy, functioning impairment ranges from mild to severe. Two individuals with the same medical diagnosis—"athetoid cerebral palsy"—may be as different as day and night in their ability to function.

Medical terms tell the educator little, if anything, about a child's special educational needs. Educators who work with children who have physical disabilities should be aware, however, of the various disabling conditions in order to understand the nature of the disorder and any particular educational implications of the disability. Educators must also be cognizant of the jargon used by other professionals who work with children with physical disabilities. Just as we educators have a tendency to use our own "education-ese," other members of a child's interdisciplinary team use their own language at times. In order to understand written reports and to converse knowledgeably both with other professionals and with parents, teachers need to become familiar with these primarily medical terms.

In the next section, we will discuss some of the more common physical disabilities found in school-age children. The disabilities have been grouped as neurological disorders, musculoskeletal disorders and diseases, and other disabilities (see Table 7.1). Remember that within each of the areas, the conditions described may be anywhere on a continuum from mild to severe disability.

NEUROLOGICAL DISORDERS

Neurological disorders are caused by damage to, or a defect or deterioration of, the central nervous system (brain and/or spinal cord). A disorder involving the central nervous system is one of the most common disabling conditions in children. It presents the most complex situation for educators because an intact central nervous system is crucial for adequate functioning of other systems of the body.

Children with central nervous system disorders often have impairment in learning ability as well as in physical functioning. A child with damage to the brain may have problems in many different areas: motor or mental retardation; learning, speech and language, emotional, or perceptual disabilities; or convulsive disorders. A child with damage to the spinal cord may have problems with sensation, movement, and paralysis of certain parts of the body.

Neurological impairments explored in this section are cerebral palsy, spina bifida, convulsive disorders, and poliomyelitis.

Cerebral Palsy

Cerebral palsy will be encountered often by teachers working with children who have motor impairments. The term is used to describe a disability with a wide range of definitions, causes, treatment procedures, characteristics, and functional difficulties.

TABLE 7.1

PHYSICAL DISABILITIES

Neurological	Musculoskeletal	Others
Cerebral palsy	Muscular dystrophy	Congenital malformations
Spina bifida	Arthrogryposis	Cystic fibrosis
Convulsive disorders	Legg-Perthes	Sickle cell anemia
Poliomyelitis	Osteogenesis imperfecta	Hemophilia
	Juvenile rheumatoid arthritis	Juvenile diabetes mellitus
	Scoliosis	Asthma
		Rheumatic fever

Definition. Numerous clinical definitions of cerebral palsy have appeared in the literature. Some are very specific:

> Any disorder that is characterized by a nonprogressive motor abnormality, with or without sensory impairment and/or mental retardation, due to injury or disease of the brain that is manifested before the fifth birthday.
> (Malamud, Itabashi, & Castor, 1964, p. 271)

Other definitions are much more general and all-inclusive:

> Cerebral palsy is a general term used to designate any paralysis, weakness, incoordination, or functional deviation of the motor system resulting from an intracranial lesion.
> (Keats, 1965, p. 6)

Although various authors include different specifics in their definitions, most generally make some reference to the brain and/or the central nervous system and some degree of motor dysfunction. For the purposes of this chapter, J. Bartram's (1969) definition will be used:

> The term "cerebral palsy" designates a group of nonprogressive disorders resulting from malfunction of the motor centers and pathways of the brain characterized by paralysis, weakness, incoordination or other aberrations of motor function which have their origin pre-

natally, during birth or before the central nervous system has reached relative maturity.
> (p. 1311)

Thus, **cerebral palsy** is a group of disorders that is nonprogressive and that involves brain dysfunction and impaired motor function.

There are three main periods when cerebral palsy may occur: prenatal (before birth), perinatal (around the time of birth), and postnatal (after birth). Though the causes of cerebral palsy are certainly interesting topics to pursue, it is beyond the scope of this section to deal in depth with these causes. References at the end of the chapter are recommended for those interested in a deeper understanding of the etiology of cerebral palsy.

Some of the more common prenatal causes of cerebral palsy are: (1) heredity (rare); (2) maternal infection, such as German measles (rubella) or shingles; (3) fetal anoxia (lack of oxygen) due to hemorrhage, knotting of the umbilical cord, maldevelopment of the placenta, or shock due to loss of blood in the mother; (4) Rh incompatibility (today, most such cases are preventable); (5) prematurity (cause of many cases of cerebral palsy in the United States); (6) maternal metabolic disorders, such as diabetes and toxemia of pregnancy; (7) overexposure to x rays; and (8) unknown causes (such as brain maldevelopment during the first twelve weeks of pregnancy) (Bleck, 1975; McDonald & Chance, 1964).

Common perinatal causes of cerebral palsy are birth injury (trauma) and lack of oxygen

TABLE 7.2

SYSTEMS FOR CLASSIFYING CEREBRAL PALSY

Cause	Degree	Topography	Physiology
Heredity	Mild	Monoplegia	Spasticity
Maternal infection	Moderate	Hemiplegia	Athetosis
Fetal anoxia	Severe	Paraplegia	Ataxia
Rh incompatibility		Diplegia	Tremor
Prematurity		Triplegia	Rigidity
Maternal metabolic disorders		Quadriplegia	Mixed
X rays		Double hemiplegia	
Unknown			

(anoxia). Postnatal causes may be (1) head injuries; (2) brain infections and toxic conditions, such as meningitis, encephalitis, and toxic chemicals (e.g., lead poisoning); (3) brain hemorrhages or clots; (4) anoxia (e.g., when the supply of oxygen to the brain is cut off in cases of drowning or cardiac arrest); and (5) brain tumors (Bleck, 1975).

It has been estimated that 85 to 90 percent of the reported cases of cerebral palsy are congenital, that is, present at or during the time of birth (Best, 1978).

Classification. Cerebral palsy can be classified in several different ways: (1) cause (if known); (2) functional state (degree); (3) topography (according to specific limb involvement); and (4) physiology (according to movement disorder). These systems are summarized in Table 7.2. The most widely used and accepted classification systems are based on limb involvement (or topography) and physiology.

Although it would be helpful to classify the degree of severity of the conditions as well, such ratings are quite subjective and thus are not as informative as the other systems unless additional descriptors are used. The three terms used by G. Deaver (1955)—mild, moderate, and severe—are still the most definitive for classification by degree of severity. Deaver's classification may be summarized as follows:

1. *Mild*—The person can walk and talk, can care for him- or herself, appears physically normal except that fine precision of movement may be impaired.

2. *Moderate*—The individual may need treatment for speech problems, training in ambulation and self-care, and, usually, braces and other special equipment. The gait is probably different from the normal.

3. *Severe*—The person needs treatment for speech, self-care, and ambulation, but the prognosis for improvement in these areas is very poor. The individual will have little use of hands and will not be able to walk unassisted or to talk clearly.

Classification according to limb involvement (topographical classification) can be broken down as follows:

- **Monoplegia.** Only one limb is involved.
- **Hemiplegia.** Upper and lower limbs on the same side are involved.
- **Paraplegia.** Lower limbs are involved.
- **Diplegia.** Lower limbs are more seriously affected than are upper limbs.
- **Triplegia.** Three limbs are involved, usually one upper limb and both lower limbs.
- **Quadriplegia.** All four limbs are involved.
- **Double hemiplegia.** Upper limbs are more seriously involved than are lower limbs.

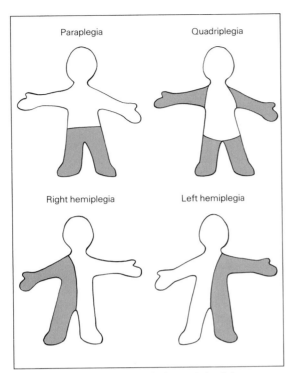

Paraplegia   Quadriplegia

Right hemiplegia   Left hemiplegia

Figure 7.1. Classification of physical disability according to limb involvement.

Monoplegia is extremely rare, and the term *double hemiplegia* is rarely used. The most commonly used terms are *left hemiplegia, right hemiplegia, paraplegia,* and *quadriplegia* (see Figure 7.1).

When considering limb involvement in cerebral palsy, it is important to keep in mind that there are degrees within each category. For example, a person diagnosed as having right hemiplegia may vary in movement and functional ability from mildly involved (can use both the right arm and leg in functional manner) to severely involved (has little or no functional use of right arm and leg).

Classification according to type of movement disorder (physiological classification) usually includes the following:

▪ **Spasticity.** Characterized by (1) involuntary contractions of the muscles when they are suddenly stretched, (2) sometimes inaccurate

and difficult voluntary motion, (3) scissoring of lower limbs caused by muscle contraction, (4) flexion of the arms and fingers.
▪ **Athetosis.** Characterized by (1) involuntary purposeless movement of the limbs, (2) involuntary motions more pronounced under stress or emotional tensions, (3) lurching, stumbling walk if ambulatory.
▪ **Ataxia.** Characterized by (1) impaired balance and sense of orientation and space, (2) weaving and stumbling gait, (3) uncoordinated movements.
▪ **Tremor.** Characterized by (1) shakiness of involved limb, particularly in attempts to use the limb, (2) a variation in constancy and pattern of movement.
▪ **Rigidity.** Characterized by (1) high levels of muscle tone, (2) lack of voluntary motion, (3) intermittent or constant resistance to movement, (4) "lead pipe stiffness."
▪ **Mixed.** Characterized by (1) usually a combination of spasticity and athetosis, (2) quadriplegia.

Extent of the Problem. It is difficult to give an accurate account of just how many children have cerebral palsy because some cases are not reported, and the incidence changes with advances in medicine, geographical location of incidence studies, classification system used, and the multiplicity of secondary handicaps. The figure most frequently given for the prevalence of cerebral palsy is .15 to .3 percent of the population. In other words, one to three children out of every thousand live births have some degree of cerebral palsy.

Spastic-type cerebral palsy accounts for the largest number of children with cerebral palsy—50 to 60 percent. Second is the athetoid type, accounting for about 15 to 25 percent. Incidence figures for the ataxic type of cerebral palsy are so varied that it would be difficult to cite a percentage. The other types (rigidity, tremor, and mixed) are infrequently diagnosed and are rarely seen in the classroom.

Associated Disabilities. In recent years, cerebral palsy has been considered to be a multihandicapping condition. Children with cerebral palsy usually have one or several secondary or associated disabilities and/or educational problems attributable to their major disability. Most frequent are speech and language disorders and mental retardation. Other problems may be vision and hearing impairment, perceptual and visual-motor disorders, sensory deficits, convulsive disorders, and social-emotional difficulties. A few of these associated disabilities will be briefly discussed below.

Speech and language disorders of some sort are found in about 50 percent of children with cerebral palsy (Bleck, 1975; Wilson, 1973). The problem may range from mild to severe—one child with cerebral palsy may have perfectly normal speech patterns, whereas another may be unable to produce any intelligible speech sounds.

Some speech disorders may be caused by breathing difficulties, auditory impairment, or paralysis of the muscles that help produce speech sounds. Children with cerebral palsy may encounter difficulties in phonation, articulation, rhythm, and linguistics.

Language deficits may also range from normal to severely impaired reception and expression. Deficiencies may exist in forming concepts, developing vocabulary, and combining words into longer phrases. These concept deficits are directly related to the degree, if any, of mental retardation. Other factors that may cause additional speech and language problems (see Chapter 6) in children with cerebral palsy are similar to those affecting the general population.*

Approximately half of the children with cerebral palsy have some degree of *mental retardation.* Incidence figures for mental retardation as a disability associated with cerebral palsy, however, are often misleading. The range varies from 30 to 75 percent, depending on what magic number is used as the cutoff point for a child to be included in the group labeled *mentally retarded*. In addi-

Cerebral palsy is a disability encountered frequently by teachers who work with children who are physically disabled. Please note, though, that these youngsters usually have intellectual abilities in the normal range. See the letters from Jenny later in this chapter. (Photo by Patricia Seibel.)

tion, many surveys conducted to determine the number of children with cerebral palsy who were also retarded were completed prior to the admittance of children with profound retardation to the public schools. Future studies should indicate higher percentages because of the higher survival rate for more profoundly involved children and because P.L. 94–142 places those children in public school settings where they can be included in the statistics.

The intelligence levels of children with cerebral palsy range from profoundly retarded to gifted; there does not seem to be a direct relationship between the severity of the physical condition and intelligence. One should never assume that a child with a severe physical disability must also have severe mental retardation.

---

*Much has been written on the characteristics of "cerebral palsy speech." Readers interested in pursuing this topic can refer to L. Travis (1971) and W. M. Cruickshank (1976a).

For example, Ginny is a ten-year-old child with severe athetosis affecting all four limbs. She cannot walk and probably never will. There is paralysis of the muscles needed to produce speech, so Ginny cannot talk. She also drools quite a lot, and her mouth hangs open. Her vision is poor, and she wears glasses. Physically, Ginny can do nothing for herself. She must be dressed, bathed, fed, and transported by others. When people first see Ginny, with the severity of her physical disability, they assume she is severely retarded.

Though Ginny is severely physically disabled, she is *not* retarded. After a system was established for eliciting a definite yes-no response from Ginny, she scored 120 on an individually administered intelligence test. With the help of adaptive equipment, Ginny can use a typewriter to do her schoolwork and an MCM-MICON communicator to interact with people. She has also learned to operate an electric wheelchair.

Because many children with cerebral palsy are limited in their ability to perform well on motor tasks often required in intelligence tests, caution should be used in interpreting test scores (IQs) for these children. Another difficulty in attempting to determine an IQ score for children with cerebral palsy is the high incidence of speech problems. When the verbal portion of an intelligence test is administered, the child with cerebral palsy may know the answer but be unable to communicate it to the examiner effectively. Furthermore, the IQ scores of children with cerebral palsy may not be as valid as the IQ scores of physically normal children. Test scores are usually suspect when they are low but rarely suspect when they are high; it is much easier to get an artificially deflated score than an inflated one for children with cerebral palsy.

Children with cerebral palsy are prone to the same kinds of *visual defects* as physically normal children, but some visual disorders seem specifically related to cerebral palsy. Some children with cerebral palsy have oculomotor defects, such as double vision, lazy eye (amblyopia), deviation of the eye in a horizontal plane (strabismus), to-and-fro movement of the eyes (nystagmus), and loss of half of the visual field of each eye (hemianopsia). Strabismus, commonly referred to as "crossed eyes," is one of the most common visual disorders related to cerebral palsy. Other common refractive errors of vision (acuity or clearness) found in children with cerebral palsy are farsightedness (hyperopia) and nearsightedness (myopia). Children with spastic-type cerebral palsy have twice as many visual acuity disorders as children with athetoid-type cerebral palsy (Caputo, 1975).

Various levels of *hearing loss* are more common in children who have athetoid-type cerebral palsy than the other types. Estimates are that about 15 percent of the children with cerebral palsy have subnormal hearing. Speech, hearing, visual, and perceptual disorders are discussed in more detail in other chapters of this text.

Convulsive disorders (seizures) are present in approximately 30 percent of the children with cerebral palsy. Children with spastic-type cerebral palsy are much more likely to have seizures than are those children with athetosis. Teachers should be aware of procedures for caring for a child during a seizure (see section on convulsive disorders later in this chapter).

Oral-dental disorders can cause many problems for the child with cerebral palsy. Difficulty in swallowing may result from paralysis or spasms of the pharyngeal muscles. Drooling, which is normal in a three-to-nine-month-old baby, may be excessive and prolonged in a child with cerebral palsy. Tooth enamel malformation often causes excessive dental cavities in the child with cerebral palsy (Bleck, 1975).

Spina Bifida

Spina bifida is a term commonly used to describe a group of disabilities characterized by one of three open defects (i.e., the neural tube is not closed) in the spinal canal due to abnormal fetal development—spina bifida occulta, meningocele, and myelomeningocele (or meningomyelocele). Incidence of this disorder is one per every thou-

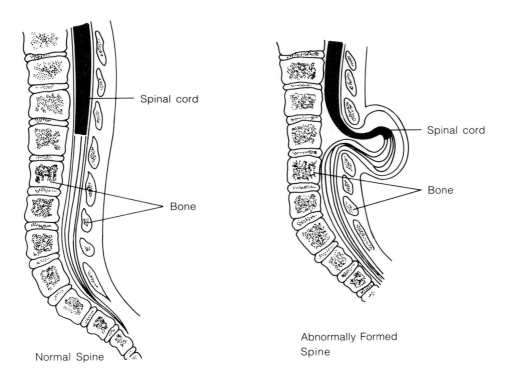

Figure 7.2. This figure illustrates a normal spine and a spine in which the vertebrae are not completely formed, resulting in an outward protrusion of the spinal cord. This disorder is termed spina bifida. (Courtesy of Spina Bifida Association of America, Rockville, MD.)

sand live births. The cause of spina bifida is unknown. From a purely medical point of view, labeling all three spinal canal defects *spina bifida* may be inaccurate, but it is a common nonmedical practice.

Spina bifida occulta is the least severe of the three conditions. One or more of the vertebrae that make up the spinal column (backbone) are not completely formed. No neurological disability occurs, because the spinal cord does not protrude. The skin over the defect may have a patch of hair or a birthmark, or it may be normal. Rarely, if ever, is treatment required.

Meningocele is an outpouching of the coverings of the spinal cord. A sac or cyst on the child's back contains spinal fluid and is covered with skin. By definition, meningoceles contain no neural elements; thus, paralysis is not usually a problem. Surgery may be required to eliminate the sac, but the child should have no further disabilities.

Myelomeningocele is the most severe form of spina bifida. The sac on the child's back contains a portion of the spinal cord and may not be completely covered by skin, permitting the spinal fluid to leak out. Depending on the level of spinal cord damage, paralysis of the lower limbs and trunk can occur. The higher up on the spinal cord the damage occurs, the more paralysis is encountered. For example, if the spinal cord is damaged at the twelfth thoracic vertebra or above, paralysis of the trunk and lower limbs will occur (Bleck, 1975).

Other disabilities associated with myelomeningocele are loss of skin sensitivity to pain, temperature, and touch; skin problems (burns and pressure ulcers); paralysis of bladder and muscles concerned with urination; bowel paralysis; and hydrocephalus (associated with mental retardation). Usually, children with myelomeningocele have all of the secondary disabilities listed above. Hydrocephalus (water brain) occurs in a large percentage of these children. An operation must be performed to relieve the pressure on the brain caused by the cerebrospinal fluid that is blocked in the brain cavities (ventricles). The sooner the hydrocephalus is corrected, the less the damage that takes place in the brain, and the higher the level of the child's intelligence is likely to be (Apgar & Beck, 1974).

The procedure used to relieve the pressure on the brain and drain the fluid is called a shunt operation. A shunt is a type of permanent drainage system consisting of a plastic tube that is inserted in the ventricle of the brain and leads into the atrium of the heart or into the abdomen so that the fluid is drained. Most children with hydrocephalus associated with myelomeningocele have some degree of mental retardation. These children often are very verbal and social, which may mask low intellectual functioning in some areas (Bleck, 1975).

Children who have paralysis of the bladder and muscles concerned with urination have a multitude of associated problems. Because the bladder is unable to respond to normal messages that it is full and time to empty, it merely fills and overflows. Problems that result are incontinence and, because the bladder also does not usually empty completely, susceptibility to many urinary infections.

It is difficult for children to participate in regular education settings when they wear diapers and often have embarrassing accidents. Surgical treatment in the form of a urinary diversion or bypass operation has been effective. Some children can successfully empty their bladders by manually pressing on the lower abdomen. This is called the Crède Maneuver (Bleck, 1975). The most recent technique, which has been very effective, is called clean, intermittent self-catheterization. This procedure can be taught to most children and allows them to empty the bladder periodically by inserting a catheter. Done properly, diapers are no longer needed, and the child stays dry and can participate in everyday activities without fear of accidents. Teachers need to be aware of this procedure and should assist students in maintaining the catheterization schedule outlined for them.

Researchers are also currently pursuing alternative solutions to incontinence in the form of electrical bladder-stimulating pacemakers (Brunner & Suddarth, 1982).

Due to lack of sensation in the afflicted area, children with myelomeningocele should be taught to inspect their skin frequently and routinely for skin breakdown. For example, they may not be able to feel irritation or pain from braces or shoes that can rub and cause pressure sores. Professionals who work with these children should remind them to shift their positions periodically and to inspect their bodies for possible damage.

Convulsive Disorders

A convulsion or seizure is a sudden alteration of brain function, beginning and ending spontaneously, that has a tendency to recur (Bleck, 1975). Some convulsions are accompanied by unconsciousness.

Convulsive disorders may occur as an associated disability with another major disability such as cerebral palsy, or they may be independent of other disabling conditions. Convulsive disorders are not specific diseases, but indicators of some abnormality of brain function. It is not uncommon for infants (six months to three years) to have seizures (febrile convulsions). Approximately 3 to 5 percent of children have this type of seizure (Baird, 1975), which may be caused by a variety of difficulties and usually does not recur.

The most frequent causes of convulsions in young infants are intracranial birth injuries such as the effects of anoxia (lack of oxygen), hemorrhage, and congenital defects of the brain. Acute infections, such as meningitis, encephalitis, and fever, are the most frequent causes of convulsions in the latter part of infancy and early childhood (Baird, 1975).

By the time children reach school age, if they have convulsions, these seizures would be of the recurring or chronic type. If a specific cause can be found for these recurring seizures, the term *symptomatic epilepsy* is used. *Idiopathic epilepsy* is the term used to describe the vast majority of seizures for which no specific cause can be found. The incidence of recurrent convulsions has not been established, though .5 to 2 percent of the population is estimated to have some degree of convulsive disorder.

Seizures may be classified in a number of ways: (1) cause, if known, (2) clinical manifestations, and (3) electroencephalographic (EEG) pattern (Baird, 1975). A more recent classification system proposes four major groupings of seizures according to the place in the brain in which the seizure originates. In this new international system, four types of seizures are: (1) partial, (2) generalized, (3) unilateral, and (4) unclassified epileptic. (See Box 7.1.) Because it will be some time before the new system is used extensively, you also need to know about the classification system now in widespread use. It groups seizures according to clinical manifestations, with the following categories: (1) grand mal, (2) petit mal, (3) psychomotor, (4) focal, and (5) myoclonic and akinetic.

Grand Mal Seizures. A grand mal (generalized) seizure sounds very dramatic. Reactions of individuals observing such a seizure for the first time are generally mixed, but the experience is usually frightening. For the person having the seizure, the experience is not as traumatic as it appears, and the child will not remember what occurred during the seizure. As with other physical disabilities, the teacher should discuss convulsive disorders with the class to prepare them for a possible seizure and to help them understand what will happen. The Epilepsy Foundation of America provides in-

formation to help teachers lead discussions. If the teacher is calm and the other students in the class understand what is happening, the incident can be treated in a routine, controlled manner.

The characteristics, length of time, frequency, and aftereffects of the grand mal seizure vary according to the individual. A typical grand mal seizure has the following stages:

1. The child may be aware that a seizure is about to occur because of some signal (aura). The child may smell an unusual odor, experience muscle twitching, have an intestinal disturbance, or just "feel funny."

2. With the onset of the seizure, the child will become stiff, lose consciousness, and fall to the ground. The face may become pale and distorted; the pupils may dilate; and, as the muscles contract, air may be forced through the vocal cords, resulting in a short, sometimes startling (for the observer) cry. Loss of bowel and/or bladder control is a possibility. This phase of the seizure, called the tonic or stiff phase, usually lasts twenty to forty seconds.

3. The clonic (jerking) phase occurs next and lasts for variable periods of time depending on the severity of the seizure disorder (usually two to five minutes). The child will become less rigid and may quiver, with arms and/or legs jerking.

4. As the seizure ends, the child may awaken in a confused state, have a headache or be quite tired, and fall into a deep sleep for variable periods of time (minutes to hours).

In addition to preparing the other children to accept such an occurrence in the classroom, teachers should follow a set procedure to ensure the safety of the child experiencing a grand mal seizure. The list of dos and don'ts in Box 7.2 should be helpful. They may seem like a lot to remember, but most are common sense and become second nature once applied.

BOX 7.1

GOODBYE, GRAND MAL

You know by now that people who work in medically related fields often seem to use terms that are unknown to, or misunderstood by, the general public. This short article is reprinted here to illustrate that (1) it takes time for old terms to be replaced by newer, more accurate, and/or more socially acceptable terms; and (2) even the professionals in a field change their minds once in a while.

No, we're not about to announce a new treatment or a new drug. We wish we were, but unfortunately the day when we shall have finally conquered epileptic seizures still seems as elusive as ever. However, we do propose to change the way we identify the most common types of epileptic seizures. We would like to pack off grand mal, petit mal and psychomotor epilepsy to the same semantic destination to which once familiar terms such as dropsy, ague, and apoplexy have already been consigned.

Instead, we propose to use Dr. Henri Gastaut's 1970 International Classification of Seizures, which reflects modern science's understanding of where in the brain the various types of seizure originate. For example, the seizures that we are all used to thinking of as grand mal and petit mal (French terms meaning, respectively, big and little sickness) are today classified as two major types of *generalized* seizures. They are called generalized because the seizure activity is distributed in a generalized way throughout the brain. The appearance of the electrical activity (as recorded by an electroencephalogram or EEG machine) is different with the two types of seizure, but the widespread involvement of the brain is the same.

According to this classification, then, a convulsive seizure (the old grand mal) is called a *generalized tonic clonic* seizure; the short lapses of attention which we used to call petit mal are now known as *generalized absence*. The word "absence" is usually given a French pronunciation, and rhymes with "Alphonse." . . .

That brings us to a third major seizure category. When it came to epilepsy which involved altered consciousness and automatic behavior, the French did not have a word for it. Or if they did, it never caught on overseas. Left to themselves, English speaking scientists came up with "psychomotor" or "temporal lobe" epilepsy to describe this common form of the disorder. However, what distinguishes these seizures from others is that they begin in one part of the brain. Hence, their classification as *partial* seizures. . . .

Will these new terms have any negative effect on the public's perception of epilepsy? How would employers react to the news that someone has partial seizures as opposed to psychomotor ones? Do generalized seizures sound better or worse than grand mal? Our feeling and our hope is that the new words, which are already being extensively used by the scientific community, are emotionally neutral, and lack the negative connotations of the past. If so, this will be a valuable bonus to our efforts to communicate more directly and accurately about epilepsy.

Source: *National Spokesman*, December, 1979, p. 2. Reprinted with permission of the *National Spokesman*, The Epilepsy Foundation of America.

Petit Mal Seizures. The second type of convulsion is **petit mal seizure.** Many seizures of this variety often go unnoticed because they typically consist of short staring spells, momentary suspension of activity, blinking of the eyes, slight twitching, and/or drooping or rhythmic nodding of the head. Seizures of this type may last a few seconds and usually no longer than thirty seconds. The child will maintain his or her position but may drop items held in the hand. The frequency of such seizures varies from one or two a month to as many as several hundred a day.

The teacher should be on the alert for possible petit mal seizures and report their occurrence and

BOX 7.2
WHAT TO DO—AND NOT TO DO—FOR A CHILD WHO HAS A SEIZURE

Do

1. *Remain calm.* If you are calm, you can handle the situation much better and set the tone for the children observing the incident.
2. *Reassure the other children* in the class as you initiate the safety procedures. Remind them of what they discussed about epilepsy—"It is not contagious; Joey will be fine; there is nothing harmful about the seizure."
3. *Ease the child to the floor,* placing him on his back with his head to one side.
4. *Clear the area* around the child of any furniture or other objects on which he might be injured.
5. *Place a soft object under the child's head.* A pillow, folded coat, or soft mat would do. This is to prevent bumps or head injuries during the clonic (jerky) phase.

6. *Loosen any tight clothing* about the child's neck.
7. *Allow the seizure* to run its course.
8. *Allow the child to rest* if he wishes after the seizure is over.

Do Not

1. Do not try to restrain the child or stop the course of the seizure. You could injure the child.
2. Do not place the child on his stomach. Injuries could occur to the face, and breathing is difficult.
3. Do not permit the child to remain seated. The potential for injury is too great.
4. Do not attempt to force anything between the child's teeth. If you have a child who is prone to biting his tongue, a soft handkerchief may be placed between the side teeth *if* his mouth is open.

any change in frequency to the appropriate medical personnel.

Psychomotor Seizures. Psychomotor seizures vary in form and are the most difficult to recognize. They usually consist of purposeful but inappropriate motor actions somewhat automatic in nature. During this type of seizure, the child may walk about, repeat some phrase over and over again, mutter incoherently, engage in lip-smacking or picking at clothing. Inappropriate emotional behavior may occur, such as verbal abuse, temper tantrums, or fear. The child usually resumes a normal activity pattern after the seizure, which may last from one to five minutes. The teacher should be aware that the child has no control over his or her inappropriate behavior at this time and should allow the episode to cease on its own.

Focal Seizures. Focal seizures may be sensory or motor. Sensory focal seizures, rare in children, result in visual, auditory, or other types of physi-

cal sensations. Focal seizures of the motor type may be a twitching of one side of the face or jerking of only one arm or leg. Rhythmic twitching or jerking of one part of the body that spreads to other specific parts of the body, usually in the same pattern from one seizure to another, has been termed *Jacksonian* seizure. Occasionally, this "Jacksonian March" is followed by a generalized seizure, indistinguishable from a typical grand mal seizure.

Myoclonic and Akinetic Seizures. The last category of convulsions is the myoclonic and akinetic seizures. **Myoclonic seizures** are characterized by brief, involuntary muscular contractions (temporary tightening of muscles). Usually, a single group of muscles is affected, causing such behaviors as sudden dropping of the head forward or backward, or the arms jerking upward. **Akinetic seizures**, sometimes called motor petit mal, inhibition, or jackknife seizures, are characterized by loss of postural tone and sudden dropping to the ground.

BOX 7.3

ON GROWING UP TIGHT

Michael B. Williams is a writer who lives in the San Francisco Bay area. This short article illustrates once again that persons with disabilities have feelings, intellect, strengths, and weaknesses—much the same as the so-called normal population.

I've always been a fan of Mary Shelley's Frankenstein's monster. To most people this minor footnote to English literature is just a tale concocted to entertain friends on a winter's eve. To me, however, Mary's brainchild provides a striking metaphor for growing up with cerebral palsy.

Up until a few years ago I considered myself a monster. I walked like a monster, lurching my way along the street, my body performing a strange visual symphony of contractions. When I attempted to speak, I sounded like a monster. All sorts of strange sounds came bubbling out of my mouth. Many people were uncomfortable at the sight of me. They either turned their heads away in fear and embarrassment or gawked in naked curiosity. I was truly a monster.

I have since discovered I'm not the monster I thought. It just lived inside of me, spawned from the culture of narrow social attitudes towards anyone who may be different and nurtured by my own sense of self-isolation.

When you grow up with cerebral palsy, chances are you grow up isolated—first in a padded cell of parental protectiveness, then in special schools that have been so thoughtfully provided for you by the state, and finally, and most completely, by your own fears. . . .

Whenever I entered a new area of experience, my mother always would pave the way for me. I always let her. After all, it was so much easier than doing it myself. I couldn't talk, she was very articulate. She always said the things I would say.

This had a subtle but profound effect on my personality. When you have someone representing you at the bargaining table of life, all you have to do is sit back and reap the benefits. As a result, I didn't develop my sense of anger and outrage until recently. All I had to do was sit there and be Mr. Nice Guy while my mother took care of the flack coming down on me. . . .

My father died in 1966, six months after my mother. I've thought about my father a lot these past eight years. He must have been a very lonely and unhappy man. I drew much of the attention and love he rightfully deserved. My parents' marriage was over long before they died. I know this not from what they said or did, but from what they did not do and did not say. I guess both of them lacked the courage to call it quits and waited for Death to pull the last strands of a tenuous relationship apart.

Their death had a devastating effect on me. The monster was now alone in the world. He had a mouthpiece no longer. He was on his own. . . .

These first few years on my own were extremely rough. I was in a peer group situation for the first time in my life, coming to terms with my disability, having to cope with my anger and thinking things I'd never thought about before, like sex.

About my anger I can only say I repressed it to the extreme. Whenever a point of contention arose between me and the people I was living with, I'd always concede it to them out of fear. I was afraid if I became the least bit testy, I would soon have no friends. After all, who likes an angry monster?

By far the most difficult problem I've had to face has been the matter of sex. When most of the people are having successful love relationships, it is extremely painful to go to bed every night alone. Whenever a potential relationship with a woman doesn't blossom, I'm tempted to fall back on the lame excuse (pun intended) of nobody loves a monster, especially one who talks funny, moves with the grace of a wounded elephant and who drools on occasion. But then I realize that I'm just suffering the consequences of all those years I spent isolated from society. It's just the interest that's accrued from growing up tight.

Source: M. B. Williams, "On Growing Up Tight," *The Independent,* 1977, 3, 18–19. Reprinted by permission.

Children who have various physical disabilities with which convulsive disorders are associated usually have one of the five types of seizures mentioned, or a mixed convulsive disorder (combination of seizure types). Fortunately, many convulsive disorders can be effectively controlled by medication. Teachers can be extremely helpful to medical personnel when a child is placed on some type of anticonvulsant medication by watching for side effects (i.e., drowsiness) or by recording the frequency and duration of seizures while various dosages of the medication are prescribed in an effort to control or limit the seizure activity. Teachers can also be of great assistance to the child by helping others understand and accept the child's disability. Perhaps the greatest hurdle for children with convulsive disorders is the social and emotional trauma of rejection by peers and adults who are uninformed and unsympathetic about the disability.

Poliomyelitis

Poliomyelitis, more commonly known as polio, one of the most feared diseases before the mid-1950s, is uncommon today in countries where people are properly immunized with polio vaccine. From 1950 through 1954, there were 190,000 cases of polio reported in the United States, mostly in children (Steigman, 1975). With the discovery of a vaccine to prevent polio, the number of cases has dropped from 40,000 per year to 100 per year. The main reason for including poliomyelitis in this chapter is to emphasize the need for proper immunization. Although polio should be totally controlled by now, there are alarming—and increasing—numbers of children who are not being immunized and who are contracting this disease.

Poliomyelitis is a viral infection of the motor cells in the spinal cord and/or nerve tissue in the brain that results in paralysis. If the infection causes only a swelling of the cells and supporting tissues, recovery will follow. If the cells are destroyed by the virus, no recovery takes place, and the paralysis is permanent (Bleck, 1975). The bladder, bowels, sensation, and intellect are not affected by the virus, but moderate to severe resid-

ual paralysis of lower limbs and trunk and skeletal deformities may occur. After initial medical and orthopedic treatment of polio, the affected child may use canes to walk and usually attends a regular school program.

MUSCULOSKELETAL DISORDERS

Musculoskeletal conditions in children may be congenital or acquired; they usually affect the child's legs, arms, spine, or joints. Children with musculoskeletal disorders may have difficulty sitting, standing, walking, or using their hands. The causes are varied and include infectious diseases, genetic defects, developmental disorders, and accidents. Although there are numerous disabilities of this type, we will discuss only a few of the more common ones.

Muscular Dystrophy

As described by Bleck (1975), **muscular dystrophy** is "a progressive diffuse weakness of all muscle groups characterized by a degeneration of muscle cells and their replacement by fat and fibrous tissue" (p. 173). The cause of muscular dystrophy is unknown, but it has a genetic (inherited) origin. The several types of muscular dystrophy are classified according to age of onset, rate of progression of weakness, distribution of muscular involvement, and mode of inheritance (Huttenlocher, 1975).

The most common form of muscular dystrophy is the Duchenne, or childhood, form (also called progressive muscular dystrophy and pseudohypertrophic muscular dystrophy). This disability affects mainly boys; it can be traced to a sex-linked recessive gene carried by the mother and transmitted to sons. Cases of females being afflicted are rare. This disease often is not diagnosed until after the child is three years old, but a history of slow motor development is usually found. Some children who have not been diagnosed as having muscular dystrophy at the time they enter school may appear to be awkward or

BOX 7.4

DEATH EDUCATION

A subject rarely discussed in textbooks dealing with children who have physical disabilities is death education. Due to the progressive and terminal nature of some disabilities, this topic needs to be addressed. In an article entitled "What Parents and Teachers Should Know About Death Education," Robert A. Berner discusses a theory of death education and offers suggestions for helping children come to terms with the facts of death.

- A child once wrote a letter to God:

> Dear God:
> What is it like to die?
> Nobody ever told me.
> I just want to know.
> I don't want to do it.
> Your friend,
> Harry

This letter points out two important needs of children: (1) "nobody ever told me," people are reluctant to talk about death, and (2) "I don't want to do it," children feel anxiety about death.

- A challenge to teachers and parents is to put the thought and experience of death into the context of living. In this way, much of the child's fears and anxiety may be alleviated.

- Proper death education enhances the child's joy of life. Death education can reduce the child's fear of death thereby increasing the joy of living.

- Death education works to improve the quality of the child's total life span, birth, living, process of dying and death. . . .

What Can Teachers Do?

- The role of the teacher in death education is to disseminate the results of scientific studies and to facilitate the child's acceptance of death.

- What a teacher should do in any specific situation cannot be known for there are too many variables. The best thing one can bring to a terminally ill student is one's self. Every teacher, therefore, needs to clarify an individual philosophy for working with terminally ill students. . . .

What Teachers Need to Know

- The dying child goes through a number of stages before accepting death. These stages may be ex-

Source: Berner, 1977. Reprinted by permission.

clumsy and may fall frequently. Teachers should be aware of this disorder and watch for signs of muscular dystrophy, as children may be inappropriately labeled as having a learning disability or minimal brain damage. Mild mental retardation is, however, a common associated disorder in the Duchenne form of muscular dystrophy.

Because Duchenne muscular dystrophy is a progressive disorder, the child with this disease will become more and more disabled. Initially, the child will have a waddling gait, will walk on his or her toes, and will have difficulty in getting up from the floor and climbing stairs. As the child's muscles become weaker, he or she will be unable to lift the arms over the head and will usually be unable to walk by ten to twelve years of age. Many skeletal deformities occur as a result of unopposed weakness of muscle groups; these include severe curvature of the spine (scoliosis), limited forward neck-bending, and permanently bent upper limbs. Duchenne muscular dystrophy is almost always fatal, and children with the disease rarely live past the later teen years. The usual cause of death is heart failure (the heart muscle becomes too weak to function) or lung infection (the breathing muscles are weak).

Teachers should be aware of the likelihood of fatigue occurring as the child becomes progres-

perienced simultaneously; not every child experiences all of them. It is important that the child experience some of them if death is to be accepted. The stages and conjectured positive contributions are as follows:

1. *Shock and disbelief*—This serves as a temporary anesthesia holding the child's sense of self-esteem together for a brief time.
2. *Crying (sometimes hysterical)*—This usually provides the needed emotional release.
3. *Feelings of isolation and loneliness*—This may help the child feel the need for others and to experience the discomfort which alienation brings. A degree of personal untidiness may be observed at this stage.
4. *Psychosomatic symptoms*—This may momentarily deviate the child's attention from the fatal prognosis to lesser conditions.
5. *Panic*—This pushes the child to explore all possibilities and to eventually accept the fact that the dying process is occurring.
6. *Guilt feelings*—This eventually enables the child to accept the fact that nobody is to blame and that the process of dying is unlikely to be reversed.
7. *Hostility-resentment*—The child attempts to defend and protect his ego by projecting these negative feelings onto teachers, parents and friends.
8. *Resists usual routine*—The child questions the worth and complains of the difficulty in doing everyday activities in an effort to come to terms with the requirements for continued living.
9. *Reconciliation*—This very positive stage enables the child to avoid feelings of hopelessness and to begin a process of accepting the inevitability of death.
10. *Acceptance*—The child struggles to adjust to the reality that death is happening and that there is living and work yet to be accomplished. The child becomes a deeper more profound person—young in years but old in experience.

sively weaker. A rest period may be required. Teachers working with children who are terminally ill should seek assistance from other professionals in helping the child cope with the terminal nature of his or her illness (see Berner, 1977; Box 7.4).

Arthrogryposis

Some children are born with congenital stiffness of one or more joints and weak muscles, a condition known as arthrogryposis multiplex congenita, or more simply, **arthrogryposis**. Although the young child generally will have stiff knees, club feet, bent stiff elbows, and/or flexed (bent) wrists and fingers, intellectual functioning and speech are not impaired. Surgical treatment, casts, and braces can help correct some of the deformities associated with this disability. Depending on the severity of the deformities of the hand, a child may need to use adaptive equipment (e.g., a typewriter guard) for written communication.

Legg-Perthes Disease

Partial or complete destruction of the growth center at the hip end of the thigh bone is characteristic of **Legg-Perthes disease**. Boys between the ages of four and ten are most frequently affected, although the cause is unknown. Treatment may consist of absolute bedrest, special bracing, and/or surgical procedures to avoid weight bearing. The growth center usually repairs itself over a period of two or three years. Legg-Perthes is usually considered a temporary orthopedic disability.

Osteogenesis Imperfecta

Often called "brittle bone" disease, **osteogenesis imperfecta** is usually an inherited disorder that may be apparent at birth or in the first few years of life. The latter form (osteogenesis imperfecta tarda) usually has a milder course, and the tendency for the bones to fracture may disappear after puberty (Warkany & Kirkpatrick, 1975). This disability is characterized by broad forehead; triangular face; small, bowed limbs; barrel-shaped chest; and excessively mobile joints. As the child gets older, deafness may occur. Treatment generally consists of surgical procedures to correct bone deformities and bracing for ambulation. Many of these children will be nonambulatory and will need to use a wheelchair.

Juvenile Rheumatoid Arthritis

We usually think of arthritis as a disease of middle-aged or elderly adults; however, young children can contract this disease as well. Many more girls than boys are affected. **Juvenile rheumatoid arthritis** is a group of diseases characterized by inflammation of the joints. Children with this disease may have severe pain, and medication is usually prescribed. Interestingly enough, the most effective medication for treatment of the inflammation is aspirin. In addition to medication, treatment procedures include sufficient rest, use of wheelchair or crutches to ease weight bearing on inflamed joints, and maintenance of muscle tone (Miller, 1975).

Teachers should be understanding of the changeable nature of children with arthritis. The child who suffers a night of pain and awakens with stiffness may not be too sociable, pleasant, or cooperative that day in school. Prolonged sitting or maintaining any one position should be avoided, as stiffness may occur. The child should be encouraged to change positions and activities frequently.

In certain types of arthritis, vision problems are possible, and the teacher should be alert to potential difficulties. Miller (1975) reports that most children taking high dosages of aspirin will have a high-tone hearing loss while taking the medication, although hearing returns to normal when the medication is discontinued.

Scoliosis

Lateral curvature of the spine—(**scoliosis**)—may be caused by congenital, neuromuscular, or idiopathic (cause unknown) conditions. Improper formation or segmentation of the bones of the spine is an example of congenital scoliosis. Children with myelomeningocele (abnormal spinal cord development) may also have congenital scoliosis. Scoliosis is also common as an associated disability in children who have neuromuscular disorders such as cerebral palsy, muscular dystrophy, or spinal cord injury.

The most common type of scoliosis is idiopathic and is found most frequently in adolescent girls. Deformity may be mild to severe, and treatment, depending on severity, consists of exercises, bracing, or surgery with fusion of the spine.

Teachers can help keep neuromuscular scoliosis from becoming severe by proper positioning of children and by alerting the appropriate medical personnel if they notice the beginnings of a curved spine. Some scoliosis can even be prevented if everyone who works with the child from infancy ensures proper positioning at all times. Tips for proper positioning are presented later in this chapter.

OTHER DISABILITIES

There are many other physical conditions that may limit a child's motor functioning. Congenital malformations, accidents, diseases, and health impairments common to school-aged children will be described in this section.

Congenital Malformations

Congenital malformations of the heart and hips are the most common disabling conditions in this group of disorders. Some defects may be hereditary or may arise during pregnancy due to abnormal fetal development or diseases or other conditions present in the mother. Congenital malformations may occur by themselves or in association with other major disabilities.

Congenital malformation of the heart or the major blood vessels leading to and from the heart occurs in approximately 1 percent of all babies born in the United States (Apgar & Beck, 1974). Until recently, many infants with congenital heart defects died at birth or shortly thereafter, but with advances in surgical procedures, many of these children now survive and lead normal lives. Depending on the severity of the condition, children with congenital heart disease may have restricted physical activities.

Congenital dislocation of the hip, if discovered early, can usually be treated effectively by splinting before the child is old enough to walk. If the defect is not discovered until a child begins to walk, treatment is less satisfactory, and impaired motor functioning may occur. Treatment consists of traction, casting, and bracing until the hip socket grows properly, or reconstructive surgery, depending on the severity of the dislocation and age of the child.

Other congenital malformations may affect the extremities (i.e., congenital amputation or webbed fingers), the head and face, or any organ or body part.

Diseases

Cystic Fibrosis. A hereditary disease, **cystic fibrosis** is characterized by chronic pulmonary (lung) disease and pancreatic deficiency. The child with cystic fibrosis may have frequent and prolonged respiratory infections, persistent cough, wheezing, frequent and perhaps bulky bowel movements (often foul in odor due to excretion of undigested fats), and abnormal mucus secretion. Cystic fibrosis is a progressive disease, with the average age of death around fifteen to twenty years. Cystic fibrosis is the most common fatal hereditary disease among young Caucasians. It is much less frequent in blacks and rare in oriental populations.

Treatment may consist of a modified diet to decrease fat intake, salt tablets, postural drainage of lungs (the child is placed in different positions to drain various areas of the lungs), and administration of antibiotics to fight infection.

Professionals working with children who have cystic fibrosis should remember that (1) the persistent cough cannot be controlled but is not contagious; (2) the child may have an increased appetite and should be permitted to take additional portions; (3) physical stamina may be impaired; and (4) the child may be absent frequently because of infection. An attempt should be made to treat the child as normally as possible (Harvey, 1975).

Sickle Cell Anemia. A hereditary blood disease, **sickle cell anemia**, which gets its name from the "sickle" shape of the red blood cells, predominately affects black persons. About 10 percent of blacks in the United States have sickle cell trait (that is, they carry one abnormal recessive gene) and are carriers of the disease, although rarely do carriers suffer any symptoms of the disease (Apgar & Beck, 1974). If both parents have sickle cell trait, their child will have sickle cell disease, although children with one parent who has sickle cell trait may also inherit the trait. There is no known cure, and death usually occurs before the age of twenty.

Characteristics of the disease are anemia (insufficiency of red blood cells); swelling of the hands, feet, and joints; bouts of severe pain (sickle cell crises) in the abdomen, legs, or arms; impairment of liver function; loss of appetite; painful, slow-healing sores; and general weakness. Frequent complications of sickle cell anemia are enlargement of the muscular part of the heart, pneumonia, and respiratory infections.

Teachers should be aware that children with sickle cell anemia characteristically drink more water than do other children and may need to urinate more frequently. Various types of crises or episodes may occur in children with sickle cell

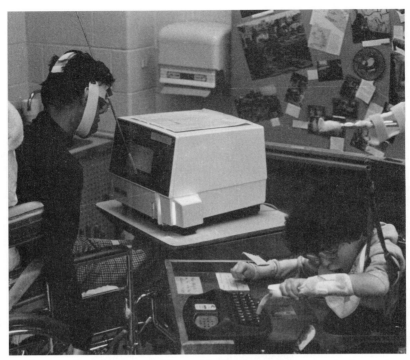

Academic independence in children with physical handicaps can be fostered by using adaptive devices such as head sticks, arm slings, and self-instructional systems. (Photo by Patricia Seibel.)

disease. A vaso-occlusive episode occurs when sickled red cells deprive tissue of adequate blood flow and pain results. Another type of episode, an aplastic crisis, occurs when, for some unknown reason, the body fails to manufacture red blood cells. Outward signs of this crisis may be weakness, lethargy, and fainting when standing (Bleck & Nagel, 1982). Teachers should watch carefully for signs of sickle cell episodes. These crises usually require treatment by a physician if they are severe and persistent. Allowances should be made for prolonged periods of absence, usually due to infection and/or hospitalization.

Hemophilia. In the hereditary disease of **hemophilia**, the blood clots very slowly or not at all. This disorder almost always occurs in males and is transmitted through a sex-linked recessive gene carried by the mother.

Children with hemophilia may suffer from swollen joints and recurring joint bleeding, resulting in crippling joint disease. Excessive bleeding may occur from minor cuts or lacerations, bruises, bumps, or falls. When a child with hemophilia has a bump or bruise, internal bleeding can occur, and medical help should be obtained.

Treatment for hemophilia consists of replacement of blood to prevent pain, disability, or life-threatening hemorrhage. In recent years, plasma concentrates have been developed to replace the deficient blood-clotting factors when a bleeding episode occurs. Pilot programs in self-treatment and home management of bleeding episodes strongly suggest that early treatment of these episodes reduces disability, deformity, and the need for hospitalization (Pearson, 1975). Unfortunately, this type of treatment is extremely expensive and therefore unavailable to many.

Because internal bleeding might occur, children with hemophilia should be instructed to examine their bodies for and to report immediately any cuts, bumps, or bruises. It is difficult not to be overprotective of children with hemophilia, but professionals should allow them to lead as normal a life as possible. These children should not be involved in any form of contact sport or any noncontact sport where they may be hit by an object (e.g., baseball). However, exercise is important, and normal physical activities such as calisthenics, swimming, and hiking should be encouraged.

Juvenile Diabetes Mellitus. Yet another hereditary disorder is **juvenile diabetes mellitus**, in which sugar (glucose) cannot be used normally by the body because of the failure of the pancreas to produce insulin. A child with undiagnosed diabetes drinks large amounts of liquid, eats excessive amounts of food, loses weight, develops tiredness and weakness, and may eventually go into coma. With the injection of insulin (the usual treatment for juvenile diabetes), these symptoms will disappear, and the child can learn to lead a healthy, normal life. Children with diabetes will have to follow a special diet and should have a certain amount of daily exercise.

Some monitoring of the child's physical activity is advisable, and after a half-hour of play, the child should eat a small snack to recover the lost energy. Teachers should be aware of the symptoms of an insulin reaction (too much insulin) and the symptoms of too little insulin, so that proper treatment may be administered.

The symptoms of an insulin reaction occur very rapidly and may include headache, nausea, vomiting, irritability, blurred vision, profuse sweating, fast heart rate, shallow breathing, cold hands and feet, and possibly a graying of the triangle formed by the nose and mouth. The administration of concentrated sugar (such as sweetened orange juice, soda, or fruit-flavored hard candies) should terminate the insulin reaction in two or three minutes (Christiansen, 1975). If the child becomes unconscious, do not induce any liquid, but rather seek professional medical assistance immediately.

Symptoms of too little insulin come on gradu-

ally. They include malaise, fatigue, warm and dry skin, excessive thirst and hunger, and deep breathing. The remedy for too little insulin is the administration of insulin. Most children with diabetes can be taught to administer their own medication so that they can function independently and lead normal lives.

Closely related to diabetes is hypoglycemia, a condition in which the body produces too much insulin. The child may experience symptoms similar to, but not as severe as, insulin shock. The child who has hypoglycemia may need snacks during school hours but should limit his or her intake of carbohydrates (Berdine & Blackhurst, 1985).

Other Health Impairments

Allergies. A child who has an allergy is sensitive to environmental substances that may have no effect on other individuals. Substances may include pollen, dust, food (such as strawberries), animals (such as cats), and drugs (such as penicillin). Contact with this substance results in a reaction, such as sneezing and watery eyes, or an irritation, such as a rash. The cause of the allergy is typically identified by a physician using the results of skin tests coupled with information gathered from an analysis of the child's medical history, home environment, and diet (Gearheart & Weishahn, 1984). Typically, treatment involves medication and minimizing exposure to the offending substances.

Students with allergies usually participate fully in educational programs. The teacher may be of assistance in identifying the substance to which the child is allergic. In addition, the teacher should carefully monitor the child's behavior, noting and reporting any difficulties to the school nurse and parents.

Asthma. A chronic allergic condition, **asthma** is characterized by wheezing, coughing, and difficulty in exhaling air. The causes of asthma are not fully understood, but allergens (offending substances causing an allergic reaction) seem to be the major culprit. Emotional factors can trigger an asthmatic attack, but they are not the cause of asthma in children. Some children can precipitate an attack and sometimes do so in an attempt to control family members and others.

Treatment for asthma usually consists of procedures for preventing episodes and treating acute attacks. Elimination of offending substances from the child's environment, reduction of the child's sensitivity to certain allergens (by hyposensitization injections), breathing exercises and postural drainage of the lungs, and prompt treatment of respiratory infections are methods of preventing asthmatic attacks.

To the extent possible, the teacher of an asthmatic child should try to eliminate allergens in the classroom. Once it has been ascertained what the allergic substances are, the alert teacher can eliminate or greatly reduce the child's contact with these substances. Exercise is important for the child with asthma but may induce wheezing if it is too strenuous. Games requiring endurance (e.g., running, football) should be avoided; short bursts of physical activity are much better for the child with asthma.

Mild attacks of asthma in the classroom may be controlled by having the child sit and rest, breathing in an easy and regular pattern, with little or no attention from the teacher or other students (Harvey, 1975).

Rheumatic Fever. An inflammatory disease that occurs after a strep infection, **rheumatic fever** is characterized by high fever, painful swelling of joints, skin rash, and inflammation of the valves and muscles of the heart. When the disease runs its course, all symptoms usually disappear. However, permanent heart damage may occur, and the child's physical activity may be restricted. Rheumatic fever may recur, and medical treatment is necessary in an attempt to prevent strep infections and permanent damage.

Sexually Transmitted Diseases. Much public attention has focused upon the increasing number of individuals who have **sexually transmitted diseases** (STDs), including gonorrhea, syphilis, herpes, and acquired immune deficiency syn-drome (AIDS). Unfortunately, age is an irrelevant factor in the transmission of these diseases; therefore, it is possible that teachers will have in their classrooms children and youth who have STDs.

Gonorrhea and **syphilis** are transmitted most frequently through sexual contact with an individual who has the disease, although newborns may be infected *in utero*. Both diseases are treatable, particularly in their early stages, through the use of antibiotics such as penicillin and tetracycline. Strains of gonorrhea that are more resistant to penicillin may be treated with ampicillin (Holmes et al., 1984).

Herpes Simplex Virus II is another STD of a more serious nature. Although its symptoms can be treated with ointments, herpes cannot be cured. As with gonorrhea and syphilis, it is transmitted via sexual contact with an infected individual. Newborns may acquire it during passage through an infected birth canal. The major symptom of herpes is the development of painful, fluid-filled blisters that break to form a crusty sore. These blisters occur two to twenty days after exposure to the virus, last approximately two or three weeks, and heal without a scar. Teachers should be aware that herpes symptoms can recur due to a number of factors, including moisture, sunburn, fatigue, traumatic events, and stress, and should take care to minimize the child's exposure to them. During school hours, teachers can ensure that the child keeps the affected area clean and dry and washes his or her hands frequently (Corsaro & Korzeniowsky, 1980).

A very common sexually transmitted disease is called **chlamydia**. It does not get as much press as herpes, gonorrhea, and syphilis, but it affects more Americans every year than any of the others. In fact, chlamydia is twice as common as gonorrhea and affects both sexes. Symptoms appear one to five weeks after exposure; they may be mild or severe and include a burning sensation when urinating, discharges from both males and females, and pain in the lower abdomen. Unfortunately, infected people often have no symptoms but can still transmit the disease. If left untreated, chlamydia may lead to serious infection and inflammation and can result in sterility in either sex.

Fortunately, the condition is relatively easy to diagnose and treat.

Perhaps the most serious of all STDs is **acquired immune deficiency syndrome.** By May 1986, three hundred U.S. school children had contracted AIDS (Weiner, 1986). Although it does not in and of itself cause death, AIDS does destroy the body's ability to fight off disease. It is transmitted in three ways. The first method of transmission is through sexual contact: 17 percent of U.S. school-age children who have AIDS contracted it in this manner. The second method of transmission is through blood or blood products: 5 percent of school-age children who have AIDS contracted it by sharing needles used to inject drugs; 42 percent developed it after receiving transfusions as part of treatment for hemophilia. Finally, AIDS can be transmitted perinatally, that is, during pregnancy, birth, or shortly after (possibly through breastfeeding): 17 percent of children with AIDS contracted the disease in this manner (Weiner, 1986). It is important to note there is no documentation of AIDS being transmitted through casual contact such as shaking hands, sharing dormitory spaces, or other close but not intimate physical contact.

AIDS among school-age children has raised serious issues for school authorities. Recall that P.L. 94–142 guarantees to all children a free, appropriate education in the least restrictive environment; the Buckley Amendment guarantees confidentiality. A number of authors and agencies have developed guidelines to ensure that these rights are protected but not at the expense of noninfected children (Black, 1986; Center for Disease Control, 1985; Pennsylvania Easter Seal Society, 1985; Price, 1986; Weiner, 1986). Their recommendations are summarized in the following list:

1. Decisions should be made by a multidisciplinary team that includes the following members: parents, educators, school principal, school nurse, physician, public health official, and, when possible, the child.

2. Most children with AIDS will benefit from regular class placement. The advantages offered in this setting outweigh the risks to their own health and the apparently nonexistent risk of infecting peers or staff.

3. Be aware that age of the learner will have an impact upon placement. Older children are capable of attending better to their own hygiene.

4. Be aware that, regardless of age, children in more advanced stages of the disease may be less able to take care of themselves independently. Thus, a more restricted environment may be warranted.

5. A more restrictive setting should be considered for children who lack control of their body secretions or who display biting behavior.

6. A more restrictive setting should be considered for students who have lesions that are oozing and uncoverable.

7. School personnel coming in contact with children who have AIDS should exercise caution in dealing with the child's body fluids and excretions. They should wash their hands frequently and wear gloves if there are any cuts on their hands.

8. Routine procedures for handling blood or body fluids should be established, regardless of whether children with AIDS are in attendance.

9. Confidential records should be maintained. The number of people who are aware of the status of the child's health should be kept to a minimum and include only those needed to ensure proper care.

10. Programs to increase awareness of AIDS and its transmission should be developed.

Teachers can be instrumental in the detection of sexually transmitted diseases, especially with very young children. As will be explained in Chapter 14, an alarming number of children are victims of sexual abuse. Teachers should be aware of signs that indicate a child may have been molested and report suspected cases to the authorities (Baker, 1984). Subsequent investigation will

TABLE 7.3

ESTIMATED INCIDENCE OF PHYSICAL AND HEALTH IMPAIRMENTS IN TEN STATES

State	Number of Children with Physical Impairments*	Percentage	Number of Children with Other Health Impairments*	Percentage
California	6,963	1.85	12,498	3.32
Florida	2,094	1.28	2,257	1.38
Illinois	1,382	.67	1,072	.52
Maine	394	1.49	349	1.32
Maryland	783	.89	902	1.04
Michigan	4,024	2.68	0	0.00
Minnesota	1,371	1.69	845	1.04
North Carolina	953	.87	1,407	1.29
Oregon	597	1.45	463	1.12
Texas	3,916	1.39	6,391	2.26

*Based on special education enrollments of students ages three to twenty-one years.

probably include a medical examination that verifies the presence or absence of any sexually transmitted diseases. With older students, teachers can take part in efforts to prevent occurrence of STDs. By using a health curriculum approved by school officials and parents, teachers can provide students with the information they need to prevent these diseases from occurring or to seek early treatment in the event they do contract them.

Other Health Impairments. Other health impairments that may limit a child's activity are tuberculosis, usually as inflammation of the lungs but possibly affecting other organs as well; inflammation or degeneration of the kidney (nephrosis and nephritis); inflammation of the colon (colitis) or lower small intestine (ileitis); liver disease (hepatitis or cirrhosis); and cancer (particularly leukemia).

Incidence of Physical and Health Impairments

Statistics from the 1985–86 school year indicate that .12 percent of children between the ages of three and twenty-one years, or 47,477 students, are physically handicapped. In addition, there are 50,478 students with other health impairments in the United States, which translates to approximately .13 percent of the school-age population (Education of the Handicapped, 1986). Table 7.3 lists numbers and percentages of students who have physical or health impairments as reported by ten states.

FUNCTIONAL DOMAINS

It is difficult to speak in general terms about children with physical disabilities because there is such a wide range of physical and mental abilities in this group. The major goal of professionals working with these children should be to alter their environment so that they can lead a life as normal as possible. A brief review of the behavioral characteristics of the population as a whole may prove useful.

Cognitive

As we have seen, a child with a physical disability may range from profoundly retarded to gifted and talented. The important point for professionals to remember is that a severe physical disability does not necessarily mean a severe mental disability.

A high spinal cord injury paralyzed this young man from the neck down. He is able to achieve some independence by using a mouth-activated page turner and a chin control device. (Photo by Dick Brown. Courtesy of *Centre Daily Times.*)

Every effort should be made to adequately assess the cognitive abilities of these children regardless of the severity of their physical disability. Formal and informal testing procedures should be utilized.* There are special assessment devices available for children with special needs, and teachers should be aware of these tools. For example, the Pictorial Test of Intelligence (PTI) (French, 1964), an intelligence test for children between the ages of three and eight, requires no verbal response. This test would be extremely useful for severely physically disabled children, as they could point to the correct answer or focus their eyes on their responses.

Motor

Like the cognitive domain, the motor functioning of children with physical disabilities ranges from severe to minimal involvement. Children with motor difficulties should be encouraged to do as much for themselves as is physically possible. There is a tendency for adults and other children to do everything for children with disabilities and to treat them differently than the other children in the class.

Frequent changes of position are important for children with motor difficulties, and physical activity should be encouraged if not contraindicated by their particular disability. The physical therapist is usually in charge of the child's physical activities or serves as a resource person.

Special adaptive equipment may be needed to help the child to function as normally as possible, to maintain the current level of physical functioning, and to prevent physical deformities (e.g., scoliosis). Motorized wheelchairs with various devices for operating them have proven to be valuable mobility aids for the disabled. Children may learn to use head-sticks, tongue-switches, breath-controlled switches, or other special devices to control the movement of their electric wheelchairs.

Other adaptive equipment used by the physically disabled includes standing tables, prone

---

*E. Hatch, J. Murphy, and S. J. Bagnato (1979) present a comprehensive overview of evaluation of handicapped children in language that is easy to understand.

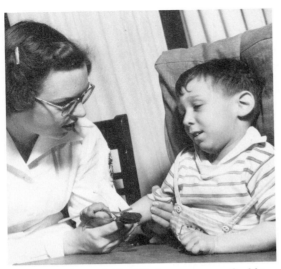

A teacher helps a child while he attempts to feed himself using a hand brace to provide support. (Courtesy of National Archives.)

The finish line is in sight! This child is dependent upon crutches and braces, but his physical problems are not going to stop him. (Photo by Janet Carlin. Courtesy of the New Jersey Tournament of Champions.)

boards, corner seats, wheelchair inserts, special feeding equipment, typewriter guards, and wedges (see Northall & Melichar, 1975; Robinault, 1973). Various types of bracing (orthoses), artificial limbs (prostheses), crutches, walkers, and wheelchairs may be used to assist in ambulation. A checklist for teachers to evaluate the fit and function of specific equipment may prove helpful (see Frederick & Fletcher, 1985; Venn, Morganstern, & Dykes, 1979).

Language

Various types of adaptive equipment are available to assist the child with a severe speech impairment to communicate with others. Special language or communication boards can be made that allow the child to point to or look at the picture, symbol, or word he or she wishes to communicate. Many electronic communication aids are available for use by the physically disabled. Some of these devices produce a printout; others use a matrix with a traveling light that can be stopped on the desired response; and others actually produce an artificial voice that says the desired word, phrase, or sentence (see Vanderheiden & Grilley, 1976). As illustrated in Box 7.5, the importance of establishing an effective communication system for the child with a physical disability cannot be overemphasized.

Social-Emotional

Children with physical disabilities have the same social and emotional problems as other children of similar ages. Learning to live with their disability is an added burden for them. The attitudes of family, friends, teachers, classmates, and others will have a great effect on these children. If others are accepting and understanding of their disabilities, children are more likely to feel good about themselves and have fewer adjustment difficulties.

Certain emotional reactions are inevitable for the child with a physical disability. The child may wish he or she were "normal" and could do all of the things other children do. It is difficult, if not impossible, to predict a specific child's reaction to

A physical therapist assists youngsters in developing motor skills. (Photo by Patricia Seibel.)

disability. A child with a mild disability may have more difficulty adjusting than a child with a severe disability. As is true with all children, professionals must look at each child individually and offer support wherever it is needed.

EDUCATIONAL CONSIDERATIONS

Educational Placements

Children with physical disabilities can be found in all types of educational settings, from education in the home to regular school classrooms. Like children with other handicapping conditions, children with physical disabilities should be educated in an environment as close to "normal" as possible. Determination for educational placement must be based on a comprehensive assessment of each child and his or her individual needs.

It cannot be stressed too strongly that a physical disability, by itself, is no reason for special class placement. In terms of the general school curriculum, children with physical disabilities have the same needs as other children. They may need special help or apparatus to make a response, but they can benefit from the same instructional practices and curriculum as other children. In short, physically disabled children need *access* to the school classroom.

Placement in regular classrooms is often quite appropriate. Individual education programs (IEPs) for these children often include an array of *related services* to be provided along with the recommended placement. Special transportation,

BOX 7.5

HI-MY-NAME-IS-JENNY

Children with physical disabilities who have severe communication and ambulation difficulties nonetheless have a desire and a drive for independence. One of the most difficult responsibilities of adults working with these children is to allow them to do things for themselves. In addition, we need to find ways to help children communicate their feelings. Just because some children cannot talk, write, or walk doesn't mean that they don't feel.

The letters that follow were written by Jenny Lowe, a young woman who has cerebral palsy. Because Jenny can't speak or walk, she has found other ways to tell people how she feels. And her message certainly comes through. Jenny was ten years old when she wrote the first letter (see Figure 7.3). Although her typing skills were not well developed, she expressed her feelings clearly.

Jenny at age ten. (Photo by Patricia Seibel.)

```
Hi-my-name-isØJenny.

And-I!mℓhandecaped..,

I-ℓhave-ℓaØeletrﬗickℛk-chair...

And-I-ⅢliⅨke-it-very-muchⅩ!

And-I-do-meney-more-thⅨings,...'

When-ⅨⅩℤI'm-mad-lookØout!

Sometimes-I-Øget-sad-because-I'm-handecape

Before-IⅩℏad-this-chⅺℊaire-I-couldn't-do,

ⅉℛℛthe-things-I-doℊnow...

In-August-ℕI-got-my-chair-and-I-was-ⅈⅆ

taℏrabowl!!

I-got-better-ansℤd-better...

After-a-wile-I-took-my-chairℐe-home..
```

Figure 7.3. Jenny's first letter. (Reprinted by permission.)

The second letter was written when Jenny was fifteen (see Figure 7.4). Her typing skills have certainly improved and her maturity is obvious.

My name is Jennifer Lowe. When I was born, I was born
with a conditøion called) (erbel Palsy. I don't look upon my
condition as a burdeyn, rather as a gift. I'm "nonverble"
I communicate with a wonderful device called a headlight. A
headlight is a simple light attached to an elastic
                                                        band.
I point to letters with that. I also use   a headstick which is a
        stick connected to a piece of plastic which is ajustable. I point,
        write and type with my headstick.   I go to schoolat Pioneer. I like
        it very much, but sometimes it can be a chore .

            At school I have a class called Speech, there I work with
        talking aides. Some have direct selection, or scanning devices.
        One kind of voice is a man's this is frustrating to me.   Another
        device is the Cannon Communicator. The Cannon is like a pocket type-
        writer, from it comes a tickertape which you read.

            I have many goals in life, one of these such goals is to get
        the right chair that suits me. Another of my goals is to get out on
        my own.

            What I have just written is telling somewyat about my life
        and the devices I use. I have used many divices I have not written
        about, and many yet   to use.

Figure 7.4. Jenny's second letter. (Reprinted by permission.)

(continued)

(continued)

We are fortunate to be able to keep in touch with Jenny! The third letter that appears here was written as she started college. It is clear that technology has made a big difference in her life.

Life was extremely hectic before my speech therapist, Chris Botti, wrote a grant to the Assistive Device Center for my Apple IIe computer. Since I became a freshman in high school, I started writing considerably more. I was put into a situation where it was easier to use a computer than my electric typewriter. The computer allowed me to change my text with just a few hits as well as to save it on a disk for future use and reference.

In order to use the Speech Department's Apple IIe, I had to use it during my speech period. A period is only a half an hour long. This put a tremendous amount of pressure on me. I'm the type of a person who has her work done on time, if not early. Consequently, I had to push myself to finish a product.

Being affected by cerebral palsy, the only body part which works exactly how I desire is my head. Therefore, I use a headstick to do all of my typing. This caused many headaches. The combination of pressure to get my work done on time and the constant banging on keys gave me bad headaches.

Midsemester, I took a creative writing course at a community college. Of course, I was required to hand in writing assignments. Once again, I had to use the speech department's computer. As you can plainly see, I had an immense need for an Apple IIe computer.

Chris Botti wrote to the Assistive Device Center to get a grant for my Apple IIe computer. The grant was approved. I got an Apple IIe of my own.

My Apple IIe helps me immensely. I don't feel so much pressure to get things done in such a rush. There really wasn't room for a third computer in the speech department. Chris allowed me to have it in my home. Really, it makes sense. My computer is in my bedroom. It makes life a lot easier. Now, when I have a writing assignment, I do it in the privacy of my own room. A tremendous amount of pressure has been lifted off my chest.

The computer not only helped me with my school writing, but also with my personal writing. Personal writing is one of my more enjoyable pastimes. I have written many letters and poems using the computer. Letter writing can be a very time-consuming activity. However, with the ability to save text on disk, I can stop whenever I have a chance. Therefore, my computer gives me freedom and much ease in my academic and personal writing.

Figure 7.5. Jenny's third letter. (*Assistive Device News*, Vol. IV, No. 1, 1987. Elizabethtown Hospital and Rehabilitation Center, Elizabethtown, PA 17022. Reprinted by permission.)

adaptive physical education programs, speech and language therapy, provision of an aide at certain times of the day (for example, at lunch and snack time to help the student eat) are some of the related services that are typically part of the IEP for physically disabled children.

Many children with physical disabilities require some degree of physical and/or occupational therapy that provides therapeutic exercise, gross and fine motor training, ambulation, or functional living skills. Children in a regular school setting could be provided these services in a manner similar to speech and hearing therapy. Sometimes, intensive therapy is indicated, and for a period of time, a special class or even a special school might meet the child's needs more effectively.

Architectural Barriers. Architectural barriers should not be an excuse for excluding children with physical disabilities from regular public school programs. Section 504 of the Rehabilitation Act of 1973 requires that any program or activity receiving federal assistance may not exclude any qualified handicapped person. Any structural changes necessary to ensure *program accessibility* must be accomplished. New buildings must be designed and constructed to be accessible to the handicapped.

This doesn't mean that all existing buildings must be altered to provide accessibility to all persons with handicaps. For example, some school districts have adopted the *magnet school* concept, in which each high school concentrates on a specific course of study. One school may offer a curriculum for students interested in creative arts, another may focus on preparing students to pursue careers in the sciences, another may be oriented to business study, and yet another may offer a general, or traditional, curriculum for both college-bound and vocational students. Suppose Betty, a student who uses a wheelchair, aspires to become an engineer. She should be attending the high school that has the science careers curriculum, but there are many stairs in this particular school building. The school district must find a way to provide Betty with access to the curricu-

This photograph illustrates the impact that architectural barriers can have on the mobility of individuals who are physically handicapped. (Photo by Dick Brown. Courtesy of *Centre Daily Times.*)

lum she needs. For instance, ramps or elevators may have to be installed. If this same school district had two high schools that offered the science careers curriculum, one barrier-free and one not, Betty could *not* choose to attend the school that was not barrier-free in order to force the school district to make it accessible because the science

Figure 7.6. International symbol for access for the handicapped.

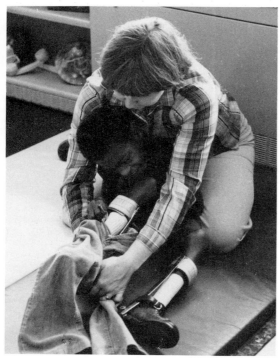

One of the functions of teachers of children with physical handicaps is helping them acquire self-help skills. (Photo by Patricia Seibel.)

program would be accessible to her already in another high school in the district.

Teachers of students with physical disabilities should remember to investigate potential field trip sites to ensure that they are accessible. Are the doorways wide enough to accommodate wheelchairs? Are the public restrooms accessible to a person in a wheelchair? Will steps be a problem? Is there an area nearby where students who are disabled can disembark? (See Figure 7.6.)

Barrier-free environments are often discussed in relation to the needs of people who are physically disabled, but those with other disabilities can also experience accessibility problems. For example, people who are blind may require braille instructions in elevators, bus stops, restaurants, and other public places. They are routinely permitted to take guide dogs in places where dogs are otherwise prohibited. Public libraries are providing access to their holdings by having available some of the technology described in Chapter 4. Similar accommodations are made for individuals who are deaf in order to provide them with access to programs. At the arts festival held annually in one town, individuals who are hearing impaired may go to the central information booth and obtain the services of an interpreter. Colleges and universities that receive federal funds are required to provide sign language interpreters so that all programs are as accessible to students who are deaf as they are to any other students.

Teaching Strategies. Teaching strategies and techniques are no different for children with physical disabilities; sound teaching principles are the same for all children. Teachers should be aware of specific learning problems that disabled children may have in addition to their physical disabilities (e.g., language deficits, mental retardation), but diagnostic-prescriptive teaching (discussed in Part III of this book) is applicable for all. There is no special curriculum for children with physical disabilities, though additions to the regular curriculum may be necessary to teach certain self-help skills, ambulation training, and leisure skills, and more emphasis may be placed on prevocational training.

Mainstreaming. Teachers need to think about the needs of all children when there is a child with a physical disability in the regular classroom. The nonhandicapped children should be helped to understand the special needs of the child with a physical disability. Special lessons and experiences may be used to increase their sensitivity and help them develop positive attitudes (see Box 7.6.). Nonhandicapped children are likely to have many questions, and some fears, about the physical condition and feelings of the child with the disability. Questions such as the following are not unusual:

- Is it "catching"?
- How did it happen?
- Can she play?
- Does it hurt?
- Will he get better?

Teachers should discuss these questions with the children before a child with a physical disability joins the class. Whether they are followed up and discussed with the child present would depend on the particular child.

Positioning. A disability such as cerebral palsy, muscular dystrophy, or spina bifida limits the individual's ability to complete even the simplest tasks. Therefore, a major consideration for teachers dealing with children who are physically disabled is the identification and use of positions that maximize participation in the environment. Proper positioning prevents contractures; lessens abnormal muscle tone; enhances respiration, digestion, and circulation; prevents pressure sores; heightens visual and auditory awareness; and facilitates interaction with the environment.

Teachers are encouraged to consult with the child's physical therapist regarding therapeutic positioning. First, the therapist observes the student in his or her usual position and notes any abnormal patterns such as "scissored" legs. Second, the therapist identifies positions that will reverse abnormal patterns or movements. Finally, the therapist analyzes the effect of gravity upon the student's body so that gravity can be used to promote good positioning (Utley & Meehan, 1982). For each student, the therapist identifies positions that maximize participation in the educational program. For example, he or she may recommend a prone position that involves use of a wedge, which encourages spontaneous head lifting and development of shoulder strength. Another position is side-lying, which allows eye-hand activities and proper spine alignment.

Teachers of students with physical disabilities should understand the contribution of proper positioning to an educational program. In addition to learning the positions described, they should become familiar with appropriate sitting and standing positions and with methods for lifting, carrying, and transferring students with physical disabilities (see Parette & Hourcade, 1986; Utley & Meehan, 1982).

COMPUTER-ASSISTED INSTRUCTION AND TECHNOLOGY

A physical disability may limit the range and strength of a movement or it may add unwanted, uncontrolled movements. Similarly, it may impose limitations on expressive communication skills (Foulds, 1982). Throughout this chapter, we have referred to devices that enable youngsters with physical disabilities to compensate for these limitations. Many are already well known to the average citizen: motorized wheelchairs, crutches, braces, and artificial limbs. Recent advances in technology have had a major impact upon the number and variety of these devices and their ability to promote motoric and communicative functioning. This in turn facilitates placement of children with physical disabilities into the least restrictive environment.

Devices that influence motor functioning include those that minimize the need for the individual to exert a physical effort. Such devices may be joysticks, voice activation devices, and breath control switches that can operate wheelchairs or

BOX 7.6

HEY, WHAT'S IT LIKE TO BE HANDICAPPED?

Children without obvious disabilities are often curious about children who are disabled. They are also usually quite accepting of each other once their curiosities have been addressed. The direct approach to handling questions is often the best.

Eight-year-old Melody has just met her new neighbor, Mark, an 11-year-old boy who has cerebral palsy. Melody is fascinated with Mark's wheelchair and interested in his unusual way of speaking and, like all kids, she's full of questions:

Melody: (Looking over the wheelchair) Hey, you sick or something?

Mark: No. I got cerebral palsy.

Melody: What?

Mark: Cerebral palsy. CP.

Melody: Oh, I get it. CP. (She pauses.) Hey, what's CP?

Mark: It's something you're born with. It means you can't walk or talk so good.

Melody: You don't ever walk?

Mark: No, but I get around real good in my wheelchair—I call it my cruiser.

Melody: But how do you play, or go to school, or have any fun?

Mark: I go to school in a bus just like you do. But my bus is different. It has this real neat lift that picks me and my chair right up and puts us in the bus. And I play all kinds of things. You know, cribbage, and Monopoly, I do puzzles, and I love to play checkers . . .

Melody: Checkers!! CHECKERS!! I just love to play checkers. Come on! Let's go on up to my apartment and we can play . . . Oh, I mean well uhhhhhhhhhh . . .

Mark: What's wrong?

Melody: Well, I mean . . . Well. Hey, can I catch CP? I mean my Mom's gonna get real mad if I come down with what you got.

Mark: No, Melody, you can't catch CP. It's something you're born with. It's all right if we play checkers together.

Mark and Melody are not real children. They are large, muppet-like puppets designed for use with regular class children to demonstrate what it's like to be handicapped and to illustrate the nature of positive peer relationships between disabled and nondisabled children.

When handicapped children enter classrooms with normal children, the disabled child often feels tense and conspicuous, while the nondisabled majority are often anxious about how to treat a child in a wheelchair, or a blind, deaf, or retarded classmate.

With the trend toward mainstreaming of handicapped children well established, such problems are on the rise and educators have begun to recognize the need for the careful orchestrating of the quality of life in classrooms where handicapped children are included with their nonhandicapped peers.

"Just because we have this new Public Law 94–142," says one regular class teacher, "normal children didn't become more tolerant, loving, and understanding overnight." And for this reason a number of curriculum approaches have been developed which involve children in simulated experiences with handicapping conditions, encounters with the aids and appliances which handicapped people use, and discussions with handicapped people themselves.

Source: B. Aiello, "Hey, What's It Like to Be Handicapped?" *Education Unlimited,* 1(1979), 28–31.
Reprinted by permission.

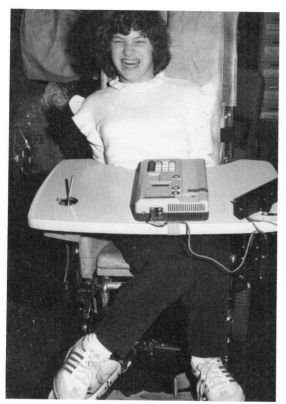

Belle Beauvais is a senior in high school in Michigan. Because of cerebral palsy, she has very limited use of her arms, legs, and voice. She is able to control her wheelchair and to communicate with the aid of sophisticated electronic aids developed by Michigan State University's Artificial Language Laboratory. (Photo by G. P. Cartwright.)

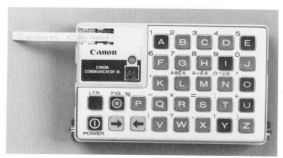

The Canon Communicator. This portable electronic communication aid weighs just 10.5 ounces. (Courtesy of Canon, Inc., Tokyo, Japan.)

turn appliances and lights on or off. Other devices enable individuals with physical disabilities to regain functioning or maximize the level of function they currently possess. Examples include robotic arms, which facilitate completion of hygiene and eating routines. Recent advancements also include the development of electrodes that are attached to or implanted in paralyzed limbs to stimulate functioning (Todd, 1986).

Devices that facilitate expressive communication skills generally fall into four categories. The first category includes devices that are nonelectronic and represent low technology. Use of these devices does not result in a permanent product; therefore, they require the presence of all conversation partners. An example is the Bliss Board, which requires the individual with the disability to point to various items. The second category includes electronic devices that do not produce any written or vocal output. An example is the Zygo 100, a device that uses light to scan a series of items. The third category contains high technology and includes devices that produce either vocal or written output for immediate or future use; an example is the Canon Communicator. The final category contains programmable high technology. In addition to producing output, these devices can be programmed to store and reproduce lengthy utterances. Examples include the Touch Talker and Light Talker by Prentke Romich, Inc. Box 7.7 illustrates the tremendous impact that these communication devices have had upon the lives of people with physical disabilities.

SUMMARY

A physical disability may or may not be a handicap to a person. A handicap refers to environmental or functional demands placed on a person with a disability as he or she interacts in given situations. A handicap is the effect a disability has on an individual's functioning in specific circumstances. Many of the environmental factors that

BOX 7.7
THE EYETYPER

The EyeTyper. (Courtesy of Sentient Systems Technology, Pittsburgh, Pa.)

The EyeTyper is a direct selection keyboard operated by eye movement. The user sits 15 to 20 inches from the EyeTyper. Sixty keys are arranged around a centrally located camera lens on the unit's front panel. The user looks at the desired key, gazing at the center light for one-half to three seconds. When the light increases in brightness, the EyeTyper has accepted the entry. The entry appears on the display area below the keyboard. The word display is two 40-character lines.

The EyeTyper is available for the IBM Personal Computer and the Apple IIe. The EyeTyper has a RS-232C port which permits the system to be used with a printer, a voice synthesizer, an external remote display or a microcomputer keyboard. The system can be attached to and powered by an electric wheelchair.

Source: Courtesy of *Communication Outlook.*

create handicaps for people with physical disabilities, even severe disabilities, can be modified so they can function.

Children with physical disabilities may have neurological, musculoskeletal, or other disabling conditions. Their cognitive, motor, language, and social-emotional abilities range from normal or above to severely and profoundly impaired. The most common disabling conditions in children are disorders of the central nervous system. Because an intact nervous system is important for adequate functioning of other systems in the body, these cases are often quite complex, and children are likely to have associated disorders. Cerebral palsy, the disability encountered most

often by teachers, has been considered a multihandicapping condition in recent years because the children usually have one or several associated problems.

Most nonsensory physical disabilities are diagnosed by medical doctors and described in medical terms. These terms are of little use to teachers in pointing to special educational needs, but professionals, including teachers, should be aware of various physical disabilities in order to understand the nature of a disorder, to understand and use written reports, to converse meaningfully with parents and other professionals, and to be aware of educational implications of the disability.

Convulsive disorders may be associated with another major disability (for example, cerebral palsy) or may occur independently. In addition to preparing other children in the classroom to accept the occurrence of a seizure, classroom teachers should know procedures for ensuring the safety of the child experiencing a seizure. Many convulsive disorders can be controlled by medication. Teachers need to watch for side effects in children on medication and report any seizures that may occur.

A main job of professionals working with children who are physically handicapped is to alter the environment so they can function and lead lives as normal as possible. Various types of adaptive equipment can help the child with a physical disability become as independent as possible, maintain current levels of physical functioning, and prevent physical deformities. Motorized wheelchairs with special devices to control them; feeding equipment; special furniture for standing, sitting, and so on; special typewriters; and communication aids are but a few of the types of adaptive equipment. Generally speaking, special teaching techniques are not required.

As with other exceptional children, placement for children with physical handicaps should be in the least restrictive environment. A physical disability, by itself, is no reason to exclude a child from the regular classroom. Nor are architectural barriers a reason for excluding children with physical disabilities from regular public schools. Decisions about placement must be based on a comprehensive assessment of each child.

A variety of related services such as transportation, adaptive physical education, physical and occupational therapy, and speech and language therapy are often required for children with physical disabilities. Required related services should be specified in the IEP.

Suggestions for Further Reading

Aiello, B. (no date). *The child with cerebral palsy in the regular classroom.* Washington, DC: American Federation of Teachers.

Teachers who have students with cerebral palsy in their classrooms will be particularly interested in this pamphlet. Sections in the text deal with (1) what it's like to have cerebral palsy, (2) preparing children for a handicapped classmate, (3) classroom considerations, and (4) resources. The pamphlet is available from the AFT Teachers' Network for Education of the Handicapped, 11 DuPont Circle, N.W., Washington, DC 20036. Request Item #444.

Best, G. (1978). *Individuals with physical disabilities: An introduction for educators.* St. Louis, MO: C. V. Mosby.

Best's book is a basic introductory text on individuals with physical disabilities. The chapters are divided into two major sections: (1) characteristics of disabilities and disability-related services and (2) learning and educational concerns. Articles in the chapter on postschool and adult alternatives are written by individuals with physical disabilities; they represent personal viewpoints and provide interesting insights into the world of the disabled.

Bigge, J., (1982). *Teaching individuals with physical and multiple disabilities* (2nd ed.). Columbus, OH: Merrill.

The primary focus of this comprehensive text is on the individual with a physical disability and not on the disability itself. There are brief descriptions of various medical aspects of disability and associated secondary disorders, but the majority of the chapters deal with issues such as psychological aspects, self-care, life experience programming, leisure, and work. This text is an excellent overall resource that should prove helpful to professionals and parents alike.

Bleck, E., & Nagel, D. (1982). *Physically handicapped children—A medical atlas for teachers* (2nd ed.). New York: Grune and Stratton.

Bleck and Nagel deal effectively and, in most instances, simply, with the various medical aspects of disability. In addition, most chapters include a short section on the educational implications of each disability. Especially well-written chapters include the sections on cerebral palsy, normal motor development in infancy, muscular dystrophy, and spina bifida.

This is an excellent resource for teachers and other professionals seeking detailed medical information about individuals with physical disabilities.

Finnie, N. (1975). *Handling the young cerebral palsied child at home.* New York: E. P. Dutton.

Special educators working with children whose physical disabilities are so severe as to require almost total care for their physical needs will find this book invaluable. The title is somewhat misleading, because the basic principles for positioning and handling the young child with cerebral palsy are the same for older children as well. Based on the Bobath approach to physical therapy—Neurodevelopmental Treatment (NDT)—Finnie's book is considered the teachers' and parents' primary guide book.

Self, P. C. (Ed.). (1984). *Physical disability: An annotated literature guide.* New York: Marcell Decker.

This text is a guide to the literature for professionals working with individuals who are physically disabled. It includes chapters on mobility, barrier-free design, independent living, social and psychological impact of a physical disability, medical concerns, and legal rights.

Todd, S. P. (Ed.). (1986). *Rehabilitation R&D Progress Reports 1986*. Washington, DC: Veterans Administration.

This is a comprehensive summary of rehabilitation research and engineering in the United States and abroad. Practitioners may be particularly interested in the sections discussing communication methods and environmental controls for individuals who are severely disabled.

Vanderheiden, G. C., & Krause, L. A. (Eds.). (1983). *Nonvocal communication source book*. Madison, WI: Trace Research and Development Center.

Descriptions and photographs of a variety of communication aids.

Wright, B. A. (1983). *Physical disability—A psychosocial approach* (2nd ed.). New York: Harper & Row.

This text is written in a nontechnical manner and is intended for use by students, professionals, individuals with disabilities, and the general public. It examines problems encountered in the social environment by people with physical disabilities.

Relevant Journals

The American Journal of Occupational Therapy
The official journal of the American Occupational Therapist Association, Rockville, MD. Published thirteen times a year, it presents new approaches and techniques of practice, development, theory, research, and professional trends.

Archives of Physical Medicine and Rehabilitation Literature
The official journal of the American Congress of Rehabilitation Medicine and the American Academy of Physical Medicine and Rehabilitation, Chicago, IL. Published monthly, it presents reports of original research and clinical experience in physical medicine and rehabilitation, diagnosis, and therapy.

Closing the Gap
A bimonthly newsletter ($15.00) designed to keep the reader up to date on research and programming for the microcomputer and the handicapped. The organization, headed by parents of an exceptional child, also conducts workshops for special education teachers. (Route 2, Box 39, Henderson, MN 56044.)

Communication Outlook
A quarterly newsletter, published jointly by the Artificial Language Laboratory at Michigan State University and the Trace Center for the Severely Communicatively Handicapped at the University of Wisconsin, dealing with the use of technology to assist handicapped people who have communication disorders. (Michigan State University, East Lansing, MI 48824.)

Handicapped Americans Report
This newsletter is published six times a year by Capitol Publishers, Arlington, VA. It keeps readers informed of proposals, legislation, programs, and grants affecting Americans who are handicapped.

CHAPTER 8

Mental Retardation

Did You Know That . . .

- children with low intelligence are not necessarily mentally retarded?

- some children are so physically and mentally impaired that accurate measurement of their intelligence is impossible?

- children with mild retardation are more like normal children than like severely retarded children?

- there are dozens of causes of mental retardation?

- great strides are being made in the prevention of mental retardation?

- most persons with moderate retardation live at home or in small community group homes and not in institutions?

- more minority groups (e.g., Hispanic, black) children than white children are classified as retarded?

- most children who are retarded grow up to be independent, self-supporting adults, no longer regarded as retarded?

- over thirty definitions of mental retardation have been proposed?

Although we may be reluctant to admit it, our images of people who are mentally retarded tend to be based on stereotypes. Sometimes, the stereotypes are quite accurate; other times, they are not. At the root of our stereotypes is the fact that few of us have had much direct contact with people who are retarded. We may believe that most people with retardation are similar to those we've met. Actually, those citizens sometimes labeled *retarded* are a diverse group who may exhibit a greater range of behavior than the so-called normal population. There is a vast difference in the abilities and disabilities of those who are mildly retarded and those who are profoundly retarded. Many children who have been labeled mildly retarded during their school years grow up to be productive, hard-working adults; the label *retarded* no longer applies to them.

In Box 8.1, we present a case study of a young man (we will call him Kevin) who was once labeled retarded. You will note that his present occupation and behavior belie that label. Included in the box is a series of general principles that can be derived from studying many cases of this sort. As you read this case study, see how Kevin compares with your own mental image of persons who are retarded.

MENTAL RETARDATION DEFINED

The story of Kevin illustrates the fact that some people who are retarded can get along quite well and become productive citizens. Kevin may or may not fit your own image of someone who bears the label *mentally retarded*. In this chapter, you will read other case studies of individuals with retardation who bear little resemblance to Kevin in terms of what they can do. Persons who are more severely retarded need varying amounts of care throughout their lives. With such extremes of behavior it should be clear that mental retardation is not a unilateral concept. Persons who are mentally retarded can exhibit quite different kinds of behavior and adaptivity, and because of this variability, it is quite difficult to define mental retardation. Many different definitions have been proposed. Indeed, we reviewed over thirty different ones (Cartwright & Cartwright, 1978); however, we will spare you the total array of definitions. We gave the U.S. Congress definition in Chapter 3. Here, we present the most commonly used definition—the one prepared by the American Association on Mental Deficiency (AAMD):

Mental retardation refers to significantly subaverage general intellectual functioning resulting in or associated with concurrent impairments in adaptive behavior and manifested during the developmental period.

(Grossman, 1983, p. 11. Used with permission.)

Criteria

According to the AAMD definition, three criteria must be met before a person should be classified as mentally retarded:

1. Subaverage general intellectual ability, and
2. Deficits in adaptive behavior,
3. Manifested during the developmental period.

General Intellectual Ability. The first of these criteria, **general intellectual ability**, refers to mental ability, what is commonly spoken of as intelligence. For purposes of this definition, general intelligence must be measured by an individually administered intelligence test. The two most widely used tests are the Stanford-Binet Intelligence Test and the Wechsler Intelligence Scales for Children. In practice, "significantly subaverage general intellectual functioning" means an IQ score below 68 on the Stanford-Binet scale or below 70 on the Wechsler scales. The AAMD classification system categorizes intellectual functioning into four levels of retardation: mild, moderate, severe, and profound.

Adaptive Behavior. The second criterion, **adaptive behavior**, is

the effectiveness or degree with which the individual meets the standards of personal independence and social responsibility expected

of his/her age and cultural group. Expectations vary for different age groups, deficits in adaptive behavior will vary at different ages. These may be reflected in the following areas.

During infancy and early childhood in:
1. Sensorimotor skills development
2. Communication skills (including speech and language)
3. Self-help skills
4. Socialization (development of ability to interact with others)

During childhood and early adolescence in areas 1 through 4 and/or:
5. Application of basic academic skills in daily life activities
6. Application of appropriate reasoning and judgment in mastery of the environment
7. Social skills (participation in group activities and interpersonal relationships)

During late adolescence and adult life in areas 1 through 7 and/or:
8. Vocational and social responsibilities and performance

(Grossman, 1983, pp. 1, 25. Used with permission.)

Two scales that can be used to measure adaptive behavior are the AAMD Adaptive Behavior Scale and the Vineland Maturity Scales. These scales assess an individual's effectiveness in the communication, motor, affective, and independent functioning domains. (Note the correspondence with the developmental domains introduced in Chapter 3.) The AAMD manual on classification and terminology (Grossman, 1983) devotes numerous pages to illustrations of the highest levels of adaptive behavior that can be expected at several age levels with mild, moderate, severe, and profound mental retardation. One such example is reproduced in its entirety in Table 8.1. The left column of the table lists age levels in three-year intervals and the four retardation levels. The behaviors in the right column indicate the *highest* levels of behavior usually found at a particular age and retardation level. For example, some six-year-old children with mild retardation can be expected to feed themselves with a spoon or fork; to

BOX 8.1

CASE STUDY—KEVIN

Once they are out of school, most people who are mildly retarded are absorbed into society and are more a part of, than apart from, the mainstream of society.

With proper education, people who are mildly retarded can become tax-paying, contributing citizens rather than wards of the state.

People with lower intelligence have lessened ability to generalize; a routine job keeps the number of decisions that must be made to a minimum.

Successful job performance depends as much on good work habits as on basic ability to do the job.

More people with mild retardation come from families in lower-income brackets than in high-income brackets.

Lack of oxygen during breech birth is a common cause of retardation.

Developmental delays are often associated with retardation.

Children with mild retardation are more like their normal peers in physical development than in mental development.

Kevin is now twenty-four years old and is starting his third year as an employee of the Lathrop drugstore chain. He makes slightly more than $18,000 per year as a driver for the firm. He has a modest savings account, a small life insurance policy, and a five-year-old car. He participates in the firm's health insurance and retirement plans, as well as the payroll savings plan. He lives with his parents but hopes to have an apartment of his own within the next year. Because he is single, he pays a bit more income tax than he feels is fair, and one of his favorite diversions is complaining about the income tax and other deductions that reduce his weekly paycheck.

Kevin's job is an important one for the firm. The firm purchases large quantities of prescription drugs, which it then disperses to its twelve affiliated pharmacies within a forty-mile radius of the main store. It is Kevin's job to deliver pharmaceutical orders to the twelve branch stores on a daily basis. The job is fairly routine; the same route is covered each day, and all the goods are prepackaged and labeled. Although the driving is routine, the responsibility is not. Kevin knows that people's lives may depend upon the safe delivery of the drugs. Absolute dependability is essential. Kevin's work record is exemplary; in his two years as driver, he has never been late to work and has missed only four days of work because of illness.

Kevin comes from a family of modest means. His father was a miner for thirty years before he was permanently disabled with black lung disease. His pension is adequate to support a fairly comfortable existence in a modest two-bedroom home, which is now owned by the family. Kevin has never lived anywhere but in the home of his parents. As an only child, he has enjoyed the extra attention that often comes in single-child homes.

Kevin's early years were relatively uneventful. The doctor told his mother that Kevin seemed to be doing fine shortly after his birth in the breech position. Presumably, though, the breech birth shut off Kevin's oxygen supply for a brief time. The lack of oxygen caused some mild brain injury and his subsequent mild mental retardation. Kevin walked and talked a little later than some children, but not so late as to cause his parents and doctor alarm. His physical development was quite satisfactory, although he did not develop into the athlete his father desired.

---

dress themselves with a little help; and to hop, skip, and ride a tricycle. Children who are moderately retarded should be able to do the same things, but only after they reach age nine. By age fifteen, some individuals who are profoundly retarded may be able to achieve the same behaviors as the six-year-old youth who is mildly retarded.

Manifestation During Developmental Period. The third criterion of the AAMD definition, *manifestation during the developmental period,* means that the problem of retardation is observed before the individual reaches eighteen years of age.

A critical element of this definition is that low IQ is a necessary, but not sufficient, condition for

Although he was classified as mildly retarded when he was in school, Kevin is an independent, self-supporting citizen as an adult. (Photo by Joseph Bodkin.)

Most children with mild retardation are so diagnosed after they are in school and start having academic problems.

In junior and senior high school, most classwork is focused on functional, useful skills.

At the end of the second grade, Kevin still was not reading. The school principal decided to retain Kevin in the second grade for another year. A year later, he was examined by a school psychologist, who found that Kevin was functioning in the slightly retarded range. His IQ was reported as 70, and Kevin was assigned to a class for children who were educable mentally retarded for the next year.

(continued)

the diagnosis of mental retardation. Similarly, poor adaptive behavior alone is not sufficient for such a diagnosis. An individual must have deficits in *both* intellectual functioning *and* adaptive behavior to be considered mentally retarded. A deficit in either aspect alone is *not* sufficient grounds for the diagnosis of mental retardation.

CLASSIFICATION SCHEMES

Discussions of definitions lead inevitably to schemes or ways of classifying children. Because the label *mentally retarded* does not adequately reflect the heterogeneity of persons so diagnosed.

(continued)

Routine, repetitive operations can be learned by people who are retarded because the nature of the task requires repetition, and thus considerable practice takes place.

The label *retarded* may penalize youngsters because some people (e.g., shop teachers, driving instructors) may fear for the safety of the individual and not give the youngsters ample opportunity to participate in programs.

Proper training and lots of practice enable youngsters who are mildly retarded to acquire useful skills.

Inability to get along with fellow workers and poor work attitude rather than lack of ability to do the job are the leading causes of job terminations of persons who are retarded, much as they are in the "normal" population.

Vocational rehabilitation and other social agencies provide services to older persons who have mental retardation or other handicaps.

Kevin remained in special classes for the rest of his school career. His special education teachers concentrated first on basic academics and later on vocational awareness and job preparation. By the time he reached high school, he was attending certain classes with his nonretarded peers. His performance in gym class was indistinguishable from the rest of the class. He did not fare very well in wood shop or machine shop, but he did do well in the bindery operations of the printing class. He stayed in the print shop for two years and became quite accomplished in several types of bindery operations.

There was some resistance to Kevin's enrollment in driver training. He had considerable difficulty with the manual of rules provided by the state licensing bureau. His special education teacher rewrote part of the manual in simpler language and tutored him on the rules. Kevin was able to master the rules quickly when they were presented to him as real situations rather than as words in a book. The performance portion of driver training went quite smoothly, although his instructor took extra time to assure himself that Kevin was especially good at defensive driving. Kevin passed the driver's test on the second try.

Kevin's first job was part-time work in a large printing plant. The pay was not very good, but he learned a few painful lessons about getting along with his fellow employees. Kevin continued to work with his vocational rehabilitation counselor and to study the want ads each day. When the job with Lathrop drugs came up, the counselor assisted Kevin in applying for the job and in taking the test for a chauffeur's license. After a short training period in which Kevin rode with an employee who knew the route between the various stores, Kevin was on his own. He was well on his way to becoming an independent, self-supporting citizen.

more precise and descriptive subgroups have been derived over the years. There are at least two classification systems you should know about: the AAMD and the system used extensively in American schools.

The AAMD system, as we saw, consists of four levels of retardation: mild, moderate, severe, and profound. Of course, youngsters with measured IQ in any of the four levels would not be diagnosed as retarded unless they also showed deficits in adaptive behavior.

The other common classification system was used widely in American schools up through the 1970s, but it is gradually being replaced by the AAMD system. This scheme contains three subgroups: **educable mentally retarded (EMR), trainable mentally retarded (TMR),** and **severely and profoundly handicapped (SPH)** or **severely and profoundly impaired (SPI).** Traditionally, youngsters whose IQ scores ranged from about 50 or 55 to 75 were labeled as educable mentally retarded. Youngsters in the IQ range from about 30 or 35 to 55 were called trainable mentally retarded. Youngsters with IQs of about 30 or lower were labeled as severely and profoundly impaired. Table 8.2 compares IQ scores as measured with the American schools and the AAMD systems. Because the correspondence between the two systems is so great, we will discuss just one system—AAMD—in the rest of this chapter.

TABLE 8.1

EXAMPLES OF ADAPTIVE BEHAVIOR

Age and Level of Retardation	Behavior
6 years: MILD 9 years: MODERATE 12 years and above: SEVERE 15 years and above: PROFOUND	*Independent functioning:* Feeds self with spoon or fork, may spill some. Puts on clothing but needs help with small buttons and jacket zippers. Tries to bathe self but needs help. Can wash and dry hands but not very efficiently. Partially toilet trained, but may have accidents. *Physical:* May hop or skip. May climb steps with alternating feet. Rides tricycle (or bicycle over eight years). May climb trees or jungle gym; plays dance games. May throw ball and hit target. *Communication:* May have speaking vocabulary of over 300 words and use grammatically correct sentences; some speech may be indistinct sometimes. If nonverbal, may use many gestures to communicate needs. Understands simple verbal communications, including directions and questions ("Put it on the shelf." "Where do you live?"). May recognize advertising words and signs (Ice Cream, STOP, EXIT, Men, Ladies). Relates experiences in simple language. *Social:* Participates in group activities and simple group games. Interacts with others in simple play ("store," "house") and expressive activities (art and dance).

Source: Adapted from H. J. Grossman (ed.), *Classification in mental retardation.* Washington, DC: American Association on Mental Deficiency, 1983, pg. 205. Used with permission.

Mild Retardation

Of the total group of persons who are mentally retarded, those with mild retardation are by far the largest subgroup, representing 85 to 87 percent of the total population. Children who are mildly retarded are being taught in regular classes to a much greater extent than was the case just a few years ago. If you are a regular elementary teacher, it is likely you will have one or more children with mild retardation in your class, at least for part of the school day.

As a group, children with mild retardation are virtually indistinguishable physically from their nonretarded peers, although statistically they may be slightly smaller and have a few more physical disorders than does the general population. These physical characteristics, though, do not in themselves represent a diagnostic or identification sign, as they often do with the more severely handicapped. On the whole, youngsters with mild retardation are slightly below average in such developmental skills as walking and talking, as well as in such self-help skills as dressing and eating

(Stevens, 1964). Normal children, however, also display variation in development, so a single developmental delay must not be considered a sure sign of mental retardation.

Children with mild retardation are not usually formally identified until after they have been in school a year or two. The first signs of subaverage general intellectual functioning are often noted as the teacher compares that child's academic progress with the progress of the other children in the class. If a child is in school with many youngsters from disadvantaged homes and the overall academic achievement of most of the students is low, then the child may not be identified as retarded at all, or not until he or she encounters severe academic difficulty later on in school. On the other hand, a child with a mild handicap who is enrolled in a class composed primarily of bright or average youngsters will be identified more rapidly. Thus, variations in expectations due to cultural or community conditions may be a factor in the diagnosis of mental retardation.

In terms of most variables, individuals with mild retardation, as a group, will be slightly below

TABLE 8.2

IQ SCORES* AND THE AAMD AND THE AMERICAN SCHOOLS CLASSIFICATION SYSTEMS

AAMD Levels	Stanford-Binet IQ Score ($\bar{X} = 100$; SD = 16)**	Wechsler IQ Score ($\bar{X} = 100$; SD = 15)**	American Schools Subgroups
Mild	68–53	70–56	Educable
Moderate	52–37	55–41	Trainable
Severe	36–20	40–26	Severely and profoundly handicapped
Profound	19 and below	25 and below	

*On individual tests such as the Stanford-Binet and Wechsler.
**$\bar{X}$ (mean) is an average score of 100 points. SD (standard deviation) refers to variability. On the Stanford-Binet, 68 percent of the population fall within one standard deviation, or 16 points, of the mean. That is, 68 percent of the population have IQ scores between 84 and 116 on the Stanford-Binet, or between 85 and 115 on the Wechsler.

the normal population (Stevens, 1964). However, a curious phenomenon exists when children who are mildly retarded reach adulthood: They are usually no longer considered retarded (Mac-Millan, 1982; Robinson & Robinson, 1976). They are quickly absorbed into the community at large and become self-supporting citizens. At this point, you might wish to refer back to the case study of Kevin, who was classified as mildly retarded at one point in his life.

Though there is no known cause of the retardation in most children with mild mental retardation (Berlin, 1978), there are hypotheses. We know that a disproportionate number of children who are mildly retarded come from lower-class and ethnic minority families. As D. L. MacMillan points out, it would be easy to blame poor language models and lackluster environmental stimulation for the retardation, except that the *majority* of children who come from such environments are not retarded. Nevertheless, in the absence of any identifiable physiological or genetic defects, or disease-induced retardation, environmental factors are still considered to be likely causes, even though the etiology of the retardation cannot be specified with certainty (MacMillan, 1982).

Moderate Retardation

Individuals who are moderately retarded make up about 6 to 10 percent of the total population of persons with retardation. They often fit common stereotypes of the mentally retarded. There are noticeably more physical problems in this group, although not nearly as many as are present in the severely and profoundly handicapped groups (Stevens, 1964). Certain physically identifiable syndromes appear in the moderately retarded; the most noticeable of these is Down syndrome. Persons who are moderately retarded can become semi-independent, and institutionalization is rare (unless physical handicaps or illness are present and specialized medical care is required). Communication can be adequate for most basic needs, and basic reading and arithmetic skills can be obtained. A few of these individuals can become self-supporting; most will require at least some lifelong supervision. Many live in small homes with groups of three to eight other persons with moderate retardation and work in community-supported sheltered workshops (Litton, 1978).

The case study in Box 8.2 tells a little about Karen, who is moderately retarded. You will note that Karen attended public schools. Although she

This child with Down syndrome is developing fine motor skills by manipulating the puzzle pieces. (Courtesy of HDS/U.S. HHS.)

was taught mostly by special education teachers, she did have the chance to interact with other teachers and nonretarded children at recess, during lunch, and so on.

Severe Retardation

Individuals who are severely retarded score roughly between 20 and 35 on a Stanford-Binet Intelligence test and represent about 3.5 percent of the total group of people who are retarded. Clearly, this group has serious intellectual problems and needs life care and close supervision. Many people in this category will spend at least a portion of their lives in an institution. The more severely affected and those with medical problems probably will be served in a public or private residential institution, whereas those in the upper portion of this group probably can be served in smaller, community-based residential facilities.

There is a strong negative correlation between IQ level and presence of organic brain pathology, central nervous system impairment, and other handicapping conditions (e.g., cerebral palsy,

blindness, deafness) (Berlin, 1978; Robinson & Robinson, 1976). That is, as one proceeds down the scale into lower and lower IQ ranges, the incidence of other handicapping conditions and/or brain injury increases. H. F. Dingman and G. Tarjan (1960) and N. H. Robinson and H. B. Robinson (1976) estimate that approximately 200,000 to 400,000 people fall into this group, or about 3 percent of the total population of individuals who are retarded. The combination of related physical handicaps, slobbering or tongue thrust, peculiar shifting gait in ambulatory cases, and general lack of social amenities make these individuals highly visible. Attention to cosmetics, neatness, and facial expression can help persons in this group be more socially acceptable.

Individuals who are in the higher-functioning range of severe retardation may be trained to do work under close supervision in sheltered workshops or work activity centers. Most should be able to acquire self-help skills if other physical handicaps do not prevent it. Language is decidedly limited, but certain basic communication skills can be achieved (Litton, 1978).

The case study in Box 8.3 describes some of the behaviors and activities of Daniel, a fifteen-year-old youth with severe retardation. Like Karen, Daniel attended school in a regular public school, although his interaction with nonretarded youth and regular teachers was minimal. Still, he became a part of the school as, quite gradually, other teachers and students began to understand and accept him.

Profound Retardation

Persons who are profoundly retarded score below 20 on standardized intelligence tests. Only about 1 percent of the entire range of persons with retardation are profoundly impaired. In many cases, the IQ score is unobtainable or estimated. In almost all cases, organic brain pathology and physical handicaps are present (MacMillan, 1982; Robinson & Robinson, 1976). Expressive speech and language skills are extremely limited, if present at all. Blindness, deafness, cerebral palsy,

BOX 8.2
CASE STUDY—KAREN

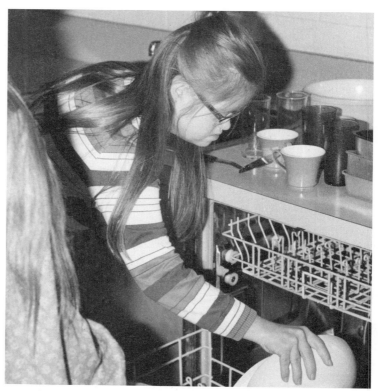

Karen has learned important self-help skills living in a group home with several other women who are moderately retarded. (Courtesy of Association for Retarded Citizens.)

Children with Down syndrome are less likely to be in institutions now than a decade ago.

A much higher percentage of children with Down syndrome and other forms of mental retardation are born to mothers over the age of thirty-five than to younger mothers.

In past years, most people with Down syndrome spent their lives in institutions for the retarded. Fortunately, Karen, now age twenty-four, has led a more normal life. Karen is the third child in a family of three children. She came rather late: Her mother was thirty-nine years old when she was born, and Karen was twelve years younger than the second-born child. Only a day or two after Karen's birth, the doctors informed her parents that she had Down syndrome, or as the condition was usually called at that time, mongolism. The doctors said that Karen almost certainly would be re-

Children with Down syndrome cut across all social classes and income levels.

Parents often receive contradictory information and advice from a variety of sources.

Raising children who are handicapped is often a difficult, emotionally draining experience.

Today, it is much more socially acceptable to include children with handicaps in normal activities than it was twenty or thirty years ago.

Good, consistent training and emotional support on the part of parents can be of enormous assistance to the developing child.

Academic skills usually approximate what would be found in a child of similar *mental* age.

The trend—indeed, the law—is toward provision of services to persons with handicaps in as normal an environment as possible.

Adults who are moderately retarded can learn to travel about their home community with safety and reliability.

Many adults who are moderately retarded can become semi-independent and economically self-sufficient.

Small group homes afford psychological as well as physical support.

The future for individuals who are retarded is enhanced by acceptance and understanding by the community at large.

tarded. Some of her parents' friends suggested that Karen be institutionalized immediately, before her parents formed too strong an attachment to her.

Karen's parents, both well-educated, were stunned by the information and bewildered by the different opinions and pessimistic prognoses passed on by friends and people in the hospital and local agencies. Eventually, they decided that Karen had the right to be treated like any other child, and they decided to keep her at home.

Karen's parents will be the first to tell you that they often had second thoughts about their decision. There were long bouts of illness, stares from strangers, difficulties in finding the right babysitters, and very slow progress in academics during the school years. In balance, though, the decision to keep Karen at home instead of in an institution was a wise one. Karen was usually fun to be with, she really had no more behavior problems than any other child, and her smiles seemed brighter.

Karen went to a special private preschool sponsored by the local Association for Retarded Citizens (ARC). Then she spent most of her public school life in special classes sponsored by the local school district. By the time she reached high school age, her language and reading levels approached those of a second grader. She learned to read "survival" words and to follow directions and ask questions for information.

Two years ago, Karen moved into a small group home with five other women who are moderately retarded. They are supervised by house parents, but they are responsible for care of themselves and their rooms, and they share the cooking. Monday through Friday mornings, Karen and another resident take the bus across town to the sheltered workshop sponsored jointly by the ARC and the state Vocational Rehabilitation Agency. Karen works all day and earns enough money to pay for her clothing, her lunch, her bus fare, and entertainment. She earns about 50 percent of what a nonretarded worker might make, only because she doesn't work as fast, not because of discrimination.

Karen feels good about herself and is very happy with the relative stability afforded by the semi-sheltered situation. Karen's parents, who are in their sixties and at the point where continuing responsibility for Karen would be quite burdensome, are now reassured that their daughter is well cared for. They are relieved that Karen is at least semi-independent and that her future seems secure and bright.

BOX 8.3

CASE STUDY—DANIEL

In contrast to mild retardation, severe retardation is usually diagnosed very early in a child's life.

The more severe the retardation, the more pronounced the developmental delays.

Children who are profoundly retarded are often placed in some specialized residential facility during their first year of life.

Physical impairments are almost always associated with severe retardation.

In the late 1970s, court rulings and state and federal laws acted in concert to deinstitutionalize persons with handicaps and to house and educate them in less restrictive environments.

State and local resources are being used more and more to establish small community-based facilities for persons with retardation and other handicaps.

Before Daniel was one year old, it was obvious that he had serious delays in his development. His vision and hearing seemed within the normal range, but there were problems in other areas. He did not babble, he did not attempt to sit up, and he seemed to have trouble swallowing. He was almost totally unresponsive to his environment. Shortly after his first birthday, Daniel was placed in a residential institution. His parents visited him about once a month, but Daniel gave little evidence of recognition.

After four years in the institution, Daniel was able to walk, but by then it was determined that he had moderate physical impairments due to cerebral palsy. By age ten, Daniel was clearly pleased when his parents and other brothers visited him on what were now weekly visits. Once a month, Daniel spent the weekend at home. His language had progressed to the point where he could say a few words, but the cerebral palsy interfered with his speech to a considerable extent.

When Daniel was twelve, the state welfare department was ordered by a federal judge to close the institution in which Daniel was placed. Daniel's parents were given the option of keeping Daniel at home and receiving some help on a daily basis or placing Daniel in a small group home with four or five other youngsters about the same age who were severely retarded. The group home would have a set of houseparents and other staff people who would be there twenty-four hours per day. After much thought and discussion, Daniel's parents brought him home to live with them.

At age fifteen, Daniel still is not fully toilet trained; he wears extra-heavy underpants when he goes on visits with his parents or goes to school. He

epilepsy, and physical anomalies are the rule rather than the exception (Stevens, 1964). Motor development is quite limited, and most persons with profound retardation are nonambulatory. Quite prevalent are such aberrant self-stimulating behavior patterns as head banging; rocking; grinding of teeth; and self-mutilation, such as biting of hands, arms, or lips. Such stereotypical behavior, however, is not congenital. Most such behaviors can be controlled by paying adequate attention to the children and by providing appropriate training.

The incidence of additional physical handicaps and central nervous system involvement is so high that normal statistical probabilities are extremely inaccurate for this group. For example,

Robinson and Robinson (1976) report that, statistically, we would expect to find only fifty-seven profoundly retarded people in the United States. That is, because intelligence follows the normal bell-shaped curve, we would expect very, very few children to have IQs near zero. Census reports and other information, however, have led experts to estimate that there are actually over 100,000 such people in the United States. The discrepancy in these two figures results from the fact that serious trauma to the brain almost always causes mental retardation.

The case study in Box 8.4 presents eight-year-old Dawn, who is profoundly retarded. Dawn will need lifelong care in an institution that can provide for her medical as well as her personal needs.

The impact of a youngster with severe retardation on the dynamics of family life is enormous. In some cases, the presence of a child with a handicap may bring a family closer together; in others, the presence of the child may tear the family apart.

The public schools are being asked to provide appropriate education to all children, no matter how serious their handicap. The social and economic impact on the schools is unsurpassed in the history of education.

Until the late 1970s, very few teachers were trained to work with individuals who are profoundly retarded. Many teachers were asked to perform tasks for which they had not been trained.

As more large institutions are closed down, there will be increased demands for small group homes (community living arrangements).

can feed himself, but he still needs more practice so that he doesn't make too much of a mess. He helps a bit in dressing but is incapable of doing the entire job. Obviously, the extra care that Daniel requires places a great burden of responsibility on Daniel's parents and siblings. In all likelihood, these responsibilities will continue throughout Daniel's life, even though with continued training he probably will be able to perform most of the tasks by himself.

A bright spot in Daniel's day is when he boards the special yellow bus and goes to school. Daniel goes to a special class in which six other youths with severe and profound retardation are enrolled. The class is in a regular junior high school, and Daniel spends time with other nonretarded children in assembly programs and at lunch. Instructional objectives for Daniel include toilet training, normalization (helping to walk with a more conventional gait and keeping his arms down at his sides instead of curled up in front of him), communication skills, and self-feeding.

Once a month, Daniel spends the weekend in the group home with several other youngsters who are retarded. This **respite care** (temporary care, such as for a weekend or a week or two) has two purposes. First, the placement of Daniel in the facility gives his parents a break from the total care and allows them to take brief trips. Second, the weekends prepare Daniel for his eventual return to a small group home. When Daniel's parents are too old to continue his daily care, he will be able to make the transition back to a group home without too much difficulty.

INCIDENCE OF RETARDATION

A perfectly logical question is: How many people in the United States are mentally retarded? Logical, yes, but an extremely difficult question to answer, especially if we look at the entire age range from birth through adulthood. Textbooks usually report a figure of about 3 percent and interpret it to mean that in a school district of a thousand children, thirty will be mentally retarded. Of the thirty, about twenty-six would fall in the mildly retarded range, three in the moderately retarded range, and one in the severely and profoundly retarded range. It is important to note,

however, that this national estimate is based solely upon IQ criterion. Nonetheless, applying the 3 percent figure to the estimated U.S. population (all ages) in 1985 would result in the figures in Table 8.3.

MacMillan (1977) made an extensive study of the problems of counting or estimating the number or percentage of individuals classified as mentally retarded. He suggests that, although 3 percent is a good estimate of the number of people who are now or have been classified as mentally retarded at some point in their lives,

the number of persons considered mentally retarded at a single point in time . . . is closer to 1% of the general population. The difference

BOX 8.4
CASE STUDY—DAWN

Most children with profound retardation receive nearly all their care in group homes or institutions.

Profound retardation is almost always accompanied by serious physical, physiological, and/or metabolic problems.

Serious physical problems may prevent accurate measurement of intelligence.

Group homes and institutions depend greatly on volunteers and others who are paid very little.

The prognosis is not good for Dawn, age eight. She has spent all her life in a state institution for people who are mentally retarded. The cause of her profound retardation is not known for sure, but doctors feel that something happened to her mother early in the pregnancy—a fall, perhaps, or a drug reaction. Profound retardation accompanied by serious physical problems, including cleft palate, were obvious at birth. During her first year, it was determined that Dawn was also blind and deaf. Thus, the belief that massive brain damage occurred in the early months of pregnancy was given additional credence.

Although she is eight years old, Dawn's size is that of a four-year-old. She has no speech and no mobility. Her IQ is not measurable. She almost certainly will need total care throughout her life. Her life expectancy is quite short.

Mrs. Arnold, seventy-two years old, is a nearly constant companion to Dawn: She is a foster grandmother. Although she is paid a minimum wage to bathe, feed, and care for Dawn eight hours a day, Mrs. Arnold receives more than money in return. Mrs. Arnold is alone in the world, and caring for Dawn is a source of strength for her. Dawn knows Mrs. Arnold and enjoys her presence. Their mutual dependency gives meaning to the lives of both people.

---

between these two figures is largely due to the fact that children who are classified as EMR by the schools are not considered mentally retarded before they enter school or after they leave it.

(MacMillan, 1977, p. 73)

The work of MacMillan (1982), Robinson and Robinson (1976), C. D. Mercer (1973), and others suggests the following conclusions regarding numbers and percentages of persons who are retarded.

1. More minority group children (e.g., black, Hispanic) than white children are classified as retarded, perhaps because of language differences and conscious or unconscious racial discrimination.

2. More males than females are classified as retarded because of sex-linked genetic problems and perhaps because of differing role expecta-

tions for boys and girls. (Sex-linked genetic problems are those linked to the X or sex chromosome carried by males. See Robinson and Robinson, 1976, for a full discussion of genetic problems.)

3. There are more children with profound retardation in the 0 to 5 age range than in older age ranges because these youngsters usually have related physical problems and thus shorter life expectancies.

4. If both IQ level and adaptive behavior are used as criteria for identifying people who are retarded, the percentage of people with retardation in the population drops below 3 percent.

5. There is an upsurge in identification of children with mild retardation during the early school years. Their adaptive behavior may be adequate for the home and neighborhood; however, they suddenly run into problems

TABLE 8.3

ESTIMATES OF NUMBERS OF PERSONS WITH RETARDATION IN 1985

	All Ages	Under 21 Years	Over 21 Years
Estimated Total U.S. Population	240,000,000	96,000,000	144,000,000
3 Percent Estimate	7,200,000	2,800,000	4,400,000
Levels of Retardation			
Mild (IQ 52–67) About 89%*	6,408,000	2,492,000	3,916,000
Moderate (IQ 36–51) About 6%*	432,000	168,000	264,000
Severe (IQ 20–35) About 3½%*	252,000	98,000	154,000
Profound (IQ below 20) About 1½%*	108,000	42,000	66,000

*Percentage of the population of individuals who are mentally retarded.

when they encounter the academic programs in most schools.

6. There is a decline in the number of people classified as mentally retarded in the immediate postschool years. With the pressures of academic competition behind them, most people who are mildly retarded are absorbed into the community at large, become self-supporting citizens, and are no longer identified as retarded.

As with the AAMD definition, the United States Office of Education (USOE) definition considers deficits in both intellectual functioning and adaptive behavior in describing mental retardation. Using these two criteria, the Education Department reports that, throughout the fifty states, there are approximately 595,600 students with mental retardation. This accounts for approximately 14.48 percent of all students with disabilities and 2 percent of the entire school-age population. Table 8.4 presents special education enrollment figures for the 1985–86 school year for ten states. Note the wide range in the percentages reported, with Oregon identifying only 4.41 percent of its special-needs students as retarded

and North Carolina reporting a figure of 20.87 percent. These figures highlight the uncertainty of our knowledge regarding the incidence of retardation. We turn our attention to causal factors in the next section.

THE CAUSES OF MENTAL RETARDATION

In 1964, H. Stevens indicated that the etiology of 75 percent of the cases of mental retardation was not known. More than two decades later, in spite of a tremendous amount of research into the causes of mental retardation, the percentage of persons with retardation for which the cause was unknown remains essentially the same. C. M. Berlin (1978) suggested that between 65 and 75 percent of all cases of mental retardation are not classifiable by cause. D. P. Hallahan and J. M. Kauffman (1986) indicate the percentage of unknown causes of mental retardation may be between 85 and 94 percent.

In general, a child with mild retardation is more likely to come from a lower socioeconomic

TABLE 8.4

ESTIMATED INCIDENCE OF MENTAL RETARDATION IN TEN STATES

State	Number of Children with Retardation	Percentage of Children with Retardation*
California	25,860	6.88
Florida	20,488	12.54
Illinois	20,519	9.96
Maine	4,131	15.57
Maryland	6,832	7.84
Missouri	16,040	10.69
Minnesota	12,314	15.19
North Carolina	22,854	20.87
Oregon	1,822	4.41
Texas	25,538	9.05

Source: *Education of the Handicapped, 12,* 1–2.

*Based on special education enrollments of students ages three to twenty-one for the 1985–86 school year. In other words, 6.88 percent of all California children enrolled in special education were classified as mentally retarded.

level than is a nonretarded child. (However, let us hasten to add that the majority of children from low-income homes are of average intelligence.) The reason for this correlation is not clear, and the topic is quite controversial. Charges of racism and cultural bias are matched with charges of ignoring evidence, rejecting scientific principles, and "wearing rose-colored glasses." The fact remains that there is a disproportionate number of retarded youngsters in minority and low-income groups. The next decades may show whether or not fairer treatment of minorities will lower the apparent incidence of mild retardation in these groups.

On the other hand, severe retardation does not respect social class or income level: Youngsters with severe and profound retardation can be found more equally distributed across income lines (Blackman, 1983). Although the specific cause of *severe* retardation can be isolated in most cases, specific causation can be attributed in very few cases of *mild* retardation.

Indeed, literally scores of causes of mental

retardation are known. H. J. Grossman (1983) groups causes of mental retardation (and some examples) as follows:

1. *infections and intoxications:* congenital syphilis, rubella, Rh blood incompatibility, intoxicants

2. *trauma or physical agent:* birth injury, postnatal trauma, anoxia

3. *metabolism or nutrition:* galactosemia, hypoglycemia, PKU

4. *gross brain disease:* neurofibromatosis, tuberous sclerosis, tumors

5. *unknown prenatal influence:* cerebral malformation, microcephalus, hydrocephalus

6. *chromosomal abnormality:* Down syndrome, Turner syndrome, Klinefelter syndrome

7. *gestational disorder:* prematurity, small size, postmaturity

8. *psychiatric disorder:* retardation following psychosis or other psychiatric disorder, with no evidence of cerebral pathology

9. *environmental influences:* psychosocial disadvantage, sensory deprivation, severe neglect

10. *other conditions:* blindness, deafness (contributing factors), mental retardation with ill-defined or unknown etiology

The next section describes some of these causes in detail.

Infections and Intoxications. Severe birth defects are possible among children whose mothers were exposed to infections and intoxications while they were pregnant. You are probably familiar with congenital rubella, or German measles. This infection was mentioned previously as a causal factor in hearing impairments, but it can also cause mental retardation. Syphilis, a sexually transmitted disease described in Chapter 7, can pass through the placenta and damage the central nervous system of an unborn baby. Toxoplasmosis is carried by raw meat or fecal material and can cause retardation, convulsions, microcephaly (small head), and hydrocephaly (excessive amounts of cerebrospinal fluid in the skull). Other infections resulting in mental retardation may occur after birth. An example is encephalitis, which may develop following certain childhood diseases or vaccines.

Intoxications during pregnancy may also cause retardation. Pregnant women who use drugs or consume excessive amounts of alcohol may place their unborn children at risk for the development of a number of problems. Intoxicant-related retardation may also occur later in life. For example, the lead contained in the sweet-tasting paint chips ingested by young children may result in retardation. Fortunately, legislation has outlawed the use of lead as an ingredient in household paint.

Trauma.   Trauma can occur during pregnancy or delivery and after birth. During pregnancy, the fetus may be exposed to irradiation or suffer hypoxia (a lack of oxygen). Problems occurring during delivery include breech birth (as with Kevin in Box 8.1), which may reduce oxygen to the baby or place inordinate amounts of pressure on the brain. A delivery that is extremely fast or slow alters the time available for the baby's skull to mold properly. Injuries during infancy, such as a fractured skull, may also cause retardation.

Metabolic Disorders.   A disorder in which mental retardation is a prime feature is phenylketonuria or, as it was known in earlier years, phenylpyruvic oligophrenia (PKU). M. L. Batshaw and Y. M. Perret (1981) describe the syndrome as "blond hair, blue eyes, profound mental retardation, hyperactivity" (p. 382). Fortunately, this syndrome, which is the result of an inborn error of metabolism, is readily diagnosable at birth by means of a simple procedure and is treatable. If the condition is diagnosed shortly after birth, the

full impact of the syndrome can be prevented by placing the infant on a special diet. Infants so treated have a very good chance of achieving normal intellectual functioning.

Mental Retardation Syndromes.   If you continue with the study of exceptionalities in children and adults, sooner or later you will encounter the concept of syndromes. A syndrome is a "combination of physical traits or malformations that are inherited in the same way and carry a similar prognosis. . . . In most cases, no specific treatment is available to correct these defects" (Batshaw & Perret, 1981, p. 377). There are dozens of syndromes associated with mental retardation, most of which can be identified only by trained medical and genetic specialists. We will discuss one syndrome to illustrate the concept.

The most commonly recognized mental retardation syndrome, and the one with which you most likely already have some experience, is called **Down syndrome.** Batshaw and Perret (1981) describe the external symptoms of the syndrome as "hypotonia (poor muscle tone), short stature, mental retardation, small nose and low nasal bridge, upward slant to the eyes, short stubby fingers, simian crease, ventricular septal defects" (p. 378). In past decades, Down syndrome children were generally institutionalized; today, however, institutionalization is the exception rather than the rule. Although mental retardation is almost always present, it is usually in the mild to moderate range and the prognosis for self-care with some supervision is very good.

In over 90 percent of the cases, the cause of Down syndrome is attributable to Trisomy 21 (an extra chromosome at location 21). In almost all cases, this condition (and about a hundred other conditions) can be diagnosed during pregnancy through the use of such prenatal diagnostic techniques as amniocentesis, sonography, and fetoscopy (see Box 8.5). Over the years, much evidence has been amassed indicating that the age of the mother is a prime factor associated with the birth of a Down syndrome child: The older the mother,

BOX 8.5
PRENATAL DIAGNOSTIC PROCEDURES

Every year, advances are made in medical techniques for studying and diagnosing potential fetal problems early in pregnancy. The most commonly used of these procedures, amniocentesis, is carried out during the second trimester of pregnancy by inserting a needle through the mother's abdomen and withdrawing about an ounce of the amniotic fluid that surrounds the fetus. Examination of the fluid and the fetal cells within the fluid through a variety of tests and growth cultures may reveal biochemical or chromosomal disorders.

Fetoscopy is a procedure that permits direct viewing of the fetus by inserting a flexible fiber-optic device through the abdominal wall. This procedure also allows the physician to take blood samples from the placenta to aid in diagnosing certain blood diseases.

Sonography, also known as ultrasound, uses sound waves with computer enhancement to produce an outline of major body parts such as spine or head. This technique has the safety advantage of not violating the placenta, and it carries fewer risks than do conventional x-ray procedures.

A fourth procedure is chorionic villi sampling. It can be performed between the eighth and tenth weeks of pregnancy and involves sampling some of the tissue surrounding the fetal placenta. This sample is analyzed to determine the presence of genetic blood disorders such as sickle cell anemia.

The benefits of these procedures are enormous. In some cases, preventive medical or therapeutic procedures can be initiated to ward off or minimize the effects of a diagnosed condition. In other cases, when such intervention is not possible, counseling of the parents can help them make decisions about how to care for the youngster if the suspected disability becomes a reality.

the more likely she will deliver a child with Down syndrome. The risk increases dramatically with age; the incidence for women ages twenty to twenty-five is about one in two thousand, whereas the rate for women forty-five years old is one in thirty-two (Batshaw & Perret, 1981).

Recently, however, new evidence suggests that Down syndrome is not exclusively related to the age of the mother. In a series of important publications, K. I. Abroms and J. W. Bennett (1981a,b; 1983) report some interesting findings showing that in 25 percent of the cases of Down syndrome, the extra chromosome is attributable to the sperm of the father. Men ages forty-one and older have increased risk of fathering Trisomy 21 Down syndrome children, regardless of the age of the mother.

Although not as common as Down syndrome, there are two other syndromes of which you should be aware: Klinefelter syndrome and Turner syndrome. Klinefelter syndrome affects males and is characterized by mild retardation, the development of female secondary sex characteristics, small male genitalia, and eventual sterility. Turner syndrome, which affects females, is characterized by bowleggedness and failure to develop secondary sex characteristics at puberty.*

ADDITIONAL PROBLEMS OF CHILDREN WITH RETARDATION

As we have seen, the characteristics of individual children with retardation will differ depending on the age of the child and the severity of the retarda-

---

*Fortunately, the most debilitating conditions are extremely rare, and it is unlikely that you will encounter many of them. For further information on this topic, we refer you to Robinson and Robinson (1976), Batshaw and Perret (1981), and Abroms and Bennett (1981).

This youngster has Down syndrome. With proper, early education, such as that illustrated by this special education class, youngsters with Down syndrome need not be institutionalized and can be expected to lead productive, if somewhat sheltered, lives. (Courtesy of Association for Retarded Citizens.)

tion. In this section, we will deal briefly with some of the characteristics you as a teacher are most likely to encounter, especially those related to the four functional domains (cognitive, motor, communication, and social) introduced earlier.

Cognitive Domain

Recall that the area in which children who are retarded differ most from other children is in the cognitive or intellectual domain. In many ways, the intellectual problems of children with retardation are reflected in lessened rate and capacity for learning (for acquiring new concepts and information). Our discussion of cognitive characteristics of youngsters with retardation stresses learning, especially in those situations in which youngsters with mild or moderate retardation are most likely to be first noticed: school and academic situations. Furthermore, this discussion is geared to children who are mildly or moderately retarded. Children with severe and profound re-

tardation usually are not taught traditional school subjects; they are taught more fundamental hygienic, social, and survival skills. Children with mild retardation progress at a rate about 50 to 70 percent that of normal children; children with moderate retardation progress at about 30 to 50 percent of the rate of normal children.

The description of the learning characteristics of any child or group of children will vary depending on the definition of learning that is used. There is little agreement among learning specialists as to the most useful definition of learning, and we will not become embroiled in this controversy. Instead, we will attempt to give you some idea of the most striking differences in learning ability between normal children and children who are mildly retarded.

We don't want to give you the impression that retardation or level of intelligence is fixed at birth and never changes. We must be careful not to assume that because a child has been labeled *mentally retarded,* there is a ceiling on the child's capabilities. To do so may result in lowered expectations for the child. Not too many years ago, it was assumed that children with moderate retardation could never learn to read. Sure enough, children at that level never learned to read—*simply because no one taught them to do so.* Today, basic reading skills are taught to many, if not most, children with moderate retardation.

Therefore, as you read the following characteristics of the learning ability of children with mild or moderate retardation, keep in mind that we are talking about groups of children. Some individual children may be stronger or weaker on these characteristics. There is no line dividing the highest-achieving groups of children who are retarded from the lowest groups of "normal" children. Deciding where to draw the line between normal and abnormal is the subject of federal regulations as reported in Part I of this book, and it requires use of the assessment procedures explained in Part III.

1. *Rate of learning.* The most striking difference in the learning characteristics of normal children and children who are retarded is that the

Basic academic skills are more likely to be included in the curriculum for students with mild or moderate retardation. (Courtesy of HDS/U.S. HHS.)

latter do not learn as fast. In general, children who are retarded take longer than normal children to reach the same level.

2. *Level of learning.* Children who are retarded do not seem to be able to go as far in the learning and schooling process as normal children. They simply are not successful in academic fields, although they may excel in other areas such as athletics, mechanics, or the arts.

3. *Rate of forgetting.* Once information has been learned, children who are retarded will tend to forget it sooner than do normal children, if they do not have the opportunity to practice what they have learned. With frequent intermittent practice, children who are retarded will retain and remember information once they have learned it. For example, they rarely forget their own names, simply because they use them often.

4. *Transfer of learning.* Children who are retarded often have trouble transferring learning from one situation to another. A skill or concept may be learned and applied appropriately in a given situation but applied inappropriately or not at all if the situation is slightly changed or if an entirely new situation arises.

5. *Concrete versus abstract learning.* Most authorities agree that children who are retarded perform better on learning tasks that are straightforward and concrete rather than highly abstract.

6. *Incidental learning.* Children who are retarded often do not acquire information that is peripheral or incidental to the main point of attention. They do not seem to be able to handle as many different pieces or kinds of information at one time as normal children can. Consequently, information not directly relevant to the task being performed may not be acquired.

7. *Learning set.* The ability to profit from experience and to generalize is poor for individuals who are retarded. Therefore, it takes more time for them to form a learning set (a systematic method of solving problems). When tackling a problem, we use a series of steps to

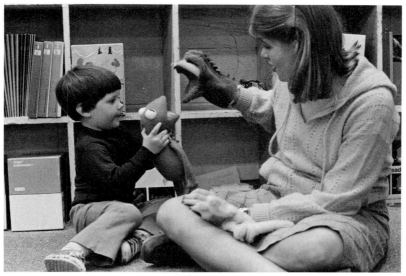

Early language stimulation and training are important for the development of young children who are retarded. (Photo by James Lukens.)

reach a solution. After a number of successful experiences with the same general series of steps, we come to use that series whenever we are in a problem-solving situation. Children who are retarded often have difficulty acquiring a learning set. However, once they have acquired one, children who are retarded can solve problems in much the same manner as normal children.

Language Domain

Language ability and other intellectual abilities are highly correlated. Therefore, children with retardation who are weak in intellectual skills will have more difficulty learning language than will children of normal intelligence. Similarly, academic or intellectual tasks that are dependent on language or verbal learning will often be difficult for children who are retarded. Of particular concern to teachers is that many children with retardation may fail at certain tasks they are capable of performing simply because they do not understand the directions.

Consider the cases of non-English-speaking children. Clearly, a child who does not speak English and who is asked in English to carry out a particular task may have great difficulty doing it. The problem is particularly acute when the child is being given an intelligence test in a language he or she doesn't understand. A perfectly normal, capable child may have great difficulty scoring in the normal range of intelligence if the test is in a language other than the child's native one. Having scored in the retarded range, such a child may then be classified as retarded and placed in a special facility or class for the retarded. Hundreds of Spanish-speaking children were labeled as retarded in California some years ago because they did not perform well on an intelligence test administered in English. It took a court decision to stop the practice. Now such tests must be administered in the native language of the child being tested.

One of the early warning signs to which parents should be particularly sensitive is delayed language, both expressive and receptive. Due to the high correlation between cognitive and language abilities, severe language delays may be a sign that a child is not progressing at a satisfactory

All children need training to help them respond appropriately in social situations. (Courtesy of College of Human Development, The Pennsylvania State University.)

rate. Psychologists, learning disability specialists, and speech/language pathologists are trained to assess the severity of language problems, even in very young children. With early diagnosis of a problem in the language domain, specialists can help a child to develop in this vitally important area. Strengthening language and social skills is an excellent way to help children who are mildly and moderately retarded fit more easily into the mainstream of society.

For more severely retarded children who seem to be unable to develop meaningful oral communication skills, it may be helpful to teach some basic survival and self-help signs. For example, many severely retarded children with no oral abilities have been taught to make simple manual gestures to express such needs as "drink" and "toilet."

Social Domain

Social skills and the ability to get along with other people are just as important to youngsters who are retarded as they are to other children. These skills become even more critical when the mildly retarded person begins to compete for a living with other persons. In fact, as will be discussed in subsequent chapters, social skills are a critical factor in maintaining employment. In general, there is no physiological reason for people with mild retardation to be any different socially from anyone else. The differences between young children who are retarded and their normal peers seem to be related to behavior; that is, children with mild retardation act like normal children who are younger in chronological age. Children who are retarded exhibit the same ranges of behavior and emotion as other children. Some are extremely well adjusted; some are not.

Differences that do emerge are often situational. A child with retardation placed in an unfamiliar situation is likely to respond just like any other child: with bewilderment, fear, anxiety, and so on. However, a child who is retarded may not have as great a capacity to generalize and so may view as foreign situations that other children might see as variations on a familiar theme.

MacMillan (1977) summarizes the important

Children who are mildly or moderately retarded may excel in areas requiring physical abilities. (Courtesy of Library of Congress.)

ideas about social-affective and personality development in children who are retarded in the following manner:

> In general, there is no support for the position that personality dynamics in the mentally retarded operate any differently than they do in nonretarded persons. What does stand out is the fact that the retarded are often exposed to situations with which they are ill-prepared to deal. (p. 415)

Such lack of preparation may cause these children to make inappropriate responses in social situations more often than do their normal peers. Children who are retarded may not fully comprehend what is expected of them and may respond inappropriately not so much because they lack the particular response required as because they have misinterpreted the situation.

Carefully planned training programs can help people who are retarded acquire appropriate response repertoires and can make them more socially acceptable. Such acceptance and proper social relationships are critical because the main reason people who are mildly retarded lose work is that they have difficulty with social aspects of the job, especially good work habits and ability to get along with fellow workers—the same problems faced by "normal" individuals. This area is known as "social skills" training and is covered in Chapter 13.

Motor Domain

Physical development and ability is the domain in which youngsters who are mildly retarded most resemble their intellectually normal peers. Physically, these youngsters are virtually indistinguishable from other youngsters. Many excel at sports (although the popular notion that there is a high incidence of retardation among gifted athletes is a myth). In contrast, the first thing many people notice about people who are profoundly retarded are the physical handicaps that almost always accompany profound retardation.

As a group, children who are mildly retarded tend to walk and talk later than other children, to grow up to be slightly shorter, and to be more susceptible to physical problems and illnesses than are other children. The more retarded the child, the more likely it is that he or she will be late in attaining major developmental milestones. It is important to note, however, that some normal children too are slow to begin walking and talking, so do not put too much faith in a single developmental lag. Children show a wide range of variability and individuality in such areas as gross motor skills, language development, and the like. Thus, the descriptions above should be treated only as generalizations. Remember that a child should not be labeled as having a particular disability such as mental retardation simply on the basis of one symptom or behavior associated with that disability.

IDENTIFICATION AND DIAGNOSIS OF MENTAL RETARDATION

Though children with severe retardation are almost always identified before they reach school, teachers often play the key role in identifying children who are mildly handicapped. As a teacher, you will need to be on the lookout for children who may have handicaps as yet unidentified. What should you look for?

The major clues, of course, are delays in the cognitive and language domains. Major cognitive activities such as arithmetic and reading usually prove difficult for these youngsters. Gross and fine motor skill problems are not as useful as indicators of mild retardation as are problems in the cognitive and language domains. In essence, you should be alert to children who deviate from the rest of the group in the characteristics we have been discussing. The following are factors to be considered when you suspect a child of being mildly retarded.

1. IQ score on intelligence test (usually a group test)

2. ability to function in learning situations found in most classrooms

3. developmental comparisons with others of the same chronological age

4. social adaptability

Ideally, behavioral descriptions in each area, along with any group test scores, should be prepared by the teacher who suspects a problem. The descriptions are used in a referral or request for more detailed examination of a child.

Teachers are *not* expected to make definitive diagnoses of mental retardation (or any other handicap). Diagnosis of a condition or causes of a condition or of specific educational problems related to mental retardation are the concerns of those who specialize in working with the mentally retarded. However, teachers *are* expected to be

alert for possible problems. Teachers are in an excellent position to observe children on a continuing basis in a variety of situations and can often note differences in children that should be studied more intensely.

Legal Issues. Some sticky legal issues are involved in the official declaration that a child is "legally mentally retarded." Different people in different counties and states are legally authorized to certify a child for purposes of welfare, cost reimbursements, admission to state institutions or special classes, tax relief, and the like. The specialist with whom you are most likely to work in a school situation is a certified school psychologist. School psychologists usually play important roles when a decision must be made as to whether a child will be placed in a special class. P.L. 94–142 specifies that no single individual will make diagnostic and placement decisions. Rather, such decisions are to be made by a team of professionals, in consultation with parents. IQ alone is not a sufficient determiner of special class placement. Identification and diagnostic procedures have been modernized and are now much fairer for children, especially minority children. Biennial reevaluations and annual progress reviews are required. All decisions affecting classification of a child as handicapped, educational placement of the child, and even short- and long-range goals and objectives are committee decisions and do not rest in the hands of a single individual.

The high visibility of the clinical and legal professions in this field reflect the need for all of us to be alert to the legal rights of children and to the variety of medical and nonmedical preventive and counseling procedures available.

Multidisciplinary Approach and Clinical Genetics. Those who provide prenatal care, nutrition, after-hospital care, home-health visitor follow-ups, and the services of the many disciplines represented in the schools and public agencies are all necessary and valuable members of the team that can deliver multidisciplinary expertise to the child and the family. Among recent developments that may have direct impact on us is the service delivery concept described by K. I. Abroms (1981). Dr. Abroms presents a compelling case for educational personnel to serve key roles in referring families and helping them locate a variety of services, particularly in the area of genetic screening and counseling. Clinical geneticists can help parents of children with handicaps answer questions that often arise: What can be done now? Is the condition catching (infectious)? Will my children pass the condition on? If we have another child, will he or she be handicapped? Such genetic counseling is but one facet of the total family-service delivery network. Other facets include social skills training, well-baby clinics, prenatal care, and financial counseling. The importance of the network is most obvious for children and youths who are more severely handicapped. However, the concept is consistent with the philosophy and the legal mandates expressed in P.L. 94–142, which calls for multidisciplinary assessment of children with handicaps.

A child who is mentally retarded can be mainstreamed in a regular classroom for certain activities. (Courtesy of U.S. Department of Health and Human Services.)

EDUCATIONAL IMPLICATIONS FOR CHILDREN WITH RETARDATION

Placements

Given the extremely wide range of behaviors exhibited by children with retardation, it is not surprising that they receive their education in a variety of settings. Similarly, no one teaching strategy or technique is used with all youngsters who are retarded. The major determinants for placements and teaching techniques are the types of behavior usually associated with different *levels* of retardation: the more serious the retardation, the more likely the child is to be educated in specialized settings with specialized techniques.

In general, children with mild retardation are educated in levels 3, 4, 5, 6, or 7 of Deno's Cascade of Services (see Figure 2.1, Chapter 2). P.L. 94–

142 requires that children who are retarded be educated with nonhandicapped children to the greatest extent possible. For children with mild retardation, this usually means regular classes with supportive services or part-time regular class attendance and part-time resource room or special class attendance. Typical placement for children with moderate retardation is in level 3 (full-time special class), with some children in level 2 (special day school) and a few in level 4 (part-time regular, part-time special class). Children who are severely and profoundly retarded usually are placed in levels 1, 2, or 3, with those who are profoundly retarded more likely to be found in level 1 (full-time residential school).

Teaching Implications

In general, the more restrictive environments (levels 1, 2, and 3) are associated with lower-level life goals (that is, expectations that youngsters may not achieve personal independence). Youngsters with profound retardation who are placed in full-time residential facilities are there because it is the best judgment of a professional team that those youngsters do not have the potential to be self-sufficient citizens and that they will need physical care and supervision throughout their lives. Children with mild retardation are educated in the least restrictive alternatives (levels 5, 6, and 7) because it is believed they have the potential to become fully independent.

Similarly, the range of available instructional strategies for educating children who are profoundly retarded is extremely limited compared with what can be used successfully with children who are mildly retarded. Conditioning and repetition are the predominant instructional strategies for children with profound retardation. By contrast, techniques that can be used to teach children with mild retardation include direct instruction, modeling, education games, inquiry, programmed instruction, and peer tutoring. In short, just about all the techniques that can be used with nonretarded children can be used with children who are mildly retarded.

Children with Mild Retardation. Before we discuss strategies and instructional issues related to teaching children who are mildly retarded, remember that the long-range goals for these children should be *total normality* in behavior, appearance, and self-sufficiency. There is no reason these children cannot become independent, self-supporting citizens when they reach adulthood—provided, of course, that they receive appropriate education experiences.

A decade ago, the expectation for youngsters with mild retardation was not so optimistic, and many people believed that most of these youngsters could never be totally independent, contributing citizens. With these lowered expectations came constraints. During the 1960s, typical place-ment for children with mild retardation was the self-contained special class, with the youngsters taking recess and even lunch with only their own class and not with their normal peers. Virtually by definition, life goals, and therefore, teaching goals and strategies, were different for youngsters with retardation than for normal youngsters. The belief that these youngsters could *not* achieve became a self-fulfilling prophecy, and the youngsters did not achieve as well in special classes as had originally been hoped. The special classes provided social as well as academic isolation in many cases.

Typical placement a generation ago has now become atypical. Today, we believe that children who are mildly retarded can become self-supporting citizens, and we try to teach them accordingly. Most are educated in regular classes alongside their nonretarded peers, if not for their entire school day, at least for a good portion of it. Even some academic subjects may be taught in small groups that include both children who are retarded and their normal peers. Full integration is achieved in all nonacademic settings.

The cognitive and language domains are the areas in which teachers need to be most sensitive to the needs of children with mild retardation. You must structure the learning situation so that ambiguities are kept at a minimum. You should perform a specific task analysis of what you want a child to do, then arrange a carefully sequenced set of activities to help the youngster move slowly but positively toward each intermediate goal. Don't expect large logical leaps to understanding; save that expectation for the occasional child who is gifted. Be specific, be precise, be supportive—just as you would be with any child.

Youngsters with mild retardation *can* reach academic goals, although they may take longer to do so than their normal classmates (MacMillan, 1982). Therefore, because there are only so many hours per week available for instruction, you will need to be especially careful that what you choose to do in those few hours is directly related to *functional* goals. You should place maximum emphasis on functional achievement in areas that can help the youngsters become financially and socially independent adults. For example, once basic reading skills are obtained, you should stress reading for information, following directions, filling out applications, reading newspapers for information and employment, and the like, rather than trying to teach the finer aspects of literary criticism. Keep in mind, however, that you will have to work toward constructive use of leisure time, so reading for pleasure should not be overlooked.

Objectives and teaching strategies in the language domain should be aimed at helping youngsters achieve *functional* literacy. You should stress *basic communication,* both oral and written, with the goal that these youngsters can become independently functioning members of society. In writing, for example, you should concentrate on essential areas such as filling out forms and applications, and writing brief business letters. Friendly letters might be a second level of priority, creative essays or poems a distant third. Oral reports on narrow topics are not as critical as other forms of communication: telephone skills, job interviews, asking questions for information, and the like. Similarly, basic, everyday math should be taught so the youngsters can join the rest of the world in coping with checkbooks and tax forms. You should concentrate on utilitarian arithmetic and measurement concepts rather than more advanced mathematics.

Children with Moderate Retardation. The predominant educational placement for youngsters with moderate retardation is a special class within a regular school. In most cases, these children live at home and attend nearby public schools, much the same as their normal peers. Because most of these children are ambulatory, no special transportation is necessary. The range of appropriate educational objectives and teaching strategies, however, is more limited for these youngsters than it is for youngsters who are mildly retarded.

Youngsters with moderate retardation may spend some of their school day in special classes and some of their day with their normal peers. Opportunity for interaction should be planned; in fact, it is required by law. Certainly, such activities as recess and lunch will be with nonhandicapped

Full participation in recreational activities is as important for children who are retarded as it is for nonretarded children. (Courtesy of Association for Retarded Citizens.)

children. In addition, other nonacademic involvements such as physical education, the arts, assemblies, sports, and recreation can be provided without too much difficulty.

If you are a special class teacher of children who are moderately retarded, your job will be to teach *functional* skills in all the domains. You should strive to help these youngsters look and act as normal as possible, so that they can be accepted in society. Direct instruction should be devoted to such areas as good grooming, personal habits and hygiene, work habits, and social skills. Career training is a must; for adolescents you should focus upon the skills and work habits necessary to work successfully in sheltered workshops and, perhaps, to compete in the open job market. Sheltered workshops provide opportunities for young people with handicaps to learn good work skills and to earn wages in an environment that is accepting of their limitations. Eventually, some persons with moderate retardation may be able to secure jobs outside sheltered workshops; others will remain in sheltered workshops for their entire working lives.

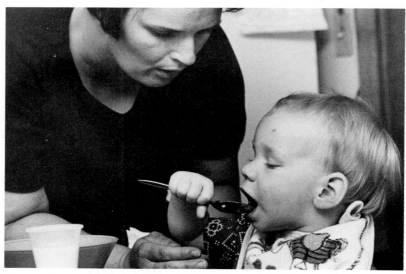

The teacher provides training in self-feeding to a child who is moderately mentally retarded. (Courtesy of Library of Congress.)

In teaching children with moderate retardation, you should always be concrete, direct, and repetitious. If your objective is to have a youngster be able to make beds, for example, you should give explicit instructions, using actual beds, and have the youngster practice with the kinds of beds he or she will be expected to make. Oral instructions on how to make beds or pictures of someone making beds will not suffice.

Children with Severe and Profound Retardation. Only a few years ago, 90 to 95 percent of this group would have lived in institutions and received only the little schooling available within the confines of the institution. P.L. 94–142 and other recent legislation and court rulings have changed all that. It is now the exception that youngsters with severe retardation are totally deprived of education or are educated entirely within the walls of a residential institution.

Although these youngsters almost always lived in very large public institutions in past years, their usual residence now is in small, community-based facilities if not in their own homes (see Box 8.6). Classes for youngsters with severe and pro-

found retardation (also called SPI—severely and profoundly impaired) may be found in most public school districts today, although small districts may band together to form cooperative arrangements for services because the number of SPI children in a single small district can be as few as one or two children. Often, these children must be transported in special vehicles that can accommodate wheelchairs. Such vehicles are staffed by a driver and an aide, who are responsible for carrying youngsters up and down flights of stairs and placing them safely in the vehicles. Classrooms for SPI youngsters usually include special toilet facilities. Indeed, a legitimate educational objective for SPI youngsters is control of bowels and bladder, as many are unable to control their bodily functions.

The primary objective for this group of youngsters is self-care, including rudimentary communication of their needs. The primary teaching strategies are repetition and simple conditioning. Establishment of routines is critical to allow good habit training to take place. With higher-functioning adults, it is reasonable to expect that they will be able to dress, feed, and toilet themselves properly and that they will benefit from simple

Training in vocational skills is critical for youths and adults with moderate retardation. (Photo by Stephen Coon. Courtesy of *Centre Daily Times.*)

work activities within a sheltered workshop. Individuals with profound retardation probably will not be so fortunate and will need close supervision and care throughout their lives. In both cases, though, there is ample evidence that they can make improvements through careful training procedures.

Technology and Computer-Assisted Instruction

A review of major special education journals indicates that technology and computer-assisted instruction (CAI) specifically designed for youngsters with retardation are just beginning to emerge. However, as R. D. Kneedler (1984) suggests, individuals who are retarded are benefiting from advances made in technology and CAI designed for individuals with other disabilities.

Technological devices used by people with communication disabilities are also appropriate for individuals whose communication skills are limited by the level of retardation or the presence of additional handicaps. Educators are advised to consider the reading, language, and spelling skills of the individual for whom the device is intended.

Self-help skills can also be monitored by technological devices that allow individuals with retardation to feed and bathe themselves.

The features of CAI make it ideal for use by learners who are retarded. Programs are patient and provide immediate feedback and reinforcement of student efforts. Programs include tutorials and drills to provide additional practice in targeted skills. M. A. Thomas (1981a) identifies a language training program for individuals with severe retardation. J. R. Seagrave and G. Seagrave (1982) and J. L. Terpenning (1982) developed reading programs suitable for individuals with mild retardation. Thomas (1981b) describes four programs developed for persons with mild or moderate retardation: time telling, coin identification, functional word recognition, and matching of sizes, shapes, and colors. Finally, computer video games have also expanded the recreational opportunities available to individuals with retardation.*

---

*R. A. Sedlak, M. Doyle, and P. J. Schloss (1982) describe programs in which individuals with retardation were taught to play video games.

BOX 8.6
A NINE-YEAR-OLD CHILD WRITES ABOUT MENTAL RETARDATION

This book report by a nine-year-old girl provides insight into her view of normalization. It also serves as an example of the use of literature as a means of making children sensitive to individual differences.

**Welcome Home, Jellybean
by Marlene Fanta Shyer**

This book is about a retarded girl, named Geraldine, and her family. Gerri, as Geraldine is called, comes home from the training center where she has spent her life of 13 years. Her mother is thrilled, but Gerri's father and brother Neil don't know *what* to think.

Why is Gerri coming home after 13 years? Because the training center finally got her toilet-trained, and Gerri's mother thought she should come home. So the family drove down to the training center to pick Gerri up. When they got there, the people at the training center were eating lunch. Neil and his parents tried to get a peek in the dining room. Well they did, and they saw rows and rows of people with big, white bibs and only a spoon and a plate of baby food in front of them. They waited a while, then decided to pack Gerri's things for her. When they got to her locker, Neil's mother exclaimed, "Where are her clothes? Where's her radio? Where are all her *things*?" And the attendant answered casually, "Oh, lots of things get stolen here." Then Neil's mother got very mad. I don't

blame her! How would you feel if your daughter had been living in this place for 13 years?

Well, this is just the beginning. Gerri learns, like she learns to say "sock" and what sounds like "shew" and also "bobbidge," which means garbage. Also, Gerri learns to eat solid foods.

And, Neil and his parents learn a few things about Gerri. She can be frustrating, which is why Neil's father moves away in one part of the story. She also has ways of letting the frustration out, like banging her head on the wall and pulling down curtains.

When Neil's dad moves away, Neil decides to stay home. But, something happens and Neil just *has* to go with his Dad. Neil gives a presentation at school and right in the middle Gerri ruins it. So the next morning Neil calls his dad and tells him to pick him up. Quick! But, as Neil was leaving, Gerri said something that made him want to stay. She said, "Neil." She had said his name! She had never ever said it before.

If I was Neil I think I would try to understand Gerri and help her to learn. But sometimes I would get very frustrated and wish that Gerri had never been born. But, even with the problems, I think it was best for Gerri to come home.

by Cathy, age 9

Source: *Welcome Home, Jellybean* by Marlene Fanta Shyer was published by Scholastic Book Services, a division of Scholastic Magazines, Inc., New York, in 1978.

SUMMARY

To be considered mentally retarded, a child must have (1) significantly subaverage general intellectual functioning and (2) deficits in adaptive behavior that are (3) manifested during the developmental period (birth to age eighteen). Subaverage intellectual functioning usually refers to general intellectual ability, especially as measured by an individually administered intelligence test such as the Stanford-Binet or the Wechsler scales. Adaptive behavior refers to the degree to which the individual meets the standards of personal independence and social responsibility expected of his or her age and cultural group.

Four levels of retardation are recognized: mild, moderate, severe, and profound. These four levels cover the same range of retardation as the levels often identified by the American public schools: educable, trainable, and severely or profoundly mentally retarded.

The largest group of individuals with retardation are those who are mildly retarded. The specific cause is not known in most cases of mild retardation. Most children with mild retardation can become independent adults if they receive adequate school programs. Often, their retardation is evident only in the school situation. More and more of these youngsters are being educated partially or totally in conventional education programs and settings.

Youngsters and adults with moderate retardation often fit the stereotypes of people who are retarded. They have lower intelligence (IQ of 35 to 55) and more physical problems. Most of them can become semi-independent, and institutionalization is seldom required. Usually, children with moderate retardation are educated in special classes and special settings.

Youngsters with severe retardation do not possess the adaptive behavior skills that would enable them to be independent or even semi-independent as adults. Their IQ levels of about 20 to 35 place them in the lowest 3 percent of the retarded population. The most severely handicapped of this group, especially those with medical problems, may be best served in an institution, preferably a small, community-based facility. Others may live at home or with several other adults with retardation in a group home.

People with profound retardation have very few adaptive behavior skills; either they are untestable or they test below 20 on general intelligence tests. Almost all of them have serious physical and medical problems. Their medical requirements, aberrant behavior, and lack of mobility usually dictate that their education and living arrangements be quite specialized. Very few of these youngsters are integrated into public school settings, although special arrangements are made for them by the public schools.

Four major sources are likely to identify individuals who are mentally retarded: parents, family doctors, public agencies, and teachers. However, only specialists, such as psychologists, social workers, and specialized physicians, after *full* examination of the child, can make the final diagnosis of retardation.

Given the wide range of behaviors exhibited by children with retardation, educational placement and teaching strategies are usually specific to the different levels of retardation. Generally, children who are more severely retarded are placed in special settings, and the range of alternate teaching strategies is limited. Children with moderate retardation are most frequently placed in special classes within regular schools and receive training in skills that will help them function on a semi-independent level in adulthood. Children with mild retardation have the greatest range of opportunities for educational placement, career options, and teaching strategies. Educational programs for these children are often more like those for the nonhandicapped than like those for any other level of retardation. Technological advances have improved communication and self-help skills, and CAI has promoted the development of academic and recreational skills.

Suggestions for Further Reading

Abroms, K. I., & Bennett, J. W. (Eds.). (1981). *Issues in genetics and exceptional children*. San Francisco: Jossey-Bass.
Genetics and the impact of genetic problems on children are presented succinctly in a highly readable but professional style by ten specialists in the field.

Batshaw, M. L., & Perret, Y. M. (1981). *Children with handicaps: A medical primer*. Baltimore, MD: Paul H. Brooks Publishing Company.
This book was written for nonmedical people who are interested in basic medical aspects of mental retardation and related disabilities.

Blackman, J. A. (Ed.). (1986). *Medical aspects of developmental disabilities in children birth to three* (2nd ed.). Iowa City, IA: University of Iowa Press.
This text summarizes health information useful to all professionals working with children with developmental disabilities. It highlights those aspects of a handicap that affect an individual's day-to-day functioning.

Drew, C. J., Logan, D. R., & Hardman, M. L. (1984). *Mental retardation: A life cycle approach* (3rd ed.). St. Louis, MO: Times Mirror/C. V. Mosby.
This is a comprehensive, readable introductory text to the field of mental retardation designed for professionals in psychology, educational psychology, special education, sociology, education, rehabilitation, and social work.

Grossman, H. J. (Ed.). (1983). *Classification in mental retardation*. Washington, DC: American Association on Mental Deficiency.

This book discusses the most widely accepted definition of mental retardation. The AAMD classification system is presented in detail, and many illustrations of various levels of adaptive behavior are given. A statistical reporting system is recommended with the purpose of standardizing the way in which mental retardation statistics are collected, maintained, and reported. A detailed glossary of terms related to mental retardation is included.

MacMillan, D. L. (1982). *Mental retardation in school and society* (2nd ed.). Boston: Little, Brown.

This text, which was designed primarily for educators, emphasizes classification, issues, trends, and child characteristics as they relate to problems in education of children with mental retardation.

Neisworth, J. T., & Smith, R. M. (Eds.). (1978). *Retardation: Issues, assessment, and intervention*. New York: McGraw-Hill.

Seventeen experts in various fields relating to mental retardation contributed chapters in this comprehensive text. Coverage includes literary perspectives, classification, sociological issues, learning, biology, identification, assessment, education, family, and residential placements.

Robinson, N., & Robinson, L. (1976). *The mentally retarded child: A psychological approach* (2nd ed.). New York: McGraw-Hill.

This edition continues the excellent and thorough coverage of virtually all aspects of mental retardation that made the 1965 edition a classic. The well-documented book deals with etiology, syndromes, services, theories, and problems of the mentally retarded from birth through adulthood.

Relevant Journals

American Journal of Mental Deficiency
Mental Retardation

These two journals published by the American Association on Mental Deficiency, Washington, DC, are sent to all members of the organization. *American Journal of Mental Deficiency* publishes exacting research articles on all aspects of mental retardation. *Mental Retardation,* the official journal of the association, publishes a wide range of articles dealing with issues in serving mentally retarded children and adults.

Education and Training of the Mentally Retarded

This journal is published four times a year by the Division on Mental Retardation, a subdivision of CEC, Reston, VA. It features data-based articles relevant to the education of persons with mental retardation.

CHAPTER 9

Learning Disability

Did You Know That . . .

- it took an act of Congress to define both the concept of learning disability and ways to determine whether or not a child has a learning disability?

- there is more controversy among experts in the field of learning disabilities than in any other field of special education?

- thirty-eight definitions of learning disability have been proposed?

- ninety-nine different characteristics of children with learning disabilities have been identified?

- no one teaching procedure or test is useful with all children who are learning disabled?

- people such as Tom Cruise, Susan Hampshire, Bruce Jenner, Woodrow Wilson, and Winston Churchill had learning disabilities?

- more boys than girls are identified as learning disabled?

You might think that the writing sample in Figure 9.1 is the product of a not-so-well coordinated six-year-old. In fact, it was written by a ten-year-old boy, Tom R. Tom is a sandy-haired, slightly freckled young man who comes from an upper-middle-class home. His parents are college educated, and there is no evidence that Tom has had any birth injuries or childhood diseases that would affect his writing. Unfortunately, Tom's reading is no better than his writing; he reads more like a six- or seven-year-old than a ten-year-old.

Is Tom mentally retarded? No. In fact, Tom excels in math reasoning and has scored in the 120 range on an individualized intelligence test. Is he emotionally unstable to the extent that a mental problem interferes with his reading? Well, maybe, but he is well liked by teachers and other children. His parents report that he gets along well with others and doesn't show any other symptoms of disturbance.

Tom is not mentally retarded. He is not emotionally disturbed. He is not physically handicapped. Tom is learning disabled.

Nancy, who is nine, seems to lack the ability to

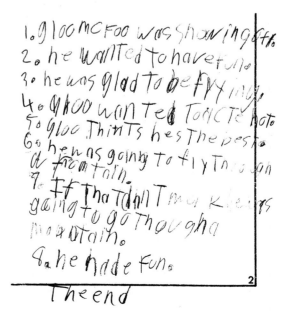

Figure 9.1. Sample of writing by a child with a learning disability.

concentrate on school work for more than a very few minutes. She is constantly on the move: out of her seat most of the time and frequently bothering other children. When she does concentrate, she fixates on relatively insignificant details, such as the border of a picture instead of the picture itself. She is very awkward on the playground. She neither throws nor catches balls with the accuracy and coordination of other girls her age. She often impulsively hits other children for no apparent reason.

Like Tom, Nancy is learning disabled. She is not doing well in certain academic areas in spite of the fact that she scores in the average range on individualized intelligence tests. This chapter introduces you to children like Nancy and Tom, children who have learning disabilities but who can't be lumped into specific categories.

THE DEFINITION PROBLEM

Learning disabilities have carried many labels. Among them are

> attention deficit disorder
> clumsy child syndrome
> perceptual handicap
> brain injury
> minimal brain dysfunction
> dyslexia
> dyslogic syndrome
> learning disorder
> educational handicap
> mild handicap
> neurological impairment
> hyperactivity
> hyperkinesis

Many more terms, both lay and professional, could be added. In 1972, William Cruikshank published a list of some forty terms that had been used to describe or refer to what is now usually called the child with specific learning disability. R. W. Vaughan and L. A. Hodges (1973) collected thirty-eight different definitions of the term *learning disability*. We will spare you all the various

definitions but will direct your attention to the one most commonly used.

In 1968, the National Advisory Committee on the Handicapped (NACH) studied the problem of learning disability and proposed a definition. This definition has been roundly criticized and nearly all learning disability specialists disagree with some parts of it. Nevertheless, the NACH definition, with slight variation, is now part of the federal laws governing the education of handicapped youngsters. Furthermore, the NACH definition or variations thereof is the definition used in the majority of state laws affecting education of the handicapped (Mercer, Forgnone, & Wolking, 1976). The NACH definition of **learning disability**, as it now appears in the federal regulations governing P.L. 94–142, is:

> "Specific learning disability" means a disorder in one or more of the basic psychological processes involved in understanding or in using language, spoken or written, which may manifest itself in an imperfect ability to listen, think, speak, read, write, spell, or to do mathematical calculations. The term includes such conditions as perceptual handicaps, brain injury, minimal brain dysfunction, dyslexia, and developmental aphasia. The term does not include children who have learning problems which are primarily the result of visual, hearing, or motor handicaps, of mental retardation, or emotional disturbance, or of environmental, cultural, or economic disadvantage.
> (U.S. Office of Education, 1977a, p. 42478)

As previously mentioned, many people have criticized this definition. For example, D. O. Hammill and colleagues (1981) identified three areas of concern. First, they believe use of the word *children* may suggest a learning disability that cannot be found among older students and adults. Second, they suggest that the inclusion of labels may be confusing and controversial. Finally, they note, the "exclusion clause" may imply that a learning disability cannot occur concomitantly with other handicapping conditions. While acknowledging problems with the federal definition, H. S. Adelman and L. Taylor (1986) also defend it on the basis that it has generated funds and facilitated personnel and program development so that a large number of youngsters with learning problems now have access to special assistance.

Other definitions have been proposed. For example, in 1981, representatives of six professional societies formed a joint committee and attempted to redefine learning disabilities. The new definition acknowledged the heterogeneity of the population, reintroduced the concept of minimal brain dysfunction, and minimized the effect of environmental factors (Kirk & Kirk, 1983; McLoughlin & Netick, 1983; Hammill et al., 1981). It is worded as follows:

> *Learning disabilities* is a generic term that refers to a heterogeneous group of disorders manifested by significant difficulties in the acquisition and use of listening, speaking, writing, reasoning, or mathematical abilities. These disorders are intrinsic to the individual and presumed to be due to central nervous system dysfunction. Even though a learning disability may occur concomitantly with other handicapping conditions (e.g., sensory impairment, mental retardation, social and emotional disturbance) or environmental influences (e.g., cultural differences, insufficient/inappropriate instruction, psychogenic factors), it is not the direct result of those conditions.

(Hammill et al., 1981, p. 336)

The controversy surrounding definitions, however, has had only a modest effect on the field, at least in terms of prevalent practices and state and federal regulations. Thus, the federal definition continues to be the most widely used and accepted definition.

CAUSES OF LEARNING DISABILITIES

Just as there are many labels and definitions for learning disabilities, there are many suspected causes, which can be classified into five general categories: biological, biochemical, maturational, genetic, and environmental.

Biological Causes. Despite the lack of conclusive evidence, brain injury has been cited frequently as a cause of learning disabilities. Other terms are used interchangeably with brain damage, such as minimal brain damage, minimal brain dysfunction, and minimal brain injury. In addition to the lack of objective evidence, subjective reactions to these labels mitigate against their use. These terms suggest to professionals and parents that intervention may be useless because the effects of brain injury are irreversible.

Biochemical Causes. The absence of proof of neurological damage has led some authorities to suspect a biochemical cause of learning disabilities. C. Hughes (1987) suggested that an imbalance in neurotransmitters may affect learning and behavior. Adelman and Taylor (1983) hypothesized that neural impulses are firing too rapidly to permit the brain to process incoming information.

There are two other possible biochemical causes. First, a metabolic deficiency may render the body unable to metabolize certain vitamins. Second, the body may have allergic reactions to certain foods or substances within foods. Both conditions may cause a chemical imbalance within the brain that decreases the ability to learn (Feingold, 1975; Weiss, 1982).

Genetic Causes. The prevalence of learning disabilities among relatives of children with learning disabilities has led many investigators to suspect a genetic link (Critchley, 1970; Halgren, 1950). For example, results of studies involving twins indicated that identical twins are more likely to experience reading problems than are fraternal twins (Hermann, 1959; Norrie, 1959).

A genetic cause of learning disabilities certainly warrants further investigation; however, we must remember how difficult it is to separate the contributions of heredity and environment to the development of an individual. As C. D. Mercer (1987) asked, "Does 'like father, like son' refer to the father sharing his genes or sharing his house with his son?" (p. 63).

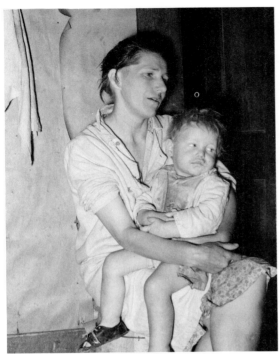

Environmental factors, including poor diet, smoking, and alcohol and drug abuse, are cited as contributors to the development of learning disabilities. (Courtesy of Library of Congress.)

Maturational Causes. Behavioral and learning features of children with learning disabilities frequently resemble characteristics displayed by younger nonhandicapped children. This had led some authorities to suspect that learning disabilities result from delays in the development of the neurological system (Goldstein & Myers, 1980), though the cause of the delay is not known.

Environmental Causes. Environmental factors are frequently cited as contributors to the development of learning disabilities. These factors include inadequate diet, radiation, fluorescent lighting, television tubes, smoking, and alcohol and drug use (Hardman, Drew, & Egan, 1987; Mercer, 1987). On a more surprising note, another environmental factor may be poor teaching: S. E. Englemann (1977) estimated that as many as 90 percent of all the students with learning disabilities were mistaught.

EXTENT OF THE PROBLEM

Estimates of the numbers or percentages of children with learning disabilities vary, largely because of different definitions of learning disability and different methods of screening and identifying children. According to J. J. Gallagher (1976), children who are truly learning disabled "are relatively rare, certainly less than one percent of the population" (p. 204). On the other hand, J. Tucker, L. J. Stevens, and J. E. Ysseldyke (1983) report that some estimates range as high as 20 percent of the school population. Estimates usually run in the 2 to 3 percent range. In 1976, federal regulations governing reimbursements to states for educating youngsters with learning disabilities placed a 2 percent "cap" on allocation of funds. That meant the federal government, in effect, estimated that only about 2 percent of the nation's youth at any one time were learning disabled to the extent that they required special services. In 1977, the cap was removed, and no specific percentage of federal funds is now set aside for the learning disabled. Enrollment figures for the 1985–86 school year released by the U.S. Office of Education indicate that of the 39,330,000 children in public schools, 1,843,964 were learning disabled. This accounts for 4.8 percent of all students and 44.74 percent of all students with disabilities. These percentages vary with state, as illustrated in Table 9.1.

M. M. Gerber (1984) has suggested that these high percentages are causing serious administrative concerns because of financial ramifications. These high, conflicting percentages are no doubt the result of the significant definitional and assessment problems plaguing the field of learning disabilities. The overlap between some youngsters with emotional disturbances and some youngsters with learning disabilities is so great that absolute diagnosis and classification are difficult, if not impossible. Similarly, there is an overlap between children who are low achievers and some children who are learning disabled, so that children in the former group are often misclassified as learning disabled. Sometimes, parents pressure school personnel to classify their children as learning

TABLE 9.1

ESTIMATED INCIDENCE OF LEARNING DISABILITIES IN TEN STATES

State	Number of Children with Learning Disabilities	Percentage of Children with Learning Disabilities*
California	211,861	25.41
Florida	64,463	39.44
Illinois	92,983	45.15
Maine	9,870	37.20
Maryland	44,424	50.97
Missouri	63,878	42.57
Minnesota	37,181	45.86
North Carolina	47,675	43.55
Oregon	25,045	60.66
Texas	153,268	54.31

Source: *Education of the Handicapped, 12,* 1–2.
*Based on special education enrollments of students ages three to twenty-one years for 1985–86 school year. In other words, 25.41 percent of all California children enrolled in special education were classified as having a learning disability.

disabled rather than retarded or disturbed. The reason? The classification "learning disabled" is much more socially acceptable.

As we have stated elsewhere in this book, definitions determine numbers of children with a problem. J. Lerner (1981), in discussing the numbers of children with learning disabilities, states: "The number of children identified as learning disabled is largely dependent upon the definition that one uses and the identification procedures one implements" (p. 16). In other words, if you use very specific and stringent criteria, you are less likely to identify a lot of children as learning disabled than if you used more loosely worded, less demanding criteria.

As you read through this chapter, keep in mind that specific learning disabilities can be quite severe and that underachievement is about the only universal characteristic of children with learning disabilities. We want you to view learning disability as a serious problem that should receive specialized attention. One may argue that blindness or deafness is more serious and debilitating to the child or that mental retardation is the most pervasive problem. To a child who has a severe learning disability, and to that child's parents, however, the problems are serious and frustrating.

Much additional research and attention must be given to this puzzling and difficult problem.

CHARACTERISTICS OF CHILDREN WITH LEARNING DISABILITIES

No one set of characteristics or behaviors will be found in all children who have been identified as learning disabled. Some children present patterns of disability primarily in the *cognitive* domain, with specific problems in reading, arithmetic, or even thinking. Others have problems in the *social* domain—relationships with others, self-concept, or inappropriate behaviors. Still others have problems in the *language* domain. They have trouble expressing themselves in oral or written form or processing language. Finally, many youngsters with learning disabilities show problems in the *motor* domain, in gross motor skills, in psychomotor or perceptual-motor skills, or in some combination thereof. Most commonly, clusters of characteristics occur in different children.

Certain characteristics grouped together may

BOX 9.1
WAYS TO RECOGNIZE A CHILD WHO IS LEARNING DISABLED

Children with learning disabilities may exhibit any combination of characteristics in the classroom that inhibit "learning efficiency." Such characteristics usually reflect some discrepancy between the child's age and the way he or she acts. Below are listed some examples.

Classroom Behavior

Moves constantly
Has difficulty beginning or completing tasks
Is often tardy or absent
Is generally quiet or withdrawn
Has difficulty with peer relationships
Is disorganized
Is easily distracted
Displays inconsistencies in behavior
Seems to misunderstand oral directions

Academic Symptoms

Reading
Loses place, repeats words
Does not read fluently
Confuses similar words and letters
Uses fingers to follow along
Does not read willingly

Arithmetic
Has difficulty associating number with symbol
Cannot remember math facts

Confuses columns and spacing
Has difficulty with story problems
Fails to comprehend math concepts

Spelling
Uses incorrect order of letters in words
Has difficulty associating correct sound with
  appropriate letter
Reverses letters and words (mirror image)

Writing
Cannot stay on line
Has difficulty copying from board or other source
Uses poor written expression for age
Is slow in completing written work
Uses cursive writing and printing in same
  assignment

Verbal

Hesitates often when speaking
Has poor verbal expression for age

Motor

Displays poor coordination
Has problems of balance
Confuses right and left
Lacks rhythm in movements, loses sequence
Has poor muscle strength for age

Source: *Today's Education,* Journal of the National Education Association, 1977, 66(4), 42.
Reprinted with permission.

form symptom clusters or syndromes. The symptom clusters are not arbitrary; they have emerged over the years through the observation and research of those who work closely with children. However, there are different ways of slicing the pie, so to speak, and specialists with differing orientations may prefer to organize their perceptions in different ways. For example, C. D. Mercer (1979) identifies six clusters or subgroups within

the domain of problems faced by all children with learning disabilities:

1. academic learning difficulties
2. language disorders
3. motor disorders
4. social-emotional problems
5. perceptual disorders
6. memory problems

L. A. Shepard, M. L. Smith, and C. P. Vojir (1983) reported that the label *learning disabled* (LD) in no way guarantees that characteristics of children so labeled will be similar to those suggested by Mercer. They also found, however, that "fewer than half the sample (of 800 LD children) had characteristics that are associated in federal law and professional literature with the definitions of learning disabilities" (p. 328). They concluded that "the label applied for the purpose of providing services cannot be assumed valid" (p. 328).

In the absence of clearly definitive research to the contrary, we believe it is useful to consider learning disability in relation to the four developmental domains that are used as an organizing vehicle throughout most of this text. The domains, in fact, are represented in the Mercer analysis and the Shepard et al. study. We will now relate those domains to the predominant characteristics associated with children who have specific learning disabilities.

Cognitive Domain

The 1977 federal definition of *specific learning disability* favors an academic/cognitive orientation. The first sentence of the definition refers to problems in the use of spoken or written language and problems in listening, thinking, reading, spelling, or doing mathematical calculations. The emphasis on academics reflects the belief that problems experienced by children with learning disabilities are largely academic ones and are not due to low intelligence.

As an example of a child who has a specific learning disability in the cognitive domain, consider Jane Y. Jane is ten years old and tests out in the normal intelligence range for ten-year-old girls, has had good schooling, and gets along well with her parents and peers. Her arithmetic reasoning is good, right at the beginning fifth-grade level. Her physical abilities and coordination are good, and she has an excellent fund of general information. Unfortunately, she cannot read, at least not at the level she should be reading. She can now understand a few sight words and has

learned enough tricks to get herself to exits and rest rooms. Overall, though, her reading is about what you'd expect of a beginning first grader.

Jane's case is a classic example of a specific learning disability. Reading problems are common among children with learning disabilities, so common, in fact, that reading disability is the only common thread linking the large majority of these children.

As we note in this chapter, assessment of children with learning disabilities and subsequent intervention strategies can be approached from different philosophies ranging from the atomistic behavioral style to the holistic, cognitive style. All approaches, however, acknowledge that reading generally is a problem for most children with severe learning disabilities. Mercer (1979) reports that most children with learning disabilities have reading problems and that the history of the field of learning disabilities was built around the common thread of reading problems. The term *dyslexia* is virtually synonymous with reading disability. As defined by T. H. Bryan and J. H. Bryan (1978), **dyslexia** is:

> a syndrome in which a child has unusual and persistent difficulty in learning the components of words and sentences, in integrating segments into words and sentences and in learning other kinds of representational systems, such as telling time, directions, and season. (p. 207)

Be warned, however, that, as is the case with learning disability, dyslexia comes in many forms. Children labeled as dyslexic are *not* all alike, so do not assume that dyslexia refers to a single unifying characteristic or a well-defined set of characteristics (White & Miller, 1983).

Reading problems are common and varied in the school-age range; don't assume that a child should carry the label *learning disabled* just because he or she is having some minor reading problems. A good rule of thumb is that a child who is reading one year or more below grade level should be referred to a reading specialist for evaluation.

Individual instruction in word recognition is essential for some children who are learning disabled. (Photo by Joseph Bodkin.)

Research in the area of mathematics is far less prevalent; however, existing data suggest some students with learning disabilities may display severe deficits in mathematics. D. Johnson and H. Myklebust (1967) indicated there might be two types of math disorders: an inability to process auditory and visual information and an inability to perform arithmetic calculations. Of course, reading difficulties may cause or compound these difficulties. A youngster who is unable to read the math problem in the first place will have a difficult time identifying the correct solution.

Other problems exhibited by children with learning disabilities include spelling, punctuation, and grammar. Poor handwriting also is common among children who are learning disabled, but this may be more a function of poor psychomotor skills than an academic problem.

Whether the problem is reading, arithmetic, or some other (less common) academic area, the critical dimension is the *discrepancy* between the area in question and both the other areas and the general intellectual level. If a child is doing poorly in *all* academics, has generally depressed language ability, and behaves more like a younger child, one might suspect a general, not specific, learning disability: mild mental retardation. If the problem is a serious one and is restricted to a single academic area, then it is more reasonable to suspect a specific learning disability. Academic retardation is the key: There is a discrepancy between what the child should be doing and what he or she is actually achieving.

Language Domain

Problems in both receptive and expressive language are often seen in children with learning disabilities. **Receptive language** is the ability to receive and understand language. **Expressive language** is the ability to express oneself verbally. A given child may have expressive language problems, receptive language problems, or both.

According to S. A. Kirk, J. J. McCarthy, and W. D. Kirk (1968), there are several aspects to the measurement of both receptive and expressive language problems. They have developed the Illinois Test of Psycholinguistic Abilities (ITPA) as a tool to help diagnose language problems. For example, one of the ITPA subtests is Auditory Reception, the ability to understand the spoken word in the form of questions. Children are asked to respond with a *yes* or *no* to such questions as "Do violins walk?" or "Do ponies shave?"

Another subtest is Auditory Sequential Memory, which tests the ability of the child to repeat digits when they are presented orally. The ITPA and related psycholinguistic approaches were widely used in the 1960s and early 1970s. However, critics have pointed out that additional research is required before tests such as the ITPA can be as useful as general intelligence tests such as the Stanford-Binet (see, e.g., Sedlak & Weener, 1973; Arter & Jenkins, 1979; Sternberg & Taylor, 1982).

Clearly, language problems significantly affect the functioning of a great many children. Consider for a moment that boy who almost never follows all your directions. You may say, "John, after you sharpen your pencil, finish your arithmetic problems. Then get out this week's spelling list and make a list of the words you misspelled."

Learning to follow directions is important for youngsters who are learning disabled. (Photo by Joseph Bodkin.)

John may sharpen his pencil and then do a variety of other things, not one of which is what you asked him to do. One response to this situation is to wring your hands and say "That boy simply *refuses* to do what I say. I know his hearing is good; he was tested just last month." Another possibility, however, is that the boy doesn't *understand* those directions, or that he is unable to remember the directions when they are given to him all at once.

Some specialists in the area of learning disabilities would prefer not to separate the language domain from the cognitive domain, arguing that language is a cognitive process, an argument that is undeniably true. However, we support studying language as a separate entity in order to give language disorders more visibility. This view is shared by the writers of the 1977 federal definition of learning disability.

Motor Domain

Motor problems—fine motor, gross motor, and perceptual motor skills—are quite commonly associated with specific learning disability. In the 1940s and 1950s, poor motor coordination, clum-

siness, awkward gait, and the like were taken as proof that a child had a brain injury. Classes for children who were brain-injured or those with minimal brain dysfunction were established to help children with motor problems. What was originally viewed as a unitary problem is now viewed as a multifaceted problem. According to D. K. McIntosh and L. M. Dunn (1973), specific learning disability "is not one unitary syndrome but rather an umbrella that covers a wide variety of children with many different learning problems" (p. 586).

General coordination problems are often reported in clinical studies and parent reports as characteristic of children with learning disabilities. Examples of problems in this gross motor area are delays in the development of such skills as crawling, walking, or throwing; or difficulty with smooth execution of such acts as throwing, skipping, or walking a balance beam. Some authorities (e.g., Barsch, 1976; Kephart, 1971) believe that following certain corrective exercise and movement routines would enhance not only motor development but academic learning as well.

Fine motor skills, such as drawing, writing, and using scissors, are often poorly developed in

Some youngsters who are learning disabled have eye-hand coordination problems. Tasks such as the one shown here (putting round pegs in round holes) give youngsters practice in this skill. (Photo by Joseph Bodkin.)

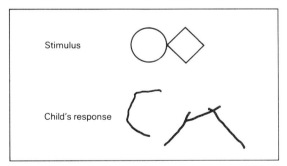

Figure 9.2 Example of design copying by a child with a perceptual-motor problem.

children with learning disabilities. Fine motor skills are highly related to **perceptual-motor skills**; in other words, children with learning disabilities often have great difficulties copying designs or tracing patterns—skills that require coordination between the hand and the eye. Figure 9.2 illustrates the work of a child who has a perceptual motor problem.

Working with children in the motor domain was prevalent through the 1960s and 1970s and even to the present day, presumably because the problems seem so apparent and crucial to traditional school functioning. Much of the evaluation and subsequent instruction in the area has been related to work carried out by Marianne Frostig. Her Developmental Test of Visual Perception and the programs that emanated from her tests have been widely used (Frostig & Horne, 1964; Frostig, Lefever, & Whittlesey, 1964). As is the case with the ITPA, however, there is little evidence for the effectiveness of this approach (Myers & Hammill, 1976; Reid & Hresko, 1981).

Social Domain

Two frequently reported characteristics of some children with learning disabilities are related to the social domain: emotional *lability* and *impulsivity*. **Lability**, the opposite of stability, refers to frequent abrupt changes in mood and temperament. **Impulsivity** refers to a lack of control over impulses. Some children with learning disabilities are likely to strike out at other persons or things with no provocation or to suddenly emit a sound at an inappropriate time.

Some experts include **hyperactivity** in the social domain, although others place it in the motor domain. Regardless of how it is categorized, hyperactivity continues to be a frequently cited characteristic of children who are learning disabled. Related characteristics include recklessness, low tolerance for frustration, aggressiveness, poor perception of social and interpersonal expectations, and inappropriate behavior.

C. D. Mercer (1981), W. H. Berdine and A. E. Blackhurst (1985), and D. P. Hallahan and J. M. Kauffman (1986) report the following as prevalent problems that affect some, though not necessarily all, children with learning disabilities:

dependency, insecurity
distractibility
perseveration (inappropriate repetition of
  behavior)
disruptive behaviors

withdrawal
hyperactivity
social perception problems
inconsistent behavior
irritability
antisocial behavior
poor self-concept
learned helplessness
external locus of control

R. Algozzine (1979) reviewed numerous studies and summarized the perceptions of children with learning disabilities by parents, teachers, and other children. His analysis is shown in Table 9.2.

IDENTIFICATION OF CHILDREN WITH LEARNING DISABILITIES

As there are many different definitions of learning disability, there are many philosophical orientations toward identifying and teaching children with learning disabilities. Obviously, if you believe that hyperactivity and perceptual-motor problems are the main characteristics of children who are learning disabled, you will want to use an evaluation procedure that identifies hyperactivity and/or perceptual-motor skills. If you believe that language problems are central to the identification of learning disabilities, you may use evaluation tools that assess the development of language skills. Thus, identification of children as learning disabled depends on which definition, orientation, and evaluation procedures are used. Furthermore, there are varying methods of teaching the children so identified.

The Federally Mandated Approach

Clearly, some consistency is needed to identify children who are learning disabled. And the massive increases in federal funds for special education that became available in the late 1970s (and

TABLE 9.2

PARENT, TEACHER, AND PEER PERCEPTIONS OF LEARNING DISABLED (LD) CHILDREN

Parent Perceptions of LD Children

Attempts to dominate peers	Less cooperative than siblings
Unable to receive affection	Has poor perseverance
Has poor impulse control	Inconsiderate of others
Anxious	Less tactful than siblings
Less able to organize than siblings	Has poor judgment

Teacher Perceptions of LD Children

Less able to cope with new situations than peers	Less socially acceptable to others than peers
Less accepting of responsibility than peers	Hyperactive
Angry and hostile	Has more problems with parents than peers do

Peer Perceptions of LD Children

Less popular/more rejected than other children	Worried and frightened
Does not have a good time	Not neat and clean
Not very good looking	Nobody pays much attention to him or her

Source: Adapted from R. Algozzine, "Social-Emotional Problems." In C. Mercer (ed.), *Children and Adolescents with Learning Disabilities.* Columbus, Ohio: Charles E. Merrill Publishing Co., 1979; used with permission.

that remained available through the 1980s) have made it imperative that commonalities in definitions and procedures across school districts and states be agreed upon.

After much study and debate, some procedures for evaluating specific learning disabilities were published in the Federal Register in December 1977. These procedures, coupled with the federal definition of learning disability, define a process that must be followed in evaluating children for specific learning disability. Failure to carry out this process would result in a violation of state and federal laws and could result in civil court action as well as loss of state and federal funds for education.

First, let's review the basic principles for evaluating all children with handicaps:

1. Tests and other evaluation materials must be given in the child's native language or other mode of communication.

2. No single procedure can be used as the *only* criterion for determining the appropriate education program for a child.

3. The evaluation must be conducted by a multidisciplinary team, including at least one teacher or other specialist who is knowledgeable in the area of suspected disability.

The following additional procedures are required in evaluating a child suspected of having a specific learning disability:

1. Additional team members. Each multidisciplinary team in addition to other members must include (a) the child's regular teacher, and (b) at least one person qualified to conduct individual diagnostic examinations (e.g., school psychologist, speech-language pathologist, or remedial reading teacher).

2. Criteria for determining the existence of a specific learning disability.
   (a) A multidisciplinary team may determine that a child has a specific learning disability if:
      (1) The child does not achieve commensurate with his or her age and ability levels in one or more of the areas listed below, when provided with learning experiences appropriate for the child's age and ability levels; and
      (2) The team finds that a child has a severe discrepancy between achieve-

ment and intellectual ability in one or more of the following areas:
      (i) Oral expression;
      (ii) Listening comprehension;
      (iii) Written expression;
      (iv) Basic reading skill;
      (v) Reading comprehension;
      (vi) Mathematics calculation; or
      (vii) Mathematics reasoning.
   (b) The team may not identify a child as having a specific learning disability if the severe discrepancy between ability and achievement is primarily the result of:
      (1) A visual, hearing, or motor handicap;
      (2) Mental retardation;
      (3) Emotional disturbance; or
      (4) Environmental, cultural, or economic disadvantage.

3. Observation.
   (a) At least one team member other than the child's regular teacher shall observe the child's academic performance in the regular classroom setting.
   (b) In the case of a child of less than school age or out of school, a team member shall observe the child in an environment appropriate for a child of that age.

4. Written report.
   (a) The team shall prepare a written report of the results of the evaluation.
   (b) The report must include a statement of:
      (1) Whether the child has a specific learning disability;
      (2) The basis for making the determination;
      (3) The relevant behavior noted during the observation of the child;
      (4) The relationship of that behavior to the child's academic functioning;
      (5) The educationally relevant medical findings, if any;
      (6) Whether there is a severe discrepancy between achievement and ability which is not correctable without special education and related services; and

(7) The determination of the team concerning the effects of environmental,
cultural, or economic disadvantage.

(c) Each team member shall certify in writing
whether the report reflects his or her conclusion. If it does not reflect his or her
conclusion, the team member must submit a separate statement presenting his or
her conclusions.

(U.S. Office of Education, 1977b, p. 65083)

The procedures listed above are thorough, and
most important, they assure fairness in the process. If the procedures are followed carefully, it is
extremely unlikely that a child will be mislabeled.

The Discrepancy Approach

Although the idea of discrepancies between actual
and potential achievement is not included in the
NACH or United States Office of Education
(USOE) definitions of learning disability, the **discrepancy approach** probably is one of the more
significant developments in recent years. It is included in the federal regulations for evaluations
of children. This approach compares the actual
performance of a particular child in each of the
various academic areas (e.g., reading, written
language) with the performance that might be
expected based on the child's mental age, chronological age, and instructional history. A discrepancy means that there is an unevenness or
divergence in a child's academic performance
compared with that child's intellectual potential.
For example, a ten-year-old child with normal
intelligence (say, 100 on the Stanford-Binet scale)
would be expected to achieve at approximately
the fifth-grade level, provided she or he had
no physical problems and had been exposed to
normal home and school environments. Though
different groups of children display different patterns of ability, and though there are differences
among children (interindividual differences) and
within children (intraindividual differences), as
Mercer (1979) stresses, it is the discrepancies in

classroom achievement that set children who are
learning disabled apart. This is the common
denominator.

TYPICAL PLACEMENTS FOR CHILDREN WITH LEARNING DISABILITIES

The predominant mode of placement for children
with learning disabilities is a resource room in
conjunction with regular class instruction. Most
children who are learning disabled spend part of
their time in a regular class and part of their time
in a resource room. In fewer cases, these children
are served by an itinerant teacher who visits a
particular child regularly. Somewhat less popular
than the resource room but considerably more
prevalent than the itinerant teacher is the special
class for children who are learning disabled. By
definition, the special class is less desirable than
the resource room because it is more restrictive,
and the child is not able to interact with peers in a
regular class setting. Special classes usually consist of the children with more severe academic
and/or behavior problems. Occasionally, children
who are disturbed are placed in classes that are
called learning disabled classes; in that case,
learning disabled is simply a euphemism, a more
socially acceptable label than *emotionally disturbed*.

The resource room teacher is required to be a
teacher of teachers as well as a teacher of children.
A prime role of the resource room teacher is to
consult with regular class teachers who have
youngsters with learning disabilities in their
classes. In many cases, the resource room and
regular teachers consult frequently and plan programs that cover both the resource room and
regular class (see Figure 9.3). Ideally, activities
that take place in the resource room reinforce and
amplify activities that occur in the regular class.
To be as effective as possible, a resource room
program depends on excellent cooperation between a child's regular teacher and the resource
room teacher.

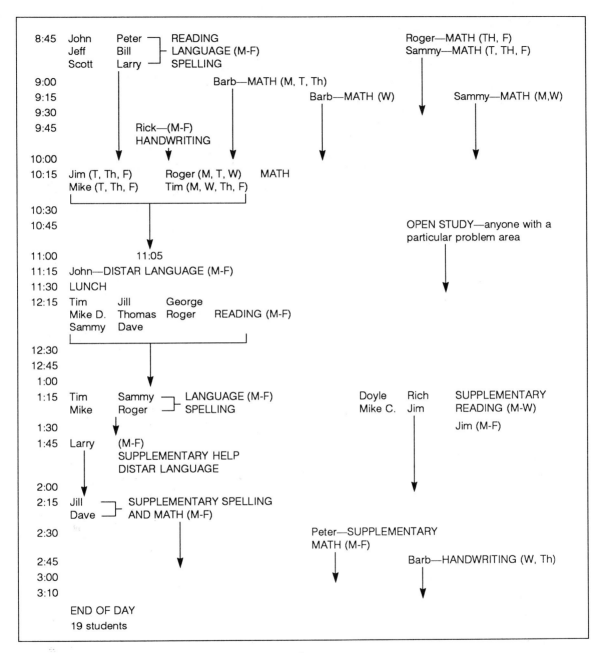

Figure 9.3. Example of schedule for resource room teacher.

Small-group instruction is as important for acquiring social skills as for acquiring academic skills. This resource room is an ideal setting for a teacher to work closely with a small group of children. (Photo by Joseph Bodkin.)

The resource room teacher may work individually with a given child on a daily basis to assist the child in doing work required in the regular class. In another case, the resource room teacher may work to extinguish certain undesirable behaviors that interfere with the child's success in the regular class. In still other cases, the resource room teacher may help children achieve basic skills (usually reading) that will help them be more successful in the regular class.

THE CONTROVERSY OVER EDUCATING CHILDREN WITH LEARNING DISABILITIES

No other area in special education is as full of controversy as learning disability. For more than twenty years, there have been seemingly endless discussions (shouting matches, in some cases) over such issues as whether children with learning disabilities have brain injuries, or whether their problems are largely perceptual. Some authorities argue that all children, including those who are retarded and disturbed, can have specific learning disabilities. Others argue that, by definition, children with learning disabilities have normal or above-average intelligence. There has been considerable debate over whether children with learning disabilities should receive training in basic processes, such as visual or auditory perception (the **process training** approach), or whether they should be trained in specific behavioral or academic skills (**skill training** or task analysis approach). Finally, some experts in the field maintain that learning disability is just a more socially acceptable term for underachievement than mental retardation or emotional disturbance.

There are two major reasons for the controversies. First, the field of educating children with learning disabilities is relatively new and thus has problems of definition. Second, because the field is relatively new, it does not have a strong empirical (research) base. In other words, there are a lot of opinions but not much research to back them up. We will not attempt to resolve the controversies, but we think you should know about them.

You will have to make up your own mind about which position(s) to take.

The major controversies concern:

1. intellectual level of children with learning disabilities

2. brain injury

3. perceptual-motor problems

4. process training versus skill training

5. underachievement

Intellectual Level of Children with Learning Disabilities

One controversy is whether children who are retarded may also have specific learning disabilities. Some experts maintain that children with learning disabilities must be of normal or better intelligence; children with an IQ lower than 75 are retarded, not learning disabled. This point of view stems in part from the NACH (and USOE) definition of learning disability as not *primarily* due to mental retardation or other handicaps. This notion is endorsed by some parent groups; psychologically, it is easier to accept the idea that your child is learning disabled (with a normal IQ) than to admit that the child is retarded or disturbed.

Samuel A. Kirk, long associated with the study of learning disabilities, clearly supports the notion of normal intelligence when he states that children with learning disabilities are "normal in sensory, emotional, and intellectual abilities" (Kirk, 1972, p. 68). He also differentiates between a child who is retarded and a child who is learning disabled in the following way: "The mentally retarded child is relatively retarded in all abilities, while the learning disabled child is retarded or defective in some abilities but relatively normal in other abilities" (Kirk, 1976, p. 260).

On the other hand, a "blue ribbon" committee of specialists in the area of learning disabilities, assembled to write a definitive paper on learning disabilities in conjunction with a large federally funded project, took a strong stance for the inclu-sion of all levels of intellect in the definition of learning disability. According to Cruickshank (1976b) "The committee members . . . stated that the term [learning disabled] refers to children at any age and noted that the problem is to be found in individuals of *all levels of intellectual capacity*" (p. 114). Cruickshank also stated that the exclusion of children with retardation from specialized teaching situations because of definitional problems "is an unnecessary tragedy, and the situation must be rectified quickly" (p. 106). Finally, speaking for the body of specialists that believes children who are retarded should not be excluded from the group of youngsters who can have learning disabilities, Cruickshank asserted that separation of children with mental retardation from children with learning disabilities on the basis of IQ is illogical; learning disabilities can be present in children and youth of any age and any intellectual level.

Brain Injury

A second area of controversy is whether children with learning disabilities have central nervous system dysfunction. As we mentioned earlier, it was assumed that the learning problems of the child with a learning disability were caused by brain injury. In recent years, however, that assumption has been replaced with the assumption of central nervous system dysfunction and not necessarily damage to brain tissue. In any case, the question of brain injury or central nervous system dysfunction is academic. Knowledge of such presumed causation does not help the classroom teacher instruct a child. Furthermore, state and federal regulations do not require proof of central nervous system dysfunction to diagnose or classify children with learning disabilities.

Cruickshank (1976b), an early researcher in the relationship between brain injury and learning problems, has modified his position somewhat: "I see absolutely no value in the term *minimal cerebral dysfunction*. . . . Furthermore, such terms as *hyperactive, hyperkinetic, organic,* and their counterparts—including *brain injured*—are

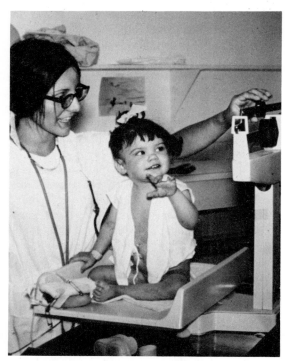

A normal child undergoing a routine medical examination. Examinations such as this are essential to identify any physical problems a child might have. Some children may exhibit no sensory or neurological problems but still have a learning disability. (Courtesy of the Department of Medical Photography, Children's Hospital, Columbus, Ohio.)

less than satisfactory and are characterizations for the most part, rather than being definitive of the problem per se" (p. 112).

Professor James J. Gallagher made extensive studies of children with brain injuries during the late 1950s and 1960s, concluding that trying to make a definitive decision of whether a child has a slight injury of the brain tissue is begging the question. The real issue for the educator is how to deal with a child who has a learning problem. Gallagher writes:

The concept of minimal brain injury for these children is *not* useful because of the difference between our concept of *disease* model and *disorder* model. In the disease model, useful in

some phases of medicine, the discovery of the cause of the disease is tantamount to discovery of the proper treatment. Discovery of the cause of measles brings forth a vaccine to cure measles. However, in a disorder model the cause does *not* relate directly to treatment, and learning disabled children represent a disorder in the same way that a hearing problem is a disorder. Therefore, discovering the physical cause of the problem, for example, brain injury, does not tell the educator what to do or how to do it. Such discoveries may be very important for eventual insight into brain structure and function, but the educator wants and needs an educational diagnosis stressing the *current* strengths and weaknesses the child may have in information processing. (Gallagher, 1976, p. 205. Used with permission.)

The quotation from Gallagher is important in two respects. First, it encapsulates what we believe to be the current predominant position on the relationship between brain injury and learning disability: The presence of a learning disability is not contingent upon an implicit or explicit diagnosis of brain injury. Second, it addresses the concept of the medical or disease model, which proposes treatment of a problem based on identification of the underlying cause of the problem. The medical model has not proved especially valuable in educating children with handicaps.

Federal regulations governing learning disability do not include brain injury as a cause of learning disability but indicate that learning disability might encompass brain injury. As reported by J. A. McLoughlin and A. Netick (1983), however, many people close to the field of learning disability insist that learning disability is a result of central nervous system dysfunction or brain injury.

Perceptual-Motor Problems

A third controversy centers on perceptual disorders. Some authorities (e.g., Cruickshank, 1976b) maintain that perceptual problems are the heart of the issue; that is, the learning problems of children who are learning disabled are the direct result of perceptual or perceptual-motor problems. This position is well represented in a definition that emerged from a federally funded project directed by Professor Nicholas Hobbs of Vanderbilt University. The extensive project, which covered all aspects of the classification of exceptional children, resulted in two volumes of commissioned papers and a third volume, *Futures of Children,* that analyzes the papers. The committee that dealt with the definition of specific learning disability proposed the following:

> *Specific learning disability,* as defined here, refers to those children of any age who demonstrate a substantial deficiency in a particular aspect of academic achievement because of perceptual or perceptual-motor handicaps, regardless of etiology or other contributing factors. The term *perceptual* as used here relates to those mental (neurological) processes through which the child acquires his basic alphabets of sounds and forms.
>
> (Wepman et al., 1975, p. 306)

Other learning disability experts do not attach such importance to the perceptual dimension (Haring & Bateman, 1977; Mercer, 1987; Wallace & McLoughlin, 1979). D. D. Hammill and N. R. Bartel (1978), for example, state that "a considerable and contrary body of research is steadily accumulating that strongly suggests that this [perceptual-motor] approach has little or possibly no educational value" (p. 342).

The United States Congress is permissive on the topic of perceptual problems; that is, a diagnosis of learning disability is not dependent on discovery of perceptual problems. P.L. 94–142 regulations indicate that the term *learning disability* includes, among others, "such conditions as perceptual handicaps, brain injury, minimal brain dysfunction. . . . " (U.S. Office of Education, 1977a, p. 42478). On the other hand, federal regulations do not require that evaluation of perceptual problems be made in determining whether a child should be identified as having a learning disability (U.S. Office of Education, 1977b).

Process Training Versus Skill Training

Some early leaders in the field of learning disabilities believed that specific learning disabilities were *not* peculiar manifestations of mental retardation or emotional disturbance, that learning disabilities presented a distinct problem, and that techniques designed for use with normal children or groups of children with other handicaps usually were not appropriate for children with learning disabilities. They believed that the observed learning disability was the result of a dysfunction in a basic ability or process, such as visual or auditory perception or perceptual-motor skills. In other words, a problem or dysfunction in a basic process such as visual perception inevitably would cause a problem in an academic area (e.g., reading) that was highly dependent on the basic process. The simplicity of this cause-effect approach was attractive to many; its relationship to the medical model gave it some additional credibility.

Proponents of this approach believed that clinical tests could be constructed to diagnose problems in the basic processes or abilities. Then programs could be developed to help children overcome or compensate for the problems in the basic processes and thereby overcome or alleviate their learning disabilities. This approach has become known as the process training (or ability) model. As an example of this approach, consider the work of S. A. Kirk, who conceptualized an approach to helping youngsters with learning disabilities. First, he designed a test to measure several problem areas related to information processing. The test, *Illinois Test of Psycholinguistic Abilities,* or ITPA (Kirk, McCarthy, & Kirk, 1968), had an immediate and prolonged effect on the diagnosis and education of children with learning disabilities (see the "Language Domain" section in this chapter). The next step was to develop for individual children specific programs based on the weakness in the processes measured by the ITPA. S. A. Kirk and W. D. Kirk (1971) and E. H. Minskoff, D. Wiseman, and J. G. Minskoff (1972) developed procedures for teaching chil-

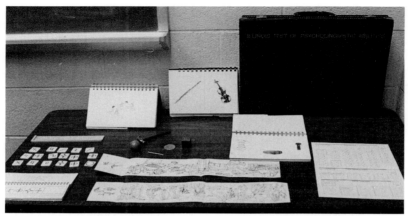

The Illinois Test of Psycholinguistic Abilities measures several aspects of language functioning. (Photo by Joseph Bodkin.)

dren (based on the ITPA model) that were directed at improving the basic processes or abilities evaluated by the tests. The basic process of auditory association, for example, would be enhanced by a program or materials that help a child organize and relate concepts presented orally. Similarly the *Marianne Frostig Developmental Test of Visual Perception* (Frostig, Lefever, & Whittlesey, 1964) was soon followed by the *Frostig Program for the Development of Visual Perception* (Frostig & Horne, 1964).

In strong contrast to process training is *skill training*. The skill training or task analysis model does not deny that basic abilities such as visual perception exist. Rather, proponents of the skill training mode assert that (1) it is difficult to obtain valid and reliable measures of the basic processes or abilities, and (2) it is not necessary to measure or train these hypothesized basic abilities in order to teach children with learning disabilities.

Advocates of the skill training method (e.g., Engelmann, 1969; Haring & Bateman, 1977; Hammill & Bartel, 1978; Stephens, 1970) go directly to the skill in question and do not speculate about the presence of an underlying process problem. The approach is quite behavioral; the specific academic behavior in question (e.g., inability to distinguish between *b* and *d*) is studied, and attempts are made to teach the child the specific skill, not to teach to the possible underlying process. (A detailed discussion of these direct instruction/task analysis methods is presented in Chapter 16).

The controversy between the process training model and the skill training model has been intense, especially during the 1970s, when numerous critical essays, research studies, and reviews were produced.* Skill training has emerged as the more popular approach and, in our judgment, has considerably more research evidence to support it.

Underachievement

The ambiguous definitions, along with variability in screening and assessment procedures, turn out to be beneficial to children but troublesome to the field of special education. The benefit to children is that children with mild problems are often identified as learning disabled. Once they are identified, they become eligible for extra help and special instruction. The troublesome part is that sometimes too many children are identified as learning disabled, and it becomes extremely costly to provide special services to all.

---

*For some lively reading, see, for example, Minskoff, 1975; Newcomer, Larsen, & Hammill, 1975; Ysseldyke & Salvia, 1974; Hammill & Larsen, 1974, 1978; Lund, Foster, & Mc-Call-Perez, 1978; Sedlak & Weener, 1973; Arter & Jenkins, 1979; Kavale, 1981; Sternberg & Taylor, 1982.

Some authorities maintain that we have not been able to define the characteristics of children with learning disabilities to the extent that identification of such children is accurate and reliable. Indeed, apparently the only characteristic common to children with learning disabilities is underachievement, and many other children have a similar problem (Ysseldyke et al., 1983; Ysseldyke & Algozzine, 1983). Louis Bates Ames (1983) reports that a large percentage of children referred to the Gesell Institute as learning disabled were underachieving (or placed at too high a level in school). J. McLeod (1983) suggested that the term *learning disability* be replaced with the concept of underachievement.

Other authorities, such as Cruickshank (1983) and H. R. Myklebust (1983), argue that the concept of a specific learning disability must be recognized and that the problem is much more complex than simple underachievement.

Once again, the concept of severity must be considered. It seems to us that very mild forms of learning disability are, in fact, indistinguishable from underachievement, mild emotional disturbance, or mild mental retardation. There is evidence, though, that with very severe cases of specific learning disability, we are dealing with a phenomenon that cannot be explained by the mechanism of simple underachievement.

If all these various definitions, approaches, and controversies seem confusing to you, be assured that you are not alone in your concern. There *are* definitional problems and disagreements that have not been resolved and may never be resolved to the satisfaction of everyone. However, the result of all the debate has, in fact, been the provision of *more* services for *more* children who need help.

Tactual stimulation by tracing figures is often used to teach numbers and letters to children who are learning disabled. (Photo by Joseph Bodkin.)

TEACHING CHILDREN WITH LEARNING DISABILITIES

As we have stressed many times, children must be treated as individuals, and an individualized approach to instruction must be employed. Just because a child is labeled learning disabled, there is no one technique you should automatically use. We have devoted an entire chapter, Chapter 16, to generic teaching methods—techniques that are not limited to one particular handicap but that can be used with individual children with many different handicapping conditions. Your own philosophical orientation toward learning disabilities will have a great influence on your choice of teaching strategies and techniques.

If your persuasion favors skill training, you probably will be particularly interested in learning about specific diagnostic and teaching techniques in the academic areas of reading and arithmetic. You might also wish to deal with study skills, memory, and attention problems. Numerous sources of information will give you rather precise instructions in how to deal with these problems. Chapter 16 presents information about direct instruction, the technique employed by most advocates of skill training. It is in the cognitive domain that skill training is most widely used (see particularly Haring & Bateman, 1977; Hammill & Bartel, 1978; Mercer, 1979; Wallace & McLoughlin, 1979; Stephens, 1970).

Those who favor the process approach will

Reading specialists and resource room teachers often work with youngsters who are learning disabled on a daily basis. (Photo by Joseph Bodkin.)

take comfort in the fact that numerous programs and techniques have been developed for problems in the motor and language domains. Much interest has been shown in the perceptual-motor process training area, largely stemming from the work of A. Strauss and H. Werner (1942) and Strauss and L. Lehtinen (1947). According to Mercer (1979), their work provides "the basic premise of the perceptual-motor orientation: motor learning is a prerequisite to higher order learning" (p. 273). Those favoring the motor learning aspect of perceptual-motor training include N. C. Kephart (1960), R. H. Barsch (1976), and B. Cratty (1969). The visual perception aspect of perceptual-motor training is represented by the works of G. Getman (1976), Frostig (1976), Frostig and D. Horne (1964), and B. Van Witsen (1979).

In the area of linguistic process training, the most well-known programs are based on the work of Kirk (see Kirk & Kirk, 1971; Minskoff, Wiseman, & Minskoff, 1972).

Given that the majority of youngsters with learning disabilities have reading problems, consideration should be given to finding ways other than reading to help these children acquire new

concepts and information. In some cases, techniques used for teaching visually impaired youngsters might be used. Obviously, these approaches will place much greater emphasis on a child's auditory skills. To many LD youth, the miniature cassette recorder is a constant companion and is used as a substitute for taking notes and reading. Often, volunteer agencies will make cassette recordings of assignments for learning disabled as well as blind children. Talking Books, a national agency, provides this service as well. The use of aurally presented materials at a faster-than-normal speech rate can be effective and is possible with an inexpensive compressed-speech device. B. J. D'Alonzo and S. H. Zucker (1982) report that by using this procedure, considerable time can be saved with no loss in comprehension.

Conversely, students with auditory reception problems might be well served through the use of approaches used with hearing impaired children. For example, S. S. Reilly and D. Barber-Smith (1982) obtained excellent results using captioned films with students who had learning disabilities.

Boxes 9.2 and 9.3 present suggestions for teaching students with learning disabilities. You may find them useful in your own classrooms.

BOX 9.2

WAYS TO TEACH STUDENTS WITH LEARNING DISABILITIES

The following suggestions are appropriate for students with *auditory* or *visual* problems:

- Seat such students in the front of the room.
- Have each of them work with a student buddy who can help them with directions and information they don't understand. Give written as well as oral directions for all assignments. You can give written directions on the chalkboard or on a calendar or in a course outline.

The following suggestions are appropriate for students with *auditory* problems:

- Use visuals—maps, slides, charts, pictures—with lectures.
- Summarize key points in each lesson in introducing and again in concluding the lesson.
- Give students a written outline for each unit of study.
- Help students with material they need to memorize by suggesting mnemonic devices.
- Use tapes for individual instruction and make tapes of your lectures that students can listen to.

The following suggestions are appropriate for students with *visual* and *visual-motor* problems:

- Use reading materials at appropriate grade levels.
- Allow such students to tape lectures, discussions, and directions rather than take notes.
- Give short written assignments.
- Give oral tests whenever appropriate.
- On written tests, provide a variety of test items: matching, multiple choice, short answer, true/false.

- Provide a variety of assignments: models, demonstrations, diagrams, tapes, slides, oral presentations.
- Give students copies of other students' classnotes.
- Give students brief written outlines of reading assignments.

Ways to Evaluate LD Students

Students can demonstrate what they've learned from a unit of study in many ways other than taking a typical test. They might—

- Make a transparency to illustrate an idea from the unit.
- Prepare a glossary of special words and their definitions from the unit.
- Draw a cartoon or cartoon strip expressing an idea from the unit.
- Adapt the information in the unit for a simple play or skit.
- Make a collage or a picture sequence related to the various ideas studied in the unit.
- Construct a bulletin board display.
- Write or tape a news commentary on a subject related to the unit.
- Interview someone who is knowledgeable about the topic under study and record the interview for presentation to the group.
- Keep a journal of new information learned in the unit each day.
- Prepare a research paper.
- Prepare a slide, filmstrip, or videotape presentation for the group.

Source: *Today's Education,* Journal of the National Education Association, 1977, 66(4), p. 48.
Reprinted with permission.

Holistic Approach. Over the past quarter century, specialists in learning disabilities have used a variety of approaches for educating children with specific learning disabilities. Regardless of the particular philosophy, the predominant mode has been to concentrate on very specific skills or behaviors, often the behaviors most in need of remediation. An alternative approach that has come to the fore in recent years has attracted a large number of advocates. This approach is referred to as a

BOX 9.3
WALKING THE LD TIGHTROPE

The excerpts that follow are taken from one of the most widely reprinted articles about learning disabilities. Corrine Bloomer, a former classroom teacher, presents information about learning disabilities that is relevant to classroom teachers in her article entitled "The LD Tightrope."

LD Children in the Classroom

Although the LD child's handicaps may be hidden, they can be extremely debilitating. The child doesn't learn many things by chance the way other children do. He or she needs to be specifically taught, and the regular classroom teacher is likely to have the major responsibility for the instruction.

Let's assume you have identified a child whom you feel is not learning as well as she or he should and who exhibits some of the characteristics [of learning disabled children.] . . . If possible, refer the child to the appropriate professional for an evaluation. This may be the psychologist and/or learning disability specialist. If "expert" help is not available or will be long in coming, don't wait. You can do a great deal to help the child learn.

It isn't always easy to isolate problem areas, but careful classroom observation can help you learn where the breakdown in the learning situation is occurring. If you *can* determine specific strengths and weaknesses, you will be better able to plan appropriate educational tasks. The following questions will serve as a guide:

1. Is the student able to concentrate *and* look *and* listen to gain information?
2. Does the student have difficulty or avoid responding orally or in writing?
3. Can he or she integrate, organize and remember information for use at a later time (process)?
4. Does noise, movement or visual stimuli distract the student?
5. Does the student learn best by doing, seeing or listening, or through a combination of the three?
6. Does the student fidget a great deal during certain learning situations? This might indicate anxiety about doing some tasks. Squinting or tilting of the head may indicate an eye problem.

Student attitudes also provide clues. The learner who is reluctant or refuses to try a task is really telling you that he or she can't cope with it or feels insecure about succeeding at it. Some students set expectations that are too high and become anxious about their performance in school. These may or may not be LD children. (*One symptom does not mean a child is learning disabled.*)

Classroom Aid

Once a classroom teacher has recognized a child's problems, with or without professional assistance, there is much that can be done. Some suggestions are:

cognitive or holistic approach to learning disabilities. It is exemplified in the work of D. K. Reid and W. P. Hresko (1981), who state that the holistic approach "is child-centered rather than curriculum-centered and . . . that complex skills cannot be dismembered into component parts and still retain their integrity" (p. 46). They also point out that "totally new teaching strategies are not required. A cognitive approach assumes only that

those we have developed will be used more effectively and that stress will be given to assisting the learning disabled in structuring their own approach to learning" (p. 51).

There is no dearth of programs and materials for teaching children with learning disabilities. Indeed, there is an enormous array of materials, ranging from complete curricula down to ditto exercises. Once again, keep in mind that no single

1. Teach the child through his or her strengths to provide successful learning experiences. If Johnny learns best by looking, include a visual component.
2. Bypass activities that require the child to use his or her deficit area in order to eliminate repeated failures. If Johnny can't write his work well, let him do it orally.
3. Work with deficit areas only after a pattern of success has been established.
4. Define and specify the concepts to be learned to eliminate possible confusion. Teaching a concept is different from teaching a skill. Relate new concepts to previous material whenever possible. For example, when you teach the silent "e" rule, relate it to other rules concerning silent vowels. Often the LD child cannot draw general conclusions.
5. Make the child aware of goals *and* their achievement. Point out what was achieved yesterday, what is achieved today and what can be achieved tomorrow. This gives a sense of success.
6. Establish clearly defined short-term goals that can be reached and that will foster progress and build self-confidence.
7. Provide immediate feedback on performance. Nothing is more defeating for a child than to have to redo papers from the previous day.
8. Use a positive approach to correction. Suggest the child find another or better answer rather than simply calling a response wrong.
9. If the child fails to make progress with a new approach or activity, drop it for the time being.
10. Do not try to teach something that the child can't or won't learn.
11. Select materials and techniques that have not been used before. Try starting one year below the child's present level.
12. Use concrete materials as much as possible.
13. Make learning fun by involving the child in games that allow him or her to move, feel, hear and see. A child who gets actively involved in the learning situation learns faster than a spectator to it.
14. Provide for seeming overlearning of skills. The LD child usually needs more exposure to an experience than other children.

We know that a significant number of tomorrow's adults are now so-called LD children. We also know that without help, children grow up taking their problems with them. Classroom teachers have been providing successful individualized instruction for years. They have made and are continuing to make dynamic and crucial contributions in educating LD children. There isn't time to wait for more research or clearer definitions. We can help them now.

program will solve the problem of how best to teach all children with learning disabilities.

Technology and Computer-Assisted Instruction

Technological advances promoting the education and treatment of children with learning disabilities have not emerged. This is not surprising, given that a learning disability does not affect communication skills or limit limb usage to the extent a physical disability does. On the other hand, many strides have been made in the development of computer-assisted instruction suitable for students with learning disabilities. R. D. Kneedler (1984) divided these programs into two categories: those that provide drill and practice and those that modify learning styles.

Drill and Practice Programs. Drill and practice programs address both reading and math skills. Programs such as *Cloze-Plus, Comprehension Power* (both by Milliken), and *Syllasearch* (produced by DLM) provide practice in letter and word recognition, vocabulary, and comprehension skills. Basic math skills are highlighted in commercially available programs such as *Math with Student Management Program* (produced by Radio Shack), *Academic Skill Builders in Math* (by DLM), *Basic Skills in Math* (by Love Publishing Company), and *Math Sequences* (by Milliken).

A third academic area that may be improved as a result of computer-assisted instruction is language arts, specifically, written composition. Many children with learning disabilities have an extremely difficult time producing compositions that are clear, concise, and well organized and that use correct grammar, spelling, and punctuation. Word-processing programs and equipment motivate students with learning disabilities to write. Editing is possible without the tedious process of recopying. Spell checkers circumvent difficulties with spelling (MacArthur & Shneiderman, 1986).

Learning Styles. The use of computers has the potential for altering the learning styles of children with learning disabilities by promoting active participation, maintaining attention, and enhancing problem-solving abilities (Kneedler, 1984).

Other Approaches

Other techniques for treating children with learning disabilities are not directly dependent upon teacher action; however, they typically require the teacher take the role of a monitor. These methods include special diets and drug and vitamin therapy.

The Feingold Diet (Feingold, 1975) is based on the premise that the presence of a learning disability is an allergic reaction to salyiclate, a natural or synthetic compound found in food colors and flavors. B. F. Feingold developed a diet that eliminates foods containing salyiclates. Although Feingold (1976) reported data documenting the favorable impact of this diet on youngsters

with learning disabilities, other authors have reported less favorable results (Kavale & Forness, 1983). Should a child in your class be placed on such a diet, you may be expected to monitor his or her eating habits.

It is also possible that a child with a learning disability may be placed on a drug therapy program that reduces or eliminates those behaviors that interfere with learning. This may be particularly true for children identified as displaying attention deficit disorders, or ADD (more commonly known as hyperactivity). Some of the drugs traditionally used are presented in Table 9.3. Side effects of these drugs are presented in Table 9.4. As a teacher of such a child, you may be expected to monitor behavior and report any changes to parents and medical personnel.

Finally, a child with a learning disability may be involved in megavitamin therapy. This involves massive doses of vitamins to minimize ADD and related learning problems. No empirical support for this approach, however, has appeared in the professional literature.

SUMMARY

Of all the problems that educators face in teaching youngsters with handicaps, learning disabilities are most puzzling. Specific learning disabilities as a category of handicap, or a label, is quite a recent phenomenon, dating only from the 1960s. Children with learning disabilities are difficult to teach, and the frustration that results is shared by both teacher and child. The characteristics of children with learning disabilities are so varied, and the disagreements among "experts" so pronounced, that it took an act of Congress merely to provide a common definition of the problem and to standardize procedures for evaluating these children. The regulations covering P.L. 94–142 define specific learning disability as "a disorder in one or more of the basic psychological processes involved in understanding or in using language, spoken or written, which may manifest itself in an imperfect ability to listen, think, speak, read,

TABLE 9.3

DRUGS COMMONLY USED TO TREAT LEARNING DISABILITIES

Generic Name	Trade Name	Classification
Methylphenidate	Ritalin	Stimulant
Amphetamine	Benzedrine	Stimulant
Dextroamphetamine	Dexedrine	Stimulant
Pemoline	Cyclert	Stimulant

Source: Gadow, 1986.

TABLE 9.4

SIDE EFFECTS OF STIMULANTS

Common	Rare	Rarer	Rarest
Insomnia	Drowsiness	Involuntary muscle movements	Hallucinations
Loss of appetite	Change in appearance		Psychosis
Headache			Seizure
Stomach ache			Increased blood pressure
Moodiness			Increased heart rate
Irritability			

Source: Gadow, 1986

write, spell, or to do mathematical calculations."

There is no such thing as a typical child with a learning disability. Some years ago, ninety-nine different characteristics of children with learning disabilities and thirty-eight different definitions of the term *learning disabled* were identified. Just about the only commonality among these children is that they all seem to have trouble in school. The trouble may be in cognitive areas, in behavior, in interactions with others, in language, or in motor learning.

Numerous tests and teaching techniques have been developed for youngsters with learning disabilities. Unfortunately, no one test or teaching strategy is useful with all such children. As with all youngsters, the best teaching is a combination of different materials, varied teaching techniques, and a trained, sensitive teacher.

Suggestions for Further Reading

Gadow, K. D. (1986). *Children on medication, Volume 1: Hyperactivity, learning disabilities, and mental retardation.* San Diego: College-Hill Press.
This is a well-written reference guide to the use of drugs with children.

Hammill, D., & Bartel, N. (1978). *Teaching children with learning and behavior problems.* Boston: Allyn and Bacon.
This book is a succinct, well-developed text that goes right to the heart of the issue of teaching: Eight of the nine chapters deal directly with how to teach children math, reading, spelling, and writing; how to manage classroom behaviors; and how to select educational materials and resources.

Lerner, J. W. (1981). *Learning disabilities* (3rd ed.). Boston: Houghton Mifflin.
Janet Lerner's fine book has become something of a classic. It is designed for specialists in related fields who want an overview of learning disabilities, as well as for regular

teachers who need information and understanding about children with learning disabilities in their classes.

Lovitt, T. C. (1982). *Because of my persistence, I've learned from my children.* Columbus, OH: Merrill.

Tom Lovitt is an experienced teacher who has spent a lot of time in school settings. More important, perhaps, he writes in such an engaging way that it really is hard to put this book down! He relays many anecdotes about the fun, and frustration, of working with children.

Mann, L. (1979). *On the trail of process.* New York: Grune and Stratton.

This scholarly work is subtitled *A Historical Perspective on Cognitive Processes and Their Training.* Much of the controversy in the field of learning disabilities deals with the issues of whether cognitive processes *can* be trained and, if so, *how* the training should occur. Professor Mann's book is an exhaustive treatise on this topic. He starts with the writings of the great philosophers, moves through the Middle Ages, and provides an extensive review of psychological and, to some extent, medical and sociological research up through the 1950s.

Mercer, C. D. (1987). *Students with learning disabilities* (3rd ed.). Columbus, OH: Merrill.

This comprehensive text balances theory with practice and is informative and relevant to the needs of both practitioners and parents.

Reid, D. K., & Hresko, W. P. (1981). *A cognitive approach to learning disabilities.* New York: McGraw-Hill.

The newer holistic approach to teaching children with learning disabilities is the subject of this comprehensive text. In many examples, traditional approaches are contrasted with cognitive and humanistic approaches.

Wiederholt, J. L. (1974). Historical perspectives on the education of the learning disabled. In L. Mann & D. A. Sabatino (Eds.), *The second review of special education.* Philadelphia: JSE Press.

Wiederholt's review of the development of the field of learning disabilities provides an ideal historical perspective. In some respects, he continues the "trail of process" started by Lester Mann. He has worked with, talked with, and interviewed the pioneers in the field. He traces the origins of the field to different sources in the nineteenth century and brings us up to the mid-1970s.

Relevant Journals

Academic Therapy
This journal is published five times per year by the DeWitt Reading Clinic. It contains many practical suggestions for teachers.

Learning Disability Quarterly
This is the official journal of the Division for Children with Learning Disabilities, a subdivision of CEC, Reston, VA. It includes review articles and reports of basic and applied research. It is published four times a year.

Journal of Learning Disabilities
This journal is published ten times a year by PRO-ED. It also features review articles and empirical reports.

Journal of Learning Disabilities, 1983, *16*(1).
The problem of defining learning disability is the ostensible focus of this special issue of the leading journal in the field. In reality, the issue goes far beyond definitions and reveals a great deal about the politics, problems, and opinions among the learning disability experts.

Learning Disabilities Focus and *Learning Disabilities Research*
These are both published twice a year by the Division of Learning Disabilities, a subdivision of CEC, Reston, VA. *LD Focus* translates research into practice.

CHAPTER 10

Emotional Disturbance

Did You Know That . . .

- there is deviant behavior in the repertoires of normal children and normal behavior in the repertoires of children who are disturbed?

- children displaying aggressive behavior patterns are less likely to experience good social adjustment and enjoy mental health as adults?

- similar deviant behaviors exhibited by different students are not necessarily caused by the same events?

- historical events originally producing a student's emotional problems may or may not influence that student's current emotional problems?

- children who are withdrawn are more likely to obtain and maintain employment and stay out of prisons and mental health facilities as adults?

- emotional maladjustments are seldom the result of an isolated traumatic event?

- parents can provide assistance to their children who are emotionally disturbed, without extensive training?

- more boys than girls are labeled "emotionally disturbed"?

What is it like to teach children who are emotionally disturbed? The introductory part of this chapter consists of a series of excerpts from a teacher's log that give you the feel of that experience (see Figure 10.1). The setting is a special class located in a regular elementary school. The eight children in the group have a variety of problems. The teacher is working on behavior control and academic skills so they can eventually be placed in a regular class, where they would be unable to function now. Notice that the teacher is very practical in approaching the child, Amy. She does not use theoretical explanations that have no direct implications for classroom management. Rather, she uses an approach that involves identifying and altering immediate events associated with the occurrence of disruptive behavior. She observes Amy's behavior, looking for patterns and counting instances of behaviors in her search for an approach that works. Once she settles on an approach, she monitors it, watching the effect on Amy's behavior and changing it when necessary to get desired results. Amy's behavior is similar to that exhibited by children labeled *emotionally disturbed.*

After reading part of Amy's story in the teacher's log excerpts, you should have a sense of the extraordinary consistency and degree of individualization required to teach a child with moderate to severe behavior problems.

THE NATURE OF THE PROBLEM

The federal definition of emotional disturbance provided in P.L. 94–142 (see Chapter 3) focuses on deficiencies in five areas. These include: (1) educational development, (2) social and interpersonal responses, (3) behavioral adjustment, (4) emotional adjustment, and (5) adjustment to school-related events. Despite these guidelines, specialists disagree considerably about definitions, classification schemes, causes, treatment, and the extent of the problem. They do not even agree on the use of the term *emotional disturbance.*

On one point there is agreement, however: Once you've seen a child with an emotional disorder, you know you've seen a child with a problem. Specialists may disagree about explanations and recommendations for treatment of the problem, but they do agree that *there is a problem.* As one writer put it, "Such children etch pictures on one's memory that are not quickly erased" (Kauffman, 1977, p. 15).

Labels and Definitions

Many labels are used as general terms for emotional and behavior problems. A study conducted by K. A. Kavale, S. R. Forness, and A. E. Alper (1986) highlights the diversity of labels. They examined 322 studies appearing in thirty-four journals and reported that thirty-one terms were used to label children who are emotionally disturbed. The following are the terms most frequently found in the professional literature:

emotionally disturbed
behavior disorders
socially maladjusted
emotionally handicapped
maladaptive behavior
psychologically disordered
character disorder
social deviant
delinquent

The two most commonly used terms are *emotionally disturbed* and *behavior disorders.* We will use the term *emotionally disturbed* in our discussions of this handicapping condition. The general problems with labels discussed in Chapter 3 apply in this case, and you should exercise caution in using them.

Descriptions of children labeled emotionally disturbed are usually not very positive. For example:

So many of our children have never before been a partner in a satisfying human relationship, they are unable, at first, to form personal relations of any kind.
(Bettelheim, 1950, p. 36)

The emotionally disturbed child is a socialization failure. Underlying all of the specialized terms and complex diagnostic labels used to describe him is the implication that his behavior, for whatever reason, is maladaptive according to the expectations of the society in which he lives.
(Hewett, 1968, p. 3)

Essentially, teachers have defined emotionally disturbed children as those who behave in ways that are considered harmful or inappropriate. The children do things that teachers want them to stop or, on the other hand, fail to do things that teachers think they ought. This would mean, of course, that *all* children are emotionally disturbed, and in a way that is true—all children do most of the things emotionally disturbed children do. The difference is that emotionally disturbed children exhibit behavior that goes to an extreme: they are too aggressive or too withdrawn, too loud or too quiet, too euphoric or too depressed. Furthermore, they exhibit these extreme behaviors over a long period of time, not just for a short while. In addition, disturbed children tend to exhibit behaviors in strange contexts—there is often nothing wrong with what they are doing, only with when and where they are doing it.
(Payne et al., 1983, p. 40)

Such children do indeed "etch pictures in one's memory." One of us still has vivid memories of emotionally disturbed children taught more than fifteen years ago:

I remember the nine-year-old from the slums of Chicago who lived in a residential treatment center for emotionally disturbed children. He did not speak. We worked together for months as I tried every technique I knew to elicit spoken language. Then, miraculously, one day he called to me across the parking lot as I was leaving, "You forgot your boots." I will always remember the frustration I felt,

Date: December 4
Amy and her mother visited for about
1/2 hr. this a.m. They will be moving
to town and she will enter my class.
I expect more information later. For
now, I know: IQ in TMR range, age 9
yrs-3 mons, several diagnostic
labels used in the past 7 yrs.--
including autistic. Her mother says
she's behaviorally disordered.

Date: January 3
Amy arrives tomorrow. Still no info.
from previous school. My plans for
the 1st day are to collect baseline
data. I expect her major problems to
be disrupting the class--will count #
of disruptions. Working definition
of disruption: any behavior that is
major and disturbs me or the other
children--hitting, pushing, throwing,
screaming, etc.

Date: January 4
What a day! The student teacher is in
shock--he's never seen a kid like
this! We won't survive any more
baseline days--need to begin intervention now. Amy had 58 major disruptions today. She hit, kicked,
choked, screamed, knocked over book-
cases, swore. When she wasn't
disrupting, she was rocking. There's
a clue. I can't use time out when
she disrupts or she'll rock. This
one will be a real challenge.

Date: January 5
Today was rough. I want to use myself as a positive reinforcer, so Pat
(aide) is going to be the restrainer.
Amy will not be allowed to rock--Pat
will restrain her. We're going to
shoot for less than 25 disruptions
per day as the initial goal. We'll
try to minimize restraining, but we
can't let her hurt other children.
Pat has instructions to step in
immediately if Amy is attacking
another child. 54 disruptions today.

Date: January 9
We're making some progress with Amy.
She had 30 disruptions today: General
plan--any major disruption is marked
on her chart. If less than 25 disruptions per day, Amy earns a star,
and 5 stars = a party for the class.
It's hard for me to remain positive
with her when she's tearing up the
place.

Date: January 15
I'm beginning to see a pattern in
Amy's behavior. So far I'm fairly
certain about two things: (1) Amy
performs well in a tutorial situation
with academic materials--she's on
task & responding appropriately to
1st grade level reading and math
lessons, (2) her behavior improves
as the week draws to a close.
Fridays are generally good days--
Mondays are ghastly!

Date: February 22
It's time for a change in strategy. I
need to be more positive with Amy,
but I've had several phone calls from
parents complaining about their
children being hurt by Amy--we've got
to keep working on that. We call it
a good day if she has less than 10
outbursts. The good days are few and
far between. 18 disruptions.

Date: February 28
We started the new "grand plan" today. Amy has a basket on her desk
with 6 plastic daisies in it. For
every disruption we take away one
daisy. If she has three daisies left
at the end of an hour, she gets to
swing. We're doing this 4 times a
day--4 one-hour blocks of time. In
4 hours today, she earned swinging
once--and it's only Wednesday.

Figure 10.1. Excerpts from the teacher's log.

Date: March 15
It's working with Amy! I think we got lucky in discovering swinging as a reinforcer--could it be that swinging is "socially acceptable" rocking? Amy earned swinging 3 of the 4 times today.

Date: March 30
A good day for Amy--only 3 disruptions today and she earned her swinging reward all 4 times. Also, we're making progress in academic areas. She can't benefit from group work yet but has made steady progress in one-to-one teaching situations. She may test in the TMR range, but I don't think she's retarded--at least not at the trainable level.

Date: April 17
Spring holidays set us back. I was right about a pattern--whenever there's an interruption (weekend, vacation, etc.) we can expect her 1st day back to be very difficult. On another note, I hear Amy's parents have an appt. at the Medical Center for a neurological exam. It's scheduled for 4/20.

Date: May 2
Received the report from the psychiatrist and the neurologist at the Medical Center today. They found no neurological damage but have changed her medication. I'm delighted to note that the dosage is being carefully monitored. She seems calmer, more in control, here these past few days.

Date: May 4
Amy's IEP Conference is scheduled next week. I feel confident about my part. I've documented her progress these past 4 mons. & feel I have realistic expectations for her next year. I expect the big problem will be in determining a placement. She still tests in the TMR range, but I don't think she belongs in a TMR class.

Date: May 9
Just as I expected, Amy's parents declined to sign off on the IEP. They are especially concerned about the TMR label. I agree. If I were called on for an opinion at a hearing, I'd have to say her behavioral problems are the primary problems. When we get her behavior under control, she can & does learn. We're having another meeting next week.

together with the joy. Joy because he had spoken at last. Frustration because there was no way of knowing what or who had finally broken through the shell of silence. Yes, these children are not easily forgotten.

As the label implies, emotionally disturbed children have a problem controlling their emotions. Their social development is not what is expected for their age; consequently, in situations in which certain social and/or emotional behaviors are required, they do not do well. They fall far short of expectations usually held for children their age.

Of the many definitions suggested for emotional disturbance, the following contains most of the important features from an educational standpoint as well as information about the severity of the problem:

Children with behavior disorders are those who chronically and markedly respond to their environment in socially unacceptable and/or personally unsatisfying ways but who can be taught more socially acceptable and personally gratifying behavior. Children with mild and moderate behavior disorders can be taught effectively with their normal peers (if their teachers receive appropriate consultative help) or in special resource or self-contained

BOX 10.1

NORMAL AND DISTURBED BEHAVIOR

The relationship between normal and disturbed behavior is striking. The following passage brings home more forcefully than many pages of well-reasoned text the dilemma we face when we try to differentiate between normal and disturbed behavior. Although some behaviors exhibited by children with emotional disturbance are so bizarre and unusual that we do not often find them in normal children, many behaviors are the same for the two groups.

Each of us contains the whole range of emotional health and disease within himself. Our nightmares, if they serve no other purpose, enable us to share the ways in which many psychotics experience life. . . . The sudden loss of temper nearly all of us have experienced gives momentary empathy with the feelings of uncontrollable rage, helplessness, confusion, guilt, and self-hate felt by the child with no impulse control. Most of us have shared a variety of neurotic symptoms: the terrifying fear of something that we know rationally should not in itself cause fear; the magical, protective cloak of knocking on wood, crossing fingers, counting to ten, holding our breath; the compulsive need to get one thing done, no matter how inane or how inconvenient, before we can do something else; the piece of work that can never be finished because it is never good enough. . . . Such illogical behavior does not mean that most of us are neurotic—only that some emotional disorder is as much a part of everyone's life as the common cold.

Source: Long, Morse, & Newman, 1976, p. 1. Used with permission.

classes with reasonable hope of quick reintegration with their normal peers. Children with severe and profound behavior disorders require intensive and prolonged intervention and must be taught at home or in special classes, special schools, or residential institutions.

(Kauffman, 1977, p. 23. Used with permission.)

There are, of course, difficulties with any definition. For instance, R. J. Whelan (1979) states that emotionally disturbed children are characterized by "behavior *excess* (that which children do too much of and shouldn't) and *deficit* (that which children should do more of but don't)" (p. 329). But how do you decide when a behavior is excessive or when there is a lack or a deficit in behavior? Let us look at some of the problems in describing emotional disturbance.

The Range and Variability of Normal Behavior. Part of the problem of defining emotional disturbance is the range and variability of normal behavior. There is deviant and unusual behavior in the repertoires of normal children, and normal behavior in the repertoires of disturbed children. The distinctions between normal and disturbed behavior are generally in *amount or degree rather than kind* (see Box 10.1). In other words, in many cases the behaviors are the same, but emotionally disturbed children perform them too often or too intensely or else not often enough or not intensely enough.

Of course, some behaviors go beyond anything considered normal. Such bizarre behaviors often involve self-stimulation behaviors and language problems. The case of Wanda, described in Box 10.2, will give you an idea of the strange behavior exhibited by some children who are emotionally disturbed.

Shifting Standards. We need standards to decide, in terms of behavior, how much is too much. In addition to intensity and frequency of behavior, it is important to know the *situation* and the *age* of the child. Behaviors that are appropriate in some

BOX 10.2
WANDA

Children who are emotionally disturbed are very different from each other and from normal children. Unlike mental retardation or hearing disability, for example, for which there are fairly standard descriptions and tests, emotional disturbance is dependent upon descriptions and interpretations of behavior. This description of Wanda lends insight into the complex problems of youngsters who are emotionally disturbed.

I was aware, of course, that emotionally disturbed children sometimes have wild fantasies, but I was not prepared for Wanda. Wanda was eleven years old when I met her. She had a tested IQ of about 160, but it didn't do her much good except, perhaps, to enrich her fantasy life. I was never able to find a topic of conversation, an area of the curriculum, a place, or a time that was free of her bizarre imaginings. She had fantasies about jeans—she "wore" special forty-pocket and hundred-pocket jeans with zippers in the front and drew stylized pictures of them. She had fantasies about the president and the governor and crucifixes and The Pit and the Pendulum, doctors, nurses, swimming pools, toilets, injections, physical examinations, Project Mercury (this was in 1962), moles (she had one on her arm that was a

microphone into which she talked and one on her leg that was a thermostat controlling her body temperature) . . . there was no end.

When she engaged in her fantasies, Wanda got a peculiar, fixed grin on her face, her eyes became glazed, she giggled, and she talked (often apparently to herself) in a high-pitched, squeaky voice. Frequently, she drew pictures with captions representing the fantasied objects and activities. Sometimes she engaged in other bizarre behaviors, such as flattening herself on the floor or wall, kissing it, caressing it, and talking to it. It was impossible to teach Wanda or to have a rational conversation with her while she was fantasizing, and she was "in" fantasy most of the time. It was impossible to predict when, during times of lucidity and reality-oriented behavior, she would suddenly enter her fantasy world again.

Mostly, Wanda had fantasies about buildings. She carried on conversations with them, and they took on human characteristics. Certain parts of buildings—doors, floors, windows, chimneys, porches, and the like—sometimes became separate entities with lives of their own. At other times, these parts of buildings were body parts to be physically examined, injected, or manipulated.

Source: Payne et al., 1983, pp. 36–37. Reprinted with permission.

situations are clearly out of order in others. If a person were being mugged, for example, the usually inappropriate behaviors of screaming, hitting, biting, kicking, and so on that could be mustered would be highly appropriate in self-defense. Or two-year-olds who hit because they have not yet learned other ways to make their anger known would not be considered to have nearly as serious a problem as ten-year-olds who know better but continue to handle social interactions by striking out and hitting when angry. The definition problem is complicated because the standards are somewhat vague to start with, and they are con-

stantly changing according to the situation and the age of the child.

Children who are emotionally disturbed are likely to display not just one but many different inappropriate behaviors and to display them frequently. To further complicate the situation, the behaviors may or may not be consistently displayed in similar situations. In some children, for example, a certain type of lesson, such as math, will almost always trigger an anxiety attack of fidgeting, inability to concentrate, confusion, and procrastination. In other children, the anxiety attack will sometimes happen with math lessons, sometimes not; it may also be related to other types of lessons, such as reading or spelling. The latter example is a more difficult situation for teachers to manage because the anxiety behaviors are not as predictable and the pattern is less obvious. One of the most frustrating problems in working with children who are emotionally disturbed is the *inconsistency* of their behavior.

Expectations of the Culture and Society. The principle of cultural relativity must be considered when deciding if a behavior is normal or disturbed. Whether or not the behavior is acceptable depends on the group norms or social situation; in other words, it is relative to the group. Behavior that is in tune with the standards or usual expectations of a particular social or cultural group is not considered abnormal—no matter how weird someone from outside the group might think it is! Over fifty years ago, Ruth Benedict (1934) described vividly the cultural relativity of behavior: "One of the most striking facts that emerge from a study of widely varying cultures is the ease with which our abnormals function in other cultures" (p. 90). She goes on to explain that it does not matter a great deal which type of abnormality we choose to illustrate this point; for whatever characteristic we choose, there are cultures in which these abnormals function at ease and without difficulty. No doubt you know that some of your own behaviors are appropriate in certain segments of society and out of bounds in others.

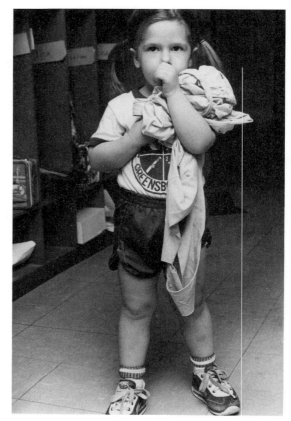

Age is an important factor in emotional disturbances. For example, thumb-sucking is a normal behavior for a two-year-old child; however, it is not an appropriate display in an adolescent. (Courtesy of Health and Human Services.)

The Measurement Problem. Emotional disturbance, or mental illness, might be defined as a lack of emotional or mental health. The problem with this approach is that there is no well-accepted definition of mental health; therefore, it is hard to describe its absence. No test yields an MHQ (mental health quotient), similar to the IQ, whereas with hearing and vision, and to some extent intelligence, accepted measuring instruments can identify those with problems. We simply do not have similar measuring devices for assessing the adequacy of emotions or personality.

The development of precise techniques for observing and recording behaviors may help solve the measurement problem. The work of applied behavior analysts who are carefully observing, documenting, and defining individuals' behaviors provides important technical procedures for all professionals. These techniques include, for example, keeping accurate records of exactly how many times a youngster screams or runs around the classroom, when such events occur, and under what circumstances. This information can often help pinpoint what precipitated the screaming or running. The techniques of describing behavior may be useful to professionals even if certain groups within the profession reject applied behavior analytic procedures as a treatment.

All children daydream and have occasional lapses of attention. Such behaviors are normal. (Courtesy of College of Human Development, Pennsylvania State University.)

Interrelationships Among Handicaps. The overlaps and interrelationships among problems were discussed in earlier chapters. As we have explained, it is possible to be handicapped in more than one way. Some children have been labeled both emotionally disturbed and mentally retarded; others have been called both emotionally disturbed and learning disabled; and so on. In some cases, different labels are used at different times. We can talk about the handicapping conditions separately in textbooks, but in dealing with real children, we have to deal with problems occurring at the same time. Obviously, the definition problem becomes even more pronounced when we recognize the interrelationships among handicapping conditions.

We have a "chicken-and-egg" dilemma. We don't know, for example, whether learning problems experienced by a child who is retarded were the cause of a failure to learn appropriate social and emotional behaviors. Perhaps the emotional disturbance disoriented the child's thinking so much that performance on an intelligence test was poor, leading to a label of mentally retarded. These are interesting problems for debate among professionals, but teachers are expected to deal with whatever behavior is presenting problems at the moment. In that respect, causation is not so relevant; knowing what will work to change behavior is more important.

Different Perspectives. Although this book is for educators, children with emotional disturbance are the concern of many other professionals as well. Police officers, various officers of the court, social workers, psychologists, medical doctors, therapists, and others also work with children who are emotionally disturbed. Each of these professionals tends to view the nature of the problem in terms of his or her own perspective—based on training, previous experience, and the service performed for the children and their families. For example, social workers are more likely to see the emotional problem within the context of the family and the school and to recommend treatment for the family as a social group. Medical doctors, on the other hand, are more likely than other professionals to view the problems in terms of illness or disease.

A number of different conceptual models are

Observation of children's behavior in natural settings such as classrooms provides important information about children's typical reactions. (Photo by Joseph Bodkin.)

used in explaining and treating emotional disturbance. Different philosophies or perspectives on the nature of the problem obviously lead to different opinions about causation, characteristics, treatment of emotional disturbance—and, of course, different definitions. Descriptions of various approaches to the problem are given later in this chapter.

Classification

Just as there are problems in defining emotional disturbance, there are complications when we try to put disturbed behavior into different categories. Most of the work in classifying disturbed behavior is based on research with adults and involves psychiatric nomenclature (manic-depressive, schizophrenic, and so on). These classification systems do not hold up well in consideration of problems experienced by children.

The emphasis has shifted over time (from the late 1950s and early 1960s to the present) from psychiatric to educational diagnosis and treatment. However, clinicians and psychiatrists continue to be interested in the problems of diagnosis and classification. Their most recent scheme is presented in the American Psychiatric Association's *Diagnostic and Statistical Manual of Mental Disorders,* Third Edition, published in 1980 (referred to as DSM-III). Disorders commonly found in children and adolescents are classified according to five major areas:

I. Intellectual
   Mental Retardation
II. Behavioral (overt)
   Attention Deficit Disorder
   Conduct Disorder
III. Emotional
   Anxiety Disorders of Childhood or
      Adolescence
   Other Disorders of Childhood or
      Adolescence
IV. Physical
   Eating Disorders
   Stereotyped Movement Disorders
   Other Disorders with Physical
      Manifestations

V. Developmental
    Pervasive Developmental Disorders
    Specific Developmental Disorders
(American Psychiatric Association, 1980, pp. 35–36)

The major problems that educators have with this approach, and with others used in psychiatry, is that the labels are not keyed to specific interventions; that is, the labels don't help teachers work more effectively with individual children.

Dimension Analysis. One approach that does seem to have merit is a dimensional classification system, now being investigated by several researchers. The dimension-analysis approach is especially important for teachers because the behaviors used to describe different types of disturbance are those typically seen in a classroom. Often, teachers use these behaviors as evidence of a problem when they screen out a child in their classroom for referral. Also, because many of these children will continue in regular classes, teachers need to learn to manage the inappropriate behaviors in the classroom situation.

G. Spivack, M. Swift, and J. Prewitt (1971) developed the Devereux Elementary School Behavior Rating Scale. From a list of more than 140 behaviors, 47 were identified that correlated with achievement and differentiated between normal and special populations. Statistical procedures that help researchers identify items that cluster together were used, and six syndromes of classroom behavior, three of which may be regarded as deviant, were identified.

One of the deviant syndromes identified is called the **underachieving syndrome.** Children who fit this pattern lack self-reliance and depend on the teacher for direction and motivation. They are unable to follow directions given in class and have difficulty deciding what to do when there is a choice between two or more things.

Another of the deviant syndromes is called the **irrepressible syndrome.** Irrepressible children are likely to be disrespectful or defiant. They may call the teacher names or treat the teacher as an equal, using first names or nicknames. They may

refuse to do what they are asked to do, with comments such as "I won't do it," or they may belittle the subject being taught, saying "Spelling is stupid." Usually, they break other rules in the classroom, too. At the same time, they are likely to be achieving at expected levels for their age.

Neither of these behavior syndromes presents insurmountable problems for the teacher; they are usually relatively easy to manage. You may even have displayed one or more of these behaviors yourself as you progressed through the elementary grades. According to the research, about 20 percent of the children in any classroom have one or more of the behaviors of the underachiever; another 15 percent present some of the behaviors of the irrepressible syndrome.

The final deviant syndrome, the **incorrigible syndrome,** describes children who are both underachievers and management problems. These children, estimated to be as many as 10 percent in a classroom, might present any or all of the following behaviors: blaming external circumstances when things don't go well (complaining that the teacher doesn't help enough or that the teacher never calls on them); irrelevant responding (telling exaggerated or untruthful stories, giving an answer that has nothing to do with the question, interrupting when the teacher is talking, or making irrelevant remarks during a classroom discussion); and creating classroom disturbances (poking, tormenting, or teasing classmates; interfering with the work of classmates; or participating in the talking or noisemaking of others). Finally, the incorrigible behavior syndrome includes inattentiveness and withdrawal from the ongoing classroom activities.

H. C. Quay (1975, 1979) and A. Von Isser, H. C. Quay, and C. T. Love (1980) identified four clusters of behaviors that seem to hang together and describe different types of disturbance on the basis of behavior ratings by teachers and parents and other information about children, including the children's responses to questionnaire items. The four clusters, or dimensions, are called: (1) conduct disorders, (2) personality disorders, (3) immaturity, and (4) socialized delinquency. Table 10.1 presents behavior traits and life

TABLE 10.1

SELECTED BEHAVIOR TRAITS AND LIFE HISTORY CHARACTERISTICS
OF FOUR DIMENSIONS OF DISORDERED BEHAVIOR

	Conduct-Disorder Dimension	Personality Disorder Dimension	Immaturity Dimension	Socialized Delinquency Dimension*
Behavior Traits	Disobedience Disruptiveness Fighting Destructiveness Temper tantrums Irresponsibility Impertinence Jealousy Signs of anger Bossiness Profanity Attention seeking Boisterousness	Feelings of inferiority Self-consciousness Social withdrawal Shyness Anxiety Crying Hypersensitivity Seldom smiles Chews fingernails Depression, chronic sadness	Preoccupation Short attention span Clumsiness Passivity Daydreaming Sluggishness Drowsiness Prefers younger playmates Masturbation Giggles Easily flustered Chews objects Picked on by others	My folks usually blame bad company for the trouble I get into. Before I do something, I try to consider how my friends will react to it. Most boys stay in school because the law says they have to. When a group of boys get together they are bound to get into trouble sooner or later. It is very important to have enough friends.
Life History Characteristics	Assaultivenesss Defiance of authority Inadequate guilt feelings Irritability Quarrelsomeness	Seclusive Shy Sensitive Worries Timid Has anxiety over own behavior	Habitually truant from school Unable to cope with complex world Incompetent, immature Not accepted by delinquent subgroups Engages in furtive stealing	Has bad companions Engages in gang activities Engages in cooperative stealing Habitually truant from school Accepted by delinquent subgroups Stays out late at night Strong allegiance to selected peers

Source: Adapted from Quay, 1972, pp. 10–15. Reprinted by permission.
*Behavior traits are not reported for this dimension; questionnaire responses are provided instead.

history characteristics for each of the four clusters of behaviors.

To be useful, behavior dimensions will have to be linked with different interventions. If researchers can demonstrate that different treatments are related to different behavior clusters, the classification system will be helpful for teachers; that is, identifying different types of disturbed behavior will indicate different special treatments. At this time, the work on dimensional analysis helps define the problem, but more research is needed before reliable matches of behavior and treatment emerge.

Severity of Behavior. Disturbed behavior can also be classified as mild, moderate, or severe. The behaviors of the child who is severely disturbed often are quite different from those exhibited by children with mild disturbance. One of the most helpful distinctions among degrees of emotional disturbance is based on who can effectively provide treatment. Children who are mildly or moderately disturbed have traditionally been described as having a neurosis. Generally, they can be managed by parents and teachers, with some special services provided by a mental-health specialist such as a clinical psychologist, counselor, or family therapist. There is usually no need to remove these children from their normal patterns of living at home and attending school during the day. Children who are severely or profoundly emotionally disturbed may be described as psychotic, schizophrenic, or autistic, and they often need intensive and prolonged specialized care. Frequently, they require the services of special teachers and are placed in special day schools or residential treatment centers, often for fairly long periods of time.

The social significance of severe behavior disorders may not be great, because the numbers are very low, but the personal significance for parents, teachers, and others who work closely with children with serious behavior disorders is profound. The teaching situation is often one-to-one. Frequently, fundamental skills of attention, language, and self-help must be taught, and teachers must deal continually with very difficult management problems. Box 10.3 describes the problems encountered by parents and school personnel dealing with a child who is severely disturbed.

Prevalence

All teachers—both special and regular educators, at preschool, elementary, and secondary levels—deal with behavior problems. No sharp line divides the persistent and pervasive problems of emotional disturbance from more transient behavior-management problems. This perplexing situation accounts in part for the widely varying estimates of the number of emotionally disturbed children. Some of the disagreements over definitions of emotional disturbance contribute to the variation in estimates.

Estimates of the prevalence of children with emotional disturbance, regardless of severity, range from less than 1 percent to as high as 30 percent. The Bureau of Education for the Handicapped has used an estimate of 2 percent for the past two decades. Teachers and other school personnel, on the other hand, identify from 20 percent to 30 percent of the school-aged population as exhibiting behavior problems (Rubin & Balow, 1978). Nearly twice as many males as females are identified as emotionally disturbed, although the ratio equalizes as they become adults (Kelly, Bullock, & Dykes, 1977). Table 10.2 presents enrollment figures for public school programs serving students with emotional disturbances in ten states. The variety of percentage rates underscores the difficulty professionals experience in identifying children with emotional disturbance.

Numbers of severely emotionally disturbed children are quite low. The U.S. General Accounting Office (1981) has reported data indicating that approximately 0.7 percent of all school-aged children in the country have been diagnosed as being seriously emotionally disturbed.

THE FOUR FUNCTIONAL DOMAINS

You might ask, "If we know that a child is emotionally disturbed, will we automatically know other characteristics of the child?" Not *automatically.* In general, we will know some other characteristics of the child, but each case must be considered separately because the existence of one condition is not a guarantee of other problems. Children who are emotionally disturbed are a heterogeneous group; they are not "cookie cutter" cases.

BOX 10.3

MARCY

Marcy is not a real child; this description is a composite portrait based on the recollections one of the authors has of working closely with youngsters who are autistic. This description illustrates the frustrations of parents and teachers trying to cope with a child who is seriously disturbed.

I had been teaching in a public school program for hearing impaired learners for two years prior to Marcy's enrollment. She was a beautiful 7-year-old child with blond hair and big blue eyes, but that's where her similarity to my other students ended. All of my training and experience did not completely prepare me for dealing with the special problems she presented.

I had been advised by the school psychologist that Marcy demonstrated "autistic-like" characteristics. She stared at lights, flapped her hands, constantly uttered the same pattern of meaningless speech sounds, had very poor eye contact, ignored everyone in her immediate surroundings, and did not respond to sound. Marcy was placed in my class with the hope that our Total Communication philosophy would provide her with an alternative form of communication.

The traditional curriculum to which my other students were exposed was out of the question for Marcy. She was not toilet trained, nor could she completely dress or feed herself. Her daily routine included training in self-help skills and developing a communication system. Teaching Marcy was diffi-cult, but we did have success using techniques such as shaping, task analysis, and lots of immediate reinforcement. As tough as my job was, I was fortunate in that an aide was assigned to Marcy full time.

Her parents did not have this luxury, however, and I really have to hand it to them. They had three other children to care for; yet they were so cooperative, attending all our meetings, offering suggestions for school programming, and following through on special programs. We found close communication between their home and the school enhanced the rate of Marcy's progress. In addition to meetings and phone calls, we had a notebook that Marcy carried in her backpack between home and school. Occasionally, the notes from her mother really made me appreciate the difficulty of living with a child who is so severely disturbed. One morning, her mother advised us that Marcy may be a little cranky due to a lack of sleep. Around three o'clock that morning, her parents heard movement in Marcy's bedroom and, upon investigation, discovered that she had soiled her bed and smeared the walls with fecal material. They made Marcy clean up the mess.

The next year, I moved to another city but still kept in contact with Marcy's parents. They had hired a college student majoring in special education to work with Marcy at home. They had also made arrangements for Marcy to stay at a residential facility every third weekend so that the family could have a "break" from the special stress they experience trying to raise Marcy.

Cognitive Development

One conclusion that can be reached easily from research reviews is that children who are disturbed, as a group, typically do not do as well in school as those who are not disturbed. They usually do not achieve academically at a level expected on the basis of either their mental or chronological age.

A look back at the descriptions of children who are emotionally disturbed and the characteristics used in the dimension-analysis classification provides a partial explanation for their academic problems. Often, their behavior in school situations is such that they do not take the opportunity to learn whatever is being presented. A child who is refusing to work, swearing at the teachers, knocking materials off other children's desks, and performing all sorts of inappropriate behaviors obviously is not a participant in in-

TABLE 10.2

ESTIMATED INCIDENCE OF EMOTIONAL DISTURBANCE IN TEN STATES

State	Number of Children with Emotional Disturbance	Percentage of Children with Emotional Disturbance*
California	9,182	2.44
Florida	17,937	10.98
Illinois	18,205	8.84
Maine	3,990	15.04
Maryland	3,704	4.25
Missouri	19,915	13.27
Minnesota	8,845	10.92
North Carolina	6,700	6.12
Oregon	2,143	5.19
Texas	20,702	7.34

Source: *Education of the Handicapped, 12,* 1–2.
*Based on special education enrollments of students ages three to twenty-one for 1985–86 school year.

struction. For some children, the pattern of failure in academic situations is so severe and long-standing that they do not have the skills to handle academic situations, and their only feasible reactions, so it seems, are to lash out in anger and frustration or to daydream and withdraw. Think how you would feel if you were expected to complete a worksheet of subtraction problems if you did not have the behavior control to pay attention to any task for longer than two or three minutes and knew nothing of the subtraction skills needed to complete the worksheet.

In order to break the failure patterns in these children, basic skills of sitting in a seat, concentrating on a task, completing a short assignment, and other tasks preparatory to the actual academic work of reading, spelling, and math are often needed. As was evident in the case of Amy, teachers must concentrate on getting the disruptive behavior under control *before* any academic work can be presented. Time that might have been spent on academic skill development is lost during efforts to bring behavior under acceptable control. It is important to remember that academic tasks can be mastered when instruction is appropriately sequenced and presented and attention is given to getting deviant behavior under control.

For some children who are emotionally disturbed, the content of the lessons presents problems. In the situations just described, the academic information was not getting through because something—such as disruptive behavior or inability to pay attention—was getting in the way. For other children, the content may get through, but the child may be unable to process it. For example, a child who has intense anxiety about animals may not be able to deal with any content involving animals. Other may "see" stimuli—letters, words, numbers—in strange and different ways, so their responses seem bizarre and inappropriate.

There are always exceptions, of course, but children who are mildly or moderately emotionally disturbed are not usually academically advanced. F. Stone and V. N. Rowley (1964) tested 116 students identified as mildly or moderately disturbed. Of these, 59 percent were academically disabled, 21 percent were functioning at grade level, and 29 percent were above grade level. J. M. Kauffman and colleagues (Kauffman, 1977) surveyed 99 children identified as mildly or moderately disturbed and found them lagging behind their normal peers by .7 years in reading, 1.6 years in spelling, and 1.7 years in arithmetic.

The situation is even more serious for children

Sitting in a chair and seeing a task through to its completion are essential steps in the development of academic skills. (Courtesy of College of Human Development, Pennsylvania State University.)

who are severely disturbed and who may not have any academic skills. In fact, the development of academic competence may not even be a priority for these children. Many display severe deficits in skills such as language, communication, self-help, and play, so those areas frequently become the focus of instruction.

Occasionally, we hear about a child with emotional disturbances who has an unusual talent. These rare cases usually involve children who are seriously disturbed, and the talents lie in one or two isolated areas. For example, there are cases on record of children with serious disturbances who have exceptional skills in memorizing music and playing the piano or who have photographic memories for scientific formulas or poetry. Unfortunately, these talents are of little help to the individual child because of the severity of the other problems.

Social and Emotional Development

Social and emotional characteristics are of primary concern in identifying and working with children who are emotionally disturbed. Children who are severely disturbed may be qualitatively different from other children because they frequently exhibit bizarre and inappropriate behaviors, such as repetitive motor behaviors, self-mutilation, and complete lack of eye contact, that are not found or are found to a lesser extent in youngsters who are mildly or moderately disturbed. The behaviors exhibited by the latter group, by contrast, are often no different from those exhibited by all children; they are simply more intense or severe and are chronic.

What are the long-term effects of inappropriate behaviors on the total development of the child? What happens when the child reaches adulthood? Again, there are exceptions, but it is highly probable that an aggressive child who is also a failure in school will have more of a problem as an adult than will a withdrawn child. Children described as conduct-disordered by Quay and as having the incorrigible syndrome by Spivack and his colleagues fit this pattern. Typically, children in these groups have significant rates of school failure. There are more males than females in this group. If they are to succeed as adults, both their aggressive, acting-out behavior and their achievement problems must be dealt with.

Other deviant patterns include withdrawn and immature behavior, which Quay and his colleagues referred to as personality disorders and immaturity problems. Just as a pattern of aggressive behavior and underachievement is a predictor of problems in adulthood for boys, a pattern of immature and withdrawn behavior together with school failure is predictive of poor adjustment in adulthood for girls. The problems related to withdrawn and immature behavior are not as obvious to society as are the problems of aggression, and treatment is not always considered as urgently. These individuals require special services to learn to manage their problems and may be treated by a physician or mental health specialist, but they

BOX 10.4
A TEACHER'S STORY

Eleanor Craig, a gifted teacher as well as an author, describes her first year of experiences teaching emotionally disturbed children in *P.S. Your Not Listening*. In the following excerpt from the book, she describes her first encounter with one of the two students who will form her class.

She asks Douglas to come in and find a chair. This is his reaction:

"Oh God!" he laughed and rocked on the floor. "Ideyah! Chayah! Ideyah! Chayah! Oh God, Oh God, what an accent! She can't even talk right. Ideyah! Chayah! Ha-ha-ha! Oh God, Oh God! You from Boston? You talk just like Kennedy!" He stood up at last. "Okay, I'll choose my chayah!" He picked up a chair and began to spin around, holding the chair out with one hand.

I headed toward him. "Put that chair down!" He twirled faster and faster. "Can't you see? Oh gosh, what a nut! What a nut! I am putting it down!" The chair shot out of his hand and slammed against the wall, leaving its impression on the cork bulletin board.

"Dizzy," he sank to the floor. "Dizzy, mmmm, dizzy," he murmured. I leaned against the wall, grateful for support. I'd had one student for ten minutes but already felt as if I'd been through a long and harrowing day. As I watched him roll on the floor, I thought of the meetings at which his problems had been described. Nothing had prepared me for this. (p. 2)

Soon the other child arrives. Ms. Craig describes the scene:

Kevin looked at neither of us. He sat rigidly with his hands folded in his lap and his head bent down. These boys had been described to me in psychological terms, but no one had suggested the incongruity of pairing so frail a child with such an overpowering classmate.

Douglas sat up now and looked at Kevin. "What's wrong with this teacher? She's retarded probably. Didn't even tell us to put our things away." He swung open the coat closet. "I'll take the first hanger. This is the other kid's." He stared at Kevin.

Kevin rose obediently, almost mechanically, and hung up his jacket. But with incredible speed, Douglas grabbed the jacket, darted across the room, and hurled it out the window. He turned to face us triumphantly. Kevin looked away. Infuriated that his victim did not react, Douglas was at his side before I could stop him. He shook Kevin's chair violently, succeeding in dumping him onto the floor. "Oh gosh, what a nut! Are you retarded or something? Get outta my seat." Kevin moved to another seat. His face was expressionless. (p. 4)

usually do not come to attention of the courts as aggressive children often do. Box 10.4 illustrates the contrasting behaviors between students who are aggressive and students who are withdrawn.

Communication Development

It is often difficult to distinguish between a social problem and a communication problem. The situation is more clear-cut for children who are seriously emotionally disturbed. In fact, their problems are considered serious because of their inability to communicate and their almost total lack of contact with the outside world. Children who are mildly or moderately disturbed, however, often communicate only too well—talking out in class, defying adults, swearing, verbally venting their emotions. Whether their excessive use of language to disrupt and control situations is a communication or a social problem may be of some interest in academic discussions, but it is irrelevant to the teacher—it is a problem that must be dealt with.

Motor Development

The discussion of motor development in children who are mildly retarded applies to children who are emotionally disturbed as well. The exception is that children who are seriously emotionally disturbed often have bizarre motor problems, such as rapidly flapping their hands or fingers, rocking, head banging, and intense rhythmic swaying. The motor behaviors of children who are mildly or moderately emotionally disturbed, however, are usually indistinguishable from the motor behaviors of normal children.

DIFFERING VIEWPOINTS ON DEFINITION AND TREATMENT

The Value of Variety

Many different approaches to the study and treatment of emotional disturbance are currently in use. Each approach has its advocates, who are often zealous in their commitment to a single point of view. The variety of approaches can cause some confusion and problems, especially for anyone who is relatively new to the field. As you read the following descriptions of different approaches, you will probably find that you are attracted to one more than others. We urge you to read carefully about those approaches that may seem less reasonable to you and to find what is unique about each, rather than searching for the one best method.

The Child Variance Project

The Child Variance Project, a major research project designed to bring some order out of the confusion surrounding the variety of theories and approaches being used to study and treat children with emotional disturbance (those at variance

with the norm) was conducted at the University of Michigan in the early 1970s (Rhodes & Tracy, 1972a, 1972b). The goal of the hundreds of specialists who participated was to examine models of disturbance and integrate and synthesize concepts about definitions, causation, and treatment. Researchers studied five schools of thought: psychodynamic, learning, ecological, biophysical, and sociological. W. C. Rhodes suggested that in finding general principles that can be used to anchor the mass of data, a certain amount of confusion occurs before order finally emerges.

> The profound insights which we owe to such giants as Pavlov, Freud, Durkheim, and others, have yielded a tremendous data pool, but have not yet eventuated in an organized, disciplined, integrated body of science. . . . If we look at the history of established sciences such as physics or biology, we might interpret this condition as an early phase in the development of behavioral science. It can be seen as a stage of fertile chaos, out of which a new, orderly system of thought will develop.
>
> (Rhodes & Tracy, 1972a, p. 13)

In the Child Variance Project, emotional disturbance was seen in three different ways: as disability, as deviance, or as alienation. *Disability* was defined as the absence of physical, intellectual, or moral competency—something was wrong with the person. *Deviance* described behavior that was noticeably different from usual expectations—something was different from the norm. Finally, *alienation* was defined as indifference or hostility in situations in which devotion or attachment had previously existed—something had been OK but went bad.

Our view of emotional disturbance makes a difference in the intervention we choose. If we view the child as disabled, the treatment would be basically biophysical and involve drugs, diet, vitamin therapy, and so forth. If we see disturbance as deviance, we would select educational treatments or psychotherapy. If we see the problem as alienation, education and psychotherapy would be used, but they would be directed to the social system rather than the individual (for example, including the family in therapy or changing the attitudes of others so that the deviant child would fit in better).

Let's turn our attention now to the descriptions of various approaches to defining and treating emotional disturbance. As you read, think about which approach you would use in a classroom situation to deal with children who are emotionally disturbed. The suggested readings at the end of the chapter will give you a more comprehensive look at the theories, interventions, and service delivery systems now in use.

The Biophysical Model

Several theories are clustered under the umbrella of the **biophysical model**. Two key ideas of this model are: (1) emotional disturbance is thought of as a physical disease, disorder, or dysfunction; and (2) the problem is viewed as being primarily within the person. Disordered behavior is thought to be caused by genetic factors, neurological damage, or biochemical problems. Opinions about the importance of the environment vary. Some theorists see biological deviations as *necessary* and *sufficient* factors in the cause of disturbance. Others argue that chemical or neurological problems are necessary, *but not sufficient,* conditions to cause the disorder. They are more interested in the role of environment, believing that environmental events may activate a predisposition to disturbance.

Causes. Theorists who belong to the biophysical group are primarily interested in genetic, developmental, arousal, neurological, and biochemical factors. Research is currently in process to determine more adequately whether emotional disturbances of various types can be inherited. There is mounting evidence, for example, that there is an inherited component in schizophrenia. But the jury is not in yet; the safest generalization at this time is that heredity alone cannot account for behavior problems.

Researchers are also studying major influences in the early development of the child that may cause problems at some future point in development. Disordered behavior might be caused by physiologically based delays in maturation during

Children who are severely disturbed spend much of their time in their own world. Communication, even eye contact, is often extremely difficult for them. (Photo by Jeff Albertson / Stock, Boston.)

infancy. For example, depending on the reaction of adults, abnormal patterns of sleep and respiration in the infant might lead to anxious or bizarre behavior later.

Arousal involves the child's natural ability to handle the level of stimulation present in the environment. Simply stated, we would say that some children's natural ability is, by coincidence, a good match for the level of stimulation in their environment, but for other children, the system may be somewhat out of balance. A placid infant may require either additional stimulation or a decrease in the level of stimulation in the environment.

Some researchers think that some seriously disturbed children use bizarre behaviors such as hand clapping, twirling, and head banging as biological "safety devices" to maintain internal balance; that is, they cannot handle too much stimulation, and the behaviors are defense mechanisms that help keep out additional input. Those researchers studying perceptual factors are looking at sensory changes that may be part of the disturbance. For example, disturbances in perception and thinking may be related to an inability to pay attention. Another group of researchers is studying neurological factors. They believe that for some children, unusual, bizarre behavior may result from a neurological dysfunction that puts the child in a different world from what we, on the outside, are able to perceive.

Other researchers are primarily interested in the chemical nature of interactions in the nervous system. It is reasonable to think that chemical processes play a role in learning and other types of behavioral change, but our knowledge of biochemical factors is very limited. An important example of success with biochemical factors is the hereditary disease phenylketonuria (PKU). The disease, characterized by severe mental retardation, is known to have a biochemical cause, and it can be treated by placing affected infants on a special diet. Other, less serious forms of emotional disturbance may also have a biophysical cause. For example, some investigators suspect minimal brain damage and allergies may cause hyperactive behavior. Others link depression and fatigue to nutritional deprivation, diabetes, hypoglycemia, and lead poisoning (Morse & Smith, 1980). With additional research, we can expect other success stories in the diagnosis and treatment of emotional problems.

Though our discussion of biologically based causes of emotional problems is necessarily very brief, one point stands out: Those who believe in the biophysical model and are now at work in research laboratories may very well make major breakthroughs in understanding and treating mental illness in the next decade.

Assessment. The purpose of assessment within the biophysical model is to identify any physical abnormalities that may hinder the child's development. Assessment is typically conducted by medical personnel including pediatricians, nutritionists, allergists, and ophthalmologists. The educator's participation is limited because he or she typically does not possess advanced medical skills. A teacher usually serves as a screening and referral agent, which requires finely tuned observation skills.

Intervention. The primary goal of intervention is to maintain or restore the health of the individual, thereby facilitating both the development of appropriate social behavior and the ability to learn. Limitations in medical knowledge may make a complete "cure" impossible; therefore, proponents of the biophysical model seek to provide the best possible compensation. Unfortunately, these compensatory techniques demand medical supervision and thus are of limited value to classroom teachers in managing the behavior of children in school situations. However, if a physician has prescribed drugs or special diets, teachers are often expected to administer them and/or monitor their effects on behavior. Sometimes, children experience side effects, such as sleepiness or sluggishness, that must be managed in the classroom.

Psychopharmacology, or drug therapy, is sometimes used with children for whom neurological factors are suspected causes of emotional disturbance. Basically, two types of drugs are used in the treatment of hyperactivity: amphetamines and tranquilizers. Tranquilizers have been used for many years with adult psychiatric patients; amphetamines are typically used with children. Some researchers have provided evidence that amphetamines such as Ritalin can reduce hyperactive behavior in children, but others disagree. There are heated debates over the value of drug therapy. Those opposed point to problems in the design of research that supposedly shows the effectiveness of the drug therapy. They also complain that physicians usually do not provide the careful supervision and follow-up that are neces-

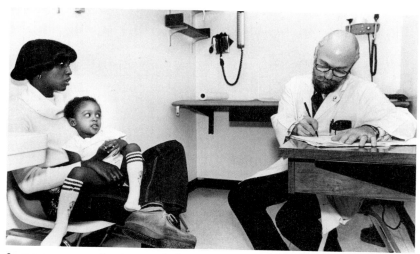

In some cases, medication may help gain control of a child's behavior. Medication levels must be prescribed and monitored by physicians. (Photo courtesy of the Department of Medical Photography, Children's Hospital, Columbus, Ohio.)

sary for effective use of drugs. Recent studies have shown that children may be receiving much more of a drug than is necessary to control their hyperactivity. Others are concerned that hyperactivity is not a homogeneous characteristic and cannot be routinely treated as such. Ethical issues must also be considered. There is concern that medication is being used to control children and promote conformity in the classroom. Another concern is that drug therapy may get at symptoms but not at the "deeply rooted" cause of the problem. For your information, Table 10.3 lists some of the more prevalent drugs used to treat children who are emotionally disturbed. Side effects of these drugs are also included.

Other interventions depend on orthomolecular therapy and nutrition. Orthomolecular psychiatry is based on the assumption that in cases of disordered behavior, bodily substances, especially those in the brain, are not at optimum levels. To treat the disorders, the biochemical balance in the body must be restored—usually by administering the needed substance. Again, this treatment is under the jurisdiction of physicians, with teachers providing information on any behavioral side effects that might be present in the classroom.

Other interventions include Feingold's (1975) diet, in which certain foods and food additives are eliminated from the diet of hyperactive children, and megavitamin therapy, in which individuals are treated with massive doses of vitamins. Neither procedure has generated strong research support thus far, but more work is under way.

The Behavioral Approach

The **behavioral approach** includes a collection of learning and behavior theories that are grouped together because of a common belief that a functional relationship exists between behavior and environmental events. The theorists believe that behavior is learned, whether it is normal or abnormal. Simply put, they reason that because abnormal behavior is learned, it can be unlearned.

Causes. Behavioral theorists study the connection between stimulus and response events. These theorists may differ, however, in their perceptions of the *process* by which the connection between the stimulus and response develops.

Most of you have probably heard of Pavlov's dog in a basic psychology course. Pavlov belongs

TABLE 10.3
DRUGS TO TREAT EMOTIONAL DISTURBANCE

Trade Name	Generic Name	Disorder	Side Effects
Ritalin	Methylphenidate	Conduct disorders Hyperactivity	Insomnia Reduced appetite
Elavil	Amitriptyline	Depression	Drowsiness Dry mouth Nausea Reduced appetite
Haldol	Haloperidol	Schizophrenia in young children	Drowsiness Nausea Slurred speech Ataxia
Mellaril	Thioridazine	Seizure disorders Hyperactivity	Initial drowsiness Phototoxicity Dizziness Irritability Enuresis
Thorazine	Chlorpromazine	Schizophrenia in school-age children	Initial drowsiness Dry mouth Weight increase Apathy

Sources: Cullinan, Epstein, & Lloyd, 1983; Gadow, 1986.

to a group of behaviorists who study **classical conditioning**. Their work is important to an understanding of emotional disturbance, especially neuroses. Just as Pavlov's dog was conditioned to salivate at the sound of the bell, people can be conditioned to be afraid of previously neutral stimuli. A famous example of how this can occur is the story of Albert, a young boy who was conditioned to fear a white rat. Originally, the child had no fear of the animal, but he did respond fearfully to a loud sound. Through continuous pairing of the loud sound (which elicited the fear) and the white rat (at first a neutral object), the child came to fear the white rat. Later, the loud sound was removed completely, but the child still displayed fear of the white rat. It took only seven pairings for Albert to show fear of the rat when it was presented alone. Furthermore, the fear generalized to other similar objects—a rabbit, a dog, a fur coat, cotton, and a Santa Claus mask. Even more interesting is that the fear occurred in different experimental situations. One of the recommended treatments for ridding Albert of his fear was reconditioning by presenting a pleasant stimulus together with the feared object so that gradually the feared object came to be associated with pleasure rather than fear.

Another group of behavioral theorists believe that people acquire new responses by observing and imitating the behavior of others, of models. In this view, people can learn new behaviors without having performed them and without receiving reinforcement. A. Bandura (1969) reported the effects of **modeling** on the development of aggressive behavior in children. Bandura's thinking suggests that abnormal behaviors may be learned by imitating the abnormal behaviors of others. His research is frequently cited in explanations of the behavior of street gangs and in criticism of aggression and violence on television.

Still another group of behavioral theorists are those who view **reinforcement** as the key concept. E. L. Thorndike is considered the father of reinforcement theory, but the reinforcement theorist best known to readers is probably B. F. Skinner (1953, 1974). Operant behaviors are responses that may not be related to any particular stimulus. Rather, a reinforcer is functional in the acquisition, maintenance, and strengthening of behaviors. Anything can be a reinforcer; we know whether or not something has functioned as a reinforcer by observing its effects on the behavior of interest. Most people think verbal praise is a reinforcer. Is it? Only if it has the effect of strengthening a behavior when given after the behavior.

The strength of a response is thought to increase with reinforcement and decrease without reinforcement. **Positive reinforcement** refers to the increased probability of a response resulting from the application, or giving, of a reinforcer. In **negative reinforcement**, removal of something unpleasant strengthens the response. Suppose a teacher knows a child dislikes oral reading. The teacher might set up a contingency specifying that whenever the child reads a page orally with two or fewer errors, there will be no further reading required that day. If the error rate goes down, signifying an improvement in oral reading, we would say that the opportunity to be released from any more oral reading functioned as a negative reinforcer. In either case—giving something pleasant or allowing escape from something unpleasant— reinforcement is at work *if* behavior improves.

Working from a behavioral perspective, T. C. Lovitt (1982) suggested six reasons for disturbed behavior:

1. poor reinforcement history
2. limited repertory of acceptable behavior
3. frustrated—can't achieve
4. poor models
5. distrust
6. upset or depressed for long periods of time

Lovitt argued that looking at these causes is relevant because they point to factors that can be remedied or removed. Although a diligent search for causes is often not very practical or productive, consideration of Lovitt's six reasons may lead to identification of a cause that leads to a cure. Lovitt suggests that no single cause can be traced for a problem behavior, but he believes one reason may set off inappropriate behavior and then other reasons may maintain or strengthen it.

Assessment. Unlike the biophysical approach, the behavioral approach does allow the teacher to be extensively involved in the assessment process. The teacher must be thoroughly familiar with the situation and able to identify, observe, and measure critical variables in the school setting. First, the teacher clearly describes the behavior under consideration. Is it excessive? Is it deficient? How often does it occur? Second, the teacher describes all aspects of the environment including events preceding and following the behavior, other people and things associated with the behavior, and probable reinforcers. Finally, the teacher describes the learner in terms of reinforcement history and any assets the child may possess that would be helpful in changing behavior (Morse & Smith, 1980).

Interventions. Perhaps the intervention most frequently associated with the behavioral approach is **behavior modification**. Actually, this term is extremely misleading. As P. A. Alberto and A. E. Troutman (1986) point out, a number of techniques may be responsible for a change in a student's behavior, including hypnosis, drugs, and psychotherapy. However, none of these techniques involves the careful application of behavioral principles to change behavior systematically. A more precise term is **applied behavior analysis**, which has been defined as "the process of applying sometimes tentative principles of behavior to the improvement of specific behaviors, and simultaneously evaluating whether or not any changes noted are indeed attributable to the process of application" (Baer, Wolf, & Risley, 1968, p. 91).

There are essentially two types of behavioral interventions: those based on **operant conditioning** and the use of reinforcement and those based

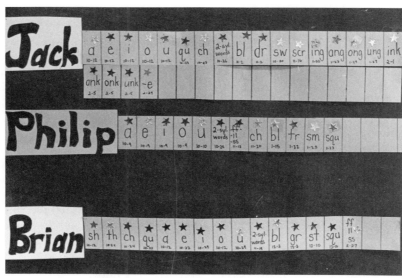

The boys' teacher believes that both competitive games and stars are positive reinforcers. Therefore, each boy's chart is added to when a new sound is mastered. (Photo by Joseph Bodkin.)

on classical conditioning techniques that involve breaking the stimulus-response bond or forming a new one. Learning theorists are described as "forever optimists" because they believe that "most human behavior is learned behavior, and learning occurs because of environmental contingencies. If one can identify the behavior and the contingencies supporting the behavior, one can change the behavior. Therefore, most maladaptive behavior can be changed into adaptive behavior" (Russ, 1972, p. 173).

Behaviorists are not much concerned with conditions within the individual. Rather, they look for ways to manipulate the environment so that new and appropriate behaviors are learned, and inappropriate behaviors are extinguished or unlearned. They emphasize the "ABCs" of behavior problems. *A* is for the *antecedents* of the behavior, the events that come before the actual behavior. Antecedents are thought of as cues, as the things that set off the behavior. *B* is for the *behavior itself*. Behaviorists are concerned with describing it precisely so there can be no doubt about whether it has occurred. *C* is for the *conse-*

quences, the events that follow the behavior and are thought to reinforce it. These ABCs are used to explain both the development of inappropriate behavior and behavior change: setting up antecedents as cues for the desired behavior, carefully describing the target behavior, and monitoring to be sure that consequences are functioning as they should.

A study of truancy intervention with three adolescents (Schloss, Kane, & Miller, 1981) illustrates these principles. An intervention program was designed based on the researchers' assessment of the positive and negative consequences associated with staying at home and going to school, respectively. The behavior of interest was defined as self-initiated school attendance. The consequences of attendance were identified based on the assessment of the positive factors related to going to school (shop classes, art classes, and athletics) and the negative factors related to staying home (home interventionist visited home with schoolwork if the youngster was ill or escorted him or her back to school or worked with parent to use prearranged sanctions if the young-

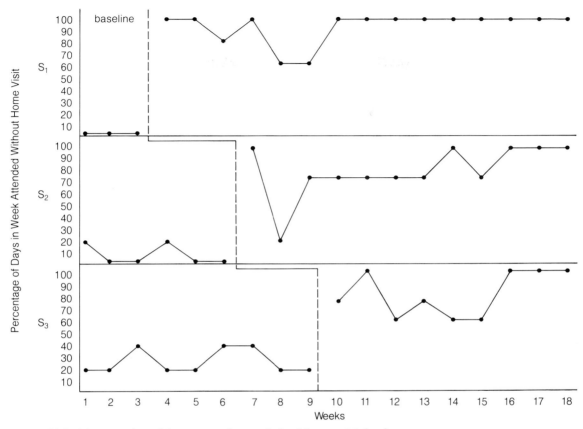

Figure 10.2. Mean number of days per week attended, without a visit by the home interventionist, across baseline and treatment conditions for three subjects. (From Schloss, P. J., Kane, M. S., and Miller, S. "Truancy Intervention with Behavior Disordered Adolescents." *Journal of the Council for Children with Behavioral Disorders,* 1981, 6, pp. 175–179. Reprinted with permission.)

ster was truant). The graphs in Figure 10.2 present the results. Note that after a flurry of visits by the home interventionist for each youngster (five for one, ten for another, and eight for the third), attendance improved and was at the 100 percent level for the rest of the year.

An important side effect of applied behavior analysis is worth noting. Using a functional analysis of behavior makes people more aware of various ways behaviors can be taught and controlled, often leading them to a critical examination of, and sometimes changes in, their practices. Teachers may, for example, discover that their practices

have been reinforcing inappropriate behaviors in their students. Parents may discover they have been "teaching" their children to misbehave by paying attention to (and thereby reinforcing) misbehavior.

One educational program for emotionally disturbed children that uses applied behavior analysis as a tool to develop various educational goals is the "engineered classroom" (Hewett, 1968). This method is summarized as follows: "A child can make progress in learning if a suitable education *task* provides meaningful, appropriate *rewards* in an environment which provides the

BOX 10.5
USING APPLIED BEHAVIOR ANALYSIS IN THE CLASSROOM

Applied behavior analysis has proven to be a very effective method of helping youngsters deal with problem behaviors. This box presents the techniques of applied behavior analysis quite clearly.

An interesting demonstration of the use of behavior modification to manage a case of severe separation anxiety can be seen in a 1975 case study of a preschool child, the essential aspects of which are summarized below.

A four-year-old girl was placed in a preschool with a strong behavioral program because during the previous year in another program, her behavior had consisted of "chronic crying, screaming, sobbing, and withdrawal" when her mother left. The tantrum behavior persisted even with vigorous attempts to redirect her to program activities.

The plan was to eliminate the undesirable behaviors with as little distress as possible for the child. The researchers devised a procedure based on the principle of stimulus fading. What they wanted to do was to contrive (set up) a special situation in which the child would not have tantrums and then gradually to return to the real-life situation without having the tantrums return. How did they accomplish this?

They asked the mother to arrange her schedule so that she could remain at the preschool for several consecutive days. The plan was to use the mother as the reinforcer for the child's nonanxious behaviors!

Since one can't administer a mother as a reinforcer in the same manner as one would give out raisins or stars, the researchers needed some way to signal the child that the mother would come and to let the mother know it was time for her to enter the classroom. A kitchen timer with a bell was chosen. The mother could hear the bell from outside the room, and it had the added advantage of being useful to time how long the child had to engage in nonanxious behavior before her mother would reappear.

First, the researchers collected baseline data for ten sessions: the number of minutes the child engaged in tantrum behaviors of crying, screaming, sobbing, etc. In the daily preschool session of 180 minutes, the average duration of the tantrum behavior was 152 minutes—the girl really did spend most of each day crying and screaming.

On the day the "treatment" was used for the first time, the girl was observed carefully for any slight pause in crying. When that happened, the kitchen timer was sounded and her mother came into the

Source: J. Neisworth, R. Madle, and K. Goeke, "Errorless Elimination of Separation Anxiety: A Case Study," *Journal of Behavior Therapy and Experimental Psychiatry, 6,* (1975), 79–82.

structure necessary for efficient application of his resources and which defines the relevant task-reward contingencies" (Kameya, 1972, p. 194).

Applied behavior analytic procedures have made it possible to maintain many children with emotional disturbance in regular classrooms. G. Wallace and J. M. Kauffman (1978) provide an extensive list of social-emotional problems commonly found in school situations, together with examples of tested activities for managing them. They point out that successful application of these activities to any particular child depends on his or her special needs and individual characteristics. An example of a program designed to meet the unique behavior displayed by a preschooler is presented in Box 10.5.

Two behavioral procedures related to classical conditioning are useful. The first, **reciprocal inhibition,** involves inhibiting anxiety by establishing a competing response. Essentially, the procedure is to have the stimulus that elicits the anxiety occur in the presence of a pleasant stimulus so that a bond between pleasure and the anxiety-eliciting stimulus is established. Systematic de-

room and played with her. The mother left after a prearranged period of time, but she told her daughter she would return again, as soon as the timer sounded. When the mother left, the crying started again, but this time a teacher told the child to listen for the timer to ring. After ten seconds of quiet listening, the timer was sounded, and the mother returned.

Gradually the amount of time the child did not cry increased and the length of time the mother stayed to play decreased. During the next three days, these procedures were repeated twelve times. Soon the researchers were satisfied that the kitchen timer was functioning as a signal that the mother was coming. Now the problem was to have the child engage in more appropriate interactions with her classmates and teachers rather than just standing quietly waiting for the bell to ring. Again, they contrived the situation so that the little girl was near, and eventually interacting with, other children or involved in activities when the bell rang. After only six days of this procedure, the girl was interacting with other children and *never* displaying the tantrum behaviors. By the seventh day of treatment, the researchers decided the child could proceed happily through the day without the presence of her mother.

Thinking they had the problem under control, they put the timer away.

Unfortunately, this was moving a little too far too fast. The absence of the ticking timer disturbed the child, and she cried for thirty-five seconds. When she quieted, the timer was reintroduced (though the mother did not appear). During the next three hours, the timer was faded gradually, placed in locations that were progressively farther away from the child. This fading procedure was successful. Less than two weeks following the collection of baseline data, the child was playing and learning in the preschool and was virtually indistinguishable from the other children. She no longer needed the reinforcement of her mother appearing or the timer ticking. To make the ending to this story even happier, the mother reported that similar problems in other settings had significantly decreased. The mother learned some new ways of managing behavior in the process, too.

sensitization is one type of reciprocal inhibition. Patients are taught a method of deep muscle relaxation because they will use the relaxation response in the treatment. Then the anxiety-eliciting stimulus is presented in various intensities ranging from "almost neutral" to "very intense." If patients continue the relaxation in the presence of gradually increasing intensities of the stimulus, they should eventually be able to cope with the anxiety-producing stimulus; they will have been conditioned to have a relaxation response in its presence instead of an anxiety response.

Consider the case of a person who has an intense fear of bees. In the desensitization process, the bees might be presented first in pictures, then dead and under glass, then in a hive behind glass, then alive but in a container, and eventually flying about in the same space as the patient. At each step, the bond between the bee stimulus and the relaxation response must be well established before the patient moves to the next level of intensity.

Aversion therapy is another behavioral technique, sometimes used in programs for smokers or alcoholics who are interested in quitting. Alcoholics might be given drugs that induce nausea when alcohol is presented. In this way, they are conditioned to have an aversion to alcohol because of the association of nausea and alcohol.

Teachers have had considerable success using applied behavior analysis to eliminate abnormal behaviors and teach children new and adaptive social behaviors. Those who are not in the behaviorist camp complain that the intervention merely changes the symptoms, not the root cause of the problem. Behaviorists argue that if other symptoms do arise, they can be treated with the same success.

We have now come full circle through a behavioral perspective on causes and interventions for disturbed behaviors. Did you notice that the same concepts are used to explain the development of both abnormal behavior and new, appropriate behaviors? The interventions based on modeling and operant conditioning can be used by regular and special teachers with a multitude of behavior problems in children who are seriously disturbed, as well as in children who are moderately or mildly disturbed. The interventions based on classical conditioning are applicable only to certain types of problems and should be used by specially trained therapists.

The Psychodynamic Approach

The **psychodynamic approach** has its roots in the work of Sigmund Freud (1949) and psychoanalytic theory, but it has evolved into something more than psychoanalysis. Psychodynamic theorists incorporate concerns about environment and experience along with explanations of the internal dynamics of personality development.

Causes. Two major concepts are essential to understanding the psychodynamic approach. One concerns biological predispositions and individual differences in such characteristics as temperament, energy, curiosity, and motivation. The second involves interaction between the child and his or her environment. The child grows within a network of interpersonal and environmental interactions. Because of biological predispositions and the individual pattern of these interactions, each child's growth process can vary. The results are a spectrum of interaction possibilities ranging from smooth and easy to stressful, or from successful to inability to cope. As you might expect, children who are emotionally disturbed experience interactions that are mostly stressful and unsuccessful.

Because individuals in the child's environment (especially parents) are often blamed for problems that may develop later in life, the significant participants in the interaction process should be studied—parents, relatives, care-givers, parents' friends, siblings, teachers, and peers. The peer group becomes more important as the child gets older and moves into social circles beyond home and neighborhood. Although it may be simple and popular to blame parents for a child's emotional problems, the sphere of influence is much greater than the parents and includes the child himself as well as society at large. As C. Cheney and W. C. Morse (1972) state, "The *child himself* with his unique set of biological givens, clearly represents a significant participant in the interactions which shape his growth" (p. 274).

According to Freud, personality is made up of three major systems: the *id,* the *ego,* and the *superego.* The id is the source of energy, and the ego is the mediator between the id and the realities imposed by the external world. The superego, which represents the moral development of the child, incorporates the norms, expectations, and values present in society. Because psychodynamic theorists are interested in the interactions between the individual and the environment, their work has centered on understanding the ego and its effect on personality development.

Freud's theory delineates stages of maturation of the child and the child's ability to deal with reality. Freud's idea was that children go through predictable stages of psychosexual development characterized by the part of the body that is the primary source of pleasurable activities. For the infant, the mouth is the primary pleasure zone (the oral stage). The anal and phallic stages follow. Supposedly, if development during these stages is normal, the child emerges as an adult with an adequate personality. Freud believed that feelings and emotions had a biological basis and played a primary role in development. His developmental sequence is based on the resolution of internal conflicts at various stages, but even fairly normal passage through the stages involves considerable stress. Abnormal behavior is described as fixations at the various stages. A mild disturbance within this developmental framework is called a **neurosis**. Examples include phobias, hysteria, and obsessive-compulsive behavior. A more severe disturbance is called **psychosis** and includes a withdrawal from reality (Morse & Smith, 1980). Relationships between the early stages and consequences for later development are summarized by B. B. Wolman (1960):

> If oral gratification has been overabundant, the individual may turn into a sanguine optimist who is overly dependent upon the world to care for him. . . . If gratification in the oral period has been insufficient, the individual may become depressive and pessimistic. In either case he is characterized as having oral interests: eating, drinking, smoking, kissing, and talking. . . . Conflicts during toilet training can lead to fixations at . . . the anal stage. Freud . . . noted three related traits of the anal character: orderliness (everything must be clean and in place), obstinacy (immovability, defiance), and parsimony (tightness in money, speech, etc.). . . .

(Cited in Rezmierski and Kotre, 1972, pp. 203–205. Used with permission.)

Freud's daughter, Anna, coined the phrase **defense mechanisms** to describe the ways people act (ego control) to keep psychic energy (id) in check. Defense mechanisms are very much a part of some descriptions of disturbed behavior. Those who work from a psychodynamic theory often use the defense mechanisms as the basis for intervention. For example, therapists try to get the person to remember what has been repressed, or forced into the unconscious, so it can be discussed on a conscious level and consequently eliminated. Other defense mechanisms that appear in case histories of children who are disturbed include

(1) denial—a kind of fantasizing to keep out unpleasant "real" information; (2) projection—attributing an impulse to some other person or object; (3) regression—returning to an earlier stage of psychosocial development when demands of the current level are not manageable; and (4) sublimation—substituting a more socially acceptable activity for a desired activity.*

By and large, the psychodynamic theorists who followed Freud emphasized the ego and studied the environment because it has an important influence on ego development. Erik Erikson built upon the stages of development proposed by Freud, but his stages are more psychosocial than psychosexual. He proposed eight important stages of development based on eight life crises (Erikson, 1968). Erikson's view of the development of abnormal behavior within these eight crises is similar to Freud's in that he believes that even normal progression through life is likely to entail some emotional problems and that problems at an early stage can have a negative impact on later development.

Another psychodynamic theorist, Carl Rogers (1961), is interested in the child's experience as it appears to the child. For Rogers, emotional disturbance is a discrepancy between the child's experience and the child's self-concept. According to Rogers, the human organism has an inherent desire to grow and actualize itself (Rogers calls this the actualizing tendency) and tries to select experiences likely to achieve that goal. A regulatory system providing feedback about the way in which the organism satisfies needs is also included in Rogers's theory.

Assessment. Assessment is typically supervised by an individual skilled in psychodynamic theory; however, it may involve the cooperation of other professionals including a psychologist, a social worker, and a neurologist. A teacher may be interviewed or asked to provide observational data regarding academic performance or social status. School records may be examined to obtain scores on intelligence and projective personality tests.

---

*C. Brenner (1955) provides further information about defense mechanisms.

Those who work from a psychodynamic approach often use play therapy to treat children who are disturbed. (Courtesy of HDS/U.S. HHS.)

Interventions. Therapists working from the psychodynamic perspective emphasize the early years of development, critical periods and stages of growth, and the biological origin of aspects of personality. For these reasons, internal conditions receive much attention. Some interventions assume that individuals are predisposed to be normal and use these normal growth processes (e.g., the self-actualizing tendency) in intervention. Many interventions focus on the development of appropriate ego controls. Working with families becomes a part of this type of intervention, too. Often, the family meets as a group to talk about problems. The overall goals of family therapy are improvement of child-rearing skills of parents and coping skills of all family members.

Advocates of the psychodynamic approach maintain that stress within the school environment must be minimized for children. One way to minimize stress is to emphasize cognitive skills, with the idea that academic accomplishments will improve self-concept and, as a side effect, improve the child's ability to cope with life situations. Instructional materials are carefully selected to reduce anxiety and fear of failure. Later, children may be helped to confront their emotional problems more directly.

The traditional "talking out" therapies are a part of the psychodynamic approach to intervention. Many of these techniques involve a one-to-one discussion between child and therapist with the goal of helping the child understand both feelings and actions. This approach conjures up images of the therapist's couch, but for young children the couch is often a playroom, and **play therapy** is the approach. Play therapy capitalizes on the natural tendency of the young child to engage in "let's pretend" and fantasy. By playing with toys and talking casually with the therapist, the child deals with his or her feelings and problems. **Reflective listening** techniques, in which the therapist helps children verbalize emotions they are experiencing, are used in play therapy and other counseling sessions. Phrases such as "You must have felt very angry when . . . " and "It must have been upsetting for you to hear that . . . " are examples of reflective listening.

An important contributor to intervention derived from a psychodynamic base is Fritz Redl. His proposals have had a great impact on preventive mental hygiene, management of behavior problems in classroom situations, and treatment of children who are emotionally disturbed in special settings such as residential schools and camps. Redl's work has as a central theme the development of ego controls and other support techniques. **Life space interviewing** (LSI), also called reality interviewing, was developed by Redl (1959) as a kind of counseling that takes place in real situations (when the behavior problem occurs) rather than in special counseling sessions. Redl's thinking is that children in conflict are more likely to accept and use help while they are in the throes of a crisis than if they must wait several days to talk with their therapist. Because LSI capitalizes on real-life events, whoever is with the child when he or she experiences a problem must be prepared to function as a reality therapist. But LSI is a very sophisticated technique and requires special training. In situations where disturbed children are educated in regular classes, there may be a crisis teacher, skilled in LSI, available in the resource room. In a crisis, the child would be sent to work with the crisis teacher (Morse, 1976). The crisis teacher is usually also trained in remedial education techniques and provides educational help at times when regular classroom work is too demanding.

Special methods have been developed to help parents and classroom teachers use interviewing techniques such as reflective listening and other methods similar to LSI in family and classroom situations. B. Guerney (1964) proposed filial therapy, a procedure in which parents are taught to use play therapy at home with their children. W. Glasser (1969) developed a type of reality interviewing similar to LSI for use by regular classroom teachers. Working with the entire class as a group, teachers lead classroom meetings designed to develop feelings of involvement and responsibility. The meetings, which are conducted regularly, may be any of three types: (1) open-ended meetings, in which any topic may be discussed; (2) social problem-solving meetings, in which children may bring up for discussion problems they are experiencing or in which the group may discuss behavioral problems of

general interest; and (3) educational diagnostic meetings, in which the children talk about educational goals and problems. Because the meetings usually take place every day, it is possible to exploit real-life events with the group. Magic Circle is a similar set of classroom group discussion procedures (Palomares & Ball, n.d.).

R. Dreikurs (1968) and R. Dreikurs and L. Grey (1970) proposed democratic discussion techniques for use between parent and child and teacher and child. Dreikurs believes it is important to understand what goals *the child* is trying to accomplish with misbehavior. If parents get used to thinking about what the child is trying to accomplish with the misbehavior, they can use four principles to talk about conflicts with the child: (1) mutual respect; (2) pinpointing the real issue—the one related to the child's goal, not the surface problem; (3) reaching agreement; and (4) participating in decision making. The family council is the vehicle used to arrive at solutions to family problems, and discussion at the family council should be in accordance with the four principles.

Interventions with a psychodynamic base emphasize helping children talk about their problems and providing emotional support so that the children feel someone (often parents and teachers) cares and will help them learn to handle their feelings and manage behavior. With these expectations for parents and teachers, special training programs are needed to help them acquire the reflective listening and other discussion skills. For children who are more seriously disturbed and require more intensive therapy, such as LSI, parents and teachers may be asked to support the efforts of experts.

Sociological and Ecological Theories

We are part of many groups: families, neighborhoods, schools, churches, and so on. Proponents of a sociological perspective are concerned with the manner in which humans behave in each of these groups. Sociologists are interested in the individual's reaction to the varying amounts of control each group attempts to exert upon his or her behavior. Ecologists are also interested in social forces as they interact with the internal forces that motivate the individual.

Causes. Sociologists study emotional disturbance from a variety of perspectives; we are interested here in their view of deviance and its relation to disturbance. There is a general agreement among sociologists that: "(1) Mental illness involves breaking the rules that regulate ordinary social interactions; (2) Mental illness is an open-ended category of deviance; many examples of deviance are considered mental illness because they do not fit other more specific categories of deviance" (DesJarlais, 1972, p. 270). Theories of deviance are concerned with rule breaking and its consequences, which are usually different for children than for adults. As children become socialized, they need to learn about rules, but more errors in rule breaking are tolerated in children because it is thought they do not yet totally understand the rules.

A major contribution of the ecological theorists is that they do not treat emotional disturbance as a concept in and of itself. Rather, they talk about disturbance or mismatch within the ecosystem—the system of relationships between organisms and environment. The ecological theorists use observation in real-life settings as a tool in studying human behavior. This approach to disturbance is highly multidisciplinary and often overlaps with other theories, as the child is seen as *acting upon* the environment and *being acted on* by the environment.

Assessment. The sociologist conducts an assessment by focusing upon the environment rather than the individual identified as disturbed, looking for conditions that promote inappropriate behavior. Areas of study include the identification of the mainstream culture, the history of social change, agents of social control, and major institutions in a society and their strengths and weaknesses. The sociologist also studies the relationship between the school and society. During an interview, a teacher may provide general infor-

mation regarding the manner in which cultural values are transmitted to students or the degree to which values of racial and ethnic minorities are represented in the curriculum. Specific information regarding a student may address membership in a racial or ethnic minority, socioeconomic status, and academic potential in relationship to members of the majority group.

Assessment from an ecological perspective focuses upon the student and the behavioral demands of all the environments in which he or she functions. A teacher may be asked to describe his or her own academic demands and to identify ways in which the child's behavior is disruptive in the school setting.

Interventions. In the review of sociological and ecological approaches provided in the Child Variance Project, some interventions are focused on the child, whereas others are focused on the school and natural community or involve some kind of artificial community or group intervention.

The remedial interventions involve teaching the child coping skills so that behaviors will be a better match with expectations in the environment. Community and school interventions are based on the assumption that the problem resides in the environment more than in the child; so the environment should be changed. Residential schools for children with emotional disturbance are examples of interventions based on creating artificial environments. These interventions involve attempts to change the child by using special environments.

Some interventions are similar to the artificial community in that they attempt to maintain the child within his or her normal or natural environment but set up an artificial group to affect change in behavior and attitudes. Morse's (1976) crisis teacher concept is based on providing a special person to intervene within the normal school environment. Project ReEd (Hobbs, 1966) is an excellent example of intervention based on the environmental perspective. In this project, intervention is directed toward changing both the child and the environment. The environmental components are family, school, and community,

TABLE 10.4
A SUMMARY OF FIVE PERSPECTIVES

	Biophysical Model	Behavioral Model	Psychodynamic Model	Sociological Model	Ecological Model
Cause	Genetic factors, neurological damage, or biochemical problem	Environmental events, or antecedents and consequences of behavior	Effect of interactions between child and significant others on personality development and resolution of internal conflicts	Breaking rules that govern social interactions	Mismatch between child and environment
Assessment	Conducted by medical personnel; teacher serves as a screening and referral agent	Teacher observes and identifies critical events in the environment, defines target behaviors, and identifies reinforcers	Conducted by qualified psychologist; teacher gives observational data	Teacher provides information on how cultural values are transmitted to children and representativeness of minority values in curriculum	Teacher may identify his or her academic demands and ways in which child's behavior is disruptive in school setting
Intervention	Teacher monitors drug or diet therapy, notes side effects, and makes modifications in daily schedule if required	Systematic application of applied behavior analytic principles (positive reinforcement, extinction, time-out, overcorrection, etc.)	Teacher selects low-stress curriculum and materials; trained teachers may conduct play therapy, reflective listening bibliotherapy	Teach individual coping behavior to match environmental expectations	Teacher changes physical organization of classroom (e.g., carrels); teacher uses effective materials, predictable rule enforcement, motivational feedback

and the cause of the problem is seen as the interaction between child and environment. Advocates of the ReEd approach feel it is necessary to remove the child from the environment for a time in order to change both child and environment before they are brought back together. In this sense, the ReEd project is concerned with the entire ecosystem. Children live in special residences and work with teacher counselors, while mental-health consul-tants also work with the teacher counselor. At the same time, social workers are responsible for maintaining contact with the child's family and the child's previous teacher. Normalization is the goal, however, and the child spends only as long as necessary in the special facility. As soon as the participants—child, family, school—are reeducated to work with each other, the child is gradually reintroduced into home and school.

Summary of the Child Variance Project

Those who study and treat the problems of emotional disturbance will benefit greatly from the research and writing emanating from the Child Variance Project at the University of Michigan. Table 10.4 summarizes widely differing viewpoints on causation, identification, and treatment of emotionally disturbed children. But through the Child Variance research and other, similar projects, important anchors are provided so that those working in the field can see how their views and approaches fit in to the overall pattern of knowledge about emotional disturbance. Reading about contrasting approaches can help you sharpen your understanding of the approach you favor. In the long run, *having a point of view and using it consistently* is more important than which point of view you have. There is no such thing as the "one best method."

ADDITIONAL EDUCATIONAL CONSIDERATIONS

Previous sections have described a variety of educational interventions useful for students exhibiting emotional disturbance. Teachers are advised to study carefully the different perspectives, then select and consistently implement strategies exemplifying the approach they believe will offer the greatest benefits to their students. There are, however, two additional considerations affecting the education of children who are emotionally disturbed. One is the use of suspension and expulsion. The other is the use of technology and computer-assisted instruction.

Expulsion and Suspension

Students with emotional disturbance obviously are more likely than their normal peers to exhibit behaviors that conflict with standards considered acceptable to public school personnel. Students who consistently do not meet these standards are usually punished through traditional methods that may include suspension and expulsion. At this point, it may be useful to review some of the information presented in Chapter 1 regarding suspension and expulsion of students with handicaps. As you may recall, a student with a handicap is entitled to due process prior to removal from a public school program. The following sections discuss use of suspension and expulsion with students who are handicapped.

Suspension. Suspension means exclusion from school for a period from one to ten consecutive school days. It constitutes a change in educational placement and parents have to be given a written notice prior to suspension. Parents have a right to a due process hearing, and no suspension may occur pending completion of the hearing. When a disciplinary program is so severe that an emergency suspension is required, regulations permit a suspension without written notice. Immediately afterward, the school must provide written notice and a due process hearing must be held as promptly as possible. A student may be suspended up to three days in an emergency situation; however, any student with an IEP or pending evaluation may not be suspended for more than ten days cumulatively in a school year unless homebound instruction or other alternative education is provided.

School staff must determine whether the misconduct is the result of the student's handicapping condition as defined by the rules and regulations that govern the administration and operation of special education. If this is indeed the case, the student's program must be reviewed by members of the multidisciplinary staff team within three school days of the misconduct. Recommendations should be written into the IEP. If parents disagree, a due process hearing can be held. A student may be suspended even if the misconduct is the result of a handicapping condition if his or her presence poses a danger to him- or herself, to other students, or to school staff, or if the student's conduct is so disruptive over a lengthy period that normal classroom activities cannot continue. Examples include an assault, or a threat to an activity, which endangers the health, safety, or welfare of those in the school (e.g., carries a weapon, sells drugs).

In-School Suspension. In-school suspension constitutes an exclusion from all or part of the educational program; however, the student attends school during that time. It is treated as a change in educational placement if, during in-school suspension, the school is unable to adhere to the IEP. In this case, in-school suspensions are governed by the same considerations as other suspensions. In-school suspensions of more than ten consecutive days require implementation of due process procedures.

Expulsion. Expulsion represents exclusion from school for a period exceeding ten school days including permanent expulsion from the school enrollment. It is considered a change in educational placement. Any expulsion must be a result of the process followed for any recommendation for a change in educational placement for a handicapped student. Specifically:

1. Evaluation or reevaluation should be conducted.

2. A multidisciplinary team must determine all data collected concerning the student.

3. The multidisciplinary team must determine the relationship of the handicap to the student's behavior and whether the behavior is a manifestation of the handicap.

4. The team should consider whether a change in IEP or placement would result in a change in the student's behavior.

5. If the recommendation is for expulsion, written notice should be issued to the parents with reasons for expulsion. They should be advised of their right to due process.

6. If a student's conduct is a result of his or her handicap, the program is reviewed and another placement is recommended or additional services are provided. All due process

protection must be accorded the youngster throughout these proceedings.

7. If a student's presence poses a danger to him- or herself or to other students or staff, the school may request an emergency change in placement.

8. Students should not be without an alternate educational program for more than ten days.

Technology and Computer-Assisted Instruction

A review of recent literature indicates that, with few exceptions, there is very little research and development of technology and CAI specifically designed for youngsters who are emotionally disturbed. However, it is possible that these youngsters may benefit from techniques and programs designed for children with other disabilities.

Technology. There are some technological advances that may have implications for students who are emotionally disturbed. Earlier in this chapter, we described the social deficits typically displayed by these children. A videodisc player may be useful in the development of appropriate social skills because it can search for and present sequences containing actual social situations. Additional screens are selected on the basis of the student's response and illustrate the consequences of a decision (Lindsey, 1987; Thorkildson, 1984).

Another technique useful for children with emotional disturbance is biofeedback. This technique uses physiological recording equipment to measure and report inner physiological activity. We are aware of a sixteen-year-old student named Scott for whom this technique was a tremendous success. He had a history of highly aggressive responses to any denial of a request. First, he practiced muscle relaxation exercises in the presence of his teacher. Next, she taught him how to use a portable biofeedback machine. Scott practiced his relaxation exercises while sensitive electrodes were attached to various areas on his head. During these sessions, Scott's teacher instructed him to imagine a request being denied. These requests were first for items that only mildly interested Scott. As he progressed, however, the items became much more valued. A green light on the front of the machine indicated when Scott was maintaining a relaxed posture; a red light indicated tension. Eventually, Scott was able to accept denials of actual request with a minimum of fuss.

Computer-Assisted Instruction. Earlier in this chapter, we described the academic difficulties encountered by children with emotional disturbance. Certainly, it is appropriate to use a well-designed software program that provides drill and practice in an academic skill in which a learner is experiencing difficulty such as math, reading (Carmen & Kosberg, 1982; Furst, 1983), or writing (Lindsey, 1987). In fact, it is possible that CAI may motivate the youngster who is apathetic, if not averse, to developing academic skills. Indeed, limited research involving use of CAI with individuals who are emotionally disturbed suggests they are motivated to interact with computers (Goldenberg, 1979; Kleiman, 1981; Lindsey, 1987; Warger, Murphy, & Kay, 1985).

SUMMARY

Specialists disagree considerably among themselves about definitions, classification schemes, causes, treatment, and the extent of the problem of emotional disturbance. As might be expected, there are a variety of different terms used to describe the problem and numerous treatment strategies have been proposed. The two terms used most often are *emotionally disturbed* and *behavior disorders*. On one point there is agreement, however: Once you have seen a child with an emotional problem, there is very little doubt that the child has a problem.

Descriptions of children with emotional disturbance are full of words with negative connotations: failure, unsocialized, aggressive, angry, withdrawn, destructive, maladaptive, unhappy, and so on. In the mild and moderate cases, the behaviors exhibited are not different in kind from those exhibited by the general population; the problem lies in the intensity and chronic nature of the behaviors. Those individuals who are severely emotionally disturbed have in their repertoire bizarre and unusual behaviors not found in others. Making a decision about whether behavior is deviant depends on a number of considerations. The intensity as well as the frequency of the behavior must be taken into account. The age and developmental level of the individual as well as the standards and typical expectations of a particular social or cultural group are also relevant. Behavior that is acceptable in some situations is not acceptable in others.

There are difficulties involved in classifying disturbed behavior. Research conducted with adults who are disturbed has been used to develop a system of psychiatric nomenclature, but this classification scheme does not generalize to the problems of children. Furthermore, psychiatric labels are not helpful in education because they are not keyed to specific intervention plans. The dimension analysis approach to classification may eventually be helpful to teachers. In this approach, researchers try to isolate and describe different patterns, or clusters, of disturbed behavior. They hope that eventually they will be able to link treatment procedures with the behavior pattern descriptions. On the basis of research already completed, it is possible to reliably identify a youngster as having a behavioral syndrome (exhibiting many of the behaviors that cluster together in that syndrome). Work is now under way to match teaching and other treatment procedures with the behavior syndromes.

At least five major theoretical positions on emotional disturbance were identified in the Child Variance Project. Those who subscribe to each point of view have different ideas about causation, description, and definition of the problem and appropriate interventions.

Those who take the biophysical approach believe that the major part of the problem lies within the individual. They are interested in genetic, developmental, arousal, neurological, and biochemical factors as explanations of disturbed behavior. Most of the interventions associated with the biophysical model must be prescribed and supervised by medical professionals. Teachers are expected to monitor the child's behavior in the classroom and report on side effects, behavioral changes, and so on.

The behavioral approach is embraced by those who believe that behavior is learned, whether it is normal or abnormal. They believe that because abnormal behavior is learned, it can be unlearned. Behaviorists are interested in a functional analysis of behavior and concentrate their efforts on describing behavior and arranging environmental events to change behavior. Causation and treatments are based on both the classical conditioning and the operant conditioning models. Behaviorists believe that the antecedents of the behavior (events coming before the behavior), the behavior itself (with an emphasis on precise description and recording), and the consequences (events following the behavior) are all important in the development of inappropriate behavior as well as in the teaching of appropriate behavior.

Psychodynamic theorists incorporate concerns about environment along with explanations of internal dynamics of personality development. These theorists emphasize the importance of the early years, certain critical periods of development, and the biological origin of aspects of personality. Intervention is sometimes based on the "talking-out" concept of psychotherapy. For young children, play therapy and other expressive therapies replace the more adult stereotype of the patient on the couch. Working with families in counseling situations is an important part of the treatment, too.

Sociologists consider emotional disturbance within the broader context of deviance and rule breaking. A related theory, ecological theory, involves the study of emotional disturbance within the ecosystem, the interrelationships between organisms and environment. Interventions based on these two theoretical positions involve looking at the child within the school and natural community or arranging for an artificial group or community for a specified period of time. Intervention is aimed at changing both the child and the environment.

Other educational considerations include suspension and expulsion. Students with emotional disturbance are more likely to engage in behaviors that would result in either suspension or expulsion. However, federal laws clearly specify the conditions under which these techniques are used with students who are emotionally disturbed.

Finally, technology and CAI may be quite beneficial to children with emotional disturbance. In addition to enhancing academic skills, technology and CAI may promote social development.

The enormous variety of explanations about disturbed behavior and the differing treatments proposed can be a source of confusion to those new to the field. But variety can be an asset rather than a liability. There is a lively exchange of ideas among those working in the field, and research is stimulated when such variety exists. These conditions are likely to pay off in new and more workable approaches for teachers working with disturbed children.

Suggestions for Further Reading

Alberto, P. A., & Troutman, A. C. (1986). *Applied behavior analysis for teachers*. Columbus, OH: Merrill.
This is an extremely informative, well-written textbook. It describes in detail applied behavior analytic procedures useful for classroom teachers. All the procedures are clearly, and sometimes humorously, illustrated.

Apter, S. J., & Conoley, J. C. (1984). *Childhood behavior disorders and emotional disturbance*. Englewood Cliffs, NJ: Prentice-Hall.
This book attempts to clarify a very confusing field. Although it focuses on what teachers of students with emotional disturbance need to know, it contains information useful to parents and a wide range of professionals.

Gadow, K. D. (1986). *Children on medication, Volume 2*. San Diego, CA: College-Hill Press.
This is an excellent book that describes in very clear language what parents, teachers, administrators, and other interested individuals should know about the use of medicine to treat epilepsy, emotional disturbance, and adolescent disorders.

Kauffman, J. M. (1981). *Characteristics of children's behavior disorders* (2nd ed.). Columbus, OH: Merrill.

This book, like the 1977 first edition, is a comprehensive treatment of the subject of emotionally disturbed children. There are four major sections: major concepts and history, origins of disordered behavior, types of disordered behavior, and rationale for intervention. The material is especially well documented.

Kerr, M. M., & Nelson, C. M. (1983). *Strategies for managing behavior problems in the classroom.* Columbus, OH: Merrill.

This is a practical behavior approach to dealing with emotionally disturbed children. It is packed with helpful examples and illustrative material. The emphasis is on data-based management for all behavior problems, including those that are severe.

Morse, W. C., & Smith, J. (1980). *Understanding child variance.* Reston, VA: The Council for Exceptional Children.

This is similar to a programmed textbook. It presents historical development, relevant names and terms, concept of deviance, causal factors, assessment, and treatment from each of the five perspectives on treating children with emotional disturbance.

Rhodes, W. C., & Head, S. (Eds.) (1974). *A study of child variance, Volume 3. Service delivery systems.* Ann Arbor, MI: University of Michigan Press.

This, the third and final volume of findings of the "Conceptual Project on Emotional Disturbance," provides information on the history and structure of the educational, legal-correctional, mental-health, and social welfare delivery systems, as well as case studies. Contributions of religious institutions and descriptions of alternative delivery systems are included.

Rhodes, W. C., & Paul, J. L. (1978). *Emotionally disturbed and deviant children: New views and approaches.* Englewood Cliffs, NJ: Prentice-Hall.

Historical and new perspectives derived from the "Conceptual Project on Emotional Disturbance" are presented. An excellent presentation on the philosophy of deviance is provided. Behaviorist, psychoneurological, sociological, ecological, existential, and atheoretical perspectives are represented.

Rhodes, W. C., & Tracy, M. L. (Eds.) (1972). *A study of child variance. (Volume 1, Theories; Volume 2, Interventions).* Ann Arbor, MI: University of Michigan Press.

These two volumes, along with Volume 3, edited by Rhodes and Head, present the major findings of the "Conceptual Project on Emotional Disturbance." Volumes 1 and 2 provide extensive descriptions and reviews of literature on the major theoretical foundations and related treatments and interventions for dealing with the emotionally disturbed.

Relevant Journal

Behavioral Disorders

This journal is the official organ of the Council for Children with Behavior Disorders, a subdivision of CEC, Reston, VA. It is published quarterly and includes position papers and reports of applied and basic research.

CHAPTER 11

Gifted
and Talented

Elisa Klein
University of Maryland

Did You Know That . . .

- some people readily identified as adults who are gifted and talented would have been passed over if they had tried to get into a special program for the gifted as children?

- there is very little agreement on a definition of giftedness or on a method of identifying children who are gifted?

- although many people are able to realize their extraordinary abilities without benefit of special programs, a dismaying amount of talent may go unrecognized because we fail to provide appropriate educational services?

- a longitudinal study of about 1,500 children who were gifted, begun in 1921, has continued for over sixty years?

- although the stereotypes of gifted children as sickly, antisocial, and "bookish" still exist, most research indicates that these children are, for the most part, healthy, popular, and well adjusted emotionally?

I magine this hypothetical situation: You are a member of a team of school personnel consisting of teacher, school psychologist, administrator, special educator, and supervisor of programs for students who are gifted. The team is meeting to select children to participate in special programs for learners who are gifted. These programs include a variety of opportunities, such as full-time classes, part-time classes in particular subject areas, acceleration (skipping all or part of a grade), and afternoon or Saturday special-interest classes. The school district has no fixed set of criteria for determining entrance into the program; selection is based on a majority vote after consideration of a variety of factors for each child including, but not limited to, the following:

individual intelligence test results
achievement test results
creativity test results
social skills evaluations
teacher recommendations and evaluations
parent interviews
child interviews

Enrollment is limited because of budgetary restraints, so selection must be carefully made. Among the applicants, you are to consider the following children.

Elaine Hawkins. Dancing has always been important to Elaine Hawkins—she considers dancing to be both the personal and vocational goal in her life. Mature-looking for her age and attractive, Elaine once dropped out of school at age ten by claiming to be sixteen years old! Her rebelliousness and stubborn attitude have always caused her problems in school, although she is an excellent teacher of young children. Elaine's other interests include reading and visiting art and history museums. She is very outspoken and radical in her political beliefs. Her IQ and creativity scores are slightly above average, social and academic scores slightly below. Elaine's parents are divorced.

Sam Edder. Sam Edder did not begin to speak until he was three years old. He has always had trouble with school, remaining withdrawn and unsociable. He was even removed from school at one time because of his emotional instability. His test scores are all below average except for his performance on creativity measures, which shows some potential. Other than reading intently and playing a musical instrument, Sam seems to have few interests and expresses little in the way of personal or vocational goals. Sam's parents are of European descent, with high school educations.

Bill Ridell. Bill Ridell has never spent much time in school. He started late because of illness and was withdrawn several times due to continued sickness. He has been labeled "backward" by school officials. He has suffered from a variety of ailments and is going deaf. Although his creative performance shows some promise, Bill's IQ score is low (81), as are his scores on other achievement indices. However, Bill enjoys building mechanical things, has good manual dexterity, and would like someday to be a scientist or railroad mechanic. Although Bill's mother is well educated, his father has had no formal schooling and is unemployed.

William Gunther. A Cherokee Indian whose parents participate in reservation activities, William Gunther has attended reservation school all his life. He has been described by his teachers as a prankster who dislikes school, and he has a reputation for damaging school property. William is interested in horse riding and roping, and he hopes to become a member of a circus or wild west show. He also shows a special skill in history and is well known for his sense of humor. William's IQ and creativity test scores are far higher than his performance on achievement and social measures, but all are within the average range.

William Horn. William Horn is every teacher's "ideal student." Well adjusted, a good organizer and leader, highly self-motivated, and attractive in appearance and personality, William has interests ranging from athletics (basketball) to academics (mathematics). In fact, he eventually wants to be a mathematics teacher. William's parents both completed college and have many interests and hob-

This gifted student completed her B.S., M.S., and Ph.D. degrees in Biochemistry in four years. (Photo by David Mengle. Courtesy of Pennsylvania State Public Information.)

bies of their own. William's IQ has been assessed at 159, with social, academic, and creative assessments indicating comparable abilities.

Mary Hall. At age eleven, Mary Hall is 5′8″ tall and 98 pounds—tall, skinny, painfully self-conscious. Due to a spinal defect and other ailments, Mary has been in and out of hospitals and has spent a lot of time in bed. She lives with her grandmother, both parents having died when she was younger. Mary's scores on intelligence tests, achievement measures, creativity tests, and the like have been decidedly average. School has never held much interest for her. She often withdraws into daydreams. At the same time, Mary likes being the center of attention and seeks this often. Mary's particular abilities seem to revolve around helping other people, especially those less fortunate than she. She is compassionate and patient with the aged, young children, and the poor.

Which of these students would you admit to the gifted program? Any? All? On what bases would you make your decisions: IQ scores, teacher recommendations, student interviews? ▪

How would you justify your choices to the child's parents? the local school board? the child?

The preceding scenarios are adapted from a "simulation game" developed by John Rader (1977; adapted with permission). The purpose of the game is to help those who work directly with children who are gifted to get a feel for some of the considerations involved in identifying giftedness and selecting children who would best benefit from specialized educational intervention. The game gives a good indication of what it is like to identify children who are gifted and talented. Although this is only a game, the case studies are based on the lives of real people. To satisfy your curiosity, let us reveal the true identities of the applicants for the gifted program:

Elaine Hawkins: Isadora Duncan
Sam Edder: Albert Einstein
Bill Ridell: Thomas Edison
William Gunther: Will Rogers
William Horn: Bill Bradley
Mary Hall: Eleanor Roosevelt

All of these eminent people have made or continue to make significant contributions to our society. Their giftedness and talents cut across a spectrum from humor (Will Rogers) to art (Isadora Duncan) to athletics (Bill Bradley) to politics and humanitarianism (Eleanor Roosevelt) to science and technology (Albert Einstein and Thomas Edison). Yet many of these people would have been passed over if, as children, they had tried to get into a program for gifted students. Edison's IQ (estimated) was only 81, Will Rogers was labeled a behavior problem, and Einstein was considered withdrawn and a slow starter. Obviously, these people were able to make their mark in life without benefit of a special program. Many people with special abilities do. Others, however, need the benefit of some type of educational intervention to fully realize their potential. Helping children who are gifted is an important aspect of being a teacher.

What does it mean to be gifted? Or talented? What is creativity? Although we all may have our own ideas of what a person who is gifted is like,

when it comes right down to deciding on a general definition and the means to identify giftedness, there is very little agreement. As a group, children who are gifted seem to have few common personal, social, physical, or cognitive characteristics. Some researchers and educators have even suggested that there is so much heterogeneity in this group it is not worthwhile to catalogue any common traits.

The heterogeneity apparent in the preceding case studies certainly does not help us in an attempt to figure out just what giftedness is about. These studies are helpful, however, because they disprove the stereotype that children who are gifted are all alike. From these brief anecdotal descriptions we have learned that among learners who are gifted:

1. There are wide-ranging differences in IQ as well as creativity, achievement, and social skills. For example, the difference in IQ scores for Thomas Edison (81) and Bill Bradley (159) is 78 points. There is also evidence of both average and superior creativity.

2. There are wide differences in physiological characteristics. Children who are gifted may be very attractive and mature like Isadora Duncan, or ungainly and self-conscious like Eleanor Roosevelt.

3. Personality and behavior characteristics run the gamut from introverted (Albert Einstein) to extroverted (Will Rogers), from ideal student (Bill Bradley) to behavior problem (Will Rogers).

4. Abilities include not only intellectual superiority but also mechanical and athletic skills and leadership qualities.

5. Children who are gifted come from a variety of backgrounds.

Some Historical Notes

Attention to the education of individuals who are gifted can be traced back to Plato, who encouraged specialized education for those outstanding children who would eventually become the leaders of Greece (Reynolds & Birch, 1982). In the United States, evidence of special programming is found as far back as 1868, and the first public school for gifted children was established in Worcester, Massachusetts, in 1901 (Passow et al., 1955). Since that time, the needs of children who are gifted have received varying attention, dependent in part on the social and political climate or movement of the moment (e.g., the Cold War, the compensatory education movement). Concern about Russia and the "space race" at the end of the 1950s, for example, led to widespread interest in and special programming for children who are gifted, particularly in the sciences.

In 1972, the United States Office of Education published findings of a study of available educational opportunities for children who are gifted and talented. The results were striking. Although between 2 and 5 percent of the school population are gifted, many of these children are not being challenged through specialized educational programs of any sort. Indeed, in filling out a questionnaire distributed to school principals, over 50 percent of those responding reported they had *no* children who were gifted in their schools! Obviously, either teachers did not know what to look for in terms of talent and creativity or children who were gifted were performing so far below their potential that they were not easily identified.

Changes in both public and federal attitudes toward the needs of other exceptional children may spill over to provide a focus on the problems of children who are gifted as well. P.L. 94–142 does not mandate specialized attention to children who are gifted, nor does it provide money for programs or services for these children. Individual states may elect to provide services to the gifted using state money.

According to a 1977 survey (Council for Exceptional Children, 1978), 84 percent (forty-three) of the states had some type of written policy dictating educational programming for children and youth who are gifted and talented. As of 1980, forty-six states reported that they had educational programs for these children, and forty-five state departments of education employed a

specific person responsible for education of the gifted (Reynolds & Birch, 1982).

In this chapter, we consider some of the major issues surrounding children who are gifted and talented. We examine definitions, characteristics, and origins of giftedness; identification of children who are gifted; and educational provisions for them. As you read, keep in mind the case studies used in the simulation game and see if your perceptions of these "children" change as you learn more about the topic.

DEFINITIONS OF GIFTEDNESS AND TALENT

There is a great deal of confusion and disagreement when it comes to establishing a definition of giftedness and talent. Children who are gifted may demonstrate ability, or potential for ability, in so many areas and with such a wide range of skills that it is difficult to reach any sort of consensus as to an acceptable definition. For instance, does giftedness mean only a superior, general intellectual ability, or does it include such diverse skills and talents as artistic ability, specific academic aptitude, creativity, leadership and social skills, and athletic prowess? What is the lower limit in the determination of giftedness?

Over the past few decades, the conceptualization of what it means to be gifted has extended from an operational definition that specifies a lower-limit IQ to broad definitions that include a wide range of exceptional behavior to multidimensional views of intelligence.

Attempts have been made to outline categories and types of definitions. For example, L. Lucito (1963) suggested five classes of definitions:

1. *Ex post facto definitions* based on demonstrated outstanding achievement or eminence in a particular endeavor

2. *Intelligence test definitions* based on a specific IQ score on an individually administered intelligence test

3. *Social definitions* based on socially approved abilities, such as artistic talent

4. *Percentage definitions* based on the requirements of society for a certain number of gifted individuals to perform specific roles

5. *Creativity definitions* based on creative behavior and/or performance on creativity measures

Are these classifications useful? Ex post facto definitions, while interesting in a historical sense, do not really have much relevance in a discussion of children who are gifted. Although Mozart's career as a musician started when he was three years old and included composing by the time he was four (Pressey, 1955), most cases in which an ex post facto identification has been used involve individuals who have achieved prominence over the course of a lifetime. In the following discussion, we will consider several types of definitions: IQ, creativity and talent, social/percentage needs, expanded, developmental, and legislative.

IQ Definitions

The use of IQ scores to determine giftedness originated at a time when schools focused on a narrow, strictly academic curriculum (Newland, 1976). Lewis Terman, whose long-term study of bright children (see Box 11.1) influenced the entire field for many years, identified participants on the basis of IQ scores of 140 or above on the Stanford-Binet intelligence test. Of the almost 1,500 children who became subjects in the study, more than 80 had IQ scores of above 170, and the average score was 150 (Terman, 1954).

In the 1960s, the American Personnel and Guidance Association recommended that "the academically talented student is one who receives a score of about 115 or over on a Stanford-Binet intelligence test or falls above a similar point on one of the Wechsler Intelligence Scales" (cited in Reynolds & Birch, 1977, p. 217). Distinctions have also been made between *levels* of IQ scores. P. Witty (1967) cites three such levels, as suggested by Gallagher:

This young girl has a musical talent that she enhances by regular practice. (Courtesy of Department of Health and Human Services.)

1. the **academically talented**, who make up 15 to 20 percent of the school population, or those with IQ scores above 116

2. the **gifted**, comprising between 2 and 4 percent of the population, or those with IQ scores above 132

3. the **highly gifted**, approximately .1 percent of the school population, or those with IQ scores above 148

The estimated percentage of children who are gifted in the general school population will be discussed shortly. If we were to determine giftedness solely on the basis of IQ scores, however, the incidence would be that reflected in Table 11.1.

Today, school districts that identify students who are gifted on the basis of IQ scores usually set the lower limit somewhere between 120 and 135.

BOX 11.1

LEWIS M. TERMAN, 1877–1956

A commitment to identifying, studying, and advocating educational intervention for children who are gifted can be traced to the same person who revolutionized intelligence testing in the United States in the early part of this century: Lewis M. Terman. Terman's influence in both psychology and education is still felt today.

Terman completed his Ph.D. in psychology at Clark University. At the turn of the century, Clark was the foremost graduate program in psychology, and many of those who had a profound effect upon American psychology either taught at Clark or received their degrees there: G. Stanley Hall, Raymond Cattell, John Dewey, and Arnold Gesell among others. From the very beginning, Terman was interested in mental testing; his dissertation was an experimental study comparing bright and slow students on a variety of tests. Terman became convinced that intelligence was greatly influenced by genetic endowment.

After several other appointments, Terman became a professor at Stanford University, where he was to remain for the rest of his career. First as a professor in the Education Department and later as chairman of the Psychology Department, Terman contributed to the national reputation of both departments.

The first version of the Stanford-Binet intelligence test in 1916 firmly established Terman at the forefront of the field of mental testing. The Stanford-Binet was a revision of the original mental scale developed by the French psychologists Binet and Simon. Terman standardized the Stanford-Binet on American school children. In 1921, Terman embarked upon a complex longitudinal study of children who are gifted. Using a lower limit IQ of 140, Terman's associates identified about 1,500 school children who were gifted on the west coast. The study continued after Terman's death in 1956, and the most recent set of data were collected in 1982. The researchers examined questions related to intelligence, such as stability of IQ. They also measured characteristics such as health, personality, hobbies

Lewis M. Terman. (Courtesy of News and Publications Service, Stanford University.)

and interests, and socioeconomic and cultural background. The children were subsequently reassessed at college age, young adulthood, and mid-life. Special studies continue on the career success of gifted women, marital satisfaction, and so on.

Terman used the data base to strengthen his belief that intellectual abilities are primarily inherited. Subsequent research has questioned the exclusive emphasis on a "native" explanation for high intellectual ability. Yet Terman's genetic view of giftedness dominated the field for many years.

Several points from Terman's view of the gifted and gifted education are summarized here.

1. Giftedness is primarily based on a high rate of general intelligence, as opposed to specialized talent or creativity.
2. Identification of children who are gifted should occur at an early age in order to facilitate placement into special educational programs.
3. Children who are gifted should receive special instruction in the schools. Depending upon available resources, specially trained teachers, individual programs, acceleration, or enrichment are some of the ways these children may be helped.
4. Individuals who are gifted have made and will continue to make a great contribution to society.

Source: Seagoe, 1975.

TABLE 11.1

GIFTED CHILDREN IN THE SCHOOL POPULATION, BASED ON IQ SCORES

IQ Score	Approximate Incidence
130	2 in 100
140	1 in 1,000
150	1 in 10,000
160 and above	1 in 100,000

J. Zettel (1979) surveyed state definitions and provisions for these children and found that thirty-eight states included very high general intellectual ability as an important criterion for identifying students as gifted and talented. The most common cut-off point was an IQ score of 130 or above.

The use of IQ as the sole criterion to define or identify giftedness is becoming rare. Although there is a strong correlation between intelligence test scores and academic achievement, giftedness may encompass far more than high achievement; in fact, many children with extraordinary abilities may not do well on intelligence tests. Moreover, the many criticisms leveled against IQ tests with respect to testing culturally different children make these tests even more suspect as sensitive indicators of giftedness. Finally, as we shall see in our subsequent discussion, a high score on an intelligence test may not reflect certain types of cognitive abilities that other measures can assess more accurately.

Creativity and Talent

As schools began to include a broader range of studies (such as arts or vocational programs) in the curriculum, definitions of giftedness based solely on IQ scores were seen as being too limited. As just noted, the IQ test cannot be faulted as an accurate predictor of academic achievement. However, when researchers in creativity pointed out that creativity is not necessarily confined to high intellectual achievement, the success of in-

TABLE 11.2

GUILFORD'S STRUCTURE OF THE INTELLECT: DIMENSIONS AND CATEGORIES

Dimension	Categories
Operations	Cognition
	Memory
	Convergent production (or thinking)
	Divergent production (or thinking)
	Evaluation
Content	Figural/visual
	Symbolic
	Semantic
	Behavioral
Products	Units
	Classes
	Relations
	Systems
	Transformations
	Implications

telligence tests as the sole form of identification was called into question. J. P. Guilford was especially instrumental in changing conceptions of giftedness to include creativity. He asserted that creativity extended far beyond what is commonly considered *general* intelligence (Guilford, 1950, 1967) and developed a model known as the Structure of the Intellect (SOI). The model represents intelligence as made up of a set of factors or abilities rather than one generalized dimension (Guilford, 1959, 1967). The model is composed of three dimensions, within which 120 factors related to the content, the process, and the products of intellectual and creative activity are classified. Each factor results from a combination of one category from each of the three dimensions. (See Table 11.2 and Figure 11.1.)

For many years, Guilford has been involved in developing a battery of tests designed to assess each of the 120 factors. It will be easier to understand how the three dimensions intersect if we look at a few examples. For instance, as teachers, we are often interested in the type of intellectual

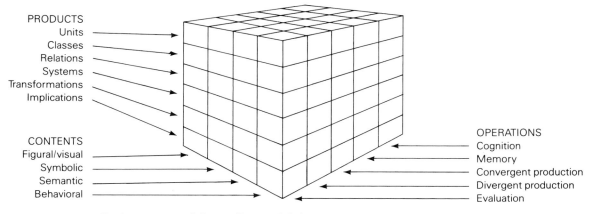

Figure 11.1. Guilford's Structure of the Intellect model. (From J. P. Guilford, *The Nature of Human Intelligence*. New York: McGraw-Hill, 1977; used with permission.)

activity that involves the *process of cognition* (recognition or discovery acquisition), *symbolic content* (configurations with meaning such as words, letters, or numbers), and *unit products* (discrete bits of information). According to Guilford (1959), the cognition of symbolic units (or the ability to recognize symbols that carry specialized discrete bits of information) could be assessed through such techniques as scrambled words ("Make a word out of these letters: HWTCA; OSHES"). If we wanted to examine cognition of semantic rather than symbolic units, verbal comprehension measures such as a vocabulary test ("What does *handball* mean?") would be appropriate. A very different sort of process would be divergent thinking, where we would be looking for a variety of responses. For example, divergent thinking in symbolic units might be measured through word fluency tests ("How many words can you think of that end in 'ly'?").

About the same time that Guilford was developing the SOI model, E. Torrance (1962) and J. Getzels and P. Jackson (1962) suggested that creativity is an important component of giftedness and may be made up of abilities far different from those measured by intelligence tests. Guilford (1950) stated that intelligence tests measure convergent thinking (the narrowing down of alternatives to discover one correct answer), but it is

divergent thinking that is important to creative thinking and productivity. Factors involved in divergent thinking include sensitivity to problems, fluency, novel ideas, flexibility, ability to synthesize, ability to analyze, ability to reorganize or redefine, complexity, and evaluation. Torrance (1962) described **creative thinking** as "the process of sensing gaps or disturbing elements, forming ideas concerning them, testing those hypotheses; and communicating the results, possibly modifying and retesting the hypotheses" (p. 16).

Getzels and Jackson (1962) compared children who received high scores on intelligence tests with those who received high scores on creativity tests. They found distinctions in terms of abilities, personality, attitudes, and other characteristics, suggesting that creative children may be different from high-achieving children. Identification solely through the use of IQ tests thus may net the high achievers but not the creative individuals.

Is creativity different from talent? These labels may be purely arbitrary distinctions. *Talent* seems to be used more in reference to a specific skill or achievement, whereas *creativity* has been used in a broader sense. Both creativity and talent, however, often connote a set of abilities entirely different from those commonly associated with intellectual giftedness. This connotation can severely

An individually administered intelligence test is often used to assess the intelligence of very bright children. (Photo by Joseph Bodkin.)

limit perceptions of what giftedness is all about, as children who are gifted may be highly creative in a wide variety of areas, including science, mathematics, arts, athletics, and so on. According to Getzels and Jackson (1978),

> Despite the growing body of literature concerning intellectual processes which seem closely allied to the general concept of "creativity," we tend to treat the latter concept as applicable only to performance in one or more of the arts. In effect, the term "creative child" has become synonymous with the expression "children with artistic talents," thus limiting our attempts to identify and foster cognitive abilities related to creative functioning in areas other than the arts. (p. 75)

Attempts to define creativity thus helped broaden notions of giftedness beyond the traditional IQ-based parameters. At the same time, however, the research on creativity generated a new set of problems, most centering on the difficult nature of assessment. Although Guilford, Torrance, and others have developed tests of creativity, its defining characteristics elude rigid categorization and standardized measures, and educators who rely on psychometric tests to identify talent often miss the truly creative individual.

Social/Percentage Needs

Another way to define and identify children who are gifted is based on the belief that there are certain functions in society that require people who are gifted and talented to perform them. T. E. Newland (1976) suggests that new definitions of giftedness should be derived from these societal needs, at least in terms of the school's responsibility to educate children who are gifted. He states that "if X percent of the present [U.S.] working population were involved in high level roles, the schools [would be] obligated to regard at least that percentage of the general population as needing to be prepared to fulfill these kinds of roles" (p. 12). Given this criterion, Newland comes up with a figure of 8 percent of the school population needed to be trained for such "major social responsibilities." This figure translates into children with IQ scores above 120 to 125.

Expanded Definitions

Concerns about the limitations of IQ-based or similarly restricted definitions served to expand the meaning of giftedness to include other parameters such as specific aptitudes or skills. A sampling of some of these "broad" or expanded definitions of **gifted** and **talented** is presented here.

[The] term giftedness encompasses those children who possess a superior intellectual potential and functional ability to achieve academically in the top 15 to 20% of the school population; and/or talent of high order in such areas as mathematics, science, expressive arts, creative writing, music, and social leadership, and a unique creative ability to deal with their environment.
(Fliegler & Bish, 1959, p. 409)

The talented or gifted child is one who shows consistently remarkable performance in any worthwhile line of endeavor. Thus we shall include not only the intellectually gifted, but also those who show promise in music, the graphic arts, mechanical skills, creative writing, dramatics and social leadership.
(Havighurst, 1958, p. 19)

[The gifted child is] any . . . whose performance in a potentially valuable line of endeavor is consistently remarkable.
(Witty, 1953, p. 256)

J. Renzulli (1978) has suggested that giftedness comes from an interaction of three important clusters of traits: above-average ability, high levels of task commitment, and high creativity (see Figure 11.2). These may be applied to any area of performance.

You can see that these expanded definitions attempt to incorporate all the dimensions of giftedness already discussed: intellectual ability, academic achievement, creativity and talent, and socially sanctioned endeavors. They reflect educators' growing attempts to view giftedness as multidimensional and subsequently to identify exceptional children with a wide range of abilities.

Although it has already been noted that a majority of state departments of education and local school districts still depend primarily on intelligence tests and achievement measures in determining who enters their gifted programs, we shall see that broader conceptions of giftedness have been incorporated into the legislative view.

Legislative Definitions

The 1972 study by the U.S. Office of Education delineated guidelines for the definition and identification of gifted and talented students. That definition, presented here, has been adopted by many states.

Gifted and talented children are those identified by professionally qualified persons who, by virtue of outstanding abilities, are capable of high performance. These are children who require differentiated educational programs and/or services beyond those normally provided by the regular school program in order to realize their contribution to self and society. Children capable of high performance include those with demonstrated achievement and/or potential ability in any of the following areas, singly or in combination:

1. general intellectual ability
2. specific academic aptitude
3. creative or productive thinking
4. leadership ability
5. visual and performing arts
6. psychomotor ability

It can be assumed that utilization of these criteria for identification of children who are gifted and talented will encompass a minimum of 3 to 5 percent of the school population.

Evidence of gifted and talented abilities may be determined by a multiplicity of ways. These procedures should include objective measures and professional evaluation measures which are essential to components of identification.

Professionally qualified persons include such individuals as teachers, administrators,

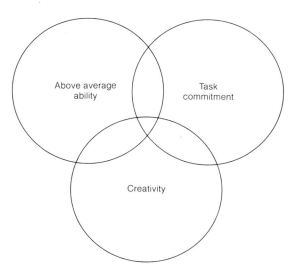

Figure 11.2. Renzulli's definition of giftedness. (Renzulli, J. What makes giftedness? Re-examining a definition. *Phi Delta Kappan,* 1978, *60*(3), 180–84. Used with permission.)

school psychologists, counselors, curriculum specialists, artists, musicians, and others with special training who are also qualified to appraise pupils' special competencies.

(Marland, 1972, pp. ix–x)

These guidelines became the basis for a definition of giftedness and talent that was incorporated into The Elementary and Secondary Education Act (P.L. 95–561, Title IX, Part A) in 1978 (Sellin & Birch, 1980).

How do these federal guidelines differ from previous definitions? One major difference is that the definition is operational to some extent; that is, it includes certain objective criteria for identification of children who are gifted and talented for the purpose of educational intervention. It delineates the minimum percentage of the school population to be considered, specifies who would do the evaluating, and outlines the types of measures to be used.

Another difference is that the definition emphatically states that children with *potential* abil-

ity should be sought out. Thus, children who are gifted include not only those who have already demonstrated their talents but also those who for some reason have unrealized potential. This distinction is important for learners who are underachievers, handicapped, culturally different, or disadvantaged, who may not be readily identified through regular means. We discuss the characteristics of these "special" groups in the next section.

Finally, this definition includes talent in psychomotor ability, leadership ability, and the performing arts, areas that were sometimes ignored in earlier conceptualizations. The federal guidelines are broad enough to encompass a wide range of abilities and talents while at the same time specific enough to delineate criteria for identification.

CHARACTERISTICS OF CHILDREN WHO ARE GIFTED: FACT OR FANCY?

Consider the following excerpts from *Wonderland,* a novel by Joyce Carol Oates (1971).

> His memory was not very good . . . both Hilda and Frederich could remember pages and pages of detail. They were strange children; they had been written up in newspapers and magazines, Jesse had discovered. They were extraordinary and Jesse was ordinary, only ordinary. (pp. 95, 96)
>
> From the rear of the house, from the "music room," came the short, choppy, blunt notes of a piano, Frederich's playing. Every day Frederich sat at the handsome grand piano, picking out notes, shading in small intricate spots on a piece of paper, as Jesse had been told. A page of Frederich's music was incredibly elaborate and also messy—there were hundreds of notes, some shaded in carefully, very deeply with a dark lead pencil, others

hardly more than scrawls, with many erasures and areas that had been crossed out so roughly that the paper had torn. . . . Jesse had not known what to make of Frederich at first. But now he understood that Frederich had a "gift," a "talent" and that this set him apart from other boys. (p. 97)

Like Frederich [Hilda] spent most of her time with her "work." She was a mathematical genius, Jesse had been told. Mrs. Pedersen had tried to explain the kind of work Hilda did, but Mrs. Pedersen herself did not really understand. "Some things she works out on paper, but most of it she does in her head. I don't begin to understand it," Mrs. Pedersen had said. . . . Neither Hilda nor Frederich attended school. Frederich, years ago, had received a high school diploma, having received perfect scores on specially administered New York State Regents examinations without taking courses, but he had no interest in leaving home in order to attend college. Anyway, Mrs. Pedersen said that no one could teach Frederich anything. If he wanted to learn something he simply learned it on his own. And his musical compositions were his own, uniquely his own; no professor of music could help him. Hilda, though four years younger, had received perfect scores on the mathematical sections of the same exams, but she had failed the other sections and had shown no interest in improving her grades. For health reasons she did not attend school. Professors at nearby universities had invited her to study with them, but she had always declined.

(p. 107; © 1971 by Joyce Carol Oates. Used by permission of Vanguard Press.)

Do Hilda and Frederich fit your image of children who are gifted? How many times have we heard that child "geniuses" are antisocial, in poor health, timid, preoccupied with their work, dependent on their families? How often are these children portrayed in literature and newspapers as oddities of one kind or another?

We have seen from the character sketches at the beginning of the chapter, and from the many definitions discussed, that these exceptional children may exhibit as wide a range of characteristics and behaviors as the general population. True, Mary Hall (Eleanor Roosevelt) was awkward and sickly, but Elaine Hawkins (Isadora Duncan) was attractive, self-confident, and graceful. Similarly, Hilda and Frederich may fit into the stereotype of reclusive "strange children . . . written up in newspapers and magazines," but there are countless other children who have normal childhoods. It is interesting that these stereotypes are so prevalent when a majority of the research conducted thus far seems to indicate the exact opposite: Children who are gifted are, in general, healthy, popular, and emotionally well adjusted. Although we must caution once again against making blanket statements because of the heterogeneity of this group, we can at least clear up some of the misconceptions by discussing characteristics of children who are gifted.

Cognitive Domain

To restate the obvious, most children who are gifted function at a high level of cognition. This high level may be reflected in typical academic skills such as a retentive memory and fluency with symbol systems (such as mathematics and reading). However, their cognitive abilities often extend beyond traditional academic skills to include more abstract processes such as hypothetico-deductive reasoning. Thus, the teacher may find that that child who is gifted is not only already several pages, chapters, or books ahead of the group but is also not content to leave facts alone. For example, in a regular lesson in social studies, while other children seem content to memorize names and dates, the student who is gifted often goes beyond to ask why, to relate past events to later outcomes, to wonder "what if," to evaluate what transpired. He or she may often become impatient with the pace of the class. The student who is gifted may express thoughts that are often highly creative, but they may throw the unprepared teacher off guard.

If we think back to some of the characteristics of creativity suggested by Guilford (1950), we find many of these included in the cognitive repertoire of children who are gifted: flexibility, fluency, creation of novel ideas, analytical ability, and so on. Some of the abilities of these children that fall within the cognitive domain include the following:

- asks many questions; is often not satisfied with "simple" answers
- has a good memory; is often exceptionally facile at retaining numbers and other symbols
- begins to read at an early age and is often several grade levels above age-mates
- likes to experiment, hypothesize, test out new ideas
- has good reasoning ability; understands quickly
- has a strong vocabulary

Social and Emotional Domain

Probably one of the most persistent stereotypes about children who are gifted is that they are socially inept and emotionally unstable. It is curious that such a stereotype has lingered despite a great deal of evidence to the contrary. The Terman longitudinal studies (Goleman, 1980; Terman, 1954; Sears, 1977; Terman & Oden, 1947) showed that, as a group, individuals who are gifted tend to be more emotionally stable, mentally healthy, and socially skilled than the general population. J. J. Gallagher (1975b) found that they are usually popular among their age-mates, although this may taper off during the secondary school years. Of course, as with any other segment of the population, there are some creative and talented people who have social and emotional problems.

Why is emotional stability common among individuals who are gifted? Studies done on the relationship between giftedness and personal and social characteristics seem to indicate that the same abilities to cope with the environment, solve problems, and seek out new ideas that are important to cognition also serve to enhance emotional

well-being. Some general personal, social, and emotional characteristics of children who are gifted include the following:

- is a leader in many social situations; enjoys decision making and assumes responsibility for the group
- is cooperative; adjusts easily
- has a good sense of humor; is quick to point out incongruities in situations
- is sensitive to the needs of others
- has an advanced level of moral behavior and sense of justice
- maintains a positive self-image and a high level of self-awareness
- is emotionally independent and stable

Physical Characteristics

Hand in hand with the perception that a child who is gifted is emotionally incompetent is the stereotype of a weak, sickly child sitting at home concocting elaborate chemistry experiments while the other children in the neighborhood play softball. Not so! Once again, prevailing perceptions and reality do not quite mesh. Physically, the child who is gifted is no weaker, less athletic, or more sickly than his or her peers. In fact, when physiological measures have been examined (for example, in the Terman longitudinal study), researchers have found that these children tend to be slightly stronger, larger, and more healthy than the norm.

IDENTIFICATION OF CHILDREN WHO ARE GIFTED

Our discussion of children who are gifted thus far has emphasized the diverse range of skills and abilities of the group. How, then, do we go about identifying that part of the population we call gifted? In 1984, the estimated number of children who are gifted in the school population was between 1.5 and 2 million; this did not include those of preschool age. Identification methods must be comprehensive enough to screen such a large target population while at the same time sufficiently detailed to focus on specific abilities. Several points must be considered when selecting identification techniques.

First, the purpose of identification must be determined. Identification has been used primarily to place children in special programs; therefore, the type of program will greatly influence the method of identification. For instance, acceleration or enrichment of traditional academic subjects most likely warrants identification through achievement measures and intelligence tests. A special program in the arts, on the other hand, requires procedures such as a review of portfolios or compositions, auditions, interviews, and so on.

Second, the relative merit of various identification and screening methods should be evaluated. In a classic article, C. Pegnato and J. Birch (1959) outlined two criteria for evaluating measures on the basis of their effectiveness (How well does the method locate all children who are gifted?) and their efficiency (What is the ratio of the actual group of gifted to those initially selected for screening?).

J. Renzulli, S. Reis, and L. Smith (1981) discuss the effectiveness and efficiency of traditional procedures (group and individual intelligence tests and achievement measures) with the case study approach. The case study method includes these measures: aptitude and achievement test information, ratings by teachers, school records, parent ratings, and student self-ratings. The authors conclude that no single evaluation procedure should be used across the board. Rather, a variety of sources of information should be used to identify youngsters who are gifted and talented.

Sources of Identification

The most common procedure in the identification process is to initially screen large groups of children during the course of regular assessment and evaluation in the schools. These assessments include group-administered measures such as intelligence, aptitude, and achievement tests. Children receiving scores above a certain cut-off point or percentile are then individually tested to determine if they qualify for specialized educational programs.

This traditional method has been greatly augmented and expanded in recent years. Table 11.3 outlines the wide variety of methods that can be used to begin the identification process. For instance, parents may contact the guidance counselor, teacher, or school psychologist and request individual testing. Teachers and other personnel may recommend children on the basis of class performance, anecdotal information, or observation.

How efficient are these methods? The best approach is to base selection on examination of several *kinds* of evidence. Though individual intelligence tests do successfully isolate high academic achievers, identification of those who show promise in artistic, psychomotor, or leadership areas may require a combination of work samples, peer nominations, parent interviews, and teacher ratings.

The identification of children who are gifted and who are from disadvantaged or different cultures is somewhat more complicated. L. L. Schwartz (1984) and E. Bernal (1979) suggest that the identification procedure be broad enough to incorporate the particular types of performance considered valuable by the culture or community. Community support and assistance should be enlisted, especially because these children may not be spotted initially through school performance measures.

Locating young children who are gifted also may require an adjustment of the traditional methods, not only because they may not yet be participating in an educational program but also because their disparate abilities may not be tapped by the standard psychometric tests. Parent interviews and anecdotal records are especially reliable when combined with a selective battery of various subtests from intelligence and achievement measures.

TABLE 11.3

SOURCES AND LEVELS OF IDENTIFICATION OF THE GIFTED

	Sources			
Level	**Tests/Assessments**	**Teachers/School Personnel**	**Parents**	**Child**
Group	Intelligence tests Achievement measures Aptitude tests	Teacher ratings Classroom observations	Parent-teacher associations Community groups	Peer nominations
Individual	Intelligence tests Creativity measures Specialized testing Recitals Auditions Special academic tests	Teacher: Ratings (learning motivation, creativity, leadership; see Martinson, 1973) Anecdotal records Recommendations Observations School psychologist/counselor: Ratings Anecdotal information Observation Other school personnel: Librarian Physical education Arts	Parent interviews Anecdotal records Ratings	Child self-ratings Interview Creative Products: Work samples (autobiographies, artistic pieces, portfolio, performance, experiments) Leadership qualifications Other

Young Children Who Are Gifted

They say as a child
I appeared a little bit wild
With all those crazy ideas
I knew I was a genius
What's so strange if you know
That you're a wizard at three
I knew this was meant for me

From the song "Twisted" by Annie Ross and Wardell Gray. © 1965 Prestige Music. Used by permission.

Finding and characterizing children when they are very young and gifted presents something of a problem. For the most part, children are identified as gifted sometime during the elementary school years as they come into contact with structured learning situations and are compared with other children the same age. However, as more children participate in some form of early intervention (day care, preschool, play groups, and so on), identifying giftedness at a younger age becomes more possible. Moreover, increased public knowledge about what these children are like

Advanced language skills may be indicative of high levels of intellectual ability. (Photo by Joseph Bodkin.)

may serve to alert parents to look for these characteristics in their young children.

Very young children may exhibit a diverse range of talents and abilities (see Box 11.2). For instance, there are many documented cases of children who walked, talked, and read at an extraordinarily early age. In the early part of this century, L. Hollingworth (1926) reported several interesting case histories of children with very high IQs (180 and above) that reveal their truly accelerated development. For example:

From her eighth month she used a paper and pencil, drawing recognizable figures. . . . She taught herself her letters from street signs and books, and could print them all before she was three, and during the next few months would write letters of several pages of her own composition, having the words, of course, spelled for her. (pp. 224–225)

At 12 months he could say the alphabet forward, and at 16 months could say it backward and forward. His parents had no idea he could reverse the alphabet until one day he announced that he was "tired of saying the letters forward" and "guessed he would say them backward." The concepts of "forward" and "backward" were thus developed by the age of 16 months. At 12 months he began to classify his blocks according to the shape of the letters on them, placing A V M W N and other pointed letters together, Q O C D and other letters with loops together, and so forth. . . . (pp. 250–251)

Other young children may show different sorts of talents, such as agility in dancing, drawing, social leadership, or creativity in question asking and problem solving. H. Robinson, W. Roedell, and N. Jackson (1979) note that young children who are gifted often have their own set of problems. For example, they may be able to read at a fourth-grade level but not have the fine motor coordination to hold a pencil and write. Or they may have many good ideas and creative inventions but be frustrated with the time available to carry these out because they still need a nap in the afternoon! The University of Washington has a preschool program for children who are gifted (Robinson et al., 1979) that takes these disparities into account in both identification and intervention. We will discuss some of the problems of identification of and intervention with children who are gifted in the following section.

Hard-to-Identify Gifted Children

When children must contend with a variety of problems or disabilities, their unique talents and gifts may be difficult to discover. Traditional identification procedures are all too often too narrowly focused on the "norm" (middle class, with no special problems or disabilities) to pick out these children. Although most children who have participated in educational programs for the gifted have come from advantaged backgrounds, there are many other children who are disadvantaged or have a disability. One of the findings of the Office of Education study (Marland, 1972)

BOX 11.2

SAMPLE OF THE WORK OF A CHILD WHO IS GIFTED

In the piece of creative writing by a five-year-old gifted child reproduced here, notice the use of vocabulary and the complex and compound sentences. Notice also the sense of excitement the young writer is able to convey.

Jousting Tournaments

When a jousting tournament begins, a herald goes from castle to castle announcing the tournament. Squires start cleaning and polishing their master's armor. Tailors make surcoats and gay gowns for the ladies. Knights practice with their swords and lances, and pages pretend with wooden swords. In a few days, the tournament will be held! People start coming to the castle that is holding the tournament. Rooms are found for spectators to sleep in. If they don't find rooms, they set up tents. Today's the day! The tournament is being held today! The knights are up at dawn. Squires help put on armor. The herald goes around collecting knights from their tents. Pretty soon they form a parade. The knights charge in the lists. A lance hits a shield—bang! A knight is thrown off a horse. It happens again and again. Ladies throw scarves and ribbons to their favorite knights. The knight who has broken the most lances receives a garland of flowers on his head by The Queen of Love and Beauty.

The End

---

was that many of these children were not being identified by traditional methods. A. White (1976) notes that approximately 2 to 5 percent of children who are gifted are also handicapped.

E. Torrance (1971) and E. Bernal (1979; Bernal & Reyna, 1975) have urged educators, psychologists, and parents to be alert for characteristics other than those present in the "typical" child who is gifted. For example, children from other cultural backgrounds (e.g., Mexican-American, Native American) may have quite different sets of talents. What is clever and creative for a child in the barrio or on the reservation, where different value systems are in operation, will not be the same as for the child who grows up in the suburbs. Furthermore, language differences often hinder performance when children are not tested in their native tongue. Torrance (1971) recommends that teachers and others be aware of the following characteristics in children who are gifted and culturally different:

1. high nonverbal fluency and originality

2. high creative productivity in small groups

3. adeptness in visual arts activities

4. high creativity in movement, dance, and other physical activities

5. high motivation from games, music, sports, humor, and concrete objects

6. language rich in imagery (p. 75).

Similarly, those who are handicapped with a physical or learning disability may not evidence their talents quite as soon or in the same manner as other children who are gifted (see Box 11.3). For example, children who are hearing impaired obviously will not have the verbal fluency commonly associated with giftedness, but they may display unique perceptual abilities or psychomotor talents. J. R. Whitmore (1981) estimated there may be 120,000 to 180,000 youngsters who are gifted *and* handicapped. These numbers are based on the expectation that at least 2 percent of all children with handicaps could be gifted. Whitmore attributes problems in identifying these learners to developmental delays that hinder performance on early aptitude measures. In addition,

BOX 11.3

RAY CHARLES—A MAN OF MANY TALENTS

Giftedness or a unique talent may be difficult to detect in individuals who are disabled or who come from culturally different or impoverished backgrounds. The life of Ray Charles exemplifies this point.

> When Ray Charles performs, his voice dominates you with its feeling of pain and hope—a reflection of his impoverished youth. Today, he is a renowned vocalist, pianist, writer, and composer. And, if that isn't enough, he is also referred to as a "living legend." . . .

While Charles is grateful for forty years of success, he can never forget the bad days. Ray Charles Robinson was not born blind, only poor. It was not until he was seven that glaucoma, compounded by the effects of poverty, left him completely blind. His love of music did not suffer, however, and he studied piano and voice at a special school for the blind.

Life has offered Ray Charles many challenges. "I've been hearing the blues all my life," he says. "People should never be bitter about anything. They should go out and learn to keep fighting for themselves."

Ray Charles has created an inspiring variety of music. It has been a great achievement, but it is his intense humanity and humility that communicate to his audiences.

> You figure anytime the public will support any artist, no matter who, for 40 years the way

Ray Charles, the "living legend," has attained a high status in the world of music despite his disability. (Columbia photo by Ron Keith. Courtesy of Joseph Curreri.)

they've stuck with me, I think I owe them something . . . , I owe them my best. And now I give them even more of myself. When it gets to the point where I can't give my best, I'll quit because they've taken care of me a long time. I had it instilled in me as a child—you always give your best, or don't give at all.

Source: Curreri, J. (1985). Ray Charles creates new variety of music. *Accent on Living, 30,* 66–68. Used by permission of Joseph Curreri.

a handicapping condition may render a child unable to demonstrate superior abilities.

The child who is gifted but underachieving presents something of a paradox. Although intelligence tests, achievement measures, parental interviews, and anecdotal records show superior abilities, the underachiever has a poor record when it comes to in-class performance. A variety of factors could contribute to underachievement, including fear of failure, boredom, emotional immaturity, and family problems. Counselors and teachers should be careful to encourage the underachiever without constantly using test scores as a source of chastisement.

David, age two, can read simple words and enjoys spelling with his magnetic letters. (Photo by Joseph Bodkin.)

ORIGINS OF GIFTEDNESS

The question of the contributions of heredity and environment to intelligence has been a continual source of debate. The debate has particular importance in a discussion of children who are gifted, for two reasons. First, it helps us gain a perspective on where cognitive ability might come from and what it is. Second, it helps determine intervention strategies. For example, if environmental factors do not appear to influence intelligence to a great degree, special educational programming, both compensatory and enriched, may not have much of an impact.

Interest in children who are gifted and their education was strongly influenced by Terman's contention that intelligence is primarily genetically determined (Seagoe, 1975). This genetic view was seconded by A. Jensen (1969), who argued that as much as 70 percent of the variability in intelligence is due to heredity. Jensen further asserted that there were strong racial differences in intelligence, and that black children

have lower levels of the cognitive abilities necessary for successful school performance.

Needless to say, such a contention stirred up a great deal of controversy. Other psychologists were quick to point to research indicating that it is the environmental context within which children live that makes the strongest impact on cognitive ability. For example, the quality of interaction between parent and child may have a profound effect on intellectual stimulation. In disadvantaged settings, factors such as the quantity and quality of interactions and lack of environmental stimulation (e.g., books, games, discussions, family outings), as well as physiological factors such as poor nutrition, all contribute to lower intellectual performance and achievement. Research aside, it seems logical that a black child raised as a second-class citizen in a white society, attending white-run schools, taking white-oriented intelligence tests, is likely to grade lower. The influence of genetics is not ruled out; rather, the interaction between heredity and environment is stressed. By recognizing the contributions of both, we can turn to educational programming as a means to enrich the lives of disadvantaged as well as advantaged children who are gifted.

A Developmental Perspective on Giftedness

It is important to consider briefly how the abilities of children who are gifted grow, change, and develop over time. Many conceptualizations have failed to define the underlying processes related to giftedness, and descriptions of characteristics of children who are gifted merely scratch the surface.

Several researchers, however, have speculated on just what abilities or processes are especially important for bright children. M. C. Reynolds and J. Birch (1977) suggest that "the chief [component of cognition] that characterizes the gifted and talented is the heightened ability to manipulate systems and particularly to manipulate systems made up of symbols" (p. 209). And according to J. J. Gallagher (1975a), "The ability to manipulate internally learned symbol systems is perhaps the sine qua non of giftedness" (p. 10).

As Reynolds and Birch go on to point out, this ability is relevant not only to academic areas such as mathematics but also to musical composition (musical notes) or dance (dance labonotation). Other processes that may be important in the development of giftedness are generalization, conceptualization, memory, motivation, and the ability to discover relationships between objects and events (Newland, 1976). The multidimensional view of intelligence depicted in Guilford's Structure of the Intellect model may provide a developmental perspective on the processes essential to gifted and creative activity.

More recently, some researchers have argued that it is time to move away from the predominantly trait-specific, psychometric-based conceptualizations of giftedness that have characterized most research and practice. D. Feldman (1982) recommended that giftedness be examined within a developmental framework. From this perspective, exceptional talent may be seen as resulting from an interaction between inherited abilities and environmental opportunities.

PARENTS, TEACHERS, AND CHILDREN WHO ARE GIFTED

Two parents related: "We started out in kindergarten with our child in the public schools, and [our] child was labeled a problem in kindergarten because when the teacher asked him to go over and turn on the light, he'd say, 'would you like to know how the light switch works?' and this sent the teacher right up the wall, so he was labeled a behavior problem."
(National Public Radio Broadcast, 1976, p. 16)

Last year . . . [Mr. and Mrs. Smith] of suburban Chicago tried to get the local public school to accept their son, Jeffrey, as an early entrant for the following fall. Only four years old, Jeffrey was extremely verbal and could already read and do arithmetical calculations. The teacher who examined Jeffrey turned down the request for early entrance. She acknowledged that Jeffrey could read, but said that he had no comprehension of what he was reading.

So Jeffrey, who is now five years old, will be starting school this fall. While he was waiting to be old enough to begin kindergarten, Jeffrey spent a good part of each week in the public library pursuing personal research projects in astronomy and geography.
(Maeroff, 1977, p. 31)

A highly gifted child, ten years old, was considered strange and not very bright. She was always at odds with her teachers. During one lesson she was reproached for grinning and was told by her teacher "to rub off the grin from her face." She took out an [eraser] and rubbed her mouth! She was promptly sent out and came to [the counselor]. During their talk, she complained bitterly that "schools for teachers should teach would-be teachers to understand the minds of children, and should not select teachers who have no sense of humor."
(Butler-Arlosdroff, 1978, p. 4)

These anecdotes show that teachers can misunderstand the needs of the child who is gifted. Stories abound of teachers who resent or ignore these children. Their parents are often portrayed as pushy and overindulgent. Are these characterizations realistic?

Probably not. However, the literature on children who are gifted is replete with such stories. Teachers and parents may be bewildered when it comes to meeting the needs of this child. Teachers are busy attempting to cope with the demands of the larger group or with the exceptional child experiencing developmental delays rather than with precociousness. Consequently, parents may think that their child is neglected and even resented by educators and may see themselves and school personnel on opposite sides of the issue, fighting over the educational future of the child. However, parents, teachers, and other school personnel can work together. Teachers often do not have enough knowledge or training about giftedness to be able to identify all kinds of exceptional children and determine the appropriate type of intervention. Parents often forget that teachers must attend to the group first and individual children second. By recognizing each others' responsibilities and priorities, adults can complement each other and help the child who is gifted at the same time. How can this be accomplished? At the outset, it is essential to understand three points:

1. Adults must realize that the needs and behavior of the child who is gifted will affect parent, teacher, and administrator differently. The creative remarks, suggestions, and inventions that are a source of enrichment and fulfillment at home may be seen as an interruption in the classroom when the teacher is moderating the demands of twenty-five children. Conversely, teachers may be delighted, challenged, and stimulated by the very same interactions that parents feel incapable of dealing with.

2. The influence that these children have on separate individuals may be different from the influence they have on the constellation of significant adults as a whole. Parents and teachers are undoubtedly the most significant adults in the child's life. Combined with the broad, albeit less noticeable, influence that the school superintendents, state and federal legislators, and others have on decisions affecting children who are gifted, this group becomes fairly complex. Adults must decide where their influence and concerns intersect, and how they might best work together.

3. Finally, it is important to be aware of the nature of reciprocal interactions between child and adult. Adult-child interaction is bidirectional; that is, just as adults affect children, so do children affect adults. This influence of children upon adults in turn affects adults' subsequent interactions with children.

A partnership of parents, teachers, and administrators may occur at several levels. Individual parents concerned about their child may meet privately with the child's teacher and the principal. Parents may form a group in which they can discuss ideas about working with their children, problems they might have, potential resources,

and the like. They can work to get the community to take an interest in children who are gifted by offering seminars or lectures on giftedness, or by arranging field trips, independent study opportunities, and so forth. Parents and teachers can work together on the local parent-teacher association or at the state level by organizing a lobby to look out for the interests of the gifted at the state department of education. Teachers can help parents by explaining the curricular modifications that are being used and by offering suggestions and support for activities at home.

EDUCATIONAL INTERVENTION: AN OVERVIEW OF PROGRAMMING

An array of different educational provisions is available for children who are gifted and talented. As is emphasized throughout this chapter, some children may need special educational programming so that they are challenged and stimulated to reach up to and beyond their potential. Arguments against such special programming have been based largely on the contention that special attention for children who are gifted may create a meritocracy, or an elite class of students. J. J. Gallagher and P. Weiss (1979) counter by noting that we already have special programs in the form of medical schools, law schools, ability tracking in elementary and secondary school, special sports programs for basketball and football stars, and so forth. By exploring all types of differential programming and using available resources more fully, educators can reach a wider spectrum of children who are gifted and talented. Although Thomas Edison and Isadora Duncan discovered and used their extraordinary talents without benefit of special educational programs, many children do not. Table 11.4 explores some of the rationales for differential educational programs for children who are gifted. In most cases, such programs are supported by state and local funds rather than federal monies.

TABLE 11.4
NEED FOR DIFFERENTIAL EDUCATIONAL PROGRAMMING FOR THE GIFTED

Reason for Need	Potential Results of Differential Programming	Possible Types of Differentiation
1. **Cognitive development** Failure to achieve potential Possible regression Necessity for early intervention Lack of higher-level thinking skills, challenge, stimulation	1. Prevention of loss of creative critical thinking Stimulation of higher-level thinking skills	1. Enrichment in regular classroom Individualized instruction Specialized programs in subject areas Some acceleration depending upon age of child, availability of programs
2. **Creative development** Lack of chances for creativity in regular classroom Pressure to conform and produce typical work	2. Acceptance of creative, unusual, divergent thinking products Stimulation of creative processes	2. Activities that encourage creativity in regular classroom Special programs in arts, sciences, creative writing, etc. Full-time differentiation
3. **Sociopersonal adjustment** Delinquency Drop-out Underachievement Need for group interaction	3. Feeling of confidence, acceptance Challenging atmosphere may help underachiever, lower drop-out rate, prevent delinquency Promotion of peer interaction	3. Changes in content and method of presentation to be more challenging Some individualization but also strong group interaction with other gifted children
4. **Benefits to teacher/classroom** Need for specialized teaching strategies Teacher may feel threatened Problems for rest of class	4. Regular teachers may feel less threatened May be able to spend more time with gifted if other needs met by special program May help develop more effective teaching strategies	4. Training for regular classroom teacher Special teacher or program

Available Options

Just as educational options for youngsters with handicaps exist on a continuum, so too does programming for children who are gifted (see Figure 11.3). B. R. Gearheart and M. W. Weishahn (1984) divide these options into three categories: ability grouping, acceleration, and enrichment. Ability grouping, as described by B. Clark (1979) includes six different arrangements:

1. *Regular classroom with a cluster.* Here, a child who is gifted is grouped with other students within the class who also are bright.

2. *Regular classroom with pullout.* Youngsters who are gifted remain in their assigned classroom for most of the school day. However, they are occasionally "pulled out" for participation in specific activities geared toward their interests and abilities. This option closely resembles the resource room option of Deno's Cascade (Deno, 1970).

3. *Individualized classrooms.* All students in this classroom, regardless of their ability levels, participate in educational activities designed to meet their individual needs.

4. *Special class with some integration.* This option closely resembles level 4 of Deno's Cascade (Deno, 1970). Here, students who are gifted spend part of their instructional day in classrooms with teachers specifically trained in ed-

BOX 11.4
UNUSUAL PROGRAMS FOR CHILDREN WHO ARE GIFTED

A wide variety of special programs exist for children who are gifted, running the gamut from after-school, Saturday, or vacation special-interest courses to full-time private schools. Although these options once were available primarily for children at the upper elementary or secondary school levels, recently programs for preschool, kindergarten, and early elementary school have been developed as well. Three examples of the diversity in programming may be cited: the preschool gifted program at the University of Washington; the Calasanctius School, a private program in Buffalo, New York; and the Study of Mathematically Precocious Youth (SMPY) at Johns Hopkins University in Baltimore, Maryland.

A long-range study of young children who are gifted and their families included a special preschool program at the University of Washington (Robinson, Roedell, & Jackson, 1979). The study had three components: a strong identification segment, the preschool program itself, and guidance and counseling services for parents. The preschool curriculum was based on a high degree of individualization combined with many opportunities for group interaction. The development of large and small motor skills was emphasized as well. This was considered an especially important component of the curriculum because young children who are gifted may have superior cognitive skills such as reading but lack the eye-hand coordination necessary for attendant skills such as writing. Other areas included in the curriculum were group decision making and the development of social skills.

The Calasanctius School (Gerencser, 1979) in Buffalo was established in 1957 as a private program offering children who are gifted something beyond the traditional modes of acceleration or enrichment. Although originally only for upper elementary and secondary level boys, Calasanctius now is coeducational and has extended its program to the preschool years.

The Calasanctius curriculum attempts to integrate rigorous and intensive instruction with ample opportunities for discussion, experimentation, and independent study. Subject matter is often sequenced over several years. For instance, the Historical Studies Program, a six- to seven-year examination of the history of civilization, incorporates individual historical time periods such as the Middle Ages or American Civilization within the overall context of civilization. Students participate in weekly colloquia, or round table discussions, instead of the traditional public school–style assemblies. Independent study in an area of academic and professional interest is encouraged through a three-year seminar program, and practical learning experiences are gained through extended field trips.

Children with extraordinary mathematical reasoning abilities can be placed in a variety of accelerated programs under the auspices of the Study of Mathematically Precocious Youth (SMPY) at Johns Hopkins University (Stanley, 1979). Begun in 1971, SMPY has attempted to develop and implement a large-scale identification/intervention program for children (usually in seventh through ninth grades) who have superior skills in mathematics and might not have the opportunity to explore these skills in regular school programs. Potential participants take the mathematics section of the Scholastic Aptitude Test (SAT-M); almost half achieve higher scores than the average high school senior. Depending on their scores, interests, locations, and schedules, students are placed in a suitable accelerated program. This may include a special SMPY mathematics class (taught by a college professor in the evenings or on the weekend), a three-week course in the summer, the skipping of an entire grade in all subjects or in mathematics only, part-time college work or early entrance to college, or college credit through Advanced Placement examinations. Some students take part purely as an extracurricular interest; others have combined several of these options to graduate from high school at a very young age and enter college with a portion of their mathematics credits already earned.

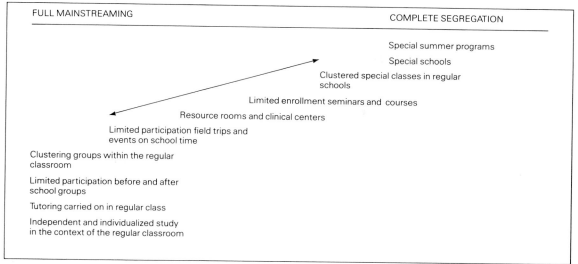

| FULL MAINSTREAMING | | COMPLETE SEGREGATION |

Special summer programs

Special schools

Clustered special classes in regular schools

Limited enrollment seminars and courses

Resource rooms and clinical centers

Limited participation field trips and events on school time

Clustering groups within the regular classroom

Limited participation before and after school groups

Tutoring carried on in regular class

Independent and individualized study in the context of the regular classroom

Figure 11.3. The continuum of options for the education of children who are gifted. (From M. C. Reynolds and J. W. Birch, *Teaching Exceptional Children in All America's Schools*. Reston, Va.: Council for Exceptional Children, 1982, p. 212; used with permission.)

ucation of the gifted. The remainder of the day is spent in the regular classroom.

5. *Special class.* Students receive instruction in self-contained classes for children who are gifted, with minimum interaction with peers who are not gifted. This placement corresponds to level 5 of Deno's Cascade (Deno, 1970).

6. *Special schools.* According to Gearheart and Weishahn (1984), this is the approach most frequently taken in larger cities where there are more students who are extremely gifted or who possess very special talents.

Acceleration, the second category discussed by Gearheart and Weishahn (1984), involves techniques that facilitate rapid movement through regular public school grades. Examples include early school entrance, skipping grades, telescoping grades (that is, completing three grades in two years), and advanced placement.

Finally, enrichment involves supplementing the school program with components not traditionally included in a regular curriculum. R. H.

Swassing (1985) suggests that children who are gifted should first master basic skills, then participate in activities designed to capitalize on their special abilities. These activities may include "field trips, library work, art projects, history projects, science experiments, music activities, producing a journal, and creative writing" (Swassing, 1985, p. 11).

Technology and Computer-Assisted Instruction

Technological advances have had more of an effect on the lives of children with physical or learning disabilities than on the lives of children who are gifted. The advent of computer-assisted instruction, however, has benefited both groups of children. As will be discussed in Chapter 16, CAI offers a range of options, from drill and practice activities to problem solving and simulation. These latter activities appear most suitable for children who are gifted because they provide greater opportunities for intellectual development. A. Dover (1983) summarized empirical reports of CAI effectiveness with learners who are gifted. She reported the positive impact of CAI upon the development of cognitive skills such as abstract thinking (Stein, 1981), problem-solving skills (Caputo, 1981; Zuber, 1980), and logical thinking (Berger, 1981; Zuber, 1980). In addition, investigators have reported that exposure to CAI improved affective performance of students who are gifted (Charp, 1977; Milner, 1974; Spencer & Baskin, 1981).

In addition to immediate gains, use of CAI with students who are gifted may have long-range benefits for society in general. These students probably have the greatest potential for contributing to the development of technology and the advancement of CAI (Kneedler, 1984). Capitalizing on this potential requires continued exposure to computer-assisted instruction that is suited to the unique characteristics of students who are gifted. According to Dover (1983), such instruction should include more sophisticated software, a professional commitment to the development of enrichment programs that involve computers, and the development of computer competencies by teachers of youngsters who are gifted.

SUMMARY

Children who are gifted and talented have exceptional abilities or potential in such a wide variety of areas that it is difficult to come up with a comprehensive definition of giftedness.

Giftedness and talent may refer to superior intellectual ability, problem-solving skills, artistic ability, leadership, social skills, or athletic prowess. Traditional evaluations have used intelligence tests as the sole criteria for identifying giftedness. This has changed as definitions of giftedness have expanded to include a variety of dimensions, including creativity.

Creativity often is associated with giftedness. The dimensions of creativity are so diverse that one theorist postulates that creativity and intelligence are not unitary phenomena but rather consist of as many as 120 factors. Other theorists agree that creativity and intelligence may be made up of a variety of attributes such as sensitivity, fluency, flexibility, complexity, and abilities to synthesize, analyze, reorganize, and evaluate.

In recent years, attempts to define giftedness have extended beyond IQ measures and creativity research to more expanded definitions that encompass a variety of abilities and talents. This expanded approach is reflected in the legislative definition adopted by the United States Office of Education and used by many states as an official definition. Researchers have suggested that more attention be directed to the underlying developmental processes that may contribute to giftedness and talent.

Despite popular beliefs, research evidence shows quite clearly that children who are gifted are not pale, sickly, bespectacled bookworms who are unhappy and keep to themselves. On the contrary, they are generally slightly happier, healthier, more popular, and more emotionally stable than are children who are not gifted.

A multiple method/multiple criterion approach to identifying children who are gifted is preferred to a single-test approach. Although an individual intelligence test usually identifies high achievers, other approaches are necessary to identify children who are underachievers or who have artistic, social, leadership, or athletic abilities.

Traditionally, the most common forms of special programs for children who are gifted have been acceleration (grade skipping) or some type of enrichment. Other education programs are quite diverse and can include full- and part-time special classes; resource rooms; individualization and acceleration by content area; special programs in the arts, sciences, writing, and the like; advanced placement courses for college-bound youngsters; summer programs; special schools; special trips; and community internships.

Suggestions for Further Reading

Barbe, W., & Renzulli, J. (Eds.) (1981). *Psychology and education of the gifted* (3rd ed.). New York: Irvington.
A volume of collected works on giftedness, this edition updates much of the research and contains some of the

foremost work in the field. A wide range of topics is covered, including a historical overview, characteristics and identification procedures, program development, instructional approaches, and counseling and personal development.

Gallagher, J. J. (1975). *Teaching the gifted child* (2nd ed.). Boston: Allyn and Bacon.

An excellent introduction to the issues surrounding the development of educational provisions for the gifted. Gallagher presents the problems clearly and with numerous examples and offers a comprehensive examination of concerns and potential curricular modifications across a wide variety of subject matter (English, social studies) and populations (disadvantaged, underachievers).

Hollingworth, L. (1926). *Gifted children, their nature and nurture.* New York: Macmillan.

This is a detailed study of young high-IQ children, with complex anecdotal accounts of their behavior at home and in school. Hollingworth's volume is a good representative of the descriptive research about gifted children conducted in the early part of the century.

Nazzaro, J. N. (1981). *Computer connections for gifted children and youth.* Reston, VA: The Council for Exceptional Children.

This is an edited collection of articles describing the impact of computer-assisted instruction upon learners who are gifted.

Passow, A. (1979). *The gifted and talented. Their education and development.* 78th Yearbook of the National Society for the Study of Education. Part I. Chicago: University of Chicago Press.

This is a volume of papers devoted to an analysis of the past, present, and future status of giftedness and gifted education in the United States and in other cultures. Many of the important researchers in the field are represented. The Yearbook covers a wide variety of topics, such as a review of federal and state provisions for gifted education, identification and evaluation of young gifted children, an update on the Terman longitudinal study, and a Piagetian perspective on giftedness.

Swassing, R. H. (1985). *Teaching gifted children and adolescents.* Columbus, OH: Merrill.

This book addresses the key issues in the education of children who are gifted, including identification, assessment, and characteristics. It includes instructional methods and materials for four major content areas.

Relevant Journals

Gifted Child Quarterly

This research-oriented journal is published four times a year by the National Association for Gifted Children, 217 Gregory Drive, Hot Springs, AZ.

Gifted Children Newsletter

This newsletter is published by Gifted and Talented Publications, Inc., RD 1, Box 128-A, Egg Harbor Road, Sewell, NJ. There are twelve issues a year, and each issue contains information and activities for the home and school.

Journal for the Education of the Gifted

This research journal is published quarterly by the Association for the Gifted, The Council for Exceptional Children, 1920 Association Drive, Reston, VA.

CHAPTER 12

Young Children with Handicaps and Their Families

Did You Know That . . .

- parents play a pivotal role in identification of and intervention for young children with handicaps, but they must often coordinate the intervention with very little help from professionals?

- parents sometimes experience grief similar to that experienced at the death of a loved one when they learn their child is handicapped?

- there are individual differences among parents in their reactions to a child who is handicapped and in their adaptations to the child?

- fathers worry more about the future whereas mothers are more concerned about the emotional strain on the family and their ability to cope with the child's needs?

- feelings and reactions of siblings should be considered?

- for many children, especially the children of poverty, the early years represent a time of missed opportunity if they are not provided with an educational program?

- many early educators believe that educating preschoolers who are handicapped with those who are not will help them be more accepting of differences as they grow up?

- parents are effective teachers of their young children with handicaps, and many successful model programs are based in the home?

Picture in your mind's eye the people standing in front of the observation window of a hospital nursery full of newborns. You would probably see a set or two of grandparents, gazing fondly at their new grandchild. Perhaps there would be an older brother or sister standing by grandmother and making funny faces, maybe saying something like, "I can't believe I was ever that tiny!" There may be a new father at the window, grinning from ear to ear and holding up the football he has just rushed out to buy his firstborn son. Of course, there would be new mothers there—perhaps they are already comparing their children with the others that lie in nearby bassinets. Which one is the biggest? The longest? Has the most hair? The reddest face? Is sleeping most peacefully?

The birth of a child is usually a time of great joy. But the happiness and positive expectations are sometimes shattered when the child is born with a problem. Think how you would feel if you were standing in front of that nursery window having just given birth to a Down syndrome baby? Or a baby with a malformed heart or limb? You could be standing there feeling pleased as punch, but the baby may have a serious problem that has not yet been diagnosed—deafness, for example. Some of the babies may seem quite normal now, as we stand and watch them through the window, but by first grade, they may have fallen behind their age mates in learning. Why? Perhaps they have hidden genetic defects, or they will not get adequate nutrition or language stimulation, or perhaps they will be abused or neglected.

FAMILY REACTIONS TO NEWS OF A HANDICAP

It is not difficult to imagine that the parents' world is turned upside down when they learn their infant is not normal. Their dreams and hopes are shattered and they have very little in the way of information to fall back on. One parent described it this way:

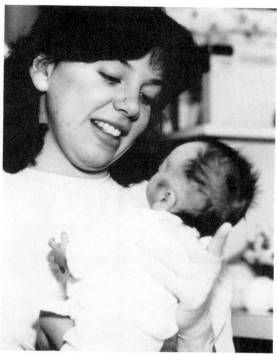

The birth of a child is usually a time of great joy. When the child has a handicap, both mother and father must deal with any discrepancy between their expectations of birth as a joyous event and the reality of a child with a handicap. (Courtesy of the Department of Medical Photography, Children's Hospital, Columbus, Ohio.)

Although parenthood is difficult, there are a number of precedents, support systems and social institutions that provide structure and reinforcement most of the time. Most parents can usually assume that their children will fit the expectations of their particular culture, grow up to be competent citizens who share in the responsibilities and benefits of the society, find satisfying and remunerative work, marry and produce children of their own, and, along the way, receive an adequate public education. These are the basic assumptions of life. As Billy's parents, my husband and I found that they did not apply. Parents of handicapped children can make no assumptions. Twenty-five years ago, the pediatrician diagnosed

Billy's retardation and gave us our only direction: "Take him home and love him. He will probably be sickly, and he will respond to music."

(Excerpt from J. B. Schulz, A parent views parent participation. *Exceptional Education Quarterly,* 1982, 3(2), 17–24. Used with permission of the publisher, PRO-ED.)

Stages of Adjustment

Upon discovering their child has a disability, parents typically react by going through a series of stages:

1. shock
2. denial
3. sadness and sorrow
4. guilt
5. rejection
6. acceptance
7. constructive action

Many authors have attempted to identify and organize these stages, resulting in slightly different sequences and labels. Generally, however, parents first experience shock. Even parents who may have suspected a problem for quite some time are still shocked when officially informed of their child's disability. Second, parents may deny the problem exists. They may cling to the belief that their child will outgrow the problem or they may "doctor shop," desperately seeking a professional opinion that will support the contention that their child is normal. Third, they will experience a sense of sadness or sorrow so deep that it nearly rivals the emotion felt upon the death of a close loved one. Fourth, parents may feel guilty, believing some aspect of their own behavior is responsible for the child's condition. Fifth, a few parents may even reject their child. This rejection could be overt and result in behavior as drastic as child abuse, or it may be covert, hidden behind statements such as "With this baby, I'm a shoe-in for sainthood." The sixth stage is acceptance, when the parents accept the child's disability and do so without feelings of guilt or anger. This stage is followed by constructive action, during which parents take specific positive steps to meet the unique challenges presented by their child's disability.

On the surface, these stages appear relatively neat and orderly. However, it should be noted that different sets of parents, or even each member of a particular couple, can vary greatly in the exact nature and intensity of their feelings, passage through these stages, and eventual degree of adjustment. Furthermore, it is not uncommon for these stages to overlap or to resurface in light of changes in the child's status.

One important difference among parents that may influence how they react to the child with a handicap concerns parental beliefs about the *cause* of the child's handicapping condition. As L. Lavelle and B. K. Keogh (1980) point out, parental feelings about causation probably affect their reactions. They state,

> The nature and intensity of some parental affective reactions may be linked to their belief that somehow they "caused" the child's handicap; other parents, however, might believe that something else caused the child's handicap or that it was an accident or an act of God. It seems reasonable to hypothesize that subsequent parental attitudes and behaviors will vary in part as a result of their views of the causes of the handicapping condition. (p. 4)

Lavelle and Keogh go on to suggest that parents' reactions might also vary depending on their views about the modifiability of the child's condition and their feelings about whether they can participate successfully in the treatment program for their child.

Mothers are especially vulnerable to adjustment problems. Perhaps because of their more immediate biological role in the birth of the child, the birth of a child has special meanings for the mother. For example, the child may be seen as a "product of love," which the mother then regards as an inadequate achievement if the child has a problem. Another view of the birth is that the child is a "gift," and the mother may feel worthless if her gift is defective. In some people's minds, the baby is seen in religious terms as a divine gift. The mother with this view might feel she is being punished if the baby has problems. Alternatively, she might feel she is being called on for special love to deal with her child who is handicapped. Also, a mother may have to deal with the possibility that her child's disability will require a lengthy hospital stay for additional medical attention. This estrangement may limit her ability to interact with and directly care for her baby. Professionals should be sensitive to this problem and provide the mother with explanations and instructions essential for a positive parent-child relationship.

The professional literature has not devoted too much attention to the relationship between fathers and newborns with disabilities. M. B. Hardman, C. T. Drew, and M. W. Egan (1987) state that the father's reactions may be more reserved. He may take upon himself the jobs of informing other family members of the birth of the child and keeping them advised of the status of the mother and the baby.

Some parent worries are linked to their roles within the family. For example, fathers are more likely to be worried about financial resources, the family budget, opportunities for their child to learn a skill and have a job, and the realism of their expectations for the child when that child becomes an adult. Mothers are more likely to worry about the emotional strain the child might put on them and on other family members, the time it will take to work with the child, and their ability (as the primary care-giver) to cope with the child's needs as well as the needs of other family members, especially the husband. Parents' fears are well founded: There is more separation and divorce among families with a child who is handicapped than among other families.

Just as parental reactions to their child's disability can vary, so too can there be variety in the reactions displayed by the child's brothers and sisters. As R. D. Kneedler (1984) points out, however, siblings are at a distinct disadvantage due to their lack of maturity. Frequently, they have many questions about the child's condition, how it will impact their lives, how to explain it to their

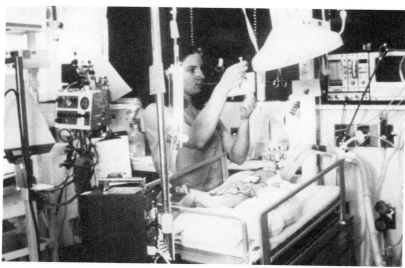

Careful monitoring is critical in the care of high-risk infants of low birth weight. For some of the infants, the risk of eye damage associated with oxygen administration must be weighed against the risk of death. (Courtesy of the Department of Medical Photography, Children's Hospital, Columbus, Ohio.)

friends, and so on. Unfortunately, they do not have access to a large group of professionals from whom they can obtain information. R. J. Simeonsson and S. M. McHale (1981) have identified some factors that do contribute to better adjustment:

1. A larger-sized family

2. the age and gender of siblings (girls frequently assume some responsibilities for caring for the child with a disability)

3. a less severe handicap

4. a handicap that is more visible and easily defined

5. good parental attitudes

The Role of Professionals

After the shock of the news that their child is handicapped, parents want information. Parents sometimes get conflicting information, which leaves them upset and confused, not knowing what to believe or think. This may be unavoidable

because a specific diagnosis is not possible and no clear-cut information can be given to the parents. Indeed, parents report having had problems securing services and gaining professional support when their children's developmental delays were due to unknown causes (Young, 1980).

Thus, the professional who first gives parents the news that their child is handicapped is sometimes the least helpful. Parents say that often they get the news but no information about care and treatment. It seems reasonable to expect that parents will be better able to accept the child and begin to adapt if the person who gives them the news is also sympathetic and has immediate suggestions for care. We should quickly note, however, that sympathetic reactions can have the opposite effect. Family, friends, and even professionals may support the parents' *denial* of a handicapping condition. Many of you may know of cases in which parents believed their child would "grow out of" a problem. Well-meaning friends and relatives, anxious to ease the parents' anxieties, may reinforce this belief and delay proper treatment.

Pediatricians

Pediatricians have primary responsibility for guiding parents through the early reactions to the news of the handicap and through the beginning diagnostic work with the child. J. Howard (1982) reports that the doctor-parent relationship often becomes strained because it is often the doctor who tells the parents about the diagnosis of the handicap. The physician is certainly right in the middle of a difficult interchange, but it is a significant transition period, and the physician needs to take an active role in helping parents move into new relationships with other professionals. For example, parents may need counseling for themselves and other family members. Or they may need genetic counseling to determine their future childbearing options. They will need information about community resources for treatment and early intervention programs. The pediatrician cannot simply provide medical information and leave it at that. Links to other specialists must be part of the pediatrician's goals in working with parents.

Pediatricians cannot rely on traditional medical models as they deal with parents of children with handicaps and with their needs. They must be more aware of child development information and more accepting of the roles of other disciplines (Guralnick, 1982). In fact, pediatrics is changing in this direction. In 1978, the Task Force on Pediatric Education studied training of physicians and recommended new emphases on developmental, behavioral, and biosocial pediatrics and on handicapping conditions and chronic illness, among others.

PARENT-CHILD INTERACTIONS

As a result of the normalization movement and other changes in social acceptance of the handicapped, parents are more likely to keep a child who is handicapped at home and be the primary care-givers. It is also more likely that parents will supervise their adolescent and adult handicapped family members.

The Social Context

As we work with parents, we must be aware of the total context within which the family exists. Many important interactions take place within the home and in the privacy of the family. The nature and quality of these interactions is partly determined by the greater social context of influences outside the home. The general public is increasingly aware of the problems of individuals who are handicapped. Thus, people may have less and less difficulty dealing with a neighbor or friend who has a child with a handicap. Parents may feel more comfortable taking their child who has a handicap for walks or on regular excursions to the park and the shopping center. Parents may feel more able to deal with children's questions about what's wrong with the baby.

Still, much of the normal conversation about child-rearing enjoyed by parents of normal children is not available to the parent of a child who is handicapped. Think about the feelings a mother of an infant who is disabled might have when other mothers are trading information and advice about their babies. The child-rearing books are written about normal children. Most parental experiences are about raising normal children. Does this wealth of written and spoken advice and support apply to children with handicaps as well? Does grandmother's remedy for teething work when your child is retarded? Which advice about selecting toys applies when your child is blind? Do the pamphlets about selecting day care make any sense when your child has a physical disability? It's no wonder that parents of children with handicaps feel they don't have child-rearing manuals to rely on. And it's no wonder parents of normal children are reluctant to offer advice and comfort.

In fact, much of the available information applies to all children—handicapped or not. The problem is that parents are not very confident about choosing, from among the helpful hints,

Imagine how you would feel as the mother of a young child who is non-ambulatory if this scene were part of your neighborhood. (Courtesy of U.S. Department of Housing and Urban Development.)

what is realistic for their child. Parents who may be naturally inclined to provide support and advice to other parents are reluctant to do so when the child is handicapped because they do not feel confident about an area in which they have no personal experience.

We know that, as a family unit, the family with a young child who is handicapped is more likely than other types of families to have many types of family problems (Embry, 1980). Some of the stress on the family is a result of the child's condition. But some of it is also influenced by the child-rearing practices and parent-child interactions that are prevalent in our culture. For example, many children with handicaps do not have normal behaviors of smiling and cooing that caregivers respond to with warmth and joy. Often, these children have behaviors, such as irritability and lack of responsiveness, that adults find difficult to deal with. This may cause the family to have problems finding babysitters or interacting naturally with neighbors. These are only a few among many possible examples of how the typical family interactions can be disrupted because of the child who is handicapped.

In short, an exceptional child requires exceptional parenting. Fortunately, there is a capacity for growth and development within the family, just as there is within the child. Parents have to learn along with their child. For example, they will have to come to terms with the child's dependency. Some dependency is realistic, especially if the child has a physical or sensory disability, but too much can stunt the development of independence. Parents of children who are handicapped may have more difficulty than other parents in encouraging a shift in primary attachment to others (for example, to the peer group as the child moves into adolescence). Parents may also have more difficulty respecting the child's need for independence and ability to make his or her own decisions, especially in the area of social relationships.

Reciprocity

Until recently, psychologists thought that influences on the infant's behavior were unidirectional: *from* the parent *to* the child. Now, however, ample research evidence suggests that this relationship between parent and child flows in two

BOX 12.1
A FATHER'S STORY

The birth of a youngster with a disability often has profound effects on the family—socially, financially, even philosophically. This story illustrates that those problems can be overcome and that parental expectations are very important.

Three and one-half years ago, the birth of my daughter Christina changed the lives of nearly everyone associated with our family. Christina has Down Syndrome. The role she plays in our family is much like that of an ordinary child. Her impact on our philosophical foundations and decision-making demands, however, has been and will continue to be considerable.

I have fears like those of any parent. Yet, there is the added concern about Christina's adjustment to new situations in her life, since her handicap does present problems not experienced by normally developing children. Because of Christina's handicap, my wife and I have different decisions to make than those of other parents. Possibly the most difficult problem is knowing what situations require more of us because of Christina's handicap and when she is simply needing normally attentive parents.

How we interact with Christina broadly defines how others may choose to respond to her. This feeling, vaguely apparent when she was born, grew stronger as Christina became more of a distinctive person to us. Her ability to let us know of her enjoyment and dependency elicited positive responses of enjoyment and concern from us. Almost from the beginning she was able to be an infant first and then an infant with a handicap. For Christina to develop her abilities to the fullest, we are convinced she must be given the opportunity to live as normally as possible.

Telling grandparents that their grandchild is handicapped is one of the first and most difficult emotional hurdles new parents face. The parents must try to steady their mercurially mixed feelings while anticipating the anger and frustration their own parents may feel when they learn that their grandchild is handicapped. We were relieved and surprised to find that both sets of grandparents were very supportive; they assured us of their concern and offered any help we might need. They did not immediately burden us with their own grief, which gave us time to get a more stable perspective on our own emotions. Only later did we find out how difficult their acceptance was. At the time, their support-

Source: From G. C. Schell, The Young Handicapped Child: A Family Perspective. *Topics in Early Childhood Special Education*, 1981, 1/3, pp. 21–27. Used with permission from PRO-ED, Inc.

directions. It is true that the adult influences the infant's behavior, but it is also the case that the infant influences the adult. Psychologists refer to this as a transactional relationship, or **reciprocity**, between parent and child (Thomas & Chess, 1977; Ludlow, 1981). In effect, this concept tells us that the infant has a role in his or her own care—that the baby causes the parent to respond in certain ways even though that baby may seem very helpless.

We alluded to the concept of reciprocity when we described ways that typical parent-child interactions are altered when the child is handicapped. C. T. Ramey, P. Beckman-Bell, and J. W. Gowen

(1980) identified four ways that mother-child interactions can be directly influenced if the child is handicapped:

1. There may be a change in the rewards that parents get from care-giving; for example, the baby may not smile or gaze at them as they expect.

2. Routine care-giving, such as feeding and bathing, may be difficult because of the child's handicapping condition.

3. Separations that may be needed for hospitalization or other treatments can disrupt the

ive attitudes freed us to focus our immediate attention on our child's needs and to begin integrating our own feelings about Christina into a plan of action to optimize her progress.

Often one member of the extended family offers special support and help. My sister-in-law Cindy has played an extraordinary role in Christina's development. From the moment she heard about Christina, there was never any doubt that Cindy had a desire to take an active part in Christina's life. Cindy is a prime motivator for Christina when difficult things need to be done. Christina walked her first steps trying to stop Cindy from leaving. She will sit still for only one person when it is time to cut her hair. Her favorite times are when Cindy babysits.

Cindy's involvement with Christina has provided us with practical and emotional benefits. We feel comfortable when we leave them together for an evening, knowing that the babysitter understands Christina's differentness. We have the satisfaction of Christina's experiencing a warm relationship with an aunt, the way nonhandicapped children do. There is also the security of knowing that if something happened to us, there is someone who would still care for Christina. Cindy's remaining an ener-getic force in our lives, as she was before Christina's birth, has helped us to feel like any family with caring and sharing relatives.

After telling our family that Christina had serious problems, informing friends was somewhat easier. Possibly the knowledge of our parents' support minimized rejection by friends. Although friends stumbled for things to say when we told them about Christina's handicap, they treated us like any other parents, expressing the same curiosity about our new child they might have expressed about other infants.

A conversation with a friend affected me more than I realized at the time. She is a ballet teacher and remarked that little girls should have an opportunity to learn to dance; she said she was looking forward to teaching Christina. It dawned on me that if others were anticipating interacting normally with our handicapped child, the least I could do was reassess my own expectations. I realized that we needed to allow her the freedom to be a child; we had to learn not to exaggerate her differentness by our own limited vision of what she would be.

normal bonding and attachment process and influence the parent-child relationship.

4. The contextual variables such as reactions of friends, financial resources, parental expectations, and marital stress may change.

Parents will also experience other influences as a direct result of the specific handicapping condition or the developmental domain in which the problem occurs. For example, if their infant has a visual impairment, they will have to adapt to the absence of eye contact. Or, if their infant is deaf, they will need to learn new patterns of language stimulation.

Professionals who work with infants and their mothers and fathers are acutely aware of the reciprocity between parent and child. The time is long past when one-half of the pair is treated and we ignore the other half. This is true for infants who are normal as well as for infants who are handicapped. The infant's activity level or temperament, for example, can make parents nervous about their child's health and development if it is different from their expectations. This, in turn, may make the parents' interactions with the baby abnormal and stressful, which, in turn, often makes the infant more active and irritable. If a family has had several children who were active babies and then have one who is quiet and placid, the mismatch between their former and current experiences may cause them to think they have an infant who is abnormal and may influence their interactions with the baby and with each other. Even if they have not had other children, their ideas of what babies should be like can influence their interactions if their baby is different from their abstract idea of baby behavior. Whatever our role with the family, we must work with the *interaction* between the parents and child in designing care and treatment.

Children do better when parents are supportive and involved and when they take part in their children's treatment and education. This is a common-sense observation, but it is also supported by research evidence (Lavelle & Keogh, 1980; Ruble & Boggiano, 1980; Tulloch, 1983). Parents' attitudes and expectations about their child and about the child's handicap can present problems that are in some ways similar to those experienced when teachers adjust their expectations for a child according to the label that child has been given. If parents view the child as troublesome and difficult, their attitudes may lead them to treat the child as troublesome. The child may then become troublesome because he or she is used to being treated as troublesome. In short, attitudes are tied to expectations, and both affect the child's development (Sameroff & Chandler, 1975).

THE RATIONALE FOR PARENT INVOLVEMENT

Parents have a unique role to play with their children who are handicapped. Their twenty-four-hour-a-day role in care and their lifelong responsibilities put them in a special situation. Professionals who work with children who are handicapped must have a genuine commitment to involving the parents; paying lip service to parent involvement will not work.

Arguments on behalf of parent involvement have been summarized by many writers (see, for example, Cartwright, 1981; Welsh & Odum, 1981; Wiegerink et al., 1980; Garwood & Fewell, 1983).

These writers agree about the major reasons for involving parents in the treatment and education of their children.

First, there are several legal mandates for parent involvement. You already know about parental roles in P.L. 94–142. Recall that parents have a pivotal role in identification, diagnosis, placement, and programming as required in P.L. 94–142. Amendments contained in P.L. 99–457 require the establishment of an Individualized Family Service Plan (IFSP) for each infant and toddler who is handicapped. The IFSP requires parent participation during its original development and at six-month intervals.

Other federal programs have mandated parent participation too. For example, Head Start regulations are permeated by requirements for parent involvement. Dr. Robert Cooke, who chaired the panel of experts that originated the idea of Head Start programs, described the child as part of the family unit and made family involvement a part of the overarching philosophy of Head Start. This philosophy was incorporated into the legislation for Head Start (O'Keefe, 1979). In addition, we should be aware that parents are consumers who pay taxes and who can and do become members of advocacy groups. Many of the legal mandates for parent involvement that exist today do so because of the strength parents have achieved through organized lobbies and advocacy groups.

Another part of the rationale for parent involvement is common sense. Parents know their children best. They spend more time with them. They have more vested interest than anyone else. They can work one-on-one and can deliver highly individualized services at low cost. They are natural reinforcing agents and they can reward behaviors in the home where these behaviors need to be applied. Improvements in parents' teaching and interaction skills are likely to benefit all family members, not just the child with handicaps who may be the initial target for parent efforts.

Finally, parents should be involved in their children's treatment and education because research has shown that when they are involved, children do better (Bronfenbrenner, 1974; Zigler & Valentine, 1979). U. Bronfenbrenner (1974) summarized the research findings in one clear sentence: "The evidence indicates that the family is the most effective and economic system for fostering and sustaining the development of the child" (p. 35). It is interesting that Bronfenbrenner's statement applies when the target of intervention is the family (the parents and the children) *as a system* rather than either the parents or the children by themselves.

ROLES FOR PARENTS

If parents are to be involved in their child's program, what should they do? How should they be involved? What roles should they play? We can think of parent roles along a continuum from least to most involvement and make judgments about which type of involvement is most likely to benefit both the child and the parent.

In practice, three assumptions guide the selection and management of parent involvement roles (Seaver & Cartwright, 1985):

1. All parents should be involved in all programs. The contacts may be no more than periodic newsletters or informal conversations as children are taken to the program. Every program builds parent involvement from this base of communication with all parents.

2. Parents will have specific needs that define the parent roles. An assessment of the parents' needs should guide the planning of their involvement.

3. Programs will have specific needs that define parent roles. Indeed, as you will see later in this chapter, some programs are based on the assumption that parents will do the teaching for their child, sometimes in the child's home.

Parents can be an *audience*. They can be passive recipients of information about their children, about child development in general, or about child-rearing. This role may be necessary and helpful, but it is not enough. Parents can also assume an active role, as *program supporters*. In this role, they perform tasks that benefit the

program—clerical work, fund-raising, advocacy work. Again, this role is fine, but it is not enough to benefit the parent and child as a pair. Another active role for parents is as learners. In contrast to the "audience" role, the "learner" role puts parents in an active situation. Still, they are not with their child and we would consider this to be only part of the total role for a parent.

Parents can be *teachers* of their children. In this case, the parent involvement is based on the parent and the child as a system or unit, and the involvement is likely to be beneficial for both parent and child. However, like everything else in life, there are trade-offs here. When parents serve as their children's teachers, they may not get the respite they need from the stress and responsibility of care-giving. Parents can burn out just as teachers can.

A similar role puts parents as *therapists* for their child. In this situation, parents are taught the principles of counseling and then become the service delivery for their child. The advantages and disadvantages of this role are similar to those of parents as teachers.

At the end of the involvement continuum is the role of parents as *decision-makers* and *policymakers*. In effect, P.L. 94–142 and P.L. 99–457 put parents in this role automatically. We maintain that, although this is a critical responsibility and one that parents should assume, even this decision-making role is not adequate unless it is coupled with some of the other roles described above. Parents need the information and skills and the opportunities to be their children's teachers and counselors as much as they need to have a right to be part of the decision-making team.

PARENTS AND PROFESSIONALS WORKING TOGETHER

Parent involvement is an area that presents some difficulties for educators. Part of the problem is that many professionals have not been trained to work with parents and are not comfortable in that role. Several recent publications include excellent

BOX 12.2

PARENTS AS TEACHERS

Marci Hanson, an expert teacher of infants who are multihandicapped, prepared a handbook for parents of Down syndrome infants as part of a special project at the University of Oregon funded by the Bureau of Education for the Handicapped. Very detailed descriptions are given so that parents can follow the recommended teaching procedures step-by-step, recording relevant aspects of their children's progress as they go through the curriculum. Parents are taught generic teaching strategies. They learn to

- specify target behaviors
- break tasks into component parts and put the parts in order
- decide about criterion levels
- find out which steps the baby can already perform
- decide where to start teaching on the task
- observe and record performance
- provide appropriate consequences

All of the teaching procedures described in the handbook were actually used in the research and demonstration project by a group of parents who have infants with Down syndrome. The research component of the project made it evident that these parents were very effective in teaching skills to their babies with Down syndrome. In fact, for many of the developmental milestones for which babies received specific instruction, the babies with Down syndrome who were taught by their parents were ahead of or had close to normal development levels expected for normal children.

Parents used the teaching procedures and curriculum in their own homes. They were encouraged to behave naturally, fitting the teaching procedures into routine daily activities. For example, mealtime was used by many parents as the natural time to teach self-feeding skills. In addition, parts of the

speech program could be taught at mealtime by having children ask for food.

The handbook contains a curriculum for the babies that follows normal developmental milestones from birth to about two years. Four areas of development are covered: gross motor, fine motor, communication, and social and self-help. An example of recommended teaching procedures for the communication component "Follows Simple Directions" is given below. Notice the level of specificity provided. Note also the tremendous responsibility given to parents for making decisions and recording information about their child's progress.

Follows Simple Directions

Developmental Milestone & Objective:
    Child will follow simple directions, such as "Come here," "Sit down," when given the direction on 8 out of 10 opportunities.
Materials: Doll
Procedure:
A. Teaching Procedure
    1. Prerequisite: Program: "LOOKS AT PERSON AND/OR ITEM."
    2. To teach the child to follow any given direction when given the verbal direction and when parent shows the behavior or gives physical gesture.
    3. Steps:
        (1) Child follows a simple direction when given the verbal direction and when parent shows the behavior or gives physical gesture.
            Example 1: Child stands up after parent directs, "Stand up," and parent shows by standing up.
            Example 2: Child comes to parent after

Source: M. Hanson, *Teaching the Infant with Down's Syndrome,* 2nd edition. Austin, Tx.: PRO-ED, 1986. Reprinted with permission.

parent directs, "Come here," and motions child to move toward parent.

(2) Child follows a simple direction when parent gives verbal direction only.

4. If necessary, define even smaller steps by adding physical prompts.
   Example: Step (1a) Child follows direction with verbal cue, demonstration, and a *slight tug* (physical prompt).

5. Teach only simple directions, such as, "Come here," "Wave bye-bye," "Give that to me."

6. One variation in teaching the child to follow the direction of bringing you something is to place the object near you, then ask the child to give it to you. Gradually move it farther and farther away until the child is following your verbal direction to get the object and bring it to you.

7. Require your child to "Come here" before being placed in chair to eat, for example. Think of a number of ways you can work this into your daily activities. Don't ask your child to come to you if you are going to punish her/him or do something the child doesn't like such as having the nose wiped or if the child is really engrossed in an activity already.

8. Do not expect the child to follow a behavior if that behavior is not in her/his repertoire. For example, don't direct the child to stand up if s/he is unable to stand.

9. Give only one command at a time.

10. Use this procedure to teach your child *location:* Come *here,* go *there,* go to the *chair,* put dolly *on the chair,* put dolly *inside* (inside a box), and so on.

11. Recommended: 10 trials per day. Some trials can be on one direction, other trials on others.

B. Consequation
   1. Praise your child for following the direction given.
   2. If child does not follow the direction, prompt her/him through the behavior. Example: raise the child to stand.

C. Data Collection
   1. Score "+" if child follows direction as specified within 30 seconds after verbal direction is given. Score "−" if child does not follow direction as specified within 30 seconds after verbal direction is given.
   2. Count and circle the number of "+'s."
   3. When child achieves correct response on 8 out of 10 of the trials for 3 days, move to the next step in the series.
   4. Use this program to teach the child to follow many simple directions.

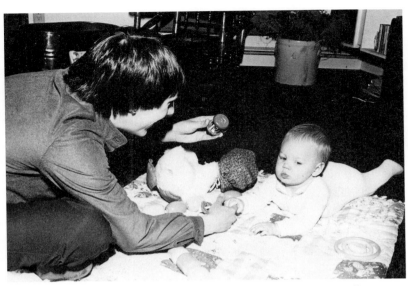

Early education for *all* children begins at home. (Photo by Joseph Bodkin.)

descriptions of the need for training to help professionals improve their working relationships with parents. The list we share with you here is a synthesis of ideas and suggestions presented by K. A. Gorham and her colleagues (1976), M. Karnes and J. A. Teska (1980), and I. H. Carney (1983).

1. Parents must be involved every step of the way; the rapport and dialogue established between parent and professional provides an essential communication base and establishes the necessary rapport between the professional and the parents and other family members.

2. Parents should be fully participating members of the treatment team; this means that professionals must be able to communicate without technical language or jargon and must give parents clear and accurate information. (This statement involves an implicit suggestion that there will be disagreements from time to time among the team members [including parents], and professionals must have practical ways to negotiate differences and resolve disputes.)

3. Professionals must be able to recognize individual differences among families and to be flexible in providing services to fathers, mothers, and siblings.

4. Programs designed for the child should help parents manage and teach the child successfully; this will involve the use of practical and realistic suggestions for care and the use of specific examples and techniques (especially those based on a behavioral approach) rather than general advice. It also involves giving parents feedback about their success with their child.

5. Professionals should help parents become a part of a support group and help them identify the community services and resources that are available, but they must also be realistic in informing parents about lack of services. Parents need to understand that the "helping professions" cannot always help.

6. Professionals should help parents dwell on the positives in their child because so many others will be dealing with the negatives. Child-rearing is a continuous problem-solving process,

Parents have made excellent progress on behalf of their children's special needs. When parents participate in policymaking, they are an especially powerful group. (Courtesy of U.S. Department of Housing and Urban Development.)

and many of the problems exist whether a child is handicapped or not. When parents begin to see this as true, they begin to see that many of their skills with other children will serve them well with the child who is handicapped.

We view parent involvement as an essential part of programs for young children who are handicapped. However, some programs experience significant parent attrition. S. W. Stile, J. T. Cole, and A. W. Garner (1979) summarized some of the research on improving parent involvement. They identified thirty-four different strategies that could be expected to improve parent involvement, with nineteen of these being strategies related to the design of the program itself. Workable options might include:

- Provide program orientation and information about what realistic outcomes are before beginning the program.
- Make clear to parents in advance the expected

extent of their participation, using a contractual agreement if necessary.
- Perform an assessment of individual needs of parents as well as individual needs of children.
- Provide activities that can be carried over into the home; these might include having parents keep records of home progress.
- Take the training to the parents' home and bring along toys and equipment on loan.
- Provide follow-up services after the initial burst of participation is over.
- Seek out successful parents and ask them to serve as trainers for new participants.
- Watch for appropriateness of reading levels in parent manuals and delete technical language from training sessions. (p. 78)

Those who work with parents of young children with handicaps must be aware of the dynamics of the family. All families experience stress, but the specific problems of families in which there is a child who is handicapped are different and more intense than are the problems

BOX 12.3
CENTRE CLIPS: PARENTS HELPING PARENTS

Parent organizations have been very successful in their advocacy efforts on behalf of groups of handicapped individuals. Sometimes, though, the little things in life result in frustrations and unhappiness. Being available with the right answer or suggestion can make a world of difference to the parents of a handicapped child. The following excerpts from *Centre Clips* illustrate one of the important services provided by parent organizations—information. Information about local events, state and national pending legislation, and other items of interest are given in this monthly newsletter published by a local ARC group.

▪ Members are urged to call the toll-free Governor's Hotline as soon as possible to help persuade the governor *not* to appeal the Pennhurst decision to the Supreme Court.

▪ Members are urged to write their local representative urging him to support House Bills 2112 and 2113 which would authorize the treatment of small group homes as "families" in all residential zones in local zoning regulations. Passage of the bills would greatly facilitate the establishment of future group homes without requiring special zoning variances. Our experience with group homes is that they have been well received by neighbors.

▪ IRS booklets most relevant to parents of children with disabilities are: Publication 17 "Your Federal Income Tax," Publication 502 "Deductions for Medical and Dental Expenses," Publication 503 "Child Care and Disabled Dependent Credit," and Publication 526 "Income Tax Deductions for Contributions." A computer singles out any taxpayer claiming high deductions so it helps to explain your child's disability and prescribed care in a letter accompanying your tax return. Other explanations and tips are on file at the local ARC office.

▪ The annual Art Show is just around the corner. It will be held at the Art Alliance Building on February 29 and March 1 and 2. Anyone—in school or out of school—interested in submitting art work should contact the ARC office as soon as possible. Volunteers are also needed to help with the show. Let us know if you can help.

▪ Ralston Purina Company has developed a cookbook suitable for group homes where independent living skills are stressed or for children and nonreading adults. Recipes are categorized as no-cook, minimal-cook, and full-cook, accommodating different skill levels. The book is available from Ralston Purina, Consumer Services, Checkerboard Square, St. Louis, MO 63188. Cost is $2.00 per copy.

▪ Twenty-three of the 25 spots available in ARC's Hobbyshops are filled, attesting to their popularity and the work of Recreation Chairmen, Dee and Tom.

▪ An Activities Calendar accompanies the newsletter. Included in this month's recreation activities were: bowling once a week; swimming two to three times per week; attending a gymnastics meet; Open Gym sponsored by the local Recreation and Parks group; a snowmobiling outing—providing the weather cooperates; Slimnastics twice a week sponsored by the local Recreation and Parks group; a birthday party; and a special family evening called "Slides Night" in which everyone is invited to bring in slides from past ARC activities.

Source: *Centre Clips,* February 1980. Reprinted with permission of Association for Retarded Citizens, Centre County Chapter, State College, Pa.

of other families. The demise of the extended family has an effect on the coping ability of families because the isolated family is left to provide special care without emotional or physical support from those usually most interested in helping—close relatives. Additional stresses occur when the family unit is not the storybook nuclear family. Recent statistics indicate that only one in seventeen children in the United States today lives in a family with mother at home, father at work, and one or two other siblings. When single parents are responsible for a child with a handicap, they experience special difficulties in finding the time and energy to provide necessary additional stimulation. Professionals must be sensitive to parents' need to deal with grief, guilt, and other emotions in reaching an acceptance of the child and the problem. Professionals should be ready with information parents need to make life decisions for the child and family.

More and more, policymakers view the roles of parents as crucial for program effectiveness. No one has put the problem in more eloquent language than Kenneth Keniston, author of a major volume, commissioned by the Carnegie Corporation Council on Children, on the future of American children. His words provide a fitting and provocative ending to this section on early childhood. Keniston (1977) tells us that never have parents been expected to assume so much responsibility in the face of such enormous pressures and lack of available services:

> Today's parents have little authority over those others with whom they share the task of raising their children. . . . The parent today is usually a coordinator without voice or authority, a maestro trying to conduct an orchestra of players who have never met and who play from a multitude of different scores, each in a notation the conductor cannot read. If parents are frustrated, it is no wonder: for although they have the responsibility for their children's lives, they hardly ever have the voice, the authority, or the power to make others listen to them. (p. 18)

PARADOXES IN EARLY EDUCATION FOR THE HANDICAPPED

The Case for Early Education

Fortunately, early childhood education experienced a significant rebirth in the 1960s. Psychologists had been gathering evidence about the value of the environment in the early years for changing the course of development. Prior to that, the prevailing point of view was that development was relatively static and fixed by heredity and that no amount of stimulation in the environment would matter much. B. Bloom (1964), J. Hunt (1961), and others wrote about the malleability of intelligence and concluded that (1) at no other time in life will learning be as easy and as rapid as it is in the early years, and (2) half of everything that is ever to be learned is learned before the age of five. Bloom and Hunt were convincing proponents for early schooling.

Projects Head Start and Follow Through. At about this same time, the political group in power was looking for a program to pacify civil rights activists and the poor. President Johnson had his "War on Poverty." In these fortuitous circumstances, **Head Start** was born in the summer of 1965 as a special summer program designed to give a boost before school to children of low-income families. It was very obvious very soon that three months or less of enrichment in the summer was not going to make up for years of deprivation, and Head Start was quickly turned into a year-round program for four- and five-year-olds.

As research about the effectiveness of Head Start received notice, there was concern that gains made during the Head Start experience appeared to "wash out" or be lost as the children moved into regular elementary schools. In the face of this evidence, Project **Follow Through** was conceived in 1968. Follow Through meant exactly what its name suggested: The educational programs and

Day care centers and Head Start programs can play an important role in the education of young children. (Courtesy of Department of Human Development, Pennsylvania State University.)

supporting services begun in the preschool years under Head Start programs were to be followed through into the early elementary years, until third grade. This meant a significant investment, because Head Start was much more than an educational program. It involved an array of health, education, and social services aimed at improving the child's physical health, emotional and social development, mental processes and skills; establishing patterns of success; improving relationships within the family; increasing the child's sense of dignity and worth; and developing responsible attitudes.

Follow-up Studies. Though the early returns on Head Start were somewhat discouraging (see, for example, Rivlin & Timpane, 1975, for a review), more recent longitudinal data seem to be impressing policymakers. Irving Lazar is coordinator of a project, started in 1975, in which those who conducted early education programs in the late 1950s and early 1960s agreed to participate in a consortium to assess the long-term effects of Head Start–type programs. Participants agreed to follow up

children they had had in their preschool programs. Without going into all the details of the study (see Darlington, 1980, and Lazar, 1979b, for specifics), we do want to report that the follow-up approach was much more effective than the group thought possible. They were able to locate and obtain data from over 80 percent of the children enrolled in preschool programs prior to 1969. The major conclusions are that Head Start children were placed in special education classes significantly less often than non–Head Start children, they were held back in grade less often, and they scored consistently higher on intelligence tests. The researchers also found that parents liked the programs, with the most frequently mentioned positive aspect being the focus on academics. In summarizing, Lazar said, "Now it is clear that a sensible program of early education can indeed prevent later school failure and reduce the need for remedial programs. None of the curricula used in these programs was exotic; all of them were effective" (Lazar, 1979a, p. 6).

As part of their follow-up on the children enrolled in the Perry Preschool Project, L. J.

Early stimulation and language training are demonstrated in this federally supported day care center. (Courtesy of Dover AFB, Dover, Delaware.)

Schweinhart and D. P. Weikart (1980) looked at life-success information at age fifteen for individuals who had been in the program as preschoolers (at ages three and four). They studied black children of poverty in Michigan and found that, under the program, the preschool children's cognitive ability improved. Even more important in the long term was the finding that, as teenagers, those same children had a greater commitment to schooling and were less likely to drop out of school. They needed fewer special education services while they were in school, and their parents reported greater satisfaction with the schooling of their children and higher aspirations for them in terms of jobs and income than did parents of control-group children. At age fifteen, youngsters who had been in the preschool program had better self-concepts and were more committed to a work ethic than were their counterparts who had not been to the preschool. In addition, there were fewer cases of teenage pregnancy and less serious delinquency in the group than would normally be expected. The researchers continue to follow these preschoolers and will issue another report

on their achievement at age nineteen. This more long-term study should help us look at what success these youngsters may be experiencing in employment, income, and family development. Only then will we know if the program planners have successfully broken the cycle of poverty that seems to feed upon itself.

A report to the Congress by the comptroller general on February 6, 1979, headed "Early Childhood and Family Development Programs Improve the Quality of Life for Low-Income Families," makes the case for early childhood education quite strongly. The major points in favor of early education, defined in the report as the prenatal period through age eight, are:

- The early years are critical in setting the course of later development.
- At no other time will as much be learned as fast.
- If development is significantly below average at age four, there are likely to be significant problems for life.
- The family is the primary influence in the

Good prenatal care, including proper nutrition, decreases the chances of physical and mental disabilities in infants. (Photo by Joseph Bodkin.)

High infant mortality rates.

Large numbers of women who receive inadequate prenatal care.

Many cases of child mental retardation that are preventable.

Large numbers of children suffering from poor nutrition.

Large numbers of children lacking immunization against preventable diseases.

Increasing juvenile crime.

Increasing adult crime and dependency on the welfare system. (p. 19)

As you might expect, the major recommendation in the report is for comprehensive services to young children and their families. Taking a strong position that the family is extremely important in the development of the child, the report calls for services to meet all needs that are critical to the development of the child, including prenatal care, health screening and referral, nutrition, educational/developmental programs, social services, mental-health services, parent involvement and education, and special services for children with handicaps.

The Role of the Federal Government

Until recently, one of the most unusual paradoxes was the limited number of programs for young children with handicaps, in spite of ample documentation of their effectiveness in reducing the impact of a disability on subsequent development (Castro & Mastropieri, 1986). For example, J. S. Payne and colleagues (1979) reported that only one-third of the preschool children identified as disabled were being served in some way. Furthermore, these children may have represented only those with obvious, severe disabilities. Other children may have had more subtle disabilities that were not detected until enrollment in public school programs. In both cases, valuable time during which problems could have been more easily remedied was lost. After recognizing the importance of involvement at an earlier age, the federal government did allocate funds for three

child's life and should be included in child development programs.

▪ Environment strongly influences the development of intelligence and is also important for the development of curiosity, social skills, and language.

(Comptroller General, 1979)

In the same report that speaks so glowingly of early education and the benefits of an adequate environment, there are data to indicate that many children suffer very negative early environments. The report states:

A number of serious problems in this country affect the development of children:

Increasing numbers of single-parent families.

early-intervention programs: Head Start, Follow Through, and **Home Start** (which is similar to Head Start except that intervention is home-based).

Head Start, the largest single federal effort on behalf of young children, received a budget allocation of $475 million in fiscal 1977 and served 349,000 children that year. The group served, however, was estimated to be only about 15 percent of those who were eligible. Gradual increases were evident, with $625 million allocated for Head Start in 1978 and enrollment expanded to about 402,000 children (about 23 percent of those eligible). For fiscal year 1979, the Head Start allocation was increased to $680 million (Comptroller General, 1979). Obviously, a substantial federal effort is under way, but there are still at least one million children, by conservative estimates, who are eligible but not receiving Head Start services.

The first federal program aimed exclusively at young children with handicaps was the Handicapped Children's Early Childhood Assistance Act of 1968, popularly known as HCEEP, or Handicapped Children's Early Education Program. Funded at the level of about $1 million the first year, HCEEP had grown to a budget of about $22 million by 1977 and has remained approximately the same since then. About 8,000 children with handicaps from birth to age five and their families receive services under HCEEP.

In the first year of HCEEP, twenty-four demonstration projects, known as the **First Chance** Projects, were funded. In the years to follow, hundreds of First Chance Projects were funded. First Chance Projects that were successful for three years were eligible to compete for outreach funding in order to disseminate their practices and materials to others working with young children with handicaps and their families. This made possible a multiplier effect: Successful methods were shared with others, who, in turn, were providing services to children with handicaps. In addition to outreach efforts, the First Chance Projects were eligible to present data regarding the effectiveness of their model before a group of researchers known as the Joint Dissemination and Review

Panel (JDRP). If they were successful in this juried review process, the models became known as *nationally validated models*, projects judged by an independent panel to be excellent projects, capable of being duplicated in other states. The first group of First Chance Projects competed in JDRP in 1975, and seven projects were selected as nationally validated models. By the end of 1979, nearly twenty HCEEP models had been selected by JDRP. Several of these models will be described later.

Economic benefits of early intervention have also been demonstrated through evaluation of HCEEP projects. W. M. Swan (1980) reported an annual per child expense for HCEEP projects ranging from $1,080 to $4,822. Even the upper end of the range can be seen as inexpensive compared to the long-term costs of institutionalization.

The Early Periodic Screening, Diagnosis and Treatment Program (EPSDT), initiated in 1968 as an amendment to the Social Security Act, is a federally supported screening program for children of poor families. The primary purpose of EPSDT is to determine if health care or related services are needed. Those receiving Aid to Families with Dependent Children (AFDC) benefits and children whose parents or guardians are receiving Medicaid and/or local or state public assistance benefits are eligible for EPSDT. Information on the effectiveness of EPSDT is sketchy, and many experts believe the program is nowhere near achieving its potential.

The 1972 amendments to the Head Start legislation (P.L. 92–424) required that at least 10 percent of Head Start slots be filled by children with handicaps. J. W. Klein and L. A. Randolph (1974) reported that about 29,000 children with handicaps were enrolled in Head Start in 1973, but they maintained that there had been children with handicaps in Head Start programs long before legislation required it. That may be true, but with the mandate came more efforts to find and enroll children who were seriously handicapped, and percentages of young children with more severe handicapping conditions in Head Start programs are inching upward each year.

The mandate for enrolling children with handicaps in Head Start makes more services available to these young children, but perhaps more importantly, the mandate supports the notion of integrating children with handicaps with normal children during their early years when attitudes and acceptance of individual differences are generally considered to be quite positive. Klein and Randolph (1974) stated the case as follows:

> There are more similarities than differences between most handicapped children and other children. Integrating handicapped and nonhandicapped children at an early age tends to foster tolerance and understanding among both groups. Learning and playing together can strengthen motivation, achievement and social competence in the handicapped child. Nearly all children can learn, although the pace and mode of their learning may differ. The general conditions for fostering optimal physical, emotional and intellectual development at an early age are similar for both handicapped and nonhandicapped children. (p. 9)

Late in 1979, the HCEEP group held a meeting in Washington, D.C., to celebrate their tenth anniversary. Dr. Ed Martin, director of the Bureau of Education for the Handicapped,* spoke to the conference participants and urged them to set a goal of education from birth for all children with handicaps. He noted that one way to do this would be to expand P.L. 94–142 so that special education and related services would be mandated for children with handicaps beginning at birth. But he also cautioned that early educators should not rely on the federal government completely, and he urged them to seek support from business, industry, unions, citizen groups, churches, and civil rights groups (*Report on Preschool Education,*

1979). Speaking from the same advocacy position, P. L. Safford (1978) wrote:

> In no other dimension of early education is the need for early education seen more sharply than in the teaching of children with special needs. The history of education for these children has been marked by active parent involvement and by lonely and heroic determination on the part of a few pioneers, often against great odds. Today there is heightened national consciousness and awareness of both the needs and the potential of children whose development may be impaired as a result of handicapping conditions—whether these conditions exist in his early environmental surroundings or within the child himself. (p. 4)

The most recent actions of the federal government involve revisions of P.L. 94–142. P.L. 99–457, The Education of All Handicapped Children Act Amendment of 1986, made specific provisions for young children with disabilities. These provisions reflect Congress' official recognition of the need to

1. minimize the potential for developmental delays experienced by infants and toddlers who are handicapped

2. reduce educational expenses by minimizing the need for special education and related services among school-age children

3. reduce the probability of institutionalization and enhance the potential for independent living

4. develop the ability of family members to meet the needs of infants and toddlers with disabilities

In response to these findings, P.L. 99–457 makes mandatory the special education programs for three- to five-year-olds that were optional under P.L. 94–142. In addition, it authorizes incentives for early intervention programs for infants and toddlers from birth to two years of age who are either at risk for delays or diagnosed as develop-

---

*Dr. Martin was subsequently named as the assistant secretary of the newly created federal Office of Special Education and Rehabilitative Services.

mentally delayed in cognitive, physical, language, speech, psychosocial, or self-help skills. The services that may be included in the intervention program consist of

family training
counseling
home visits
special instruction
speech pathology
audiology
occupational therapy
physical therapy
case management services
medical services (for diagnosis and evaluation)
early identification, screening, assessment
health services

Just as P.L. 94–142 mandated the establishment of an IEP, P.L. 99–457 mandates the establishment of an Individualized Family Service Plan, or IFSP. This plan requires a multidisciplinary assessment of the unique needs of the child and family members. Shortly after assessment, a written document is drawn up at a meeting of members of the multidisciplinary team, including the parents or guardian. This document identifies levels of performance; strengths and weaknesses; anticipated outcomes; criteria, procedures, and time tables for measuring progress; specific services; and a case manager. The IFSP is reviewed every six months to measure progress and evaluated once a year.

Measures such as those outlined in P.L. 99–457 should promote major improvements in the delivery of services to children with disabilities and their families. Furthermore, it is hoped that the delivery of these services will minimize the impact of a handicapping condition and decrease the need for additional special education and related services as the child reaches public school age.

The Case for Integration

Many early educators believe that educating preschoolers who are handicapped with preschoolers who are normal has the long-term potential for accomplishing the goals of normalization. When children are physically together and interacting informally and socially with the frequency typical of preschool programs, they may grow up to be more accepting of differences, even the most extreme ones.

The argument centers on the quality of the interactions. If these contacts are carefully planned and positive, and if they come early in life, chances are the integration will be genuine and will continue to be so as the children move together through the school years. In other words, social interactions at the preschool level may prepare children for future mainstreaming in both school and community.

For example, in a 1980 report, M. J. Guralnick studied social interactions of thirty-seven young children, ages four to six years, who were enrolled in an integrated preschool program. Both communicative and parallel play interactions were observed during free-play periods. The study revealed that children with mild handicaps and nonhandicapped children interacted more often than expected simply on the basis of availability. On the other hand, the nonhandicapped children interacted with the children who were moderately and severely handicapped less frequently than expected. This research corroborates other studies showing that children who are mildly handicapped and nonhandicapped interact well in play situations. Conclusions about social integration for young children who are more severely handicapped must await more research.

Several of the First Chance projects are designed to provide for integration of young children who are handicapped with normal young children. The HICOMP project (Neisworth et al., 1980), for example, includes a set of eight hundred objectives, sequenced according to developmental levels and grouped into four domains of development: communication, own care, motor, and problem solving. Project staff members developed an easily learned linkage system that allows preschool teachers to translate the results of developmental assessment into objectives and lesson plans from the HICOMP curriculum in a matter of minutes.

MODEL PROGRAMS FOR YOUNG CHILDREN WITH HANDICAPS

In Chapter 2, we explained that there are several ways of delivering education services to school-age youngsters. Providing similar educational, social, and health services to very young children is a relatively recent phenomenon. The federal government has helped schools, colleges, and other agencies investigate the best ways of offering, or delivering, services to very young children. Several models or approaches have achieved good success.

M. B. Karnes and R. R. Zehrbach (1977) have identified seven variations for delivery systems: home, home followed by center, home and center, center, technical assistance and consultative services, prenatal, and intervention into higher-level systems (p. 21). They also identified four critical dimensions for making decisions about program design: nature of the population to be served; geographical area and population density; theoretical base or educational philosophy to be used; and service delivery system to be used. In another publication, Karnes (1977) expanded the list to seven critical factors, adding financial resources, availability of trained personnel, and availability of physical facilities. In a review of research on successful program models, G. McDaniels (1977) isolated three general characteristics:

1. *Articulated goals.* Programs with clearly defined and carefully specified goals are the most likely to succeed, and the chances for success are increased when administrators, parents, and teachers share the same goals.

2. *Time dimension.* The earlier the intervention, the better is the general rule of thumb. In addition, there usually is not enough time to do everything well, and priorities will need to be set on use of available time.

3. *Training.* The success of the program depends on the care-giver, and the care-giver needs training to implement a specific method.

Whether they are home-based, operate in a center, or combine home and center components, programs for young children with handicaps tend to have similar goals—generally speaking, to make the children as nearly normal as possible. Objectives are typically derived from tables of normal development, and programs are usually designed so that objectives in the four developmental domains are included in a balanced program. Whereas the decisions about *what* to teach usually come from normal developmental milestones, *how* to teach is often highly specific and extremely detailed. As C. E. Kaiser and A. H. Hayden (1977) put it: "While the environment is important for the normal baby, it becomes critical for the handicapped baby. It will no longer be the case that any one of a multitude of reasonably good environments will provide a fertile learning ground. A baby with a handicap is a baby with highly specialized needs" (p. 9). They describe a teaching episode at the Model Preschool Center for Handicapped Children in the University of Washington Child Development and Mental Retardation Center that illustrates the specificity of the teaching process:

> Bert is a handicapped infant who likes to hear the radio, and he is working on "head control" in an infant learning program. Placed on his stomach, he will soon raise his head just slightly off the floor. The teacher will immediately turn on a transistor radio which will stay on until his chin touches the floor. Bert can "make" the music happen again by lifting his head and "keep it on" by maintaining his head lift. He quickly understands the "game" and works hard at keeping the music on. (p. 12)

PROGRAMS WITH PARENT INVOLVEMENT

Woven throughout this chapter is the notion that parents are the child's first teachers and that they are, in fact, very effective teachers. It should not surprise you, then, to learn that most programs for young children with handicaps somehow involve the parents. Those who are designing programs will find the National Diffusion Network Catalog, *Educational Programs That Work* (Far West Laboratory, 1980) to be particularly helpful. It includes descriptions of about seventy-five projects with a parent component. Parent programs, like the model programs described earlier, can be center-based or home-based, or they may be a combination of center and home services. Hospital-based programs are available for children whose problems are life-threatening. There are also media-based programs that involve parents and other omnibus programs that have many goals involving parents, many settings, and many modes of interacting between parent, child, and professional. Research has not yet shown us the "best fit" between a particular model and the specific needs of a single family. In the absence of that information, practical concerns such as transportation, child care for other children in the family, and scheduling of program activities to accommodate parents' work schedules influence the type of parent program chosen.

Home-Based Approaches. When parent-infant interactions are the primary goals for an intervention program, the program is often based in the home, the natural setting for parents and infants. In Box 12.4, you will find a description of one successful model program that is a home-based approach: The Portage Project. There are many others.

Although the child is seen as the focus of the home-based approach, its positive impact is heavily dependent upon the degree of parental involvement, particularly that of the mother. Typically, in a home-based program, the mother is the teacher for her child. A parent trainer visits the home, usually about once a week, and brings toys and other materials that will be used in the teaching during the upcoming week. Emphasis is usually on using naturally occurring events and materials and embedding the learning in routine family activities. Modeling, or demonstrating, of techniques and instruction in the use of record-keeping devices are often used by the parent trainer.

There are many advantages to home-based approaches. First, it is more cost-effective to work with children in their natural environment. Second, the home-based approach avoids separating children from their parents. Third, it is possible that other family members, such as siblings, will indirectly benefit from the intervention (Arenas & Ensher, 1986). Finally, a special advantage of the home as a teaching setting is that there are numerous opportunities for applying the learning to life activities. Because children with handicaps often have trouble generalizing from the specific teaching setting to other settings, this can be an important advantage. It is one thing to learn to button on a special buttoning frame; it is quite another to learn it on your own clothes.

Center-Based Approaches. Precise Early Education for Children with Handicaps (PEECH) (Karnes & Zehrbach, 1977) is a model program that is primarily center-based. Children ages three to six years are integrated with their nonhandicapped peers in a half-day preschool program. Other center-based approaches may be available through organizations such as United Cerebral Palsy, Easter Seal Society, Association for Retarded Citizens, and regional child developmental centers.

A variety of parent involvement opportunities are available, similar to what we might expect to find in a preschool for normal children: parent visits, parent conferences, group meetings of parents, and home visits. For example, the HICOMP approach described in Box 12.5 is a similar center-based means of integrating preschoolers who are handicapped with preschoolers who are nonhandicapped. Advantages of the center-based approach include the provision of an educationally structured environment that offers a wider variety of toys and other materials, other students, and specialized therapies. Disadvantages include high cost and the possibility that follow-up at home may be limited (Arenas & Ensher, 1986).

BOX 12.4
THE PORTAGE PROJECT—A HOME-BASED APPROACH TO EARLY EDUCATION

The Portage Project, based in Portage, Wisconsin, is an example of a home-based approach for educating young handicapped children. It was designed to provide for the needs of children and families in the rural areas of southern Wisconsin, but it has become one of the most frequently used models for home-based education and for rural, dispersed populations.

The approach depends heavily on the skills of parents as teachers of their handicapped young children. Parents are provided with activities for use with their preschoolers, and they keep daily records of the child's progress on individually tailored goals. Behavior modification procedures form a major part of the teaching system, and it is important for parents to follow directions carefully and consistently and to keep accurate records. Children are provided with goals that can be accomplished in one week. The teacher who visits the home brings the necessary materials, written instructions on how to teach and how to reinforce, and the forms needed to keep records for the week. Both paraprofessionals and professionals have served as teacher trainers (the name given those who make the home visits).

One of the basic components of the project is the curriculum, or instructional program, consisting of a developmental checklist and a set of 450 curriculum cards covering self-help skills, cognitive development, socialization, language development, and motor skills. The curriculum is intended for children from birth to age six. Most people are surprised to learn of the fairly limited amount of time spent by Portage staff members with an individual child. Teachers visiting the home spend only about 1½ hours per week with a child, with the expectation that parents will spend at least fifteen minutes a day working with their child. More information about the Portage Project approach is given by M. S. Shearer and D. E. Shearer (1972).

Examples of objectives and activities from the *Portage Guide to Early Education* are given in Figure 12.1.

Figure 12.1. Sample objectives and activities from the Portage Guide to Early Education. (Copyright © 1976 Cooperative Educational Service Agency 12. Reprinted with permission.)

Source: S. Bluma, M. Shearer, A. Frohman, and J. Hilliard, *Portage Guide to Early Education: Card File* (rev. ed.). Portage, Wis.: Cooperative Educational Service Agency 12, 1976. Card File samples in Figure 12.1 are reprinted with permission.

Hospital-Based Approaches. This model for service delivery, described by S. J. Bagnato, S. M. Munson, and R. H. MacTurk (1987), is for those infants with developmental problems so severe that short- or long-term hospitalization is frequently required. These problems may include cerebral palsy, spina bifida, meningitis, and brain injury. The unique needs of these children and their parents are addressed through programming developed and implemented by a variety of specialists including infant special educators, psychologists, and pediatricians.

Media-Based Approaches. Media-based projects have used television and printed materials as means of delivering instruction to parents. The parents, in turn, teach their children. The Read Project Series is a set of ten self-instructional manuals for parents of children who are retarded (Baker & Heifetz, 1976). The content of the manuals is self-help skills, play and socialization skills, and methods of dealing with problem behavior. A behavioral approach is used in the teaching suggestions, with parents learning how to select a target behavior, how to set the stage for

cognitive 42

AGE 3-4

TITLE: Points to 10 body parts on verbal command

WHAT TO DO:

1. Begin with facial parts. As you say, "Here are my eyes," point to your own eyes and have the child imitate where you point on his own body. Repeat with additional body parts including hands, feet, neck, elbow, stomach, fingers, toes, etc.
2. Stand in front of a full-length mirror with the child. Have the child move or touch a body part as you name it. "Touch your knee, wiggle your nose, etc." Reward by praising.
3. Draw two circles, one larger than the other on paper. Draw in one or two body parts and then have the child name what's missing and point to where each body part should go. Praise the child when he answers correctly.
4. Point to body parts on dolls.
5. Encourage child to say name of body part as he points to it.
6. Let child put a sticker on body part if he points to it correctly.

PortageGuide

socialization 43

AGE 1-2

TITLE: Greets peers and familiar adults when reminded

WHAT TO DO:

1. Arrange situations for the child to greet adults, by taking child to door when answering door bell.
2. Use toy phone and real phone and encourage the child to mimic you saying, "Hello, how are you?"
3. Encourage and model behavior when daddy, sisters or brothers come home by having them specifically greet the child. Praise the child when he does imitate them.

PortageGuide

learning, how to reward success, and how to record progress.

Another example of a media-based approach is Lekotek, a resource center that makes available to parents carefully selected toys that capture a child's attention and promote meaningful interactions. Parents are trained in the toy use by specialists during a visit to a Lekotek center. At the end of the training session, parents are allowed to take several toys home for a month. Although the home office is in Evanston, Illinois, Lekotek centers are located all over the United States.

A final example of a media-based approach, the Let's-Play-to-Grow Kit, available from the Kennedy Foundation, consists of a series of printed materials, films, records, and equipment that describe and illustrate the importance of play between parents and their young child with a handicap.

Combination Approaches. Many programs fall into this category. Perhaps this is because developers who worked with center-based approaches found they had to incorporate the home into their

BOX 12.5
HICOMP—A CENTER-BASED APPROACH TO DEVELOPMENTAL INTEGRATION

The HICOMP Project is one of the First Chance model projects designed around a center-based program in which children who are handicapped participate together with children who are nonhandicapped. Project directors consider HICOMP to be a comprehensive model since a continuum of components has been developed and field tested. Model components are:

COMP-Ident:
A series of find/screen alternatives for communities and agencies interested in conducting an early identification project in their locale. A range of possible early identification procedures is described, and evaluative comments are included for some methods. COMP-Ident also includes a package of materials for training staff and volunteers in basic screening skills.

COMP-Curriculum:
A sequenced listing of objectives for children ages birth to five years, grouped according to the developmental domains of communication, own care, problem solving, and motor, together with a Lesson Plan Selector. The objectives are in a format such that assessment information and child progress data can be recorded right on the curriculum; thus, the curriculum becomes a part of the child's permanent record. A sample page from the COMP-Curriculum is given in Figure 12.2. The Lesson Plan Selector is a set of field-tested generic teaching strategies, teaching settings, consequences, and evaluation strategies. A coding system indicates which strategies have been validated for certain curricular objectives.

COMP-Parent:
A manual for parents of different developmental levels designed to secure generalization between home and classroom. Instructions for planning and conducting parent meetings, home visits, and home consultation and parent training in the classroom are provided.

COMP-Training:
A means of achieving the multiplier effect by training personnel in schools and other human-service agencies to implement the HICOMP approach. Agency personnel can be trained to use all the other components: find/screen, curriculum and teaching procedures, and parent programs.

The overriding purpose of the HICOMP approach is movement toward normalization for all enrolled in the program. Brief individualized teaching episodes, based on direct instruction, are integrated with the usual preschool activities. A typical schedule for a day in the preschool is given in Figure 12.3. The schedule illustrates how direct teaching toward specific objectives for individual children is interspersed with typical preschool activities. This practice facilitates the integration of children who are handicapped and those who are normal because all children receive instruction that is appropriate to their developmental level.

Source: J. T. Neisworth, S. Willoughby-Herb, S. Bagnato, C. Cartwright, and K. Laub, *Individualized Education for Preschool Exceptional Children*. Rockville, Maryland: Aspen Systems Corporation, 1980. Sample page and schedule in Figures 12.2 and 12.3 are reprinted with permission.

Objective Number	General Objective	Pretest	Date Begun	Date Ended
M-3-1	Fundamental Movement (Gross Motor)			
M-3-1.1	Walks on tiptoe, demonstrated			
M-3-1.2	Begins a simple somersault			
M-3-1.3	Stands on balance beam with both feet			
M-3-1.4	Jumps from bottom step			
M-3-1.5	Walks up stairs, alternating feet			
M-3-1.6	Walks down stairs, alternating feet			
M-3-1.7	Walks on line on floor			
M-3-1.8	Rides a tricycle using pedals			
M-3-1.9	Stands on one foot, momentarily			
M-3-1.10	Catches large ball by holding it against body			
M-3-1.11	Jumps with both feet over low objects (1"-2" high)			
M-3-1.12	Begins to climb a ladder or jungle gym			
M-3-1.13	Slides between two objects sideways			
M-3-1.14	Ducks under objects			
M-3-1.15	Maintains balance on a variety of surfaces			
M-3-1.16	Walks up and down incline			
M-3-2	Skilled Movement or Visual-Motor or Fine Motor			
M-3-2.1	Draws circle, imitating adult			
M-3-2.2	Draws vertical line from model			
M-3-2.3	Draws horizontal line from model			

Figure 12.2. Sample page from the COMP-Curriculum. (Reprinted with permission.) (continued)

(continued)

Event	Duration	Purposes
1. Arrival at 8:45	15 min.	a. Greet children b. Discussions with parents
2. Free-choice time (with some 10-minute lessons for children whose advancement or delays require extra teacher-directed activities)	20 min.	a. To reinforce exploratory behaviors b. To reinforce appropriate social interaction and modeling behaviors c. To provide opportunities for the generalization of skills to a variety of people and settings d. To provide additional teacher-directed activities for children whose behavioral characteristics suggest such enrichment
3. Directed-activity period #1 (children meet as individuals or in groups of two to four for lesson); content: communication	20 min.	a. To teach specific skills within the communication curriculum
4. Outside recess	20 min.	a. To teach gross motor skills (e.g., riding tricycles) b. To reinforce appropriate social, language, and problem-solving skills in another situation c. To teach skills in outdoor recreation (e.g., tag games, sandbox games)
5. Toileting	5–10 min.	a. To teach toileting skills b. To provide experiences in learning toileting through observation of older children
6. Snack	15 min.	a. To teach eating skills b. To teach eating manners c. To reinforce conversation

Figure 12.3. Sample HICOMP program daily schedule. (Reprinted with permission.)

approach, and vice versa. The Parents Are Effective Early Education Resources (PEERS) Project in Philadelphia is a low-cost approach to infant stimulation and parent training (Losinno, n.d.). Parents attend group seminars and workshops on Saturdays and receive training on a variety of topics. They are then expected to provide thirty minutes of teaching each day in their home. While parents are in class, teenage volunteers work with their infants and specialists observe the babies' progress and reactions. The involvement of the volunteers is a good way to further normalization goals; it is also an inexpensive way to provide services. In addition to tips on teaching their infants, parents are given help in lifelong family planning (e.g., career planning and insurance evaluation).

Another variation that is a combination approach is the Lunch-Box Data System (Fredericks, Baldwin, & Grove, 1976). In this system, parents teach at home what is being taught at the center; messages about the child and the necessary teaching are sent back and forth between home and school in the child's lunch box. As is the case with many successful programs involving parents as teachers, precise instructions are provided to the parents about child expectations and about teaching tasks and materials.

Event	Duration	Purposes

7. Circle time (whole group lesson)	15 min.	a. To teach behaviors of attending and imitation, and language and memory within a large-group context
		b. To maximize the possibility of positive modeling behaviors by:
		  1) children learning each other's names
		  2) teachers reinforcing appropriate behaviors within earshot of all children
		c. To teach listening skills relevant to storytelling
		d. To teach skills in singing and making rhythms

8. Directed-activity period #2; content: problem solving	15 min.	a. To teach specific skills within the problem-solving curriculum
9. Directed-activity period #3; content: either motor or social skills*	15 min.	a. To teach specific skills within the motor curriculum b. To teach special skills within the social curriculum
10. Free-choice time with a variety of planned art and motor activities	25 min.	a. To provide a setting in which children may choose among activities b. To provide additional practice in gross and fine motor skills within an inside, large-group setting c. To provide additional settings for generalization of skills learned during directed-teaching activities
11. Clean-up and leaving	10 min.	a. To teach behaviors of cleanliness b. To teach behaviors of orderliness

*Motor and social skills are both taught daily, but not always within the setting of an activity period. For example, "sharing" is introduced in a directed-activity time but later is taught during free-choice time.

SIMILARITIES AMONG PROGRAMS FOR YOUNG CHILDREN WITH HANDICAPS

No matter what the handicapping condition, the setting, or the amount and type of parent involvement, successful programs for young children have the following features in common:

1. Structure is obvious in the program—both for the parents and for the children.

2. Intervention occurs early and is coordinated by someone other than the parent.

3. The approach in the program is individualized, both for the child and for the parents.

4. The concept of reciprocity between parent and child is emphasized, and the family is dealt with as a unit.

5. The long-term goals for the children are for them to function in the least restrictive environment; however, separation from their normal peers may be required to build a foundation for later integrated experiences.

A center-based approach may offer a large variety of materials and gives parents a much needed break in their routine. (Photo by Eileen Christelow/Jeroboam, Inc.)

6. Ultimate goals for parents are to prepare them to participate in making decisions and to become advocates on behalf of their child throughout the child's life.

SUMMARY

In this chapter, we have described the impact on the family of the birth of a child with a handicap. Parent-child interactions must be viewed within the overall general social context. This is a context that is becoming more accepting of handicapping conditions and people with handicaps. Therefore, parents who have young children who are handicapped may experience more openness and support among their relatives, neighbors, and friends, but they will still face significant adjustment problems.

Psychologists have documented that the interplay between parent and infant (or child) is a reciprocal one. The behavior of the parent influences the child just as the behavior of the child influences the parent. Parents' attitudes about themselves, their child, and the cause of the handicap influence their expectations for their child. Their expectations, in turn, influence their behaviors with the child.

Families with children who are handicapped are more vulnerable to stress than are other families. The adjustment and adaptation that must be accomplished by the family are significant, never-ending, and constantly in flux. It is no wonder that we find higher incidences of separation, divorce, and child abuse in these families.

Parents are the child's first teachers. For this reason and several others, a strong case can be built for genuine involvement of parents in the care and treatment of their child. There are also legislative and legal reasons for parent involvement, the most obvious of these being the mandates for parent participation in evaluation, diagnosis, placement, and IFSP planning as part of P.L. 99–457. In programs with their children, parents can assume various roles ranging from passive ones of information-receiving to active ones as teachers, therapists, policymakers, and advocates. In all types of parent involvement, we need to improve the interactions among parents and professionals.

Children who have serious and multihandicapping conditions are often identified at birth or shortly thereafter. They require very early and very sustained intervention if they are to gain independence and make developmental progress. Fortunately, P.L. 99–457 requires services for children between the ages of three and five years. It also offers financial incentives for programs for infants and toddlers.

The evidence about the value of early childhood education for enhancing the development of both normal children and children with handicaps has been mounting steadily; it is now widely accepted that the early environment is crucial to subsequent development. Many experts believe that mildly handicapping conditions are largely preventable or at least more easily remedied if appropriate educational and other services are provided during the years before public schooling.

Nevertheless, only about one-fourth of the children eligible are currently enrolled in Head Start.

The same factors that place a child at risk tend to make it more difficult for the child's family to provide for a stimulating environment. For example, problems associated with teenage pregnancy, inadequate prenatal care, poor nutrition, inadequate health care, low income, poor housing, and unemployment place the child at risk and also deplete energy and resources, so that the family is less capable at intervening positively on behalf of the child.

Head Start is the largest single federal effort for young children. Recent evidence about the long-term effects of Head Start suggest that Head Start programs were successful in keeping children out of special education. The first federal program aimed exclusively at young children with handicaps was the Handicapped Children's Early Childhood Assistance Act of 1968, popularly known as First Chance. In 1972, amendments to Head Start legislation required that at least 10 percent of the places in Head Start be reserved for preschoolers with handicaps. In addition to providing services, this requirement facilitates the integration of preschoolers with handicaps and normal children. Some researchers believe that beginning integration this early in the lives of children is likely to have long-term benefits for normalization and more widespread acceptance of individual differences.

There are a variety of model programs for infants and preschool-age children who are handicapped, but almost all are based on one of five basic delivery systems: home-based programs, center-based programs, hospital-based programs, media-based programs, or combination programs. Successful programs seem to have several ingredients in common: (1) clearly defined goals, (2) early intervention, (3) an individualized approach, (4) emphasis on the family as a unit, (5) the child functioning in the least restrictive environment, and (6) parents involved in decision-making. Parents play an important role in programs for young children with handicaps, becoming the treatment coordinator if there is no program available for their child. Often, parents are expected to deliver the educational intervention and to follow through in the home with procedures begun in a center.

Suggestions for Further Reading

Allen, K. E. (1980). *Mainstreaming in early childhood education*. Albany, NY: Delmar Publishers.
Eileen Allen has produced an excellent practical handbook for all teachers of young children. Her extensive teaching experience is revealed in the many examples, the down-to-earth presentation, and the numerous practical suggestions. The book, which is profusely illustrated, concentrates on describing the rationale and recommended teaching procedures for a developmental curriculum for children as well as modifications for children with special needs.

Blackman, J. A. (1986). *Medical aspects of developmental disabilities in children birth to three* (2nd ed.). Iowa City, IA: University of Iowa Press.
This resource book, useful for early intervention professionals, summarizes health information that may have an impact upon the day-to-day functioning of young children.

Ensher, G. L., & Clark, D. A. (1986). *Newborns at risk*. Rockville, MD: Aspen Systems.
This book is an easily understood, scholarly text that presents issues of primary importance to professionals interested in the care and treatment of young children with disabilities. It integrates theory, research, and clinical applications.

Garwood, S. G., & Fewell, R. R. (1983). *Educating handicapped infants*. Rockville, MD: Aspen Systems.
Garwood and Fewell have produced an edited book that addresses comprehensively the topic of handicapped infants. The book brings together a number of experts in infant education. The treatment of various topics is well documented with research literature as well as personal experience. Infant education is a relatively new field, and this book should provide a major resource to those who are entering it. Information in three major categories is presented: the theoretical issues in infant development, infant growth and development, and approaches to facilitating infant development.

Neisworth, J. T., Willoughby-Herb, S. J., Bagnato, S. J., Cartwright, C. A., & Laub, K. W. (1980). *Individualizing early education for handicapped children*. Rockville, MD: Aspen Systems.
Project participants in the HCEEP model called HICOMP pooled their talents to produce this practical handbook for early educators, with a complete copy of the HICOMP curriculum. Chapters on screening and assessment, linking procedures for arriving at curriculum decisions and preparing IEPs on the basis of assessment information, and formative and summative evaluation procedures are designed to help classroom teachers and others make use of

information about children. Chapters on generic teaching methods, lesson planning, and material selection and design are organized to help teachers implement the HICOMP curriculum or any similar early childhood program.

Neisworth, J. T., & Bagnato, S. J. (1987). *The young exceptional child.* New York: Macmillan.

This is an extremely useful introductory text for individuals interested in early education for children with disabilities. It presents various exceptionalities through a developmental/behavioral approach, then discusses education and treatment from a diagnostic/prescriptive perspective.

Spodek, B., Saracho, O. N., & Lee, R. C. (1984). *Mainstreaming young children.* Belmont, CA: Wadsworth.

This handy paperback volume provides a wealth of practical information about integrating the young handicapped child with his or her normal peers. The book begins with a section describing the foundations of mainstreaming. Part Two includes chapters about identification, assessment, planning and organizing the classroom, developing the IEP, and working with parents. Another major section provides suggestions for adapting the curriculum and the materials for teaching within the content areas. These curricular adjustments for young handicapped children are described for reading, language arts, social studies, science, mathematics, play, and creative expression.

Relevant Journals

Journal of the Division of Early Childhood

Published twice a year by the Division of Early Childhood, a subdivision of the Council for Exceptional Children, this journal presents review articles and applied research reports.

Topics in Early Childhood Special Education

TECSE is a new journal for early special educators, published by Aspen Systems, Rockville, MD. It was inaugurated in 1981 and is published quarterly. S. Gary Garwood, Rebecca Fewell, Allen Mori, and John Neisworth are editors, with each issue devoted to a special topic and having its own special issue editor. Important compilations with such titles as "Families of Handicapped Children," "Infants at Risk," "Play and Development," and "Curricula in Early Childhood Special Education" have already appeared.

CHAPTER 13

Adolescence and Adulthood

Did You Know That . . .

- people do not "grow out of" most disabilities?

- the number of training programs for adolescents and adults with handicaps is increasing at a faster rate than are programs for elementary-school-aged youngsters?

- more adults with handicaps live in small neighborhood group homes than in large residential institutions?

- preventing adults who are handicapped from marrying and having children is a violation of their civil rights?

- adults with handicaps have the same rights to housing, programs, and jobs as nonhandicapped adults?

- many tests to evaluate vocational skills are inappropriate for individuals with handicaps?

- the concept of normalization includes access to recreational skills?

- technology and computer-assisted instruction have opened new doors for the development of vocational and recreational skills?

An apocryphal story that occasionally makes the rounds recounts the time parents were proudly displaying their preschool children to the neighbors. The neighbors, all of whom had teenage children, nodded wisely as one of them said, "You'd better enjoy those kids while you can. Sooner or later, they'll grow up to be teenagers."

Yes, those cute little toddlers do grow up to be teenagers, and then adults. Children with handicaps grow up, too. In some cases, they "grow out of" their disabilities. More often, they do not. Most physical disabilities, such as visual or hearing impairment or paraplegia, are irreversible. With age and experience, people with disabilities often become better able to cope and to be a more integral part of society, but the basic impairment does not go away. With adulthood, societal expectations change, and those with mild academic, cognitive, social, or motor handicaps can be helped make the adjustments and acquire the skills that will help them become equal, or at least supporting, members of society. Other people with more serious disabilities, however, will require special programs, training, jobs, and housing for many years.

This chapter introduces you to the problems and successes of adolescents and adults who have disabilities of one kind or another. We deal with many topics and programs. Roughly, though, the chapter is divided into two sections: adolescence and adulthood. The adolescent period is a time when young people can still expect considerable help and advice from the public school system. It is also a time when other agencies begin to collaborate with the schools to help those with handicaps make the transition to adulthood. The rest of the chapter deals with adults with disabilities and focuses on problems that occur and services that are available after the public (or private) schools have discharged their mandated responsibilities.

ADOLESCENTS WITH HANDICAPS

The adolescent growth period is often a difficult period for the young person with no handicap; it may be doubly difficult for the young person who

Teenagers with disabilities experience pleasures and problems of adolescence similar to those experienced by all teenagers. (Courtesy of Easter Seal Society for Crippled Children and Adults of Pennsylvania.)

is handicapped. An obvious change, of course, is that teenagers take on the appearance of young adults. Physical developments place them close to the mature end of the growth curve. They look like young adults, and they are expected to act like young adults. They are expected to take on increasing responsibilities and become increasingly independent. But some youngsters who are handicapped are simply unable to take on more responsibility.

With physical maturity comes sexual maturity, at least on the physical level. Unfortunately, many youngsters with handicaps lack even basic information about sex, and some may never fully understand the changes they feel taking place within their bodies.

Finally, the peer group takes on increasing importance during the teenage years. Parents and teachers are no longer the dominant forces in these young lives; many teenagers are guided more by the peer group than by their parents. Often, of course, such guidance leads youngsters in directions that are not socially responsible.

Teenagers who are handicapped often find it extremely difficult to cope with the interactions between the handicap and the new pressures of

adolescence. Obviously, their teachers must be especially sensitive to the kinds of pressures those adolescents face. By the time the youngster who is mildly retarded or learning disabled reaches adolescence, the youngster is well aware of his or her limitations and may have developed elaborate defense mechanisms to cover them up.

For example, one of the authors taught students who were mildly handicapped and/or learning disabled in a large urban high school. There was a tacit agreement among these students, the special teachers, and the principal that the youngsters were permitted to arrive at the special class or resource room one or two minutes after the bell with no penalty. Because all the high school students knew that rooms 103 and 206 were special classes and resource rooms, it was embarrassing for the youngsters who were handicapped to be seen entering those rooms. Therefore, they hung around outside some other room until the bell rang. Then, when the halls were clear, they would duck into the special classes. Similarly, many of these youngsters would carry trigonometry or physics texts around the halls with the titles clearly showing even though they were functioning at an elementary level in math. The youngsters wanted to be a part of the greater peer group and not set apart as different. These defense mechanisms were important to the youngsters and respected by the teachers.

Adolescents with disabilities fall roughly into two groups: those who are mildly vocationally handicapped and those who are seriously vocationally handicapped. The grouping refers to the extent to which a youngster can become an independent citizen rather than to the level of severity of a specific disability.

Adolescents with Mild Vocational Handicaps. Youngsters who are mildly vocationally handicapped are those who are likely to become independent, self-supporting adults. Given appropriate counseling, career and vocational training, and perhaps compensatory skills, they should be able to compete in the open job market. Some will go to college for further education. Others will attend technical or trade schools or receive other types of postsecondary training (see Box 13.1). Even totally blind individuals and profoundly deaf people may be only mildly vocationally handicapped. If a person can hold down a job, get around the community, run a household, communicate with friends, and so on, that individual is only mildly handicapped, according to this definition.

Adolescents with Serious Vocational Handicaps. On the other hand, there are numerous individuals with disabilities for whom the prognosis for independence is not good. Individuals who are seriously vocationally handicapped are those whose disabilities are so severe or intense that they are unlikely to become self-sufficient, independent adults. People who are severely or profoundly retarded come to mind immediately. Persons who are multihandicapped or severely physically handicapped are less likely to be able to live alone and get themselves to and from a competitive job than are persons who are less seriously disabled.

In general, most of the concepts related to individuals who are seriously vocationally handicapped are generalized from studies and pro-

This young woman has become a self-supporting adult with proper vocational training. (Courtesy of Library of Congress.)

grams for persons with retardation. Concepts related to mild vocational handicaps are drawn from the learning disabilities literature. Further information about educational programs can be found here, in other disability chapters, and in the generic teaching strategies chapter (Chapter 16).

Educational Programs for Adolescents with Handicaps

Until the last few years, educational programs for adolescents with handicaps were few and far between. During the late 1950s and 1960s, efforts were made to initiate new classes and programs for elementary students with mild handicaps, but programs for youngsters who were older or more severely handicapped were almost nonexistent in public schools. Of course, until 1978, when P.L. 94–142 was put into effect, children with severe handicaps customarily were excluded from public schools; private schools and institutions served this group. Furthermore, a higher percentage of people with handicaps resided within institutions a decade or two ago than do so today. Youngsters who attended special classes in public schools often were "socially promoted" until they reached the magic age of sixteen, at which time they usually quit school and dropped from sight.

In contrast to programs for elementary-age pupils, there are astonishingly few program descriptions and relatively few research studies dealing with educational programs for secondary-age students. The major exceptions are programs for individuals who are mentally retarded. Through the cooperative efforts of schools, the Association for Retarded Citizens, and other agencies, the history of training programs, work-study programs, and work–activity center programs for persons with retardation is somewhat longer. Programs for groups with other handicaps, however, were quite limited in number until the mid-1970s. Since then, many more special programs have been arranged for adolescents and postadolescents with handicaps of every variety and level of severity. Much of the impetus has come from parent groups, including the Association for Retarded Citizens and the Association for Children with Learning Disabilities. As of September 1, 1980, special education services are required for all youth with handicaps up to the age of twenty-one. After that age, private agencies and public agencies such as vocational rehabilitation are available.

Programs for Adolescents with Mild Vocational Handicaps

By the time a youngster with a handicap reaches midadolescence (age fifteen to sixteen), it is probably too late to continue traditional developmentally based skills programs in reading, math, and the like. Instead, every effort should be made to equip the individual with specific survival skills in those areas. Functional skills development, personal counseling, and career/vocation counseling and training form the core of secondary programs for students who are mildly vocationally handicapped.

Functional skill development is designed to help a youngster survive in the open job market. For some youngsters, functional skills may be extremely basic and, in fact, may overlap the functional skills taught to students who are seriously vocationally handicapped. Others may have adequate reading, for example, but need intensive tutoring in certain arithmetic skills such as balancing a checkbook or basic measurement for cutting fabrics.

W. H. Berdine and A. E. Blackhurst (1985) and C. D. Mercer (1987) identified other functional skills needed for daily living and for social and personal competence. Daily living skills include money management, selecting and maintaining a residence, food purchase and preparation, clothing purchase and care, and community mobility. Social and personal competence skills include the development of proper personal hygiene habits, socially responsible behavior, interpersonal relationships, independence, and recreational and leisure skills. According to R. L. McDowell (1979), adolescents with handicaps need the following specific personal and social behaviors to help them function successfully in society and on the job:

1. Be able to establish eye contact if required by the situation.

2. Demonstrate respect for others and their property.

3. Be attentive to authority figures in appropriate ways.

4. Exhibit good manners.

5. Use appropriate manners.

6. Discriminate between behaviors as to time and place (i.e., recognize that certain behaviors are appropriate at different times and places).

BOX 13.1

SOME POSSIBLE ADAPTATIONS FOR SECONDARY SCHOOL
AND COLLEGE STUDENTS

Physical Handicaps/Mobility Problems

Academic Alternatives

- faculty meet with students at accessible sites
- waivers of some lab requirements
- substitutions for some course or lab requirements
- oral exams
- encourage students to consider alternate programs; e.g., study vocal instead of instrumental music, or laboratory sciences instead of field sciences

Physical Barriers/Transportation

- move a class to an accessible location
- modify entrances, halls, classrooms, etc., as required to accommodate wheelchairs, crutches
- curb cuts
- provide students with books they need until libraries are made fully accessible
- install elevators, ramps
- provide special seating at sports, cultural events for handicapped students *and* their nonhandicapped companions
- provide wheelchair lifts for vans, buses
- equip vehicles for paraplegic use

Field Trips

- select accessible sites for field trips
- provide alternate field trips
- present field trip information via film

Other

- heated sidewalks so snow, ice won't impede wheelchairs, crutches

- covered walkways between buildings
- nonslip floor surfaces in halls, classrooms, ramps
- electric-eye doors, elevators
- alternate locations for elevator, auto door controls; e.g., four feet from and at right angles to elevator, door

Visually Impaired

Academic Alternatives

- waivers of some course, lab requirements
- oral exams, presentations
- tests by braille, audio tape, Optacon, etc.
- provide readers or taped lessons

Special Equipment/Services

- optical enlargers
- portable tape recorders
- large-print books
- braillers
- talking calculators
- Optacon
- guidance devices such as Sonicguide
- training in use of special equipment

Accessibility/Mobility Facilitation

- braille elevator information
- braille maps of community, bus routes, etc.
- braille information on doorways, building directories
- auditory signals in elevators
- auditory signals at traffic lights

---

7. Achieve a reasonable balance between dependence and independence.

8. Learn to accept directions and to take orders.

9. Learn to accept and follow the work schedule established by an employer.

10. See a task through to its completion. (p. 2)

Career/vocational counseling and training help young people learn about the work world and the basic skills needed in most employment situations. For example, most jobs require a cer-

Hearing Impaired

Academic Alternatives

- written exams and presentations
- more extensive use of visual media, captioned films
- provide ready access to portable audiovisual equipment
- provide manual interpreters

Special Equipment/Services

- teletype telephones
- voice synthesizer communicators
- portable ticker tape or videotape communicators
- visual light substitution for telephone bells, doorbells, etc.
- translators to translate audio tracks of films, videotapes into transcripts

Speech Impaired

Academic Alternatives

- written instead of oral exams and presentations
- substitution of requirements
- encourage student to consider alternative courses

Special Equipment/Services

- teletype telephones
- portable communicators: ticker tape, video display

All Handicaps

Academic Alternatives

- special testing arrangements
- academic "buddy" system to fulfill lab requirements
- arranging alternate sites for field experiences
- providing different emphases within courses
- alternative methods for satisfying course objectives
- exemption from certain requirements, e.g., standard physical education
- providing adapted equipment

Living Arrangements

- providing residence hall rooms with private baths
- modifications of living quarters, toilet facilities, cafeteria, etc. as required

Accessibility/Mobility Facilitation

- providing special parking and driving privileges
- providing transportation between buildings
- providing assistance at registration
- modifying entrances, stairways as required

Employment

- affirmative action program
- faculty/job/schedule/equipment modifications

Other

- coordinator of services for the handicapped
- obligation of clubs, intramurals to accommodate handicapped students

tain clothing style, promptness, completion of assigned tasks, and getting along with fellow workers. Vocational training generally refers to training for a specific job or, more likely, job area. The Vocational Education Amendments of 1976 (P.L. 94–482) require that 30 percent of state grant funds be spent on vocational programs for youths who are handicapped or disadvantaged. Such funds can be used to train adolescents who are either handicapped or nonhandicapped in such traditional vocational areas as automotive and building trades, food services, distributive

BOX 13.2
PROJECT PROGRESS

Finding a job for an individual who has limited intellectual and social skills can be quite a challenge. Community groups such as the Association for Retarded Citizens often can be quite helpful to young adults with special needs.

PROGRESS stands for Providing Realistic Opportunities for Gainful Rehabilitative Employment Success in Society. And that's exactly what is happening for Pete Gordon. Every afternoon, he runs the paper shredder at People's National Bank of Central Pennsylvania in State College, Pennsylvania. It's a job he loves, but one he probably never would have gotten without some help from a program run by the Association for Retarded Citizens.

Pete is one of four students between the ages of 16 and 21 years old who has found a job in State College through PROGRESS, an ARC program. The program sets up interviews with students and employers who said they have a job for a person with a handicap. A job coach from ARC goes with the student to the interview and provides one-to-one supervision on the job until the student can work alone.

"Having a job coach is a big help," said Patty Gordon, Pete's mother. "It gets a foot in the door and gives the students confidence."

Employers fill out a "vocational assessment" form on each PROGRESS worker. The form details the percentage of work completed, whether the student reports to work on time, and if the worker corrects behavior when told. The jobs are permanent part time. As long as the arrangement works, the student can keep the job. Each job is 15 hours a week.

In Pete's case, the job was perfect for him, his mother said. It has given him confidence and reinforces his self-worth.

"If you could have seen his face when he got his first paycheck, that said it all," she said. "It's good for him to realize he has to be on time and he has to continue working."

For Pete, the best part of the job is running the machine. There was nothing about the job he didn't like.

"I like the whole thing," he said.

Source: Adapted from Knoski, K. (1985, April). 'Progress' job at bank fits Pete Gordon to a T. *Centre Daily Times.* Used by permission.

education, business education, personal services (beautician, hospital orderly, day care center aide), and agriculture, or in newer professions such as data processing.

According to P. J. Schloss and R. A. Sedlak (1986), a vocational curriculum for students with handicaps should include basic training in academic, social, personal, and motor skills; career information and exploration; job-seeking skills; and the development of specific job competencies. Specific skills included in each curricular area would be identified through a job-setting analysis that used the following eight steps:

1. identifying current or future environments
2. observing others perform the skill
3. developing a skill checklist
4. pretesting
5. prescribing prosthetics and modifications
6. delineating task sequences
7. conducting training
8. posttesting (p. 340)*

---

*We refer you to a demonstration of this technique described in P. J. Schloss, D. McEwen, E. Lang, and J. Schwab (1986).

Programs for Adolescents with Serious Vocational Handicaps

Goals for adolescents who are seriously vocationally handicapped lie primarily in the personal area: self-care, mobility, communication, and leisure activities. The overriding concern is fostering as much independence as possible. For individuals who are severely or profoundly retarded, adolescent programs probably will be a continuation of programs already in progress. The main emphasis will be on self-care—feeding, dressing, toileting, personal hygiene—and on communication—making needs known and simple conversations. Youngsters who are seriously disturbed will continue in programs designed to improve interpersonal relations, self-concept, and the like and will receive additional instruction in leisure and hobby-type activities.

Adolescents who are visually or hearing impaired usually are not considered to be seriously vocationally handicapped in the same sense as individuals who are profoundly retarded or seriously disturbed. Rather, it is expected that these youngsters can become reasonably independent and self-supporting if they are trained in a specific vocation. They can be blue-collar, white-collar, or professional workers.

Youngsters who are deaf-blind or multihandicapped are more likely to require continued care. Consequently, the goals for them will undoubtedly focus on fostering as much independence and self-care as possible.

Adolescents with severe physical handicaps will require prosthetic devices and aids for daily living. Fortunately, there is a remarkable array of technological aids available to help individuals with physical handicaps to be more independent. These youngsters should be taught to identify appropriate devices and trained in their use. For example, a voice-controlled computer device is available that can be "trained" to respond to a single voice and to carry out such functions as turning a light or a TV on or off, answering the telephone, turning a page in a book placed in a special holder, or even programming a computer.

Sex Education

Not too many years ago, the topic of sex education was barely mentioned with nonhandicapped youngsters and almost never with handicapped youths. Today, sex education programs are more common for both groups. If you think about it, handicapped youths may have a greater need for programs dealing with sexuality than other youngsters. Often, by the nature of their handicap, they may lead a somewhat sheltered life and may not have opportunity for frank discussions with their peers about changes in mind and body. Applying the concept of normalization to the area of sex, there is no reason why handicapped people should not have the same rights (and restrictions!) regarding sex as nonhandicapped people have. Most of the arcane laws about handicapped people being forbidden to marry are now gone. With proper preparation and a sound economic plan, the handicapped should have the same opportunity for marriage and child rearing as other people.

Over the last decade, more attention has been given to developing materials and programs about sex for use with young people who have a variety of handicaps. In addition to printed materials for youth and adults, there are films, slides, filmstrips, and cassettes for youngsters with varying handicaps. Details of these materials and programs are beyond the scope of this book, but they are readily available. An overview of sociosexual education was provided by B. Edmonson (1980). A good source for information is the Sex Information and Education Council of the United States, sponsored by the American Association for Health, Physical Education and Recreation in Washington, DC.

Career Education

The decade of the 1970s were the maturational years of an important concept called *career education*. **Career education** is a systematic program wherein an individual learns about and prepares

■ BOX 13.3

BUILDING A BRIDGE TO INDEPENDENCE

The Bryant School's Pre-Vocational Program puts moderately retarded high school seniors into jobs and provides them with a bridge to work after graduation.

In the spring of a youngster's final year in high school, thoughts usually turn to independence, jobs, and broader horizons. But not Celia Lovera's. For her, graduation loomed more as a closing door. It meant fewer learning opportunities and less time with friends. Instead of earning a wage, she would continue to be a financial burden on her parents.

Celia, moderately retarded from a case of spinal meningitis when she was three, attends Bryant School at Spokane, Washington. Originally started by a small group of concerned parents, The School for Retarded Children (later renamed Bryant) became part of the public school system in 1951 and now serves 136 profoundly, severely, or moderately retarded students in the Spokane area, ranging in ages from six to 21.

Four months before she was to graduate, something happened to brighten Celia's future. The Bryant School Pre-Vocational Program, federally funded, gave her a crack at a job in the community before she finished school.

The Pre-Vocational Program provides job-training opportunities for 16- to 21-year-old moderately mentally retarded students, but it goes beyond most placement services that connect employee and employer. The difference is a site trainer to coach the student on the job until he or she is thoroughly familiar with the requirements of the work and comfortable in the environment. In this way, the program provides a necessary bridge between the school and the community for the student.

Without this bridge, employers are hesitant to

Celia has completed a pre-vocational training program and is working regularly in the kitchen of a nursing home. (Photo by William Benish. Courtesy of Bryant School, Spokane, Washington.)

hire the mentally retarded, says Shirley Ellis, Pre-Vocational coordinator, "mostly because of their own lack of knowledge about mentally retarded persons." The mentally retarded are often passive and not likely to make demands. It is all too easy, says Ellis, for others to stereotype them as incapable of learning anything. Many people also associate mental retardation with mental illness. Both conclu-

Source: Condensed from Rowe, J. Building a bridge to independence. *American Education.* Washington, DC: U.S. Department of Education, July, 1980. Used with permission.

sions are false, but the net effect is that employers shy away from hiring anyone mentally retarded.

Students are chosen for the program on the basis of their willingness to work and their ability to get along with others. Most of them are moderately retarded, having an IQ around 50, and many read on a first or second grade level.

The program is proving that moderately retarded students are capable of learning much like other students though at a much slower pace. Some of them are quite socially aware, are interested in the opposite sex, enjoy sports, dancing, music, and movies. Others are shy. Moderately retarded students are more accepting, less critical than average teenagers.

While the moderately retarded cannot compete with the stamina and speed of their nonretarded peers, site trainer Glenda Brown—who has a daughter in Bryant—says, "There's not one of them who can't do something worthwhile."

The Bryant program now has 17 training sites at restaurants, hospitals, laundries, convalescent homes, and small manufacturing companies. Gary Tucker, for example, has been working for two months in a shop which rents and sells tuxedos. His chores include laundering, vacuuming, ironing, sorting, and placing tuxedos on their proper racks, and cleaning and spraying shoes. Gary works about 75 percent on his own, says Brown, and he plans and handles his workload well.

It's been a year since Celia Lovera took her first step into the job community. From the day she was escorted to the site by her job trainer and met the man who was to become her "boss," Celia's life has changed. She's learned to perform a number of kitchen tasks. She's also learned to get along with strangers and has made friends with people different

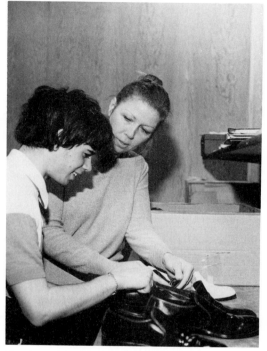

Gary is receiving on-site training as part of his pre-vocational program at Bryant School in Spokane, Washington. (Photo by William Benish. Courtesy of Bryant School, Spokane, Washington.)

from herself. And she can ride a bus alone. In fact, not too long after she started her job, Celia missed her bus connection. Rather than waiting for the next bus and being late for work, she walked the one mile to her destination—finding the way without difficulty.

BOX 13.4

BLINDNESS DIDN'T STOP HER FROM MASTERING JOB DETAILS

This story illustrates how technology can be very helpful to a blind person. It also points out that relatively minor modifications in office procedures and equipment can make a major difference in helping someone work up to his or her potential.

The visitor, momentarily lost inside the new Human Development East Building, pokes his head in the door of Room 210 and asks the secretary for directions.

She opens her braille notebook and, reading by fingertips, quickly locates the answer. The visitor, slightly astonished, mumbles a "Thank you, Miss," and leaves, back on course.

"I think I get a better chuckle from people asking me directions than anything else," says Peggy Hoover, blind for all of her 23 years. "I wonder what they're thinking when I'm looking it up in braille."

Good humor is just one of the qualities Ms. Hoover has brought to her job as secretary in the office of the Associate Dean for Continuing Education and Commonwealth Campuses in the College of Human Development.

"She's very competent, and she brings a sensitivity to others and a commitment to her work beyond that which I normally would expect," says William H. Parsonage, faculty associate in the Office and the person, along with colleague Margaret Bastuscheck, to whom Ms. Hoover is mainly responsible.

Ms. Hoover, a resident of Pine Glen, a small town 35 miles northwest of University Park, has been working for Penn State since May 1, 1979—five months after receiving her associate degree in secretarial studies from Thiel College in Greenville, PA.

Entering the Centre County job market, she found herself "looking all over the place." In her initial interview at Penn State, she was told that "they would keep me in mind for things I could do. I thought 'Snow-job time—you might as well look elsewhere.'"

Eventually she found a temporary job at the Centre County Library in Bellefonte, but was called by Penn State 20 days later to come in for an interview.

"A position had opened up," Mr. Parsonage recalls. "She applied for it, was found to be competent, and on that basis was employed."

Her first day was not easy. "I'd never want to relive it," Ms. Hoover says. "I was getting all this information about the office, and by lunchtime I felt so overwhelmed I didn't think I could ever learn all of it."

Office telephones posed another problem, for it was impossible to distinguish which of four lines was ringing from the uniform sound of the bell.

The phone company, however, adjusted the system so that each line rings in its own pitch.

Besides answering phones—a large part of any secretary's job—Ms. Hoover types correspondence, transcribing the text from cassettes, and maintains and files records, particularly those concerning part-time faculty members at Commonwealth Campuses.

The only "special" equipment she uses is an Optacon—a small machine that electronically "raises" typeface so that it can be read through sensations to the fingertips.

"The machine is invaluable," Ms. Hoover says. "I can use it for looking at personnel cards in the files

Source: *Intercom*, The Pennsylvania State University, University Park, Pa., January 31, 1980.
Reprinted by permission.

for working and living in the modern world to the maximum extent of his or her ability. Thus, career education is not limited to preparation for a job, especially when the clients are children and youths with handicaps. For some of these students, daily living in the least restrictive environment and the attainment of social fulfillment are the goals for career education. Finding a useful societal role and accepting it, whether as a paid employee or not, is an important achievement.

Career education begins in the primary years and extends through the school years. According

Ms. Hoover reads information from a braille sheet. (Photo by Scott Johnson.)

or for something as simple as telling me if I have letterhead stationery going in the right direction before I put it in the typewriter."

She also uses it to read typewritten letters from her pen-pals, many of them classmates from her 12 years of schooling at the Western Pennsylvania School for the Blind in Pittsburgh.

"It personalizes the letters and gives you some privacy because no one has to read them to you," she says.

Ms. Hoover, who says she's "pretty well adjusted by now to the basics of my job," also enjoys church activities, rock music and sports, particularly baseball and Steeler football.

Life for her is full, she says, both at work and at home with her parents and two brothers.

"Being blind does not bother me a bit," she affirms. "It's a fact of life, it's never going to change, so why sit around and feel sorry for yourself?"

—Roger Williams

to C. J. Kokaska (1983), career education differs from vocational education in that the latter focuses on training in specific technical skills whereas career education helps individuals develop to their potential *in attitude* toward not only the workplace but also their own place within society. You might say that career education helps individuals attain the attitudes and general skills necessary for success on any job (the how-to-succeed), while vocational education helps individuals learn what to do on a particular job. Career education is the job of all teachers from kindergarten on. Generally, vocational education commences at the level of junior or senior high school. Vocational education builds upon career education. Neither program alone is sufficient.

A total K–12 career education is a comprehensive system that covers a lot of ground and touches a lot of people. C. Ellington (1983) listed the four major phases of career education:

Grades 1–6	Career awareness
Grades 7–9	Career exploration and assessment
Grades 10–12	Career preparation
Ages 18–adult	Specialized training and career placement

Ellington also listed the minimum team for a successful career education program: guidance counselor, occupational specialist, work experience teacher, regular and/or special teacher, parents, rehabilitation specialist, and work evaluator. Of course, different team members will have different emphases depending on the age of the child or youth.

Kokaska (1983) identified the major components of a total career education program:

- instructional materials and techniques
- parent/family training and participation
- cooperative planning with community agencies and business
- career/vocational assessment, training, and placement
- personal counseling and decision making
- training of all teachers involved (p. 195)

It is easy to see from all this that vocational education may overlap with career education and that the regular and special education teachers must be knowledgeable about both programs.

ADULTS WITH HANDICAPS

Just as children grow up to be teenagers, so do teenagers grow up to be adults. Unfortunately for people with handicaps, reaching adulthood doesn't mean they have no more problems. If all

has gone well for individuals who are mildly vocationally handicapped, they should function fairly well in society as adults. Those who are seriously vocationally handicapped, however, will still require supervision; some will require total or near total care.

The concepts of normalization and deinstitutionalization were introduced in Chapter 1. Both concepts initially referred to helping adults with retardation lead lives as normal as possible in settings removed from the depersonalized institution. Now we will apply these concepts to all adults with handicaps. As in the lives of nonhandicapped adults, focal points in the lives of adults with handicaps are housing, employment, and leisure-time activities. These points are paramount in the normalization movement: Denying persons with handicaps of any rights, including marriage and having children, is a violation of their civil rights.

Housing

According to R. A. Madle (1978, p. 467), the range of residential alternatives that should be available for adults with handicaps includes

natural homes
adoptive homes
foster homes
group foster homes
community residences ("group homes")
apartments
nursing homes
regional centers
public or private institutions

The purpose of all these alternatives should be to provide a home for the residents in the least restrictive environment. The predominant trend in this decade is for housing that will permit adults with handicaps to live as independently as possible. Community residences (group homes) or apartments for small numbers of people are the most desirable, at least for those who do not need total or near total health and personal care.

The overarching principle governing residential decisions should be normalization. If an individual has the self-help skills and stability to be

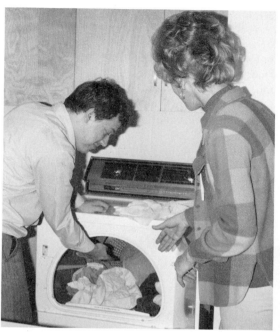

Specific instruction in personal care is important training for young adults with handicaps. (Courtesy of Association for Retarded Citizens.)

An important element of group home living is instruction in homemaking skills. (Courtesy of Association for Retarded Citizens.)

able to function in a small group setting, every effort should be made to locate or establish a group home or apartment. Location is critical. The home should be in a residential neighborhood, close enough to walk to shopping areas and recreation facilities or on a convenient bus line for ready access to those areas. Size is also critical. Group homes should be large enough to take care of six to twelve individuals, with no more than two to a room. Apartments should not exceed four tenants. Numbers larger than these suggest a "mini-institution."

Group homes are staffed by house parents or directors and other staff members twenty-four hours per day. The predominant role of staff should be educational, not custodial. The residents may need specific training in housekeeping, cooking, hygiene, transportation, and the like as they continue to seek independence.

In group homes, residents are expected to share all the chores of cleaning, cooking, and so on, while maintaining their own personal hygiene, washing their own clothing, and engaging in other individual activities.

Independent Living. Most adults with disabilities will tell you that their greatest desire is to live independently. For adults who are mentally alert but physically disabled, modifications of conventional living space and/or assistance from a personal-care attendant make independent living a possibility. Some of the adaptations that make independent living possible for people who are severely physically disabled are reported by J. Norgard (1983):

- two-van garage with power door
- kitchen with adapted appliances and controls

- adjustable counter tops
- emergency medical alert system
- pass-card-access exterior doors
- light-pressure rocker switches
- adapted door handles
- wheel-in shower
- accessible sinks and toilets
- lowered clothing rods
- fire alarm system
- intercom
- automated telephone dialing system
- heated, ice-free sidewalk

Indeed, a home with all these features, and more, has been constructed as a demonstration and resource center in Golden Valley, Minnesota, a suburb of Minneapolis. It is managed by the Courage Independent Living Center.

Berkeley, California, was a "hotbed" of political activism in the 1960s. Interestingly, in the 1970s, an equally strong activism occurred on behalf of adults with physical disabilities. Once again, albeit on a less visible national level, Berkeley was a rallying point, specifically with the establishment of the Center for Independent Living (CIL). CIL is an advocacy and support group for adults with physical disabilities. It provides counseling and information to help people with disabilities live as independently as possible.

Transportation

Another goal of adults with disabilities is to be able to move to and from their homes with a minimum of hassle. Personal mobility aids such as computer-controlled wheelchairs, and guidance devices for the blind were discussed in earlier chapters. In addition to helping individuals with handicaps acquire such personal aids, society has an obligation to provide access to public transportation as well as public buildings. As we reported in Chapter 1, sections 503 and 504 of the Vocational Rehabilitation Act of 1973 guarantee that no one be denied access to housing, jobs, or transportation simply because that person has a disability. Because of this law and because of increasing awareness of the problems of people with disabilities, some advances in transportation

access have been made during the past decade.

The most obvious advances toward a barrier-free environment are the ubiquitous curb cuts and ramps. Curb cuts permit people driving wheelchairs or using crutches to cross streets with much less trouble than they would have trying to negotiate a six-inch curb. Ramps are useful for people in wheelchairs, of course, but they also permit those using canes or crutches and people with chronic health or heart problems to gain easier entrance to buildings. Less obvious are modifications to allow all individuals easier access to public transportation. Washington, DC, has tested what are known colloquially as "kneeling buses." These buses have a pneumatic system that lowers a section of the bus to ground level, thus allowing easier entrance to people with crutches or wheelchairs or with disabilities that would not permit them to step up the twelve to eighteen inches onto a conventional bus. Other communities have adopted the "Handi-Van" concept, and special vans with wheelchair lifts are available on call, for little or no cost, to transport people with disabilities. The subway system of Washington, DC, also is accessible to people with physical disabilities.

Perhaps you have seen braille letters embossed in the metal adjacent to elevator floor indicators. This inexpensive modification permits the visually impaired to be more independent.

These illustrations demonstrate that we have made some gains in access to transportation. It is obvious, though, that we have a way to go before transportation is totally accessible to all.

Employment

Part of normalization is the "chore" of getting up and getting to work on time. Many adults with handicaps go to work every day just as nonhandicapped adults do. Part of the thrust of the Vocational Rehabilitation Amendments of 1973 was to assure that no one is denied employment because of a disability unrelated to job performance. Once again, there have been some positive results in the last decade, but there is still room for improvement. Individuals with sensory or physical disabilities are not restricted to any particular class of jobs. The range of possibilities and actual positions is wide, from the stereotypical (but archaic) newspaper vendor to corporation president, physician, and professor. A major charge to rehabilitation agencies (federal, state, and local) is to help people with disabilities obtain and maintain employment. These agencies provide specialized training and equipment as well as counseling and placement services.

Sheltered Workshops and Work Activity Centers.

Some individuals have disabilities so serious that conventional employment is not possible. Some of these people can obtain limited employment and/or work experience in sheltered workshops or work activity centers. A **sheltered workshop** employs adults with disabilities to perform a variety of jobs, many of which are subcontracted from conventional manufacturing plants, distribution companies, or other firms. The employees receive a wage, usually on a piece-rate basis, and must maintain themselves as satisfactory employees by regular attendance, promptness, satisfactory performance, and adequate relationships with other employees. Sheltered workshops provide modest wages for thousands of Americans who are handicapped.

Work activity centers are set up to assist those who cannot perform satisfactorily in a sheltered workshop or who may be able to do so with sufficient training. Although work activity centers simulate sheltered workshop employment, the wages are lower, the hours are shorter, and development of work skills and proper attitude are emphasized.

Some adults with handicaps are able to use public transportation to get to their employment. Others are transported in vans by the sheltered workshop or work activity center.

VOCATIONAL EVALUATION

A number of standardized tests are available to assist teachers and counselors in pinpointing current levels of student performance and targeting goals for vocational education. Before we discuss

them, however, we must offer a few words of caution. First, remember that many of the tests used to evaluate vocational skills are not designed to reflect the unique characteristics of adolescents and adults who are handicapped. For example, such tests may require reading and writing skills that exceed the ability levels typically displayed by learners with special needs. Second, individuals with handicaps are rarely included among the samples of people on whom these tests were standardized, which limits our ability to draw valid conclusions from test results. Despite these limitations, many standardized tests continue to be used to evaluate the vocational interests and abilities of individuals with handicaps.

Interest Inventories. It is anticipated that individuals will experience greater job satisfaction if they are employed in areas in which they have a keen interest. Therefore, a portion of vocational evaluation is devoted to the identification of a student's specific interests. The teacher can capitalize on these interests and carefully select educational activities that will motivate student participation and hopefully increase job success. Two interest inventories in particular may be useful with individuals who are handicapped. The first, the AAMD-Becker Reading-Free Vocational Interest Inventory, samples interest in eleven occupational areas by having the individual circle enjoyable activities presented via pictures. The second, the Wide Range Interest Opinion Test (WRIOT), samples interest in eighteen occupational areas by having students select from three pictures those activities that are most and least preferred. Other inventories are the Strong-Campbell Interest Inventory and the Kuder Occupational Interest Inventory. These measures, however, may have limited usefulness with individuals who are handicapped due to the problems described earlier.

Aptitude Tests. In addition to identifying areas in which a student has a keen interest, it is essential to identify those areas in which he or she has a reasonable chance for success. Therefore, a number of aptitude tests have been developed that measure an individual's potential in a number of areas, such as tool use, knowledge of mechanical principles, and eye-hand coordination. Unfortunately, many of the limitations discussed earlier in this section apply to aptitude tests as well. One additional word of caution is warranted. Aptitude tests measure an individual's *future potential*. They do not take into account the impact of subsequent instruction upon skill development. It is possible that a student who professes to enjoy clerical work may have little or no aptitude for this job. However, educational activities targeting the development of these skills may be successful. Thus, teachers should exercise caution when using aptitude tests to assist adolescents and adults who are making career choices.

An Alternative to Standardized Tests. Standardized tests may not provide all the data needed to measure job performance. For example, an opportunity may arise for an individual to secure employment at a local fast food restaurant. This could be a position in which a learner has an interest; furthermore, it may be the only employment opportunity available to the individual. The teacher may need to know how well the individual currently performs and what areas need to become the focus of instruction. A standardized test may not adequately assess an individual's ability to satisfactorily perform these skills. An alternative is to use a skills checklist (see Figure 13.1). Although gathering these types of data and teaching these skills may require administrative adjustments beyond the typical format, the results of testing as well as the impact of training may be more relevant and beneficial than traditional assessment methods.

RECENT LEGISLATION FOR VOCATIONAL EDUCATION

Vocational education for individuals with handicaps has been given a much needed shot in the arm by some recent legislative acts. They include the Job Training Partnership Act (JTPA), the Carl Perkins Act, and recent amendments to P.L. 94–142.

The Job Training Partnership Act. The Job Training Partnership Act of 1982 (P.L. 97–300) replaces and improves the Comprehensive Employment Training Act. Its purpose is to expand the role of private industry and business in the employment of youth and adults who are disadvantaged. Fortunately, benefits are extended to all those who face serious barriers to employment, including individuals who are handicapped. M. D. Sarkees and J. L. Scott (1985) identified services funded by JTPA:

1. job search assistance
2. counseling
3. remedial and basic skills training
4. vocational exploration
5. literacy and bilingual training
6. job development
7. preapprenticeship training
8. follow-up services (p. 10)

Although wages and public service jobs are not provided by JTPA, its funds do give each local community a great deal of flexibility in designing supported work programs for individuals with handicaps. Such programs involve location of job placements within a community, identification of social and vocational skills necessary to obtain and maintain competitive employment, skills training in community-based settings, and extensive follow-up (Lagomarcino, 1986). Measures such as these enhance the ability of individuals with handicaps to function effectively within the community.

The Carl Perkins Act. The Carl Perkins Act of 1984 has two broad, interrelated goals. Economically, the act targets the improvement of the skills of individuals in the labor force and the preparation of adults for job opportunities. Socially, the act seeks equal opportunities for all adults in vocational education (Terry, 1985). This act places high priority on those individuals, includ-

Thorough vocational evaluation and training help youngsters acquire needed vocational skills. (Photo by Joseph Bodkin.)

ing people who are handicapped, who have traditionally been underrepresented in vocational programs. B. Cobb and D. E. Kingsbury (1985) summarize the services now mandated for individuals who are handicapped:

1. supplemental services in regular rather than separate vocational education programs

2. information regarding local vocational education opportunities

3. assessment of interests, abilities, and needs

4. activities focused on guidance, counseling, and career development

5. counseling to enhance transition from school to employment

6. adapted curriculum, instruction, equipment, and facilities

Amendments to P.L. 94–142. Finally, P.L. 99–457, the Education of the Handicapped Act Amendment of 1986, makes specific provisions for secondary education and transitional services

for youths with handicaps. The amendment budgets $8.1 million in 1989 to fund grants to local and state educational agencies and to JTPA. These funds may be used to conduct demographic studies and develop strategies and demonstration models that promote the transition of youths with handicaps to postsecondary education, vocational training, competitive employment, continuing education, and adult services.

These provisions reflect a recognition of the difficulties confronting youths with handicaps who are completing their academic careers. With up to an 80 percent jobless rate reported among adults with handicaps, it is imperative that we develop programs that facilitate a successful transition from schools to community living (Will, 1984). The transition process includes a range of options regarding career choices, independent living arrangements, social life, and economic opportunities. Because the presence of a disability may adversely impact the transition process, parents and all professionals concerned with the long-term outlook for a youngster with a handicap must make a concerted effort to design and implement a transition-enhancing program well in advance of the student's high school graduation. An organized, comprehensive plan will facilitate the acquisition of skills necessary to function effectively in community settings.

LEISURE-TIME ACTIVITIES

The concept of normalization requires that individuals with handicaps be afforded the same opportunities available to nonhandicapped individuals in the areas of housing and training. This concept can be extended to include the development of leisure skills. However, as M. Bender, S. A. Brennan, and P. J. Verhover (1984) have noted, leisure skills for individuals who are handicapped may not develop spontaneously and may require individualized and direct learning experiences. Toward this end, there has been a sharp increase in the training of specialists to assist handicapped

Area	Skill		Prompt				
			P	M	V	C	Na
M	1.	Stands in front of register					
S	2.	Smiles at customer					
S	3.	Greets customer					
S/L	4.	Asks to take customer's order					
S/L	5.	Describes item upon customer request					
R	6.	Locates item on register					
M	7.	Presses corresponding register key					
L	8.	Suggests any special item					
L	9.	Repeats order to customer					
L/Ma	10.	Tallies order					
L	11.	Asks "for here or to go?"					
M/S	12.	Identifies cost with social amenity					
M	13.	Gets tray/bag of appropriate size					
M	14.	Gets items in the following order: beverages, sandwich/breakfast, cookies/pies, fries/hashbrowns, ice cream					
L/S	15.	Orders special grill items					
M	16.	Places item on tray/in bag (heavy items on bottom)					
M	17.	Provides condiments at customer request					

Figure 13.1. Skills checklist for fast food restaurant counter work. (Courtesy of M. Smith, P. Schloss, and C. Schloss.)

persons in the pursuit of physical education and recreation activities. Creative and productive use of leisure time and improvement of skills in each of the developmental domains (motor, communication, cognitive, social) are the goals of this new wave of professionals. Their services are badly needed and much appreciated by other groups who work with children and adults with handicaps.

Active use of leisure time is especially impor-

tant for those persons who do not have full-time jobs; their days would be long and empty without recreation. In addition to professionals such as therapeutic recreation specialists and adaptive physical educators, parent and advocate groups such as the Association for Retarded Citizens provide a variety of special activities for adults with handicaps. Bowling, swimming, hayrides, picnics, slide shows, and birthday and holiday parties, as

Area		Skill	Prompt				
			P	M	V	C	Na
S	18.	Obtains money from customer					
Ma	19.	Counts money given					
M/Ma	20.	Presses corresponding register keys					
M/R	21.	Presses "amount tendered"					
M/Ma	22.	Places money into appropriate sections					
Ma	23.	Identifies change due by reading register					
Ma	24.	Selects bill/coins representing correct change					
Ma	25.	Gives change to customer, identifying amount					
R/P	26.	Presses "print" upon customer request for receipt					
M	27.	Gives tray/bag to customer					
S	28.	Thanks customer and asks him/her to come again					
S/L	29.	If necessary, asks customer to wait for special order					
all	30.	Repeats procedure with next customer					
S/L	31.	Informs customer when special order is ready					
M	32.	Gives special order to customer					
S	33.	Thanks customer for waiting					
M	34.	Assists other crew members when not busy					

Checklist Key

Curriculum Area   Prompt

L — Language   P — Physical
M — Motor   M — Model
Ma — Math   V — Verbal
S — Social   C — Cue
R — Reading   Na — Not Applicable

well as individual hobbies, are arranged and encouraged.

The program known as Horseback Riding for the Handicapped is an excellent example of a leisure-time activity that has great therapeutic as well as recreational value. The program is staffed mainly by volunteers and offers training and experience in recreational horseback riding to children and adults who have a wide array of dis-

abilities. Originally known as Equine Therapy, the program was started in Europe. Today, there are programs in almost all the fifty American states, some sponsored by 4-H, others by local riding clubs.

Although these programs are a step in the right direction, one problem is that recreational activities for individuals with handicaps are planned and supervised by others. In their absence, it is unlikely these programs would continue. More recently, emphasis has been placed on the development of skills by individuals with handicaps that enable them independently to select and participate in leisure activities available within the community. These programs minimize the involvement of "outsiders" and can therefore continue in their absence.*

TECHNOLOGY AND COMPUTER-ASSISTED INSTRUCTION

Developments in technology and computer-assisted instruction have had an impact upon the adjustment of youths and adults with handicaps. Technological advances have included the development of many devices that assist in the maintenance of suitable employment. For example, laser canes enable individuals with visual impairments to maneuver safely to, from, and about the workplace. Microprocessors act as notebook, data processor, computer terminal, and calculator. Standup wheelchairs enable workers with physical handicaps to reach objects in high places. Telecommunication devices allow individuals with hearing impairments to use office phones. Improvements in technology have also enhanced the number and quality of leisure activities available to individuals with disabilities. For example, closed captioning now permits people with hearing impairments to enjoy many television programs.

Computers have benefited youths and adults with handicaps on a variety of fronts. First, they serve as a means for developing essential job skills. For example, interactive video allows students to practice employment interview skills. Second, an increasing number of employment opportunities require competence with computers. Individuals unable to perform tasks requiring physical stamina may seek positions within areas such as computer programming and word pro-

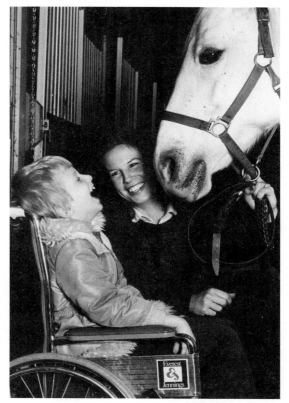

Horseback Riding for the Handicapped. Who's enjoying the first encounter more—the instructor or the student? (Photo by Scott Johnson. Courtesy of Pennsylvania State University.)

cessing. Finally, computers expand the number of available leisure options. For instance, computer games are a popular recreational activity among individuals with retardation (Sedlak, Doyle, & Schloss, 1982).

ADVOCACY

Laws, court cases, and compassion for other human beings are some of the reasons for the many positive changes that have occurred on behalf of individuals with disabilities in the past quarter-century. Another force, and perhaps the prevailing force behind the litigation and legislation, is a

---

*We refer you to a program described by P. J. Schloss, M. A. Smith, and W. Keihl (1986).

BOX 13.5

JOHN ROSSITER

John Rossiter is a senior at Kent State University, majoring in personnel and business management. He is anticipating entering the job market and is preparing for employment interviews. Cerebral palsy has affected his mobility and communication skills, so a wheelchair enables him to get around. An augmentative communication system with a synthe-sized speech output helps him communicate. This system will be particularly useful during job interviews when nervousness may make his speech even more difficult to understand. Rossiter hopes prospective employers will be able to look beyond his speech limitations and appreciate his knowledge and expertise.

Source: The college campus scene (1985, Fall). *Current Expressions*, pp. 1, 4. Information courtesy of Prentke Romich Company.

---

dedicated group of advocates. **Advocates** are people who expend a great deal of time and energy trying to help children and adults with handicaps get along in school and society. Advocates take on the establishment. They are the ones who "sit in" in the governor's office to make sure he or she (and the rest of the populace) are aware of the problems, discrimination, and prejudices faced by people who have disabilities. Some of these advocates are parents or relatives of people with handicaps. Some are professional people intimately involved in providing services to disabled individuals. And some are disabled themselves (see Box 13.6).

Advocacy is now a big business. Some advocacy groups have very large budgets that are used to instigate court suits or to lobby for changes in legislation. Many groups have full-time, paid staff members—lawyers, lobbyists, writers. Some receive state and federal funds. Others do not accept government funds and exist on donations. Some groups are active only in the political arena. Others exist only to provide medical or other services to children and adults with disabilities.

SUMMARY

The difficulties encountered by youngsters with handicaps may increase when they reach adolescence. The interactions of disabilities and the problems of adolescence are intense. These youngsters must cope not only with their handicaps but also with peer pressure, sexual maturity, and rapid growth.

Youngsters who are mildly vocationally handicapped are those who are most likely, given appropriate training, to become independent, self-supporting adults. Youngsters who are seriously vocationally handicapped, on the other hand, are those whose disabilities are so severe or intense that they are unlikely to become economically or socially independent.

Programs for adolescents who are mildly vocationally handicapped focus on functional skill development, personal counseling, and career/vocational counseling and training. Programs for adolescents who are seriously vocationally handicapped are primarily of a personal nature: self-care, mobility, communication, and leisure activities.

As with children and adolescents, the major goal for adults with handicaps is normalization—in housing, employment, and leisure time activities.

Vocational evaluation is conducted with both adolescents and adults to measure current levels of performance, target program goals, and monitor progress. Although a number of norm-referenced instruments are available, they may be of limited usefulness with individuals who are handicapped; criterion-referenced measures may afford a more appropriate alternative.

BOX 13.6

GEORGE ALDERSON, ADVOCATE

George Alderson writes his column with the help of a home computer. (Courtesy of the Altoona *Mirror* from a story by Jeff Montgomery, staff writer.)

George Alderson is a syndicated columnist who lives in Altoona, Pennsylvania. His column, titled "Handicapped—Handicapable" appears in nearly a hundred newspapers throughout the United States. Over 3.5 million people read his columns, which cover an incredible territory of information of interest to, and useful for, individuals with disabilities. The columns range from folksy, almost homespun philosophy to tips on getting around in a wheelchair to hard-hitting action plans for making positive changes on behalf of people with disabling conditions.

He has strong opinions about a lot of things. One of his prime interests is the language used when describing or referring to people who happen to drive wheelchairs or use crutches. I know he would chide me if I referred to someone as "confined to a wheelchair" or as a "cripple." He believes that the individual comes first, and the disability second. It is better to say "the person who uses a wheelchair" or the "person who has a disability."

George is an information source and does a lot of information exchange—obtaining information from someone in Maine and passing it on to someone else in Indiana. He has been a driving force in making state parks more accessible to the handicapped and in passing a law to make parking easier for people with handicaps.

George knows of what he speaks. He lost a leg a few years ago, and his wife has had rheumatoid arthritis since early in life. Look for his column, or drop him a line in care of Columbia Features, P.O. Box 295, Altoona, PA 16603. If you include a stamped, self-addressed envelope, he may respond via a letter written on his personal computer. Yes, George decided a word processing and filing system controlled by a computer was the way to go. And he didn't touch a computer until he was past the age of sixty!

A well-rounded individual has appropriate leisure skills. However, such skills may develop among individuals with handicaps only as a result of carefully designed and implemented instructional programs. Technology and CAI have promoted the development of leisure skills as well as vocational skills.

Advocacy has done much to promote appropriate programs for individuals with handicaps. The involvement of advocates, coupled with recent legislative acts such as JTPA, the Carl Perkins Act, and amendments to P.L. 94–142, has had great effect on the lives of individuals with handicaps.

Suggestions for Further Reading

Bender, M., Brannan, S. A., & Verhoven, P. J. (1984). *Leisure education for the handicapped.* San Diego: College-Hill Press.

This text provides a rationale for programs targeting the development of leisure skills by individuals with handicaps. It provides an extensive taxonomy on leisure education and specific leisure learning units.

Brolin, D. E. (1982). *Vocational preparation of retarded citizens.* Columbus, OH: Merrill.

This book is one of the few that focus specifically on the vocational training of retarded adolescents and adults. In addition, it discusses planning and improving normalization services for retarded persons.

Hale, G. (1979). *Sourcebook for the disabled.* New York: Paddington Press.

An extremely informative 288-page, large-format paperback that contains a wealth of information about independent living for people with physical disabilities. The book covers such topics as adapting the home, communication, walking aids, transportation, personal needs, sex, employment, rehabilitation, and recreation.

Miller, S. R., & Schloss, P. J. (1982). *Career-vocational education for handicapped youth.* Rockville, MD: Aspen Systems.

Miller and Schloss provide a thorough and comprehensive text that covers virtually all facets of career and vocational education for mildly handicapped youth. They give practical classroom techniques based on sound theory and practice. They also describe exemplary programs for secondary-school-aged handicapped youth.

Rusch, F. R. (1986). *Competitive employment issues and strategies.* Baltimore, MD: Paul H. Brooks.

This edited volume reviews the research in human services fields related to the employment of individuals with handicaps.

Sarkees, M. D., & Scott, J. L. (1985). *Vocational special needs.* American Technical Publishers.

This text consists of twelve modules, each covering a specific area related to vocational special-needs education. Topics include referral, assessment, IEP development, curriculum modification, and transition.

Schloss, P. J., & Schloss, C. N. (1983). *Strategies for teaching handicapped adolescents.* Austin, TX: PRO-ED.

This is a book of program forms useful in the implementation of a functional curriculum in programs for learners with severe disabilities. Forms are included for such areas as mathematics, reading, language, behavior management, and vocational education.

Weiss, L. *Access to the world.* (1983). The Complete Traveler, 199 Madison Avenue, New York, NY 10016.

This book (as well as the Hale book) is illustrative of the new breed of publications useful to handicapped individuals. It is written to help those with disabilities cope with public transportation and with hotels and restaurants around the world.

Relevant Journals

Career Development of Exceptional Individuals

This is a CEC journal published four times a year. It includes primarily applied research reports describing effective strategies for promoting vocational competence among students with handicaps.

The Journal for Vocational Special Needs Education

This journal is the official organ for the National Association of Vocational Education Special Needs Personnel. It is published three times a year and includes articles on teacher preparation, program design, student characteristics, methods and materials adaptation, and cooperative work arrangements.

CHAPTER 14

Special Groups

Did You Know That . . .

- there are over 65,000 children who are multiply handicapped or deaf-blind whose functional levels range from total independence to need for total care?

- children with different cultural and linguistic backgrounds often confront many situations in school similar to those faced by handicapped children?

- an estimated 2 million children suffer physical abuse, neglect, sexual abuse, and emotional abuse and neglect each year?

- recent studies reveal that approximately 23 percent of youngsters between the ages of twelve and seventeen have serious drinking problems and that over half of all teenage deaths are related to alcohol or to other drugs?

- half of the individuals arrested in the United States for serious crimes are under the age of twenty, and among that group is an overrepresentation of mentally retarded, learning disabled, and behaviorally disordered young people?

- about 1 million teenage girls get pregnant each year, and about half of them are under the age of eighteen?

So far in this text, we have been talking about those children with sensory impairments, physical disabilities, learning difficulties, and behavior problems in traditional school settings whose educational needs are to be met according to the provisions in P.L. 94–142, the Education for All Handicapped Children Act of 1975, and more recently in P.L. 99–457, Education of the Handicapped Act Amendments of 1986. Two groups of children we have not yet discussed in detail are the multiply handicapped and the deaf-blind. These children, because of the complex nature of their impairments, usually require very intensive individualized instruction that precludes their participation in many or all regular classroom activities. Still, it is important to be aware of the potential these children hold when they are provided early stimulation and appropriate instruction to spur language, motor, and social development. Some youngsters with concomitant handicaps do master the cognitive, personal, and social skills basic to participation in regular education programs. If they take their places in regular classrooms, teacher attitudes have an enormous effect on their success.

Experienced teachers and others knowledgeable about the activities of young people in schools today will quickly point out that our discussion has made no mention of several other large groups of children and youth whose needs and problems, although not addressed in P.L. 94–142, are attracting more and more concern from medical, legal, and social service personnel as well as from school personnel. One such group that has increased significantly in both size and heterogeneity is made up of children from culturally different families and families whose dominant language is not English. Other groups that have also increased in size and variability in recent years are abused and neglected children, abused and neglected handicapped children, chemically dependent youths and drug and alcohol abusers, youngsters in trouble with the law, and pregnant girls below age nineteen.

The purpose of this chapter is to increase your awareness of these various special groups of children. We do not mean to create new categories for special education, or to suggest that new ones should be created; we simply want to point out that these groups of students are already in many regular school classrooms and bring with them some very special problems and needs. We also raise some questions regarding the teacher's responsibility, either legally or simply as a concerned human being, to provide or secure help for these children and their families.

CHILDREN WHO ARE MULTIPLY HANDICAPPED

According to the definition used in P.L. 94–142, **multiply handicapped** refers to "concomitant impairments (such as mentally retarded–blind, mentally retarded–orthopedically impaired, etc.), the combination of which causes such severe educational problems that they [children] cannot be accommodated in special education programs solely for one of the impairments" (U.S. Office of Education, 1977a, p. 42478).

In comparison to other groups of children enrolled in special education programs, the number of children who are multiply handicapped is small. That fact contributes to the difficulties some school districts face in ensuring for these children appropriate programs in the least restrictive environment and in locations where opportunities exist for integration in meaningful activities with nonhandicapped children. For example, a child who has no vision, who is cerebral palsied, and who functions at the profoundly retarded level probably will need special class placement and intense instruction on a one-to-one basis in, among other things, self-help skills such as feeding and toileting. This child may be one of only two or three such children in a geographically large and sparsely populated rural school district. To equip and staff a special class adequately and assure that necessary related professional personnel are available to assist the teacher as well as the students, school districts sometimes work together to operate cooperative programs. But the location of the class may mean that stu-

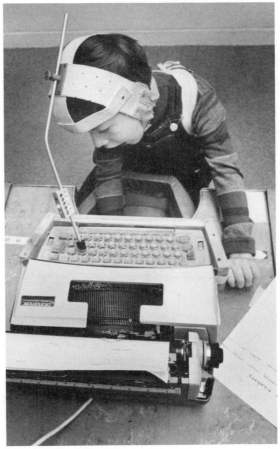

Communication is a difficult problem for most children who are multiply handicapped. This child laboriously types out a message on a typewriter with a headstick. (Photo © George Bellerose/Stock, Boston.)

dents spend considerable time each day traveling to and from their class, time that cannot be spent with family or with peers or in activities complementary to the school program.

In the days before the passage and implementation of P.L. 94–142, many of these multihandicapped children were excluded or "excused" from attending school. One rationale was that they could not profit from education in the traditional sense of the word. Many were placed in institutions where they lived out their lives doing very little.

Incidence

In 1984, the number of children reported under P.L. 94–142 and P.L. 89–313 as multiply handicapped was 67,189. The previous year, the count was 65,241. Note, however, that accurate determination of the numbers of multiply handicapped youngsters is extremely difficult because of the methods used to count those children actually receiving services, the federal and state regulations mandating only unduplicated counts, and the differences from state to state and even within a state regarding services for children in the three-through-five age group. For example, a four-year-old child who is spastic cerebral palsied, has low vision, and does not have a mode of communication may be in a class for physically handicapped youngsters yet receive help from a teacher of visually handicapped children and consulting services from a speech and language pathologist. That child, because of the placement, however, may be counted only as physically handicapped. Although this classification, in part, represents an accurate reflection of the child's needs, what is lost is the information useful for projecting personnel needs, space and facility requirements, and related services typically required by children with a mix of problems. In some areas, that same child might not even be in a public school program. In other areas, the child might be in a class for children with communication disorders, receive itinerant services for vision, be seen regularly by the physical therapist, and be classified only as having communication disorders or speech and language disorders.

Causes

The causes of multihandicapped conditions in children are many and can be quite complex. Some are genetic problems that lead to severe defects in body structures and/or function prior to birth. Diseases like encephalitis or meningitis and others that attack the central nervous system (as rubella can do when a pregnant woman is exposed during her first trimester) can result in a mix of sensory impairments, cardiac defects, and ortho-pedic problems. Injuries or anoxia during or soon after birth can cause damage. In many cases, the causes are not clear, but the marks they leave are.

Although few of these children may enter regular classes to participate in academic activities, many do attend regular schools where their special classes are provided.

Educational Considerations

Instruction for children who are multiply handicapped must be tailored to each child's particular needs. Certainly, communication skills and language development comprise a part of the program for many physically involved and low-functioning children. Some children who do not have control of speech musculature use language boards with pictures and/or words that meet communication needs in various environments.

Social development is also important. Horizontal patterns of social interaction with age peers who may or may not be handicapped are presently receiving more emphasis than in past years when more attention went to vertical patterns between child and care-givers and teachers (Sailor & Guess, 1983). Both patterns need to be developed in environments where interactions come naturally and with purpose.

Self-help skills are essential so that, as children who are multiply handicapped become adults, they can be as independent as possible. And developing leisure-time skills, recreation interests, and community-living skills are particularly important curriculum components at the secondary level, as are sex education and vocational preparation to the extent possible. Some multiply handicapped individuals can master the tasks necessary for independent living to some degree while others need constant care and supervision.

Perhaps the best way to illustrate the severity of problems that face teachers and parents of children who are multiply handicapped is to introduce you to Carla and her family.

Carla is eight years old. She spends most of her waking hours in a wheelchair equipped with pillows and ties to hold her fragile body securely.

On her legs she wears braces, and on her head she wears a helmet. Her arms and head are constantly in motion, and her left hand is contracted inward with her fingers locked in a fist. Carla does not speak, but she makes sounds that can be interpreted as pleasure or anger by those who work with her. On a tray attached to her chair rests a language board with pictures and words placed in five rows of four columns. Carla points with her right hand to a picture or word in response to questions. She still must be fed her meals, but she is learning to chew and swallow solid foods with much less spilling and drooling than a year ago. She startles at loud noises or unexpected bumps.

Carla attends a special class in a regular elementary school in the school district adjacent to her own district of residence. Her school program includes physical therapy, speech therapy, language instruction, fine-motor activities with her right hand to develop skills prerequisite to typing, and arithmetic. She enjoys being with the other seven children in her class and particularly likes to go outside to watch the recess activities. Frequently, Carla's aide pushes her wheelchair in tag games and in relay races. Carla lives at home with her parents, two older brothers, and grandmother.

Carla presents a challenge to her teachers. She has potential but no effective or efficient mode of communication at present. She has developed some muscle control for eating and pointing but not enough for speaking or picking up small objects. She tries hard but tires easily. Carla is learning, slowly but surely. Her teachers see progress in small steps after weeks and months of effort.

Consider Carla's parents. Both work at full-time jobs and are concerned about the limited time they have at home as a family. They are anxious about Carla's future and what plans they should make to assure that she will have appropriate and loving care when they are gone. And they worry about their older boys, too. With all the hospital bills and extra equipment Carla has needed, little money has been left for college savings, scout camp, or other things Carla's parents would like to provide their sons. The boys, ages twelve and fifteen, help care for their sister as much as they can when at home, and they talk freely about her with their friends, who treat her like any other member of the family when they come to visit. Carla's parents, who wonder what will happen as all three children grow older, value the assistance and support they receive from other parents of children who are handicapped in their local parents' group.

Carla's needs and those of her parents are similar to those of other children who are multiply handicapped and their parents: instruction based on assessment of specific communication, motor, social, and self-help skills; related services to assure an appropriate education program for each child; and support services for families with well-informed and sensitive personnel who can help parents deal with their concerns, long-range plans, and day-to-day routines. Parents need to be regarded as equal partners with special knowledge about their child, and their relationship with professionals in education and other areas must be based on mutual respect if the child is going to benefit from their interactions.

DEAF-BLIND CHILDREN

Children who are called deaf-blind are those with "concomitant hearing and visual impairments, the combination of which causes such severe communication and other developmental and educational problems that they cannot be accommodated in special education programs solely for deaf or blind children" (U.S. Office of Education, 1977a, p. 42478). These children require early identification, skilled assessment, careful sequencing of instruction based on assessment data, and consistency in management and care.

Incidence

Fortunately, the number of deaf-blind children is small, although their needs are great. In 1985, there were approximately 2,600 deaf-blind children between the ages of three and twenty-one reported to the U.S. Department of Education (U.S. Bureau of the Census, 1986).

Helen Keller and Anne Sullivan. (Courtesy of Library of Congress.)

Estimates of the size of the school-age group vary from 5,000 to 30,000. In 1980, there were approximately 1,000 deaf-blind children enrolled in special education programs, almost without exception in special classes full-time (U.S. Bureau of the Census, 1982). One difficulty in obtaining even a close estimate of the number of youngsters in this group is related to how these children are accounted for administratively. Some may be in programs for severely and profoundly retarded children, some in programs for multiply handicapped, and some, because limited motor function may be viewed as the dominant problem, in programs for physically disabled children. For this reason, figures are not very reliable, which makes long-range planning for facilities and professional staff difficult.

Causes

By 1976, more than five thousand deaf-blind children had been located by the network of federally funded regional deaf-blind centers in the United States. Many children in this group were victims of the German measles epidemic of the 1960s (Dantona, 1976). Other factors contributing to, but not necessarily the sole cause of, the combination of deafness and blindness are complications related to prematurity, genetic defects, accidents prior to or during the birth process, irradiation, physical abuse after birth, and complications of diseases such as encephalitis or meningitis.

Educational Considerations

Many of the children called deaf-blind actually have low vision, which they must be taught to use, and some useful hearing, which instruction and bilateral amplification may enhance. Even so, teachers who choose to work with these children face a real challenge to their ingenuity, skill, and patience. For every great success, there are many lesser accomplishments, even though the effort expended by both the children and their teachers may be as great as that of Anne Sullivan and Helen Keller.

Consider fourteen-year-old Luke, who is a residential student at a state school for the blind. He has had heart surgery, orthopedic surgery, and eye surgery. He wears leg braces and now walks independently. His glasses aid him in traveling around his school, but he has little clear central vision for discriminating fine detail. Most of the ten signs Luke uses spontaneously are related to eating, toileting, dressing, and going outside. He understands at least twenty-five more signs, which his teachers use in combination with the spoken word. Luke dresses himself, takes care of his personal needs, eats at the table with few spills, and is showing progress in the pre-vocational training program. His greatest needs at present are more language and greater competence in a mode of communication.

Although Luke and others who have even less vision and hearing may never enter your class as students, they may enter your thoughts as you contemplate the broad range of programs the education system must offer to meet its obligation to

BOX 14.1

RICHARD KINNEY, 1923–1979

For many people, the idea of living without seeing and hearing brings thoughts of overwhelming despair and conjures up images of a dark and silent oblivion. But then, those people probably have not ever heard of Richard Kinney.

Born in 1923, Richard Kinney lost his sight at age seven and his hearing during his years at Mt. Union College in Ohio. Armed with determination, zest for life, and the encouragement of friends and family, he later completed his college degree, the third deaf-blind person in history ever to do so. He went on to Hadley School for the Blind in Winnetka, Illinois, to teach and later to become its president. Kinney traveled throughout the world as educator, author, and lecturer. He and his wife, who also was blind, had one son.

Richard Kinney's poetry perhaps most clearly expresses the richness he found in life that prompted him to lead others out of their inner silence and darkness. Two of his poems are reproduced here.

Invitation

Through rain and rainbows let us walk
And pause and ponder as we talk
Of beauty, burning like an ember,
That you see . . . and I remember.

Let us lean against the sky
Westward where the echoes die,
Each sound that your quick ear gives
Sifted for me through silent sieves . . .

Once upon a sunshine-dappled day,
I heard a blind girl, musing, say,
"I cannot see the stars, but I
Enfold within my soul a sky!"

So if the sky enfolding you
Bends close about us, then we two
Walk with a sky within, without . . .
Heavens about us, *all* about!

And every bird-enchanted breeze
Gathers us treasures from the seas!
And every flower from the life-lush sods
Fountains us nectar from the gods!

Dream upon dream, our pulses beat
With dust and stars beneath our feet—
With stars and dust that, overhead,
Beckon to worlds unlimited. . . .

Through veils and vistas let us walk
and pause and ponder as we talk
Of beauty that we'll share together
All in the rain and rainbow weather.

Poor Robin

How did it happen? No one knows.
Hopping across the lawn she goes
With one wing drooping, I suppose
She'll never fly again. The sky
Must seem to her so very high
When other robins hurry by,
Singing, with buoyant wings a-whir,
On homely tasks, bustle and stir,
Joys that will never be for her. . . .
Yet as I muse in pity, she
Goes hopping onward merrily,
To pause at length by the small fir tree.
From ground to lowest bough she springs
And mounts toward heaven without wings—
One branch at a time, she hops and clings.
Now nestlings waken from their naps:
I am confounded—Well, perhaps
She's never heard of handicaps.

Source: Poems by Richard Kinney are included in L. M. Crist, *Through the Rain and Rainbow: The Remarkable Life of Richard Kinney*. Nashville, Tenn.: Abingdon Press, 1974. Poems reprinted with permission of Hadley School for the Blind, Winnetka, Ill.

provide a free, appropriate education for all hand-icapped children.

There are those who would question the amount of effort, time, and money spent on the education and care of deaf-blind and other children who are severely multiply handicapped. Their questions really demand a thoughtful consideration of priorities, values, and attitudes toward human life. The degree to which society withholds from some of its members that which can help them develop to their maximum is a reflection of the values that society attributes to human life per se. Do only those who achieve taxpayer status "count"? Are those who will need some kind of supervision or personal care most of their lives worth less (in effect, worthless)? We do not think so.

That there are upper limits to the possibilities of growth in each life no one can deny. But it seems likely that these limits are movable by virtue of the capacities of reflection, for self-objectification, and to a degree by breadth of education, and by the effort an individual may put forth. From the ethical and theological points of view the stretching toward this limit, whatever it is, is as much of a triumph for a life of slight potential as for a life whose potentials are great.

(Allport, 1978, p. 88)

CULTURALLY DIVERSE GROUPS

Have you ever hurt
    about baskets?
I have, seeing my grandmother weaving
    for a long time.
Have you ever hurt about work?
I have, because my father works too hard
    and he tells how he works.
Have you ever hurt about cattle?
I have, because my grandfather has been working
    on the cattle for a long time.

Have you ever hurt about school?
I have, because I learned a lot of words
    from school,
And they are not my words.*

What happens when a child enters a class-room and his or her words are not those of the others in the class? We could explore this question from the child's point of view and look at the uncertainty he or she feels. We could consider the question from the teacher's perspective and talk about attitudes and expectations, teaching strategies, second language acquisition, or language structure. We could also discuss how this child's classmates might respond. All of these perspectives are important when we think about children with diverse cultural backgrounds in schools.

Most discussions of cultural diversity occur within the context of concern for ethnic backgrounds or primary languages of groups of individuals. Although both ethnic and language background are important considerations, other factors also contribute individually and in combination to the way we act, react, and interpret the actions and words of others. For example, within the American macroculture, we can classify groups not only by ethnicity and language but also by socioeconomic status, gender, religion, age, and exceptionality (Gollnick & Chinn, 1986). Each of these microcultures could be further examined for characteristic features; for instance, in terms of socioeconomic status we could look at annual income, accumulated wealth, occupation, educational level, prestige, and power. In terms of age, we can subdivide into infancy, childhood, adolescence, early adulthood, middle age, and old age.

Manifestations of each of these microcultures can also be observed for variations in clothing, housing, patterns of etiquette, values, and language; the latter could be examined both for the particular language and language elements and

---

*Written by an Apache child in Arizona. Found in *Many Voices: Bilingualism, Culture, and Education* by Jane Miller. London: Routledge & Kegan Paul, 1983, 15. Used with permission.

for the other aspects of oral-verbal communication described in Chapter 6. For this brief introduction to the complex topic of cultural diversity among children with sensory, physical, behavioral, and/or learning handicaps, we will focus on general ideas, attitudes, and activities.

You are probably familiar with the analogy of the United States as a melting pot where people who enter from different countries are assimilated into the patterns and norms of their new land. Another way to view the great diversity in our country is to think of a mosaic where each culture contributes

Diversity of talents, values, and interests are found among children of all racial and ethnic groups. (Courtesy of HDS/U.S. HHS.)

> its own unique tiles, with their distinctive glaze and sharp edges, to the mosaic. Examined too closely, a mosaic presents a discordant picture of poorly, even oddly, juxtaposed individual units strangely cemented together. Yet, on balance, this technique, when viewed from a reasonable distance, presents a complete picture, the total amounting to far more than the sum of the parts.
>
> (Carter, 1982, p. xi)

This view seems to enhance the task of the special education teacher and others working with children who are handicapped from culturally diverse backgrounds. We can zero in on special needs, and we can also step back to see the richness the child brings and can add to the instructional setting. A. Hilliard (1980) has observed that although the term "*cultural diversity* encourages us to see differences, it does so without any implicit message of inequality." *Cultural minority* means fewer in number; *cultural diversity* means distinctive work views, values, styles, and languages of different groups of people.

Within the culturally diverse groups, we can find even more diversity if we distinguish, to the extent possible, among indigenous groups, established groups, and new groups. Some examples from the U.S. population would be Native Americans, black Americans, and Asian Americans (Churchill, 1986). Children who are handicapped or gifted can be found in any of these groups as well as in the majority culture. For instructional purposes, the teacher's concern must be the instructionally relevant attributes of each student, whatever the "group." As Hilliard (1980) has emphasized,

> The thing that matters is how a child's culture is regarded by those who are charged with his or her care. A child's culture (i.e., world-view, values, style, language) is frequently used as a marker to target the child for a different treatment than the children of those who hold power in a society. It is the educator's professional responsibility to see that this does not happen. (p. 586)

Major Groups

Various groups are represented in our present American mosaic, and, in 1975, the Federal Interagency Committee on Education listed some of the larger groups, as shown in Table 14.1.

Blacks. Black Americans make up the second largest discernible racial group in the United States today and account for approximately 12 percent of the total population. Within this group, as within all the others including the white group, there exists great heterogeneity.

Along with Hispanics and Native Americans, black Americans have suffered severe economic deprivation over the years. Although a larger proportion of black young people are finishing secondary school now than did even a decade ago, the relative gains in education have not been accompanied by the anticipated relative economic gains. Unemployment and underemployment still are higher among black Americans than among white Americans (Gollnick & Chinn, 1986).

One manifestation of culture we mentioned earlier is language, and some researchers have pointed to the use of black English, sometimes referred to as *ebonics,* as a factor that contributes both to the slow assimilation of some black Americans into the mainstream of society and to assessment of performance in school. Others have maintained that the close relationship between ethnic minority membership and dialect and teacher perceptions, attitudes, and expectations complicate the question of how much black English might or might not interfere with evaluation of performance in school. The controversial issue of how to handle dialects in instructional settings presents a continuing challenge to educators who acknowledge the legitimacy of dialects but who also recognize the disadvantages in certain situations, such as in some social and vocational settings, associated with the use of nonstandard English (Gollnick & Chinn, 1986). Although we have introduced the topic of nonstandard dialects in this discussion of black English, the issue relates to the use of nonstandard dialects by all other cultural minority groups as well.

TABLE 14.1

UNITED STATES POPULATION (ESTIMATED) BY MAJOR ETHNIC AND LINGUISTIC GROUPS, 1985

Cultural Group	Population (rounded)
White	180,600,000
Black	26,000,000
Hispanic	14,600,000
Asian/Pacific Islander	3,600,000
Native American	1,400,000
Other	260,000

Source: U.S. Bureau of the Census (1983). *1980 census of population.* Volume 1, Chapter C, Part I, 1-280.

Hispanics. People of Hispanic origin make up the third largest cultural group, about 7 percent of the total U.S. population today (see Box 14.2). Within this group are people who report their ethnic background to be Puerto Rican, Mexican, and Cuban as well as Central and South American (Stock, 1987a). Individuals in this group can be of any racial group, which makes past census data based on self-report of ethnic origin subject to questions about accuracy because of the way questions were asked and responses coded. Recent changes made by the Bureau of Census should help to alleviate some of these problems in the future.

The Spanish language, the second most frequently used language after English in the United States, might seem to be the major cultural feature of Hispanic Americans; yet, wide differences in linguistic, nonlinguistic, and metalinguistic aspects of the Spanish that individual members use separate the subgroups in significant ways. Among those who speak Spanish, of course, are those people, including some Hispanic Americans, for whom Spanish is the second language. The nonlinguistic or nonverbal aspects of Spanish affect how clearly speakers of different Hispanic backgrounds communicate not only with each other in Spanish or English but also with non-Hispanic Spanish speakers and monolingual En-

Bilingual education is more than teaching two languages; it includes teaching social customs and lifestyles of other cultural groups—in this case, Hispanic. (Photo © Elizabeth Crews.)

TABLE 14.2

PUBLIC ELEMENTARY AND
SECONDARY SCHOOL ENROLLMENT
AND ENROLLMENT IN BILINGUAL
PROGRAMS: 1980

Cultural Group	Enrollment (thousands)	Bilingual Enrollment	
		Number	Percentage
White	29,180	50	.2
Black	6,418	7	.1
Hispanic	3,179	643	20.2
Asian American	749	116	15.5
American Indian	16	16	5.2

Source: U.S. Bureau of the Census, 1982, p. 151.

glish speakers. Knowing only the words and knowing both the words and the culture that imbues the words with connotations and tradition are not the same.*

Children from Hispanic families come to school with varied repertoires of experience, expectations, and hopes. Each teacher these children meet plays some part in determining how these children develop as the school years go by. Given that the Hispanic group is the fastest-growing minority cultural group in the United States today, teachers must pay attention to their own repertoire of experiences with and expectations and hopes for these children.

Asians/Pacific Islanders. Among the Asian and Pacific Island group are included Chinese, Japanese, Philippine, Korean, Vietnamese, Indian, Indonesian, Thai, Laotian, Cambodian, Malaysian, Samoan, Guamanian, and Native Hawaiian persons. Except for the last group, these individuals

may arrive in the United States with little or no knowledge of English. In some communities, adult education programs or church organizations offer courses in English as a second language. Children of these families may arrive at school and need to learn English before they are able to participate in any of the regular school programs.

Many Asian American children who come to school with little knowledge of English are enrolled in bilingual education programs (see Table 14.2). Bilingual education programs make use of both the native language and English for instruction. Those bilingual programs that take a *maintenance* approach try to help the students function effectively in the two languages and cultures. Those that take the *transitional* approach aim to use the native language initially but then phase in English as soon as possible so English becomes the language for instruction and exchange (Gollnick & Chinn, 1986).

Native Americans. The American Indian and Alaskan Native group make up one of the smallest segments of the minority population in the United States, comprising less than 1 percent of the total

*For an enlightening discussion of this topic, the reader is directed to *Non-Verbal Communication in Puerto Rico* by C. J. N. Curt (1984).

BOX 14.2

HISPANIC AMERICANS: A BRIEF PROFILE

A first step toward recognizing the special needs of a child whose ethnic and/or language background differs from the backgrounds of other children in the school is to learn something about the culture from which the child comes and the language that child uses when not in school. People of Hispanic origin make up the third largest cultural group in the United States today and in some parts of the country comprise the largest percentage of youngsters in the school district. Are you ready to meet the needs of special learners of Hispanic origin?

Hispanics, the fastest growing minority group in the United States, represent immigrants and their descendants from many countries, even different continents. There is among them cultural and racial heterogeneity. Some Hispanics trace their descent from the original Spanish colonists, others are descendants of African slaves first brought to the Caribbean islands or to Mexico, and there have historically been patterns of intermarriage between these populations as well as with indigenous American populations and other immigrant groups. Regardless of their origin, the Hispanic population is a rapidly growing proportion of the national population due to immigration and high birth rates. The Census Bureau projects that by the year 2050 Hispanic people will be 30.5 percent of the population.

The Hispanic population increased from 4.5 percent of the U.S. population in 1970 to 6.4 percent in 1980 (April, 1970—9.1 million; April, 1980—14.6 million). The major national groups identified in the U.S. Census reports are of Puerto Rican, Mexican, Cuban and "other Spanish/Hispanic" origin. . . .

Eleven states accounted for 89 percent of the Hispanic population. Five Southwestern states (New Mexico, Texas, California, Arizona, Colorado) are home to the majority of Hispanics. . . .

The Hispanic population of the Southwest is 86 percent Mexican origin. The Puerto Rican–origin population is concentrated in the urban Northeastern cities, with growing representation in major Midwestern cities. The Cuban–origin population is concentrated in Florida, with a secondary concentration in the New York City–New Jersey metropolitan area. Many of the "other Spanish" are found in New Mexico and Colorado, as "Hispano," traditionally thought to be descendants of Spanish colonists. . . .

The 1980 Census reports four million Hispanic

Source: Stock, L. (1987). Hispanic Americans: A brief profile. *Journal of Visual Impairment and Blindness, 81* (6), 262–263. © 1987 by the American Foundation of the Blind. Used with permission.

U.S. population (Bird, 1977; Stock, 1987b). Among the almost eight hundred different tribal groups, language, customs, lifestyles, and religious beliefs vary widely and influence the daily lives of tribal members to a greater or lesser extent.

Though gathered into one cultural group with the Native American Indians, the Alaskan Natives present very diverse microcultures. The Eskimos, who make up the largest subgroup, live mainly in the north along the Arctic Ocean and to the west along the Bering Sea. The Aleuts, a branch of the Eskimos on the Aleutian Chain and Alaska Peninsula, together with the Alaskan Indians found primarily in the interior along the river valleys and in southeastern Alaska, form the rest of the Alaskan Native group.

The Native American Indian tribes are concentrated in states west of the Mississippi but are also found in the East (see Box 14.3). Over half live in urban areas. Most of those in rural areas live on one of the 250 Indian reservations set apart by the federal government.

Indian education was viewed as a federal responsibility rather than a state obligation before

households in the U.S. Most (75%) were husband-wife families and 19 percent were families headed by a female. The majority of Hispanic children under 18 years of age were living in a family setting, three-fourths living with both parents. Family situations do differ by the type of Hispanic origin. Families of Mexican background are larger (4.07 persons) and less likely to be headed by a woman, while 40 percent of Puerto Rican families are headed by women. These differences can often be traced to variations in patterns of migration. . . .

. . . Even though the Spanish language is common to Hispanics, there are differences. For example, the Spanish language spoken among Puerto Ricans differs from that spoken among Mexicans or Cubans. There are differences in words in the vocabulary, pitch of voice and patterns of language. Cultural patterns also vary widely, and while many Hispanic-Americans are Catholics, there are differences in the religious practice of the Catholic faith from group to group. The religious practice of Hispanics from the Caribbean has been influenced by African traditions. Hispanics originally from Central America have been influenced, in part, by Indian traditions.

Educational attainment by young Hispanics has been improving. In 1983, 58 percent of young Hispanics (23 to 34 years old) were high school graduates, compared to 45 percent in 1970. However, 40 percent of Hispanics (of all ages) did not go beyond the 8th grade, compared to 18 percent nationally. Only 20 percent went on for college training, compared with 32 percent nationally. Differences of educational attainment among young adults according to place of origin exist based on the class composition of the particular group. Seventy-one percent of Cubans were high school graduates, compared to 53 percent of Mexican and 55 percent of Puerto Rican individuals. . . .

The latest population statistics show the Hispanic population in the U.S. to be fast-growing, young and very diverse in nature. While the Hispanic group lags behind the general population in average education and employment rates, many gains have been made in the past decade. The growing numbers and attainments of Hispanics will mean an increased demand for better education, employment and training programs, housing and family services.

the enactment of the Indian Citizenship Act of 1924. In subsequent years, greater state involvement was encouraged, and the secretary of the interior was authorized to contract with states and territories to provide education programs in addition to those operated by the Bureau of Indian Affairs (BIA). In 1972, Congress passed P.L. 92–318, the Indian Education Act (Title IV of the Education Amendments of 1972), which requires active participation of the parents of Indian children in both planning and operating school programs. The provisions of P.L. 94–142 that apply to

children who are handicapped under state and local education agency jurisdiction similarly apply to American Indian and Alaskan Native children who are handicapped under the jurisdiction of the secretary of the interior. In order for adequate and appropriate services to be available for children who are handicapped among this minority group, attention needs to be directed to the improvement of policies and practices within the BIA to ensure the efficient use of funds and development of services, the development of cooperative agreements among BIA schools and social

BOX 14.3

NATIVE AMERICANS: A BRIEF PROFILE

Native American Indians are an indigenous group in the United States along with Alaskan Natives. Teachers must be aware of special tribal customs and behaviors that indicate respect if they want to work effectively with Native American children and youth with special needs and with their families.

Once the *only* inhabitants of the land that is now the U.S., Native Americans (using any of several possible definitions) today make up a tiny proportion—less than 1 percent—of the U.S. population, but a growing number. There were in 1980 about 1.6 million Native Americans, up sharply from less than 1 million in the 1970 census. Once in control of their destiny, later generations of Native Americans are among the most socioeconomically deprived ethnic groups in the nation. Nevertheless, there is continuing strength and pride in the richness of tribal cultures, and linguistic diversity still exists.

The majority of today's Native American population lives west of the Mississippi River, where five states alone account for over 40 percent of the population: Arizona, California, New Mexico, Oklahoma, and Washington. Also, many of the 283 "federally recognized" tribes (as defined by the Bureau of Indian Affairs) are scattered through the Midwest and East, for example: Eastern Cherokees (North Carolina); Choctaws (Mississippi); Creeks (Alabama); Seminoles (Florida); Penobscots, Passamaquodies and Narragansetts (New England); Rappahannocks and Chickahominies (Virginia); Oneidas, Onondagas, Tuscaroras, Mohawks and Tonowandas (New York) and Menominees and Chippewas (Wisconsin).

Over half of Native Americans counted in the 1980 Census lived in cities. . . .

Some Native Americans live on farms, but most who are counted as "rural" live on one of the 250 reservations which range in size from the huge Navajo Reservation covering portions of Arizona, New Mexico, Colorado, and Utah (where over 104,000

Navajos reside) down to small California "rancherias" with fewer than 10 inhabitants. In 1980 the federal government held "in trust" 52 million acres of Native American land, as reservations or other acreage.

English is the primary language spoken by Native Americans, although about 30 percent of them speak an indigenous language; . . . Estimates vary, but well over 100 languages are believed to be in use. . . .

The plight of Native Americans in the areas of employment and income is dismal. On most reservations job development has failed to occur due to geographic isolation, lack of skilled labor, and the absence of capital investment. And where lands have been exploited for their natural resources, they have then been depleted, and abandoned by investors. . . .

Poor nutrition and housing have contributed to a tuberculosis rate more than six times the national average in 1980. Contaminated water supplies make Native Americans 70 times more likely than Whites to suffer from dysentery. Rates of influenza and pneumonia are three times the national average. Native Americans are 10 times more likely than White Americans to have strep throat; eight times more likely to get hepatitis; and almost four times more likely to get mumps, chicken pox and whooping cough. The Native American suicide rate in the 1980's was six times greater than any other ethnic group in the United States. There is a growing drug abuse problem. The alcoholism rate among Native Americans and the death rate from cirrhosis of the liver are the highest in the nation. However, mortality and morbidity have been decreasing for the past 30 years. Thus, as noted earlier, despite their many social problems, the Native American population is increasing.

Native American leadership in emerging social and political action movements holds promise for improving the social and health conditions of their peoples.

Source: Stock, L. (1987). Native Americans: A brief profile. *Journal of Visual Impairment and Blindness, 81* (4), 152. © 1987 by the American Foundation of the Blind. Used with permission.

service programs and local and state schools and institutions, the recruitment and training of adequate numbers of teachers and other school personnel who are not only qualified to work with children who are handicapped but who also can work well with children of other cultural backgrounds, and the strengthening of advocacy groups and activities (Ramirez & Smith, 1978).

Awareness of some of the problem areas teachers may face when working with Native American children is essential if teachers are to be successful with these children whose traditional behavior differs from that of most children of the dominant white culture. The following are some suggestions for teachers and others to keep in mind in an attempt to prevent misunderstandings and misinterpretations of behavior due to cultural differences:

1. Do not expect direct eye contact.

2. Do not probe deeply when asking questions.

3. Develop a tolerance for silence.

4. Do not reprimand or praise a Native American in front of others.

5. Make your handshake gentle.

6. Use demonstration of actual skills or techniques.

7. Be sensitive to the Native American client's perception of time and scheduling.

8. Respect importance of the extended family.

9. Avoid condescending statements, stereotypes, and generalizations.

(Taken from Orlansky, M. D., and Trap, J. J. (1987). Working with Native American persons: Issues in facilitating communication and providing culturally relevant services. *Journal of Visual Impairment and Blindness, 81* (5), 151–55. © 1987 by the American Foundation for the Blind. Used with permission.)

Cultural Differences in School

In Table 14.2, we can see the cultural makeup of the 1980 public elementary and secondary school enrollment as well as the enrollment of those students in bilingual education programs. Germane to this discussion is the number of children from these various cultural groups in bilingual *special* education (but we found no figure to report). The purpose of bilingual special education is to "meet the academic, sociocultural, and psychological needs of non-English-speaking handicapped pupils who cannot meet performance standards normally expected of a comparable group of English-speaking handicapped pupils" (Plata & Santos, 1981, p. 98). Box 14.4 contains a set of questions designed to help the special educator plan for the assessment, placement, instruction, and/or physical management of special education children in bilingual programs.

Teachers who have had students from other racial and cultural backgrounds in their classes will no doubt echo the question raised by K. S. Chan and R. Rueda (1979) as to why some "minority children demonstrate the ability to think, act, and be motivated appropriately in activities out of school, yet do not demonstrate these same behaviors in school" (p. 427). Their contention is that, for some children, a conflict may exist between the child's development in his or her cultural setting and the prerequisites for school— what is referred to as the "hidden curriculum"— because

1. Educators presume the development of rudimentary cognitive skills.

2. Educators anticipate that children will be motivated to attend and perform well in school.

3. Educators assume that the child has a command of standard English.

4. Upon entering school, children are expected to possess a finite set of student behaviors [that is, they know the role of student in relation to teacher]. (p. 423)

Of course, not all children of the school's dominant cultural group may arrive at school having mastered these aspects of the hidden curriculum. Perhaps we should be more concerned about the prerequisites for adjustment to school, settling into the routine, or "behaving" as defined

BOX 14.4

QUESTIONS TO DETERMINE NEEDS OF CHILDREN IN BILINGUAL EDUCATION

What do you do and where do you start when children come to school with physical, sensory, learning, or behavior handicaps—and with a primary language different from the language of instruction and little or no facility in communicating in that language of instruction? How do you determine if perhaps some of these children are gifted? Here are some questions to help school district personnel decide where to begin and what plan of action to design.

Appraisal and Assessment

1. Who will assess linguistically different students suspected of having a handicapping condition?
2. What instruments will be used to ascertain the "true" performance levels of these pupils?
3. What procedures will be used to ensure that the assessment is nondiscriminatory?
4. What competencies must appraisal personnel have to successfully assess bilingual handicapped pupils?
5. What alternative procedures will be established when there are no appraisal personnel who can speak the pupil's language?
6. Where and how will appraisal personnel be trained?
7. Who will train appraisal personnel?

Placement Decisions

1. What are the alternative program placements that will be used to meet the "least restrictive environment" criteria stipulated in P.L. 94–142 and P.L. 93–516?
2. What criteria will be used to reach a placement decision?
3. What procedures will be used to ensure that procedural safeguards are followed?
4. If special education is merited:
   a. What procedures will be used to ensure adequate parental participation in the placement process?
   b. What procedures will be used to ensure that parents adequately understand the appraisal and placement information and its ramifications?

Instructional Personnel and Materials

1. Are the teaching personnel in the placement alternatives trained to teach linguistically different handicapped pupils? If not:
   a. What procedures will ensure that there will be sufficient numbers of trained personnel in the future?
   b. Who will train the instructional personnel?
   c. Where, when, and how will they be trained?
   d. What instructional skills are needed to teach bilingual handicapped children?
2. Does the curriculum adequately and appropriately meet the learning and other needs of bilingual handicapped pupils? If not:
   a. What procedures will ensure that adequate and appropriate materials will be acquired?

Source: Plata, M., and Santos, S. Bilingual Special Education: A Challenge for the Future. *Teaching Exceptional Children,* Vol. 14 [3], December, 1981, p. 99. Used with permission of The Council for Exceptional Children.

in schools and then determine what to do when children do not demonstrate mastery of those skills. Eventually, we must face the questions about school expectations, significant cultural differences that may inhibit or prevent meeting these expectations, the role of schools in socializing students and transmitting common elements of the culture, and the degree to which expectations of the schools can or should actually change to accommodate greater diversity among students.

Teachers who have minority group children in their classes need to be sensitive to the cultural

b. Will instructional materials be developed for the bilingual handicapped pupil? If so:
  • Who will create the materials?
  • What guidelines will be used to develop instructional materials for these students?
  • What support system will be used to enhance the creation of instructional materials (time, place, supplies)?
3. What procedures will be used to ensure that all necessary parties, including parents, are involved in developing an IEP for the bilingual handicapped pupil?
  a. Have plans been established to translate information for the non-English-speaking parents/guardians during the formulation of the IEP?
  b. Are there alternative plans when translators are unavailable?
  c. Are there plans to ensure that there will be an adequate number of translators in the future?
4. What procedures will be used to evaluate the instructional program for the bilingual handicapped pupil?
  a. What kinds of evaluation will be done? Formative? Summative?
  b. What instruments will be used?
  c. Who will evaluate the program?
  d. When and how often will evaluations take place?
  e. How will the evaluation results be used?
  f. What are the essential competencies necessary for evaluators to adequately and com-

prehensively evaluate a bilingual special education program?

Physical Management

1. Are all of the instructional components required to implement the IEP accessible to the pupils?
2. Are special transportation, equipment, furniture, and storage facilities available?
3. Have ancillary personnel (bus drivers, cafeteria workers, aides, and others) received appropriate training in meeting the pupils' special needs? If not:
  a. Who will train the ancillary personnel?
  b. When, where, and how will training occur?
  c. What skills do ancillary personnel need to successfully work with bilingual handicapped students?

The self-study will probably reveal several unresolved questions in the areas of assessment, placement, instruction, and/or physical management of bilingual special education programs. Each local education agency will need to use available resources to seek practical solutions to their own unique circumstances.

differences that may contribute to difficulties in school adjustment and performance. Children can quickly sense both an attitude of contempt as opposed to an attitude of respect for differences and a willingness to explore other ways of living and learning.

The following is a list of the major goals of multicultural education programs that should provoke both thought and action on the part of professionals concerned about the cultural diversity in our schools today and about how to provide appropriate education for handicapped youngsters who also belong to other microcultures within our American society:

1. Learn basic academic skills.

2. Acquire a knowledge of the historical and social realities of U.S. society in order to understand racism, sexism, and poverty.

3. Overcome fear of differences that leads to cultural misunderstandings and intercultural conflicts.

4. Function effectively in own and other cultural situations.

5. Value cultural differences among people and view differences in an egalitarian mode rather than in an inferior-superior mode.

6. Understand the multicultural nation and interdependent world in which we live.

(From Gollnick, D. M., & Chinn, P. C. (1986). *Multicultural education in a pluralistic society,* 2nd edition. Columbus, OH: Charles E. Merrill, 255–56. Copyright © 1986 Merrill Publishing Co. Reprinted by permission.)

P. C. Chinn (1979) has observed that "enlightenment in cultural diversity and a careful study of the idiosyncrasies of each ethnic group, coupled with sound special education techniques, will provide a basic foundation for meeting the needs of these children" (p. 536). So, what will happen to the child who is handicapped who enters the class and uses "different words"? It depends in large part on the teacher.

The United States is regarded as an affluent nation, but hundreds of thousands of our children suffer from the effects of poverty and neglect. (Courtesy of HDS/U.S. HHS.)

ABUSED AND NEGLECTED CHILDREN

▪ A nine-month-old boy is brought to the emergency room with the shape of an iron burned into his back (he "walked" under the ironing board and knocked it off).

▪ A ten-month-old girl with second- and third-degree scalding burns on her feet, buttocks, and perineum "fell into the bathtub filled with hot water."

▪ Pathology reports confirm diagnosis of venereal disease in a seven-year-old girl.

▪ X rays show fresh, partly healed, and old spiral fractures in arms and legs of a three-year-old boy.

▪ A nine-year-old girl refuses to change into gym clothes; later examination reveals welts and stripes on upper arms and back from beatings with a belt and power cord.

▪ Fourteen-year-old Joe is deaf and blind, has no speech, and does not walk. He screams if touched.

▪ Etc., etc., etc.

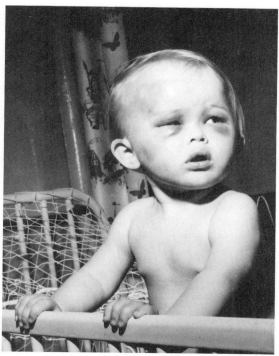

In most states, public health officials are required by law to report all cases of suspected child abuse. (Courtesy of Wide World Photos.)

Incidence

The National Center on Child Abuse and Neglect estimates that more than 1 million children suffer physical, emotional, and sexual abuse and neglect by a parent or care-giver each year. Because of reporting procedures and difficulties involved in obtaining unduplicated counts, exact figures are not known. In addition, evidence suggests that many cases of abuse and neglect go unreported, even though all fifty states have laws against child abuse.

The U.S. Census Bureau, in its 1986 report for 1984, recorded more than 1,700,000 reported victims of maltreatment, over 2.5 times the number reported in 1976 (U.S. Bureau of the Census, 1986). Estimates of the number of cases of sexual abuse, based on the actual number of cases re-

ported and on factors that inhibit such reporting, range from 45,000 to over 1 million (Morgan, 1985). Over 700,000 children in the United States do not receive adequate food, clothing, or shelter each year. Approximately 2,000 children, most under the age of four years, die each year from abuse and neglect (Bird, 1977; McNeese & Hebeler, 1977; Morgan, 1985). The number of children whose lives are damaged by emotional abuse is unknown, partly because incidents are difficult to document and because single incidents that might be observed may not appear to be very significant in isolation (Morgan, 1985). But the cumulative effects can be devastating, as Box 14.5 suggests. As for the abuse and neglect of children who are handicapped, evidence suggests that both occur "in at least the same proportion" as among other children (Morgan, 1987, p. 43).

Although concern over the plight of abused children has existed for years, only recently has the topic been openly discussed, have suspected cases of abuse been reported to the authorities, or has much effort been made to salvage the bodies and lives of the victims. In the early 1970s, however, a child named Mary Ellen came to the attention of some church workers in her community who, unsuccessful in getting help from other agencies or the authorities, approached the Society for the Prevention of Cruelty to Animals for help because the child was being beaten regularly by her adoptive parents. The Society was able to have her removed from their home on the grounds that such beatings constituted cruelty to animals and Mary Ellen was a member of the animal kingdom (Rose, 1980). Soon after, groups that now make up the Society for the Prevention of Cruelty to Children were founded throughout the country.

Definitions

The term **battered child syndrome** was first used in 1962 to describe children with serious and frequent injuries accompanied by discrepancies between clinical findings and the explanations

BOX 14.5
EMOTIONAL ABUSE: DO YOU GET THE FEELING?

The following excerpt is taken from Sharon Morgan's book entitled *Children in Crises: A Team Approach in the Schools* in which she discusses many of the difficult situations that children today frequently must face: separation and divorce, death of a loved one, depression and attempts at suicide, and abuse and neglect. In her chapter on abuse and neglect, we are introduced to Stacy, age eight. As you read selected portions of this incident between Stacy and her mother, what impression of their relationship do you get? How would you document it for a third party?

"Well, what do you think? Isn't your mother gorgeous? Could have been a movie star, you know! People tell me all the time how I look like Jane Fonda or Faye Dunaway. 'Course you came along and I had to give up all my plans and get married—have a baby. Anyway, I do still have a terrific figure!" . . .

Stacy was only half listening as she stooped in the bathtub, clutching her feet with her hands. She was not sitting all the way down in the tub yet—the water was too hot. She looked up at her mother thinking about what she had just said. Yes, her mother was very pretty. Stacy even thought she was the most beautiful lady in the whole world, especially when she was fixin' up to go out someplace.

She stared at her mother who was all dressed up and ready to go out and see people and have a good time.

A funny feeling came over Stacy as she compared in her mind how extremely different they were. She thought of herself and how ridiculous she looked and felt. There was her mother all dressed with makeup and hair in place, looking very beautiful. And Stacy naked in the bathtub, hunched over with her bare bottom in the air—scrawny, hair half wet, and hanging in her face. She wished her mother would leave the bathroom and let her be alone. She hated looking like that even in front of her mother.

"Put some more cold in the water, Mamma. It's too hot! I can't sit down—the water burns."

"How many times have I told you not to call me Mamma! Or Mommy. Or Mom! None of that stuff! Are you completely dense? Call me by my name like everybody else. My name—as you know—is Rita! My mother named me after her favorite movie star, Rita Hayworth—just the most gorgeous woman in Hollywood in her day, the most popular pinup of the soldiers during World War II. Don't kiss and hug and hang all over me, either. You're too big for that! Take your bath like I told you. You're holding up the show. I don't intend to be late and you aren't either. I've got plans, have someplace to go tonight. And you—you're going to your dad's for the weekend." . . .

She felt a trickle of tears run down the side of her

Source: Morgan, S. R. (1985). *Children in crises: A team approach in the schools.* San Diego, CA: College-Hill Press, pp. 117–124. Used with permission.

provided by parents (Kempe et al., 1974). Various types of abuse and neglect have been recognized since then, with some kinds being more difficult to confirm than others (McNeese & Hebeler, 1977). **Physical abuse** refers to nonaccidental injuries of a child, which are most frequently the result of beatings and burns. **Physical neglect** is viewed as willful failure to provide the basic medical attention, nourishment, clothing, supervision, and housing necessary for sustaining healthy life.

Sexual abuse, both assaultive (with injury) and nonassaultive, is any sexual activity between an adult and a child. *Emotional abuse* and *neglect,* which are even more difficult to define or document (McNeese & Hebeler, 1977), typically involve signs that are "hazy, indistinct, and obscure," as the incident between Stacy and Rita in Box 14.5 suggests (Morgan, 1987, p. 28). The National Committee on Prevention of Child Abuse characterizes **emotional abuse** as " . . . excessive, aggres-

nose. Nothing she felt made a difference to her mother. She wouldn't dare tell her what she was just thinking. Her mother didn't seem to care that the water was so hot—that her feet and hands had turned as red as a lobster. In fact, Rita had not stopped staring at herself in the mirror long enough to notice Stacy's misery.

Stacy's feelings of rage dissolved into great sadness. Her chest ached and throbbed and felt like the heaviest part of her body. She considered what she had just wanted to shout at her mother and gave more thought—she really did not hate her mother; she loved her. Her mother really did not do bad things to hurt—hardly even gave her spankings, and when she did, they didn't even hurt at all. She just didn't pay attention to how Stacy felt or what she wanted. She wanted her mother to love her—that's what she wanted most of all. She wished her mother would take her out of the tub and wrap her in a towel and hug her and rock her. . . .

"Hot baths are good for a person. Gets all the dirt out of your pores. The stink, too, I might add. You did that nasty thing at school again today. I'm telling you, Stacy, I don't want that school calling me again to come and get you because you wet yourself. You're a big girl now—eight years old is far too big to still be having those accidents. God, sometimes I wonder just whose child you are! You certainly are

nothing like me. My dear own mother used to say what a beautiful, perfect child I was. I certainly never did such nasty things." . . .

Stacy listened to her mother rave on and on about her numerous failings. She was still not sitting down in the tub—still clutching her red feet because the water was too hot. She thought about what happened that day at school and she felt embarrassed. She couldn't think clearly about the whole confusing incident. It left her mind feeling numb because she didn't understand how it happened. School was mostly something to be endured. Things always seemed to go wrong at school and she didn't understand how they happened. Like this thing today. . . .

"Do I have to go to Dad's? Can I have a babysitter instead? I wish Gram was here! There isn't anything to do at Dad's house. Could I stay home this weekend with you?"

"No, you cannot have a babysitter! I can't afford it! These days, kiddo, my poor dear dead mother wouldn't want anything to do with you. Thank God she can't see how you've turned out. She would be real disgusted with you, Stacy—just as I am. I need the weekend to myself, can't have you around all the time or I might start acting as crazy as you do!" . . .

Do you get the feeling? . . .

---

sive, or unreasonable parental demands that place expectations on a child beyond his or her capabilities. . . . constant and persistent teasing, belittling, or verbal attacks. . . . failure to provide the psychological nurturance necessary for a child's psychological growth and development—no love, no care, no support, no guidance" (cited in Morgan, 1985, p. 129).

For legal purposes, the Child Abuse Prevention and Treatment Act of 1974 (P.L. 93–247)

defines **child abuse and neglect** as "the physical or mental injury, sexual abuse or exploitation, negligent treatment, or maltreatment of a child under the age of eighteen or the age specified by the child protection law of the State in question, by a person who is responsible for the child's welfare, under circumstances which indicate that the child's health or welfare is harmed or threatened thereby, as determined in accordance with regulations prescribed by the Secretary" (P.L. 93–

247 as amended by P.L. 95–266, April 24, 1978, Sec. 3).

D. F. Kline (1977) has pointed out that this definition should appeal to educators "since it flows from a sense of what children are, what they need, and what they may become" (p. 15). "What they may become" warrants particular attention because studies show a tendency for abused children to become abusing parents (McCaffrey, 1979; Johnson & Morse, 1974; Morgan, 1987). In fact, one source estimates that 85 percent of abused children will become abusing parents (*Facts about Child Abuse and Neglect,* n.d.). Although rather shocking, the idea of abused children becoming abusing parents should not be too surprising, because that role model of parenting may be the only one available for the abused child. Speaking of the importance of early attachments and affiliations, G. W. Allport (1978) has observed that "love is not easily commanded or offered by one whose whole life has been marked by reactive protest against early deprivation" (p. 33).

Identification

The need for early identification of victims of child abuse and neglect is essential to break the vicious cycle of hurt, damage, and waste. Poor child-rearing practices, stress, isolation, unrealistic expectations given a child's level of physical and mental development, ignorance of child care procedures, serious marital discord, abuse as a child, low self-esteem, physical or mental illness, and crises surrounding separation or divorce can all contribute to abusing parental behaviors (McCaffrey, 1979; McNeese & Hebeler, 1977; Soeffing, 1975; Morgan, 1987).

Because teachers spend concentrated periods of time with children, they are in ideal situations to pick up signs of abuse and neglect, provided they know what to look for. Table 14.3 lists some of the behaviors and signs that might raise suspicions.

M. C. McNeese and J. R. Hebeler (1977) have stressed that prerequisites to an incident of abuse are "a *child* who is difficult to manage (or is merely considered difficult by parents), a *parent* or *fam-*

ily that has the potential to abuse, and a *stressful event* that precipitates the abuse" (pp. 5–6). We might think that a handicap would result from the abusing treatment of a parent or, in some cases, a relative or babysitter. M. Soeffing (1975) has pointed out, however, the need for additional research on the characteristics of a child that might cause or increase the risks of abuse in some family and stressful situations. Her concern is the seemingly higher risk of abuse and neglect that handicapped children carry.

B. C. Rose (1980), in her discussion of the abusive family, has also pointed to the vulnerability of children who are handicapped to abuse. She elaborated on the major elements identified as contributing to abusive behavior: "a parental history of abuse or neglect as part of the parent(s)' childhood, parental feelings of isolation and loneliness, unstable marital relationship, and inappropriate expectations for the abused child" (p. 4).

More recently, Morgan (1987) has focused on the numbers of children who are handicapped who are victims of abuse and neglect. Although it is not possible to answer with much certainty the question of which comes first in most cases, the handicapping condition or the abuse or neglect that leads to the condition, it is possible to show with the data available that some youngsters were first handicapped and then abused, and some were abused and subsequently became handicapped.

Reporting Suspected Abuse

All states have some form of law making it mandatory to report child abuse. Failure to report in some states carries fine or imprisonment. Figure 14.1 shows a sample report form that can be used if nothing is available in the local school. Many school districts have formal procedures to be followed when suspected cases of abuse or neglect are identified. All fifty states now provide for immunity for those who report suspected cases of child abuse in good faith (Rose, 1980). Not all states, however, define abuse and neglect in exactly the same way (Morgan, 1985).

Teachers frequently are not aware of what role

TABLE 14.3

SIGNS OF POSSIBLE CHILD ABUSE AND NEGLECT

Emotional

1. Self-destructive behavior
2. Apathy, depression, and withdrawal
3. Academic failure
4. Developmental delays
5. Hyperactivity, tantrums, and conduct disorders
6. Pseudo-maturity
7. Lacks trust
8. Rigid, compulsive, and disorganized
9. Feelings of inadequacy and poor self-esteem
10. Role reversal—the child takes care of the parent
11. Excessive fantasy
12. Fearful and hypervigilant
13. Lacks creativity
14. Poor peer relations or peer dependence
15. Lacks familial attachment
16. Gender confusion
17. Lacks empathy
18. Excessive anxiety and night terrors
19. Oblivious to hazards and risks

Physical

1. Physical trauma that cannot adequately be explained—bruises, cuts, broken bones, burns, etc.
2. Behavioral and psychological signs
   a. Passive—"frozen watchfulness"
      hypervigilant
      pseudo-adult behavior
   b. Aggressive—hostile
      self-hate
      poor impulse control
   c. Regressive
   d. Problems with interpersonal relationships—lonely
      isolated
      unhappy

Sexual

1. Physical injuries to the genital area
2. Sexually transmitted diseases
3. Difficulty urinating
4. Discharges from the penis or vagina
5. Pregnancy
6. Fear or aggressive behavior towards adults, especially their own parents
7. Sexual self-consciousness
8. Sexual promiscuity and acting-out
9. Inability to establish appropriate relationships with peers
10. Running away, stealing, and using alcohol or drugs
11. Withdrawal, regressive behavior, or behavior that makes the child look retarded
12. Seems to use school as a sanctuary by coming early and not wanting to go home
13. Complaints of frequent nightmares
14. Indirect hints that they are afraid to go home or afraid of someone in particular at home

Source: Morgan, S. R. (1987). *Abuse and neglect of handicapped children.* San Diego,
CA: College-Hill Press, pp. 32–33, 35–38, 41. Used with permission.

Sample Letter 1: Report

Oral Report Made To: _____ Date: _____ Time: _____   _____

Child's Name: _____ / _____ / _____   _____

Age: _____ Birthdate: _____ Gender: _____   _____

Child's Address: _____ Phone: _____   Reporter: _____ Signature: _____

Person Involved: _____   Position: _____

Address: _____ Phone: _____   Address: _____ Phone: _____

Father's Name: _____ Mother's Name: _____

Address & Phone If Different From Child's: _____   Witness(es) to Report: _____

_____   Position: _____

_____   Address: _____ Phone: _____

Signs & Symptoms: _____   Date: _____ Time: _____

_____

_____   Copies: 1.   Principal

_____   2.   Counselor

_____   3.   School Nurse

              4.   File

Child's Oral Report: _____   Additional Witness(es) To Child's Condition: _____

_____   _____

_____   Address: _____ Phone: _____

Figure 14.1. Sample abuse report form. (Source: Morgan, S. R. (1987). *Abuse and neglect of handicapped children.* San Diego, CA: College-Hill Press, pp. 118–119. Used with permission.)

they can play (or they have not contemplated the role they should play) when incidents of abuse and neglect are suspected. The following steps are suggested as a way to start and might be developed into a school or district inservice education program (McCaffrey, 1979, pp. 48–49).

1. Recognize abuse or neglect.

2. Talk with children or their parents.

3. Make a report.

4. Understand the role of agencies offering health care, child care, homemaker service, and other family services.

5. Develop school policy if none exists.

6. Analyze available school resources.

7. Plan a school-based program for those children identified.

8. Work collaboratively with other agencies on the prevention and treatment of child abuse and neglect.

CHEMICALLY DEPENDENT YOUTH

Incidence

Drug and alcohol use and abuse have reached new highs among the total population in recent years and have spawned large groups of children and adults from all social, economic, and age levels whose daily functioning falls subject to the priorities of drink and drugs. Close to 10 million adults are considered to be alcohol abusers, and one in ten American workers is a serious problem drinker or alcoholic (Garner, 1979). Indications are that more and more people are selecting alcohol as the drug of choice over other drugs (Alibrandi, 1978; U.S. Bureau of the Census, 1986, p. 106). And evidence shows that many are eventually finding it necessary to seek treatment for drug and alcohol abuse. In 1980, over 181,000 people were under some form of treatment for drug abuse in 3,449 treatment programs across the country.

Even more alarming are reports that alcohol consumption among youth has increased over 300 percent in recent years. Studies indicate that as many as 23 percent of all young people between the ages of twelve and eighteen have serious drinking problems (Horton, 1985). Drinking and use of drugs have filtered down into the activities of shocking numbers of preteens as well. The average beginning age for drinking alcohol among U.S. youngsters is now twelve years five months. And the increasing number of young people who drink regularly, frequently, and in excess are likewise increasing their chances of addiction, accidents, and death (Horton, 1985).

In 1982, almost 27 percent of the twelve-through seventeen-year-olds surveyed in a study by the National Institute on Drug Abuse reported having tried marijuana, and over 11 percent reported themselves to be current users. Over 65 percent of those surveyed had tried alcohol, and 27 percent considered themselves to be current users. In that same year, among the eighteen-through twenty-five-year-old group surveyed, over 27 percent were current marijuana users. Approximately 95 percent had at least tried alcohol, and 68 percent were current users (U.S. Bureau of the Census, 1982, p. 123; 1987, p. 106).

Those young people caught up in the use of drugs often bring the effects of their habits with them to school in the form of hangovers, nonfunctional behavior, preoccupation with locating a source for the next dose, and efforts to enlist others into the ranks of users. Teachers need to be informed about signs of drug and alcohol abuse and dependency and to be able to recognize those who need specialized help from medical and legal authorities. One fact sometimes overlooked is that giving alcohol to minors or intoxicated individuals is illegal, as is possession of certain drugs.

Drug Categories

There are four basic categories of drugs, each having a different major effect on an individual's senses and behavior.

1. **Stimulants.** Stimulants increase alertness, reduce hunger, produce a feeling of well-being, and reduce fatigue. If these drugs are taken in large quantities over long periods of time, users can become dependent upon stimulants such as amphetamines and must then increase the amounts ingested or injected to produce the "highs" they seek.

2. **Depressants.** Depressants are sedatives, substances that reduce the activity level of the brain and muscles. Barbiturates and alcohol are depressant drugs. The alcohol in alcoholic beverages is ethyl alcohol, C_2H_5OH, a flammable, colorless fluid. Overdoses of depressants can cause death, with the basic heart functions and breathing rate so slowed that the individual falls into a deep sleep and never wakes up. Other substances that produce the relaxing effects users seek in excess include glue, paint thinner, and other volatile materials. Continued excessive use can lead to impaired liver

function, malnutrition, blackouts, bizarre behavior, and death.

3. **Hallucinogens.** Drugs such as LSD, STP, and peyote produce alterations in the senses of time, color, space, and sound. The effects may range from ecstasy to extreme depression, with the possibility of flashbacks or unanticipated return "trips" and severe alterations in mental function and personality.

4. **Narcotics.** Narcotics relieve pain and blunt the senses. In large quantities, they can cause euphoria or stupor. Users can become physically and psychologically dependent on them and can build up tolerance so increased amounts are necessary to produce the same effects. Although narcotics can be ingested, most users inject their doses. Once users reach the dependency state, many suffer malnutrition because these drugs reduce appetite. Overdoses are frequently fatal. Withdrawal symptoms can reach severe proportions twelve to sixteen hours after the last dose. Heroin, morphine, marijuana, cocaine, and opium are narcotics.

Increase in Drug Use

Explanations for the increased rates of drug use and alcoholism among youth cover social aspects, physiological aspects, and combinations of the two. Although some studies have suggested that there may be biochemical differences between alcoholics and nonalcoholics, excessive problem drinking may also be linked to a social structure that encourages drinking and use of drugs to ease pressures and discomfort; to the feelings of guilt often generated by excessive use; and to what the individual is taught, or not taught, about drinking at home and at school (Alibrandi, 1978; Horton, 1985). Peer pressure, lowered self-esteem, and, often but not always, trouble in the family leading to unhappiness and fighting have been linked to drug and alcohol abuse. But even in the "best" of families, some young people find paths to drugs

and alcohol. Even outstanding amateur and professional sports figures, whom many young people and people young-in-heart have admired, have had their lives ruined, and sometimes terminated, as a result of drug abuse.

Another indication that drug and alcohol use is on the increase is the number of babies born with **fetal alcohol syndrome (FAS)**. Characteristics of this syndrome fit into three major categories: mental retardation, growth deficiencies in both height and weight, and unusual facial features. Some children with FAS also have joint and cardiac problems (Furey, 1982). Because a major result of FAS is mental retardation, early identification and intervention are important so these children can develop to their maximum potential. Just as important is education for the general population regarding the risks to babies of pregnant women who consume alcohol. Prevention is the ultimate cure.

Role of the Teacher

What is the teacher's role in drug and alcohol problems? What kind of model does the teacher present? What attitudes toward drug use and abuse does the school reflect? Answers to these questions have bearing on what means, if any, a school will adopt to deal with the drug problems of its youth.

Certainly, recognition of the behavioral signs of children with problems is an initial step. The following is a list of some signs of possible drug abuse that may alert teachers and other school personnel to students nearing the abuse stage of alcohol and drug use.

decline in academic performance and physical coordination
frequent absenteeism
lack of interest in extracurricular activities
conflicts with authority figures
problems with peers
new peer relationships
evidence of self-destructive behavior

One popular means of treating drug and alcohol abuse is group therapy. (Photo by Peeter Vilms/Jeroboam, Inc.)

avoidance and distancing
depression
lack of energy
impulsive behavior
lack of concern about personal well-being and hygiene
obvious signs of intoxication
evidence of a troubled home life

(Horton, L. (1985). *Adolescent alcohol abuse*. Bloomington, IN: Phi Delta Kappa Educational Foundation, pp. 18–21. Used with permission.)

The Drug Abuse Education Act of 1986 should stimulate the implementation of more abuse prevention programs to keep young people from getting caught up in drug use for purposes other than medication. Education programs aimed at potential alcohol abuse stress "the advantages of abstinence or controlled drinking along with teaching the early warning signs of alcohol abuse" (Horton, 1985, p. 36). Other goals for prevention programs appear in the following list, which states that students should

1. Realize it is not essential to drink.

2. Understand they have a choice about whether or not they will drink alcoholic beverages.

3. [Be] aware that no social situation requires that they drink.

4. Know it is always correct to refuse a drink if they don't want it.

5. Refuse to accept that excessive drinking (or any drinking) indicates adult status, virility, or masculinity for males and glamour for females.

6. Learn that uncontrolled drinking is an illness that can and should be treated as early as possible.

7. Know that one is never too young to become an alcoholic.

8. Understand that safe drinking depends on complex physiological and psychological factors including healthy attitudes, good self-esteem, and emotional maturity.

(Horton, L. (1985). *Adolescent alcohol abuse*. Bloomington, IN: Phi Delta Kappa Educational Foundation, p. 37. Used with permission.)

Drug education programs have earned both praise and scorn, depending upon the approaches taken. To some, teaching children to drink "properly" seems as ludicrous as teaching children to eat sugar "properly" to avoid diabetes (Alibrandi, 1978, pp. 59–60). R. H. Blum and his associates (1972), at the end of their study of 211 families from different ethnic and socioeconomic backgrounds, concluded that

drug education does not consist in the mere accumulation of scientific or historical data. These are components, but the essence is faith in a certain way of living. Youth who suffer no drug risks have discovered that the values worth living by are self-respect and respect for others and kindness and responsibility to the family and to oneself. The democratic concepts of freedom, self-expression, individuality, and equality are noble only when they are predicated on the primary injunction to consider "we" and "thou" before "I." When this injunction is not learned or is ignored, these concepts become weapons used by individuals who pursue power and gain. Drug education is then a family process which transmits the age-old wisdom, "Love thy neighbor as thyself." (p. 305)

TEENAGE PREGNANCY

An estimated 12 to 13 million teen and preteen girls in the United States are sexually active (Klein, 1978). One in 10, or over 1 million, will become pregnant. Over 20 percent of all live births in 1980 were to unmarried women, and over 90,000 of those babies were born to girls under the age of fifteen (U.S. Bureau of the Census, 1986, 1987). Teenage pregnancies happen in all ethnic and socioeconomic groups.

The alarming increase in teenage sexual activity resulting in a teenage pregnancy rate among the highest in the world (Klein, 1978) has reached epidemic proportions in this country (McLean et al., 1979). Factors associated with teenage pregnancy and delivery include prematurity, higher infant mortality rate, and congenital neurological impairments such as deafness and blindness (Schinke, Gilchrist, & Small, 1979), all of which contribute to make pregnant teenagers and their babies major high-risk groups (Wallace, 1979; Anastasiow, 1983). Furthermore, many teenage mothers who are poor grow poorer as graduation from high school passes them by. Few of these young mothers have had adequate preparation for parenting. Most are too young to have many marketable skills. If the girl marries, there is a great possibility the marriage will end in divorce within several years. These factors, coupled with problems associated with establishment of a home, have led to the recognition of the need for schools to offer programs that deal with family planning, responsibilities of family members, the nature and demands on time of child care, and normal child development.

Factors Contributing to Increase

Growing concern over these numbers of "children bearing children" (McLean et al., 1979) has prompted a variety of explanations, many of which point to social pressures coming from peers, media, and sales promotions. L. Klein (1978) suggests that "we profess chastity as an ideal, but sex for profit and fun is flaunted everywhere in contemporary society. We exhibit, stimulate, and excite youth and deny and criticize the response" (p. 1154). Klein (1978) and the staff at Emory University School of Medicine, in their studies of early adolescent childbearing, have listed numerous factors they view as contributing to the increase in teenage promiscuity and pregnancy; among them are

- social attitudes that to be popular is to be sexually active
- failure to provide teens with sex education, family life education, and education for parenthood
- failure (for legal, financial, and moral reasons) to provide birth control and family planning services aimed at teens
- failure to provide early pregnancy detection and subsequent prenatal care

Other contributing factors are adolescent needs for caring, for something to love, for a reason to be needed, for more attention, and for independence. These needs may be expressed as a rebellion against family norms, a declaration of independence, or a way to get out of school. Values within the family structure may not be sufficiently strong or clear to counteract the pressures some teenagers feel to do what "everyone else" is doing. It must be recognized, too, that more adults today do not view premarital sex as "wrong."

A teacher may be the one person a girl who thinks or knows she is pregnant approaches for advice or for help. It is essential that teachers be aware of their own reactions to this situation and be able to control their own feelings in order to provide the assistance requested or to arrange for referrals to appropriate health-care agencies.

Education Programs

Some schools have offered special programs for pregnant girls in an effort to keep them in school and to teach them about child development, infant and child care, and family management. Most of these programs provide for some type of follow-up after delivery to help the young mother manage her new responsibilities (Helmrich, 1981). This is important because only a small percentage of the babies born to girls in the fifteen-to-nineteen age range are put up for adoption.

If one goal of current sex education programs is to reduce teenage pregnancy, it appears that few programs have been very successful or else few teenagers have participated. Attempts have also been made to provide sex education programs that will decrease the amount of teenage sexual activity and pregnancy. S. P. Schinke, L. D. Gilchrist, and R. W. Small (1979) have suggested four major components of an education program to increase responsible sexual behavior among adolescents:

1. accessible and relevant information on human sexuality, reproduction, and birth control

2. accurate comprehension of information

3. use of that information in making own decisions and choices

4. development of behavior skills to carry out those decisions in social situations (p. 84)

Klein (1978) has stressed that sex education and information must be presented "in a context of human values. The validity of abstinence and the postponement of first and subsequent sexual activity must be a component of educational programs" (p. 1154). Girls must be taught that "No" is *a,* and in the minds of many, still *the,* correct response to overtures that might lead to sexual activity outside the bonds of marriage.

Whether we approve of sexual activity among unmarried teens and preteens or not, the fact is that such activity goes on. Teachers need to sort out their own attitudes and values before trying to influence or advise their students regarding their responsibilities to themselves and others as sexual human beings.

JUVENILE DELINQUENCY

I have found delinquent boys and girls, but I have also found the woods full of delinquent men and women, and some of them holding high positions.
(Gates, 1907, p. 995)

So observed a highly respected speaker at an NEA convention back in 1907. The title of his address, "The Training of the Incorrigible," which was assigned to him, reflects an attitude toward a segment of the school-age population that many people would share today.

The first reform school for delinquent youth was opened in Chicago in 1855; the first special classes for disobedient, truant, and incorrigible boys in the 1870s in New Haven, Connecticut; and the first juvenile court in 1899 in Chicago (Nazzaro, 1977). One of the first programs for delinquent youngsters with handicaps was opened in Elmira, New York, in 1876. The schools and courts have had long years of experience with those labeled juvenile delinquents.

C. M. Nelson, R. B. Rutherford, and B. I. Wolford (1987), in what is described as the first book that deals with special education and the criminal justice system, report that of those arrested in the United States for serious crimes such as larceny, burglary, and aggravated assault, half are under the age of twenty. A particularly disturbing fact they explore in their book is that, among the juveniles under the supervision of corrections, there is an overrepresentation of handicapped youngsters, particularly those with mild to moderate high-prevalence handicaps: mental retardation,

Adjudicated juvenile delinquents are youngsters who have been found guilty of one or more crimes; some youngsters receive open-ended sentences to juvenile centers or reform schools. (Photo © Jerry Berndt/ Stock, Boston.)

learning disabilities, and behavior disorders. The criminal justice system faces great challenges in providing appropriate education for all of the juveniles under its supervision, particularly those who require special education.

Definitions of Delinquent Behavior

Just who are juvenile delinquents? Those whose behavior deviates beyond the limits society at large and schools in particular will tolerate? Those who break laws or customs? Those who get caught? Those who are adjudicated? Is the term a diagnostic category that explains why a juvenile acts a certain way? What does a juvenile delinquent become when he or she reaches age eighteen?

The definition and label issue complicates an already complex and growing problem that is increasing in both urban and rural areas. Juvenile delinquency has been called "an intrinsic part of modern industrialized societies" (Clarizio & McCoy, 1976, p. 281).

But we still need to define the term. L. J. Carr (1950) has pointed out that juvenile delinquency may mean one thing morally, another thing legally, another practically, and still another statistically. *Webster's* defines the term *delinquent* as "failing or neglecting to do what duty or law requires; guilty of a fault or misdeed." The legal definitions, although they vary from state to state, hold fairly closely to the dictionary definition and view the **juvenile delinquent** as "a person under a specific age who violates any state or local law, or commits any act that would be considered a crime if committed by an adult" (Kvaraceus, 1971, pp. 7–8). Also frequently included are acts related to the juvenile's status as below age: truancy, running away, and incorrigibility.

Clinically, the juvenile delinquent is "a young person who habitually resolves his personal-social problems through overt aggressive behavior which dominant society finds bothersome and contrary to its identified values" (Kvaraceus, 1971, p. 7). From the juvenile's point of view, the behavior may be purposeful and functional in coping; from society's point of view, it may be intolerable.

In practice, we find the term *juvenile delinquent* applied in a variety of ways, summarized by H. F. Clarizio and G. F. McCoy (1976, p. 282; based on Carr, 1950; used with permission):

1. *Legal delinquents:* All youth committing antisocial acts as defined by law

2. *Detected delinquents:* All detected antisocial youth

3. *Agency delinquents:* All detected antisocial youth reaching any agency

4. *Alleged delinquents:* All apprehended antisocial youth brought to court

5. *Adjudged delinquents:* All antisocial youth legally "found" delinquent by court action

6. *Committed delinquents:* All adjudged delinquents committed to an institution

From the legal point of view, we can see that any juvenile who "breaks the law" has committed a delinquent behavior. But how many acts must be committed, or how serious must one act be, to warrant the label *juvenile delinquent* to identify an individual? Many youngsters in the course of reaching age eighteen commit a delinquent act. W. C. Kvaraceus (1971) has emphasized the danger inherent in labeling the one-time offender a juvenile delinquent: "Having been adjudicated a delinquent, the youngster may now know how he is expected to behave. Thus, instead of preventing delinquent behavior, the school and community can unwittingly help produce and contribute to it" (p. 20).

Related to the problem of definitions and labels is the question of number: How many juveniles are delinquent? A variety of factors influence the number actually reported as well as the interpretation of that number. Not all states consider the same acts as crimes. Types of cases and ages of juveniles over which the courts have jurisdiction vary from state to state. In addition, the availability of community child-welfare agencies has a significant bearing on how many cases are entered into the courts (Clarizio & McCoy, 1976).

Factors Related to Delinquency

Many factors can affect the incidence of delinquent behavior. Among them are age, the peak being about seventeen; sex, with more boys involved than girls, although the number of girls is increasing; family stability, with degree and consistency of supervision playing a part; socioeconomic status, to some unknown extent; race and ethnicity; urban-rural differences; intelligence, also to some degree not clearly evident; and some individual constitutional factors (Clarizio & McCoy, 1976).

Many causes have been suggested for the pattern of delinquent behavior evident in some juveniles. Kvaraceus (1971) has cited three major

Some delinquent youngsters must be incarcerated for serious crimes against society. When they reach the age of eighteen, they are transferred to adult correctional facilities. (Photo © Jeff Albertson/Stock, Boston.)

sources of influence: (1) subcultural and cultural forces that have to do with what is the norm for behavior in the juvenile's peer group, (2) pathological and psychological forces, and (3) community attitudes that may fluctuate from region to

BOX 14.6
FROM ONE WHO TURNED BACK

In trouble at school, not interested in class work, a good fighter, a member of a rowdy gang that drank heavily—Eddie was well on his way to becoming a first-class delinquent. He did have a few things in his favor, though. He had stayed away from drugs, and he had grown up in a home where reading was common. Many of Eddie's friends could not read at all. Eddie could; in fact, he enjoyed reading but chose not to do most of his school assignments except for a quick pass through a book before a test. Even so, his grades were satisfactory and he graduated from high school.

Eddie wanted to go to college in his home town so he could be near his friends, but a concerned uncle let it be known that Eddie could live with him and his wife if he wanted to leave home and go to the state university. Eddie finally did just that. There were plenty of rough days—and nights—as Eddie adjusted to living in new surroundings under new rules that were consistently enforced.

It worked. No one can be certain of all the factors that turned Eddie around—his own growing up, his academic abilities not really exercised until college, his new surroundings, absence of his school gang friends, a clearly defined set of limits for his behavior, or the influence of new ideas and new challenges. Today, Eddie is a college professor. He has his Ph.D. and is teaching in the Department of Criminal Justice at a large university.

Eddie has prepared this word of advice for teachers who are confronted with adolescents who seem to be traveling the road he started and from which he was diverted:

- The first thing an educator should remember is that the delinquent adolescent is an adolescent first and a delinquent second.
- Adolescents in general are very difficult to work with, and delinquent adolescents present an even greater challenge. Delinquency is a serious problem, and educators serve a critical function in prevention and rehabilitation.
- Teacher goals should include fewer dropouts, fewer suspensions, and fewer court referrals. Educators must be prepared to deal with disruptive and delinquent behavior in the classroom quickly and forcefully, but in a manner that is oriented toward improving the youth and his or her self-concept.
- Applying the label *delinquent* only tends to reinforce already unacceptable behavior. Of course, not all delinquent behavior can be handled in the classroom. School administrators and parents must be mobilized if there is to be any serious progress made in preventing and correcting delinquent behavior.*

*Reprinted by permission.

region and time to time. D. S. Elliott and H. L. Voss (1974) have proposed four conditions critical for development of delinquent behavior: (1) the juvenile's real or anticipated failure in school, (2) perceived or real extrapunitiveness, (3) normlessness, and (4) extensive exposure to delinquent persons or groups. Clarizio and McCoy (1976) have described the characteristics generally found among delinquents, including impulsivity, aggressiveness, and irresponsibility.

The typical juvenile in a correctional institution has been described as having a record of foster care placement, truancy, school failure, drug or alcohol abuse, poor self-concept, poor impulse control, and emotional problems (*Programs for the Handicapped,* 1983, p. 4). Many of them, as was mentioned earlier, display evidence of mental retardation, emotional disturbance, and learning disability.

Role of the Schools

You may be wondering what this discussion has to do with control in school of youngsters who disrupt the instructional program and whose behavior is intolerable even if not strictly delinquent. Some would give to the schools both the blame for causing and the responsibility for eliminating delinquent behavior among juveniles.

Clearly, one way to eliminate juvenile delinquency from schools would be to suspend or expel those who commit delinquent acts. That would solve the school problem to some extent, but it would not deal with the larger societal problem. Kvaraceus (1971) has warned against expecting the schools to do more than is realistic, given that some of the forces fostering delinquent behavior lie outside the school: "The school is not a hospital, it is not a clinic, it is not a community warehouse for disturbed or disturbing children and youth, nor is it an adolescent ghetto or limbo. The unique and special role of the school is to be found in its teaching-learning function aimed at agreed-upon objectives" (p. 2).

What should be the role of the teacher who meets juvenile delinquents in the classroom? A teacher should make learning happen, identify those students at risk because of behaviors that are common among delinquents, and work with other school and community personnel to help those juveniles who remain in school. Not all juveniles whose behavior is delinquent ought to remain in school (Clarizio & McCoy, 1976; Kvaraceus, 1971); for those who can and do, however, the classroom teacher can function in three major areas:

1. *Prevention.* Figure 14.2 is a checklist teachers may find useful in screening out students whose behavior indicates they might need help. In many school districts, referrals go to the counselor or school psychologist.

2. *Instruction.* High-quality systematic instruction by concerned teachers, clearly defined objectives, a noncompetitive learning environment, appropriate materials and curriculum, concern for individual differences, and stress on the consequences of behavior for some students will keep school from being an alienating place. Of course, providing that kind of instruction and setting may require that some changes be made in the traditional school program—perhaps for the benefit of all students.

3. *Cooperation.* For some students, work-experience programs help link the school to the real world. For others, group or individual counseling helps. Remedial instruction is beneficial for some, whereas removal from the school setting may be necessary for others. The teacher must be able to share relevant information and plan with the concerned professionals from the school and community who are also working for the best interest of each student.

Teachers and other school personnel who work with delinquent juveniles may find themselves in close contact with agents of the criminal justice system: the police, the courts, and corrections. As the relatively new field of correctional special education develops and programs are designed to provide basic education, social skills, and marketable job skills for youthful offenders, new opportunities should emerge for special education teachers attracted to the task of meeting the needs of incarcerated young people with handicaps.

It should be noted that the majority of those students labeled as juvenile delinquents turn into law-abiding adults (Clarizio & McCoy, 1976). Nevertheless, delinquent behavior during the adolescent years continues to be a serious challenge to society, to the criminal justice system, and to the educational system.

Yes	No	?	Factor
( )	( )	( )	1. Shows marked dislike for school
( )	( )	( )	2. Resents school routine and restriction
( )	( )	( )	3. Disinterested in school program
( )	( )	( )	4. Is failing in a number of subjects
( )	( )	( )	5. Has repeated one or more grades
( )	( )	( )	6. Attends a special class for retarded pupils
( )	( )	( )	7. Has attended many different schools
( )	( )	( )	8. Intends to leave school as soon as the law allows
( )	( )	( )	9. Has only vague academic or vocational plans
( )	( )	( )	10. Has limited academic ability
( )	( )	( )	11. Is a seriously or persistently misbehaving child
( )	( )	( )	12. Destroys school materials or property
( )	( )	( )	13. Is cruel and bullying on the playground
( )	( )	( )	14. Has temper tantrums in the classroom
( )	( )	( )	15. Wants to stop schooling at once
( )	( )	( )	16. Truants from school

Figure 14.2. Delinquency proneness checklist for teacher use, based on school factors differentiating delinquents from nondelinquents. (Source: W. C. Kvaraceus, *Prevention and Control of Delinquency: The School Counselor's Role.* Hanover, New Hampshire: TSC, 1971, p. 44. Reprinted by permission.)

SUMMARY

We have called your attention to two groups of children whose instructional needs are so extensive that most require educational placements outside the regular classroom setting for at least some, if not all, of their school years: the multiply handicapped and the deaf-blind. In an effort to emphasize the special needs of other students not considered under provisions for handicapped children, we have briefly described the child from a different cultural and/or linguistic background, the plight of the abused and neglected child, the abuser of drugs and alcohol, the child who is pregnant, and the juvenile delinquent.

We have tried to stimulate your thinking about the diversity among school children, the factors related to that diversity that can affect school performance, and the responses school personnel can make when meeting with youngsters from any of these groups.

Our intent has not been to create new categories for special education, but to make you aware of the diversity of talents, values, and interests that are found among children of school age. Being aware is the first step toward responding to the particular needs of these children.

Suggestions for Further Reading

Alibrandi, T. (1978). *Young alcoholics.* Minneapolis, MN: Comp-Care Publications.

Alibrandi minces no words in this highly readable discussion of alcoholism among children and youth, what fosters it, signs to watch for, and one approach to treatment. This book is informative reading for high school students as well as adults.

Churchill, S. (1986). *Education of linguistic and cultural minorities in the OECD countries.* San Diego, CA: College-Hill Press.

This analytical summary of the major findings of a cross-national study presents finances, organization, and governance of and public policy issues surrounding education for linguistic and cultural minority groups. Data were gathered from fifteen of the member and associate member nations of the Organization for Economic Cooperative Development, among them the United States, the United Kingdom, Canada, and Australia. Churchill reports on policies affecting education of indigenous groups such as Native Americans, Maoris, and Lapps, as well as established minorities such as the Acadian French and "new" minorities including resident or guest workers and immigrants in the various countries. This book, while focusing on a much broader topic than special education for handicapped youngsters in the United States, should pique the curiosity of any reader interested in cross-cultural education, international issues, and comparative education. It also should stimulate much thought about what constitutes an appropriate education in a pluralistic society.

Curt, C. J. N. (1984). *Non-verbal communication in Puerto Rico.* Cambridge, MA: Evaluation, Dissemination and Assessment Center.

Carmen Judith Nine Curt's short collection of papers, presentations, and case studies offers the reader a refreshingly original introduction to the importance of nonverbal communication when speakers of different languages and cultures meet to exchange ideas verbally. She illustrates her points with interesting examples from her experiences in the Anglo and Puerto Rican cultures. She stresses the value of learning to switch cultural channels and to appreciate the richness and diversity of our own as well as other cultures.

Gollnick, D. M., & Chinn, D. C. (1986). *Multicultural education in a pluralistic society.* Columbus, OH: Merrill.

Gollnick and Chinn look at culture from a very broad perspective and examine the microcultures we all belong to a greater or lesser extent. After an introductory chapter that explores how we learn culture, various manifestations of culture, the macroculture and microcultures in the United States today, the concept of cultural pluralism, and the major objectives of multicultural education, the authors devote chapters to socioeconomic status, ethnicity, language, gender, religion, exceptionality, and age. A final chapter suggests strategies for multicultural education and elements that teachers should consider in efforts to use students' cultural backgrounds as part of educational programs. These elements include textbooks and instructional materials, curriculum, teachers' behaviors in the classroom, and the overall school climate.

Horton, L. (1985). *Adolescent alcohol abuse.* Bloomington, IN: Phi Delta Kappa Educational Foundation.

This short paperback presents a concise discussion of the growing problems of adolescent drug abuse. Along with information about numbers of problem drinkers and specific behaviors that suggest an individual might have problems with alcohol and/or drugs, the author talks about why many adolescents abuse alcohol and other drugs and what

role the school can play in education, prevention, and treatment. The author stresses the problems caused by the ambiguous, confusing, and at times contradictory attitudes displayed toward alcohol and drug use in American society.

Lash, J. P. (1980). *Helen and teacher: The story of Helen Keller and Anne Sullivan Macy.* New York: Delacorte Press.

Written by a Pulitzer Prize–winning author, this story of Helen Keller and her teacher and companion, Anne Sullivan Macy, reveals intense relationships nourished by closeness, dependence, and mutual experiences as well as by desires for independence, autonomy, and individual achievement.

Morgan, S. (1987). *Abuse and neglect of handicapped children.* San Diego, CA: College-Hill Press.

In this short five-chapter book, Morgan outlines factors that can contribute to our attitudes toward children who are handicapped and that can set the stage for our treatment of handicapped children and youth. She then describes what emotional, physical, and sexual abuse and neglect are and lists signs of each. After a discussion of the relationships between abuse and neglect and handicapping conditions, with some thought-provoking comments about children who are in residential and institutional settings, Morgan focuses on characteristics of adults who abuse children, showing how heterogeneous they are as a group but how they share an inability to cope appropriately with stressful situations. In the final chapter, Morgan identifies some of the issues related to child abuse and neglect, with special mention of the very serious problem of false accusations against teachers and care-givers and suggestions as to how they can protect themselves. Checklists for documentation, along with toll-free child abuse hot-line numbers for each state, are provided in the appendices.

This is not an "enjoyable" book; rather, it is a good introduction to a serious problem that requires further study leading to prevention, to treatment of both victims and perpetrators, and to the alleviation of the social factors that may contribute to its existence.

Morgan, S. (1985). *Children in crisis.* San Diego, CA: College-Hill Press.

In this at times depressing and frightening book, the reader is introduced to the difficult and painful situations in which more and more children find themselves today, situations over which they have little or no control and from which few emerge unscathed: family separation and divorce, loss through sickness or death of a loved one, child abuse and/or neglect, and mental illness, including depression to the point of suicide. The author opens her discussions of the various situations with vignettes that breathe life into the objective data and theoretical explanations of causes, coping mechanisms, complications, contributing factors, and conclusions that follow. Pointing out the disproportionately large number of handicapped children who are abused or neglected, Morgan raises the question of cause and effect: Are handicapped children more vulnerable to abuse, or are children handicapped as a result of abuse?

This book makes a good, albeit unsettling, introduction to Morgan's more recent book, described above. Both books should be of particular interest to teachers, counselors, psychologists, and others who work with handicapped children.

Nelson, C. M., Rutherford, R. B., & Wolford, B. I. (Eds.) (1987). *Special education in the criminal justice system.* Columbus, OH: Merrill.

This text is one of the few, if not the only, books presently available that addresses the special education needs of juvenile offenders who are handicapped. Part I provides background information about the criminal justice system (police, courts, and corrections), handicapped offenders in the system, and special education legislation as it affects correctional education. Part II discusses the characteristics and problems of mentally retarded, learning disabled, and behaviorally disordered offenders. Part III describes functional assessment and the functional curriculum that students should have in correctional settings and examines issues related to preparation for transfer from correction facilities to public schools. This book should be of great value to professionals in special education and the criminal justice system as they attempt to deal with handicapped juveniles entering the criminal justice system.

Sowell, T. (1981). *Ethnic America: A history.* New York: Basic Books.

Sowell offers a good overview of the major ethnic groups that make up the American mosaic. He describes how and why American ethnic groups from Europe, Asia, Africa, and Latin America have developed as they have and suggests implications that give the reader a clear picture of the "unity and diversity" that can be found in our present American society.

Yoken, C. (1979). *Living with deaf-blindness: Nine profiles.* Washington, DC: The National Academy of Gallaudet College.

The book introduces six men and three women, ages twenty-three to seventy-one, who are deaf-blind. All had sufficient communication skills to tell their own stories to the author through writing, speech, typing, fingerspelling, signs, or combinations of modes. Their stories make the reader vividly aware of the frustrations, concerns, and needs of deaf-blind persons, especially in the areas of mobility and communication. The book is good reading for the teacher or other professional who wants to work with deaf-blind individuals but who has had little direct experience with any member of this group.

Relevant Journals

Adolescence
An international journal published quarterly by Libra Publishers, 4901 Morena Blvd., Ste. 207, San Diego, CA 92117.

Bilingual Journal
Published quarterly by the Evaluation, Dissemination, and Assessment Center of Lesley College, 49 Washington Avenue, Cambridge, MA 02140.

Children Today
A bi-monthly interdisciplinary publication of the Department of Health and Human Services, Office of Human Development Services, 200 Independence Avenue, S.W., Room 356-G, Washington, DC 20201.

Elementary School Guidance and Counseling
This journal is published four times a year by the American Association for Counseling Development, 5999 Stevenson Avenue, Alexandria, VA 22304.

International Journal of Child Abuse and Neglect
A quarterly publication of Pergamon Press, Journals Division, Maxwell House, Fairfax Park, Elmsford, NY 10523.

Journal of Alcohol and Drug Education
Published three times a year by the Alcohol and Drug Problems Association of North America, c/o MICAP, Box 10212, Lansing, MI 48901.

Journal of American Indian Education
This journal is published three times a year by the Arizona State University Center for Indian Education, Farmer 302, Tempe, AZ 85287.

Journal of Association for Persons with Severe Handicaps
Published quarterly by the Association for Persons with Severe Handicaps, 7010 Roosevelt Way, N.E., Seattle, WA 98115.

Journal of Black Studies
This journal is put out quarterly by Sage Publications, 275 S. Beverly Drive, Beverly Hills, CA 90212.

Journal of Correctional Education
Published quarterly for the Correctional Education Association by the Center for the Study of Correctional Education, University of Wisconsin—Stout, Monomonie, WI 54751.

Journal of Multicultural Counseling and Development
This journal is published four times a year by the Association for Counseling and Development, 5999 Stevenson Avenue, Alexandria, VA 22304.

Suicide and Life-Threatening Behavior
A quarterly publication of the American Association of Suicidology, put out by Guilford Publishers, 200 Park Avenue, S., New York City, NY 10003.

Organizations for Parents and Professionals

Alcoholics Anonymous
P.O. Box 459
New York, NY 10017

Association for Counseling Development
5999 Stevenson Avenue
Alexandria, VA 22304

The Association for Persons with Severe Handicaps
7010 Roosevelt Way, N.E.
Seattle, WA 98115

Association of American Indian Affairs
95 Madison Avenue
New York, NY 10016

Correctional Education Association
1400 20th Street, N.W., Ste. 1100
Washington, DC 20036

National Clearinghouse on Alcohol Information
P.O. Box 2345
Rockville, MD 20852

National Clearinghouse for Bilingual Education
1555 Wilson Blvd., Suite 605
Rosslyn, VA 22209

National Council on Alcoholism
73 Third Avenue
New York, NY 10017

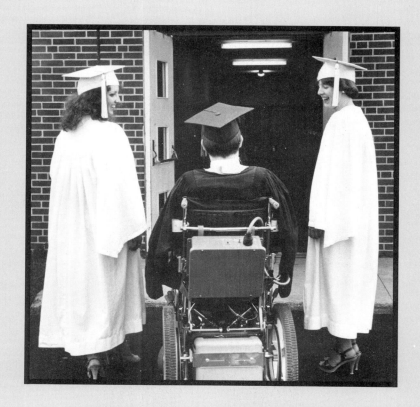

Part III is designed to draw the facts and theories together and give readers specific skills in dealing with people who are atypical. This part covers basic information that is generic to many situations and to many people with disabilities.

Identification, Assessment, and Teaching

CHAPTER 15

Identification and Assessment

Did You Know That . . .

- assessment is an integral and never-ending part of instruction?

- assessment is the link (or bridge) between identification and intervention?

- teachers can develop their own informal assessment procedures?

- regular educators have an excellent record of success in the initial identification of children with problems?

- intensive diagnosis is not needed for all children, only for those who are screened out of the total group as possibly having some problem?

- although teachers can engage in a wide variety of assessment activities, there are certain assessment procedures they are not allowed to administer?

- teachers and others who use assessment procedures need to be informed consumers and select the procedures wisely?

Remember Linda, the child who was introduced at the beginning of this book? We described her as frequently inattentive, often leaving her seat and interrupting other children. She seems bothered by the teacher's questions and has a certain testy manner about her. Her schoolwork is spotty, and she often misses assignments. She's becoming a topic of conversation among her classmates. Some of them call her "dummy"; others are unwilling to join her reading group or play with her. Some of her classmates tease her, and she cannot deal with that at all. She is often found daydreaming. In short, her behavior is mildly annoying and quite puzzling.

When we first introduced Linda, we posed several questions: Is she emotionally disturbed? Mildly mentally retarded? Is her poor school performance a result of an inability to read? Of a learning disability? Is she hard of hearing? Or is she of superior intelligence and finding this particular classroom a miserable, boring experience? If you were Linda's teacher, what *actions* would you take to help her? How would you *find answers* to these questions? Where would you begin?

This chapter and those that follow will help you take the important background information presented in Parts I and II and *do* something with it. The information that has been presented in the first two parts is the foundation for action. But unless you see how that important information can be *put to use,* you will not be able to have an impact on the lives of special children.

We believe that everyone has an influence on the lives of exceptional children. Special educators and other specialists have obvious and important roles. But other people are important as well. Regular educators should recognize the tremendous potential they have for initial screening and identification efforts. Special children cannot be served until they are found, and regular educators have an excellent record of identifying and assessing the problems of children who may not yet be identified as exceptional. With recent attitude changes and more acceptance of the concept of normalization, along with the legal mandate for the least restrictive environment of P.L. 94–142, more and more regular educators are working in concert with special educators to teach exceptional children. Regular educators are often the sole providers of educational services for children who are mildly handicapped.

THE IDENTIFICATION MODEL

As part of a series of research projects beginning in 1969, we designed a model to help teachers make intelligent decisions about children. It was extensively field tested by thousands of teachers (Cartwright & Cartwright, 1972a, 1973). The model specifies what teachers need to know and how they are to behave. It is designed in flowchart form because the specific sequence of the actions and systematic consideration of alternatives are every bit as critical as the actions themselves. The Decision Model for Identification of Exceptional Children is given in Figure 15.1.

Screening Children. The first two steps in the model require that the teacher evaluate all the children in the classroom in order to identify those who exhibit deviations from normally expected behavior. Evaluation of children is a continuous process and should be an integral part of the total educational effort. Information about normal behavior and possible abnormal behavior in each of the functional domains is used for **screening** children in terms of deviations. By continually monitoring children's progress, teachers can be alert to problems that might interfere with development in any of the functional domains.

The identification model is especially appropriate for teachers and other professionals who work with preschool and primary grade children who may not yet manifest clear-cut signs of atypical behavior. In these cases, teachers and parents should watch for subtle clues to incipient problems. They need to be sensitive to what certain behaviors may suggest as well as what they may *not* suggest.

Several skills and understandings are crucial to successful performance of the first two steps in the model. Especially important are understanding (1) the relative nature of "normality" in terms

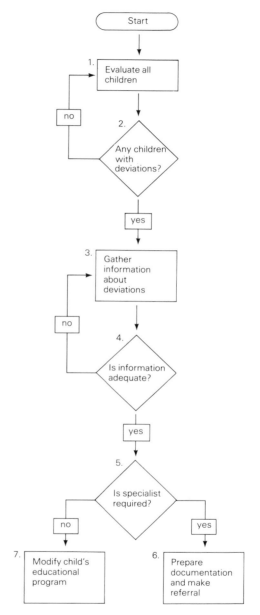

Figure 15.1. Decision Model for Identification of Exceptional Children.

of sociocultural factors and societal and educational expectations; (2) inter- and intraindividual differences; (3) the results of group tests; and (4) the continuous and circular nature of the screening process.

If the answer to the question, "Are there any children with deviations?" is negative, the continual evaluation and progress monitoring of all children simply continues. The cyclical nature of the screening process is indicated by the arrow pointing back to the first step in the model. If the answer is affirmative, then the child in question has been screened out of the total group for a closer look—the arrow points ahead to the third step and the task of diagnosis.

Collecting Data. In the third step, the teacher and other specialists gather precise information as to the nature and extent of any differences. Successful implementation of this step requires knowledge of methods of data collection and interpretation that emphasize appraising each child in terms of deviations noted during screening. The nature of the data will depend on the nature of the deviation in question.

In order to get a complete picture of the child, various sources of information should be incorporated in the diagnostic process. The child and his or her parents are important sources of information. A variety of tests, checklists, and rating scales, both commercially available and teacher-made, can be administered. Teachers can visit the home and interview parents. Special situations can be arranged, and the child's responses to tasks can be observed and recorded.

When a considerable amount of information has been collected, the time has come for consideration of the question posed at the fourth step in the model: "Is information adequate?" A "no" response at this point results in returning to step three to continue data collection.

Evaluating Data. Tentative completion of the third step enables the teacher to evaluate the data and make the decisions called for in steps four and five. Necessary skills for evaluation include interpretation of educationally relevant data. Teachers must also have information about the specialists who can be expected to provide various types of intensive diagnostic services for children.

Deciding About Referrals. When an affirmative answer is given at step four, the teacher should proceed to the next decision block and decide whether **referral** is in order. To decide, the teacher asks: Have I exhausted all sources of information available to me in my role as a classroom teacher? Can I make educational plans for this child on the basis of information currently available? Do I need more information before I make educational plans for this child?

When the decision is for referral, the teacher proceeds to step six and prepares the necessary documentation. When the decision for referral is negative, the teacher accepts responsibility for modification of the child's educational program within the regular classroom setting.

It is important to note that even if the decision is to refer the child to a specialist, the teacher will not receive feedback from the specialist immediately and will need to modify the child's educational program in the interim. Whether a referral is made or not, the information collected for screening and diagnosis is the basis for planning instruction.

The Identification Model shows a *formal* action of referral that involves a specialist to carry out further diagnosis. We want you to be aware that a great deal of *informal* consultation with specialists goes on at each step in the model. Typically, teachers consult with specialists such as speech therapists, school nurses, resource room teachers, and their classroom teacher colleagues as they proceed with their routine evaluation. You will see how these informal consultations work in the case study presented in Chapter 17.

The referral step in the model relates to requirements of P.L. 94–142. At the point of referral, formal procedures for notifying parents about the intent to evaluate the child would be instituted. Parent involvement in terms of permission to conduct the evaluation and participation in the decisions about placement and IEP development and approval would follow.

HUMAN DEVELOPMENT FOUNDATIONS

In seeking individuals who require special attention, we need to know what reasonable expectations are at various ages and stages of development.

Parents can provide valuable information about their children's development. (Photo by Joseph Bodkin.)

Information about human growth and development becomes a yardstick—a standard by which to judge whether a particular observed behavior, or pattern of behaviors, is normal or unusual.

Principles of Development

Development is continuous and interrelated. Domains of development are often discussed as separate entities, but each domain is a part of the whole. A cumulative influence operates in that every change—no matter how small or how specific—influences the total in some way. When changes are gradual, as most are, it is easier for the total organism to adapt and stay in a kind of developmental balance. If changes are dramatic, the balancing act is much more difficult.

Development proceeds from the simple to the complex. Each of us, with our incredibly complex systems and parts, began as a single cell. The organism is able to integrate increasing numbers of simple cells into a total pattern of harmonious functioning at each point in development. The whole organism adapts to support the newly developed and more complex parts. Think of the increasing complexity in the motor domain over a period of four to five years. The infant begins to walk with shaky, halting first steps—one or two at a time. By first grade, these simple first steps have developed into walking, running, hopping, jumping, and maybe even skipping and galloping.

Development proceeds in an orderly fashion and follows certain established growth patterns. Predictable growth patterns can be seen in prenatal as well as postnatal development. Development proceeds from head to toe and in an inward to outward direction. Growth does not occur evenly, with all body parts growing at the same time and at the same rate. Similarly, we do not expect all abilities typical of a particular age group to emerge at the same time. Development in infancy is rapid compared with the slower rates of development in middle childhood and adolescence.

Individual Differences

Tables of normal development that can be found in most child development texts present helpful information. The tables show typical characteristics at each age level within each domain of development and should be viewed as benchmarks. A birthday does not signal the emergence of a whole new set of skills. Rather, the skills emerge gradually, with most children of a certain age level having accomplished many of the skills during that year.

Children grow in many different ways—not just up—and not all at the same rate. Each person is unique. Even identical twins, who have the same biological endowment, develop into unique individuals.

Developing children become increasingly different from each other. At birth, individuals appear to be more alike because there are not many behaviors on which to show differences. But anyone who has spent time in a newborn nursery will assure you that some individual differences are present even at birth. Greater individual differences become apparent as both the number of behaviors and opportunities for differences to show themselves increase. In general, the range of differences increases with increasing age. As we grow older, the difference between the lowest point, or least amount, of development and the highest point, or greatest amount, of development for a characteristic increases with increasing age.

Just as individuals differ in *which behaviors* are exhibited, they also differ in the *rate* of acquiring behaviors. Some are faster, some are slower. Some are faster in one domain than in other domains. In addition, each individual's rate of development varies from time to time. Even within the same child, development is sometimes fast, sometimes slowed down. An infant may develop more rapidly than expected in the motor domain, for example, crawling and standing and walking before most age-mates. This same infant may perform just about as expected in the language and social-emotional domains.

When we speak of variations of growth *within* the same person, we are speaking of **intraindividual differences**. When we make comparisons *among* individuals, we are working with **interindividual differences**. When we compare any given individual with the average for a characteristic, we are also making an interindividual comparison. In the brief example of the infant given above, the statement that the infant was progressing faster in the motor domain than in the language and social-emotional domains described intraindividual differences—within the same child, the rate of development was different in different domains. We also described interindividual differences: The child was doing better than most other children of the same age in the motor domain but was about the same as other children in language and social-emotional development.

In effect, this entire book is concerned with the detailed analysis of individual differences. There are numerous references to similarities and differences among children in areas such as vision, hearing, motor control, language development, intellectual development, emotional health, and so on. We have spoken frequently of the relative nature of normality in an area. When it is clear that a child has a disability or handicap, we have encouraged you to look within the child for patterns of strengths and weaknesses to provide direction for your work with the child. In the final analysis, classroom teachers must deal daily with individual differences between and within children in order to perform successfully.

THE NEED FOR INFORMATION

Teachers and others who work with children, whether exceptional or not, continually use information to make decisions. We use information for

- *Screening.* We note some surface clues that signal something may be wrong.
- *Diagnosis.* We check out our suspicions by probing deeper to determine if a problem exists, what that problem is, and perhaps even why it exists.
- *Program planning.* We plan for instruction and supporting services on the basis of what we know about the child and about various instructional approaches and services.
- *Placement.* We decide what type of program and setting are most suitable for the child and whether to group children, and if so, how.
- *Progress checking.* We monitor the child's progress continuously so we can modify our

ideas about the nature of the problem or the appropriateness of our approach to it.

Definitions of Assessment and Evaluation

The process of gathering the information used in reaching each of the different types of decisions is referred to as **assessment**. Note that it is a process, not a single finite task. Also note that the information has an intended use. **Evaluation** is another term that refers to the same process of gathering information and using it in making decisions. Both terms imply a judgment and decision-making process as well as information gathering. These terms can be used interchangeably; here, we will use the term *assessment*.

J. Salvia and J. E. Ysseldyke (1987), in their comprehensive book about assessment in special education, go one step further: "Good assessment procedures take into consideration the fact that anyone's performance on any task is influenced by the demands of the task itself, by the history and characteristics the individual brings to the task, and by the factors inherent in the setting in which the assessment is carried out" (p. 5). This suggests that we must look at what the children do on a variety of tasks and in a variety of settings and relate these findings to their total functioning.

Other special educators have a similar concept of assessment. G. Wallace and S. C. Larsen (1978) include a special chapter on ecological assessment in which they advocate looking closely at the environment as well as at the child. M. Walkenshaw and M. Fine (1979) define assessment as "the study of an individual in an educational context, focusing on the quantitative and qualitative appraisal of his/her abilities, learning capacities, and emotionality as they relate to the child responding appropriately to the demands of the environment" (p. 8). Walkenshaw and Fine use the familiar analogy of the blind men and the elephant in emphasizing the need for a comprehensive view of the child and the assessment process:

In that tale, upon examining different parts of the elephant, each of the blind men argued with surety for his definition of the total elephant. Of course, each definition had been derived from a different perspective and produced entirely different definitions. In assessment, if an individual starts with a narrow frame of reference the resulting view of the problem will be restricted and considerably biased. (p. 5)

We agree that a comprehensive and integrated approach to assessment is in order.

ASSESSMENT— AN INTEGRAL PART OF TEACHING

A major aspect of the model for identification of exceptional children (Figure 15.1) was the circularity at each step. The arrows at each decision block always point forward to a new action or back to the previous step so that consideration is continuous; the process is never-ending. Teachers do not have to go out of their way to use the model because it is based on actions that are a routine and natural part of the educational process. The principles of assessment reinforce the basic theme that assessment is an integral part of teaching and learning.

Various authors break down assessment into slightly different steps, but the same ideas are present in each scheme. Assessment is not a collection of tests or procedures; it is a process guided by several generally accepted principles:

1. Priority should be given to determining and clarifying what is to be assessed. — *Know what questions you are asking.*

2. Tests and other assessment procedures should be selected in terms of the purposes to be served. — *Choose the procedure most likely to answer the question.*

3. A variety of assessment procedures is required in order to have comprehensive assessment. — *Be sure you have a complete answer to the question.*

4. Assessment procedures can be misused; proper use depends on an awareness and understanding of their limitations as well as their strengths.

   Understand that some answers may be in error.

5. Assessment involves using information as well as gathering it; it is a means to an end, not an end in itself.

   Use the information to answer the question.

   (Adapted from Gronlund, 1976)

The principles illustrate that assessment and instruction are closely tied together. Whether the task is teaching or assessment, first priority is given to specifying the objectives—*What* is to be taught? *What* is to be assessed? An answer to one question provides an answer to the other.

The three key characteristics of assessment procedures are reliability, validity, and usability. Reliability refers to the dependability of assessment, validity to the truthfulness component of assessment, and usability to the practical matters surrounding the use of the assessment procedure. Validity is the sine qua non of assessment because, if we are not getting the answers we need, it doesn't matter in the least how dependable they are or how easy they are to get.

TYPES OF ASSESSMENT

In the sequence of actions that make up the evaluation process, certain procedures are used to gather information. Which procedures should we use? The answer is found in the purpose of the assessment—what needs to be known? Descriptions of tests and other assessment procedures appropriate for answering various types of questions about learners can be found in general assessment textbooks such as those listed at the end of the chapter. Readers should consult more specialized resources for information about issues and special problems in assessing youngsters with handicaps.

Current and Historical Information

Salvia and Ysseldyke (1987) argue that current information has certain obvious advantages, but they point out that without some historical information, an adequate understanding of the events and experiences related to present functioning is not possible. Figure 15.2 shows current and historical information collected by means of tests, observations, and judgments. Note that the information gathered currently is under the control of the evaluator who can determine what information is to be collected, how it will be collected, and if and how it will be verified. Historical information has limitations because it is not known (1) if important information was missed, (2) if it was verified, and (3) what the situations or conditions under which it was collected were. When historical information is collected on the basis of recall by parents, for example, the unreliability of memory must be considered.

Maximum Versus Typical Performance

Assessment procedures can be classified according to their intended use in determining typical or maximum performance (Cronbach, 1970). Procedures designed to determine a person's abilities are called measures of *maximum* performance. The purpose is to find out what people can do when they are trying their very best. By contrast, procedures that measure *typical* performance are used to determine what the person usually does in normal or routine situations. The distinction is that measures of typical performance tell us what individuals *will* do, whereas measures of maximum performance are supposed to tell us what they *can* do.

A good example of maximum versus typical performance assessment involves learning to drive a car and having to pass a test to be awarded a driver's license. The test that is usually given to ascertain the individual's understanding of the laws and regulations governing operation of a motor vehicle elicits maximum performance.

TYPE OF INFORMATION   TIME AT WHICH INFORMATION IS GATHERED

Current   Historical

	Current	Historical
Observations	Frequency counts of occurrence of a particular behavior Antecedents of behavior Critical incidents	Birth weight Anecdotal records Observations by last year's teacher
Tests	Results of an intelligence test administered during the assessment Results of this week's spelling test given by the teacher	Results of a standardized achievement-test battery given at the end of last year
Judgments	Parents' evaluations of how well the child gets along in family, neighborhood, etc. Rating scales completed by teachers, social workers, etc. Teacher's reason for referral	Previous medical, psychological, or educational diagnoses Previous report cards Parents' recall of developmental history, of undiagnosed childhood illnesses, etc.

Figure 15.2. Sources of information. (From *Assessment in Special and Remedial Education* by John Salvia and James E. Ysseldyke. Copyright © 1987 by Houghton Mifflin Company. Reprinted by permission of the publisher.)

Whether or not that same person follows those same laws and regulations while routinely operating a motor vehicle—in other words, typical performance—may be quite another story!

Placement, Formative, Diagnostic, and Summative Assessment

N. E. Gronlund (1976) and P. W. Airasian and G. J. Madaus (1972) differentiate among placement, formative, diagnostic, and summative assessments. Distinctions among the four categories are related to the way the assessment process is tied into the instructional process. *Placement* assessment is undertaken for the purpose of determining the entry level behavior in a sequence of instruction. The monitoring that takes place while the instruction is under way is *formative* assessment. If any difficulties occur during the instruction, the procedure used to uncover the difficulties is called *diagnostic* assessment. Finally, the assessment of achievement at the conclusion

of the instructional sequence is called *summative* assessment.

Although we agree with the logic underlying the classification scheme proposed above, some of the terms are used in a slightly different way in special education. We use the term *placement* to refer to the decision about the setting in which the child will be educated—regular class, resource room, special class, and so on. We use the term *diagnostic assessment* to refer to the decision about an appropriate entry level in an instructional sequence as well as any procedures used to probe learning difficulties that may be uncovered during instruction.

In our view, three phases of assessment occur after the placement decision has been made: (1) diagnostic—conducted prior to initial instruction and, if instruction was unsuccessful, prior to recycling; (2) formative—conducted during instruction to assess progress on objectives and monitor the instructional process; and (3) summative—conducted at the completion of an instructional unit, semester, or term.

Criterion-Referenced and Norm-Referenced Assessments

Another way of classifying assessment procedures is in terms of how the results are interpreted. Basically, there are two ways of interpreting performance: (1) **criterion-referenced assessment**, which describes the child's performance in terms of the specific behaviors demonstrated; and (2) **norm-referenced assessment**, which describes the child's performance in comparison to some known group.

Norm-referenced assessment is tied to interindividual differences. The intent is to compare the performance of one person with that of the group. The emphasis is on relative standing of individuals rather than on absolute mastery of content. The standard varies depending on the performance of the group. For instance, in a group of poor readers, a child who might be just average compared to other groups could well be the best in the class. If the comparison group shifts to a group of reading "superstars," this same "average reader" could well be the worst in the class. The child has not changed—only the standard has! In other words, in order to interpret the reading performance of the child, we must know something about the reading performance of the group. Standardized achievement tests that yield information such as percentile ranks, stanines, or standard scores are examples of norm-referenced assessment procedures. Other nontest assessment procedures can also be norm-referenced if the information they yield is interpreted in light of a person's relative position within a group. Table 15.1 presents commonly used norm-referenced instruments.

Norm-referenced tests are very useful when the purpose of testing is screening or program evaluation. They are also valuable in making placement decisions and in determining student's potential in a given program or curriculum. However, norm-referenced tests have several limitations to their usefulness. First, they do not provide useful information for instructional purposes. Second, they have limited diagnostic potential from a skill-training perspective. Third, special-needs students are often underrepresented or unrepresented in the norm group. Fourth, these tests have been determined to discriminate against minority students (Anastasi, 1976). Furthermore, norm-referenced tests require substantial amount of administrative time.

Criterion-referenced assessment procedures are tied to intraindividual differences and measure a person's development of particular skills in terms of absolute levels of mastery. That is, they are designed to assess the individual's standing with respect to a particular criterion. In this case, the standard is the criterion behavior; and the concern is whether the child can perform the behavior, not how he or she compares to a group. You can think of this type of assessment as yielding results of a yes-no nature: Yes, the child can perform the behavior; no, the child cannot. Note that the standard does not vary as it does with norm-referenced assessment. The standards in criterion-referenced assessment are often derived directly from the instructional objectives and can be stated in terms of frequency of exhibiting the behavior or accuracy of the performance. For example, a teacher who says that a child completed a group of single-digit, whole number addition problems with 90 percent accuracy or that a child stays in an assigned seat 90 percent of the time during reading class is making a criterion-referenced statement.

Curriculum-Based Assessment

Curriculum-based assessment (CBA) simply measures the level of achievement of a given student in terms of the expected curricular outcomes of the school. The essential measure of success in education is the student's progress in the curriculum of the local school. CBA has several advantages over the traditional assessment methods, some of which have been outlined by S. L. Deno (1985):

- *Improved communication.* CBA provides data on student performance that clearly, simply, and meaningfully relates to educational decisions. In special education, this need for effective communication is extremely important

TABLE 15.1
COMMONLY USED NORM-REFERENCED TESTS

Intelligence Tests

McCarthy Scale of Children's Abilities
Slosson Intelligence Test
Stanford-Binet Intelligence Scale
The Wechsler Scales

Intelligence Tests for Special Populations

Arthur Adaptation of the Leiter International Performance Scale
Blind Learning Aptitude Test
Columbia Mental Maturity Scale
Pictorial Test of Intelligence
Test of Non-Verbal Intelligence
The Nebraska Test of Learning Aptitude

Academic Achievement Tests

Basic Achievement Skills Individual Screener
Brigance Diagnostic Inventories
California Achievement Test
Gates-MacGinitie Reading Tests
Iowa Tests of Basic Skills and the Tests of Achievement and Proficiency
Metropolitan Achievement Tests
Peabody Individual Achievement Test
SRA Achievement Series
Stanford Achievement Test Series
Wide Range Achievement Test

Adaptive Behavior Tests

AAMD Adaptive Behavior Scale
Vineland Social Maturity Scale
Vineland Adaptive Behavior Scale

---

because of the critical nature of decisions being made about students.

▪ *Increased sensitivity.* CBA data are sensitive to growth in student performance over relatively short durations. This enables a teacher to frequently evaluate the effectiveness of efforts to solve a child's achievement problem.

▪ *Improved data base.* CBA improves the data base for making educational decisions for several reasons, all of which relate to the fact that measures of student achievement may be obtained frequently.

▪ *Peer referencing.* CBA procedures make it possible for teachers to obtain a normative perspective on student performance by sampling regular classroom peers.

▪ *Cost-effectiveness.* CBA procedures are cost-effective because they do not require purchase of additional test materials. CBA requires a fraction of the time to administer when compared to achievement tests.

CBAs are usually given at the beginning of the school year, with the results being used to place students in appropriate curriculum settings and to identify specific skills each student needs to learn. All or part of a CBA may be readministered immediately following instruction on a topic to assess skill mastery. Following mastery, CBAs may be used periodically throughout the year to measure long-term retention. A CBA can be developed for any type of curriculum material; separate CBAs are developed for each subject area. The steps involved in developing and using CBAs have been given by C. S. Blankenship (1985) and include the following:

1. List the skills presented in the materials selected.

2. Examine the list to see if all important skills are presented.

3. Decide if the resulting, edited list has skills in a logical order.

4. Write an objective for each skill on the list.

5. Prepare items to test each listed objective.

6. Prepare testing materials for student use, presenting the items.

7. Plan how the CBA will be given.

8. Give the CBA immediately prior to beginning instruction on a topic.

9. Study the results to determine which students need further practice and which students have mastered the topic.

10. Readminister the CBA after instruction and study the results.

11. Periodically readminister the CBA throughout the year to assess for long-term retention. (p. 234)

ASSESSMENT—THE BRIDGE BETWEEN IDENTIFICATION AND INTERVENTION

P.L. 94–142 Mandates

Many of the mandates in P.L. 94–142 concern obtaining and using information. Some requirements speak to how the information will be gathered, others specify how and by whom the information will be used. The requirement for **Child Find** mandates screening and follow-up diagnosis, where indicated, in order to find and serve exceptional children. It stipulates that evaluation must be done in a nondiscriminatory manner and that procedural safeguards are to be applied at every step in the identification, diagnosis, and placement process. Development of the individualized education program depends on assessment at present functioning levels, and methods of evaluating child progress are required as part of the IEP.

Teachers' Responsibilities

Classroom teachers must exercise responsibility in the assessment process in many ways. The decisions that lead to referral for further assessment are based on information collected by the classroom teacher. Often, teachers devise their own procedures for collecting this information, but sometimes they use commercially available tests.

Consulting Specialists. If, in applying the Identification Model, a teacher finds that additional, more specialized information is needed to make decisions about placement and instructional programming, the child would be referred to a specialist for further assessment. The assessment is frequently conducted by a team of specialists: school psychologist, social worker, educational diagnostician, medical doctor, and others. When a child has not yet been diagnosed, and a variety of diagnoses are possible, those involved must be open-minded and prepared to assess comprehensively in order to find the general problem area. Then they can proceed with more specific diagnostic procedures that will yield necessary in-depth information in a specific functional domain.

Information gathered by specialists is communicated to the classroom teacher who may be responsible for preparing the IEP. Even though classroom teachers may not routinely administer some of the specialized assessment procedures, they need to know what is being assessed and how to interpret the results in order to make good use of the information in planning the child's future educational experiences.

Assessment of children's problems is often a complex process that requires the skills of many different professionals. (Photo by Joseph Bodkin.)

Drawing Inferences from Data. Because different people are likely to make different inferences from the same set of behaviors, it is essential that teachers and other diagnosticians report their findings in terms of specific behaviors. If a test has been used, adequate information about the test should be given so that the person receiving and using the results knows what the score means. Similarly, if teacher-made devices have been used, information about each assessment device itself must be shared with anyone using the results so that the specific behaviors sampled are known. Knowing that the child received a score of six on the "ABC Block Test" means nothing unless the teacher also knows what the test is designed to measure, which behaviors are sampled, how it is scored, how the results are to be interpreted, what reliability and validity information is provided, and so on. Very specific recording and reporting of behavior helps to eliminate some of the different conclusions that might be drawn about the children.

Specific guidelines for reporting and interpreting test results have been provided by J. A. McLoughlin and R. B. Lewis (1981). These include the following:

1. Use referents or guideposts when reporting data.

2. Group data by major skill areas.

3. Begin a discussion of each area with a statement of the current level of performance.

4. Divide the discussion in each area into appropriate subdivisions.

5. Specify the mastered and unmastered skills in each academic and behavioral area.

6. Analyze the data on an intraindividual basis, as well as on an interindividual basis.

7. Indicate the nature of a task by rewording the names of subtests or giving examples of the task, whenever necessary.

8. Report the same kind of scores as much as possible.

9. Use standard scores or percentiles when comparing test performance.

10. Report a student's performance in ranges, indicating the meaning of the numerical scores.

11. Indicate other test scores and data to corroborate findings.

12. Use correct and incorrect student responses and other examples to illustrate a learning problem or style.

13. Whenever learning performance in one area seems to be affecting performance in another area, indicate the relationship.

14. Integrate information about educational and noneducational correlates at the appropriate point. (pp. 503–506)

Linking Assessment Information to Curriculum Planning. The concept of linking assessment information to curriculum planning is well accepted in the abstract. The procedures for ensuring the link from assessment information to teaching objectives and lessons is often not well documented. Several special educators have begun to define the procedures required to build these links (Bagnato, 1981; Bagnato & Neisworth, 1979). Furthermore, they have tested their ideas using protocol materials with teachers and have documented the effectiveness of their suggested procedures. The steps required to build the assessment-curriculum linkage are:

1. Identify those developmental deficits that require more intensive diagnosis.

2. Match assessment devices according to curriculum characteristics and content (i.e., choose an assessment procedure that has items similar to the type of objectives in the curriculum).

3. Determine developmental levels in major areas of functioning (e.g., assess in the four developmental domains).

4. Identify developmental ceilings in each domain (i.e., find the point in the hierarchy of items at which the child just barely passes and then fails items higher in the sequence).

5. Match the tasks represented by the developmental ceilings to objectives in the curriculum for each developmental domain (e.g., a test item of "attempts cube tower" that was failed would translate to a curriculum objective of "practices stacking two cubes," and a failed test item of "speaks three to four words" links to the curriculum objective of "uses words in speech").

Essentially, S. J. Bagnato and J. T. Neisworth have adapted norm-referenced scales and used them as criterion-referenced procedures. Used in this way, the items the child fails indicate what that child needs to learn. The procedure works because early childhood curricula and assessment procedures for young children include similar developmental areas and use similar behavioral tasks.

Assessment of exceptional youngsters often appears to be a negative process—it seems as if we are concentrating on what's *wrong* with the child. It is true that we are searching for problems, but we are also discovering what's *right* with the child. Then we can work with both types of information—the problems and the assets—to help the child make progress. We must also be aware that

there are special problems involved in assessment of learners who are handicapped. Several excellent reviews of the issues embedded in assessment are available and we recommend them to you if you wish further study.* Special considerations about assessment of various handicapping conditions are included in the chapters in Part II.

CHOOSING ASSESSMENT PROCEDURES

The *purpose* of the assessment is the key to answering questions about *what* and *how* to assess. Time spent clarifying the type of information that is needed will pay important dividends. Considerations will include questions such as:

1. What are the gaps in the information we have about the child?

2. Is the information collected thus far such that a comprehensive picture of the child's functioning in all domains is available?

3. What suspicions about the child's problems are beginning to form and will require further checking?

4. What sketchy information needs to be confirmed or disproved?

5. Have various sources of information been used in the process of gathering information: parents? peers? child? other professionals?

6. Is the information collected thus far of a general or specific nature? Are we ready to become more specific?

7. Will we be expected to participate in a decision about whether to label a child in some way?

8. Do we know enough about the child's present

---

*See Page, 1980; Brooks-Gunn & Lewis, 1981; and Ysseldyke & Algozzine, 1982.

level of functioning to place him or her in a curriculum?

9. Do we know enough about the child's past successes in learning to make decisions about useful methods and materials?

10. Has adequate attention been given to factors in the environment that may be contributing to the problem?

All of these questions and others can be answered through the use of assessment. Information derived from assessment is necessary both for identification and for intervention. In fact, the same general procedures are often used in both cases; the decisions to be made may differ, but the same principles, cautions, and procedures apply. Careful attention should be given to the technical characteristics of the test. Professionals whose job it is to administer tests should be prepared to choose carefully among those available. And those who use the results of tests should make it their responsibility to be informed consumers as well.

Reviewing Published Assessment Procedures

Comprehensive reviews of commonly used assessment instruments are provided by Salvia and Ysseldyke (1987) and Wallace and Larsen (1978). Not all published instruments are included (an impossibility considering the thousands that are on the market), but representative examples in various categories have been chosen, and the descriptions provided are quite thorough. Salvia and Ysseldyke (1987) review procedures in the following categories: assessment of intelligence using both individual and group tests; assessment of sensory acuity, oral language, perceptual motor skills; and assessment of personality. They also review academic achievement; screening devices; diagnostic tests in reading, math, written language, and adaptive behavior; and assessment of school readiness. Wallace and Larsen (1978) include many nontest assessment procedures in the following categories: early childhood, perceptual, spoken language, word analysis, reading compre-

hension, spelling, written expression, arithmetic, and career education. Descriptive information about published assessment devices also can be found in many other evaluation texts (some suggestions are listed at the end of this chapter).

A publication edited by O. K. Buros (1974) entitled *Tests in Print* provides titles of tests, grade or age levels included, publication dates, special comments about the test, information about the different types of scores provided, authors and publishers, and an indication as to whether the particular test has been reviewed in a series of related publications edited by Buros, the *Mental Measurements Yearbooks*. A 1974 publication by the American Psychological Association, *Standards for Educational and Psychological Tests,* includes helpful information about selecting and using standardized tests. Finally, the catalogs produced by test publishers provide descriptions of tests and other assessment procedures, and the manual accompanying each procedure provides additional, more technical information.

Teacher-made Assessment Procedures

Assessment procedures should be chosen or designed so as to achieve a good match between the special characteristics of the procedure and the behaviors about which information is needed. If we need information about the types of errors children make as they decode phonetically regular words, an error analysis procedure is called for. If we need summary information about children's achievement in a science unit, a teacher-constructed criterion-referenced achievement test is called for. If we are interested in work-study students' interactions with peers on the job, a carefully structured interview with the employer may be required.

Special Considerations. Adaptations of test items and procedures may be necessary if children do not have the **enabling behaviors** required to respond. Items should elicit the behaviors intended (recalling information, seeing associations, finding the meaning), and we should guard

Even though this young child who is gifted cannot print the letters, he can demonstrate spelling skills using magnetic letters. (Photo by Joseph Bodkin.)

think of *desirable* criterion levels. For example, addition is usually taught before multiplication; some programs set criterion levels as high as 95 percent accuracy on addition before teaching multiplication. However, it is not absolutely essential to have such high accuracy on addition in order to begin to understand multiplication. It is certainly possible, and many teachers consider it quite desirable, to introduce multiplication while continuing to increase the accuracy of addition. If we insist that all children attain rigid criterion levels that are not essential prerequisites to the next steps in the program, we may be contributing to further developmental delays. Characteristics of the child, the objectives, and the instruction programs should be accounted for in setting criterion levels.

against test situations in which children are prevented from making a response because they do not have other, extraneous behaviors required to make the response. For example, a child with cerebral palsy may not be able to hold a pencil (an enabling behavior) to answer a test item *but still may know the answer.* Ways should be found to help children display responses.

Teachers should be creative in adapting tests for special groups. Children who cannot read can listen to questions and point to pictures, make X's, draw lines, or give answers orally. Children whose motor skills prevent them from responding can use devices to point to answers, nod their heads, or give answers orally. Questions can be presented pictorially rather than in written form.

Criterion Levels. It is not necessary to set the same criterion for every task, or for every learner. When learning is viewed as cumulative, children need not always reach a specific criterion level on one set of objectives before going on up the task ladder. In some task hierarchies, there are *necessary* criterion levels; at other times, we should

Parent and Peer Appraisal and Self-Report Techniques

Some information about individuals is best gained by simply asking them (self-report) or those who know them—peers or family (parent and peer appraisal). Such methods are especially useful for determining a child's interests, attitudes, and personal adjustment. These methods of gaining information assume that the person giving the information is being as honest and accurate as possible.

The **interview** is a dialogue between two people: the interviewer (who is attempting to gain information) and the interviewee (the person giving the information).

Questionnaires and inventories are somewhat like written interviews. A **questionnaire** presents individuals with a set of questions to which they respond in writing. The questions may be purely factual or they may be personal, asking respondents how they think or feel about some matter or what they think they would do in a given situation.

A **sociometric technique** involves asking the individuals in a group to indicate (either orally or in writing) those group members with whom they would prefer to be associated in a given situation. This technique is a way of determining how a group is socially structured. It indicates those who are socially accepted or rejected by the others in the group. This information can be very helpful to teachers in understanding the behavior of their pupils.

OBSERVATION

Perhaps the most valuable assessment skill for the classroom teacher is **observation** and the recording of information about children. Most of the information about children that is of interest to us is *not obtainable in any other way than through observation* (Cartwright & Cartwright, 1984).

There are literally hundreds of thousands of behavioral events in any classroom every day! Clearly, no one can capture them all. However, the efficiency of collecting observational data can be improved by *making observation a habit,* a routine part of what you do as a teacher. Teach yourself to capitalize on any and all opportunities to observe. This will have many positive effects: Observing will not be a novelty in the classroom, the teachers' observations will be unobtrusive, and the information obtained will be more typical of actual behavior of the children.

Purpose is the key to setting up an appropriate observational situation. If the purpose is carefully described, answers to questions such as the following will be obvious.

- Who will make the observation? If the purpose requires some information about how the teacher interacts with the child, it may be necessary to call in another observer.
- Who or what will be observed? Sometimes, apsects of the environment as well as the behavior of the child and/or the teacher will be of interest.
- Where will the observation take place? For many behaviors, it will be important to be sure that a variety of situations are represented in the observational records.
- When will the observation occur? Usually,

both planned and incidental opportunities for collecting observational data will be used.
- How will the observations be recorded? A variety of reporting forms are in use.

Recording Observations

An observation that is not recorded is lost. A handy supply of a variety of general forms used to record results of observations will greatly improve the efficiency of the process and be a kind of "insurance" that important observational information will not be lost or forgotten.

One of the simplest and most direct types of observation is to look for certain behaviors and record their frequency, rate, and/or duration. The results can be graphed to get a "picture" of the behaviors of interest. Even though simple, this procedure is very powerful because it is straightforward and direct and thus likely to yield quite reliable and valid information.

There are several different methods for recording data. One method is frequency recording, used to determine the number of occurrences of discrete behaviors. Frequency recording is appropriate for behaviors that have discrete start and stop times. Responses that are of a relatively constant duration and intensity are also suitable for frequency measurement. Because frequency recording involves simply counting the number of times a response occurs, it may be the most practical measure available to the classroom teacher. Some behaviors, however, cannot be recorded by simple counting, so other means must be employed. Duration recording can be used for behaviors that extend over a period of time. To collect duration data, the recorder enters the time the behavior begins and ends; the difference between these times is the duration for one episode. Latency recording is used to assess the period of time that elapses from some cue to the time the learner engages in the target behavior. The data collected from these methods are somewhat limited for most classroom purposes because they require a substantial amount of observation time. Another observation technique is interval recording, useful for behaviors that do not have obvious start or stop times and that may occur over a period of time. Interval data are collected by dividing a time period into short intervals (e.g., from five to sixty seconds). The responses can then be scored as occurring or not occurring during each interval.

A variety of aids are available that improve accuracy as well as efficiency of observation because a behavior is recorded at the time it is observed rather than when it is convenient to write it down. Index cards, small notebooks, clipboards, and copies of various recording forms can be kept at various places in the classroom so that something to use for a record of the observation is at hand just about anywhere a teacher might be. Portable tape recorders can be left running in certain key locations to unobtrusively capture children's conversations. Many observational situations involve tallying frequencies of behaviors or time-sampling procedures. A variety of inexpensive counters and timers—golfer's wrist counter, kitchen timer, supermarket counter, parking meter timer—are available for these situations. Simple shorthand or coding systems can be devised to record quantities of information rapidly. Photographs, movie films, and videotapes can also be used if the equipment is available.

Because one of the problems with observation is that the information is fleeting (the behavior is performed and then it is gone), the observer must work quickly to record the results of the observation to document what the child did. Some innovative procedures have been proposed to help record behaviors. These procedures are termed *permanent product measures* and involve having some type of physical evidence remain after the behavior has been performed (Halle & Sindelar, 1982). For example, if we are interested in the child's walking ability, we might rub chalk on the soles of the child's shoes, have the child walk across the carpet, and then observe the footprints on the carpet to check for number of steps taken, number of inches steps are out of alignment, and so forth. Or, if we were interested in the child's eating success, we might weigh the food tray and bib before the meal and then weigh them again after the meal. The difference in weights would, of course, tell us how much food the child had eaten.

Record Forms

A **checklist** consists of a list of expected behaviors, characteristics of performance, or desired attributes of a product, together with a space for recording whether the items were present or absent. Some checklists are designed so that a series of behaviors can be ranked (dated) in the order or sequence of their occurrence. A simple *yes* (behavior or characteristic is present) or *no* (behavior or characteristic is absent) is all that is required to record information on the checklist. Some checklists allow for the notation that a skill is emerging by providing a *sometimes* response. The items on the checklist are developed from the criteria for successful performance or for an acceptable product.

One of the advantages of using checklists is that a great deal of information can be recorded very quickly. However, the behaviors (or characteristics of a performance, or desired aspects of a product) must be known in advance.

Participation charts are similar to checklists in that they are used to record the presence or absence of behaviors. They are especially useful when many learners are being observed simultaneously and when *participation* in some activity is the behavior of interest. Participation charts consist of a list of names of learners and space to tally each time each learner participates. The format can even be set up so it corresponds to the seating arrangement in use during the activity (see the participation chart for a spelling game shown in Figure 15.3).

Many times, we are interested in more than whether or not a behavior occurred; we want to know *how well* it was performed. In these situations, **rating scales** are appropriate record-keeping forms. Rating scales are similar to checklists in that the expected behaviors, characteristics of performance, or aspects of a product appear on a list. They differ from them in that the observer is asked to rate the quality or frequency of the performance.

Brief factual accounts of events are called **anecdotal records**. In preparing an anecdotal record, we try to "freeze" the event in a "word picture" of the incident. The idea behind anecdotal records

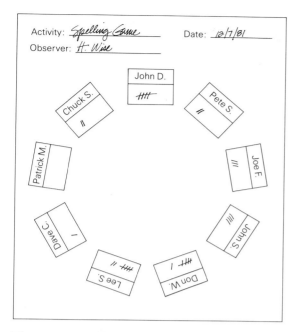

Figure 15.3. Participation chart. (From C. A. Cartwright and G. P. Cartwright, *Developing Observation Skills,* McGraw-Hill, 1984, p. 97; used with permission.)

is to be factual; interpretations are left off the record form. Anecdotal records are best used for unanticipated behaviors, incidents, or events. Because the behaviors are unanticipated, the record form must be open-ended. A general format with spaces for date, time, name of child, and setting should be available; the rest is up to the teacher, who needs to be alert to unanticipated behaviors of interest. Even though behaviors recorded on the anecdotal record are unanticipated, they are not insignificant. A single behavioral event may not be especially important, but several anecdotes forming a pattern are relevant, and anecdotal records are a way of ensuring that they are included in assessment of children.

Testing with Computers

Testing was seen as the original educational application of computers. With the large memory capacity of computers, thousands of questions could be stored, then randomly selected, adminis- tered, and scored, and the results could be permanently recorded. Computer testing, however, has progressed beyond group testing to individual diagnosis and prescription. For example, Auburn University programmed a battery of tests for appraisal of LD students and then used the information to assist in IEP development (Martin, 1981). In many schools, following testing, a student profile of strengths and weaknesses is developed, analyzed, and matched to appropriate teaching materials. The computer continually reviews and updates a child's program, monitoring progress toward skill acquisition. The computer enables both formative and summative evaluation of a child's educational progress.

SUMMARY

Exceptional children cannot be served unless they are found. The process of planning and providing educational programs and related services begins with the identification of the child as one who needs special attention. Teachers need to use the information that is continually being generated in the classroom to identify and screen out any children suspected of having problems. Once a child has been screened out as a possible problem, more specialized assessment is required to determine if there really is a problem, and if so, to pinpoint the difficulty.

There is a gap to be bridged between identification and intervention. That bridge is assessment—the process of gathering information to use in decisions about children's educational programs. Teachers need specific information to describe children's strengths and to help identify appropriate instructional strategies and techniques.

One of the major responsibilities of the teacher is gathering information, which is then used for screening, diagnosis, placement, program planning, and progress checking. The process of gathering the information used in reaching each of the different types of decisions is assessment.

Several principles of assessment provide guidelines. The first step in the assessment process is clarifying what is to be assessed, so the procedure most likely to answer the question can be chosen. There may be more than one answer to the question, or it may be necessary to ask several related questions; this will require a variety of procedures so that comprehensive assessment takes place. The information gathered through assessment must be used to make decisions— assessment is a means to an end, not an end in itself.

Assessment procedures have been classified according to several dimensions. Some experts draw a distinction between current and historical data, noting that it may be important to have both to reach a full understanding of a problem. Assessment can also be thought of in terms of assessing maximum versus typical performance.

Another way of classifying assessment procedures is in terms of the way the results will be used. If we describe the child's performance in terms of specific behaviors demonstrated, we are using criterion-referenced assessment. If we compare the child's performance in terms of relative position in some known comparison group, we are using norm-referenced assessment. Assessment may also be thought of as diagnostic (conducted prior to instruction to determine where to start or to pinpoint problems in unsuccessful instruction), formative (conducted during instruction to monitor the process and assess progress on objectives), or summative (conducted at the end of instruction). An emerging technique in assessment is curriculum-based assessment, which measures the child's achievement in terms of curriculum expectations.

Numerous commercially available assessment devices cover such dimensions as general intelligence, screening, infant assessment, academic achievement, adaptive behavior, perceptual-motor skills, and language. In spite of what seems to be an overabundance of assessment devices, many teachers soon learn that precise, direct instruction often requires developing specific assessments for their own class or group of children or even for one particular child. Teacher-made assessment devices usually are criterion-referenced, whereas commercially available instruments traditionally are norm-referenced.

Interview, questionnaire, and inventory procedures are followed to find out certain types of information usually available only from the respondent. These self-report techniques are useful for determining the interests, attitudes, and perhaps personal adjustment of children and parents.

Direct observation is a valuable assessment skill for teachers, because much important information about children can be obtained only through observation. Some methods of data collection include frequency, duration and latency, and time interval recording. Careful planning requires advance answers to such questions as: Who will be observed? What will be observed? Where and when and for how long will the observation take place? Efficient and consistent observation procedures will assure that the behaviors were actually seen and that two or more observers will agree on the behavior that occurred. Checklists, rating scales, and anecdotal records also can be useful tools to assist teachers in assessing areas of behavior where changes have occurred or where changes are needed. Recently, computers have been used to assess efficiently students with handicaps.

Suggestions for Further Reading

Bertrand, A., & Cebula, J. P. (1980). *Tests, measurement, and evaluation: A developmental approach.* Reading, MA: Addison-Wesley.
A chapter entitled "Assessing Children with Special Needs" is included in this general text on measurement and evaluation written for the classroom teacher. Principles of growth and development are recommended as the foundation for teachers in making evaluation decisions. The authors argue that tests are not inherently bad for children even though they have been maligned recently by some writers. The usual information on the nature of the evaluation process, the role of objectives in evaluation, use and interpretation of the results of standardized tests, observation, and teacher-made tests is included. The material is organized according to developmental domains in keeping with the authors' philosophy. A timely discussion of major issues in testing and evaluation is included.

Cartwright, C. A., & Cartwright, G. P. (1984). *Developing observation skills* (2nd ed.). New York: McGraw-Hill.
Many behaviors of interest and importance to teachers are most appropriately assessed using observation procedures. The authors provide a rationale for extensive use of obser-

vation and present numerous examples of appropriate uses. In addition, suggestions are given for observing the behavior of teachers and assessing the instructional environment through observation. Several how-to-do-it chapters deal with behavior tallying and charting, checklists, participation charts, rating scales, and anecdotal records.

Coladarci, A., & Coladarci, T. (1980). *Elementary descriptive statistics: For those who think they can't.* Belmont, CA: Wadsworth.

In fewer than one hundred pages, the authors present essential information about descriptive statistics in an understandable and entertaining manner. This paperback book is intended for those who need to produce and/or use descriptive statistics. Ways of organizing and presenting new data, including construction of graphs, are described. Chapters also are devoted to determining the average and variability, understanding derived scores, and describing relationships. Many realistic examples make the book very readable.

McLoughlin, J. A., & Lewis, R. B. (1981). *Assessing special students.* Columbus, OH: Merrill.

This book provides a clear, comprehensive guide to the assessment of students who are mildly handicapped. A strong education orientation toward assessment is maintained throughout the book. The book provides both an understanding of assessment and the practical skills necessary to successfully assess students so you can teach them as well. It covers the technical aspects of administering, scoring, and interpreting formal tests as well as skills for designing and using informal techniques. A strength of the book is its balanced coverage of formal and informal assessment. Many useful sample test profiles, checklists, and illustrations provide a practical and handy resource to use in the classroom.

Salvia, J., & Ysseldyke, J. E. (1987). *Assessment in special and remedial education* (4th ed.). Boston: Houghton Mifflin.

This is one of the few comprehensive texts on assessment specifically for special education. Part One is an overview of assessment, with a description of basic considerations in psychological and educational assessment of students. It also includes fundamental legal and ethical considerations in assessment. Part Two addresses basic measurement concepts. Part Three includes descriptions and technical comments on tests of general achievement, intelligence, perceptual-motor skills, sensory functioning, language, personality, and readiness. Part Four deals with the application of assessment information. This is an excellent sourcebook for information about published assessment procedures.

Swanson, H. L., & Watson, B. L. (1982). *Educational and psychological assessment of exceptional children: Theories, strategies, and applications.* St. Louis, MO: C. V. Mosby.

This book discusses major issues in the field of measurement and presents information on the basic qualities of tests. It also deals with social issues such as the appropriate use of testing and assessment of minority children. Strategies that view the child as a problem solver are introduced, as is a basic framework to guide the reader's own course of thought and action, step by step.

Related Journal

Diagnostique

This journal is published by the Council for Educational Diagnostic Services, a division of The Council for Exceptional Children. It publishes articles on diagnosis covering a range of exceptionalities. Articles on reliability and validity of educational tests and measurements are frequently included.

CHAPTER 16

Generic Teaching Strategies

Did You Know That . . .

- no single method, no one style of education, no single grouping arrangement, no one set of materials is suitable for all?

- the range of educational environments is greater for children who are handicapped than for those who are nonhandicapped?

- level of severity of handicap is as important as type of handicap in planning for instruction and placement?

- learning is not efficient when behavior is not under control?

- there are probably as many different techniques of teaching as there are talented teachers?

- a teacher's philosophical orientation toward handicapped children influences the type of instructional strategies the teacher will use?

- direct instruction procedures help to individualize instruction for each child?

- computer-assisted and computer-managed instruction is assuming an important place in education?

I f you were to select one thousand children who are handicapped and one thousand children who are nonhandicapped at random from all the children in the United States and to compare the two groups, you would find that the children and youths in both groups cry, laugh, talk, listen, ask and answer questions, and so on. By definition, however, the children labeled *handicapped* would exhibit some of these behaviors at an excessive rate (such as a youngster who is emotionally disturbed crying too often) or a deficit rate (such as a child with a learning disability failing to answer questions).

Children who are handicapped exhibit a much greater range of behaviors than do the nonhandicapped. Children who are handicapped are identified as and called handicapped because their behaviors are different from those of the so-called normal group. Consider, for a moment, what you might find in our random group of children who are handicapped.

First, you might be struck by the fact that some of these youngsters are so retarded and physically disabled that they cannot walk, talk, or even feed themselves; they are totally dependent on others for all their needs. On the other hand, you might encounter a few youngsters who are physically and socially indistinguishable from the group that is normal; in fact, they may have intelligence scores much above average and be planning on careers as doctors, lawyers, or other professionals whose livelihoods depend upon keen intellect and good judgment. Upon closer examination, however, you might find that all of these children are seriously learning disabled and lag far behind their classmates in reading although perhaps not in other academic subjects.

Look again, and you may find very bright children whose vision is so impaired that they can barely distinguish light from dark, children with hearing impairment who prefer to communicate with their hands rather than through more traditional methods, children with physical disabilities who require mechanical or human assistance to turn the pages of their calculus texts, children who excel in the arts or in athletics but who can't keep up with other children in more academic subjects, fearful youngsters whose days are spent trying to avoid interactions with other people . . . the list could go on and on.

FACTORS INFLUENCING CHOICE OF TEACHING STRATEGIES

It is the responsibility of the public schools of America to educate all the children—not just the "normal" children. Obviously, no one method, no one style of education, no one grouping arrangement could provide adequate education services for all these diverse problems. Thus, it is no surprise that teachers have come up with a variety of techniques, environments, even philosophies in an effort to provide every child with a free, appropriate public education.

Children who are handicapped receive their education in a variety of settings; in fact, the range of educational environments is probably greater for the handicapped than for the nonhandicapped. No one setting is used for all children who are handicapped, even those bearing the same categorical label. Similarly, no one teaching strategy or technique is used with all youngsters with handicaps, even if they have a common label.

Throughout this book, we have tried to point out teaching ideas and techniques that are useful for children with specific problems. Each disability chapter contains some considerations for teaching children with a particular disability, and this chapter offers some generic teaching strategies. But there are many more strategies and methods available than we could list in a single chapter. It simply is not possible in one chapter, or even in one book, to deal in depth with all possible teaching strategies and methods that can be used successfully with all children who are handicapped. Therefore, we must be quite selective in this chapter, which introduces a variety of teaching ideas and strategies that are not limited to any one disability group. We hope you will be sufficiently interested in some of these ideas to follow them up on your own or in other courses.

Type of Handicap. The techniques and materials used to teach children with one type of handicap may be quite different from those used for another handicap. You wouldn't use the phonics approach to teach reading to youngsters who are profoundly deaf, for example. Similarly, you would not try to teach children who are totally blind to read conventional textbooks (unless you were using an electronic reading aid), nor would you expect a youngster who is seriously physically disabled to participate routinely in all aspects of a standard physical education program.

Level of Severity. Aside from the rather obvious modifications in teaching strategies that would be required in the three cases just mentioned, you will find that level of severity of a handicap is as important as type of handicap in planning instructional strategies and placement for children with handicaps. The more serious the disability, the more likely that a child will be educated in a special setting. In addition, the range of workable teaching strategies is much smaller for youngsters who are severely disabled.

Age. Another important factor in matching instruction to a learner's characteristics is the student's age level. Generally speaking, young students are most likely to benefit from a developmental orientation. Instructional experiences designed to provide the student with basic skills necessary for success in school through the secondary level often become the primary focus of the curriculum. Once at the secondary level, the student is more likely to benefit from a functional approach to curriculum development. This may involve identifying community settings (e.g., work, recreational, leisure, residential) in which the student is expected to participate. Curriculum objectives are then drawn from the skills necessary for success in these settings.

In general, children with mild handicaps are educated in levels 3, 4, 5, 6, or 7 of Deno's Cascade of Services (see Figure 2.1, Chapter 2). The emphasis of late has been to place as many children who are mildly handicapped as possible in full-time or part-time *regular* classes with supporting services. Typical placement for children who are moderately handicapped is in level 3, full-time special class, with some children in level 2 (special day school) and a few in level 4 (part-time regular, part-time special class). Children who are severely and profoundly retarded, children who are severely disturbed, and children who are seriously physically handicapped usually are placed in levels 1, 2, or 3, with children with profound retardation most likely to be found in level 1 (full-time residential school).

BEHAVIOR MANAGEMENT

Many children who are handicapped have serious problems in behavior control and may need help in controlling outbursts of aggressive or irrelevant behavior or in attending to appropriate cues in academic or social situations. A legitimate, very important job for teachers is designing **behavior management** or training programs to help children manage their own behavior. A child's behavior must be appropriate for a given situation, or little learning will take place. A child cannot learn to read if bizarre behavior patterns prevent her or him from becoming involved in the learning situation. Once the child can control the behavior, then learning should be more efficient.

For youngsters who are seriously emotionally disturbed or severely retarded, academic instruction, per se, is meaningless; control of behavior is the foremost goal. For youngsters who are disturbed, the problem is bizarre or inappropriate behavior, and the major goal for all who work with them is to help them interact with others in socially appropriate ways. For youngsters who are severely and profoundly retarded, the major goal is to help them become more self-sufficient in daily routines of hygiene, nourishment, and so on.

Thus, skills in behavior management are much more critical for teachers of the handicapped than for teachers of children who are nonhandicapped. Planning a behavior-management program for a child with a handicap has much in

One of the goals for children with developmental delays is to help them become as self-sufficient as possible. (Courtesy of Department of Agriculture.)

common with planning an instructional program for a child who is handicapped. The commonalities include:

- carefully delineating the behavior the child is to display at the conclusion of the program; the behavior can be academic (such as matching pictures and words) or social (such as maintaining eye contact with the teacher)
- identifying the current level of achievement or behavior in the area to be taught
- selecting an instructional strategy or behavior management plan
- selecting or developing instructional supporting materials
- keeping precise records of the child's progress toward the instructional or behavioral goal

Discipline. At first glance, you might think that behavior management is a form of discipline. It is if you think of discipline as habit training. It is not if you regard discipline as punishment. Generally, we will regard **discipline** as a method for maintaining an environment conducive to learning and for managing the behavior of students.

Discipline is a very large topic that can be approached from many different perspectives. For example, C. H. Wolfgang and C. D. Glickman (1980) present three diverse views, or psychological models, that can be called on to deal with disciplinary problems:

1. *noninterventionist*—humanistic and psychoanalytic thought

2. *interventionist*—experimental, behavioral psychology

3. *interactionist*—social, Gestalt, and developmental psychology

Each of these models or theories has guidelines and suggestions for dealing with discipline. The various procedures for dealing with discipline and disruptive behavior include values clarification, behavior modification, social discipline, teacher-effectiveness training, and transactional analysis. Find a position with which you are comfortable, and try out procedures and suggestions based on that position. Of course, you could be eclectic and use ideas from more than one theoretical position.

Classroom Management. Closely related to discipline is **classroom management**, the manipulation of the classroom environment to facilitate active engagement of students toward achievement of academic and social goals. C. S. Englert and C. C. Thomas (1982) report three variables that are important for classroom management:

1. active teaching and interacting with students in small groups

2. clear rules and procedures

3. effective monitoring of group work and seatwork activities

According to Englert and Thomas (1982), successful classroom management procedures include teacher positioning in the room, frequent direct observation of each child, appropriate praise, and circulation among students between lessons. The physical arrangement of the classroom is also an important consideration in the total management plan (Schloss & Sedlak, 1986). Disruptive movement between activities should be minimized, and the teacher should have all students in his or her visual field at all times. The seating arrangement should discourage formation of high- and low-ability clusters, so that the teacher's attention is spread equally within the classroom. Emphasis on these relevant attributes contributes significantly toward smooth functioning within the classroom and is conducive to increased student learning.

THE DIAGNOSTIC TEACHING MODEL

Academic instruction and classroom management differ not so much in basic procedures and planning as in the specific objectives to be accomplished. They are highly similar in the systematic way in which they must be applied.

The Diagnostic Teaching Model (Cartwright & Cartwright, 1972b; Cartwright, Cartwright, & Ysseldyke, 1973; Ward et al., 1973) describes a scheme for planning, implementing, and evaluating a program of diagnostic teaching or behavior management. By treating the child as an individual with specific and potential learning abilities, diagnostic teaching can be effective in helping each child develop. The Diagnostic Teaching Model has these purposes: (1) to prevent learning problems; (2) to correct existing problems; (3) to enhance learning assets. The model, shown in flowchart format in Figure 16.1, illustrates one way to develop a diagnostic teaching program. Each of the rectangular shapes represents a step in the program. Each of the diamond shapes represents a decision that must be made in using the program. The arrows show the direction the teacher should move in planning and executing

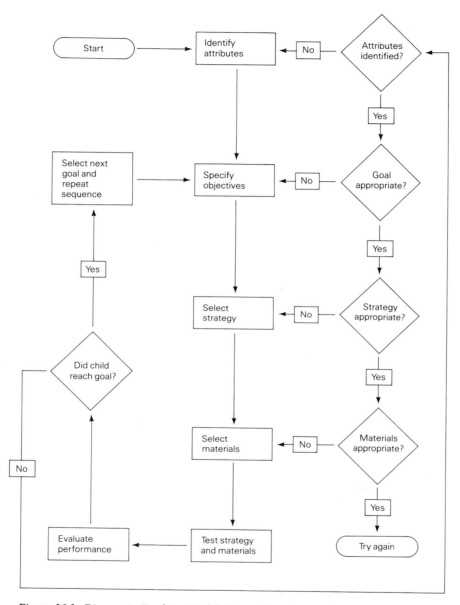

Figure 16.1. Diagnostic Teaching Model. (From G. P. Cartwright and C. A. Cartwright, "Gilding the Lily," *Exceptional Children,* 1972, *39,* 231–234.)

the steps and decisions of the Diagnostic Teaching Model.

Identifying the Relevant Attributes of the Child. The first step in the Diagnostic Teaching Model involves identifying the relevant attributes

(or characteristics) of the child. Relevant attributes are those related to the specific behavior of interest to the teacher. For example, noticing that a child is not interacting with the other children, the teacher might identify relevant behavior by (1) observing for a number of days to see which situations prompt this behavior, (2) recording frequency of the behavior, and (3) observing the other children's behavior toward the first child.

There are several things to remember when identifying attributes:

1. The more information known about the child, the greater the probability that all of the child's relevant attributes will be identified.

2. Some relevant attributes may not be obviously related to the learning situation. For example, an emotional problem may be interfering with a child's reading.

3. The search is begun by looking for the relevant characteristics that seem to be most logically related to the situation. However, other areas must be explored until all information is collected.

Specifying Teaching Objectives. The second step is specifying teaching objectives. In simple terms, this means stating what the child should be able to do after completing the learning experience. Objectives should be carefully selected to meet certain rules:

1. Objectives should be stated in terms of observable behavior.

2. Objectives should meet the child's needs.

3. Objectives should be stated in simple, small steps.

4. Objectives should build to a larger goal.

The actual objectives selected for development in the special education program are closely related to the abilities and disabilities of the student. In Chapter 3, we discussed four domains of instruction. One or more of these domains may be emphasized for students with varying disabilities. For example, skills in the *motor* domain may be stressed for students who are orthopedically impaired, health impaired, multiply handicapped, or visually handicapped. Skills in the *social* domain may be promoted for learners who are seriously emotionally disturbed. Skills in the *communica-*

tion domain are likely to be developed for youngsters who are deaf, deaf-blind, speech impaired, or visually handicapped. Finally, individuals who are mentally retarded or learning disabled may require a special curriculum in the cognitive domain. In all cases, selection of objectives will depend in large part upon the curriculum being used in the school or school district.

Selecting the Instructional Strategy. Once an objective or cluster of objectives has been selected, the next step in the model is selecting the instructional strategy and management procedures. These strategies are the activities chosen by the teacher to lead the child to the stated objectives. Several factors should be considered in the choice of a strategy:

1. The strategy should begin at the child's present level.

2. The strategy should ensure that the objectives will be met.

3. The strategy should stimulate the child.

4. The strategy should proceed in small steps.

5. The strategy should be a match between the relevant attributes of the child and the desired objectives.

Selecting Appropriate Materials. The next step in the model is making and/or selecting appropriate materials to reach the stated objectives. These are the actual materials the student will use. Often, the teacher has a large variety of resources from which to choose—books, films, manipulative objects, and so on. Sometimes, however, teachers will have to develop their own materials.

Evaluating the Program. The diagnostic teaching program is ready to be tested with the child (the next step) when the relevant attributes are identified and the objectives, strategy, and materials have been selected. When the program has been completed by the child, the teacher must evaluate whether or not the objective has been reached. There is no magic formula to tell the teacher exactly which objective to specify or

BOX 16.1

POINTS TO REMEMBER

Here are a number of common sense suggestions you can use when teaching or working with children, adolescents, or adults who have disabilities.

. . . When you meet a person who has a disability

- Remember that a person who has a disability is a *person*—like anyone else.
- Relax. If you don't know what to do or say, allow the person who has a disability to help put *you* at ease.
- Explore your mutual interests in a friendly way. The person likely has many interests besides those connected with the disability.
- Offer assistance *if asked* or if the need seems obvious, but don't overdo it or insist on it. Respect the person's right to indicate the kind of help needed.
- Talk about the disability if it comes up naturally, without prying. Be guided by the wishes of the person with the disability.
- Appreciate what the person *can* do. Remember that difficulties the person may be facing may stem more from society's attitudes and barriers than from the disability itself.
- Be considerate of the extra time it might take for a person with a disability to get things said or done. Let the person set the pace in walking or talking.
- Remember that we all have handicaps; on some of us they show.
- Speak directly to a person who has a disability. Don't consider a companion to be a conversational go-between.

- Don't move a wheelchair or crutches out of reach of a person who uses them.
- Never start to push a wheelchair without first asking the occupant if you may do so.
- When pushing a wheelchair up or down steps, ramps, curbs, or other obstructions, ask the person how he or she wants you to proceed.
- Don't lean on a person's wheelchair when talking.
- Give whole, unhurried attention to the person who has difficulty speaking. Don't talk for the person, but give help when needed. Keep your manner encouraging rather than correcting. When necessary, ask questions that require short answers or a nod or shake of the head.
- Speak calmly, slowly, and distinctly to a person who has a hearing problem or other difficulty understanding. Stand in front of the person and use gestures to aid communication. When full understanding is doubtful, write notes.
- When dining with a person who has trouble cutting, offer to help if needed. (It may be easier to ask if the person would prefer to have the food cut in the kitchen.) Explain to a person who has a visual problem where dishes, utensils, and condiments are located on the table.
- Be alert to possible existence of architectural barriers in places you may want to enter with a person who has a disability; watch for inadequate lighting, which inhibits communication by persons who have hearing problems.

Source: From pamphlet entitled *Points to Remember.* Reprinted by permission of the National Easter Seal Society, Chicago, IL.

which teaching methods and materials to select. Therefore, the "test" for a diagnostic teaching program is to try it with the child to see if it works.

Because the objective is stated in terms of observable behavior, the teacher can easily determine if the child's performance matches the per-

formances specified in the objective; in other words, *criterion-referenced assessment* should be used.

If the child has reached the stated objective, the teacher specifies the next objective and goes through the sequence again. This means that a new strategy and new materials will be selected to reach a new objective. If the child does not reach the specified objective, the teacher must analyze the program, asking questions at each step of the model. After this thorough examination, if the child fails to reach the specified goal a second time, the teacher should seek help from a resource teacher, guidance counselor, supervisor, or specialist in the field to determine why the program has failed.

THE MANY FACES OF INSTRUCTION

The rest of this chapter is devoted to an overview of some of the approaches and instructional strategies that can be used with children who are handicapped. No one approach is guaranteed to work with all children or even with all children with a particular handicap. You should choose approaches that are compatible with your own beliefs. We do believe, however, that a systematic approach is best and that the best teacher is one who plans carefully, keeps precise records of a child's progress, and is highly sensitive to each child's needs and capabilities.

Clearly, fewer teaching strategies can be used with children who are profoundly retarded than with children of average intelligence. The less serious the handicap, either mental or physical, the more diverse and numerous the strategies that can be used. In general, we would recommend that no strategy be *automatically* excluded from use with any groups of children with handicaps.

Remedial and Compensatory Education

You may have come across the terms *remedial education* and *compensatory education*. For purposes of this chapter, we will distinguish between the two. Technically, **remedial education** refers to the process of improving or correcting skill in a particular area or field. For example, remedial reading might be defined as increasing reading comprehension and speed by giving the student specific instruction in improved reading techniques and in eliminating poor reading techniques or habits. *Remedial* implies cure or restoration, the raising of a person's skills to a normal or near-normal level.

Compensatory education is based on a different premise: Because some outside force may prevent a person from acquiring normal or near-normal skills in some area, the person must be given skills in another area as compensation. *Compensatory* refers to counterbalancing, substituting for, or offsetting one skill with another. An example of compensation from biology is the counterbalancing of a weak organ or function by the extra or excessive development of another structure or organ.

Special education uses both remedial and compensatory strategies to help youngsters with handicaps adapt to the demands of society. Both techniques may be used for a single type of handicap. In fact, teaching techniques are not easily sorted into two piles: remedial and compensatory. Age of child and purpose of instruction will define a technique as remedial or compensatory.

Obviously, some compensatory techniques are required for children who are blind. Total blindness prevents a child from learning to read in the conventional fashion, so an intensive remedial reading program would be useless. Instead, the child needs other communication techniques to compensate for the inability to read conventional print: braille, perhaps, or a "reading machine" such as the Optacon or Kurzweil.

Similarly, captioned films and television programs, manual language techniques, and teletype telephones are not remedies for a person who is deaf; rather, they are techniques used to compensate for the lack of ability to hear and understand conventional speech sounds.

A great many compensatory techniques have been developed to help people with physical handicaps. Wheelchairs and crutches are obvious examples, but there are many other **assistive devices** ranging from quite simple gadgets designed to assist in dressing and toileting to elaborate

The Kurzweil reading machine, a compensatory reading device for children and adults who are blind. (Courtesy of Martha Stewart-Kurzweil Computer Products.)

computer-based devices that can accept voice commands and execute many different complex operations.

With all handicaps, there should be a balance between remedial and compensatory techniques. Eventually, though, as youngsters reach the secondary-age level, attention should be placed on the fullest development of functional skills that will be most useful in adulthood. At this point, efforts must be made to help youngsters compensate for weaknesses that have been resistant to change through remedial techniques. This approach is especially appropriate for those youngsters with a mild handicap (e.g., the learning disabled) who are likely to become self-supporting citizens if they can compensate for certain weak areas (e.g., reading).

Direct Instruction

According to N. G. Haring and N. D. Gentry (1976), **direct instruction** is "the direct measurement of a pupil's performance on a learning task

and the accompanying arrangement of instructional programs and procedures for each child" (p. 109). The key components are systematic assessment, instruction, and evaluation. The system is designed to individualize instruction for each child while keeping in mind the many demands placed on a teacher's time. The following steps are included in direct instruction:

1. assessing pupil performance

2. setting goals

3. systematic planning of instructional or management programs

4. selecting or preparing instructional materials

5. specifying instructional procedures

6. arranging motivational factors

7. evaluating student progress
   (Haring & Schiefelbusch, 1976)

Note the high correlation of these steps with the Diagnostic Teaching Model developed by G. P.

The direct-instruction approach to teaching depends on careful analysis of the task to be learned. (Photo by Joseph Bodkin.)

Cartwright and C. A. Cartwright (1972b) and presented in detail earlier in this chapter. As is the case with our model, most of the steps in the direct-instruction model focus on planning instruction (setting the stage) and collecting relevant information about the child (or children). The actual implementation of the instruction—interaction with the child or small group—is critical, of course, but the implementation will be successful only if there has been proper planning.

P. J. Schloss and R. A. Sedlak (1986) describe in detail the procedures involved at each step. The first step in the planning is an assessment, conducted by the multidisciplinary team, which should provide the educator with information on the instructional strategies to be used with each student. Educators may collect additional information through informal tests. Having established learner needs, goals must be set in clear, well-defined terms, appropriately sequenced and adequately matched to student behavioral and learning characteristics. Careful planning of the instructional and management program is essential for effective teaching practice. Programs must

be planned to the last detail, but at the same time, they must be flexible enough to accommodate changes in a variable classroom environment. The educator must have several alternatives available in case the preplanned instruction cannot be implemented.

Appropriate materials aid instruction and must also be chosen with care. Some factors that influence this choice include the age and ability of the student, the motivational quality associated with the material, the applicability of materials to the learning principles and student evaluation, and the flexibility, durability, and attractiveness of the materials.

The next step is to determine and then apply instructional procedures. This includes presenting information to students in a logical and sequential manner. While presenting new material, it is important to establish student attention, to provide numerous explanations, to ensure that the nature of the presentation is consistent with expected performance, and to ask frequent questions to judge student comprehension. After this phase of instruction, students practice skills under the guidance of the instructor, who provides prompts. These prompts gradually become less intrusive and less frequent as the learner exhibits competency and, finally, works independently. Establishing a system of reinforcements is necessary to promote the occurrence of skill objectives and should be matched to student characteristics.

The final step requires evaluation of student performance to determine progress toward stated criteria. Through evaluation, specific problems can be pinpointed and modification directed at remediating the error that may be obstructing learning at any step of the program.

In essence, the direct-instruction approach advocates selecting precise, measurable objectives for each child and setting up instructional environments and procedures in such a way that both the child and the teacher know exactly what is to be learned and what criteria will be used to judge the learning. Advocates of the direct instruction approach have developed numerous approaches and techniques; the following is a sample of some of them:

Children engaged in independent activity, after having received instruction and guided practice. (Courtesy of Department of Health and Human Services.)

1. Work with small groups of children.

2. Pitch the lesson to challenge the lowest-functioning child.

3. Place the lowest-functioning child in the *center* of a small group of children.

4. Give immediate feedback to children's responses.

5. Use short, simple demonstrations.

6. Present one unambiguous concept at a time.

7. Give adequate practice so that a newly acquired skill is *overlearned*.

8. Use graphs, charts, and the like so the child can see daily or weekly progress.

(Ward et al., 1973; Engelmann, 1969; Becker, Engelmann, & Thomas, 1971; Haring & Schiefelbusch, 1976; Stephens, 1970)

You may also encounter the concept of *structured instruction*—"carefully organized manipulation of environmental events designed to bring about prespecified changes in learners' perform-

ance in skill areas of functional importance" (Lloyd & Carnine, 1981, p. viii). You should regard the concepts of direct instruction and structured instruction as essentially equivalent.

Task Analysis

Closely related to direct instruction and the Diagnostic Teaching Model is **task analysis**. In fact, task analysis is essential to the direct-instruction approach. You may run across references to this term or to the *task analytic approach,* so we are including this brief overview as added information.

Task analysis involves breaking down learning tasks into their component parts so that the skills involved in performing the task can be identified. **Prerequisite skills** (skills the child must have before another behavior can be performed successfully) must be identified.

Central to task analysis is the idea that learning is cumulative—skills build upon one another. Thus, learning tasks are analyzed into particular behaviors so that the learning hierarchy can be applied to the classroom situation. Once an appropriate behavioral objective for the student has been defined, it must be determined whether the child possesses the prerequisite skills necessary to achieve the objective. Task analysis is used to determine the skills necessary to ensure the proper sequencing of instruction and the diagnosis of special needs.

Sequencing Instruction

Writing objectives correctly is an important step in task analysis because precise objectives are necessary for precise sequencing of instruction. A well-written objective for a task contains a condition, a criterion, and a terminal behavior. In breaking down a task into its component parts, it is important to remember that no essential step can be omitted.

Enroute (or enabling) **behaviors** are the prerequisite skills necessary for the successful completion of a **terminal behavior**. The identification of enroute behaviors is accomplished by working backward from the terminal behavior, asking: What skills must the child have in order to perform this task?

$$\begin{matrix} \text{task} \\ \text{analysis} \end{matrix} = \begin{matrix} \underline{\text{analyze}} \\ \text{terminal} \\ \text{behavior} \end{matrix} \text{ to } \begin{matrix} \underline{\text{identify}} \\ \text{enroute} \\ \text{behaviors} \end{matrix} \text{ to } \begin{matrix} \text{terminal} \\ \text{behavior} \end{matrix}$$

In this way, a hierarchy of skills is built. The implication of the task analysis for instructional sequencing is obvious. If a child can perform none of the enroute behaviors in the hierarchy, he or she should be taught the easiest behaviors first. Instruction must begin at the child's level in the skill hierarchy.

Determining whether the learner is ready to learn a new task or to begin the next level of instruction is an important aspect of sequencing instruction. Task analysis has a very practical way of defining *readiness*: When a child has mastered the prerequisite skills, then she or he is *ready* to learn a particular task (perform the terminal behavior).

Once a set of enroute behaviors has been established for a particular terminal objective, it can be determined what enroute behaviors a child already can perform. These are called *entry behaviors*. Readiness is determined by the entry behaviors a child has for a particular task. The major concepts of task analysis are listed here; the list serves as a convenient summary of the steps involved in carrying out a task analysis.

1. Task analysis involves breaking down learning tasks into their component parts so that skills involved in performing the task can be identified.

2. Precise objectives are necessary for precise sequencing of instruction.

3. Enroute or enabling behaviors are the prerequisite skills necessary for the successful completion of a terminal behavior.

4. Entry behaviors are enroute behaviors a child can already perform.

5. When a child can perform all the enroute behaviors, he or she is ready to learn the terminal behavior.

Perceptual-Motor Training

The Diagnostic Teaching Model, direct instruction, and task analysis are major instructional approaches that can be applied to children with a wide variety of problems. These approaches assume that changes in the learning environment must be made to enhance or to capitalize upon a child's strengths. Rather than trying to make changes in the child, educators should adapt the environment.

However, some education professionals, especially in the area of learning disability, believe that changes in the environment are necessary but not sufficient for learning to occur in some children. They believe that basic changes in a child's abilities or processes must occur as well. Consequently, they address themselves to techniques that deal with underlying processes rather than academic products. Such is the case with **perceptual-motor training**.

Perceptual-motor and eye-hand coordination problems are often linked to the reading and writing problems of both children who are mildly retarded and children who are learning disabled. One popular approach to teaching children with mild handicaps has been to concentrate on their perceptual problems: gross motor skills, fine motor skills, form perception, memory sequencing, visual and auditory discrimination, and the like. The reasoning is that problems in these areas, especially in discrimination and sequencing, prevent the acquisition of higher-level skills, such as reading. To teach reading, you first must correct or remediate the underlying perceptual or perceptual-motor problems.

Perceptual-motor training is quite controversial; there are radically divergent opinions on the utility of the approach. For example, two noted authorities in the field of learning disability have this to say about perceptual-motor training: "Personally, we very rarely recommend the use of

Practice in eye-hand coordination tasks is an important element in perceptual-motor training. (Photo by Joseph Bodkin.)

perceptual training; and when we do, it is never for the purpose of improving children's academic skills or of making them more educable for academic work" (Hammill & Bartel, 1978, p. 341). On the other hand, Marianne Frostig, who has devoted much of her life to the development of methods of testing and teaching children with visual perception problems, claims that perceptual training alleviates not only perceptual problems and their academic correlates but behavioral deficits as well, especially lack of attention (Frostig, 1976; see also Sedlak & Weener, 1973; Arter & Jenkins, 1979). In any case, perceptual-motor training of one kind or another is widely used with children who are mildly handicapped, especially those labeled as learning disabled, and you should know about the general approach.

The theory behind perceptual-motor training states that satisfactory auditory and visual perception skills are essential for successful acquisition of academic skills, especially reading and writing. As D. D. Hammill and N. R. Bartel (1978) point out, some first-grade children are classified as having perceptual-motor problems on the basis of

certain screening tests. These children receive special perceptual training exercises to the exclusion of more conventional academic work until they have shown a certain amount of improvement in the perceptual exercises. Then they are introduced to more formal academic work. Unfortunately, the authors point out,

> The tests of perception do not seem to relate to measures of academic ability to any meaningful degree; and the use of the [perceptual training] activities with children has not been demonstrated to produce either better school performance or perceptual-motor growth itself. On the contrary a considerable and contrary body of research is steadily accumulating that strongly suggests that this approach has little or possibly no educational value.
> (Hammill & Bartel, 1978, p. 342)

According to D. A. Sabatino (1972), there are four common types of perceptual problems that may affect children:

1. **Visual discrimination**—ability to distinguish sizes, shapes, etc., of symbols and letters

2. **Auditory discrimination**—ability to differentiate among sounds (e.g., beginning or ending consonants of common words)

3. **Visual memory**—ability to retain or recall visual symbols, shapes, letters, etc.

4. **Auditory memory**—ability to retain or recall sounds and combinations of sounds

Numerous tests and exercises are available to help children with these problems. Some of these training activities concentrate on eye movement and focusing and on eye-hand coordination: tracing, copying designs, map making, bead patterning, dot-to-dot or follow-the-numbers exercises, jigsaw puzzles, and so on. Activities designed to help with auditory problems include rhythm exercises, rhyming word games, vocal imitations, sound localization and identification, and so on. Most textbooks dealing with methods of teaching children with learning disabilities provide detailed activities covering all the various perceptual problems (see, for example, Hammill & Bartel, 1978; Van Witsen, 1979; Wallace & McLoughlin, 1979).

Other Strategies

There are probably as many different techniques of teaching as there are talented teachers. Some of the more popular strategies are discussed briefly here.

Modeling. In its basic form, **modeling** is simply asking a child to imitate or model what you or someone else demonstrates. It is especially good for youngsters who have difficulty understanding verbal instructions or who have trouble remembering a series of verbal instructions. Although modeling can be used in relatively few academic situations, it can be a very effective technique in the affective and motor domains.

Inquiry. Inquiry is instruction by asking a series of specific and leading questions. Children are led to an understanding of concepts through careful questioning procedures. The learning comes through the application of the youngsters' own words and statements as they are gradually expanded to include a new concept.

Peer Tutoring. Peer tutoring, or instruction of one child by another, is helpful to both the tutor and the tutee. Both can acquire additional cognitive or academic skills as well as cooperative skills. Of course, you must structure the situation quite carefully: The tutor must be trained, special materials prepared, and an appropriate location for the tutoring session secured.

Art, Dance, and Music Therapy. These therapies involve the use of artistic exercises in the visual or performing arts to help children achieve personal, social, or academic growth. Specialists in each of these areas work closely with teachers to coordinate academic or other classroom objectives with activities developed by the therapists.

This adult who is handicapped is following the model established by her instructor. (Courtesy of Association for Retarded Citizens.)

Therapists work with groups or with individual children in a variety of settings. Activities are modified according to the disabilities and needs of the children.

Horticulture Therapy. Horticulture therapy and education is a program in which youngsters with disabilities are taught to care for living plants. Children who are mildly, moderately, or severely handicapped with a range of disabilities can be helped through their own work with flowers, plants, and shrubs. Advocates of this program point out that some of the basic needs in life are made clear and that youngsters with disabilities learn responsibility and independence through caring for their own plants.

Equine Therapy. Development of self-confidence and ability to manipulate one's environment are the goals of horseback riding for the handicapped.

Media-Based Instruction. Media-based materials—films, tapes, videocassettes, and the like—

A fourth-grade girl acts as a tutor for this six-year-old girl. (Photo by Dick Brown. Courtesy of *Centre Daily Times*.)

This child listens to a set of taped instructions and carries out a variety of activities. (Photo by Joseph Bodkin.)

can be used by individual children or with small and large groups of children. The educational film has continued to be improved, and it is now possible to get short, single-concept films as well as more comprehensive presentations. Children can use film cartridges or videotapes to view short films when and as often as they wish. Teacher-made worksheets in conjunction with teacher-prepared cassette tapes can be directed precisely to the needs of a single child or a small group of children in a class. Your imagination is the only limiting factor in teacher-made media-based instruction.

Educational Games. Having fun while learning is the drawing power of educational games. Years ago, a Friday afternoon pastime or a rainy-day lunch routine was playing "hangman" on the blackboard. Spelling bees predated the McGuffey readers. Today, there are literally dozens of educational publishing companies producing hundreds of games that are related in some fashion to the acquisition of specific skills or concepts. Educational games range from relatively simple and

inexpensive playing-card-based word and number games (like Lotto) or letter-matching games to electronic games and microcomputers. The attraction of games is enhanced when you consider that many of them require cooperative efforts by the participants. Games can be structured so that affective objectives such as cooperation and general improvement of social skills can be met.

Programmed Instruction. This form of instruction burst onto the education scene in the late 1950s and early 1960s with promises of rapid and permanent changes in schooling practices for all youngsters. These sweeping changes did not occur, however, and interest in the technique waned. Nevertheless, the basic principles upon which **programmed instruction** were built remain sound: careful analysis of the task(s) to be learned; small, incremental steps to lead the learner from little or no knowledge to mastery; self-pacing and perhaps self-monitoring by the learner; and revision of the material based on analysis of trials by many learners. Of all the handicapped groups, deaf children have received the most programmed instruc-

Identification of constellations has been made into an exciting game by the creative teacher of these fourth-grade students who are gifted. (Photo by Joseph Bodkin.)

tion. Let us hope that the best of programmed materials (e.g., the Sullivan reading series) remain, and the rest are forgotten.

Computer-Assisted and Computer-Managed Instruction. A logical successor to programmed instruction, computer-assisted and computer-managed instruction is rapidly assuming a place in education. Much developmental and remedial instruction will be carried on with the assistance of computers before the end of the century.

Computer-assisted instruction (CAI), as discussed throughout the text, refers to the use of computers to provide direct instruction to learners. Typically, specific instructional programs are stored within the computer's memory. A learner sits at a computer terminal, often a televisionlike device with an attached keyboard. The computer displays information to the learner and asks questions. The learner responds by pressing keys or pointing to an answer on the video display screen. The computer evaluates the learner's response and congratulates the learner on the correctness of the response, gives the learner additional infor-

mation, branches the learner to another section of the program, or responds in some variation of the above alternatives. Under the control of the computer program may be graphic and color displays, slides, audio tapes, films, videotapes, and the like. Learners are guided through the programs by the computer. Computer-assisted instruction has taken on many forms; however, it consists primarily of electronic delivery of instruction through drill and practice, tutorials, games, or simulations.

- Drill and practice implies repetition of factual knowledge. This form of CAI helps the learner maintain or overlearn skills or facts already acquired. Math facts and spelling words are two areas of heavy use of the computer, but other specific academic areas such as reading to improve word-decoding skills have been successfully developed for CAI (Spring & Perry, 1981). The computer can continually generate mathematics problems and check responses for students who need additional practice. This teacher time-saver eliminates hours of ditto preparation and correction.

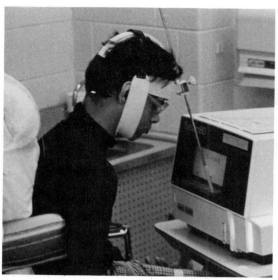

This young man is using a head-stick to answer questions posed by the programmed audio-visual device. (Photo by Patricia Seibel.)

The use of computer-based instruction devices, such as this microcomputer, continues to increase in both elementary and secondary schools at a rapid rate. (Photo by Eileen Young. Courtesy of the Ohio Department of Education, Division of Special Education, Martin W. Essex School for the Gifted; and the Department of Human Services Education, The Ohio State University.)

▪ Tutorials teach new academic content and may contain a drill and practice aspect. The tutorial mode of CAI is designed to help a learner acquire new facts or skills. Tutorials utilize the patience of the computer to teach, reteach, and teach again. A tutorial may vary from student to student because the computer analyzes student responses and alters the tutorial accordingly. Branching and reinforcement strategies provide an individualized program for each learner. Research indicates that computers have been used to teach spelling, writing, reading, math, language arts, and social and vocational skills to a variety of students with handicaps (Howe, 1981; Halworth & Brebner, 1981; Spring & Perry, 1981; Watkins & Webb, 1981).

▪ Games imply arcade-type activities with an instructional intent and outcome. They can be used to develop both motor and social skills. Arcade activities are highly motivating; students strive to complete other activities to be allowed to play the games and then work hard

to improve their scores. Critics note the depersonalization of computer games but forget that it is one area where handicapped students can interact with nonhandicapped peers both in the classroom and through phone lines (Apple Computer, Inc., 1980).

▪ Simulations present situational experiences that provide learning environments previously inaccessible to handicapped students. Sometimes, simulations are content specific, enabling a student to participate in chemistry, physics, or biology laboratory experiments without requiring manipulation of equipment. Other simulations have a problem-solving format, requiring knowledge of environmental conditions unfamiliar to the students. In either situation, simulations provide experiences associated with higher-level cognitive skills (Bennett, 1982).

Computer-managed instruction (CMI) is a much broader concept than CAI. In theory at least, CMI is a system of instruction whereby a broad instructional plan for a learner or group of learners is implemented with a great deal of assistance from a computer. The computer serves as a record keeper and directs students to a variety of possible learning experiences designed to help them reach the next scheduled or planned objective. For example, a student could be directed to review a certain single-concept film, or read pages 68–102 in Textbook A, or complete assignment sheet 13C. In CMI, instruction may or may not be offered directly by the computer.

Teachers may also find computers helpful as management tools. Computers can play a significant role in activities such as planning an IEP, managing school resources, and coordinating increasing costs and program needs. Computers enable better planning and more accurate reporting, and represent an efficient management tool. Specifically, they can assist teachers in the following ways:

1. generate IEPs

2. generate report cards

3. generate quarterly student reports

4. score tests

5. record and analyze behavior observations

6. recommend appropriate activities for students

7. describe diagnostic materials

8. report on student due process status

9. remind when notices are due

10. report student achievement and evaluation status

11. store information on health history

12. store information on community resources

Computers can also be useful to administrators in the following ways:

1. reimbursement computation according to state and federal formulas

2. counts of students screened, assessed, placed, and reviewed

3. generation of standardized reports

4. reports of compliance with P.L. 94–142

5. child counts cross-referenced by class, teacher, school, and handicap

6. records of testing and reports

7. personalized mailings to parents and service providers

8. lists of incomplete information on student records

9. audit trails for program placement and review

Software Selection. In utilization of the computer for effective CAI, the hardware is not as critical as the selection of well-designed software. Software (often called courseware) should be purchased only after a complete evaluation process similar to the following:

1. critique of the sequential text

2. analysis of size of steps between presentations of new concepts

3. assessment of reading levels

4. determination of adequacy of reinforcements

5. analysis of amount of required student response

6. determination of value of accompanying teacher documentation

7. analysis of consistency with goals and objectives of program

8. determination of personalized element in interaction

9. assessment of adequate use of redundancy and drill

10. analysis of organization and implementation of program materials
(Grimes, 1980; Hannaford & Sloane, 1981)

Unless the courseware is adequate for the individual student's needs, computer time is ineffective.

Courseware can be teacher prepared or commercially prepared. Some software is designed specifically for the special-needs student. One program with proven effectiveness is the ILIAD system for deaf students, which enables the child to specify the lesson content, after which the computer designs the precise individualized lesson (Bates & Wilson, 1981). Many teachers have chosen to develop their own software because commercially prepared programs that require substantial typing are often inappropriate for physically handicapped students, and the content or reading level is frequently not congruent with the student in need of the material. As a result of this, regional centers have been established to help teachers with software development (Chiang, 1978; Arcanin & Zawolkow, 1980). Lessons developed by these centers are categorized and stored in library fashion for other teachers' access.

Word Processing. Teacher acceptance of mainstreamed handicapped students has increased as a result of student use of *word processing*. This computer function enables a student to submit legible work by typing homework, term papers or projects, and tests with easy alteration through editing. English teachers are discovering that composition from nonhandicapped pupils using word processors improves because chunks of text can be repositioned, making it easier for students to rewrite assignments. Because of this, handicapped students are being more creative and finding writing exciting, an improvement over past devastation and frustration (Beckerman, 1983). If a student is both physically handicapped and nonverbal, word processing might be his or her sole communication source. Note-taking is an impossible task for an individual unable to grasp a pencil or whose muscles become exhausted. Classes can be taped and then transcribed with the aid of a word processor to help the student recall the material covered. Use of word processing facilitates placement in the least restrictive environment without interrupting daily activities.

Numerous commercial software packages are available for word processing. It is advisable to select a program that does not require multiple-key input to activate commands but has adequate file storage or is similar to a student's home system.

SUMMARY

Children with handicaps receive their education in a variety of settings and with a variety of techniques. Considering that some children who are handicapped are extremely bright and college-bound, whereas others are so profoundly retarded that they have virtually no communication or motor skills, it is not surprising that no single teaching setting, strategy, or technique can be used with all. The more serious the handicap, the fewer are the teaching strategies that can be used. In fact, level of severity is nearly as important as type of handicap in planning instructional strategies.

It is necessary for teachers to help many youngsters manage their behavior so they can respond appropriately in learning situations. Planning behavior-management programs has much in common with planning instructional programs. The Diagnostic Teaching Model identifies those commonalities and assists teachers in making critical decisions in the planning and implementing of instructional and behavior-management programs. The following are key components in the Diagnostic Teaching Model: identify relevant attributes, specify objectives, select strategy and materials, test, and evaluate performance. In general, the direct instruction/task analysis approach is favored by the Diagnostic Teaching Model, although objectives in all domains can be addressed.

Remedial education refers to the process of improving or correcting skill in a particular area. Compensatory education refers to substituting or counterbalancing a weak skill or area with a stronger skill or area. For example, people who are blind are taught braille to compensate for their inability to read conventional print.

Included in this chapter are brief discussions

of generic teaching strategies that are widely used with children who are handicapped: direct instruction, task analysis, perceptual training, modeling, inquiry, peer tutoring, media-based instruction, educational games, programmed instruction, and computer-based instruction.

Suggestions for Further Reading

Alberto, P. A., & Troutman, A. C. (1986). *Applied behavior analysis for teachers.* Columbus, OH: Merrill.

This book provides information on behavior management in a systematic, organized manner. The authors explain the concept and principles governing applied behavior analysis in a way that teachers find easy to implement in the classroom. Each component of planning, implementing, and evaluating a program has been clearly described.

Cartwright, C. A., Cartwright, G. P., Ward, M. E., & Willoughy-Herb, S. (1981). *Activities, guidelines, and resources for teachers of special learners.* Belmont, CA: Wadsworth.

A collection of individual and group activities, lists of print and nonprint resources, and suggestions related to generic teaching skills are covered in this easy-to-use reference book.

Lloyd, J., & Carnine, D. W. (Eds.) (1983). Structured instruction: Effective teaching of essential skills. *Exceptional Education Quarterly, 2*(1).

This special issue includes seven articles that cover the teaching of reading, arithmetic, and communication as well as vocational and community living skills.

Schloss, P. J., & Sedlak, R. A. (1986). *Instructional methods for students with learning and behavior problems.* Boston: Allyn and Bacon.

This book addresses the nature of differential curricula and instructional strategies. Through their concern for individual assessment, instructional goals and objectives, and data-based educational procedures, the authors deal directly with hands-on problems of the special education teacher. Teachers will appreciate the translation of theory to classroom plans and activities.

Thiagarajan, S. (1979). Designing instructional games for handicapped learners. In E. Meyen, G. A. Vergason, & R. J. Whelan (Eds.), *Instructional planning for exceptional children.* Denver: Love Publishing.

This article for the classroom teacher explains how to design, produce, evaluate, modify, and adapt instructional games for the classroom.

Thomas, C. H., & Thomas, J. L. (1980). *Meeting the needs of the handicapped: A resource for teachers and librarians.* Phoenix: Oryx Press.

This resource contains articles that address the problems of handicapped students, and offers suggestions for solving those problems. Also included is information about selection of instructional materials, producers of materials, and organizations and publications related to the handicapped.

Turnbull, A., & Schutz, J. B. (1979). *Mainstreaming handicapped students: A guide for the classroom teacher.* Boston: Allyn and Bacon.

This book is not so much a guide to mainstreaming as an effective guide to individualization of instruction for children who are mildly handicapped. It covers the IEP process; teaching reading, arithmetic, social studies, science, art, and music; behavioral change; and integration of children with handicaps into regular classes.

Van Witsen, B. (1979). *Perceptual training activities handbook* (2nd ed.). New York: Teachers College Press.

Over 250 ideas, activities, games, and exercises are provided in this handy paperback publication designed for teachers as an aid in planning programs to help children develop sensory skills. The book is squarely in the perceptual training camp but will be useful to teachers of most preschool and elementary-age youngsters who are mildly handicapped.

CHAPTER 17

Coordination of Services

Did You Know That . . .

- "helping" professionals do not always help?

- many families with children who are handicapped have been "referred around" from one agency to another, with the end result that parents end up coordinating the package of services their child needs?

- classroom teachers are often the first to spot mildly handicapping conditions when the child begins to experience problems in school?

- parents and children have a legal right to privacy?

- regardless of the mandates of P.L. 94–142, it is people who make the decisions—their values and attitudes toward the concepts embedded in the law will make it or break it?

- a student can attend the multidisciplinary team meeting?

- a due process hearing can be emotionally draining and requires extensive preparation?

- computers can be used as efficient management tools?

I n response to a questionnaire sent to the parents of children who are handicapped, one parent wrote:

> The doctors have to be reeducated to *care*. We found in too many instances we were given a diagnosis and no recommendations, no help. The doctors did not know what was available and made no attempt to help. Once a diagnosis was made, we were left on our own to find help. When we'd ask for help, we'd be told, "Nothing can be done and there is no help." This happened with two different pediatricians and two different neurologists. We found our help from other parents and our own pocket. These "professionals" tested, prodded, and billed us, but did not help us. (Gorham et al., 1976, p. 158)

Unfortunately, the experience of these parents is far too typical. Time and time again, K. A. Gorham and colleagues point to situations in which parents are dealing with a "'helping' professional who does not help" (p. 157). We, the authors, and you, our readers, are members of "helping" professions. The indictment embodied in the parent's comment is not easy to admit to.

When a child's problem is serious, it is often discovered at an early age; the person who becomes the bearer of the bad news and recommends referral to a specialist is usually the family doctor. Many doctors, however, are ill equipped to coordinate information from several specialists and manage treatment packages that may involve an array of services in addition to medical care. The tendency is for the child and the family to be referred from one specialist or agency to another, with the parents left with the responsibility for coordinating the information and deciding where to go or what to do next.

Less serious or less obvious problems may not be uncovered before the child enters school. In this case, the regular classroom teacher may be the first person to suggest to parents that something is wrong or different about their child. The regular classroom teacher also may have trouble

A young child's regular classroom teacher may be the first person to suspect that the child has a learning problem. (Photo by Joseph Bodkin.)

dealing with specialists. Even though teachers are often most knowledgeable about the child's behavior in normal, everyday school situations, they are sometimes excluded from the diagnostic process. Changes are occurring as a result of P.L. 94–142, but the problems are far from fully resolved.

The major purpose of this chapter is to present information about referral and the problems involved in follow-through and in coordination of services. In this way, you will complete the book with a comprehensive understanding of the processes of identification, intensive diagnosis, and coordination of services, including educational programming. Prospects for solving many of the problems involved in referral and planning for intervention have improved since passage of P.L. 94–142. Thus, we encourage you to embrace an attitude that says:

I DO have responsibility for these children.

and

I CAN make a difference.

REFERRAL PROCEDURES

One of the decisions presented in the Identification Model in Chapter 15 indicated that, for some children, there would come a time when the teacher would have to determine whether a referral for more intensive, specialized assessment would be in order (see Figure 15.1). How does a teacher decide if a referral is needed? And how is the referral handled?

Criteria for Referral

There is no checklist of standard criteria indicating whether a referral is needed. It would be nearly impossible to construct such a checklist because of the highly individualized nature of the assessment process for each child. However, some guiding principles can help teachers make decisions (see Figure 17.1). What is needed is to reach a balance between a situation of "diminishing returns" and the tendency to "pass the buck." What do we mean?

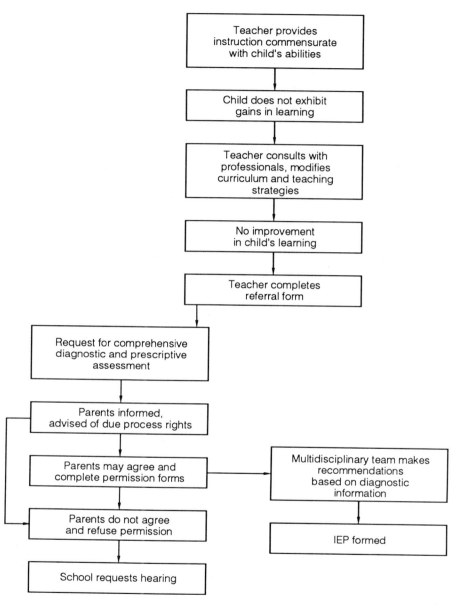

Figure 17.1. Referral procedure.

By "diminishing returns," we are referring to situations in which teachers have nearly exhausted their own professional resources—the child is not getting any better even though the teacher has collected a great deal of information and has tried a number of different strategies, none of which seems to be working. By not "passing the buck," we mean that the teacher's attempts to solve the problem should be genuine, and the teacher should feel satisfied that he or she is not simply trying to get rid of responsibility for the child by passing the case on to someone else.

Here we must insert a caution against painting every situation either black or white. There is probably no absolutely clear-cut decision or perfect time for referral. The decision to initiate referral usually happens gradually, on the basis of a number of informal consultations with other teachers, parents, and professionals. Furthermore, let us stress once again that referral itself does not necessarily confirm the existence of a particular condition. In fact, it may prove the opposite. What is important is for parents and teachers to find out for sure what the situation is.

At this point, let's return to the case of Linda, who was introduced at the beginning of the book. When you look at Figure 17.2, you will notice that a series of communications about Linda is implied in the note from Linda's teacher, Evelyn Crosby, to Janet Payne, the school nurse. According to the note, Evelyn is beginning to detect a pattern and needs advice from Janet about how to proceed.

Teacher Responsibilities

If it is decided that the child should be referred for more intensive diagnosis, teachers should follow whatever procedures have been set up in their school district to ensure procedural safeguards under P.L. 94–142.* It is the teacher's responsibility to summarize all information that has been gathered up to the time of referral. The information should be forwarded to the professional who will assume responsibility for the child's case. Completion of a set of referral forms provides a way of summarizing and organizing the data generated in the classroom. An example of a set of referral forms, the teacher referral statement, is included in this chapter. Many school districts have developed similar referral forms.

Several points about the teacher referral state-

ment are noteworthy. Usually, children with problems are described in terms of those problems; there is a tendency to concentrate on what the child is *unable* to do. The teacher referral statement, however, is constructed so that the teacher describes the child in terms of what he or she *is able* to do. The focus is on describing the conditions under which the child can perform.

Furthermore, in addition to providing a means of documenting the need for referral and of collating information about the child, the forms can be put to other uses. They serve as a check on the adequacy of information obtained about a child. In completing the forms, the teacher may find that information needed to answer questions, make a rating, and so on is lacking, and the teacher may have to continue to collect information about the child before completing the referral forms. In this way, a check on the adequacy of the information already obtained about a child and guidelines about what specific additional information is needed are provided. Referral forms also can be used as guidelines in planning and implementing a child's educational program. A teacher may reach the decision that the child does not need to be referred for intensive diagnosis. In this case, it is the teacher's responsibility to use the information gathered as a starting point for planning modifications in the child's educational program.

All school systems have some established procedures for referrals, and teachers should be knowledgeable about these procedures. Usually, as in Linda's case, some informal consultation occurs within the school. In some districts, special consultants may not be available in all schools but rather travel from school to school within the region. In such cases, the consultation may have to be more carefully scheduled.

The classroom teacher should work with resource people in the school to determine if resources within the classroom have been fully used and if any additional resources exist within the school building. If the teachers and resource consultants decide that additional information about the child is needed, a request for comprehensive diagnostic and prescriptive assessment would be

---

*Some of the information about P.L. 94–142 that was introduced in Part I is repeated here because it is particularly relevant to the referral process.

FROM THE DESK OF
EVELYN CROSBY

9/30

Janet,

Please stop by my room when you have a few minutes. I've been watching Linda more closely & am really convinced something *is* wrong. I think I'm beginning to see a pattern —

1. She volunteers to answer questions only when I'm facing her directly.

2. When I'm at the back of the room she watches what Susan beside her does before getting started.

3. This morning I purposely stood by the windows & spoke rather quietly about a schedule change. Linda continued reading, then noticed me & seemed to be straining to see? hear? understand? She started to get her jacket for recess when it was time to go to the auditorium for the

Figure 17.2. Note from Linda's teacher, Evelyn Crosby, to Janet Payne, the school nurse.

assembly — which I'd announced earlier.
She seemed surprised at the change when
she finally figured out what was
happening.

4. At recess during the usual game of Red
Rover, Linda didn't run when her
name was called. The other children on her
team started yelling + pushing her
and she finally started after several
of them gave her a shove.

    She doesn't seem confused or ask
me to repeat or watch what others
are doing ———— 1. when she comes to my desk
                2. when she's looking right
                   at me
                3. when she's working in a
                   small group
Help! What do you think?
Have you had a chance to test her
again? Is there anything I should
know from her health record? What
next? Her parents and I are really
concerned about her school problems.
                    Evelyn

made, usually to a district office such as pupil personnel services. In Linda's case, her teacher, Evelyn Crosby, has decided a referral is needed and has contacted the principal, Kurt Sampson (see Figure 17.3). He indicates that an official request would be required but suggests that the parents be telephoned immediately.

Some special educators and assessment specialists recommend that parents be invited to discuss the child's case informally before they receive written notification through the mail (Losen & Diament, 1978). A more effective partnership between school officials and parents may result if parents are not caught off guard by a request for special assessment. Because parents will also need to be involved in an eventual placement decision that is part of the IEP, any procedure that will foster trust and open communication between parents and school personnel is recommended. Guidelines for planning and conducting conferences with parents are provided in the next section.

Parent-Teacher Conferences

Planning the Conference. Parents can provide valuable information regarding their child's behavior, educational concerns, perceived strengths and weaknesses, and management practices. However, teachers often find planning and participating in parent conferences a source of great anxiety. Parents, too, may express reluctance and exhibit negative attitudes based on prior experiences with such conferences. They often think they accomplished very little or develop feelings of guilt from these conferences. A few measures can help remedy such a situation. For example, advance planning of conferences should ensure that conference objectives are met. Some steps that can be followed to facilitate such preparation include selecting a site, sending advance notice, giving a copy of the agenda to parents, studying the student's school file, making notes of pertinent information, understanding the purpose of the conference, listing information to be included, having work samples available, and listing positive aspects of student performance.

Conducting the Conference. Some suggestions have been made by B. J. Price and G. E. Marsh (1985) for conducting a parent-teacher conference:

1. When conducting the conference, select a site that has privacy, a comfortable temperature, and an informal seating arrangement so that communication is not inhibited.

2. Conduct the conference in a relaxed manner, and begin on a friendly note. Do not initiate conversation by discussing the problem. Rather, begin with an opening remark, introduce participants, and explain their roles and the purpose of the meeting.

3. Be straightforward while providing information about the child's program, progress, and evaluation and while explaining the purpose of the meeting. Use jargon-free, simple language, and be as specific and precise as possible.

4. Listen carefully to parents and communicate your interest in what they have to say. Provide several opportunities for input from parents and other participants.

5. Follow the format specified for the conference to avoid losing sight of the purpose of the conference.

6. End the conference with a summary of what has been disclosed and recommendations for follow-up activities.

Procedural Safeguards

Regardless of specific procedures within a school, the classroom teacher must be prepared to share whatever is known about the child, according to the requirements set forth in P.L. 94–142. Both teachers and parents have certain responsibilities in protecting the rights of children and parents. Essentially, parents have the right to expect that due process will be followed throughout the screening, assessment, and programming phases of their child's case. Parents must be kept continually and accurately informed about what is hap-

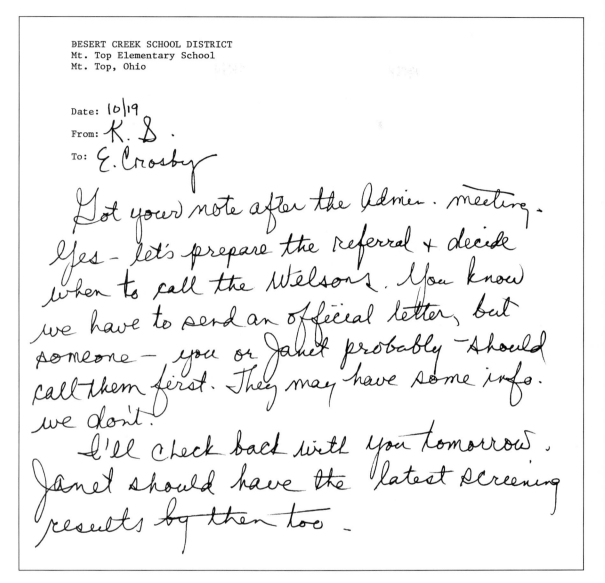

DESERT CREEK SCHOOL DISTRICT
Mt. Top Elementary School
Mt. Top, Ohio

Date: 10|19

From: K. S.

To: E. Crosby

Got your note after the Admin. meeting.
Yes — let's prepare the referral + decide
when to call the Wilsons. You know
we have to send an official letter, but
someone — you or Janet probably should
call them first. They may have some info.
we don't.

I'll check back with you tomorrow.
Janet should have the latest screening
results by then too —

Figure 17.3. Note from Kurt Sampson, the principal, to Evelyn Crosby.

pening to their child at each step in the process. As a final recourse, they have the right to an impartial hearing if they think these rights have been violated or if they disagree with the decisions made about their child.

Let's consider how concerns for these parental rights and responsibilities are translated into ac-

tion. The teacher has the right and the responsibility to continually evaluate the progress of all children in every domain. This routine evaluation does not require any special parental permission. However, once it is decided that there might be something different about the child and further assessment is suggested, parental permission

Parent-teacher conferences are an essential part of the planning process for establishing and maintaining programs for youngsters with disabilities. (Photo by G. P. Cartwright.)

must be obtained. Specific procedures vary somewhat from state to state, but in general, parents must be sent a notice (in their native language) that describes the tests and other assessment procedures that are proposed. The notice must also contain information about who will perform the assessment and how the results of the assessment will be used. A parental permission form should be included with the notice so that written permission is provided before the assessment begins. Figures 17.4–17.7 describe this process for Linda.

Evelyn Crosby and Janet Payne have worked together to fill out a referral form (see Figure 17.4) for Linda. After receiving the referral form, the director of special services organizes the assessment and completes the form notifying Linda's parents of the intent to conduct an evaluation. Finally, the principal sends a letter to Linda's parents (see Figure 17.5) and includes the Notice of Intent to Conduct an Evaluation (see Figure 17.6) and a Parental Permission Form (see Figure 17.7).

If parental permission is not secured, the school district may request a hearing to corrobo-

rate their opinion that a further evaluation is necessary for the future well-being of the child. Parents may also request a hearing on the matter if they do not agree that further assessment is needed. In most cases, informal conferences are planned in an attempt to resolve differences, concerns are worked out amicably, and no hearing is required. Note, however, that an overwhelming number of requests for hearings come from parents in disagreement with a school system proposal regarding identification, evaluation, or placement of their handicapped child. Hearings can often be emotionally draining for school personnel and parents. In addition, hearing requirements put considerable pressure on school personnel, who have to prepare to testify in support of the educational proposals they have made, organize relevant materials, and contact appropriate witnesses.

After Assessment

Once the evaluation has taken place, what happens to the results of this more specialized diagnosis? Who participates in further decisions

Teachers should provide information they have gathered about a child to the referral agency. (Photo by Joseph Bodkin.)

Federal and state laws require that parents be informed about planned changes in the school placement of their children and that they must give their permission for the school to evaluate their children. (Photo by G. P. Cartwright.)

about the child? Again, specific procedures vary from state to state. In compliance with P.L. 94–142, states have required school districts to set up special interdisciplinary teams or committees to make recommendations based on the diagnostic information. In New York State, for example, each school district is required by law to have a committee on the handicapped. The committee meets regularly to make recommendations to the board of education and to parents regarding children who need special education services. "The Committee must include the following people: a school psychologist, a teacher or administrator of special education, a physician, a parent of a handicapped child who lives in the district but is not employed by the district, and may also include other people appointed by the board of education" (State Education Department of New York, 1978, p. 3).

The composition and role of the New York State Committee on the Handicapped is in keeping with several provisions of P.L. 94–142: that a full and individualized evaluation of each handicapped child's educational needs must take place

before a child is placed in a special education program, that evaluation must include information about all areas pertinent to the suspected disability and must be made in a way that is not racially or culturally discriminatory, and that evaluation must be performed by a multidisciplinary team of professionals designated by the school district.

As noted earlier, each state sets up certain standards and procedures for the diagnostic process under the general guidelines of P.L. 94–142. The states, in turn, have chosen to make each school district responsible for

▪ ensuring that all tests and other assessment procedures are provided and administered in the native language of the child (unless there

REFERRAL FOR EVALUATION

ORIGINATOR: School personnel (including a teacher), a parent, a judicial officer, a social worker, a physician, a person having custody of the child, any other person including a school age child who may ask for a referral through any one of those listed above.

PURPOSE: To begin the evaluation process.

SEND TO: Special Education Administrator. Mr. Ken Tryan, Director
Special Services

Date: **10/21/79**

STUDENT

1. NAME: __Wilson__ __Linda__ __Jo__
               Last   First   Middle

2. ADDRESS: __356 Wagonwheel Way__
             Number   Street

   __Mt. Top__   __Ohio__   __01234__
      City   State   Zip Code

3. TELEPHONE: _____
          Area Code   Number

4. BIRTH DATE: __3__ / __17__ / __72__ 5. GRADE: __2__
        Month   Day   Year

6. CURRENT EDUCATIONAL PROGRAM:

   ☒ Regular   ☐ None   ☐ Special Needs   ☐ Other

PARENT

1. NAME: __Wilson__ __Robert and JoAnne__
             Last   First   Middle

2. ADDRESS: __356 Wagonwheel Way__
             Number   Street

   __Mt. Top__   __Ohio__   __01234__
      City   State   Zip Code

3. TELEPHONE: _____
          Area Code   Number

4. PRIMARY LANGUAGE OF THE HOME:

   ☒ English   ☐ Other   Specify _____

IS THIS AN INITIAL EVALUATION?   ☒ Yes   ☐ No

SPECIFIC REASONS FOR REFERRAL

Please indicate the specific reasons and/or situations which make you feel that an evaluation is needed.

1. *Classroom observations 9/20 – 10/20 Linda never once volunteered answers during*

Figure 17.4. Referral form for Linda.

reading or math class. When Mrs. Crosby
called her name + made certain she was
2. watching her before asking a question,
Linda responded correctly each time
she was called on. During work periods
she interrupted other children to ask for help.
3. Linda frequently comes up to Mrs. C's desk
to ask what she is supposed to do.
The other kids tease her about this +
she often gets upset.
4.
She does much better with written
rather than oral directions.

Hearing screening — failed.

ATTEMPTS TO RESOLVE

Please indicate all attempts to resolve each of the above listed reasons within the current
educational program. This should include what was done, for how long, and by whom.
Attempts to resolve should follow the sequence of reasons listed above.

1. Mrs. Crosby either stands by Linda's
desk or looks directly at her when
giving instructions. Although Mrs. C.
2. has discovered some strategies that
seem to work with Linda, she thinks
perhaps something more could be
3. done. We suspect a hearing problem
but think there might be more
to it. Mrs. C. has been checking with
4. Linda to be sure she knows what to
do so Linda won't need to bother
other children for help.

DESERT CREEK SCHOOL DISTRICT

Mt. Top Elementary School
Mt. Top, Ohio

October 21, 1979

Mr. and Mrs. Robert Wilson
356 Wagonwheel Way
Mt. Top, Ohio 01234

Dear Mr. and Mrs. Wilson:

Enclosed is the official request form we ask you to complete and return to us so we can begin the individual evaluation of your daughter, Linda. As Mrs. Crosby explained during her telephone conversation with you last week, she has noted a pattern over the last few weeks of what appeared to be inattentive behavior but what upon closer observation seems more like difficulty in hearing under certain circumstances. Mrs. Payne, our school nurse, obtained results during her hearing screening last week that indicate further hearing evaluation is advisable.

We will keep you informed and will arrange a meeting with you to discuss the evaluation results. We understand that you wish to have Linda examined at the Bell Hospital Audiology Clinic rather than at Cavern County Clinic. Please ask the Clinic to send a copy of their report to Mrs. Janet Payne at Einstein Middle School, 35 Cirque Blvd., in Mt. Top as soon as possible.

If you have any questions, please feel free to call me. We want to do our best to assure that Linda has an educational program that is appropriate for her.

Sincerely yours,

Kurt Sampson, Principal
Mt. Top Elementary School

cc: E. Crosby
H. Paulson
K. Tryan

Enclosures

Figure 17.5. Letter from school principal to Linda's parents.

NOTICE OF INTENT TO CONDUCT AN EVALUATION

ORIGINATOR Mr. Ken Tryan, Director, Special Services

PURPOSE: To inform parents that a referral for an evaluation has been made and to inform parents of their rights.

Date 10/21/79

Dear Parent:

_____ Evelyn Crosby, Linda's teacher _____,

recently filed a form requesting that your child Linda _____, be evaluated by this office. A copy of the request as filed is enclosed for your review.

The evaluation procedures and their associated instruments that will be used in each of the following areas are:

Intelligence: WISC-R

Achievement: PIAT and KeyMath Diagnostic Arithmetic Test and Woodcock Reading Mastery Test

Behavior:

Physical: Parents prefer to arrange for audiological testing.

Other: Auditory Discrimination Test.

The findings of the evaluation will be used by the following people to develop a set of program recommendations for your child.

Name	Title
Helena L. Paulson	Supervisor, Program for H.I.
Evelyn Crosby	Classroom Teacher, Grade 2
Arlene G. Bell	Teacher of Hearing Impaired

It is very important that you be aware of and understand that you have the following rights:

1. To review all records related to the referral for evaluation.
2. To review the procedures and instruments to be used in the evaluation.
3. To refuse to permit the evaluation (in which case the local education agency can request a hearing to try to overrule you).
4. To be fully informed of the results of the evaluation.
5. To get an outside evaluation for your child from a public agency, at public expense if necessary.

Your child's educational status will not be changed without your knowledge and written approval.

Enclosed is a Parent Permission Form which must be completed by you and returned to this office within 10 school days.

Should you have any questions please do not hesitate to call me.

Yours truly,

Name Ken Tryan

Title Director, Special Services

Telephone Number 999-0001

Enclosures:

Figure 17.6. Notice of Intent to Conduct an Evaluation.

PARENTAL PERMISSION FORM

Name of Director of Special Education:___Ken Tryan___

Address:___Rhodes High School, Administrative Wing___

___5 Morraine Lane, Mt. Top, Ohio___

I am in receipt of the Notice of Intent to Conduct an Evaluation for my child,___Linda___. I understand the reasons and the description of the evaluation process that you provided and have checked the appropriate box below.

☐ Permission is given to conduct the evaluation as described.

☐ Permission is denied.

_____
Parent's Signature

_____
Date

Figure 17.7. Parental Permission Form.

is some reason that it is clearly not possible to do so)
- using tests and other assessment procedures that have been validated for the specific purposes for which they will be used
- ensuring that tests are administered by a trained professional who will work according to the instructions provided by the author and publisher of the test
- selecting and administering all tests so as not to be racially or culturally discriminatory

(Research for Better Schools, 1978, p. 3)

In addition, use of a single procedure as the sole criterion for determining placement is prohibited.

The law and the federal and state regulations to implement it are specific about the contents of

the information that must be provided to parents *in writing* in a classification as handicapped and a decision that special education services will be required. Written notification must be provided if any of the following conditions apply:

- The child will be classified as handicapped and in need of special education.
- There is a change in the child's current classification or current special education program.
- The child is to be continued in the current special education program for another year.

Parents must receive a detailed description of the recommendations of the **multidisciplinary team**. They must be told about the tests and other assessment procedures that were used in reaching

A due process hearing allows parents and school personnel to share concerns and to make plans for appropriate educational programs. (Photo by G. P. Cartwright.)

any decision. They must be told that they have the right to examine and receive copies of their child's records. The notification must also explain that the parents have the right to an independent evaluation for their child, at public expense, if they disagree with the findings of the committee. Finally, parents must be informed of their right to a formal hearing, conducted by an impartial officer, to challenge the recommendation. They must be told how to go about setting up such a hearing, how to obtain legal counsel, and how to appeal the outcome of the hearing.

In Linda's case, things have been happening on schedule. Linda's parents signed and returned the form permitting the evaluation to take place. They also took her to the Bell Hospital Audiology Clinic as they had planned. The clinic forwarded the results of the hearing evaluation to the school district (see Figure 17.8). In the meantime, the school evaluation took place as scheduled, and the results were gathered and used to discuss the need for special services and prepare an IEP for Linda (see Figures 17.9 and 17.10). It was discovered that Linda did have a hearing loss and that a hearing aid would help her considerably. Other tests indicated that, although Linda was below

grade level in reading by nearly a year, her math performance was just slightly below grade level; her general intelligence assessment indicated average ability.

Now that Linda's hearing problem has been discovered and she is learning to use her hearing aid, instruction in reading and speech and language, as well as in other areas of the curriculum, might be more successful. Evelyn Crosby must be careful, though, that she monitors Linda's progress carefully to be sure there are no other problems interfering with Linda's performance in school.

Preparing the IEP

Before the passage of P.L. 94–142, it was often argued that elaborate screening and assessment procedures were used *in place of* intervention. Those arguing for P.L. 94–142 believed that parents were strung along with the idea that something was being done for their child even though all that was really happening was the accumulation of information in a filing cabinet in some agency. We are not naive enough to suggest that such situations don't exist today, but they certainly are much less likely now that the provisions

Name Linda Jo Wilson   Date 10/28

Age 7-7

Audiologist K. A. Ito

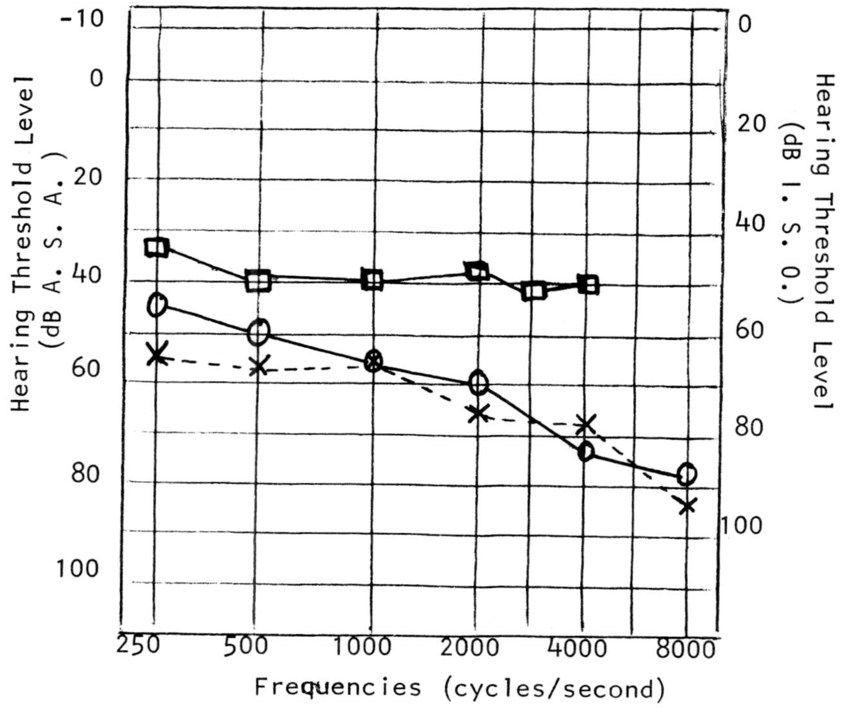

Air conduction O - Right X - Left   Bone conduction [- Right] - Left

Aided in Right - □

Comments: Child was cooperative and composed.

Figure 17.8. Results of Linda's hearing evaluation.

Information about present levels of functioning

Intelligence: WISC-R Performance 114
                        Verbal 102
                        Full Scale 110

Reading: Woodcock Reading Mastery Test, Grade Score 1.4
           Linda performed relatively well on the word comprehension
           and passage comprehension components of the Woodcock.
           She had great difficulty with word identification and word
           attack and her score, overall, reflects her almost non-
           existent skills in word analysis.

Math: KeyMath Diagnostic Inventory, Grade Score 1.9
        Performance in math operations indicates Linda adds and subtracts
        two digit numbers with no regrouping. She does not multiply
        but can divide by two when she has objects or pictures to manipu-
        late. She identifies coins and tells time by the quarter hour.

Language and Speech: An analysis of a sample of Linda's spontane-
                       ous language shows that she uses declarative,
                       negative, question, and imperative sentence
                       patterns. Her articulation test reveals prob-
                       lems with /tr/; /t/ in final position; and some
                       difficulty with /g/ in the medial position.
                       Testing was done face to face.

Emotional maturity: Linda got along fine with the examiner in the
                      testing situation. Her teacher reports she has
                      some difficulties in class, especially with other
                      children teasing her and getting impatient with
                      her when she does not seem to know what to do next.
                      She appears on the brink of tears at times before
                      beginning a new assignment, but when instructions
                      are given directly to her she has no trouble
                      following what to do. She often watches others
                      and copies what they do.

Hearing: Linda has a moderate bilateral sensorineural hearing loss
           according to the report received from the Bell Hospital
           Audiology Clinic. Auditory discrimination during the Clinic
           tests was 60% for the right ear and 65% for the left and
           improved to 85% with a hearing aid in her right ear. Discrim-
           ination improved to 90% when she was in a position to lip read.

(continued)

Figure 17.9. Excerpts from Linda's IEP.

INDIVIDUALIZED EDUCATION PROGRAM PLAN

Student's Name: Linda J. Wilson

Birth Date: 3/15/72

Present Date: 11/22/79

Grade/Program: Grade 2/Regular class

Teacher(s): Mrs. Evelyn Crosby

School: Mt. Top Elementary

Primary Assignment(s)	Date Started	Expected Duration of Services	Special Media or Materials
Regular class (with language instruction and speech and hearing therapy)	9/79 (11/79)	1979-80 school yr.	

Reason for Assignment(s): Moderate hearing loss in speech range

Services			
Language Instruction	11/79	ongoing	
Speech and hearing therapy	11/79	"	

Dates for review and/or revision of the Individualized Education Program Plan:

5/1/80

Person responsible for the maintenance and implementation of the Individualized Education Program Plan:

Arlene G. Bell, Teacher of hearing impaired children for Region 28

Figure 17.9 (*continued*)

Instructional Area: ___Hearing___

Annual Goal: ___Linda will learn to insert and remove her hearing aid, check parts (molding, battery, settings) for proper fit and operation, and make necessary adjustments in settings.___

SHORT-TERM OBJECTIVE	INSTRUCTIONAL METHODS MEDIA/MATERIAL TITLE(S) (OPTIONAL)	EVALUATION OF INSTRUCTIONAL OBJECTIVES	
		TESTS, MATERIALS EVALUATION PROCEDURES TO BE USED	CRITERIA OF SUCCESSFUL PERFORMANCE
1. Linda will a. insert aid properly b. remove aid properly c. check battery, molding, and settings d. adjust settings for different environmental noise backgrounds		1. a-c. Ms. Bell will have Linda attempt tasks and provide instruction as necessary.	1. a-c. successful performance for 5 consecutive times classroom teacher will have Linda check under her supervision at least once a week d. succesful conversation in cafeteria, playground, classroom, and office

Figure 17.9 (*concluded*)

EDUCATIONAL PLAN: REQUEST FOR PARENT'S APPROVAL

ORIGINATOR: Special Education Administrator. Ken Tryan, Director, Special Services

PURPOSE: To present the proposed educational objectives to the parents and obtain their approval for the recommended placement.

Name of Special Education Administrator: __Ken Tryan__

Address: __Rhodes High School, Administrative Wing__

__5 Morraine Lane, Mt. Top, Ohio__

Date: __11/22__

Dear Parent:

    The evaluation of your child has been completed. All papers relevant to the evaluation, including the actual results of each assessment, are available for your inspection. All school reports, files, and records pertaining to your child are available to you for copying.

    Your child's educational plan and placement and the services that will be provided to attain the prescribed objectives of the plan are described in the enclosed forms. Please review this information carefully.

Do you approve of the proposed educational objectives? ☒ Yes   ☐ No

Do you approve of the proposed educational placement? ☒ Yes   ☐ No

Signature: __Robert Wilson__   Date: __11/22__
                Parent

    If you have not approved this plan, we would like to discuss this with you informally sometime during the next 30 days. During this period you have the right to meet with any member of the evaluation team or with the entire team to try to resolve any differences. If we cannot resolve any disagreement informally, then you have the right to obtain a hearing before an impartial officer. During any period of disagreement over placement, your child will continue in his present educational placement.

    If you have signified that you accept the plan as presented, your child's proposed educational program will start immediately after receipt of this form.

Sincerely yours,

__Ken Tryan__
Special Education Administrator

Figure 17.10. Request for parents' approval of educational plan.

of P.L. 94–142 are in place. The law requires that decisions be made, that the assessment be handled properly, and that the information be used as the basis for planning placement, special services, and instructional programming.

After all assessment information has been collected and analyzed, the placement, specification of special services needed, and educational program guidelines are determined by the **IEP team.** This team consists of a representative of the school district (such as the principal), the child's teacher (perhaps the one who made the referral in the first place), one or both of the child's parents (or, in some cases, a court-appointed parent surrogate), and, where appropriate, the child. If the evaluation has been completed for the first time, a member of the multidisciplinary evaluation team is also included on the IEP committee. If a member of the assessment team is not included, someone else who is familiar with the assessment procedures used with the child must be present.

Student Participation. Because the term *whenever appropriate* is not usually defined by policymakers, students are seldom included in their own educational planning. The decision to involve the student should be based on individual characteristics. The following considerations, provided by E. B. Gillespie and A. P. Turnbull (1983), can assist parents and teachers in deciding if a student could benefit from involvement in the multidisciplinary team meeting:

1. *Communication*—Does the student understand conversation conducted in simple language and does he or she express preferences and interests?

2. *Comfort*—Will the student feel comfortable if a nonthreatening environment is maintained? How will the student react if disagreements occur?

3. *Interest*—Does the student understand the purpose of the meeting and nevertheless wish to attend? Will student involvement be beneficial?

If the student will be participating in the conference, all members of the IEP team should be informed, and school personnel should work with the parents to help the student prepare for the meeting. During the meeting, whenever possible, the student should be asked to share some information about her- or himself (age, class, and so on). The meeting should be conducted in an informal manner, and suggestions should be phrased positively with an emphasis on the student's strengths. When student or parent makes a contribution, it should be reinforced, discussed, and included whenever feasible. As the IEP takes shape, all persons present should understand and agree with the decisions made. The student and parents should be asked to sign the IEP and provided with a copy. After the meeting is concluded, the student should be told that his or her participation was valuable.

Resources for Parents. Many states, school districts, and parent organizations have prepared materials to help parents understand and exercise their rights (for example, see Figure 17.11). Rights entail responsibilities, and parents must do their "homework" and come to meetings prepared with information to offer as well as questions to ask. *Your Child's Right to an Education,* a booklet prepared to guide parents of children who are handicapped in New York State (State Education Department of New York, 1978), encourages parents to think about the program being proposed for their child. They are provided with a list of questions and concerns that many parents might have if they were attending an IEP planning meeting. For example,

- What do the test results show about the child's abilities?
- What goals have been set for the child?
- What services will be provided to the child in order to reach the goals?
- What type of physical education program will be provided?
- What regular classroom experiences will be available to the child?

A PARENT/CITIZEN SURVEY: IMPROVING SERVICES FOR CHILDREN IN SPECIAL EDUCATION

Public Law 94–142 (The Education for All Handicapped Children Act of 1975) is a federal law which provides for a free and appropriate public education for all handicapped children regardless of the degree or type of handicap. This law also requires that a written educational program (IEP) be developed for each child to meet his/her unique educational needs.

This questionnaire is designed to find out about the parents' views concerning one aspect of this law—the Individual Educational Plan (IEP). We value the amount of time and help you are about to give. Keep in mind that your help could improve services for children throughout the country. As one example, we plan to produce a handbook for parents on how to participate more successfully in the IEP process.

School Building _Mt. Top Elem. School_

School System _Desert Creek_

Parent's Name _Mr & Mrs Robert Wilson_

Address _356 Wagonwheel, Mt Top OH 01234_

        Street   City   State   Zip

Child's Age _7_   Sex: M ___ F _✓_

What is your child's *primary* handicapping condition?

hearing loss

Is your child in a public school?   Yes _✓_ No ___
If NO, what type of school? i.e., parochial, private, state

_____

Your phone number (would be held confidential) could be helpful to us if we want to follow up.

_____

Area Code   Number

Please answer the following questions after you have attended the meeting at which your child's IEP was developed for the coming school year.

Parts and Procedures of the Individual Education Plan

Please Circle your answer

1. The IEP meeting was held within 30 days following evaluation of my child. If NO, please check when the IEP meeting was held following the evaluation: (Yes)   No

2 mos. later	3 mos. later	4 mos. later
5 mos. later	6 mos. later	never

2. The information from my child's evaluation before the IEP was fair and useful for planning a program for my child.   (Yes)   No

3. The following were present at the IEP meeting:

My child   Yes (No)

Child's teacher   (Yes) No

School representative (other than child's teacher)   (Yes) No

Parent or Guardian   (Yes) No

Other _____

4. The IEP for my child contained the following items:

annual goals   (Yes) No

short-term objectives   Yes No

specific service(s) to be provided   (Yes) No

present level of performance   (Yes) No

date services were to begin   (Yes) No

ways to check my child's progress   Yes No

special materials, equipment or media   Yes (No)

percentage (%) of time in regular class placement   *NA* Yes No

place for me to indicate my approval   (Yes) No

Figure 17.11. Parent-citizen survey form.

educators informed me of how the IEP was to be developed and what would be in it (Yes) No

5. The description of my child's present educational performance in the IEP included information in all four of these areas: *same as her others in her class*

self-help skills (personal maintenance) Yes No

academic skills (reading, math, etc.) Yes No

social behavior (how s/he gets along with others, etc.) Yes No

physical skills (coordination, running, etc.) Yes No

6. There were major areas of educational needs for my child which were ignored during the IEP meeting. Yes (No)

7. The short-term objectives are written as specific steps my child will achieve in the next three months or more. (Yes) No

8. The short-term objectives did seem closely related to the annual goal(s). (Yes) No

9. The annual goal(s) in the IEP did not fully meet the educational needs of my child. Yes (No)

10. The IEP clearly stated what specific service(s) my child would be receiving. (Yes) No

11. The dates for the beginning of services for my child were quite clear. (Yes) No

12. I know when the IEP services will end for my child. ? Yes No

13. The service(s) for my child in the IEP was determined by what was available rather than what was needed (for example: if a certain service was known to be needed but the final decision was made based on what the school district currently had). Yes (No)

14. A specific date was set for reviewing my child's progress under this IEP. (Yes) No

15. The method of checking my child's progress in the IEP included:

how it would be checked   Yes No

when it would be checked   Yes No

who would be responsible for making sure it's done   Yes No

16. Some regular class placements for my child were considered during the IEP meeting. *all the time* Yes No

17. Every attempt was made by educators to provide services for as much time as possible in a regular classroom. NA Yes No

18. A completed copy of the IEP was:

made available to me to look at Yes No

made available to me to keep (Yes) No

19. The IEP for my child was completed before the meeting with me. Yes (No)

What Were Your Feelings About the Following:

20. Educators presented information during the IEP meeting in understandable language. (Yes) No

21. I was given the opportunity to ask questions about points I didn't understand regarding the IEP. (Yes) No

22. I was encouraged to contribute significant information to my child's IEP. (Yes) No

23. The IEP that was developed seemed to fit my child's needs. (Yes) No

24. Educators provided information that helped me understand the IEP process. (Yes) No

25. I felt like a fully participating member with the educators during the planning of the IEP. (Yes) No

(continued)

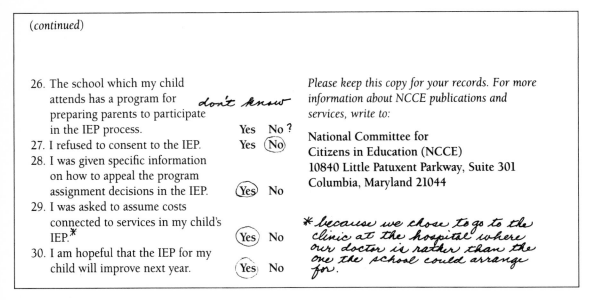

Figure 17.11 (*concluded*). Reprinted with permission of the National Committee for Citizens in Education, Columbia, Maryland 21044.

- What extracurricular activities will be available for the child to participate in?
- How do the other children in the class react to the child?
- What behavior problems have been displayed by the child?
- How is the teacher handling these problems?
- How often will the child's progress be checked?
- When will a report on the child's progress be received?

(From State Education Department of New York, 1978, p. 9)

There is also Closer Look, a federally funded service for parents of children who are handicapped that provides parents with information about services as well as about their rights. Closer Look produces radio, TV, billboard, and poster ad campaigns about finding and serving children who are handicapped (see Figure 17.12). Another means of keeping parents informed and involved is Pennsylvania's project CONNECT, which includes a telephone hot-line service. Parents are invited to call the toll-free number with questions about services and procedures. Project staff members "connect" with information about locally available service options.

Another helpful guide for parents, and for teachers, is *The Special Education Handbook* (1986). This handy manual offers a wealth of practical information about legal requirements established by federal legislation, including the evaluation process, requirements for a team approach to evaluation, understanding test results, and parents' right to a second opinion. Specific tips are given for parents about working with school personnel to plan the IEP. For example, elements of appropriate goals and objectives include the following:

- *The desired behavior or skill.* Use terms that are specific and observable to describe what you expect your child to accomplish.
- *The conditions under which the behavior is to occur.* Be specific in stating when and/or where the behavior is to occur.
- *The desired level of performance.* Criteria should be observable and expressed in quantitative form.

When appropriate, the youngster should be involved in his or her IEP conference. (Photo by G. P. Cartwright.)

In addition, sample questions such as the following guide parents and educators in determining the best placement for the child, consistent with legal requirements:

- How many students are currently in this special education placement?
- Are my child's academic skill levels comparable to those of other special education children with whom he or she will be grouped?
- Is my child compatible with the other students in the placement?
- Will the placement have any harmful effects on my child?
- Will my child disrupt or impede the education of other students if placed in a regular class?
- Is the teacher's instructional style compatible with my child's educational needs?
- What resources will be available to my child in this school?
- Do one or more aides assist the teacher in this placement?
- What is the school's general climate with regard to students who have disabilities?
- Where is the school located?

- Are the school's important facilities physically accessible to my child?
- Where is my child's classroom located within the building?
- What opportunities are available for mainstreaming my youngster?
- What is my child's reaction to the placement? What is my overall reaction?
- What opportunities are available for parent participation?

MULTIDISCIPLINARY TEAMS

The idea of multidisciplinary teams for diagnosis and IEP planning was presented in the previous section. It may be helpful to consider in more detail (1) when teams are needed, (2) how team membership is determined, and (3) the responsibilities of team members.

Legal Constraints. The law mandates that referral, diagnosis, program planning, and evaluation be based on mutual agreement and decisions

THIS IS AGAINST THE LAW.

Jack Devlin is not cutting classes. He just doesn't go to school. Because the school doesn't want him. Jack's handicap doesn't fit into the school's program.

A few years ago, that would have been too bad.

This year, it's against the law. Now every child has a right to the kind of education he needs to develop his full potential. No matter what his handicap.

If you have a child who needs special education, we have information about how to get it.

Write to:

CLOSER LOOK,

BOX 1492
WASHINGTON, D.C. 20013
(a service of the U.S. Dept
of Health, Education & Welfare)

Figure 17.12. Example of a Closer Look magazine ad.

reached by a *team* so as to avoid individual decisions that may be determined by a single perspective or philosophy. Even if P.L. 94–142 did not require the involvement of a multidisciplinary team at certain points in the decision-making process, common sense tells us that a team is appropriate. The diversity of assessment procedures needed to get specific information about the problems involved makes the task nearly impossible for one person to accomplish. A special booklet on preparation of IEPs, by the Foundation for Exceptional Children (Torres, 1977), includes an excellent list of guidelines for the appointment of the team and the conduct of the evaluation. Many of the points discussed have been made already in this chapter. Reliance on the classroom teacher as an important source of information about the child's development is particularly noteworthy.

> The student's teacher should be viewed as one of the primary sources of information regarding both the child's educational and social development. The day-to-day activities in the educational setting give the teacher an opportunity to observe the child working on specific educational curriculum areas. Observations of the child's learning style, mode of interaction with others, and obvious constraints or barriers to future learning can be reviewed and documented.
> (Higgins, 1977, p. 12)

The Role of the Teacher and Other Professionals. In many cases, the classroom teacher triggers the information-gathering process. The evaluation team may be called in because of a referral by the classroom teacher, as was the case with Linda. It is incumbent upon the evaluation team to make use of the information previously gathered by the classroom teacher; there is no point in assigning a team member responsibility for redoing what the classroom teacher has already done. For one thing, it is wasted effort. But more important, the classroom teacher is in the *best* position to gather information about normal, everyday interactions and learning situations.

In addition to professionals associated with

the public schools (teachers, school psychologists, school counselors, speech therapists, educational consultants, and administrators), other professionals may be needed on the team if the case under consideration so warrants. Pediatricians, neurologists or other medical specialists, family counselors, social workers and psychologists, and occupational and physical therapists may be needed to round out the multidisciplinary team. In each case, the symptoms of the child enter into decisions about composition of the team.

Advantages and Disadvantages. A multidisciplinary team has certain disadvantages as well as advantages. Advantages have been identified by C. V. Morsink (1984) and include the following:

1. Members in a team encourage innovative ideas, creative thinking, and development of well-discussed methods of program planning, implementation, and evaluation.

2. The quality of plans developed by a group is enhanced due to several sources of expert knowledge.

3. Solutions to problems are more easily generated by members willing to share resources.

4. Team planning encourages public commitment and support for implementation.

Disadvantages identified by Morsink (1984) include the following:

1. Role differentiation may not be clear, creating uncertainty in group functioning.

2. Possessive attitudes regarding individual areas of expertise may create differences.

3. Interaction between members may not be sufficient or cordial.

4. A few members with strong opinions may dominate others.

5. Conflict of opinion may be time-consuming and nonproductive.

To ensure smooth functioning of a multidisciplinary team, roles must be well defined, and team members must remain open-minded and flexible in order for good communication to exist. The team should share common goals and not work at cross-purposes. Members must contribute to discussions and offer information and opinions relevant to the best concerns of the child. Parental involvement is especially important: With some support and guidance, parents can assume an essential role in planning and implementing their child's progress.

Suggestions for Parents and Professionals. Regardless of the mandates of P.L. 94–142, it is *people* who make the system work. Genuine respect for the rights of all concerned and for the special talents of the team members cannot be legislated—they are a matter of attitudes and values. The following list of suggestions for professionals is abstracted from a list proposed by K. A. Gorham and her colleagues. P.L. 94–142 had not yet been signed into law when their study was completed and published, and some of these suggestions for professionals are now mandated in that law. It might be argued that if such attitudes had been more prevalent in the past, the mandates in P.L. 94–142 would not have been necessary.

1. Have the parents involved every step of the way. The dialogue established may be the most important thing you accomplish. . . .

2. Make a realistic management plan part and parcel of the assessment outcome. Give the parents suggestions for how to live with the problem on a day-to-day basis, with the needs of the child, the capacities of the family, and the resources of the community all considered. . . .

3. Inform yourself about community resources. Give the parents advice on how to go about getting what they need. Steer them to the local parent organization.

4. Wherever possible, make the parents team members in the actual diagnostic, treatment, or educational procedures. . . .

5. Write your reports in clear, understandable, jargon-free language . . . the parents *must* be as well informed as you can make them. Information that they do not understand is not useful to them. . . .

6. Give copies of the reports to parents. They will need them to digest and understand the information in them; to share the information with other people close to the child; and to avoid the weeks or months of record-gathering which every application to a new program in the future will otherwise entail.

7. Be sure the parents understand that there is no such thing as a one-shot, final, unchanging diagnosis. . . .

8. Help the parents to think of life with this child in the same terms as life with their other children. . . .

9. Be sure that the parents understand the child's abilities and assets as well as his disabilities and deficiencies. What the child *can* do is far more important than what he cannot do. . . .

10. Warn the parents about service insufficiencies. Equip them with advice on how to make their way through the system of "helping" services. Warn them that they are not always helpful. Tell them that the child has a *right* to services. Tell them to insist upon being a part of any decision making done about their child.

11. Explain to the parents that some people with whom they talk (teachers, doctors, professionals of any kind, other parents) may dwell on negatives. Help train the parents not only to think in positives but to teach the other people important in the child's life to think in positives.

(Gorham et al., 1976, pp. 183–184. Used with permission.)

Parents are ultimately responsible for their children—all their children, not just the ones with problems. Attitudes by professionals such as those embodied in the principles above will go a long way toward making parents more self-confident in rearing their children.

The Due Process Hearing. At any point in the process of evaluation, placement, and program implementation, parents may request a hearing if they disagree with the school system. Preparation for a due process hearing must begin immediately upon receipt of the hearing request. Federal regulations state that the hearing officer may disallow introduction of evidence that has not been disclosed to the other party at least five days before the scheduled hearing. Steps in the preparation include:

1. *Selecting appropriate documents.* Relevant documents should be selected from the student's records and organized in chronological order. Documents should provide the following information:
   a. child's school history
   b. documentation of the child's handicapping condition
   c. description of the programs and services being proposed to meet the child's educational needs
   d. anecdotal notes regarding the child's actions and behaviors
   e. chronology of the school system personnel's contacts with the parents

2. *Choosing and preparing witnesses.* This is a difficult process because the abilities, feelings, and fears of witnesses to testify and respond effectively under cross-examination have to be considered. Witnesses' feelings may include:
   a. anxiety, resentment, anger, defensiveness
   b. fear of defending their credentials
   c. conflict between loyalty to the school and responsibility to the child

3. *Understanding facts of the case.* Each potential witness reviews all documentation in the child's records. Witnesses should be prepared to serve as "experts" on the validity and reliability of the assessment instruments used for evaluation of the child.

4. *Prehearing briefing.* The briefing should provide an open and full discussion to reach consensus while maintaining individual professional judgment. The order in which wit-

nesses will testify should be determined. Each witness must be prepared to deal with cross-examination.

During the period before a hearing, emotions are heightened. Nevertheless, an effective working relationship must be maintained between the service providers and parents. To maintain professional behavior, school personnel should:

1. continue in their professional roles

2. avoid getting drawn into discussions about appeal issues

3. avoid communicating with parents' attorneys

4. remember that statements can be taken out of context and misconstrued

HANDLING INFORMATION ABOUT CHILDREN

We have made the point several times that assessment is a means to an end, not an end in itself. The information that is collected must be *used*. But it must be used with care and treated with appropriate safeguards.

Confidentiality

The basic principle underlying the confidentiality of information is that parents and children have a *right to privacy*. Problems often occur when school personnel and other professionals need information in order to make decisions about children's educational programs. All the people involved are interested in the future well-being of the children, but they see the situation from the perspective of their own needs. Professionals need information and often need to share it; parents want the information treated with respect and want their privacy protected. How can these conflicting needs be resolved?

What is crucial is full and open communication with parents and informed consent to collect and/or disseminate certain information about children. The 1974 Family Educational Rights and Privacy Act (P.L. 93–380), often called the Buckley Amendment, requires that any educational agency that accepts federal funds must give parents opportunities to look at and, if necessary, correct their children's school records. Furthermore, the law requires that parental consent be obtained before information is released. Students over age eighteen also have these rights to access and privacy.

Maintenance of Records

In general, information should be kept on file only as long as there is a need to use it. School records should be purged periodically to remove any information that is no longer required or accurate.

Some help in making decisions about what to include and what to retain in school records came from a conference held by the Russell Sage Foundation in 1969. (The guidelines from the 1969 conference preceded what is now mandated in P.L. 94–142.) Briefly, conferees identified three types of information: (1) Category A, the basic minimum information needed by schools—identification, grades completed, attendance records, and report cards; (2) Category B, *verified* information such as test results and medical conditions (special diets, allergies, chronic health problems, and so on) that is useful in planning for the child; and (3) Category C, information that *may* be useful. It is Category C information that requires informed consent. Assessment information being collected in order to determine if a child has a handicapping condition would fall into Category C because, at the beginning of the assessment process, it is not known which information will be useful and which will prove unnecessary.

TEACHERS AS ADVOCATES

One of the best ways for regular class teachers to believe in the concept of mainstreaming is for them to have a successful experience working with a child who is handicapped. A teacher who has had a positive experience often becomes an advocate for the least restrictive environment within the school, perhaps even working with other teachers throughout the district.

In Linda's case, Evelyn Crosby was convinced—so much so that she was called on to help convince Linda's next teacher, Mr. Krye (see Figures 17.13, 17.14, and 17.15). She also participated in an in-service program at the beginning of the next school year (see Figure 17.16).

P.L. 94–142 includes provisions governing the assessment process that give classroom teachers and parents both expanded rights and expanded duties. When parent and child interests conflict, the educator must try to achieve a compromise solution by assessing the specific needs of the family and the child. If needed resources for resolving such a situation are not available in the local community, the role of the professional is one of advocating for such services. Teachers should become involved in the advocacy process to strengthen their relationships with parents and facilitate future collaborations, because no matter how much legislation is passed or how many court decisions are handed down, parents will always be ultimately responsible for their children's welfare. All parents, not just those with exceptional children, have this responsibility, and most are not well prepared for it. Parents deserve all the help that we, as members of helping professions, can give them. Remember—

We DO have responsibility for these children.

and

We CAN make a difference.

SUMMARY

A major problem in providing a free, appropriate education for all children is coordination of services and the many different individuals who play important roles in serving children. Getting the right person to the child at the right time is one part of the problem; cooperative programs and

follow-through are others. This chapter has used information from the whole book to provide you with a fuller understanding of the processes and problems of identification, intensive diagnosis, and coordination of services, including educational programming.

Teachers, parents, and others who work with children sometimes need to seek help from others for a particular child—they need to make a referral. A referral is a clear, concise statement of a child's strengths and weaknesses and a request for assistance in dealing with the child's problems.

P.L. 94–142 requires specific safeguards to assure that a child's rights to education are not violated, that confidentiality of information is maintained, and that parents are involved in every major decision about a handicapped child's education. Most of the major decisions—evaluation, placement, program—are made by a multidisciplinary team. Thus, coordination of services among the various disciplines is crucial. Team members must work toward a common goal, and well-defined roles and good communication between members facilitates this process.

Disagreement between the school and parents regarding evaluation and placement of the child may result in a due process hearing. A hearing requires extensive preparation and is a time-consuming and emotionally draining experience.

Implementation of a child's IEP, or individualized education program, will be a cooperative effort among services with the major effort taking place at the school level. The essential elements of the IEP are primary assignment (placement), date of start of services, duration of services, present functioning levels of the child, and short- and long-range objectives for the child.

It is incumbent upon all professionals involved in placement, evaluation, and programs for handicapped children to keep parents involved. Joint efforts between parents and professionals are vital ingredients in providing a free, appropriate public education for all handicapped children. Conferences with parents can be crucial in determining outcomes regarding decisions about a child. Utmost care must be taken in planning and conducting such meetings.

DESERT CREEK SCHOOL DISTRICT
Mt. Top Elementary School
Mt. Top, Ohio

Date: May 6, 1980

From: Hugh N. Krye

To: Kurt Sampson

What's this I hear about a deaf student coming into my class next year??

Will stop by your office tomorrow to see you.

Figure 17.13. Note from Mr. Krye, Linda's third-grade teacher, to the principal.

DESERT CREEK SCHOOL DISTRICT
Mt. Top Elementary School
Mt. Top, Ohio

Date: May 6, '80

From: R. Sampson

To: Hugh Krye

Sorry I missed you ther a.m. - was called to Pupil Personnel Services re bus schedule changes.

There are a number of second graders with special needs moving up this year. We'll talk more at Fri. meeting. Meantime, if you see Evelyn, you might ask her about her class.

Figure 17.14. Response to Mr. Krye from the principal.

DESERT CREEK SCHOOL DISTRICT
Mt. Top Elementary School
Mt. Top, Ohio

Date: May 6, 80
From: K. Sampson
To: Evelyn C.

You will probably be getting some questions from some of the other teachers about Linda & Darryl & how you've managed this year.

Would you be willing to come to dept head meeting on Friday to talk about your work with the children — some general comments would be reassuring. Thanks.

Room 34   3:00pm.

Figure 17.15. Memo to Linda's teacher from the principal.

```
                    DESERT CREEK SCHOOL DISTRICT
                     Mt. Top Elementary School
                         Mt. Top, Ohio


In-service Program                              August 28, 1980
                     HEARING IS ALSO BELIEVING!
   8:30- 9:00 AM    Coffee and conversation

   9:00- 9:15 AM    Welcome
                        Kurt Sampson, Principal
                        Dr. Katurah Osbourne, Superintendent

   9:15-10:00 AM    "You may wonder why we've called you together..."
                        Ken Tryan, Director of Special Services

  10:00-10:15 AM    Break

  10:15-11:00 AM    "How do I tell thee?  Let me count the ways..."
                        Dr. Helena L. Paulson, Supervisor of Program
                            for Hearing Impaired

  11:00-11:45 AM    "The system approach:  Follow-up of referrals"
                        Harry M. Mummer, Speech Therapist

  11:45- 1:00 PM    Lunch - All art work on display was done by DCSD
                            students in special classes.

                    Professional books and catalogs on display are
                    available for loan from the professional collec-
                    tion in Room 13.

   1:00- 1:45 PM    "The way it's s'pposed to be..."
                        Arlene G. Bell, Teacher of Hearing Impaired

   1:45- 2:30 PM    "And that's the way it is - usually..."
                        Evelyn Crosby, Classroom Teacher

   2:30- 2:45 PM    Break

   2:45- 3:30 PM    Panel discussion with time for questions
                        Moderator:  Hugh N. Krye,Classroom Teacher

The MTES In-service Committee would like to thank all those DCSD
personnel who have helped with this program.
```

Figure 17.16. In-service program agenda.

Suggestions for Further Reading

Note: The readings suggested for Chapters 1 and 2 are also relevant here.

Bateman, B. (1980). *So you're going to a hearing: Preparing for a Public Law 94–142 due process hearing.* Northbrook, IL: Hubbard.
According to Bateman, this brief manual is intended to "demystify the experience" of a due process hearing and make it "more meaningful and less intimidating." There are four major sections, arranged according to the sequence of activities for such a hearing: what happens before the hearing, the prehearing conference, the events during the hearing itself, and what happens after the hearing. Major issues associated with each phase of the process are provided, and sample forms are included.

Edmister, P., & Ekstrand, R. E. (1987). Lessening the trauma of due process. *Teaching Exceptional Children, 19*(3), 6–11.
This article explains in detail the procedure of a due process hearing. It includes sections on prehearing preparation, role of case presenter/attorney, role of the witness, and preparation for testimony. It also includes a brief description of posthearing reactions. Major issues associated with each phase are provided.

Shore, K. (1986). *The special education handbook: A comprehensive guide for parents and educators.* New York: Teachers College Press.
This paperback is a detailed guide that provides parents and educators with information about legal and procedural issues associated with the child's evaluation and the development of an IEP. Furthermore, it offers suggestions for resolving conflicts with the school.

Turnbull, A. P., Strickland, B. B., & Brantley, J. C. (1982). *Developing and implementing individualized education programs* (2nd ed.). Columbus, OH: Merrill.
This excellent book for preservice teachers and professionals is a step-by-step guide to the development and implementation of IEPs. In addition to basic information, it contains practical exercises that promote application of new skills.

Relevant Journals

Exceptional Children and *Teaching Exceptional Children*
Both of these journals are published by The Council for Exceptional Children. They periodically contain articles related to IEPs, due process, multidisciplinary teams, and the like that provide important and current information on those issues.

GLOSSARY

Ability training. *See* **process training.**

Academically talented. Students with strong academic achievement; IQs above 116; upper 15 to 20 percent of the school population.

Acquired immune deficiency syndrome (AIDS). A sexually transmitted disease that reduces the body's ability to fight infections. It is fatal.

Adaptive behavior. The effectiveness with which an individual meets the standards of personal independence and social responsibility expected of his or her age and cultural group.

Adventitiously deaf. *See* **postlingual deafness.**

Advocate. An individual, such as a teacher or a parent, who works to secure better services and opportunities for people with disabilities.

Akinetic seizure. A manifestation of epilepsy characterized by loss of postural tone and sudden dropping to the ground.

American Sign Language (Ameslan). The fourth most commonly used language in the United States. A combination of sign language and fingerspelling, but with its own system of rules distinct from English.

Ameslan. *See* **American Sign Language.**

Amniocentesis. A medical procedure during which a needle is inserted through the abdomen of a pregnant woman to the amniotic sac surrounding a fetus. The fluid withdrawn is then tested to detect the presence of abnormal conditions.

Anecdotal record. Brief, factual account of events; a good means for recording unanticipated behaviors, incidents, or events. General format consists of date, time, name of child, setting, and behavior description.

Anoxia. A lack of oxygen in the blood that impairs normal tissue functioning.

Aphasia. Condition in which a person, usually an adult, has difficulty forming or comprehending symbols of language because of some type of brain damage.

Applied behavior analysis. The systematic application of principles of behavior to improve specific behaviors and the simultaneous evaluation of behavior change attributed to this application. Also known as **behavior modification.**

Arthritis. A condition which affects the joints and muscles causing pain, stiffness, and inflammation.

Arthrogryposis. A musculoskeletal disorder characterized by congenital stiffness of the joints and weak muscles.

Articulation errors. Speech problems resulting in faulty production of **phonemes.**

Assessment. Process of obtaining information about performance, through testing or other means, and using that information to make educational decisions.

Assistive devices. Compensatory materials, machines, computers, and the like used to assist physically handicapped persons; for example, wheelchairs, crutches, computer-based devices that accept voice commands.

Asthma. A chronic allergic condition characterized by wheezing, coughing, and difficulty in exhaling air.

Astigmatism. Distorted or blurred vision, usually due to irregular curvature of the cornea.

Ataxia. A form of cerebral palsy characterized by poor muscle coordination that negatively influences balance and coordination.

Athetosis. A form of cerebral palsy characterized by involuntary, jerking, and purposeless movements of the head, tongue, and extremities.

Attention deficit disorder (ADD). A condition characterized by hyperactivity, impulsivity, and inattentiveness.

Audiogram. Report of an audiometric hearing exam, indicating decibel loss at various frequencies.

Audiologist. A hearing specialist trained to administer and interpret nonmedical aspects of hearing examinations; can prescribe hearing aids.

Audiometer. A carefully calibrated instrument designed to test hearing at various frequencies and intensity levels in the range of human hearing.

Auditory discrimination. "Ability to differentiate among sounds (e.g., beginning or ending consonants of common words)" (Sabatino, 1972).

Auditory memory. "Ability to retain or recall sounds and combinations of sounds" (Sabatino, 1972).

Aura. A sensation reported by some individuals with epilepsy that is felt just prior to the onset of a grand mal seizure.

Autism. A disturbance of behavior noted in early childhood that may be characterized by self-stimulation, self-injurious behavior, or the absence of speech.

Aversion therapy. An applied behavior procedure in which subject changes habits or behaviors through induced dislike of them.

Babbles, babbling. Combination of vowel and consonant sounds repeated over and over by a baby, particularly when the baby is alone and content.

Battered child syndrome. Serious and frequent injuries of children, with discrepancies between clinical findings and explanations for the injuries given by parents.

Behavioral approach. A theory that views human behavior as learned and, therefore, amenable to change. *See* **behavior management.**

Behavior management. Training to help children manage or control their own behavior. Programs consist of carefully delineating the behavior the child is to display at the conclusion of the program; identifying the current level of achievement or behavior; selecting an instructional strategy or behavioral management plan; selecting or developing instructional or supporting materials; and keeping precise records of the child's progress toward the goal.

Behavior modification. An old term for **applied behavior analysis.** In a generic sense, it may also include procedures totally unrelated to applied behavior analysis, such as hypnosis, psychosurgery, and drug therapy.

Biophysical model. A way of describing and explaining atypical behavior in terms of a physical disease, disorder, or dysfunction.

Blind. Having either no vision or, at most, light perception but no light projection.

Blindness. "Central visual acuity for distance of 20/200 or less in the better eye with correction or, if greater than 20/200, a field of vision no greater than 20 degrees at the widest diameter" (Hatfield, 1975); no sense of vision, or light perception only (Barraga, 1976).

Braille. A system of raised dots that enables individuals with visual impairments to read using their fingertips.

Buckley Amendment. Amendment to Family Rights and Privacy Act of 1974, specifying that agencies are required to maintain confidentiality of student records and to destroy records no longer used or needed.

Career education. A systematic program wherein an individual learns about and prepares for working and living in the modern world to the maximum extent of his or her ability.

Cascade model. Seven levels on a continuum of special education services, ranging from least restrictive (regular classroom) to most restrictive (residential school).

Central auditory dysfunction. Interference with or breakdown of sound transmission along the auditory pathways in the brain stem or auditory cortex; a central hearing loss.

Central hearing loss. *See* **Central auditory dysfunction.**

Central processing unit (CPU). This section of the computer is the control mechanism. It consists of a group of silicon chips that perform a variety of control operations and transfer functions.

Cerebral palsy. A disorder due to brain damage that results in lack of control of voluntary muscles, paralysis, weakness, or lack of coordination of certain large and small muscles. Can be very mild or extremely debilitating. Often causes speech problems.

Checklist. An observational technique in which a list of behaviors, characteristics, or traits is marked as being present or absent for a child's behavior sample.

Child abuse and neglect. "The physical or mental injury, sexual abuse or exploitation, negligent treatment, or maltreatment of a child under the age of eighteen . . . by a person who is responsible for the child's welfare, under circumstances that indicate the child's health or welfare is harmed or threatened thereby . . . " (P.L. 93–247).

Child Find. Mandate of P.L.94–142 that requires screening and follow-up diagnosis, where indicated, in order to find and serve exceptional children.

Chlamydia. Most common sexually transmitted disease; affects both sexes and, if left untreated, can result in sterility. In females, 60 to 80 percent of all cases may be without symptoms.

Class action suit. A court case in which a single individual or small group of persons represents an entire class or group of persons. The results of the suit apply to all members of the predefined class or group. The 1972 PARC case was a class action suit in which the decision was rendered to affect not just the plaintiffs but all retarded children in Pennsylvania.

Classical conditioning. Presentation of stimuli that evoke an automatic, unlearned response; for example, shock or noise (unconditioned stimuli) causing involuntary, reflexive responses (unconditioned responses). A stimulus that is neutral (conditioned stimulus) is paired with an unconditioned stimulus and results in the conditioned stimulus alone evoking the response.

Classroom management. The manipulation of the classroom environment to facilitate active engagement of students toward achievement of academic and social goals.

Cleft lip. Incomplete closure of the upper lip. The cleft occurs during gestation; frequently can be closed with surgery.

Cleft palate. Incomplete closure of the hard and/or soft palate (roof of the mouth). The cleft occurs during gestation; sometimes can be closed through surgery.

Closed captioning. Captioning visible on the television screen only as the result of being hooked up to a special decoder.

Cluttering. Excessive speed of verbal output; disorganized sentence structure; slurring, telescoping, or omitting syllables or sounds.

COHI. Crippled and other health impaired; the general population of children with physical disabilities. *See* **other health impaired**.

Communication. A very broad term that refers to verbal and nonverbal methods for exchanging information.

Communication disorder. A problem in receiving auditory input, using language, or producing speech such that the process of exchanging ideas and expressing feelings is affected.

Compensatory devices. Technological aids used as tools to assist handicapped individuals to function more independently.

Compensatory education. Counterbalancing, substituting, or offsetting one skill with another, on the premise that because something prevents a person from acquiring normal or near-normal skills in one area, he or she must acquire skills in another area as compensation.

Computer-assisted instruction (CAI). The use of computers to provide direct instruction through specific programs stored within the computer's memory. The learner sits at a computer terminal that displays information and asks questions. The computer evaluates the learner's responses and then chooses the next step, providing more information, branching to another selection, or offering a variation of these alternatives.

Computer-managed instruction (CMI). Broad instructional plan for a learner or group of learners implemented with a great deal of assistance from a computer. The computer serves as a record keeper and directs students to a variety of possible learning experiences for reaching the next scheduled or planned objective. Also includes other administrative uses.

Computer program. A written set of instructions stored on a floppy disc and designed to accomplish a specific purpose. Many programming languages exist. BASIC, LOGO, and Pascal are commonly used with microcomputers.

Conductive hearing loss. Hearing loss attributable to problems in the transmission of sound from the outer ear through the middle ear.

Congenital. Present at birth. A congenital disability can be the result of disease, malnutrition, or trauma between conception and birth; chromosomal anomalies; genetic disorders; or inheritance.

Consent agreement. An agreement reached between the two opposing parties in a lawsuit. The agreement carries the force of law, and both parties agree to abide by it.

Constitutional law. One of the sources of law that regulate and mandate education and other civil issues. Interpretations of the U.S. Constitution are made by the courts and then carry the force of the law.

Courseware. Computer programs used to help students achieve educational objectives (e.g., spelling games, math tutorials, problem solving, or simulations of the sciences).

Creative thinking. "The process of sensing gaps or disturbing elements, forming ideas concerning them, testing these hypotheses, and communicating the results, possibly modifying and retesting the hypotheses" (Torrance, 1962). Expressing unusual ideas, or identifying novel uses of familiar ideas or objects.

Criterion-referenced assessment. Evaluation of performance in terms of specific behaviors demonstrated, where the expected behavior serves as the criterion; assessment of an individual's standing with respect to a particular criterion. This form of evaluation is tied to intraindividual differences.

Cued speech. A speech-based system of communication in which hand locations and shapes supplement lip movements to make the forty English phonemes distinguishable from each other.

Cultural diversity. Distinctive work views, values, styles, and languages of different groups of people.

Curriculum- based assessment (CBA). Evaluation of a child's achievement in terms of the expected curricular outcomes in a given school.

Cystic fibrosis. A disease that affects the mucous glands, resulting in respiratory and digestive problems.

Deaf. Having a hearing impairment so severe that the child is impaired in processing linguistic information through hearing, with or without amplification, and educational performance is adversely affected.

Deaf-blind. Having "concomitant hearing and visual impairments, the combination of which causes such severe communication and other developmental and educational problems that they cannot be accommodated in special education programs solely for deaf or blind children" (U.S. Office of Education, 1977a).

Deafened. *See* **postlingual deafness.**

Decibel (db). Unit of measure of sound intensity; a sound pressure ratio expressed as a logarithmic number and measured from an arbitrary reference point.

Defense mechanism. A reaction to frustration or conflict, whereby the person attempts to avoid anxiety and fails to face the true motives for his or her actions; examples include repression, clinical projection, or sublimation.

Deinstitutionalize. To remove or release patients or residents from large, impersonal institutions or residential facilities and place them in small, community-based group homes or in their own residences.

Depressants. Sedatives; drugs that reduce the activity level of the brain and muscles.

Developmental aphasia. Poor speech due to problems in processing language; inability to use language appropriately by children with otherwise intact communication systems and adequate intelligence.

Developmental domains. An educational philosophy and approach for organizing educational objectives and classifying children's problems according to four domains: cognitive, motor, social, and communication.

Diabetes. A metabolic disorder which renders the pancreas unable to secrete the appropriate amount of insulin.

Diplegia. Paralysis in which lower limbs are more severely affected than are upper limbs.

Direct instruction. "The direct measurement of a pupil's performance on a learning task and the accompanying arrangement of instructional programs and procedures for each child" (Haring & Gentry, 1976). The key components are systematic assessment, instruction, and evaluation. The method is designed to individualize instruction within the framework of the many demands on a teacher's time.

Disability. An objective, measurable, organic dysfunction or impairment (e.g., loss of a hand or paralysis of speech muscles).

Disc drive. A peripheral device used for extra external memory. It reads or stores programs from a floppy disc. Some computers may use a tape recorder instead of a disc drive.

Discipline. A method for maintaining an environment conducive to learning and for managing the behavior of students.

Discrepancy approach. Development of education programs for children (especially learning disabled children) on the basis of divergences between a child's actual and expected performances in an instructional area.

Double hemiplegia. Paralysis in which upper limbs are more seriously involved than are lower limbs.

Down syndrome. A chromosomal aberration that results in mental retardation and the following physical characteristics: epicanthic folds of the eyelids, large fissured tongue, broad and flat nose bridge, and poor muscle tone.

Drill and practice. The repetitive presentation of factual knowledge (spelling or math); assists in the maintenance of previously acquired skills or information.

Due process. P.L. 94–142 requires that a child may not be tested or placed in a special education setting unless the parents are consulted. Due process refers to certain procedures that must be followed in the event of a disagreement.

Dysgraphia. Difficulty with or inability to identify written symbols of language.

Dyslexia. "A syndrome in which a child has unusual and persistent difficulty in learning the components of words and sentences, in integrating segments into words and sentences, and in learning other kinds of representational systems, such as telling time, directions, and reasons" (Bryan & Bryan, 1978).

Echolalia. Meaningless repetition of words or sentences initially spoken by other people.

Ecological theories. A group of explanations for behavior that involves study of the interrelationships between organisms and the environment. Naturalistic observation is often the tool used to study behavior from this perspective.

Educable mentally retarded (EMR). One of three groups of retarded children classified according to a scheme once prevalent in American schools. Corresponds roughly to IQ levels between 50 and 75.

Educational technology. The educational application of machines and the programs that drive them.

Emotional abuse, neglect. Failure to provide a "loving environment" in which a child can "thrive, learn, and develop" (McNeese & Hebeler, 1977).

Emotional disturbance. A condition characterized by lack of self-control, difficulty in interpersonal relations, depression, lack of contact with reality, unexplained physical problems. Also referred to as behavior disorder. *See also* **neurosis** and **psychosis.**

EMR. *See* **educable mentally retarded.**

Enabling behaviors. Prerequisite skills necessary for the successful completion of a **terminal behavior;** the ability to perform the response required by a particular test item even though some type of handicapping condition may be present (e.g., a child must be able to hold the pencil before beginning to print).

Enrichment. Educational experiences for individuals who are gifted that extend beyond the traditional curriculum.

Enroute behaviors. Prerequisite skills necessary for the successful completion of a **terminal behavior;** identified by working backward from the terminal behavior and finding what skills the child must have in order to perform the task. Also called **enabling behaviors.**

Epilepsy. A condition of the central nervous system characterized by periodic seizures.

Error analysis. Procedure used to find out possible reasons instruction has not succeeded; involves comparing patterns of error with patterns and sequences of teaching to pinpoint program components that need to be reworked.

Evaluation. Process of gathering and using information in making decisions. *See* **assessment.**

Exceptionalities. Refers to children and youth who differ sufficiently from the norm to warrant special consideration in housing, schooling, and/or transportation. Includes gifted as well as retarded, disturbed, blind, deaf, physically disabled, and learning disabled.

Expressive language. Means of expressing oneself verbally.

Extended school year (ESY). Schooling in excess of the traditional 9-month school year. Summer programs are sometimes offered to handicapped youngsters to offset the academic losses that may occur during the summer break. *See* **regression/recoupment phenomenon.**

FAPE. *See* **free, appropriate public education.**

Farsightedness. *See* **hyperopia.**

Fetal alcohol syndrome (FAS). A syndrome affecting babies born to women who used alcohol excessively during pregnancy. These children may display retardation, brain damage, hyperactivity, facial anomalies, and heart problems.

Fingerspelling. One type of **manual communication** in which each letter of a word is represented by a hand position.

First Chance. First federal program and demonstration projects aimed exclusively at young handicapped children through the Handicapped Children's Early Childhood Assistance Act. Following a three-year period of successful model demonstration, projects were eligible to compete for outreach funding in order to disseminate their practices and materials.

Floppy disc. A memory storage item that is inserted into a disc drive. It may contain a commercially prepared program or one written by the user and saved for later use.

Fluency. The smooth flow or rhythm of speech. Major fluency problems are **stuttering** and **cluttering.**

Focal seizure. Manifestation of epilepsy that may be either sensory or motor.

Follow Through. Federally funded program used to provide compensatory education for children in the early elementary grades in an effort to continue services initiated during the preschool years by Head Start.

Free, appropriate public education. Education and related services provided at public expense, under public supervision and direction, and without charge to the individual.

Frequency. Pitch of sound, described by cycles per second (cps) or Hertz (Hz).

Functional academics. Academic instruction focusing on the development of practical skills needed to survive in the community.

Functional vision. "How people use whatever vision they may have" (Barraga, 1983).

General intellectual ability. Intelligence; mental ability; ability to acquire and use new information and concepts. Usually measured by a group or individual test.

Generalization. Process in which a skill taught under a specific set of circumstances appears in different environments or with different persons or materials.

Generic classification. A way of organizing instruction for children based on individual strengths and weaknesses. A generic system does not label a child as having a particular handicap or disability.

Genetic counseling. Discussion and information gathering with families for the purpose of determining the likelihood of producing offspring with genetically determined disabilities.

Gifted. "Those children who possess a superior intellectual potential and functional ability to achieve academically in the top 15 to 20% of the school population; and/or talent of high order in such areas as mathematics, science, expressive arts, creative writing, music, and social leadership, and a unique creative ability to deal with their environment" (Fliegler & Bish, 1959); those with IQ scores above 132, between 2 and 4 percent of the population (Witty, 1967). *See* **talented**.

Gifted and talented children. *See* **gifted** or **talented**.

Gonorrhea. Common sexually transmitted disease; responds well to medical treatment. Affects both sexes. Symptoms are specific to genital region.

Grand mal seizure. A severe manifestation of epilepsy resulting in a loss of consciousness and extreme convulsions.

Habilitation. Program of services designed to assist individuals with disabilities in improving their social, functional, mobility, and employment skills.

Hallucinogens. Drugs that produce alterations in the senses of time, color, space, and sound.

Handicap. Environmental or functional demands placed upon a person with a disability as he or she interacts in a given situation; an individual's reaction to his or her disability.

Handicapped. Those children evaluated and diagnosed as being mentally retarded, hard of hearing, deaf, speech impaired, visually handicapped, seriously emotionally disturbed, orthopedically impaired, other health impaired, deaf-blind, or multihandicapped, or as having specific learning disabilities. These children are eligible for special education and related services under P.L. 94–142.

Hard-of-hearing. Having a hearing impairment, whether permanent or fluctuating, that adversely affects educational performance; having sufficient hearing to allow successful processing of linguistic information, frequently with amplification.

Head Start. Largest single federal effort on behalf of young children funded under the Economic Opportunity Act; based on the concept of beginning early if children are going to need more than the usual education because of conditions that place them at risk.

Hearing impaired. A general term that describes both the **deaf** and the **hard-of-hearing**.

Hemiplegia. Paralysis of the limbs on one side of the body.

Hemophilia. A hereditary disease in which the blood clots slowly or not at all, characterized by swollen joints and joint bleeding, as well as by excessive external and internal bleeding.

Herpes simplex. Can cause cold sores or blisters. If it appears on the genitals, it can cause mental retardation in children born to women who contract it in the later stages of pregnancy.

Hertz (HZ). Measures the frequency or pitch of a sound.

High incidence handicaps. Those handicapping conditions that occur at rates of 2 to 3 percent in the general population; includes mental retardation, physical handicaps, learning disabilities, emotional disorders, and speech impairments.

Highly gifted. Youngsters with an IQ score above 148, who make up approximately .1 percent of the school population.

Home Start. Federally funded program for young children, similar to Head Start except that intervention is home-based.

Hydrocephaly. A condition in which excessive amounts of cerebrospinal fluid enlarge the head.

Hyperactivity. Excessive motor behavior (fidgeting, restlessness, inordinate amount of movement around class or home) with or without a clearly defined purpose.

Hyperopia. Farsightedness. The eyeball is too short, with the result that the theoretical point of best focus for nearby objects is behind the retina, and nearby objects appear less distinct than do distant objects.

IEP. *See* **individualized education program.**

IEP team. A group that plans a child's IEP; made up of a representative of the school district (such as the principal), the child's teacher, one or both of the child's parents (or, in some cases, a court-appointed parent surrogate), and, where appropriate, the child. With a first evaluation, a member of the **multidisciplinary team,** or at least someone else who is familiar with the assessment procedures used with the child, must be present.

Impairment. Tissue damage, defect, or deterioration that may result in disability or dysfunction.

Impulsivity. Lack of control over impulses; spontaneous actions with little thought to consequences.

Incorrigible syndrome. Pattern of behaviors exhibited by some disturbed children: underachievement, management problems, irrelevant responses in class, classroom disturbances, inattentiveness.

Individualized education program (IEP). A statement specifying instructional goals and any special education and related services a child may need; written and reviewed annually. Included are (1) the present educational levels of the child; (2) a statement of annual goals, including short-term instructional objectives; (3) a statement of specific services, if needed; (4) the programs; (5) the date when special services are to begin and the expected duration of these services; and (6) the tests and other requirements or information used to gauge the child's progress to determine if the instructional objectives are being met.

Input device. Generally, a keyboard, similar to that on a typewriter, used to put information into the CPU. Adaptations for the handicapped include a touch-sensitive screen, auditory input devices, light pens, and keyboard simulators.

Inquiry. Instruction by asking a series of specific and leading questions. Learning comes through application of the student's own words and statements as they are gradually expanded to include a new concept.

Instructional technology. The educational application of machines and the programs that drive them.

Intensity. Power of sounds, usually expressed in decibels; volume.

Interface. A device that permits an individual to communicate with a computer or other technological system. For example, a keyboard is an interface.

Interindividual differences. Variations *among* individuals; comparisons of a given individual with the average for a characteristic.

Interview. A dialogue between two persons: The interviewer, who attempts to gain information, and the interviewee, the person giving the information.

Intraindividual differences. Variations *within* an individual; comparisons of the rates of development in the various domains.

Irrepressible syndrome. Pattern of behaviors exhibited by some disturbed children: lack of respect, defiance, open challenges.

Itinerant teacher. A teacher who travels to a variety of schools, consulting with the teacher and providing individual instruction to a student with a handicap.

Juvenile delinquent. "A person under a specific age who violates any state or local law, or commits any act that would be considered a crime if committed by an adult" (Kvaraceus, 1971).

Juvenile diabetes mellitus. A hereditary disorder in which sugar (glucose) cannot be used normally by the body because of the failure of the pancreas to produce insulin.

Juvenile rheumatoid arthritis. A musculoskeletal disorder characterized by inflammation of the joints.

Lability. Frequent abrupt changes in mood and temperament; opposite of stability.

Lalling. An early stage of prelanguage development; also a common articulation error in older children and adults, usually involving the *l* and *r* sounds. Similar to lisping.

Language. "A set of symbols—oral or written—used by members of a social community in a fairly standardized way to call forth meaning" (Blake & Haroldsen, 1975).

Language disorders. Language delays, deviations in development, and disorders acquired after language has been established.

Language problems. Difficulties with the linguistic code, or rules and conventions for linking symbols and symbol sequences. *See* **language disorders.**

Learning disability. A disorder in one or more of the basic psychological processes involved in understanding or using spoken or written language, which may be manifested in an imperfect ability to listen, think, speak, read, write, spell, or do mathematical calculations. The term includes such conditions as perceptual handicaps, brain injury, minimal brain dysfunction, dyslexia, and developmental aphasia. The term does not include children who have learning problems that are primarily the result of visual, hearing, or motor handicaps; of mental retardation; or of environmental, cultural, or economic disadvantage.

Least restrictive alternative. *See* **least restrictive environment.**

Least restrictive environment (LRE). The federal rules for implementation of P.L. 94–142 state that handicapped youths may be educated in segregated settings only when the nature or severity of the handicap is so great that education in regular classes is not possible. Education in regular classes is the least restrictive environment for most children; full-time residential school and hospitalization are the most restrictive. *See* **Cascade model.**

Legg-Perthes disease. A musculoskeletal disorder characterized by partial or complete destruction of the growth center at the hip end of the thigh bone.

Legislation. The governmental process in which elected members of state congresses or the U.S. Congress originate and pass laws.

Life space interviewing. Counseling that takes place in real situations and at the time the behavior problem occurs. Basic objectives are to work on long-range therapeutic goals and to provide emotional support. Requires special training.

Litigation. The process in which a judge and/or jury review evidence and render a decision about a particular case or suit. Results of a court case may establish precedence and become one source of state and federal law.

Low incidence handicaps. Those handicapping conditions that occur in rates less than 1.5 percent of the general population; includes sensory impairments, multihandicaps, severe handicaps, and deaf-blindness.

Low vision. Limited distance vision but some useful near vision at a range of several feet.

LRE. *See* **least restrictive environment.**

Mainstreaming. Efforts to educate children in the least restrictive environment or educational setting; placing handicapped children in conventional schools and classes and integrating them with normal children to the maximum extent possible.

Manual communication. A system of hand symbols and signals that convey specific ideas, concepts, or words.

Mathias Amendment. Public Law 93–380, Title VI B, Education of the Handicapped Amendment (1973); requires that a state develop specific programs and provisions for the education of the handicapped in order to retain its eligibility to receive federal funds for educating the handicapped.

Measurement. Process of determining the extent or nature of something by comparison with a standard. In education, standards are often contrived by determining average performance of a group rather than through real events in a physical world, and measures are usually indirect.

Media-based materials. Films, videotapes, audio cassettes, and the like for use by individuals or with small and large groups of children in teaching whole lessons or particular concepts or themes.

Mentally retarded. Having significantly subaverage general intellectual functioning concurrent with deficits in adaptive behavior, manifested during the developmental period and adversely affecting educational performance.

Metalinguistics. Aspect of human communication that reflects the "status of communication" (Owens, 1986, p. 28), or the attitude or degree of respect and the relationship between the participants.

Microcephaly. A condition in which the head is too small to permit normal brain development, resulting in retardation.

Mildly vocationally handicapped. Likely to become an independent, self-supporting adult given appropriate counseling, career and vocational training, and perhaps compensatory or other types of postsecondary training; able to compete in the job market, hold down a job, get around the community, run a household, communicate with friends, and so on.

Minority. Persons in the United States whose origins are in the original peoples of North America, the Far East, Southeast Asia, or the Pacific Islands; black/Negro, or persons whose origins are in any of the black racial groups of Africa; Hispanic, or a person of Mexican, Puerto Rican, Cuban, Central or South American, or other Spanish culture or origin.

Mixed form of cerebral palsy. Characterized by a combination of **spasticity** and **athetosis.**

Modeling. Learning behaviors through observing others; performance of the behavior may depend on consequences associated with the action. An especially good technique to use with youngsters who have difficulty understanding or remembering verbal instructions.

Modem. A peripheral device allowing communication with other computers through telephone connections.

Monoplegia. Paralysis of one limb.

Multidisciplinary team. Group of professionals responsible for evaluating a child and making decisions about the child's education program. The team must include at least one teacher or other specialist with knowledge in the area of suspected disability.

Multihandicapped. Having "concomitant impairments (such as mentally retarded–blind, mentally retarded–orthopedically impaired, etc.), the combination of which causes such severe educational problems that they cannot be accommodated in special education programs solely for one of the impairments." The term does not include those who are deaf-blind (U.S. Office of Education, 1977a).

Multiply handicapped. *See* **Multihandicapped.**

Muscular dystrophy. "A progressive diffuse weakness of all muscle groups characterized by a degeneration of muscle cells and their replacement by fat and fibrous tissue" (Bleck, 1975).

Myoclonic seizure. Manifestation of epilepsy characterized by brief, involuntary muscle contractions.

Myopia. Nearsightedness. The eyeball is generally too long, with the result that the point of best focus for distant objects is in front of the retina, and nearby objects appear much more distinct than do distant objects.

Narcotics. Drugs that reduce pain and blunt the senses; in large quantities can cause euphoria, stupor. Can be addictive.

Nearsightedness. *See* **myopia.**

Negative reinforcement. Increasing the frequency or strength of a behavior through the removal of aversive events following the performance of the desired behavior. When an individual is allowed to escape or get rid of unpleasant, aversive conditions by performing a certain behavior, we say the behavior is under the control of negative reinforcement.

Neurological disorder. Damage to or defect or deterioration of the central nervous system. May result in a variety of physical and mental problems, including paralysis, convulsive disorders, mental retardation, learning disabilities, or speech problems.

Neurosis. Mild to moderate emotional/mental disorder. Wide range of behaviors include anxieties, phobias, and socially unacceptable tics and mannerisms. *See also* **emotional disturbance** and **psychosis.**

Nonlinguistics. Aspect of human communication process that helps convey the meaning and feeling underlying the spoken word but that is nonverbal and not part of the linguistic code.

Normalization. A humanistic movement to provide surroundings, opportunities, and programs for disabled persons much like those available to more normal children and adults.

Norm-referenced assessment. Evaluation of a child's performance in terms of relative position in some known comparison group; the standard varies depending on the performance of the group. Tied to interindividual differences.

Observation. System for gathering useful information about children by watching as objectively as possible; watching a child perform a task and recording what you see, using checklists, rating scales, anecdotal records, and so on.

Oculist. *See* **Ophthalmologist.**

Operant conditioning. A method of changing behavior in which emitted responses are controlled by the selective application or withholding of reinforcement.

Ophthalmologist. A medical doctor who specializes in the diagnosis and treatment of all defects and diseases of the eye by prescribing glasses and drugs, performing surgery, and carrying out other forms of medical treatment.

Optician. A person who grinds lenses according to prescription, fits spectacle and contact lenses, and adjusts frames.

Optometrist. A licensed nonmedical practitioner who is trained to measure refractive errors and eye muscle disturbances.

Oral communication. Communication in which speech is the main channel.

Orientation. The location of oneself within the environment and in relation to objects within the environment.

Orthopedically impaired. Having a severe orthopedic impairment that adversely affects educational performance. The term includes impairments caused by congenital anomaly (e.g., clubfoot, absence of some member, etc.), impairments caused by disease (e.g., poliomyelitis, bone tuberculosis, etc.), and impairments from other causes (e.g., cerebral palsy, amputations, and fractures or burns that cause contractures).

Orthoptist. A technician trained to carry out eye exercise programs under medical supervision.

Osteogenesis imperfecta. A musculoskeletal disorder characterized by brittle bones, especially early in life.

Other health impaired. Having impaired strength, vitality, or alertness as a result of chronic or acute health problems (such as a heart condition, tuberculosis, rheumatic fever, nephritis, asthma, sickle cell anemia, hemophilia, epilepsy, lead poisoning, leukemia, or diabetes) that adversely affect educational performance.

Otolaryngologist. Medical ear, nose, and throat specialist who provides medical and surgical treatment.

Otologist. Physician who specializes in treatment of diseases of the ear; can diagnose causes of hearing problems and recommend medical and surgical treatment.

Output device. Most often a screen similar to a TV screen; however, a printer also enables the CPU to type on paper (called hard copy) the information it sends to the user. Also, other devices such as wheelchairs or speech synthesis devices can be considered output devices.

Paralinguistics. Aspect of human communication process that suggests the attitudes or feelings of the speaker; elements include intonation patterns, stresses, rate of speech flow, use of pauses, variations in pitch and volume, and overall melody or rhythm.

Paraplegia. Paralysis of both legs.

Partial vision. Visual acuity of 20/70 or less in the better eye after correction.

Participation chart. Observation form used to record presence or absence of behaviors, consisting of a list of names of learners and space to note each time a learner participates. Especially useful when many learners are being observed simultaneously and when participation in some activity is the behavior of interest.

Peer tutoring. Instruction of one child by another in a structured situation; tutors must be trained, special materials prepared, and an appropriate location established.

Perceptual-motor skills. Those abilities that enable a child to interpret basic sounds and forms and then perform appropriate actions as a result of mental or neurological processes.

Perceptual-motor training. Approach to teaching mildly handicapped children by focusing on and remediating perceptual problems such as gross and fine motor skills, form perception, memory sequencing, laterality training, visual and auditory discrimination, and so on, that prevent the acquisition of higher-level skills such as reading.

Peripheral hearing loss. Conductive or sensorineural hearing loss, as contrasted with central hearing loss. Peripheral loss is attributable to problems in the middle or outer ear, whereas central loss refers to problems within the brain pathways or cortex.

Peripherals. These are additional attachments that operate using the CPU when connected to it (interfaced with it). Examples are a printer or game paddles.

Petit mal seizure. A seizure characterized by brief lapses in consciousness.

Phonemes. Individual distinctive sounds of speech; there are about forty phonemes in the English language.

Photophobia. Extreme sensitivity to light.

Physical abuse. Nonaccidental injuries that most frequently are the result of beatings and burns.

Physically disabled. Having nonsensory physical impairments, limitations, or health problems.

Physical neglect. Willful failure to provide the basic medical attention, nourishment, clothing, supervision, and housing necessary for sustaining healthy life.

Play therapy. A "talking-out" therapy used to help a child deal with social and emotional problems, involving arranging the environment with a variety of toys and props and allowing the child to play and talk casually with a therapist.

Poliomyelitis. Viral infection of the spinal cord and/or nerve tissue in the brain; may result in paralysis.

Positive reinforcement. The application of consequences that follow a behavior and result in increasing the frequency, duration, or intensity of that behavior.

Postlingual deafness. Severe hearing loss that occurs after the acquisition of basic language skills. People with this condition are also known as deafened or adventitiously deaf.

Prelingual deafness. Deafness that occurs prior to the acquisition of language.

Prenatal diagnosis. Medical techniques for studying and diagnosing potential fetal problems early in pregnancy.

Prerequisite skills. Skills that are necessary before one can successfully perform another behavior.

Principal. Administrative leader in a school; fosters development and implementation of regular and special education programs.

Process training. Instructional programs designed to strengthen the psychological process underlying particular academic skills.

Profile. Graphic representation of information that makes it possible to look at an individual's pattern of strengths and weaknesses; sometimes used in the process of identifying a child as exceptional.

Programmed instruction. Teaching materials based on (1) careful analysis of the task(s) to be learned; (2) small, incremental steps leading the learner from little or no knowledge about the task or skill to mastery; (3) self-pacing and perhaps self-monitoring by the learner; and (4) revision of the material based upon analysis of trials by many learners.

Psychodynamic approach. A way of understanding human behavior, derived from the work of Sigmund Freud, that emphasizes the importance of the early years, critical growth stages, and the development of appropriate internal controls.

Psychomotor seizure. The most varied in form and most difficult to recognize of all epileptic seizures; usually consists of purposeful but inappropriate motor actions somewhat automatic in nature.

Psychosis. Severe behavioral/mental disorder characterized by loss of contact with reality, inability to maintain oneself in modern society. *See also* **emotional disturbance** and **neurosis**.

Public Law 94–142. The Education for All Handicapped Children Act of 1975; a federal law that guarantees a free, appropriate public education for all handicapped children from ages three to twenty-one, regardless of the severity of the handicap.

Public Law 99–457. The Education of Handicapped Children Act Amendment of 1986. The legislative act made specific provisions for early childhood education.

Pure tone audiometer. *See* **audiometer.**

Quadriplegia. Paralysis in which all four limbs are involved.

Questionnaire. Form that presents a set of questions to which subjects respond in writing; questions may be factual or personal and might be similar to those used in a structured interview.

Random access memory (RAM). Internal memory storage that can be accessed by the user. Usually described in thousands of characters or bytes (as in 48K, 64K).

Rating scale. A list of expected behaviors, characteristics of performance, or aspects of a product that an observer rates according to quality or frequency.

Read only memory (ROM). This contains information read only by the CPU. The user cannot access it or record anything on it.

Receptive language. Means of receiving and understanding verbal or written communication.

Reciprocal inhibition. An applied behavior technique involving inhibiting anxiety by establishing a competing response.

Reciprocity. The concept of the infant influencing the adult even while the adult influences the infant.

Referral. Recommendation of a child to a specialist for further observation and/or testing.

Reflective listening. A technique in which a therapist (or parent or teacher) helps individuals verbalize emotions they are experiencing by describing, defining, or paraphrasing the client's comments; for example, saying "that must have made you angry . . . " or "you're feeling frustrated because . . . " to help the client express emotions.

Refractive errors. Common causes of reduced visual acuity, including myopia, hyperopia, and astigmatism.

Regression/recoupment phenomenon. The situation in which a handicapped youngster loses ground, or regresses, academically during the summer. Recovering, or recouping, such losses requires considerable time during the next school year. *See* **extended school year.**

Reinforcement. The application of consequences to increase the frequency or strength of a response. *See* **negative reinforcement** and **positive reinforcement.**

Related services. Transportation and such developmental, corrective, and other supportive services as are required to help a handicapped child benefit from special education. Included are speech pathology and audiology, psychological services, physical and occupational therapy, recreation, early identification and assessment of disabilities, counseling and medical services for diagnostic or evaluation purposes, school health services, social-work services in schools, and parent counseling and training.

Reliability. The consistency and dependability of the results of information-gathering processes; consistency may be over time, from one observer to another, from one form of a test to another, or within the same observer for different times and different children.

Remedial education. The process of improving or correcting skill in a particular area or field; raising skills to normal or near normal.

Resource teacher. A teacher who provides instructional services to children with disabilities in specific academic areas.

Respite care. Placing a handicapped child in a group home or other facility for a brief period of time (one day or two or three weeks) to give parents a break in, or respite from, the daily routine of caring for the child. Alternatively, providing a temporary caregiver in the child's home for a few days while the parents take a vacation.

Rheumatic fever. An inflammatory disease that occurs after a strep infection, characterized by high fever, painful swelling of joints, skin rash, and inflammation of the valves and muscles of the heart.

Rh incompatibility. The mother has Rh negative blood and the father has Rh positive, which may result in a baby being born with a disability.

Rigidity. Form of cerebral palsy characterized by high muscle tone, lack of voluntary motion, and resistance to movement.

School psychologist. Professional trained to administer individual tests and evaluate performance to determine nature of learning and behavior problems.

Scoliosis. A musculoskeletal disorder characterized by lateral curvature of the spine.

Screening. Process of administering tests in order to find children who are in need of further help or special attention; screening is often initially carried out by teachers and does not require a certified psychologist for administration.

Sensorineural hearing loss. Hearing loss resulting from problems within the inner ear.

Seriously emotionally disturbed.
1. The term means a condition exhibiting one or more of the following characteristics over a long period of time and to a marked degree, which adversely affects educational performance:
   a. An inability to learn which cannot be explained by intellectual, sensory, or health factors;
   b. An inability to build or maintain satisfactory interpersonal relationships with peers and teachers;
   c. Inappropriate types of behavior or feelings under normal circumstances;
   d. A general pervasive mood of unhappiness or depression; or
   e. A tendency to develop physical symptoms or fears associated with personal or school problems.
2. The term includes children who are schizophrenic or autistic. The term does not include children who are socially maladjusted, unless it is deter-

mined that they are seriously emotionally disturbed. (U.S. Office of Education, 1977a)

Seriously vocationally handicapped. Having a disability so severe or intense that one is unlikely to become a self-sufficient, independent adult, able to live alone, get around in the community, or be competitive in the job market.

Severely and profoundly handicapped (SPH). *See* **Severely and profoundly impaired.**

Severely and profoundly impaired (SPI). One of the three groups of children classified according to a scheme once prevalent in American schools. Corresponds roughly to IQ levels of 30 and lower.

Sexual abuse. Any sexual activity, injurious or not, between an adult and a child.

Sexually transmitted disease (STD). A disease transmitted via sexual contact such as syphilis, herpes, and Acquired Immune Deficiency Syndrome.

Sheltered workshop. A subsidized place of employment for adults with disabilities. The workers receive minimum wage or piece rate. Workshops are often sponsored by organizations such as the Association for Retarded Citizens.

Sickle cell anemia. A hereditary blood disease characterized by anemia resulting from insufficiency of red blood cells, impairment of liver function, swelling of limbs and joints, severe pain, loss of appetite, and general weakness.

Sign language. *See* **manual communication.**

Skill training. Direct instruction of children in specific skills or behaviors without dealing with possible underlying processes.

Sociological theory. An explanation of human behavior that involves the study of the rules of social interactions; a way of describing emotional disturbance in which mental illness is viewed as breaking the rules of social interactions.

Sociometric technique. Means of determining how a group is socially structured; asking individuals in a group to indicate those group members with whom they would prefer to be associated in a given situation.

Spasticity. A form of cerebral palsy characterized by involuntary muscle contractions and inaccurate and difficult voluntary motion.

Special education. Specially designed instruction, at no cost to the parent, to meet the unique needs of the handicapped child, including classroom instruction, instruction in physical education, home instruction, and instruction in hospitals and institutions (P.L. 94–142).

Specific learning disability. *See* **learning disability.**

Speech. "Medium that employs an oral linguistic code that enables one human being to express feelings and to communicate thoughts to another human being" (Eisenson, Auer, & Irwin, 1963).

Speech impaired. Having a communication disorder, such as stuttering, impaired articulation, a language impairment, or a voice impairment, such that educational performance is adversely affected.

Speech/language pathologist or clinician. Professional trained to determine the nature of speech and language problems and their treatment and remediation.

Speech problems. Problems associated with production of the oral symbols of language.

Speech synthesizer. A device that simulates the human voice enabling rapid communication for nonvocal individuals.

Spina bifida. A group of disabilities, including spina bifida occulta, meningocele, and myelomeningocele, characterized by open defects in the spinal cord.

Stimulants. Drugs that increase alertness, reduce hunger, produce a feeling of well-being, and/or reduce fatigue.

Stuttering. Abnormal or repetitive interruptions of the normal flow of speech, or prolongations of sound.

Syndrome. "Combination of physical traits or malformations that are inherited in the same way and carry a similar prognosis" (Batshaw & Perret, 1981).

Syphilis. A sexually transmitted disease that can cause retardation in a baby if contracted by the mother in the later stages of pregnancy.

Talented. "The talented or gifted child is one who shows consistently remarkable performance in any worthwhile line of endeavor. Thus we shall include not only the intellectually gifted, but also those who show promise in music, the graphic arts, mechanical skills, creative writing, dramatics and social leadership" (Havighurst, 1958). *See* **Gifted.**

Task analysis. Breakdown of learning tasks into their component parts so that skills involved in performing the task can be identified. Branching and reinforcement strategies combined with a management aspect produce effective learning.

Terminal behavior. A target behavior or objective toward which a program of training is geared. Sometimes referred to as long-range objective.

Threshold of hearing. The point at which an individual responds to sound at least half the time.

Total communication. The philosophical position regarding the development of communication skills that advocates the use of whatever enables the child who is deaf to communicate with others; also refers to the combined use of speech, signing, gestures, speechreading, fingerspelling, and even reading and writing in an attempt to extend the communication capabilities of the child who is deaf.

Trainable mentally retarded (TMR). One of three groups of retarded children classified according to a scheme once prevalent in American schools. Corresponds roughly to IQ levels between 30 or 35 and 55.

Tremor. Form of cerebral palsy characterized by shakiness in involved limb and variation in constancy and pattern of movement.

Triplegia. Paralysis in which three limbs are involved, usually one upper limb and both lower limbs.

Underachieving syndrome. Pattern of behaviors exhibited by some disturbed children: low self-reliance, overdependence on others, difficulty in decision making.

Validity. Ability of an evaluation to yield results that will serve the purposes they are intended to serve; the "truth" component of an evaluation procedure; extent to which a test measures what the authors state it will measure.

Visual acuity. A measure of the resolving, or refracting, power of the eyes to bend light rays so they come to a point of focus on the retina and enable one to see fine detail at varying distances.

Visual discrimination. "Ability to distinguish sizes, shapes, etc., of symbols and letters" (Sabatino, 1972).

Visual field. The entire area seen at one time without shifting the gaze.

Visually handicapped. "Having a visual impairment that, even with correction, adversely affects educational performance. The term includes both partially seeing and blind children" (U.S. Office of Education, 1977a); "total group of children who require special educational provisions because of visual problems" (Barraga, 1976).

Visually limited. Having useful vision for educational purposes but some limit in function under average conditions.

Visual memory. "Ability to retain or recall visual symbols, shapes, letters, etc." (Sabatino, 1982).

Vocal play. A stage in language development in which a child begins to "play" with or practice sounds. The sounds are not true words, but they are pronounced in the same way and in appropriate social or solitary situations.

Vocationally handicapped. *See* **mildly** or **seriously vocationally handicapped.**

Voice problems. Problems in the resonant quality of the voice; problems in control of pitch, timbre, volume, or quality of the voice.

Work activity center. A heavily subsidized workshop and training center for adults who are too severely disabled to find competitive employment even in a sheltered workshop. The emphasis is on training for work and social skills rather than income.

GLOSSARY OF ABBREVIATIONS

ABA	Applied Behavior Analysis		MBD	Minimal Brain Damage or Minimal Brain Dysfunction
ADD	Attention Deficit Disorder		MBI	Minimal Brain Injury
AFT	American Federation of Teachers		MR	Mental Retardation
AIDS	Acquired Immune Deficiency Syndrome		NARC	National Association for Retarded Citizens
ASHA	American Speech-Language-Hearing Association		NDT	Neurodevelopmental Training
BD	Behavior Disorders		NIEH	Neurologically Impaired/Emotionally Handicapped
CAI	Computer-Assisted Instruction		OT	Occupational Therapist
CBE	Computer-Based Education		PH	Physically Handicapped
CDC	Center for Disease Control		PI	Perceptually Impaired
CEC	Council for Exceptional Children		PKU	Phenylpyruvic Olgophrenia or Phenylketonuria
CIC	Clean Intermittent Catheterization		PMR	Profoundly Mentally Retarded
CLA	Community Living Arrangements		PT	Physical Therapist
COHI	Crippled or Other Health Impaired		SEA	State Educational Agency
CP	Cerebral Palsy		SED	Seriously Emotionally Disturbed or Socially/Emotionally Disturbed
ED	Emotionally Disturbed		SLA	Supervised Living Arrangements
EH	Educationally Handicapped or Emotionally Handicapped		SPH	Severely/Profoundly Handicapped
EHA	Education of Handicapped Children's Act		SPI	Severely/Profoundly Impaired
EMR	Educable Mentally Retarded		SPMR	Severe/Profound Mental Retardation
ESY	Extended School Year		STD	Sexually Transmitted Diseases
FAPE	Free Appropriate Public Education		TAM	Technology and Media (Division of CEC)
FAS	Fetal Alcohol Syndrome		TED	Teacher Education Division (of Council for Exceptional Children)
HI	Hearing Impaired		TMR	Trainable Mentally Retarded
IEP	Individualized Education Program		TTD	Telecommunication Device for the Deaf
IFSP	Individualized Family Service Plan		UCP	United Cerebral Palsy
IPP	Individual Program Plan		USOE	United States Office of Education
LD	Learning Disabilities or Learning Disabled		VI	Visually Impaired
LEA	Local Education Agency			
LRE	Least Restrictive Environment			

BIBLIOGRAPHY

Aaron, R. (1975). Computer-managed instruction for behaviorally disordered adolescents. *Reading Improvement, 12,* 103–107.

Abel, G. L. (1959). Problems and trends in the education of blind children and youth. In G. L. Abel (Ed.), *Concerning the education of blind children.* New York: American Foundation for the Blind.

Abroms, K. I. (1981). Service delivery networks. In K. I. Abroms & J. W. Bennett (Eds.), *Issues in genetics and exceptional children.* San Francisco: Jossey-Bass.

Abroms, K. I., & Bennett, J. W. (Eds.). (1981a). *Issues in genetics and exceptional children.* San Francisco: Jossey-Bass.

Abroms, K. I., & Bennett, J. W. (1981b). Parental contributions to Trisomy 21. In P. Mittler (Ed.), *Frontiers of knowledge in mental retardation: Biomedical aspects* (Vol. 2). Baltimore, MD: University Park Press.

Abroms, K. I., & Bennett, J. W. (1983). Current findings in Down's syndrome. *Exceptional children, 49*(5), 449–450.

Adelman, H. S., & Taylor, L. (1983). *Learning disabilities in perspective.* Glenview, IL: Scott-Foresman.

Adelman, H. S., & Taylor, L. (1986). The problems of definition and differentiation and the need for a classification schema. *Journal of Learning Disabilities, 19,* 514–520.

Aeschleman, S., & Tawney, J. (1978). Interacting: A computer-based telecommunications system for educating severely handicapped preschoolers in their homes. *Educational Technology, 18,* 30–35.

Airasian, P. W., & Madaus, G. J. (1972). Functional types of student evaluation. *Measurement and Evaluation in Guidance, 4,* 221–233.

Alberto, P. A., & Troutman, A. C. (1986). *Applied behavior analysis for teachers.* Columbus, OH: Merrill.

Algozzine, B., & Mercer, C. D. (1980). Labels and expectancies for handicapped children and youth. In L. Mann & D. Sabatino (Eds.), *The fourth review of special education.* New York: Grune and Stratton.

Algozzine, R. (1979). Social-emotional problems. In C. D. Mercer (Ed.), *Children and adolescents with learning disabilities.* Columbus, OH: Merrill.

Alibrandi, T. (1978). *Young alcoholics.* Minneapolis, MN: Comp-Care.

Allard, K. E. (1982, March). *The videodisc and implications for interactivity.* Paper presented at the Annual Meeting of American Educational Research Association, New York. (ERIC Document Reproduction Service No. ED 217 884).

Allegheny Intermediate Unit. (1982, July). *Exceptional children's program: Improved individual instruction program* (Final Report 1977–1980). (ERIC Document Reproduction Service No. ED 213 153).

Allport, G. W. (1978). *Becoming: Basic considerations for a psychology of personality.* New Haven, CT: Yale University Press.

Ambron, S. R. (1978). *Child development* (2nd ed.). New York: Holt, Rinehart and Winston.

American Annals of the Deaf. (1975, October). Report of the ad hoc committee to define deaf and hard of hearing, *120*(5), 509–512.

American Optical Company. (1976). *The human eye: A course in programmed instruction.* Southbridge, MA: Author.

American Printing House for the Blind Annual Report. (1987). Louisville, KY: American Printing House.

American Psychiatric Association. (1980). *Diagnostic and statistical manual of mental disorders* (3rd ed.). Washington, DC: Author.

American Speech and Hearing Association (ASHA). (1974). *ASHA Report, 16*(9), 544.

Ames, L. B. (1983). Learning disability: Truth or trap? *Journal of Learning Disabilities, 16*(1), 20–21.

Anastasi, A. (1976). *Psychological testing* (4th ed.). New York: Macmillan.

Anastasiow, N. J. (1983). Adolescent pregnancy and special education. *Exceptional Children, 49*(5), 396–401.

Anderson, K., & Milliren, A. (1983). *Structured experiences for integration of handicapped children.* Rockville, MD: Aspen Systems.

Apgar, V., & Beck, J. (1974). *Is my baby all right?* New York: Pocket Books.

Apple Computer, Inc. (1980). *Personal computers for the physically disabled: A resource guide.* Cupertino, CA: Author. (ERIC Document Reproduction Service No. ED 213 182).

Appleton, B. (1982). An inexpensive home eye test. *Minnesota Medicine, 65*(1), 575–577.

Arcanin, J., & Zawolkow, G. (1980). Microcomputers in the service of students and teachers—Computer-assisted instruction at the California School for the Deaf: An update. *American Annals of the Deaf, 125*(6), 807–813.

Arenas, S. A., & Ensher, G. L. (1986). Intervention in home- and computer-based programs. In G.L. Ensher & D. A. Clark (Eds.), *Newborns at risk* (pp. 215–247). Rockville, MD: Aspen Systems.

Armstrong v. Kline, 476 F. Supp. 583 (E.D. Pa. 1979).

Arter, J. A., & Jenkins, J. R. (1979). Differential diagnosis—prescriptive teaching: A critical appraisal. *Review of Educational Research, 49*(4), 517–555.

Ashcroft, S. C. (1982, February). *Evaluation and research program for the portable braille recorder (PBR): Final report* (Vol. 1). (ERIC Document Reproduction Service No. ED 207 267).

Ashton-Warner, S. (1963). *Teacher.* New York: Simon and Schuster.

Association for the Development of Computer-Based Instructional Systems. (1987). *SIG/HAN NEWS, 1*(1), 2.

Audette, D. (1982). Private school placement: A local director's perspective. *Exceptional Children, 49*(3), 214–219.

Avery, C. B. (1967). The education of children with impaired hearing. In W. M. Cruickshank & G. O. Johnson (Eds.), *Education of exceptional children.* Englewood Cliffs, NJ: Prentice–Hall.

Baer, D. M., Wolf, M. M., & Risley, T. R. (1968). Some current dimensions of applied behavior analysis. *Journal of Applied Behavior Analysis, 1,* 91–97.

Bagnato, S. J. (1981). Developmental scales and developmental curricula: Forging a linkage for early intervention. *Topics in Early Childhood Special Education, 1*(2), 1–8.

Bagnato, S. J., Munson, S. M., & MacTurk, R. H. (1987). Exceptional infants and toddlers. In J. T. Neisworth & S. J. Bagnato (Eds.), *The young exceptional child* (pp. 180–205). New York: Macmillan.

Bagnato, S. J., & Neisworth, J. T. (1979). Between assessment and intervention: Forging an assessment/curriculum linkage for the handicapped preschooler. *Child Care Quarterly, 8*(3), 179–195.

Baird, H. (1975). Acute or nonrecurrent convulsions. In V. Vaughn, R. M. McKay, & W. Nelson (Eds.), *Textbook of pediatrics* (2nd ed.). Philadelphia: W. B. Saunders.

Bajan, J. W., & Susser, P. L. (1982). Getting on with the education of handicapped children: A policy of partnership. *Exceptional Children, 49*(3), 208–212.

Baker, B., & Heifetz, L. (1976). The Read Project: Teaching manual for parents of retarded children. In T. Tjossem (Ed.), *Intervention strategies for high risk infants and young children.* Baltimore, MD: University Park Press.

Baker, C. J. (1984). Child abuse and sexually transmitted diseases. In K. K. Holmes, P. Mardh, P. F. Sparling, & P. J. Weisner (Eds.), *Sexually transmitted diseases* (pp. 116–119). New York: McGraw-Hill.

Bandura, A. (1969). Social learning theory of identificatory processes. In D. A. Goslin (Ed.), *Handbook of socialization theory and research.* Chicago: Rand McNally.

Barbara, D. A. (1965). *Questions and answers on stuttering.* Springfield, IL: Charles C. Thomas.

Barraga, N. (1964). *Increased visual behavior in low vision children* (Research Series #3). New York: American Foundation for the Blind.

Barraga, N. (1973). Utilization of sensory-perceptual abilities. In B. Lowenfeld (Ed.), *The visually handicapped child in school.* New York: John Day.

Barraga, N. (1976). *Visual handicaps and learning: A developmental approach.* Belmont, CA: Wadsworth.

Barraga, N. (1983). *Visual handicaps and learning* (rev. ed.). Austin, TX: Exceptional Resources.

Barraga, N. (1986). Sensory perceptual development. In G. Scholl (Ed.), *Foundations of education for blind and visually handicapped children and youth: Theory and practice* (pp. 83–98). New York: American Foundation for the Blind.

Barsch, R. H. (1976). Ray H. Barsch. In J. M. Kauffman & D. P. Hallahan (Eds.), *Teaching children with learning disabilities: Personal perspectives.* Columbus, OH: Merrill.

Bartel, N., & Guskin, S. (1980). A handicap as a social phenomenon. In W. M. Cruickshank (Ed.), *Psychology of exceptional children and youth* (4th ed.). Englewood Cliffs, NJ: Prentice–Hall.

Bartram, J. (1969). Cerebral palsy. In W. Nelson, V. Vaughn, & R. McKay (Eds.), *Textbook of pediatrics.* Philadelphia: W. B. Saunders.

Bates, M., & Wilson, K. (1981, September). *ILIAD: Interactive language instruction assistance for the deaf: Final report* (Report #4771). (ERIC Document Reproduction Service No. ED 219 918).

Batshaw, M. L., & Perret, Y. M. (1981). *Children with handicaps: A medical primer.* Baltimore, MD: Paul H. Brooks.

Battle v. Commonwealth, 79, 2158, 2188-90, 2568-70 (3d Cir. July 18, 1980).

Beadle, K. R. (1975). Communication disorders—speech and hearing. In E. E. Bleck & D. A. Nagel (Eds.), *Physically handicapped children: A medical atlas for teachers.* New York: Grune and Stratton.

Beadle, K. R. (1982). Communication disorders—Speech and hearing (2nd ed.). In E. E. Bleck & D. A. Nagel (Eds.), *Physically handicapped children: A medical atlas for teachers* (pp. 133–143). New York: Grune and Stratton.

Becker, W., Engelmann, S., & Thomas, D. (1971). *Teaching: A course in applied psychology.* Chicago: Science Research Associates.

Beckerman, J. (1983, February). You don't have to know the language. *The Computing Teacher, 10*(6), 23–25.

Bender, M., Brannan, S. A., & Verhover, P. J. (1908). *Leisure education for the handicapped.* San Diego, CA: College-Hill Press.

Benedict, R. (1934). Anthropology and the abnormal. *Journal of General Psychology, 10,* 59–80.

Bennett, R. E. (1982). Application of microcomputer technology to special education. *Exceptional Children, 49,* 106–113.

Berdine, W. H., & Blackhurst, A. E. (1985). *An introduction to special education* (2nd ed.). Boston: Little, Brown.

Berger, M. (1981). *Computers in your life.* New York: Thomas Y. Crowell.

Berlin, A. (1972). Hearing problems. In G. P. Cartwright & C. A. Cartwright (Eds.), *CARE: Early identification of handicapped children.* University Park, PA: Pennsylvania State University.

Berlin, C. I. (1976). Programmed instruction in the decibel. In J. L. Northern (Ed.), *Hearing disorders*. Boston: Little, Brown.

Berlin, C. M., Jr. (1978). Biology and retardation. In J. T. Neisworth & R. M. Smith (Eds.), *Retardation: Issues, assessment, and intervention*. New York: McGraw-Hill.

Bernal, E. (1979). The education of the culturally different gifted. In A. H. Passow (Ed.), *The gifted and the talented: Their education and development*. 78th Yearbook of the National Society for the Study of Education. Part 1. Chicago: University of Chicago Press.

Bernal, E., & Reyna, J. (1975). Analysis and identification of giftedness in Mexican American children: A pilot study. In B. O. Boston (Ed.), *A resource manual of information on educating the gifted and talented*. ERIC Clearinghouse on Handicapped and Gifted Children. Reston, VA: The Council for Exceptional Children.

Berner, R. (1977). What parents and teachers should know about death education. *DOPHHH Journal, 3*, 17–21.

Berquist, C. C. (1982). A methodology for validating placement of children in exceptional child education programs. *Exceptional Children, 49*(3), 269–270.

Best, G. A. (1978). *Individuals with physical disabilities: An introduction for educators*. St. Louis, MO: C. V. Mosby.

Bettelheim, B. (1950). *Love is not enough*. Glencoe, IL: Free Press.

Birch, J. W. (1975). *Hearing impaired children in the mainstream*. Minneapolis, MN: University of Minnesota, Leadership Training Institute/Special Education.

Bird, C. (1977). *What women want: From the official report to the President, the Congress, and the People of the United States*. New York: Simon and Schuster.

Black, J. L. (1986). AIDS: Preschool and school issues. *Journal of School Health, 56*, 93–95.

Blackman, J. A. (1983). *Medical aspects of developmental disabilities in children birth to three*. Iowa City, IA: University of Iowa, Division of Developmental Disabilities.

Blake, R. H., & Haroldsen, E. O. (1975). *A taxonomy of concepts in communication*. New York: Hastings House.

Blankenship, C. S. (1985). Using curriculum-based assessment data to make instructional decision. *Exceptional Children, 52*, 233–238.

Blaschke, C. L. (1982). Microcomputers in special education: Trends and projections. *Journal of Special Education in Technology, 5*, 25–27.

Bleck, E. (1975). Cerebral palsy. In E. Bleck & D. Nagel (Eds.), *Physically handicapped children: A medical atlas for teachers*. New York: Grune and Stratton.

Bleck, E., & Nagel, D. (1982). *Physically handicapped children—A medical atlas for teachers* (2nd ed.). New York: Grune and Stratton.

Bledsoe, C. W., & Williams, R. C. (1967). The vision needed to nurse the blind. *AAWB Contemporary Papers* (Vol. 1). Washington, DC: American Association of Workers for the Blind.

Bloom, B. (1956). *Taxonomy of educational objectives: The classification of educational goals*. New York: Longmans.

Bloom, B. (1964). *Stability and change in human characteristics*. New York: John Wiley.

Bloom, B., & Sosniak, L. (1981). Talent development and schooling. *Educational Leadership, 39*(2), 86–94.

Blum, R. H. (1972). *Horatio Alger's children*. San Francisco: Jossey-Bass.

Board of Education of the Hendrick Hudson Central School District v. *Rowley*, 102 S. Ct. 3034 (1982).

Bradford, E. J., & Hickey, J. G. (1982). New York City Committee on the Handicapped regarding appropriate placement of handicapped children. *Exceptional Children, 49*(6), 545–547.

Brenner, C. (1955). *An elementary textbook of psychoanalysis*. New York: International Universities Press.

Bricker, D., & Bricker, W. (1973). *Infant, toddler, and preschool research and intervention project report. Year III*. Nashville, TN: George Peabody College for Teachers, Institute on Mental Retardation and Intellectual Development.

Brinker, R. P., & Lewis, M. (1982). Making the world work with microcomputers: A learning prosthesis for handicapped infants. *Exceptional Children, 49*, 163–170.

Brolin, D. E. (1982). *Vocational preparation of retarded citizens* (2nd ed.). Columbus, OH: Merrill.

Bronfenbrenner, U. (1974). *Longitudinal evaluations: A report on longitudinal evaluations of preschool programs: Is early intervention effective?* (Vol. 2). (Publication No. OHD 74-25). Washington, DC: Department of Health, Education and Welfare.

Bronfenbrenner, U. (1975). Is early intervention effective? In H. J. Leichter (Ed.), *The family as educator*. New York: Teachers College Press.

Brooks-Gunn, J., & Lewis, M. (1981). Assessing the handicapped young: Issues and solutions. *Journal of the Division for Early Childhood, 2*, 84–95.

Brown v. *Board of Education of Topeka, Kansas*, 347 U.S. 483 (1954).

Bruininks, R. H., & Warfield, G. (1978). The mentally retarded. In E. L. Meyen (Ed.), *Exceptional children and youth: An introduction*. Denver, CO: Love.

Bryan, T. H., & Bryan, J. H. (1978). *Understanding learning disabilities* (2nd ed.). Sherman Oaks, CA: Alfred.

Budoff, M., & Hutton, L. R. (1982). Microcomputers in special education: Promises and pitfalls. *Exceptional Children, 49*, 123–128.

Bull, G. L., & Rushakoff, G. E. (1987). Computers and speech and language disordered individuals. In J. D. Lindsey, (Ed.), *Computers and exceptional individuals* (pp. 83–104). Columbus, OH: Merrill.

Burleson, D. L. (1975). *Starting a sex education program: Guidelines for the administrator. Sex education for the visually handicapped in schools and agencies*. New York: American Foundation for the Blind.

Burlington School Committee of the Town of Burlington, Massachusetts v. *Department of Education of the Commonwealth of Massachusetts*, 105 S. Ct. 1996 (1985).

Buros, O. K. (Ed.). (1974). *Tests in print II*. Highland Park, NJ: Gryphon Press.

Butler-Arlosdroff, N. (1978, June 25–30). *Training teachers towards responsibility in future education: Innovative models*. Paper presented at the First World Conference on the Future of Special Education, Sterling, Scotland.

Caccamise, F. (1974). Musts for hearing people. *American Annals of the Deaf, 119*(3), 296–297.

Capute, A. (1975). Cerebral palsy and associated dysfunctions. In R. Haslam & P. Valletutti (Eds.), *Medical problems in the classroom*. Baltimore, MD: University Park Press.

Caputo, P. (1981). Action research roundup: Higher achievement for high achievers. *Classroom Computer News, 2,* 19.

Carmen, G., & Kosberg, B. (1982). Educational technology research: Computer technology and the education of emotionally handicapped children. *Educational Technology, 22*(2), 26–30.

Carney, I. H. (1983). Services for families of severely handicapped preschool students: Assumptions and implications. *Journal of the Division for Early Childhood, 7,* 78–85.

Carr, L. J. (1950). *Delinquency control.* New York: Harper.

Carter, C. (1982). *Non-native and nonstandard dialect students: Classroom practices in teaching English, 1982–83.* Urbana, IL: National Council of Teachers of English.

Cartwright, C. A. (1981). Effective programs for parents of young handicapped children. *Topics in Early Childhood Special Education, 1*(3), 1–9.

Cartwright, C. A., & Cartwright, G. P. (1984). *Developing observation skills* (2nd ed.). New York: McGraw-Hill.

Cartwright, G. P. (1984). Computer applications in special education. In D. F. Walker & R. D. Hess (Eds.), *Instructional software: Principles and perspectives for design and use* (pp. 166–180). Belmont, CA: Wadsworth.

Cartwright, G. P., & Cartwright, C. A. (Eds.). (1972a). *CARE: Early identification of handicapped children.* University Park, PA: Pennsylvania State University.

Cartwright, G. P., & Cartwright, C. A. (1972b). Gilding the lily: Comments on the training based model for special education. *Exceptional Children, 39,* 231–234.

Cartwright, G. P., & Cartwright, C. A. (1973). Early identification of handicapped children: A CAI course. *The Journal of Teacher Education, 24*(2), 128–134.

Cartwright, G. P., & Cartwright, C. A. (1978). Definitions and classification approaches. In J. T. Neisworth & R. M. Smith (Eds.), *Retardation: Issues, assessment, and intervention.* New York: McGraw-Hill.

Cartwright, G. P., Cartwright, C. A., & Ysseldyke, J. E. (1973). Two decision models: Identification and diagnostic teaching of handicapped children in the regular classroom. *Psychology in the Schools, 10,* 4–11.

Castro, G., & Mastropieri, M. A. (1986). The efficacy of early intervention programs: A meta-analysis. *Exceptional Children, 52,* 417–424.

Center for Disease Control. (1985). *Guidelines for serving children with acquired immune deficiency syndrome (AIDS).* Atlanta, GA: Author.

Chan, K. S., & Rueda, R. (1979). Poverty and children in education: Separate but equal. *Exceptional Children, 45*(6), 422–428.

Charp, S. (1977). A statement in behalf of computers in the learning society. In *Computers in the learning society.* Congress of the United States, House Committee on Science and Technology. Hearings before the Subcommittee on Domestic and International Scientific Planning, Analysis and Cooperation of the Committee on Science and Technology. Report No. 47, Washington, DC.

Cheney, C., & Morse, W. C. (1972). Psychodynamic interventions in emotional disturbance. In W. C. Rhodes & M. L. Tracy (Eds.), *A study of child variance, Vol. 2: Interventions* (pp. 253–393). Ann Arbor, MI: University of Michigan Press.

Chiang, A. (1978). *A demonstration of the use of computer assisted instruction with handicapped children.* Arlington, VA: RMC Research Corporation. (ERIC Document Reproduction Service No. ED 166 913).

Chiang, B. (1986). Modifying public domain software for use by the learning disabled student. *Journal of Learning Disabilities, 19,* 315–317.

Chinn, P. C. (1979). The exceptional minority child: Issues and some answers. *Exceptional Children, 45*(7), 532–536.

Christiansen, R. (1975). Diabetes. In E. E. Bleck & D. A. Nagel (Eds.), *Physically handicapped children: A medical atlas for teachers.* New York: Grune and Stratton.

Churchill, S. (1986). *Education of linguistic and cultural minorities in OECD countries.* San Diego, CA: College-Hill Press.

Clarizio, H. F., & McCoy, G. F. (1976). *Behavior disorders in children* (2nd ed.). New York: Thomas Y. Crowell.

Clark, B. (1979). *Growing up gifted.* Columbus, OH: Merrill.

Cobb, B., & Kingsbury, D. E. (1985). The special needs provisions of the Perkins Act. *VocEd, 60*(4), 33–34.

Cole, E., & Gregory, H. (Eds.) (1986). Auditory learning. *Volta Review, 88*(5), 5–6.

Colenbrander, A. (1976a). *Classification of visual performance: Tentative definitions.* Unpublished paper from the Committee on Information, International Council of Ophthalmology and the Committee on Terminology, American Academy of Ophthalmology and Otolaryngology.

Colenbrander, A. (1976b). Low vision: Definition and classification. In E. E. Faye (Ed.), *Clinical low vision.* Boston: Little, Brown.

Comptroller General of the United States. (1979, February 6). *Report to the Congress: Early childhood and family development programs improve the quality of life for low-income families* (HRD 79-40). Washington, DC: General Accounting Office.

Cornett, R. O. (1975). Cued speech and oralism: An analysis. *Audiology and Hearing Education, 1*(1), 26–33.

Corsaro, M., & Korzeniowky, C. (1980). *STD: A common-sense guide.* New York: St. Martin's Press.

The Council for Exceptional Children. (1978, April). *The nation's commitment to the education of gifted and talented children and youth.* Reston, VA: Author.

Cratty, B. (1969). *Perceptual-motor behavior and educational processes.* Springfield, IL: Charles C. Thomas.

Critchley, M. (1970). *The dyslexic child* (2nd ed.). London: Heinemann Medical Books.

Cronbach, L. J. (1970). *Essentials of psychological testing* (3rd ed.). New York: Harper & Row.

Cruickshank, W. M. (1972). Some issues facing the field of learning disability. *Journal of Learning Disabilities, 5,* 380–388.

Cruickshank, W. M. (Ed.). (1976a). *Cerebral palsy: A developmental disability.* New York: Syracuse University Press.

Cruickshank, W. M. (1976b). William B. Cruickshank. In J. M. Kauffman & D. P. Hallahan (Eds.), *Teaching children with learning disabilities: Personal perspectives.* Columbus, OH: Merrill.

Cruickshank, W. M. (1977). Myths and realities in learning disabilities. *Journal of Learning Disabilities, 10*(1), 57–64.

Cruickshank, W. M. (1983). Learning disabilities: A neurophysiological dysfunction. *Journal of Learning Disabilities, 16*(1), 27–29.

Cullinan, D. C., Epstein, M. H., & Lloyd, J. W. (1983). *Behavior disorders of children and adolescents.* Englewood Cliffs, NJ: Prentice-Hall.

Curt, C. J. N. (1984). *Non-verbal communication in Puerto Rico* (2nd ed.). Cambridge, MA: Evaluation, Dissemination and Assessment Center, ESEA Title VII, Lesley College.

D'Alonzo, B. J., & Zucker, S. H. (1982). Comprehension scores of learning disabled high school students on aurally presented content. *Exceptional Children, 48*(4), 375–376.

Dantona, R. (1976). Services for deaf-blind children. *Exceptional Children, 43*(3), 172–174.

Darlington, R. B. (1980). Preschool programs and later school competence of children from low-income families. *Science, 208,* 202–204.

Davis, N. C. (1983, February). Yes, they can. Computer literacy for special education students. *The Computing Teacher, 10*(6), 64–67.

Deafness: A fact sheet. (1984). Washington, DC: National Information Center on Deafness, Gallaudet College.

Deaver, G. (1955). *Cerebral palsy: Methods of evaluation and treatment* (Rehabilitation Monograph IX). New York: Institute of Physical Medicine and Rehabilitation.

Deno, E. N. (1970). Special education as development capital. *Exceptional Children, 37,* 229–237.

Deno, S. L. (1985). Curriculum-based assessment: The emerging alternative. *Exceptional Children, 52,* 219–232.

DePauw, K. P. (1981). Physical education for the visually impaired: A review of the literature. *Journal of Visual Impairment and Blindness, 75,* 162–164.

DeSantis, V., & Schein, J. D. (1986). Blindness statistics (Part 1): An analysis of operational options. *Journal of Visual Impairment and Blindness, 80*(1), 517–522.

Des Jarlais, D. C. (1972). Mental illness as social deviance. In W. C. Rhodes & M. L. Tracy (Eds.), *A study of child variance: Vol. 1: Theories.* Ann Arbor, MI: University of Michigan Press.

Diana v. (California) State Board of Education, C-70 37 PFR (1970).

Dingman, H. F., & Tarjan, G. (1960). Mental retardation and the normal distribution curve. *American Journal of Mental Deficiency, 64,* 991–994.

Dinkmeyer, D., & McKay, G. D. (1973). *Raising a responsible child: Practical steps to successful family relationships.* New York: Simon and Schuster.

Dix, D. L. (1975). On behalf of the insane poor. In M. Rosen, G. Clark, & M. S. Kivitz (Eds.), *The history of mental retardation: Collected papers* (Vols. 1 & 2). Baltimore, Md: University Park Press.

Dodds, A. G., Clark-Carter, D. D., & Howarth, C. I. (1984). The sonic pathfinder. An evaluation. *Journal of Visual Impairment and Blindness, 78,* 203–205.

Dover, A. (1983). Computers and the gifted: Past, present, and future. *Gifted Child Quarterly, 27,* 81–86.

Dover, A. (1986). Special ed enrollment increases slowly, ed figures reveal. *Education of the Handicapped, 12*(22), 1–3.

Downs, M. P. (1976). The handicap of deafness. In J. L. Northern (Ed.), *Hearing disorders.* Boston: Little, Brown.

Dreikurs, R. (1968). *Psychology in the classroom* (2nd ed.). New York: Harper & Row.

Dreikurs, R., & Grey, L. (1970). *A parent's guide to child discipline.* New York: Hawthorn.

Dunn, L. M. (1968). Special education for the mildly retarded—Is much of it justifiable? *Exceptional Children, 35,* 5–22.

Edmonson, B. (1980). Sociosexual education for the handicapped. *Exceptional Education Quarterly, 1*(2), 67–76.

Education of the handicapped (1986, October 29). *12* (2) (newsletter). Washington, DC: Capitol Publications.

Eisenson, J. J. (1971). Speech defects: Nature, causes, and psychological concomitants. In W. M. Cruickshank (Ed.), *Psychology of exceptional children and youth.* Englewood Cliffs, NJ: Prentice-Hall.

Eisenson, J. J., Auer, J. J., & Irwin, J. V. (1963). *The psychology of communication.* New York: Appleton-Century-Crofts.

Ellington, C. (1983). Career education: People working together. *Teaching Exceptional Children, 15*(4), 210–214.

Elliott, D. S., & Voss, H. L. (1974). *Delinquency and dropout.* Lexington, MA: D. C. Heath.

Ellis, J. W., & Luckasson, R. (1986). Denying treatment to infants with handicaps: A comment on Bowen v. American Hospital Association, *Mental Retardation, 24,* 237–240.

Elstner, W. (1983). Abnormalities in the verbal communication of visually impaired children. In A. Mills (Ed.), *Language acquisition in the blind child: Normal and deficient* (pp. 18–41). San Diego, CA: College-Hill Press.

Embry, L. H. (1980). Family support for handicapped preschool children at risk for abuse. In J. J. Gallagher (Ed.), *New directions for exceptional children: Parents and families of handicapped children* (pp. 29–57). San Francisco: Jossey-Bass.

Engelmann, S. E. (1969). *Preventing failure in the primary grades.* Chicago: Science Research Associates.

Englemann, S. E. (1977). Sequential cognitive and academic tasks. In R. D. Kneedler & S. G. Tarver (Eds.), *Changing perspectives in special education.* Columbus, OH: Merrill.

Englert, C. S., & Thomas, C. C. (1982). Management of task involvement in special education classrooms. *Teacher Education and Special Education, 5*(2), 3–10.

Erikson, E. H. (1968). *Childhood and society* (rev. ed.). New York: Norton.

Ernst, M. (1977). *NAVA special report.* Fairfax, VA: National Audio-Visual Association.

Etkin, W. (1963). Communication among animals. In J. J. Eisenson, J. J. Auer, & J. V. Irwin (Eds.), *The psychology of communication.* New York: Appleton-Century-Crofts.

Etlinger, L. E., & Ogletree, E. J. (1981, October). *Calculators and microcomputers for exceptional children.* (ERIC Document Reproduction Service No. ED 202 707).

Facts about child abuse and neglect. (n. d.) Charleston, WV: West Virginia Department of Education.

Fant, L. (1977). *Sign language.* Northridge, CA: Joyce Media.

Far West Laboratory. (1980). *Educational programs that work.* San Francisco: Author.

Faye, E. E. (1970). *The low vision patient.* New York: Grune and Stratton.

Faye, E. E. (1976). Clinical definition and classification of the low vision patient. In E. E. Faye (Ed.), *Clinical low vision.* Boston: Little, Brown.

Feingold, B. F. (1975). *Why your child is hyperactive.* New York: Random House.

Feingold, B. F. (1976). Hyperkinesis and learning disabilities linked to the ingestion of artificial food colors and flavors. *Journal of Learning Disabilities, 9,* 551–559.

Feldman, D. (1982). A developmental framework for research with gifted children. In D. Feldman (Ed.), *Developmental appoaches to giftedness and creativity*. San Francisco: Jossey-Bass.

Felix, L., & Spungin, S. J. (1978). Preschool services for the visually handicapped: A national survey. *Journal of Visual Impairment and Blindness, 72*(2), 59–66.

Fewell, R. R., & Vadasy, P. (1986). *Families of handicapped children*. Austin, TX: PRO-ED.

Fincher, J. (1982). Before their time. *Science 82, 3*(6), 68–78.

The First Lady talks about drug abuse. (1983). *American Education, 19*(1), 2–4.

Fitzgerald, G., Fick, L., & Milich, R. (1986). Computer-assisted instruction for students with learning disabilities. *Journal of Learning Disabilities, 19,* 376–378.

Fliegler, L., & Bish, C. (1959). Summary of research on the academically talented student. *Review of Educational Research, 29,* 408–450.

Foulds, R. A. (1982). Applications of microcomputers in the education of the physically disabled child. *Exceptional Children, 49,*155–162.

Fraiberg, S. (1977). *Insights from the blind*. New York: Basic Books.

Frederick, J., & Fletcher, D. (1985). Facilitating children's adjustment to orthotic and prosthetic appliances. *Teaching Exceptional Children, 17,* 228–230.

Fredericks, D., Baldwin, V. L., & Grove, D. (1976). A home-center based parent training model. In D. L. Lillie, P. L. Trohanis, & K. W. Goin (Eds.), *Teaching parents to teach: A guide for working with the special child*. New York: Walker.

French, J. (1964). *The Pictorial Test of Intelligence*. Boston: Houghton Mifflin.

Freud, S. (1949). *An outline of psychoanalysis*. New York: Norton.

Frisina, D. R. (1967). Hearing disorders. In N. Haring & R. L. Schiefelbusch (Eds.), *Methods in special education*. New York: McGraw-Hill.

Frostig, M. (1976). Marianne Frostig. In J. M. Kauffman & D. P. Hallahan (Eds.), *Teaching children with learning disabilities: Personal perspectives*. Columbus, OH: Merrill.

Frostig, M., & Horne, D. (1964). *The Frostig program for the development of visual perception*. Chicago: Follett.

Frostig, M., Lefever, D. W., & Whittlesey, J. (1964). *The Marianne Frostig developmental test of visual perception*. Palo Alto, CA: Consulting Psychologists Press.

Furey, E. M. (1982). The effects of alcohol on the fetus. *Exceptional Children, 49*(1), 30–34.

Furst, M. (1983). Building self-esteem. *Academic Therapy, 19,* 22–26.

Furth, H. (1973). *Deafness and learning: A psychosocial approach*. Belmont, CA: Wadsworth.

Gadow, K. D. (1982). Problems with students on medication. *Exceptional Children, 49,* 20–29.

Gadow, K. D. (1986). *Children on medication* (Vol. 1). San Diego, CA: College-Hill Press.

Gallagher, J. J. (1975a). *Teaching the gifted child* (2nd ed.). Boston: Allyn and Bacon.

Gallagher, J. J. (1975b). What are gifted children like? In L. Crow & A. Crow (Eds.), *Educating the academically able*. New York: David McKay.

Gallagher, J. J. (1976). James J. Gallagher. In J. M. Kauffman & D. P. Hallahan (Eds.), *Teaching children with learning disabilities: Personal perspectives*. Columbus, OH: Merrill.

Gallagher, J. J., & Weiss, P. (1979). *The education of gifted and talented students: A history and prospectus* (Occasional paper #27). Washington, DC: Council for Basic Education.

Garman, M. (1983). The investigation of vision in language development. In A. Mills (Ed.), *Language acquisition in the blind child: Normal and deficient* (pp. 162–166). San Diego, CA: College-Hill Press.

Garner, G. W. (1979). *The police role in alcohol-related crises*. Springfield, IL: Charles C. Thomas.

Garrity, J. H., & Mengle, H. (1983). Early identification of hearing loss: Practices and procedures. *American Annals of the Deaf, 128,* 99–106.

Garwood, S. G., & Fewell, R. R. (1983). *Educating handicapped infants*. Rockville, MD: Aspen Systems.

Gates, W. A. (1907). The training of the incorrigible. *Journal of Proceedings and Addresses of the 45th Annual Meeting of the NEA* (pp. 995–999). Winona, MN: National Education Association.

Gearheart, B. R., & Weishahn, M. W. (1984). *The exceptional student in the regular classroom* (3rd ed.). St. Louis, MO: Mirror/C. V. Mosby.

Gerber, M. M. (1984). The Department of Education's sixth annual report to Congress on PL 94–142: Is Congress getting the full story? *Exceptional Children, 52*(3), 209–224.

Gerencser, S. (1979). The Calasanctius experience. In A. H. Passow (Ed.), *The gifted and talented: Their education and development*. 78th Yearbook of the National Society for the Study of Education. Part I. Chicago: University of Chicago Press.

Gerken, K. C. (1978). Performance of Mexican American children on intelligence tests. *Exceptional Children, 44*(6), 438–443.

Getman, G. (1976). Gerald Getman. In J. M. Kauffman & D. P. Hallahan (Eds.), *Teaching children with learning disabilities: Personal perspectives*. Columbus, OH: Merrill.

Getzels, J., & Jackson, P. (1958). The meaning of giftedness—An examination of an expanding concept. *Phi Delta Kappan, 40,* 275–277.

Getzels, J., & Jackson, P. (1962). *Creativity and intelligence*. New York: John Wiley.

Geyer, M. L., & Yankaver, A. (1971). Teacher judgment of hearing loss in children. In I. M. Ventry, J. B. Chaiklin, & K. F. Dixon (Eds.), *Hearing measurement: A book of readings*. New York: Appleton-Century-Crofts.

Gibson, J. J. (1966). *The senses considered as perceptual systems*. Boston: Houghton Mifflin.

The gifted child. (1978, October 23). *Newsweek,* 108–119.

Gillespie, E. B., & Turnbull, A. P. (1983). It's my IEP: Involving students in the planning process. *Teaching Exceptional Children, 16,* 26–29.

Glasser, W. (1969). *Schools without failure*. New York: Harper & Row.

Goffman, E. (1963). *Stigma: Notes on the management of spoiled identity*. Englewood Cliffs, NJ: Prentice-Hall.

Goldenberg, E. P. (1979). *Special technology for special children*. Baltimore, MD: University Park Press.

Goldstein, D., & Myers, B. (1980). Cognitive lag and group differences in intelligence. *Child Study Journal, 10,* 119–126.

Goldstein, H., Moss, J. W., & Jordan, L. J. (1965). *The efficacy of special class training on the development of mentally retarded children.* Urbana, IL: University of Illinois, Institute for Research on Exceptional Children.

Goleman, D. (1980). One thousand five hundred and twenty-eight little geniuses and how they grew. *Psychology Today, 13*(9), 28–53.

Gollnick, D. M., & Chinn, D. C. (1986). *Multicultural education in a pluralistic society.* Columbus, OH: Merrill.

Goodrich, G. L. (1984). Applications of microcomputers by visually impaired persons. *Journal of Visual Impairment and Blindness, 78*(9), 408–414.

Gorham, K. A., DesJardins, C., Page, R., Pettis, E., & Scheiber, B. (1976). Effects on parents. In N. Hobbs (Ed.), *Issues in the classification of children* (Vol. II, pp. 154–188). San Francisco: Jossey-Bass.

Gottlieb, J. (1981). Mainstreaming: Fulfilling the promise? *American Journal of Mental Deficiency, 86,* 115–126.

Graham, M. D. (1963). Toward a functional definition of blindness. *Research Bulletin 3.* New York: American Foundation for the Blind.

Greer, J., & Greer, B. (1986). Public domain software: New horizons for the family computer. *Exceptional Parent, 16*(6), 41–46.

Grimes, L. (1980). Computers are for kids: Designing software programs to avoid problems of learning. *Teaching Exceptional Children, 14*(2), 49–53.

Gronlund, N. E. (1976). *Measurement and evaluation in teaching* (3rd ed.). New York: Macmillan.

Grossman, H. J. (Ed.). (1973). *Manual on terminology and classification in mental retardation.* Washington, DC: American Association on Mental Deficiency.

Grossman, H. J. (Ed.). (1983). *Classification in mental retardation.* Washington, DC: American Association on Mental Deficiency.

Grumet, L., & Inkpen, T. (1982). The education of children in private schools: A state agency's perspective. *Exceptional Children, 49*(3), 200–206.

Guarino, R. L. (1982). The education of handicapped children in private schools. *Exceptional Children, 49*(3), 198–199.

Guerney, B. (1964). Filial therapy: Description and rationale. *Journal of Consulting Psychology, 28,* 304–310.

Guess, D., Bronicki, M. A., Firmender, K. H., Mann, J. M., Merrill, M. A., Olin-Zimmerman, S. J., Wanat, P. E., Zamarripa, E. J., & Turnbull, H. R. (1984). Legal and moral considerations in educating children with herpes in public school settings. *Mental Retardation, 212,* 257–263.

Guilford, J. (1950). Creativity. *American Psychologist, 5,* 444–454.

Guilford, J. (1959). Three faces of intellect. *American Psychologist, 14,* 469–479.

Guilford, J. (1967). *Nature of human intelligence.* New York: McGraw-Hill.

Guralnick, M. J. (Ed.). (1978). *Early intervention and the integration of handicapped and nonhandicapped children.* Baltimore, MD: University Park Press.

Guralnick, M. J. (1980). Social interactions among preschool children. *Exceptional Children, 46*(4), 248–253.

Guralnick, M. J. (1982). Pediatrics, special education, and handicapped children: New relationships. *Exceptional children, 48*(4), 294–295.

Halderman v. *Pennhurst State School and Hospital,* 446 F. Supp. 1295 (E.D. Pa. (1977).

Halderman v. *Pennhurst State School and Hospital,* 612 F.2d 84 (3d Cir. 1979).

Halgren, B. (1950). Specific dyslexia: A genetic study. *Acta Psychiatrica Neurologica, 65,* 1–287.

Hall, E. T. (1959). *The silent language.* New York: Fawcett World Library.

Hallahan, D. P., & Kauffman, J. M. (1982). *Exceptional children: Introduction to special education* (2nd ed.). Englewood Cliffs, NJ: Prentice-Hall.

Halle, J. W., & Sindelar, P. T. (1982). Behavioral observation methodologies for early childhood education. *Topics in Early Childhood Special Education, 2*(1), 43–54.

Halliday, C. (1971). *The visually impaired child: Growth, learning, development—infancy to school age.* Louisville, KY: Instructional Materials Reference Center for Visually Handicapped Children, American Printing House for the Blind.

Halworth, H. J., & Brebner, A. (1980, March–April). *CAI for the developmentally handicapped: Nine years of progress.* Paper presented at the Association for the Development of Computer-based Instructional Systems. (ERIC Document Reproduction Service No. ED 198 792).

Hammill, D. D., & Bartel, N. R. (1978). *Teaching children with learning and behavior problems.* Boston: Allyn and Bacon.

Hammill, D. D., & Larsen, S. C. (1974). The effectiveness of psycholinguistic training. *Exceptional Children, 41,* 5–14.

Hammill, D. D., & Larsen, S. C. (1978). The effectiveness of psycholinguistic training: A reaffirmation of position. *Exceptional Children, 44,* 402–414.

Hammill, D. D., Leigh, J. E., McNutt, G., & Larsen, S. C. (1981). A new definition of learning disabilities. *Learning Disabilities Quarterly, 4,* 336–342.

Hannaford, A. E., & Sloane, E. (1981). Microcomputers: Powerful learning tools. *Teaching Exceptional Children, 14*(2), 54–57.

Hannaford, A. E., & Taber, F. M. (1982). Microcomputer software for the handicapped: Development and evaluation. *Exceptional Children, 49,* 137–142.

Hardman, M. B., Drew, C. T., & Egan, M. W. (1987). *Human exceptionality* (2nd ed.). Boston: Allyn and Bacon.

Haring, N. G., & Bateman, B. (1977). *Teaching the learning disabled child.* Englewood Cliffs, NJ: Prentice-Hall.

Haring, N. G., & Gentry, N. D. (1976). Direct and individualized instructional procedures. In N. G. Haring & R. L. Schiefelbusch (Eds.), *Teaching special children.* New York: McGraw-Hill.

Haring, N. G., & Schiefelbusch, R. L. (Eds.). (1976). *Teaching special children.* New York: McGraw-Hill.

Harley, R. K., Henderson, F. M., & Truan, M. (1979). *The teaching of braille reading.* Springfield, IL: Charles C. Thomas.

Harrison, J. (1985). Hearing impairments. In G. Scholl (Ed.), *The school psychologist and the exceptional child* (pp. 179–202). Reston, VA: The Council for Exceptional Children.

Harrod, N., & Ruggles, M. (1983). Computer asssisted instruction: An educational tool. *Focus on Exceptional Children, 16*(1), 1–8.

Hart, V. (1980). Environmental orientation and human mobility. In R. L. Welsh & B. B. Blasch (Eds.), *Foundations of orientation and mobility*. New York: American Foundation for the Blind.

Harvey, B. (1975). Cystic fibrosis. In E. Bleck & D. Nagel (Eds.), *Physically handicapped children: A medical atlas for teachers*. New York: Grune and Stratton.

Hasazi, S. B., Gordon, L. R., & Roe, C. A. (1985). Factors associated with the employment status of handicapped youth exiting high school from 1979 to 1983. *Exceptional Children, 51*, 455–469.

Hatch, E., Murphy, J., & Bagnato, S. J. (1979). The comprehensive evaluation for handicapped children. *Elementary School Guidance and Counseling, 13*(3), 171–187.

Hatfield, E. M. (1975). Why are they blind? *Sight Saving Review, 45*(1), 3–22.

Hathaway, W. (1959). *Education and health of the partially seeing child* (4th ed.). New York: Columbia University Press.

Havighurst, R. (Ed.). (1958). *Education of the gifted*. 57th Yearbook of the National Society for the Study of Education. Part 2. Chicago: University of Chicago Press.

Hayden, A. H., & Haring, N. G. (1976). Early intervention for high risk infants and young children: Programs for Down's syndrome children. In T. D. Tjossem (Ed.), *Intervention strategies for high risk infants and young children*. Baltimore, MD: University Park Press.

Heber, R., & Garber, H. (1975). The Milwaukee project: A study of the use of family intervention to prevent cultural-familial mental retardation. In B. Friedlander, G. Sterritt, & G. Kirk (Eds.), *Exceptional infant*. New York: Brunner/Mazel.

Heinich, R. (Ed.). (1979). *Educating all handicapped children*. Englewood Cliffs, NJ: Educational Technology Publications.

Heller, H. (1983). Special education professional standards: Needs, value, and use. *Exceptional Children, 50*, 199–204.

Helmrich, D. (1981). School programs for pregnant teenagers. *American Education, 17*(6), 26–27.

Herman, K. (1959). *Reading disability: A medical study of word blindness and related handicaps*. Springfield, IL: Charles C. Thomas.

Heward, W. L. (1981, July). *Visual response system demonstration project: Final report*. (ERIC Document Reproduction Service No. ED 198 684).

Hewitt, F. M. (1968). *The emotionally disturbed child in the classroom*. Boston: Allyn and Bacon.

Heyes, A. D. (1984). The sonic pathfinder: A new electronic travel aid. *Journal of Visual Impairment and Blindness, 78*, 200–202.

Higgins, J. P. (1977). Present level(s) of performance and assessment: Some basic considerations. In S. Torres (Ed.), *A primer on individualized education programs for handicapped children*. Reston, VA: The Foundation for Exceptional Children.

Hill, E. (1986). Orientation and mobility. In G. Scholl (Ed.), *Foundations of education for blind and visually handicapped children and youth: Theory and practice*, (pp. 315–340). New York: American Foundation for the Blind.

Hilliard, A. (1980). Cultural diversity and special education. *Exceptional Children, 46*(8), 584–588.

Hobbs, N. L. (1966). Helping disturbed children: Psychological and ecological strategies. *American Psychologist, 21*, 1105–1115.

Hobbs, N. L. (1975). *The futures of children*. San Francisco: Jossey-Bass.

Hobbs, N. L. (1976). *Issues in the classification of children* (Vols. 1 & 2). San Francisco: Jossey-Bass.

Hochberg, J. E. (1964). *Perception*. Englewood Cliffs, NJ: Prentice-Hall.

Hofmeister, A. M. (1982). Microcomputers in perspective. *Exceptional Children, 49*, 115–121.

Holland, R. P. (1982). Learner characteristics and learner performance: Implications for instructional placement decisions. *The Journal of Special Education, 16*(1), 7–20.

Hollingworth, L. (1926). *Gifted children, their nature and nurture*. New York: Macmillan.

Holmes, K. K., Mardh, P., Sparling, P. F., & Wiesner, P. J. (1984). *Sexually transmitted diseases*. New York: McGraw-Hill.

Home eye test for adults gets rousing send off. (1983). *Prevent Blindness News, 8*(1), 3.

Honig, A. S. (1979). *Parent involvement in early childhood education* (rev. ed.). Washington, DC: National Association for the Education of Young Children.

Hoover, R. E. (1963). Visual efficiency as a criterion of service needs. *Research Bulletin No. 3*. New York: American Foundation for the Blind.

Hoover, R. E. (1967). Vision: The most valuable sense. *AAWB Contemporary Papers, Vol. 1*. Washington, DC: American Association of Workers for the Blind.

Horton, L. (1985). *Adolescent alcohol abuse*. Bloomington, IN: Phi Delta Kappa Educational Foundation.

Howard, J. (1982). The role of the pediatrician with young exceptional children and their families. *Exceptional Children, 48*(4), 316–322.

Howe, J. A. (1981, January). Computers can teach where others fail. *Technological Horizons in Education, 8*(1), 44–45.

Howe, S. G. (1974). A letter to the Governor of Massachusetts, June 30, 1857. In S. A. Kirk & F. E. Lord (Eds.), *Exceptional children: Educational resources and perspectives*. Boston: Houghton Mifflin.

Hunt, J. McV. (1961). *Intelligence and experience*. New York: Ronald Press.

Huttenlocher, P. (1975). Neuromuscular diseases. In V. Vaughn, R. McKay, & W. Nelson (Eds.), *Textbook of pediatrics* (2nd ed.). Philadelphia: W. B. Saunders.

International Classification of Impairments, Disabilities, and Handicaps. (1980). Geneva, Switzerland: World Health Organization.

Irving Independent School District v. Tatro, 104 S. Ct. 3371 (1984).

Israelite, N. K. (1986). Hearing-impaired children and the psychological functioning of their normal-hearing siblings. *Volta Review, 88*, 47–54.

Jan, J. E., Freeman, R. D., & Scott, E. (1977). *Visual impairments in children and adolescents*. New York: Grune and Stratton.

Jankowski, L. W., & Evans, J. K. (1981). The exercise capacity of blind children. *Journal of Visual Impairment and Blindness, 75,* 248–251.

Jensen, A. (1969). How much can we boost IQ and scholastic achievement? *Harvard Educational Review, 34,* 1–123.

Johnson, B., & Morse, H. A. (1974). Injured children and their parents. In J. Leavett (Ed.), *The battered child: Selected readings.* Morristown, NJ: General Learning Corporation.

Johnson, D., & Myklebust, H. (1967). *Learning disabilities: Educational principles and practices.* New York: Grune and Stratton.

Johnson, G. (1983). A point of view: Inconsistencies in programming. *Education and Training of the Mentally Retarded, 18,* 101–102.

Jones, J. C. (1976). *Growing children: A program in child development and parenthood.* Lewisburg, PA: Central Susquehanna Intermediate Unit.

Jones, J. W. (1965). *The visually handicapped child at home and school.* Washington, DC: U.S. Government Printing Office.

Kabler, M. L., Stephens, T. M., & Rinaldi, R. T. (1983). Extended school year for the handicapped: Legal requirements, educational efficacy, and administrative issues. *Journal of Special Education, 17*(1), 105–113.

Kaiser, C. E., & Hayden, A. H. (1977). The education of the very, very young. *Educational Horizons, 56*(1), 4–15.

Kameya, L. I. (1972). Behavioral interventions in emotional disturbance. In W. C. Rhodes & M. L. Tracy (Eds.), *A study of child variance: Interventions:* Vol. 2. Ann Arbor, MI: University of Michigan Press.

Kammerlohr, B. A., Henderson, R. A., & Rock, S. (1983). Special education due process in Illinois. *Exceptional Children, 49*(5), 417–422.

Karnes, M., & Teska, J. A. (1980). Toward successful parent involvement in programs for handicapped children. In J. J. Gallagher (Ed.), *New directions for exceptional children: Parents and families of handicapped children* (pp. 85–111). San Francisco: Jossey-Bass.

Karnes, M. B. (1977). Exemplary early education programs for handicapped children: Characteristics in common. *Educational Horizons, 56*(1), 47–54.

Karnes, M. B., & Zehrbach, R. R. (1977). Alternative models for delivering services to young handicapped children. In J. B. Jordan, A. H. Hayden, M. B. Karnes, & M. M. Wood (Eds.), *Early childhood education for exceptional children: A handbook of ideas and exemplary practices.* Reston, VA: The Council for Exceptional Children.

Kauffman, J. M. (1977). *Characteristics of children's behavior disorders.* Columbus, OH: Merrill.

Kavale, K. A. (1981). Functions of the Illinois Test of Psycholinguistic Abilities (ITPA): Are they trainable? *Exceptional Children, 47,* 496–510.

Kavale, K. A., & Forness, S. R. (1983). Hyperactivity and diet treatment: A meta-analysis of the Feingold hypothesis. *Journal of Learning Disabilities, 16,* 324–330.

Kavale, K. A., Forness, S. R., & Alper, A. E. (1986). Research in behavioral disorders/emotional disturbance: A survey of subject identification criteria. *Behavioral Disorders, 11,* 159–167.

Keats, S. (1965). *Cerebral palsy.* Springfield, IL: Charles C. Thomas.

Keith, R. W. (1976). The audiologic evaluation. In J. L. Northern (Ed.), *Hearing disorders.* Boston: Little, Brown.

Kelly, R. R. (1987). Computers and sensory impaired individuals. In J. D. Lindsey (Ed.), *Computers and exceptional individuals* (pp. 125–146). Columbus, OH: Merrill.

Kelly, T. K., Bullock, L. M., & Dykes, M. K. (1977). Behavioral disorders: Teachers' perceptions. *Exceptional Children, 43,* 316–317.

Kempe, C., Silverman, F., Steele, B., Droegemueller, W., & Silver, H. (1974). The battered child syndrome. In K. Leavett (Ed.), *The battered child: Selected readings.* Morristown, NJ: General Learning Corporation.

Keniston, K. (1977). *All our children: The American family under pressure.* New York: Harcourt Brace Jovanovich.

Kennedy, A. B., & Thurman, S. K. (1982). Inclinations of nonhandicapped children to help their handicapped peers. *Journal of Special Education, 16*(3), 319–327.

Keogh, B. K. (1986). Future of the LD field: Research and practice. *Journal of Learning Disabilities, 19,* 455–460.

Kephart, N. C. (1960). *The slow learner in the classroom.* Columbus, OH: Merrill.

Kephart, N. C. (1971). *The slow learner in the classroom* (2nd ed). Columbus, OH: Merrill.

Kettler, K. (1985). Evaluating commercial software. *American Annals of the Deaf, 130*(5), 357–360.

Kidd, J. W. (1983). The 1983 AAMD definition and classification of mental retardation: The apparent impact of the CEC-MR position. *Education and Training of the Mentally Retarded, 15,* 243-244.

Kilburn, J. (1984). Changing attitudes. *Teaching Exceptional Children, 16,* 124–127.

Kirchner, C. (1983). Special education for visually handicapped children: A critique of data on numbers served and costs. *Journal of Visual Impairment and Blindness, 77,* 219–223.

Kirchner, C. (1985). *Data on blindness and visual impairment in the United States: A resource manual on characteristics, education, employment and service delivery.* New York: American Foundation for the Blind.

Kirk, S. A. (1972). *Educating exceptional children* (rev. ed.). Boston: Houghton Mifflin.

Kirk, S. A. (1976). Samuel A. Kirk. In J. M. Kaufmann & D. P. Hallahan (Eds.), *Teaching children with learning disabilities: Personal perspectives.* Columbus, OH: Merrill.

Kirk, S. A., & Kirk, W. D. (1971). *Psycholinguistic learning disabilities: Diagnosis and remediation.* Urbana, IL: University of Illinois Press.

Kirk, S. A., & Kirk, W. D. (1983). On defining learning disabilities. *Journal of Learning Disabilities, 16*(1), 20-21.

Kirk, S. A., & Lord, F. E. (Eds.). (1974). *Exceptional Children: Educational resources and perspectives.* Boston: Houghton Mifflin.

Kirk, S. A., McCarthy, J. J., & Kirk, W. D. (1968). *The Illinois Test of Psycholinguistic Abilities* (rev. ed.). Urbana, IL: University of Illinois Press.

Kleiman, G. (1981). Microcomputers and hyperactive children. *Creative Computing, 7,* 93–94.

Klein, J. W., & Randolph, L. A. (1974). Placing handicapped children in Head Start programs. *Children Today, 3,* 7–10.

Klein, L. (1978). Antecedents of teenage pregnancy. *Clinical Obstetrics and Gynecology, 21*(4), 1151--1159.

Kline, D. F. (1977). *Child abuse and neglect: A primer for school personnel.* Reston, VA: The Council for Exceptional Children.

Kneedler, R. D. (1984). *Special education for today.* Englewood Cliffs, NJ: Prentice-Hall.

Knoff, H. (1983). Effect of diagnostic information on special education placement decisions. *Exceptional Children, 49*(5), 440–444.

Koestler, F. A. (1976). *The unseen minority: A social history of blindness in America.* New York: David McKay.

Kokaska, C. J. (1983). Career education: A brief overview. *Teaching Exceptional Children, 15*(4), 194–195.

Kolich, E. M. (1985). Microcomputer technology with the learning disabled: A review of the literature. *Journal of Learning Disabilities, 18,* 428–431.

Konopka, G. (1983). Adolescent suicide. *Exceptional Children, 49,* 390–395.

Kupfer, C. (1979). The future of eye research. *Sight Saving Review, 49*(1), 21–31.

Kvaraceus, W. C. (1971). *Prevention and control of delinquency: The school counselor's role.* Hanover, NH: TSC.

LaCour, J. (1983). Interagency agreement: A national response to an irrational system. *Exceptional Children, 49*(3), 265–267.

Lagomarcina, T. R. (1986). Community services. In F. R. Rusch (Ed.), *Competitive employment issues and strategies.* Baltimore, MD: Paul H. Brookes.

Larson, H. J. (1982, March). *Analysis of alternative management information systems appropriate for special education application.* Sacramento, CA: California State Department of Education. (ERIC Document Reproduction Service No. ED 208 617).

Lavelle, N., & Keogh, B. K. (1980). Expectations and attributions of parents of handicapped children. In J. J. Gallagher (Ed.), *New directions for exceptional children: Parents and families of handicapped children* (pp. 1–27). San Francisco: Jossey-Bass.

Lazar, I. (1979a). Does prevention pay off? *DEC Communicator, 6,* 1–7.

Lazar, I. (1979b). *Lasting effects after preschool: A report of the consortium for longitudinal studies* (DHEW Publication No. OHDS 79-30178). Washington, DC: U.S. Government Printing Office.

Leonard, L. (1986). Early language development and language disorders. In G. H. Shames & E. H. Wiig, *Human communication disorders* (pp. 291-330). Columbus, OH: Merrill.

Lerner, J. W. (1981). *Learning disabilities* (3rd ed.). Boston: Houghton Mifflin.

Lilly, M. S. (1970). Special education: A teapot in a tempest. *Exceptional Children, 37,* 43–49.

Lilly, M. S. (1971). A training based model for special education. *Exceptional Children, 37,* 745–749.

Lilly, M. S. (1986). The relationship between general and special education: A new face on an old issue. *Counterpoint, 11,* 45–51.

Lindgren, H. C. (1969). *An introduction to social psychology.* New York: John Wiley.

Lindsey, J. D. (1987). *Computers and exceptional individuals.* Columbus, OH: Merrill.

Ling, D., Ling, A. H., & Pflastier, G. (1977, May). Individualized educational programming for hearing impaired children. *Volta Review, 204*–230.

Littlejohn, S. W. (1983). *Theories of human communication* (2nd ed.). Belmont, CA: Wadsworth.

Litton, F. W. (1978). *Education of the trainable mentally retarded.* St. Louis, MO: C. V. Mosby.

Lloyd, J., & Carnine, D. W. (1981). Foreword. *Exceptional Education Quarterly, 2*(1), viii–ix.

Lombardino, L., Willems, S., & MacDonald, J. D. (1981). Critical considerations in total communication and an environmental intervention model for the developmentally delayed. *Exceptional Children, 47*(6), 455–461.

Long, N. J., Morse, W. C., & Newman, R. G. (Eds.) (1976). *Conflict in the classroom: The education of children with problems* (3rd ed.). Belmont, CA: Wadsworth.

Losen, S. M., & Diament, B. (1978). Parent involvement in school planning. *The Exceptional Parent, 8,* 19–22.

Losinno, T. (Ed.). (n.d.). *The PEERS program: An overview.* Philadelphia: Association for Retarded Citizens and Special People in the Northeast.

Lovitt, T. C. (1982). *Because of my persistence, I've learned from children.* Columbus, OH: Merrill.

Lowenfeld, B. (1971). Psychological problems of children with impaired vision. In W. M. Cruickshank (Ed.), *Psychology of exceptional children and youth.* Englewood Cliffs, NJ: Prentice-Hall.

Lowenfeld, B. (1973). Psychological considerations. In B. Lowenfeld (Ed.), *The visually handicapped child in school.* New York: John Day.

Lowenfeld, B. (1975). *The changing status of the blind: From separation to integration.* Springfield, IL: Charles C. Thomas.

Lowenfeld, B. (1981). *Berthold Lowenfeld on blindness and blind people: Selected papers.* New York: American Foundation for the Blind.

Lucito, L. (1963). Gifted children. In L. M. Dunn (Ed.), *Exceptional children in the schools.* New York: Holt, Rinehart and Winston.

Luckasson, R. A. (1986). Attorney's fees reimbursement in special education cases: Smith v. Robinson. *Exceptional Children, 52,* 384–389.

Ludlow, B. (1981). Parent-infant interaction research: The argument for earlier intervention programs. *Journal of the Division for Early Childhood, 3,* 34–41.

Lund, K., Foster, G., & McCall-Perez, F. C. (1978). The effectiveness of psycholinguistic training: A re-evaluation. *Exceptional Children, 44,* 310–319.

MacArthur, C. A., & Shneiderman, B. (1986). Learning disabled students' difficulties in learning how to use a word processor: Implications for instruction and software evaluation. *Journal of Learning Disabilities, 19,* 248–253.

MacMillan, D. L. (1977). *Mental retardation in school and society.* Boston: Little, Brown.

MacMillan, D. L. (1982). *Mental retardation in school and society* (2nd ed.). Boston: Little, Brown.

Macy, D. J., & Carter, J. L. (1978). Comparison of a mainstream and self-contained special education program. *Journal of Special Education, 12,* 308–313.

Madell, J. R. (n. d.). *Hearing health care: Pointers for parents.* New York League for the Hard of Hearing.

Madle, R. A. (1978). Alternative residential placements. In J. T. Neisworth & R. M. Smith (Eds.), *Retardation: Issues, assessment, and intervention.* New York: McGraw-Hill.

Maeroff, G. (1977, August 21). The gifted few. *The New York Times Sunday Magazine,* 30–32, 72–76.

Maher, C. A. (1983). Goal attainment scaling: A method for evaluating special education services. *Exceptional Children, 49*(6), 529–536.

Malamud, N., Itabashi, H., & Castor, J. (1964). Etiologic and diagnostic study of cerebral palsy. *Journal of Pediatrics, 65,* 270–293.

Margolis, J., & Charitonidis, T. (1981). Public reactions to housing for the mentally retarded. *Exceptional Children, 48,* 68–70.

Marland, S. (1972). *Education of the gifted and talented.* Washington, DC: U.S. Government Printing Office.

Martin, J. E., Rusch, F. R., & Heal, L. W. (1982). Teaching community survival skills to mentally retarded adults: A review and analysis. *Journal of Special Education, 16,* 243–267.

Martin, L. L. (1981, September). *Model development for a university-based learning disability clinic.* (ERIC Document Reproduction Service No. ED 201 143).

Martinson, R. (1961). *Educational programs for gifted pupils.* Sacramento, CA: California State Department of Education.

Martinson, R. (1973). *The identification of the gifted and talented* (unpublished manuscript). Ventura, CA: National/State Leadership Training Institute of Gifted/Talented.

McCaffrey, N. (1979). Abused and neglected children are exceptional. *Teaching Exceptional Children, 11*(2), 47–50.

McCarthy, M. M. (1983). The Pennhurst and Rowley decisions: Issues and implications. *Exceptional Children, 49*(6), 517–522.

McDaniels, G. (1977). Successful programs for young handicapped children. *Educational Horizons, 56*(1), 26–33.

McDermott, P. A., & Watkins, M. W. (1983). Computerized versus conventional remedial instruction for learning disabled pupils. *Journal of Special Education, 17,* 81–88.

McDonald, E., & Chance, B. (1964). *Cerebral palsy.* Englewood Cliffs, NJ: Prentice-Hall.

McDowell, R. L. (1979). The emotionally disturbed adolescent. *PRISE Reporter,* No. 3, May 1979, pp 1–2. King of Prussia, PA: Pennsylvania Resources and Information Center for Special Education.

McIntosh, D. K., & Dunn, L. M. (1973). Children with major specific learning disabilities. In L. M. Dunn (Ed.), *Exceptional children in the schools* (2nd ed.). New York: Holt, Rinehart and Winston.

McLean, J. L., & Snyder-McLean, L. (1978). *A transactional approach to early language training.* Columbus, OH: Merrill.

McLean, R. A., Mattison, E. T., Cochrane, N. E., & Fall, K. (1979). Maternal mortality study. *New York State Journal of Medicine, 79*(2), 226–230.

McLeod, J. (1983). Learning disability is for educators. *Journal of Learning Disabilities, 16*(1), 23–24.

McLoughlin, J. A., & Lewis, R. B. (1981). *Assessing special students.* Columbus, OH: Merrill.

McLoughlin, J. A., & Netick, A. (1983). Defining learning disabilities: A new and cooperative direction. *Journal of Learning Disabilities, 16*(1), 21–23.

McMahon, J. (1983). Extended school year programs. *Exceptional Children, 49*(5), 457–460.

McNeese, M. C., & Hebeler, J. R. (1977). The abused child: A clinical approach to identification and management. *Clinical Symposia, 29*(5), 1–36.

McPherson, M. G. (1983). Improving services to infants and young children with handicapping conditions and their families: The division of maternal and child health as collaborator. *Zero to Three, 4*(1), 1–6.

Me, myself, and eye: The teacher as producer. (1982). *Journal of Special Education Technology, 5*(1), 37–41.

Meeting the needs of handicapped delinquent youth. (1983). *Programs for the Handicapped, 1,* 4–5.

Mellor, C. M. (1981). *Aids for the 80s: What they are and what they do.* New York: American Foundation for the Blind.

Mercer, C. D. (Ed.). (1979). *Children and adolescents with learning disabilities.* Columbus, OH: Merrill.

Mercer, C. D. (1987). *Students with learning disabilities* (3rd ed.). Columbus OH: Merrill.

Mercer, C. D., Forgnone, C., & Wolking, W. D. (1976). Definitions of learning disabilities used in the United States. *Journal of Learning Disabilities, 9,* 376–386.

Mercer, J. R. (1973). *Labelling the mentally retarded.* Berkeley, CA: University of California Press.

Messerley, C. (1986). The use of computer-assisted instruction in facilitating the acquisition of math skills with hearing impaired high school students. *Volta Review, 88*(2), 67–78.

Millar, S. (1983). Language and active touch: Some aspects of reading and writing by blind children. In A. Mills (Ed.), *Language acquisition in the blind child: Normal and deficient* (pp. 167–186). San Diego, CA: College-Hill Press.

Miller, J. (1975). Juvenile rheumatoid arthritis. In E. Bleck & D. Nagel (Eds.), *Physically handicapped children: A medical atlas for teachers.* New York: Grune and Stratton.

Miller, J. (1983). *Many voices: Bilingualism, culture, and education.* London: Routledge and Kegan Paul.

Miller, S. R., & Schloss, P. J. (1982). *Career-vocational education for handicapped youth.* Rockville, MD: Aspen Systems.

Mills v. Board of Education of the District of Columbia, 348 F. Supp. 866 (1972).

Milunsky, A. (1977). *Know your genes.* Boston: Houghton Mifflin.

Minskoff, E. H. (1975). Research on psycholinguistic training: Critique and guidelines. *Exceptional Children, 42,* 136–144.

Minskoff, E. H., Wiseman, D., & Minskoff, J. G. (1972). *The MWM program for developing language abilities.* Ridgefield, NJ: Educational Performance Associates.

Moores, D. F. (1979). Hearing impairments. In M. S. Lilly (Ed.), *Children with exceptional needs.* New York: Holt, Rinehart and Winston.

Moores, D. F. (1987). *Educating the deaf: Psychology, principles, and practices* (3rd ed.). Boston: Houghton Mifflin.

Morgan, S. (1985). *Children in crisis.* San Diego, CA: College-Hill Press.

Morgan, S. (1987). *Abuse and neglect of handicapped children.* San Diego, CA: College-Hill Press.

Morse, W. (1976). The crisis of helping teacher. In N. J. Long, W. C. Morse, & R. G. Newman (Eds.), *Conflict in the classroom: The education of children with problems* (3rd ed.). Belmont, CA: Wadsworth.

Morse, W. C., & Smith, J. (1980). *Understanding child variance.* Reston, VA: The Council for Exceptional Children.

Morsink, C. V. (1984). *Teaching special needs students in regular classrooms.* Boston: Little, Brown.

Myers, P. I., & Hammill, D. D. (1976). *Methods for learning disorders.* New York: John Wiley.

Myklebust, H. R. (1983). Toward a science of learning disabilities. *Journal of Learning Disabilities, 16*(1), 17–18.

National Association for Retarded Citizens. (1973). *Facts on mental retardation.* Arlington, TX: Author.

National Public Radio Broadcast. (1976). *The gifted and talented: Problems of parenting.* Washington, DC: Institute for Educational Leadership.

National Society to Prevent Blindness. (1976). *Annual report for 1975.* New York: Author.

National Society to Prevent Blindness. (1977). *Signs of possible eye trouble in children* (Pub. G-112). New York: Author.

National Society to Prevent Blindness. (1979). *Annual report for 1978.* New York: Author.

National Society to Prevent Blindness. (1983a). *Annual report for 1982.* New York: Author.

National Society to Prevent Blindness. (1983b). Home eye tests get rousing send off. *Prevent Blindness News, 8*(1), 3.

Nazzaro, J. (1977). *Exceptional timetables: Historic events affecting the handicapped and gifted.* Reston, VA: The Council for Exceptional Children.

Neisworth, J. T., Willoughby-Herb, S. J., Bagnato, S. J., Cartwright, C. A., & Laub, K. (1980). *Individualizing early education for handicapped children.* Rockville, MD: Aspen Systems.

Nelson, C. M., Rutherford, R. B., & Wolford, B. I. (Eds.). (1987). *Special education in the criminal justice system.* Columbus, OH: Merrill.

Newcomer, P., Larsen, S., & Hammill, D. (1975). A response. *Exceptional Children, 42,* 144–148.

Newell, F. W., & Ernest, J. T. (1974). *Ophthalmology: Principles and concepts.* St. Louis, MO: C. V. Mosby.

Newland, T. E. (1971). Psychological assessment of exceptional children and youth. In W. M. Cruickshank (Ed.), *Psychology of exceptional children and youth.* Englewood Cliffs, NJ: Prentice-Hall.

Newland, T. E. (1976). *The gifted in socio-educational perspective.* Englewood Cliffs, NJ: Prentice-Hall.

Nirje, B. (1976). The normalization principle. In R. B. Kugel & A. Shearer (Eds.), *Changing patterns in residential services for the mentally retarded.* Washington, DC: President's Committee on Mental Retardation.

Norgard, J. (1983). The Courage Independent Living Home. *Human Development News,* August-September, p. 2.

Norrie, E. (1959). Word blindness. In S. J. Thompson (Ed.), *Reading disability.* Springfield, IL: Charles C. Thomas.

Northall, J., & Melichar, J. (Eds.). (1975). *Information system on adaptive and assistive equipment used in schools for physically handicapped children.* San Mateo, CA: United Cerebral Palsy Association of Portland, Oregon, Adaptive Systems.

Northern, J. L., & Lemme, M. (1986). Hearing and auditory disorders. In G. H. Shames & E. H. Wigg (Eds.), *Human communication disorders: An introduction* (2nd ed.) (pp. 415–444). Columbus, OH: Charles E. Merrill.

Notes on Charles Van Riper's speech correction: Principles and methods. (1978). Englewood Cliffs, NJ: Prentice-Hall.

Oates, J. (1971). *Wonderland.* Greenwich, CT: Fawcett.

O'Connell, J. C. (1983). Education of handicapped preschoolers: A national survey of services and personnel requirements. *Exceptional Children, 49*(6), 538–540.

Official Actions of the Delegate Assembly at the 54th Annual International Convention, The Council for Exceptional Children. (1976). *Exceptional Children, 43*(1), 41–47.

O'Keefe, A. (1979). *What Head Start means to families* (DHEW Publication No. OHDS 79-31129). Washington, DC: U.S. Government Printing Office.

Orlansky, M. D., & Trap, J. J. (1987). Working with Native American persons: Issues in facilitating communication and providing culturally relevant services. *Journal of Visual Impairment and Blindness, 81*(4), 151–155.

Owens, R. E., Jr. (1986). Communication, language, and speech. In G. H. Shames & E. H. Wiig (Eds.), *Human communication disorders: An introduction* (2nd ed.) (pp. 27–79). Columbus, OH: Merrill.

Oyer, H. J. (1966). *Auditory communication for the hard of hearing.* Englewood Cliffs, NJ: Prentice-Hall.

Page, E. B. (1980). Tests and decisions for the handicapped: A guide to evaluation under the new laws. *Journal of Special Education, 14*(4), 423–487.

Palmer, D. (1983). An attributional perspective on labeling. *Exceptional Children, 49*(5), 423–429.

Palmer, E. A., & Phelps, D. (1986). Multicenter trial of cryotherapy for retinopathy of prematurity. *Pediatrics, 77*(3), 428–429.

Palomares, U., & Ball, G. (n. d.). *Magic circle/interchange program* (rev. ed.). San Diego, CA: Human Development Training Institute.

Papert, S. A. (1982, October). *Information prosthetics for the handicapped* (Final Report). (ERIC Document Reproduction Service No. ED 216 500).

PARC, Bowman et al. v. *Commonwealth of Pennsylvania,* 334 F. Supp. 279 (1971).

Parette, H. P., & Hourcade, J. J. (1986). Management strategies for orthopedically handicapped students. *Teaching Exceptional Children, 18,* 282–286.

Passow, A., Goldberg, J., Tannenbaum, A., & French, W. (1955). *Planning for talented youth.* New York: Teachers College, Columbia University, Bureau of Publications.

Payne, J. S., Kauffman, J. M., Brown, G. B., & DeMott, R. M. (1979). *Exceptional children in focus* (2nd ed.). Columbus, OH: Merrill.

Payne, J. S., Patton, J. R., Kauffman, J. M., Brown, G. B., & Payne, R. A. (1983). *Exceptional children in focus* (3rd ed.). Columbus, OH: Merrill.

Pearson, H. (1975). Diseases of the blood. In V. Vaughn, R. McKay, & W. Nelson (Eds.), *Textbook of pediatrics.* Philadelphia: W. B. Saunders.

Pearson, J., Kell, R., & Taylor, W. (1973). An index of hearing impairment derived from the pure-tone audiogram. In W. Taylor (Ed.), *Disorders of auditory function: Proceedings of the British society of audiology. First conference.* London: Academic Press.

Pegnato, C., & Birch, J. (1959). Locating gifted children in junior high school: A comparison of methods. *Exceptional Children, 25,* 300–304.

Peli, E., Arend, L. E., & Timberlake, G. T. (1986). Computerized image enhancement for visually impaired persons: New technology, new possibilities. *Journal of Visual Impairment and Blindness, 80,* 849–854.

Pennhurst State School and Hospital v. *Halderman,* 451 U.S. 1 (1981).

Pennsylvania Easter Seal Society. (1986). *Program bulletin: Acquired immune deficiency syndrome (AIDS).* Middletown, PA: Pennsylvania Easter Seal Society.

Peterson, R. L., Zabel, R. H., Smith, C. R., & White, M. A. (1983). Cascade of services model and emotionally disturbed students. *Exceptional Children, 49*(5), 404–408.

Pfeiffer, S. I. (1982). The superiority of team decision making. *Exceptional Children, 49*(1), 68–69.

Phelps, L. A., & Lutz, R. (1977). *Career exploration and preparation for the special needs learner.* Boston: Allyn and Bacon.

Pietras, T. P. (1979). Teaching as a linguistic process in a cultural setting. *The Clearing House, 53*(4), 165–168.

Pines, M. (1982, March 30). What produces great skills? *New York Times,* 21–22.

Plata, M., & Santos, S. L. (1981). Bilingual special education: A challenge for the future. *Teaching Exceptional Children, 14*(3), 97–100.

Poorman, C. (1980). Mainstreaming in reverse. *Teaching Exceptional Children, 12*(4), 136–142.

Powers, D. A. (1983). Mainstreaming and inservice education of teachers. *Exceptional Children, 49*(5), 432–439.

President's Committee on Mental Retardation. (1969). *The six hour retarded child.* Washington, DC: U.S. Government Printing Office.

Pressey, S. (1955). Concerning the nature and nurture of genius. *Scientific Monthly, 81,* 123–129.

Price, B. J., & Marsh, G. E. (1985). Practical suggestions for planning and conducting parent conferences. *Teaching Exceptional Children, 17,* 274–278.

Price, J. H. (1986). AIDS, the schools, and policy issues. *Journal of School Health, 56,* 137–139.

Programs for the handicapped. (1983). Washington, DC: Special Education and Rehabilitative Services, U.S. Department of Education.

Propp, G., Nugent, G., Stone, C., & Nugent, R. (1981, August). *Videodisc: An instructional tool for the hearing impaired.* (ERIC Document Reproduction Service No. ED 200 227).

Public Law 99–457, Education of the Handicapped Act Amendments of 1986. *Congress and Administrative News,* 10-8-86, p. 1145.

Putnam, J. W., & Bruininks, R. H. (1986). Future directions in deinstitutionalization and education: A delphi investigation. *Exceptional Children, 53,* 55-62.

Quay, H. C. (1972). Patterns of aggression, withdrawal, and immaturity. In H. C. Quay & J. S. Werry (Eds.), *Psychopathological disorders of childhood.* New York: John Wiley.

Quay, H. C. (1975). Classification in the treatment of delinquency and antisocial behavior. In N. Hobbs (Ed.), *Issues in the classification of children* (Vol. 1). San Francisco: Jossey-Bass.

Quay, H. C. (1979). Classification. In H. C. Quay & J. S. Werry (Eds.), *Psychopathological disorders of childhood* (2nd ed.). New York: John Wiley.

Quay, H. C., Morse, W. C., & Cutler, R. L. (1966). Personality patterns of pupils in special classes for the emotionally disturbed. *Exceptional Children, 32,* 297–301.

Rader, J. (1977). An evaluation of a simulation on the identification of the gifted and talented. *Dissertation Abstracts International, 37A*(8), 5002.

Ragghianti, S., & Miller, R. (1982). The microcomputer and special education management. *Exceptional Children, 49,*131–135.

Ramey, C. T., Beckman-Bell, P., & Gowen, J. W. (1980). Infant characteristics and infant-caregiver interactions. In J. J. Gallagher (Ed.), *New directions for exceptional children: Parents and families of handicapped children* (pp. 59–84). San Francisco: Jossey-Bass.

Ramirez, B., & Smith, B. J. (1978). Federal mandates for the handicapped: Implications for American Indian children. *Exceptional Children, 44*(7), 521–528.

Rauth, M. (1981). What can be expected of the regular education teachers? Ideas and realities. *Exceptional Education Quarterly, 2*(2), 27–36.

Redl, F. (1959). The concept of the life space interview. *American Journal of Orthopsychiatry, 29,* 1–18.

Redl, F., & Wineman, D. (1951). *Children who hate.* Glencoe, IL: Free Press.

Reid, D. K., & Hresko, W. P. (1981). *A cognitive approach to learning disabilities.* New York: McGraw-Hill.

Reilly, S. S., & Barber-Smith, D. (1982). Expanded use of captioned films for learning disabled students. *Exceptional Children, 48*(4), 361–363.

Renzulli, J. (1978). What makes giftedness? Re-examining a definition. *Phi Delta Kappan, 60*(3), 180–184.

Renzulli, J., Reis, S., & Smith, L. (1981). *The revolving door identification model.* Mansfield Center, CT: Creative Learning Press.

Renzulli, J., & Smith, L. (1977). Two approaches to identification of gifted students. *Exceptional Children, 43,* 512–518.

Report of the Ad Hoc Committee to Define Deaf and Hard of Hearing. (1975, October). *American Annals of the Deaf, 120*(5), 509–512.

Report on preschool education (1979, December 18). *11*(25) (newsletter). Washington, DC: Capitol Publications.

Research for Better Schools. (1978). *Clarification of P.L. 94–142 for the classroom teacher.* Philadelphia: Author.

Reynolds, M. C. (1962). A framework for considering some issues in special education. *Exceptional Children, 28,* 367–370.

Reynolds, M. C., & Birch, J. (1977). *Teaching exceptional children in all America's schools.* Reston, VA: The Council for Exceptional Children.

Reynolds, M., & Birch, J. (1982). *Teaching exceptional children in all America's schools* (2nd ed.). Reston, VA: The Council for Exceptional Children.

Rezmierski, N., & Kotre, J. (1972). A limited literature review of theory of the psychodynamic model. In W. C. Rhodes & M. L. Tracy (Eds.), *A study of child variance: Vol. 1. Theories* (pp. 181–258). Ann Arbor, MI: University of Michigan Press.

Rhodes, W. C., & Tracy, M. L. (Eds.). (1972a). *A study of child variance: Vol. 1. Theories.* Ann Arbor, MI: University of Michigan Press.

Rhodes, W. C., & Tracy, M. L. (Eds.). (1972b). *A study of child variance: Vol. 2. Interventions.* Ann Arbor, MI: University of Michigan Press.

Ricker, K. S. (1981). Optical media bring biology to visually impaired students. *Science Teacher, 48*(2), 36–37.

Rivlin, A. M., & Timpane, P. M. (Eds.). (1975). *Planned variation in education: Should we give up or try harder?* Washington, DC: Brookings Institution.

Robinault, I. (Ed.). (1973). *Functional aide for the multiply handicapped.* New York: Harper & Row.

Robinson, H., Roedell, W., & Jackson, N. (1979). Early identification and intervention. In A. H. Passow (Ed.), *The gifted and talented: Their education and development.* 78th Yearbook of the National Society for the Study of Education. Part I. Chicago: University of Chicago Press.

Robinson, N. H., & Robinson, H. B. (1976). *The mentally retarded child: A psychological approach* (2nd ed.). New York: McGraw-Hill.

Rogers, C. R. (1961). *On becoming a person: A therapist's view of psychotherapy.* Boston: Houghton Mifflin.

Rose, B. C. (1980). Child abuse and the educator. *Focus on Exceptional Children, 12*(9), 1–16.

Rose, S., & Waldron, M. (1984). Microcomputer use in programs for hearing impaired children: A national survey. *American Annals of the Deaf, 129*(3), 358–442.

Rosen, M., Clark, G., & Kivitz, M. S. (Eds.). (1975). *The history of mental retardation: Collected papers* (Vols. 1 & 2). Baltimore, MD: University Park Press.

Ross, M. (1977). Definition and descriptions. In J. Davis (Ed.), *Our forgotten children: Hard-of-hearing pupils in the schools.* Minneapolis, MN: University of Minnesota Audio Visual Library Service.

Ross, M. (1981). Introduction. In M. Ross & L. W. Nober (Eds.), *Educating hard-of-hearing children.* Reston, VA: The Council for Exceptional Children.

Rowley v. *Board of Education of the Hendrick Hudson School District,* 483 F. Supp. 528 (S.D. N.Y. 1980a).

Rowley v. *Board of Education of the Hendrick Hudson School District,* 632 F.2d 945 (2d Cir. 1980b).

Ruberry, J., & Lyon, E. (1980, September). The teletypewriter and the videotape recorder: Media equipment that taps student resources. *American Annals of the Deaf, 125*(6), 674–678.

Rubin, R., & Balow, B. (1978). Prevalence of teacher identified behavior problems: A longitudinal study. *Exceptional Children, 45,* 102–111.

Ruble, D. N., & Boggiano, A. K. (1980). Optimizing motivation in an achievement context. In B. K. Keogh (Ed.), *Advances in special education* (Vol. 1). Greenwich, CT: JAI Press.

Russ, D. (1972). A review of learning and behavior therapy as it relates to emotional disturbance in children. In W. C. Rhodes & M. L. Tracy (Ed.), *A study of child variance: Vol. 1. Theories.* Ann Arbor, MI: University of Michigan Press.

S-1 v. *Turlington,* No. 78-8020 Div-CA-WPB (S.D. Fla., 1979).

Sabatino, D. A. (1972). Learning disability. In G. P. Cartwright & C. A. Cartwright (Eds.), *CARE: Early identification of handicapped children.* University Park, PA: Pennsylvania State University.

Safford, P. L. (1978). *Teaching young children with special needs.* St. Louis, MO: C. V. Mosby.

Sailor, W., & Guess, D. (1983). *Severely handicapped students: An instructional design.* Boston: Houghton Mifflin.

Salend, S. J. (1984). Factors contributing to the development of successful mainstreaming programs. *Exceptional Children, 50,* 409–416.

Salvia, J. (1980). The use of tests in schools. *Diagnostique, 7*(2), 14–20.

Salvia, J., & Ysseldyke, J. E. (1987). *Assessment in special and remedial education* (4th ed.). Boston: Houghton Mifflin.

Sameroff, A. J., & Chandler, M. J. (1975). Reproductive risk and the continuum of caretaking causality. In F. D. Horowitz, M. Hetherington, S. Scarr-Salapatek, & G. Siegel (Eds.), *Review of child development research* (Vol. 4). Chicago: University of Chicago Press.

Sarkees, M. D., & Scott, J. L. (1985). *Vocational special needs.* Homewood, IL: American Technical Publishers.

Sataloff, J., & Michael, P. L. (1973). *Hearing conservation.* Springfield, IL: Charles C. Thomas.

Scadden, L. A. (1984). Blindness in the information age: Equality or irony. *Journal of Visual Impairment and Blindness, 78*(9), 399–400.

Schein, J. D. (1984a). Cochlear implants and the education of deaf children. *American Annals of the Deaf, 129*(3), 324–332.

Schein, J. D. (1984b). *Speaking the language of sign: The art and science of signing.* Garden City, NY: Doubleday.

Schein, J. D., & DeSantis, V. (1986). Blindness statistics (Part 2): Blindness registers in the United States. *Journal of Visual Impairment and Blindness, 80*(2), 570–572.

Schell, G. C. (1981). The young handicapped child: A family perspective. *Topics in Early Childhood Special Education, 1*(3), 21–27.

Schinke, S. P., Gilchrist, L. D., & Small, R. W. (1979). Preventing unwanted adolescent pregnancy: A cognitive-behavioral approach. *American Journal of Orthopsychiatry, 49*(1), 81–88.

Schloss, I. P. (1963). Implications of altering the definition of blind. *Research Bulletin No 3.* New York: American Foundation for the Blind.

Schloss, P. J., Kane, M. S., & Miller, S. R. (1981). Truancy intervention with behavior disordered adolescents. *Behavioral Disorders, 6*(3), 175–179.

Schloss, P. J., & Miller, S. R. (1982). Effects of the label "institutionalized" versus "regular school student" on teacher expectations. *Exceptional Children, 48*(4), 363–364.

Schloss, P. J., & Sedlak, R. A. (1986). *Instructional methods for students with learning and behavior problems.* Boston: Allyn and Bacon.

Schloss, P. J., McEwen, D., Lang, E., & Schwab, J. (1986). PROGRESS: A model program for promoting school to work transition. *Career Development of Exceptional Individuals, 9,* 16–23.

Schloss, P. J., Smith, M. A., & Keihl, W. (1986). Rec Club: A community based recreational program for adults with moderate retardation. *Education and Training of the Mentally Retarded, 21,* 282–288.

Schmidt, M., Weinstein, T., Niemic, R., & Walberg, H. J. (1986). Computer-assisted instruction with exceptional children. *Journal of Special Education, 19,* 493–501.

Scholl, G. T. (1968). *The principal works with the visually impaired.* Reston, VA: The Council for Exceptional Children.

Scholl, G. T. (1973). Understanding and meeting developmental needs. In B. Lowenfeld (Ed.), *The visually handicapped child in school.* New York: John Day.

Scholl, G. T. (Ed.) (1985). *The school psychologist and the exceptional child.* Reston, VA: Council for Exceptional Children.

Scholl, G. T. (1986a). Growth and development. In G. Scholl (Ed.), *Foundations of education for blind and visually handicapped children and youth: Theory and practice* (pp. 65–81). New York: American Foundation for the Blind.

Scholl G. T. (1986b). What does it mean to be blind? In G. Scholl (Ed.), *Foundations of education for blind and visually handicapped children and youth: Theory and practice* (pp. 23–33). New York: American Foundation for the Blind.

Scholl, G. T., & Schnur, R. (1976). *Measures of psychological, vocational, and educational functioning in the blind and visually handicapped.* New York: American Foundation for the Blind.

Schreier, E. M., DeWitt, J. C., Goldberg, A. M., & Leventhal, J. D. (1987). An evaluation of synthetic speech software programs. *Journal of Visual Impairment and Blindness, 81*(2), 70–75.

Schulz, J. B. (1981). A parent views parent participation. *Exceptional Education Quarterly, 3*(2), 17–24.

Schwartz, L. L. (1984). *Exceptional students in the mainstream.* Belmont, CA: Wadsworth.

Schweinhart, L. J., & Weikart, D. P. (1980). *Young children grow up: The effects of the Perry Preschool Program on youths through age 15.* Ypsilanti, MI: High/Scope Educational Research Foundation, The High/Scope Press.

Scott, R. A. (1969). *The making of blind men: A study of adult socialization.* New York: Russell Sage Foundation.

Seagoe, M. (1975). *Terman and the gifted.* Los Altos, CA: W. Kaufmann.

Seagrave, J. R., & Seagrave, G. (1982). Dots and draw. In G. C. Vanderheiden & L. M. Walstead (Eds.), *Trace Center international software/hardware registry.* Madison, WI: University of Wisconsin.

Sears, R. (1977). Sources of life satisfaction of the Terman gifted men. *American Psychologist, 32,* 119–128.

Seaver, J. W., & Cartwright, C. A. (1985). *Child care administration.* Belmont, CA: Wadsworth.

Secord, W. A. (1986). An interview with Dr. Elizabeth Wiig. *Directive Teacher, 8*(1), 10–11, 30.

Sedlak, R. A., Doyle, M., & Schloss, P. J. (1982). Video games: A training and generalization demonstration with severely retarded adolescents. *Education and Training of the Mentally Retarded, 17,* 332–336.

Sedlak, R. A., & Weener, P. (1973). Review of research on the Illinois test of psycholinguistic abilities. In L. Mann & D. Sabatino (Eds.), *The first review of special education* (Vol. 1). Philadelphia: JSE Press.

Seeing Eye Facts. (n.d.). Morristown, NJ: The Seeing Eye.

Sellin, D., & Birch, J. (1980). *Educating gifted and talented learners.* Rockville, MD: Aspen Systems.

Semmel, D., Goldman, S. R., Gerber, M. M., Cosden, M. A., & Semmel, M. I. (1985). Survey of special education and mainstream teachers' access to and use of microcomputers with mildly handicapped students. (Tech. Rep. No. 9,0). Santa Barbara, CA: University of California.

Shames, G. H. (1986). Disorders of fluency. In G. H. Shames & E. H. Wiig (Eds.), *Human communication disorders* (pp. 243-289). Columbus, OH: Merrill.

Shames, G. H., & Wiig, E. H. (Eds.). (1986). *Human communication disorders: An introduction* (2nd ed.). Columbus, OH: Merrill.

Shane, H. G. (1987). *Teaching and learning in the microelectronic age.* Bloomington, IN: Phi Delta Kappa Educational Foundation.

Shannon, C. E. (1949). The mathematical theory of communication. In C. E. Shannon & W. Weaver (Eds.), *The mathematical theory of communication.* Urbana, IL: University of Illinois Press.

Shannon, S., & Weaver, W. (1949). *The mathematical theory of communication.* Champaign, IL: University of Illinois Press.

Shearer, M. S., & Shearer, D. E. (1972). The Portage Project: A model for early childhood education. *Exceptional Children, 39,* 210–217.

Sheely, P., & Hansen, S. A. (1983). Use of vibrotactile aids with preschool hearing impaired children: Case studies. *Volta Review, 85*(1), 14–26.

Shepard, L. A., Smith, M. L., & Vojir, C. P. (1983). Characteristics of pupils identified as learning disabled. *American Educational Research Journal, 20*(3), 309–331.

Shrybman, J. (1982). *Due process in special education.* Rockville, MD: Aspen Systems.

Siegel, I. (1976). Genetics for the clinician. In E. E. Faye (Ed.), *Clinical low vision.* Boston: Little, Brown.

Sight Saving Review, New estimates (editorial). (1979). *49*(1), 2.

Simeonsson, R. J., & McHale, S. M. (1981). Review: Research on handicapped children: Sibling relationships. *Child Care, Health, and Development, 7,* 153-171.

Simon, E. P. (1984). A report on electronic travel aid users: Three to five years later. *Journal of Visual Impairment and Blindness, 78,* 478–480.

Simpson, F. (1986). Transition to adulthood. In G. Scholl (Ed.), *Foundations of education for blind and visually handicapped children and youth: Theory and practice* (pp. 405–422). New York: American Foundation for the Blind.

Skinner, B. F. (1953). *Science and human behavior.* New York: Macmillan.

Skinner, B. F. (1974). *About behaviorism.* New York: Alfred A. Knopf.

Smith v. Robinson, 104 S. Ct. 3457 (1984).

Smith, C. R. (1986). The future of the LD field: Intervention approaches. *Journal of Learning Disabilities, 19,* 461–472.

Smith, J. (1979). *Thirty projects: A conspectus.* Albuquerque, NM: University of New Mexico.

Sobeerenberger, R. (1982). Treatment from ancient times to the present. In P. Cegelka & H. Prehm (Eds.), *Mental retardation: From categories to people.* Columbus, OH: Merrill.

Soeffing, M. (1975). Abused children are exceptional children. *Exceptional Children, 42*(3), 126–133.

Software shopper available. (1987). *SIG/HAN News, 1*(1), 2.

Sowokinos, J. W. (1986). Computers and the visually impaired kindergarten child. *Journal of Visual Impairment and Blindness, 80,* 638–641.

Spencer, M., & Baskin, L. (1981). Classroom computers: Do they make a difference? *Classroom Computer News, 2,* 12–15.

Spivack, G., Swift, M., & Prewitt, J. (1971). Syndromes of disturbed classroom behavior: A behavioral diagnostic system for elementary schools. *Journal of Special Education, 5,* 269–292.

Spring, C., & Perry, L. (1981, September). *Computer-assisted instruction in word-decoding for educationally-handicapped children.* (ERIC Document Reproduction Service No. ED 201 075).

Spungin, S. J. (1986). Corridors of insensitivity: Technology and blind persons. *Journal of Visual Impairment and Blindness, 79,* 113–116.

Stainback, W., Stainback, S., Courtnage, L., & Jaben, T. (1985). Facilitating mainstreaming by modifying the mainstream. *Exceptional Children, 52,* 144–152.

Stallard, C. K. (1982). Computers and education for exceptional children: Emerging applications. *Exceptional Children, 49,* 102–104.

Stanley, J. C. (1979). The study and facilitation of talent for mathematics. In A. H. Passow (Ed.), *The gifted and talented: Their education and development.* 78th Yearbook of the National Society for the Study of Education. Part I. Chicago: University of Chicago Press.

State Education Department of New York. (1978). *Your child's right to an education: A guide for parents of handicapped children in New York State.* Albany, NY: State Education Department, Office for Education of Children with Handicapping Conditions.

Steigman, A. (1975). Poliomyelitis. In V. Vaughn, R. McKay, & W. Nelson (Eds.), *Textbook of pediatrics.* Philadelphia: W. B. Saunders.

Stein, G. (1981). What three studies show about computer based learning: Improving problem solving skills. *Computer Classroom News, 2,* 12–15.

Stephens, T. M. (1970). *Directive teaching of children with learning and behavioral handicaps.* Columbus, OH: Merrill.

Sternberg, L., & Taylor, R. L. (1982). The insignificance of psycholinguistic training: A reply to Kavale. *Exceptional Children, 49*(3), 254–256.

Stevens, H. (1964). Overview. In H. A. Stevens & R. Heber (Eds.), *Mental retardation.* Chicago: University of Chicago Press.

Stewart, J. C. (1986). *Counseling parents of exceptional children.* Columbus, OH: Merrill.

Stile, S. W., Cole, J. T., & Garner, A. W. (1979). Maximizing parent involvement in programs for exceptional children. *Journal of the Division for Early Childhood, 1*(1), 68–82.

Stock, L. (1987a). Hispanic Americans: A brief profile. *Journal of Visual Impairment and Blindness, 81*(6), 262–263.

Stock, L. (1987b). Native Americans: A brief profile. *Journal of Visual Impairment and Blindness, 81*(4), 152.

Stone, F., & Rowley, V. N. (1964). Educational disability in emotionally disturbed children. *Exceptional Children, 30,* 423–426.

Strauss, A., & Lehtinen, L. (1947). *Psychopathology and education of brain-injured children.* New York: Grune and Stratton.

Strauss, A., & Werner, H. (1942). Disorders of conceptual thinking in the brain-injured child. *Journal of Nervous and Mental Disease, 96,* 153–172.

Stuart v. *Nappi* 443 F. Supp. 1235 (D. Ct. 1978).

Swan, W. M. (1980). The handicapped children's early education program. *Exceptional Children, 47,* 12.

Swanson, H. L., & Watson, B. L. (1982). *Educational and psychological assessment of exceptional children: Theories, strategies, and applications.* St. Louis, MO: C. V. Mosby.

Swassing, R. H. (1985). *Teaching gifted children and adolescents.* Columbus, OH: Merrill.

Swink, P., & Orioli, E. M. (1986a). *Cocaine and the family.* Daly City, CA: Krames Communications.

Swink, P., & Orioli, E. M. (1986b). *Cocaine in the workplace.* Daly City, CA: Krames Communications.

Tarver, S., & Hallahan, D. P. (1976). Children with learning disabilities: An overview. In J. M. Kauffman & D. P. Hallahan (Eds.), *Teaching children with learning disabilities: Personal perspectives.* Columbus, OH: Merrill.

The Task Force on Pediatric Education. (1978). *The future of pediatric evaluation.* Evanston, IL: American Academy of Pediatrics.

Tawney, J. W. (1979). *Telecommunications for the severely handicapped.* (ERIC Document Reproduction Service No. ED 160 070).

Tawney, J. W., & Cartwright, G. P. (1981). Teaching in a technologically oriented society. *Teacher Education and Special Education, 4,* 3–14.

Taylor, J. L. (1959). The itinerant teaching program for blind children. In G. L. Abel (Ed.), *Concerning the education of blind children.* New York: American Foundation for the Blind.

Taylor, J. L. (1973). Educational programs. In B. Lowenfeld (Ed.), *The visually handicapped child in school.* New York: John Day.

TED Executive Committee (1986, October). *A statement by the Teacher Education Division of the Council for Exceptional Children on the regular education initiative.* Reston, VA: The Council for Exceptional Children.

Teitelbaum, M. L. (1981). Teachers as consumers: What they should know about the hearing impaired child. In M. Ross & L. W. Nober (Eds.), *Educating hard of hearing children* (pp. 82–87). Reston, VA: The Council for Exceptional Children.

Terman, L. (1954). The discovery and encouragement of exceptional talent. *American Psychologist, 9,* 221–230.

Terman, L., & Oden, M. (1947). *Genetic studies of genius: The gifted child grows up* (Vol. 4). Stanford, CA: Stanford University Press.

Terpenning, J. L. (1982). Edufun. In G. C. Vanderheiden & L. M. Walstead (Eds.), *Trace Center international software/hardware registry.* Madison, WI: University of Wisconsin.

Terry, D. R. (1985). Highlights of the Carl Perkins Act. *VocEd, 60*(4), 31–32.

Thackray, J. (1982). How to score fewer racquet sport eye injuries. *Sight-Saving, 51,* 2–6.

Thomas, A., & Chess, S. (1977). *Temperament and development.* New York: Brunner/Mazel.

Thomas, C. K. (1958). *An introduction to the phonetics of American English.* New York: Ronald Press.

Thomas, M. A. (1981a). Computer-based language training: A conversation with Duane M. Rumbaugh and Mary Ann Romski. *Education and Training of the Mentally Retarded, 16,* 193–200.

Thomas, M. A. (1981b). Educating handicapped students via microcomputer/videodisc technology. *Education and Training of the Mentally Retarded, 16,* 264–269.

Thorkildsen, R. (1982, July). A microcomputer/videodisc system for delivering computer-assisted instruction to mentally handicapped students. *Proceedings of the Annual Summer Conference on Computer: Extension of the Human Mind.* Eugene, OR: University of Oregon. (ERIC Document Reproduction Service No. ED 219 867).

Thorkildson, R. (1984). *Interactive videodisc social skills program: Development and field testing of a microcomputer/videodisc based social skills curriculum for the severely emotionally disturbed child.* (Tech. Report No. G00801537). Logan, UT: Utah State University.

Todd, S. P. (Ed.). (1986). *Rehabilitation R&D progress reports 1986.* Washington, DC: Veteran's Administration.

Tooze, D. (1981). *Independence training for visually handicapped children.* Baltimore, MD: University Park Press.

Torrance, E. (1962). *Guiding creative talent.* Englewood Cliffs, NJ: Prentice-Hall.

Torrance, E. (1971). Psychology of gifted children and youth. In W. M. Cruickshank (Ed.), *Psychology of exceptional children and youth* (3rd ed.). Englewood Cliffs, NJ: Prentice-Hall.

Torres, S. (Ed.). (1977). *A primer on individualized education programs for handicapped children.* Reston, VA: The Foundation for Exceptional Children.

Travis, L. (Ed.). (1971). *Handbook of speech pathology and audiology.* New York: Meredith Corporation.

Tucker, I., & Nolan, M. (1986). Objective assessment of auditory function. In D. Ellis (Ed.), *Sensory impairments in mentally handicapped people* (pp. 218–258). San Diego, CA: College-Hill Press.

Tucker, J., Stevens, L. J., & Ysseldyke, J. E. (1983). Learning disabilities: The experts speak out. *Journal of Learning Disabilities, 16*(1), 6–14.

Tulloch, D. (1983). Why me? Parental reactions to the birth of an exceptional child. *Journal of the Division for Early Childhood, 7,* 54–60.

Turnbull, H. R. (1986). *Free appropriate public education: The law and children with disabilities.* Denver, CO: Love.

Tuttle, D. (1986). Educational programming. In G. Scholl (Ed.), *Foundations of education for blind and visually handicapped children and youth: Theory and practice* (pp. 239-253). New York: American Foundation for the Blind.

Tyrer, L. B. (1978). Complications of teenage pregnancy. *Clinical Obstetrics and Gynecology, 21*(4), 1135.

United States Bureau of the Census. (1978). *Statistical abstracts of the United States: 1978* (99th ed.). Washington, DC: U.S. Government Printing Office.

United States Bureau of the Census. (1982). *Statistical abstracts of the United States: 1982–83* (103rd ed.). Washington, DC: U.S. Government Printing Office.

United States Bureau of the Census. (1983). *1980 Census of the Population.* Vol. 1, Chapter C, Part I, 1–280.

United States Bureau of the Census. (1986). *Statistical abstracts of the United States: 1987* (107th ed.). Washington, DC: U.S. Government Printing Office.

United States Department of Education. (1984). Executive summary: Sixth annual report to Congress on the implementation of P.L. 94–142: The Education for All Handicapped Children Act. *Exceptional Children, 51,* 199–202.

United States General Accounting Office. (1981). *Disparities still exist in who gets special education.* Washington, DC: Author.

United States Office of Education. (1977a, August 23). Implementation of Part B of the Education of the Handicapped Act. *Federal Register, 42,* 42474–42518.

United States Office of Education. (1977b, December 23). Assistance to states for education of handicapped children: Procedures for evaluating specific learning disabilities. *Federal Register, 42,* 65082–65083.

United States Office of Education. (1979). *Progress toward a free appropriate public education: A report to Congress on the implementation of P. L. 94–142.* Washington, DC: Department of Health, Education, and Welfare.

Urwin, C. (1983). Dialogue and cognitive functioning in the early language development of three blind children. In A. E. Mills (Ed.), *Language acquisition in the blind child: Normal and deficient* (pp. 142–161). San Diego, CA: College-Hill Press.

Utley, B. L., & Meehan, D. (1982). *Physical management.* Unpublished manuscript, University of Pittsburgh.

Vanderheiden, G., & Grilley, K. (Eds.). (1976). *Nonvocal communication techniques and aids for the severely physically handicapped.* Baltimore, MD: University Park Press.

Van Hasselt, V. B., Hersen, M., Moore, L. E., & Simon, J. (1986). Assessment and treatment of families with visually handicapped children: A project description. *Journal of Visual Impairment and Blindness, 80,* 633–635.

Van Hasselt, V. B., Simon, J., & Mastantueno, A. (1982). Social skills training for blind children and adolescents. *Education of the Visually Handicapped, 14,* 34–40.

Van Riper, C. (1978). *Speech correction: Principles and methods.* Englewood Cliffs, NJ: Prentice-Hall.

Van Riper, C., & Emerick, L. (1984). *Speech correction: An introduction to speech pathology and audiology.* Englewood Cliffs, NJ: Prentice-Hall.

Van Witsen, B. (1979). *Perceptual training activities handbook* (2nd ed.). New York: Teachers College Press.

Vaughan, D., & Asbury, T. (1977). *General ophthalmology* (8th ed.). Los Altos, CA: Lange Medical Publications.

Vaughan, D., & Asbury, T. (1980). *General ophthalmology* (9th ed.). Los Altos, CA: Lange Medical Publications.

Vaughan, D., & Asbury, T. (1986). *General ophthalmology* (11th ed.). Los Altos, CA: Appleton-Century-Crofts.

Vaughan, R. W., & Hodges, L. A. (1973). A statistical survey into a definition of learning disabilities. *Journal of Learning Disabilities, 6,* 658–664.

Venn, J., Morganstern, L., & Dykes, M. (1979). Checklists for evaluating the fit and function of orthoses, prostheses, and wheelchairs in the classroom. *Teaching Exceptional Children, 11,* 51–56.

Vision problems in the United States: A statistical analysis. (1980). New York: Operations Research Department, National Society to Prevent Blindness.

Von Isser, A., Quay, H. C., & Love, C. T. (1980). Interrelationships among three measures of deviant behavior. *Exceptional Children, 46,* 272–276.

Walkenshaw, M., & Fine, M. (1979). Psychoeducational assessment: An integrated viewpoint. In E. L. Meyen, G. A. Vergason, & R. J. Whelan (Eds.), *Instructional planning for exceptional children*. Denver, CO: Love.

Wallace, G., & Kauffman, J. M. (1978). *Teaching children with learning problems* (2nd ed.). Columbus, OH: Merrill.

Wallace, G., & Larsen, S. C. (1978). *Educational assessment of learning problems: Testing for teaching*. Boston: Allyn and Bacon.

Wallace, G., & McLoughlin, J. A. (1979). *Learning disabilities: Concepts and characteristics* (2nd ed.). Columbus, OH: Merrill.

Wallace, H. M. (1979). Selected aspects of perinatal casualties. *Clinical Pediatrics, 18*(4), 213–223.

Wang, M. C., Reynolds, M. C., & Walberg, H. J. (1986). Rethinking special education. *Educational Leadership, 44*(1), 26–31.

Ward, M. E., Cartwright, G. P., Cartwright, C. A., & Campbell, J. (Eds.). (1973). *Diagnostic teaching of preschool and primary children*. University Park, PA: Pennsylvania State University.

Ward, R. D., & Rostron, A. B. (1985). Computer-assisted learning for the hearing impaired: An interactive written language environment. *Volta Review, 85*, 346–352.

Warger, C. L., Murphy, L. B., & Kay, B. R. (1985). The use of microcomputers with autistic adults: Planning, implementing, evaluating. *Teaching Exceptional Children, 18*, 52–56.

Warkany, J., & Kirkpatrick, J. (1975). The bones and joints. In V. Vaughn, R. McKay, & W. Nelson (Eds.), *Textbook of pediatrics*. Philadelphia: W. B. Saunders.

Warren, D. H. (1984). *Blindness and early childhood development* (2nd ed.). New York: American Foundation for the Blind.

Wasserman, S. (1982). The gifted can't weight that giraffe. *Phi Delta Kappan, 63*, 621.

Watkins, M. W., & Webb, C. (1981, September-October). Computer-assisted instruction with learning disabled students. *Educational Computer, 1*(3), 24–27.

Weaver, W. (1949). Recent contributions to the mathematical theory of communication. In C. E. Shannon & W. Weaver (Eds.), *The mathematical theory of communication*. Urbana, IL: University of Illinois Press.

Weener, P., Barritt, L. S., & Semmell, M. I. (1967). A critical evaluation of the Illinois Test of Psycholinguistic Abilities. *Exceptional Children, 33*, 373–380.

Wehman, P. (1983). Toward the employability of severely handicapped children and youth. *Teaching Exceptional Children, 15*, 220–225.

Wehman, P., & Hill, J. W. (1981). Competitive employment for moderately and severely handicapped individuals. *Exceptional Children, 47*, 338–347.

Wehman, P., & Hill, J. W. (1984). Integrating severely handicapped students in community activities. *Teaching Exceptional Children, 16*, 142–145.

Weiner, R. (1986). *AIDS: Impact on the schools*. Arlington, VA: Education Research Group, Capitol Publications.

Weisgerber, R. A., & Dehaas, C. (1980, January). *The potential of environmental sensors for improving the mobility performance of mainstream blind students* (Final Report). (ERIC Document Reproduction Service No. ED 175 203).

Weiss, B. (1982). Food additives and environmental chemicals as sources of childhood behavior disorders. *American Academy of Child Psychiatry, 21*, 144–152.

Welsh, M. M., & Odum, C. S. H. (1981). Parent involvement in the education of the handicapped child: A review of the literature. *Journal of the Division for Early Childhood, 3*, 15–25.

Welton, J. W. (1982, September). *Individualized educational program: Monitoring analysis plan* (Instructional Manual). Sacramento, CA: California State Department of Education. (ERIC Document Reproduction Service No. ED 215 487).

Wepman, J. M., Cruickshank, W. M., Deutsch, C. P., Morency, A., & Strother, C. R. (1975). Learning disabilities. In N. Hobbs (Ed.), *Issues in the classification of children* (Vol. 1). San Francisco: Jossey-Bass.

Werth, P. (1983). Meaning in language acquisition. In A. Mills (Ed.), *Language acquisition in the blind child: Normal and deficient* (pp. 77–88). San Diego, CA: College-Hill Press.

Wexler, H. (1979). Each year a million pregnant teenagers. *American Education, 15*(5), 6–14.

Whelan, R. J. (1979). The emotionally disturbed. In E. L. Meyen (Ed.), *Basic readings in the study of exceptional children and youth*. Denver, CO: Love.

White, A. (1976). Gifted among the handicapped. *Proceedings from the 2nd Annual Conference on Handicapped Gifted*. New Orleans: Association for the Gifted.

White, M., & Miller, S. R. (1983). Dyslexia: A term in search of definition. *The Journal of Special Education, 17*(1), 5–10.

White, W. J., Alley, G. R., Deshler, D. D., Schumaker, J. B., Warner, M. M., & Clark, F. L. (1982). Are there learning disabilities after high school? *Exceptional Children, 49*(3), 273–274.

Whitestock, R. H. (1980). Dog guides. In R. L. Welsh & B. B. Blasch (Eds.), *Foundations of orientation and mobility* (pp. 565–580). New York: American Foundation for the Blind.

Whitmore, J. R. (1981). Gifted children with handicapping conditions: A new frontier. *Exceptional Children, 48*, 106–114.

Wiederholt, J. L. (1974). Historical perspectives on the education of the learning disabled. In L. Mann & D. A. Sabatino (Eds.), *The second review of special education*. Philadelphia: JSE Press.

Wiegerink, R., Hocutt, A., Posante-Loro, R., & Bristol, M. (1980). Parent involvement in early education programs for handicapped children. In J. J. Gallagher (Ed.), *New directions for exceptional children: Ecology of exceptional children* (pp. 67–85). San Francisco: Jossey-Bass.

Wiig, E. H. (1986). Language disabilities in school-age children and youth. In G. H. Shames & E. H. Wiig (Eds.), *Human communication disorders* (pp. 331–379). Columbus, OH: Merrill.

Wilbur, R. B. (1976). The linguistics of manual language and manual systems. In L. Lloyd (Ed.), *Communication assessment and intervention strategies*. Baltimore, MD: University Park Press.

Wilbur, R. B. (1979). *American sign language and sign systems*. Baltimore, MD: University Park Press.

Will, M. (1984). Bridges from school to working life. *Programs for the Handicapped, 2*, 1–5.

Will, M. (1986). Educating children with learning problems: A shared responsibility. *Exceptional Children, 52*, 411–415.

Williams, M. B. (1977). On growing up tight. *The Independent, 3*, 18–19.

Willis, D. J., & Faubion, J. H. (1979). Hearing disabled children and youth. In B. M. Swanson & D. J. Willis (Eds.),

Understanding exceptional children and youth. Chicago: Rand McNally.

Wilson, J. J. (1981). Notetaking: A necessary support service for hearing-impaired students. *Teaching Exceptional Children, 14*(1), 38–40.

Wilson, K. (1982). Computer systems for special educators. In J. Dominguez & A. Waldstein (Eds.), *Educational applications of electronic technology* (pp. 1–21). Albuquerque, NM: WESTAR.

Wilson, M. (1973). Children with crippling and health disabilities. In L. M. Dunn (Ed.), *Exceptional children in the schools.* New York: Holt, Rinehart and Winston.

Withrow, M. S. (1981, November). *Auditorily augmented interactive three-dimensional television as an aid to language learning among deaf and hearing impaired children* (Final Report). (ERIC Document Reproduction Service No. ED 203 623).

Witty, P. (1953). The gifted child. *Exceptional Children, 19,* 225–259.

Witty, P. (1967). Twenty years in education of the gifted. *Education, 88*(1), 4–10.

Wolf, N. (1985, June). Lawscore: Handicapped kids, lawyers' fee bill introduced. *American Bar Association Journal,* p. 31.

Wolfensberger, W. (1972). *The principle of normalization in human services.* Toronto: National Institute on Mental Retardation.

Wolfgang, C. H., & Glickman, C. D. (1980). *Solving discipline problems.* Boston: Allyn and Bacon.

Wolman, B. B. (1960). *Contemporary theories and systems in psychology.* New York: Harper & Row.

Wood, M. (1968). *Blindness—Ability not disability* (Public Affairs Pamphlet Number 295a). New York: Public Affairs Pamphlets.

Wooding, S. L. (1980, January). Hilary's story. *Young Children, 35*(2), 27–32.

Wright, B. A. (1960). *Physical disability—A psychological approach.* New York: Harper & Row.

Wright, B. A. (1983). *Physical disability—A psychological approach* (2nd ed.). New York: Harper & Row.

Wurster, M. V. (1983). Career education for visually impaired students: Where we've been and where we are. *Education of the Visually Handicapped, 14,* 99–104.

Wyatt v. *Aderholt,* 334 F. Supp. 1341 (1971).

Young, M. (1980). *Factors influencing utilization of resources and support systems by parents of handicapped children.* Unpublished doctoral dissertation, University of California, Los Angeles.

Ysseldyke, J., Algozzine, B., & Allen, D. (1982). Participation of regular education teachers in special education team decision making. *Exceptional Children, 48*(4), 365–366.

Ysseldyke, J., & Salvia, J. (1974). Diagnostic-prescriptive teaching: Two models. *Exceptional Children, 41,* 181–185.

Ysseldyke, J. E., & Algozzine, B. (1982). *Critical issues in special and remedial education.* Boston: Houghton Mifflin.

Ysseldyke, J. E., & Algozzine, B. (1983). LD or not LD: That's not the question! *Journal of Learning Disabilities, 16*(1), 29–31.

Ysseldyke, J. E., Algozzine, B., Shinn, M. R., & McGue, M. (1982). Similarities and differences between low achievers and students classified learning disabled. *The Journal of Special Education, 16*(1), 73–85.

Zettel, J. (1979). State provisions for educating the gifted and talented. In A. H. Passow (Ed.), *The gifted and the talented: Their education and development.* 78th Yearbook of the National Society for the Study of Education. Part I. Chicago: University of Chicago Press.

Zigler, E., & Valentine, J. (Eds.). (1979). *Project Head Start: A legacy of the war on poverty.* New York: Free Press.

Zuber, R. (1980). Methodology of science, artificial intelligence and the teaching of logic to gifted children. *Gifted and Talented Education, 2,* 41–46.

AUTHOR INDEX

SUBJECT INDEX